KING EDWARD II

Edward II's alabaster effigy on a Purbeck marble tomb beneath a freestone canopy: Gloucester Cathedral, formerly St Peter's Abbey.
From a photograph by Arthur Gardner in *The Archaeological Journal* 61 (1904), reproduced in his *English Medieval Sculpture*, Cambridge, 1937.

King Edward II

Edward of Caernarfon
His Life, His Reign, and Its Aftermath,
1284–1330

ROY MARTIN HAINES

McGill-Queen's University Press
Montreal & Kingston • London • Ithaca

© McGill-Queen's University Press 2003
ISBN-13: 978-0-7735-2432-3   ISBN-10: 0-7735-2432-0 (cloth)
ISBN-13: 978-0-7735-3157-4   ISBN-10: 0-7735-3157-2 (paper)

Legal deposit second quarter 2003
Bibliothèque nationale du Québec

Printed in Canada on acid-free paper.
First paperback edition 2006

This book was first published with the help of a grant from
the Humanities and Social Sciences Federation of Canada,
using funds provided by the Social Sciences and Humanities
Research Council of Canada.

McGill-Queen's University Press acknowledges the support of
the Canada Council for the Arts for our publishing program.
We also acknowledge the financial support of the Government
of Canada through the Book Publishing Industry Development
Program (BPIDP) for our publishing activities.

National Library of Canada Cataloguing in Publication

Haines, Roy Martin
    King Edward II : Edward of Caernarfon, his life, his reign, and
its aftermath, 1284–1330 / Roy Martin Haines.

Includes bibliographical references and index.
ISBN-13: 978-0-7735-2432-3   ISBN-10: 0-7735-2432-0 (bnd)
ISBN-13: 978-0-7735-3157-4   ISBN-10: 0-7735-3157-2 (pbk)
    1. Edward II, King of England, 1284–1327.   2. Great Britain
– Kings and rulers – Biography.   3. Great Britain – History –
Edward II, 1307–1327.   I. Title.

DA230.H34 2003   942.03´6´092   c2002-905062-6

This book was typeset by True to Type in 10½/13 Times

MEMORIAE

Erici Segelberg
Universitatis Upsalensis
Theologiae Doctoris incliti,
amici sociique nostri,
in terra viventium nunc ambulantis

Contents

Preface

This book has been a considerable time in germination, many years in growth. The idea of writing a history of Edward of Caernarfon's reign occurred to me in Canada while I was engaged on a biography of Archbishop Stratford. A visiting fellowship at Clare Hall, Cambridge (1987-88), coupled with a Social Sciences and Humanities Research Council Research Grant with leave stipend (1987-90), enabled me to get to grips with much more than the preliminaries, but for some six years afterwards other commitments ensured that the skeleton structure lay unfinished on the stocks. This was due to numerous vicissitudes, not least of them retirement from Dalhousie, and a subsequent migration from Putney (London) to Somerset, carried out almost unassisted over a period of time by my wife and myself. We were then faced with settling down in a new environment, and the temporary loss of convenient access to London, Oxford, and Cambridge libraries, not to mention the distraction entailed by a large garden. There were other academic concerns, including a calendar of the episcopal register of Bishop Montacute, diversions for various articles, as well as a sheaf of biographies for the medieval section of the Oxford University Press's *New Dictionary of National Biography*, and for the *Dictionnaire d'histoire et de géographie ecclésiastiques,* many of them relevant to Edward's reign. Eventually, however, it became possible, with a great effort, to return to the task.

Social and economic factors have been subordinated to an overall narrative structure that is principally concerned with the personal and political struggles at the centre of Edward's life and reign. Despite the modern preoccupation with "cultures" I remain committed to the concept that individuals exert a significant influence on events. Furthermore, this book reflects aspects of Edward's life and times to which I have been particularly attracted and which in some instances, for instance the "afterlife" of that king, have prompted lectures or articles. These elements are of historical significance and are notably revealing in the case of Edward, as also in the cases of Isabella and Mortimer. Inevitably one has to rely on a wide range of secondary sources, but wherever possible I have followed my usual practice of getting back to the manuscripts, as will be evident from the bibliography and footnotes.

It is arguable that disproportionate attention has been paid to Edward II and his reign, whether by historians, playwrights as diverse as Marlowe and Bertolt Brecht, poets, propagandists, moralists or even, more recently, choreographers. Historical researchers have subjected every known surviving document to microscopic examination, sometimes with more ingenuity than common sense would warrant. Interpretative theories about Edward's reign, such as those involving constitutional evolution, baronial opposition, the middle party, have each had their advocates, their demolition experts, or their revisionists. Administrative, economic, social, and fiscal considerations have in their turn occupied centre stage. Even the Edward-Gaveston relationship has been regarded as explicable in terms of the ancient bond of fraternity, with the biblical David and Jonathan as remote spiritual ancestors.

By any "objective" standard Edward was a lamentable character, his reign a shambles, located uneasily between that of his father and that of his warlike but well-respected son. He was ill equipped to be a medieval king. Yet the collapse of his rule amid a welter of intrigue, the over-indulgence of unpopular favourites, and the machinations of his own queen demand a measure of sympathy or at least understanding. Many of those who in their various ways wished to oppose or supplant him were no better. One need only mention Isabella, Mortimer and Lancaster. Edward's mighty downfall from the summit of kingship, his shoddy treatment, both real and imagined, at the hands of his captors, and his brutal death, gave way to pity and the concept of martyrdom, as had recently been the fate of the earl of Lancaster. Edward was no saint, no martyr. He brought much misery to his country, but it remains a matter of opinion whether Edward III's policy of waging a large-scale war with France for a kingdom he could never possess is preferable – there was no question of its acceptability at the time. We still do not warm to weak kings or to those in a medieval context who could not win battles against long-standing foes. Contemporaries did warm to the youthful, chivalrous conqueror of the French, weighed down by the spoils of war.

Roy Martin Haines
Soundings, Curry Rivel
Feast of St Denys, 2001

Acknowledgments

Much of the background to this book was acquired during preparation of other related, even unrelated books and articles, so that my thanks are initially due to the Canada Council, the Social Sciences and Humanities Research Council, and the Dalhousie Research and Development Fund, all of which at various times did so much to make those researches possible, whether at the Vatican Archives in Rome, Montpellier, or London, Berkeley, and elsewhere in the United Kingdom. In 1987 I was invited to deliver the Bertie Wilkinson Memorial Lecture at Toronto, choosing as my topic "Edward II: A Continuing Enigma." It was an honour to pay tribute to a historian who had made extensive and detailed contributions to the subject on which I was so rashly to engage. It brought to mind many convivial roast beef banquets at Hart House in his company.

My more immediate debt is due to Clare Hall, Cambridge, for my initial visiting fellowship, which saw the inception of this book more or less in its present form, my subsequent visits there, and my acceptance as a life member in 1990. One of the great concomitant blessings was the use of the Cambridge University Library in which I examined most of the secondary sources and a number of the primary ones. It was there too that I was first introduced to the advantages of word-processing on a Macintosh computer, a mainstay ever since. To my son-in-law, Professor Alexander Jones, of the University of Toronto, an expert in such matters, I am much indebted for solving the many software hazards which afflict the inexperienced. Adrian Suggett, another of my sons-in-law, a PC hardware engineer, I am happy to thank for coming to my rescue more than once when the "machinery" proved recalcitrant or inoperative. Thanks to both of them and to Macintosh for relegating the labours which I recall in connection with earlier volumes to mere horror stories from the past.

I am, of course indebted, as before, more particularly to the Bodleian Library, British Library, Public Record Office, and the Institute of Historical Research, not to mention the many English local Record Offices. Adrian James, the assistant librarian of the Society of Antiquaries of London, has always promptly provided copies, as well as the books themselves. More recently I have been particularly grateful to have the use in Taunton of the library of the Somerset Archaeological and Natural History Society – not to overlook the ready assistance of its librarian David Bromwich – as well as of the Somerset Record Office. Those who have responded to my queries are too numerous to mention, but I would particularly like to thank Professor Seymour Phillips for sending me copies of his articles which have been most helpful in elucidating the obscurities and complexities of Irish history. Dr A.J. Taylor kindly took an interest in my researches into Edward II's "Afterlife" and, as will be seen from my first chapter, I have been intrigued by his exciting detective work on the plan and evolution of Welsh castles. He supplied me with a transcript of Darcy's expense account (PRO E101/624/14) detailing necessaries for Edward II's burial in 1327. Andrew Hughes, a fellow member of Worcester College, Oxford, whom I met from time to time in Toronto at productions of the "Poculi Ludique Societas," provided some useful and original interpretation of the modifications in the coronation rite. Cynthia Neville of Dalhousie University kindly sent me articles bearing on the Scottish situation, while another former colleague, Daniel Woolf, let me have offprints concerned with post-Reformation interpretations of aspects of medieval history. My thanks are due to the editor of the Bristol and Gloucestershire Archaeological Society's Transactions for permission to reuse in chapter 8 much of the material from my article.

Without the work of so many scholars, too numerous to mention individually, but who are so well represented in both the footnotes and bibliography, this work would have been little more than a cursory sketch. As it is, so much material is available, so many hypotheses and interpretations have been advanced, that it is difficult to pilot one's way between them and still sustain coherence, let alone readability. I trust, nonetheless, that the scope of this book will help to tie together many loose ends and to make sense of a number of conundrums. From it may well emerge a certain inevitability about Edward's downfall – but that is to confuse hindsight with insight.

Abbreviations

AASRP	*Associated Architectural Societies' Reports and Papers*
AH	*Analecta Hibernica*
AIBL	*Académie des Inscriptions et Belles Lettres*
AJLH	*American Journal of Legal History*
An. Hib.	*Analecta Hibernica*
Ann. Grace	*Jacobi Grace, Kilkenniensis, Annales Hiberniae*
Ann. Innis.	*Annals of Innisfallen*
Ann. Loch Cé	*Annals of Loch Cé 1014–1590*
Ann. Lond.	*Annales Londonienses*
Ann. Paul.	*Annales Paulini*
Ann. Ulster	*Annals of Ulster*
Ant. Jnl.	*Antiquaries Journal*
App.	Appendix
APS	*The Acts of the Parliaments of Scotland*, ed. T. Thomson and C. Innes, RC 12 vols. London, 1814–75)
Arch. Ael.	*Archaeologia Aeliana*
Arch. Camb.	*Archaeologia Cambrensis*
Arch. Jnl.	*Archaeological Journal*
ARDK	*Deputy Keeper of the Public Records in Ireland, Annual Reports* 39, 42, Dublin 1909, 1911
BBCS	*Bulletin of the Board of Celtic Studies*
BEC	*Bibliothèque de l'école des chartes*
B&GAS see *TB&GAS*	
BIHR	*Bulletin of the Institute of Historical Research* (continued as *Historical Research* , *HR*)
Biog. Cantab.	A.B. Emden, *A Biographical Register of the University of Cambridge to 1500*, Cambridge, 1963
Biog. Oxon.	idem, *A Biographical Register of the University of Oxford to 1500,* 3 vols. Oxford, 1957–59

BJRL	*Bulletin of the John Rylands Library*
Bk. Armagh	*The Book of Armagh*
BL	British Library
BRHE	*Bibliothèque de la revue d'histoire ecclésiastique*
BSFS	*British Society of Franciscan Studies*
CPMR	*Calendar of Plea and Memoranda Rolls*
CCL	Canterbury Cathedral Library
CCR	*Calendar of Close Rolls*
CChR	*Calendar of Charter Rolls*
CChW	*Calendar of Chancery Warrants 1244–1326*, London, 1927
CDI	*Calendar of Documents Relating to Ireland*
CDS	*Calendar of Documents Relating to Scotland* , vol. 3 1307-57, Edinburgh, 1887
CFR	*Calendar of Fine Rolls*
CHEL	*Cambridge History of English Literature*, ed. A.W. Ward and A.R. Waller, vols. 1 and 2, Cambridge, 1933–34
CIPM	*Calendar of Inquisitions Post Mortem*
CJH	*Canadian Journal of History*
Clyn, *Annals*	*(The) Annals of Ireland* (see Bibliography)
CMH	*Cambridge Medieval History*
CMRE	*Calendar of Memoranda Rolls (Exchequer) 1326–1327*, London, 1968
Concilia	*Concilia Magnae Britanniae et Hiberniae*, ed. D. Wilkins, 4 vols. London, 1737
CPL	*Calendar of Papal Letters*
CPMR	*Calendar of the Plea and Memoranda Rolls of the City of London*
CPR	*Calendar of Patent Rolls*
CQR	*Church Quarterly Review*
CS	Camden Society
ChS	Chetham Society
CUL	Cambridge University Library
C&WAAS	*Cumberland and Westmorland Antiquarian and Archaeological Society*
DCL	Doctor of Civil Law
DCnL	Doctor of Canon Law
DHGE	*Dictionnaire d'histoire et de géographie ecclésiastiques*
DNB	*Dictionary of National Biography*
DTh	Doctor of Theology
EC	H. Johnstone, *Edward of Carnarvon, 1284–1307*, Manchester, 1947

EcHR	*Economic History Review*
ed., edn	edited, edition
EETS	*Early English Text Society*
EHR	*English Historical Review*
EPNS.	*English Place-Name Society*
Foedera	*Foedera, Conventiones , etc.*, ed. T. Rymer, new edn, ed. A. Clarke, F. Holbrooke, J. Caley, 4 vols in 7, London, RC 1816–69
Foedera (H)	*Foedera, Conventiones etc.*, 3rd. edn, ed. T. Rymer, 10 vols., The Hague, 1739–45
GEC Complete Peerage	
	G.E. Cokayne, *The Complete Peerage*, 14 vols. London/Stroud, 1910–98
Guide	*Guide to the Contents of the Public Record Office* 1, London, 1963
HBC	*Handbook of British Chronology*, 2nd. edn, ed. F.M. Powicke, E.B. Fryde, (London 1961); 3rd. edn, ed. E.B. Fryde, D.E. Greenway, S. Porter and I. Roy, London, 1986
HCM	Hereford Cathedral Muniments
HMCR	Reports of the Royal Commission on Historical Manuscripts
HR	*Historical Research*
HantsRO	Hampshire Record Office
IAS	*Irish Archaeological Society*
IER	*Irish Ecclesiastical Record*
IHS	*Irish Historical Studies*
IJ	*Irish Jurist*
IM	*Instrumenta Miscellanea* (Vatican Archives)
IMC	*Irish Manuscripts Commission*
IS	*Irish Sword*
Itinerary EII	E.M. Hallam, *The Itinerary of Edward II and his Household, 1307–1328*, L&I Soc. 211, 1984
JBS	*Journal of British Studies*
JCLA&HS	*Journal of the County Louth Archaeological and Historical Society*
JEH	*Journal of Ecclesiastical History*
JHI	*Journal of the History of Ideas*
JMH	*Journal of Medieval History*
JnGaA&HS	*Journal of the Galloway Archaeological and Historical Society*
JRL	*Journal of the John Rylands Library*

JRSAI	*Journal of the Royal Society of Antiquaries of Ireland* and see *PRSAI*
JW&CI	*Journal of the Warburg and Courtauld Institutes*
L&I	*List and Index* (PRO material)
Le Neve	*John le Neve, Fasti Ecclesiae Anglicanae 1300–1541,* 12 vols. Institute of Historical Research, London 1962–67)
Letters	H. Johnstone ed., *Letters of Edward of Prince of Wales (1304–1305),* Roxburghe Club, Cambridge, 1931
MLR	*Modern Language Review*
MP	*Modern Philology*
MS	*Mediaeval Studies*
MS(S)	Manuscript(s)
NH	*Northern History*
NHI	*A New History of Ireland*, vol. 2, ed. A. Cosgrove, Oxford 1987
NMS	*Nottingham Medieval Studies*
n.s.	new series
o.s.	old series
OHS	*Oxford Historical Society*
P&P	*Past and Present*
PBA	*Proceedings of the British Academy*
PCAS	*Proceedings of the Cambridge Antiquarian Society*
PHE	*Political History of England,* ed. W. Hunt and R.L. Poole, 12 vols. London 1905–10
PIAS	*Publications of the Irish Archaeological Society*
PRIA	*Proceedings of the Royal Irish Academy*
PRO	Public Record Office
PROI	Public Record Office Dublin
PSA	*Proceedings of the Society of Antiquaries*
PRSAI	*Proceedings of the Royal Society of Antiquaries of Ireland* and see *JRSAI*
PSANS	*Proceedings of the Somerset(shire) Archaeological and Natural History Society*
PSAScot	*Proceedings of the Society of Antiquaries of Scotland*
RB	*Revue Bénédictine*
RC	Record Commission
RCHM	Royal Commission of Historical Monuments
RDP	*Reports Touching the Dignity of a Peer,* 5 vols. London, 1820–29
Reg.MS	*Registrum Magni Sigilli Regum Scotorum 1306–1424*

Rep.DKI	*Reports of the Deputy Keeper of the Public Records of Ireland*
RHGF	*Recueil des Historiens des Gaules et de la France*
RMS	*Reading Medieval Studies*
Rot. Parl.	*Rotuli Parliamentorum*, 1783
Rot. Parl. Inediti	*Rotuli Parliamentorum* ed. Richardson and Sayles
Rot. Scot.	*Rotuli Scotiae in Turri Londoniensi*, vol. 1, 1814
RS	Rolls Series
RSAI	Royal Society of Antiquaries of Ireland
RWH	*Records of the Wardrobe and Household*
SA	Society of Antiquaries of London
s.a.	sub anno
ser.	series
SHF	*Société de l'histoire de France*
SHR	*Scottish Historical Review*
SCH	*Studies in Church History*
SHR	*Scottish Historical Review*
SR	*Statutes of the Realm*
SS	Surtees Society
St.H.	*Studia Hibernica*
Stevenson, Documents	
	Documents Illustrative of the History of Scotland
supp. ser.	supplementary series
s.v.	sub voce
TAPhS	*Transactions of the American Philosophical Society*
TB&GAS	*Transactions of the Bristol and Gloucestershire Archaeological Society*
TC&WAAS	*Transactions of the Cumberland and Westmorland Antiquarian and Archaeological Society*
TD&GNH&AS	*Transactions of the Dumfries and Galloway Natural History and Archaeological Society*
TGLHS (Morgannwyg)	
	Transactions of the Glamorgan Local History Society
TRHS	*Transactions of the Royal Historical Society*
Trans.Thor. Soc.	*Transactions of the Thoroton Society*
WA&NHSM	*Wiltshire Archaeological and Natural History Society Magazine*
WAM	Westminster Abbey Muniments
WAS	Worcestershire Archaeological Society
WHR	*Welsh History Review*

WHS   Worcestershire Historical Society
YAJ   *Yorkshire Archaeological Journal*
YAS Rec. Ser. *Yorkshire Archaological Society*, Record Series

NOTE. Two dates linked by an X indicate a specific but unknown date between the opening and closing limits. E.g. 1305 X 1316.

John Stratford, bishop of Winchester (1323–33), archbishop
of Canterbury (1333–48). His much-damaged alabaster effigy
in Canterbury Cathedral.
Author's photograph.

Mutilated fragment of the copy of a letter to Pope John XXII from Adam Orleton, bishop of Hereford (1317–27), Worcester (1327–33), and Winchester (1333–45), complaining of his ill treatment. "Herodiana namque sevicia" – Herodian rage (line 10 from bottom).

Cotton MS Vitellius E. IV 9, fo. 19v. by courtesy of the British Library Board.

PART ONE

Edward of Caernarfon,
His Kingship, and Its Denouement

1

Formative Years, 1284–1307

Edward of Caernarfon, the fourth son and eleventh child of Edward I by his first wife, Eleanor of Castile, was born in his name-place on 25 April 1284, the feast of St Mark, and was baptized on Mayday shortly thereafter.[1] The previous year carpenters had been busily engaged upon the erection of chambers for the use of the king and queen in the castle still in course of construction.[2] It could well have been by deliberate intent that the birth took place where Roman imperial grandeur was conjured up by the nearness of Segontium (*Caer Seint*) and close to the spot where the body of Magnus Maximus was believed to have been discovered in 1283. Constantine, who set out from England to claim the purple, was thought to have been his son.[3] Edward I's pedigree allegedly stretched back to classical times and he was steeped in Arthurian legend.[4] As recently as April 1278 he and his queen had visited Glastonbury Abbey where in a remarkable ceremony, well attended by the court, he had overseen the reburial of what were purportedly the remains of Arthur and Guinevere, directing that their tomb be placed before the high altar.[5] The castle echoed these aspirations in stone. Caernarfon, it has been claimed, was intended to be "the capital of a new dynasty of English princes ... a palace-castle reflecting in its symbolism its own Roman origins and using the likeness of the Theodosian walls of Constantinople to invoke the imperial throne."[6] Of course, it also symbolized the achievements of Edward I himself.

Edward's "romantic" notions should not be allowed to obscure his essentially practical nature. We need not countenance David Powel's story that the opportunist king when at Rhuddlan sent Welsh lords to Caernarfon for the christening offering them "one that was borne in Wales and could speake never a word of English, whose life and conversation no man was able to staine."[7] At the same time it is useful to recall that the title Prince of Wales, adopted by Llywelyn ap Gruffydd in 1258, had been given legal recognition by King Henry III in the treaties of Pipton (1265) and Montgomery (1267), although for the first of these he was under duress. Thus there could have been some vaguely conceived notion of making political capital from a Welsh-born son. That the Welsh were not duped by any such manœuvre is suggested by Madoc ap Lywelyn's revolt in 1294–95, during which the far-from-finished Caernarfon Castle was overrun.[8]

THE FAMILY CIRCLE

The death on 19 August 1284 of Edward I's promising heir, Alfonso (or Alphonso) of Windsor, while still in his eleventh year, was much lamented, so the Dunstable annalist tells us. It was surely unexpected, for earlier in the same year he had been affianced to Margaret, daughter of Florence V, count of Holland, and the "Alfonso psalter" was in process of being illuminated in honour of their anticipated marriage.[9] His eldest brother John had died before Alfonso's birth while Henry, born in 1267, did not survive beyond October 1274. Small wonder that the king expressed his thankfulness by generous feeding of the poor on the birthday of Edward, the sole surviving son.[10]

The infant prince was initially entrusted to a wet nurse, Mary or Mariota Maunsel, "a burgess of Caernarfon," who is known to have fallen ill at Rhuddlan.[11] Her successor Alice, wife of Reginald de Leygrave, was later described as the king's foster mother.[12] Certainly he knew her far better than his real mother, Eleanor of Castile, the dutiful wife who was constantly at the king's side even on crusade. When Edward was only two Eleanor stayed abroad with her husband between mid-May 1286 and 12 August 1289. On the couple's return Edward and four of his five sisters were taken from Langley to Dover to meet their parents.[13] Fifteen months after her disembarkation, on 28 November 1290, the queen died of a lingering fever, possibly malaria, at Harby near Lincoln. The grief-stricken king erected stone crosses along the cortège's route. Eleanor is also remembered by William Torel's fine bronze effigy in Westminster Abbey, while the engraving in William Dugdale's *Book of Monuments* recalls that sculptor's companion figure in Lincoln Cathedral prior to its defacement in the seventeenth century.[14]

The loss of Edward's mother was followed the next year by that of his grandmother, Eleanor of Provence, who from her retirement at Amesbury in Wiltshire, where she had taken the veil in 1286, appears to have maintained a lively interest in the health and welfare of her grandson; remonstrating, for instance, against the king's plan to take him to the North.[15] By the time the old king married Margaret of France on 10 September 1299, his son was fifteen, so she must have been more like an elder sister than a mother. But he did have considerable contact with the new queen and for a while in 1299 their households merged.[16] Thus for most of his childhood Edward's immediate family was almost exclusively female. Whether this affected his subsequent sexual orientation is open to debate. As his sisters, with the exception of Mary, departed one by one to set up their own households he was left, so to speak, to the not-so-tender mercies of his father, an irascible and demanding old man of iron determination. Small wonder that in 1305 he was to write to Agnes de Valence, sister of Aymer de Valence, soon to become earl of Pembroke, to the effect that he hoped she would be "nostre bone mere," promising to behave towards her as a son should.[17]

INCREASING RESPONSIBILITIES

Following Queen Eleanor's death the county of Ponthieu passed in 1290 to her surviving son, Edward. Homage on behalf of the young man was performed by proxy in April 1291 and Edmund, earl of Lancaster, took charge in his name.[18] Three years later the county, together with Gascony, was confiscated by the French king and not returned until 1299 under the terms of the peace of Montreuil. Thereafter the Frescobaldi, Italian bankers, were responsible for raising the revenues.[19] Only in February 1301, when Edward came of age, was he in a position to act as nominal count of Ponthieu. In practice the administration was in the hands of a series of seneschals or stewards.[20]

The young Edward's first exposure to political crisis came in 1297, when a number of barons made common cause against Edward's demands and he was faced with the tough and uncompromising archbishop of Canterbury, Robert Winchelsey, acting in response to the bull *Clericis laicos* of 1296, which sought to forbid clerical taxation for secular purposes without papal consent. Following the stand taken at the Salisbury Parliament by the earls of Hereford and Norfolk, graphically depicted by the chronicler Guisborough,[21] the king made a well stage-managed appeal. On 14 July, flanked by his son and the temporarily reconciled Winchelsey, he is said to have entrusted his heir, the Lord Edward, to the archbishop and to Reginald Grey. And then, Guisborough claims, the magnates performed fealty to Lord Edward, who was acclaimed by those assembled as heir, future lord, and successor to the kingdom.[22]

It was not long after this ceremony – between 23 August 1297 and 14 March of the following year – that Edward acted as nominal regent during his father's absence abroad.[23] Deputed to advise him was a council of the archbishop-elect of York, Henry of Newark, three other bishops, the earls of Cornwall, Surrey (Warenne), and Warwick, and three barons.[24] Prior to the king's sailing on 24 August barons and prelates presented the Monstraunces, a series of articles highly critical of royal policies. The king is said to have prevaricated by claiming that he could not respond without his full council part of which was already in Flanders. Ostensibly the redress of these grievances was left to the regency and on 10 October 1297, for which date parliament had been summoned, the Lord Edward as *locum tenens* sealed the *Confirmatio Cartarum*.[25] It may be that Edward recalled this experience when, as king, he was confronted by the Ordainers.

By a charter of 7 February 1301, while the Lincoln Parliament was in session,

King Edward conferred a generous patrimony on his son, then approaching seventeen. This comprised the royal lands in Wales together with the earldom of Chester and its appendages in many parts of England. The "principality of Wales" included Anglesey in the North with the mountainous region of Snowdonia, Gwynedd, the heart of Welsh resistance to Edward's imperialism, with the four cantreds of Rhos, Englefield, Rhuvoniog, and Duffryn Clwyd. In the South were the counties of Cardigan and Carmarthen – West Wales – with the "Welsheries" of Is Aeron and Uwch Aeron. Shortly thereafter Montgomery Castle and the hundred of Chirbury in Central Wales, formerly held by the young Edward's stepmother, were added. These territories constituted a broad sweep of land facing the sea west of the Marcher lordships. Neither the term "principality" nor the title "prince" receive specific mention in the royal grant but the form of address "Prince of Wales and earl of Chester" was soon adopted. On 6 April 1301 the prince travelled to inspect his new lands and to receive the homage of his tenants and, at his father's command, that of some nine marcher lords.[26]

THE PRINCE'S HOUSEHOLD AND CURIA

We can learn something of the early years of Lord Edward from such household rolls as have survived. That covering the period from November 1292 until 12 April 1293 with its ten membranes is one of the lengthiest, and provides an interesting conspectus of the peripatetic nature, save in the winter months, of the young prince's existence. It itemizes the expenditure of each of the customary departments: seneschalcy, buttery, scullery, saucery or saltery, hall, chamber, and marshalcy or stables.[27] Between 23 November 1292 and the following 12 April Edward spent no fewer than 141 days in Hertfordshire at Langley, the manor of the king's cousin, Edmund, earl of Cornwall, a property that was to pass into his possession in 1302 and for which he was to retain a lasting affection.[28] He then moved to Mortlake, an archiepiscopal manor on the Thames outside London for just over a month, and from there to Kennington, also on the south bank of the Thames but opposite the City, where he remained for twenty-seven days. Apart from those lengthy stays he was more or less permanently on the move, sometimes as a guest at other than royal properties.[29] For instance, he stayed more than once at Otford in Kent, which like Mortlake passed into the king's hands with other temporalities of the archbishopric of Canterbury following John Pecham's death in December 1292. On another occasion he spent eleven days at Downton just over the Hampshire border in Wiltshire, presumably in the residence of the bishop of Winchester, John of Pontoise. By mid-October he was back at Mortlake.[30] On occasion Scottish prisoners or hostages were billeted upon the household, as was the case in 1297 with Edward Balliol, son of King John Balliol, Alexander, son of the earl of Mar, and Robert of Strathearn – until ordered to the Tower with his brother Gilbert.[31]

Supplementing these accounts of wardrobe and household is a unique roll containing copies of letters issued under Prince Edward's privy seal, some in Latin but most in Anglo-Norman (Old French), as convention required: some 741 items for the single year November 1304-November 1305. There are difficulties about interpreting them as indicative of the prince's habits or character. Most of the letters follow common form and represent the type of correspondence engaged in by other important laymen or ecclesiastics. What part Edward played in their composition cannot be known. It is possible that he did not see the greater number of them prior to despatch under his seal. His personal instructions were doubtless delivered *viva voce*, the regular medieval practice. Such letters seldom reveal intimate matters. Yet every now and then, there are what appear to be individual touches. The letter to Agnes de Valence has already been mentioned. Another described by its editor as "the strangest and most unconventional of all," is addressed to Louis, count of Evreux, half-brother of King Philip IV. The letter states that the prince is sending him "a big trotting palfrey that can hardly carry," together with "some misshapen greyhounds of Wales, which can catch a hare well if they find it asleep, and running dogs which can follow at an amble. ... And dear cousin," he added, "if you would care for anything else from our land of Wales, we will send you some wild men, if you like, who will know well how to give young sprigs of nobility their education."[32] Surely such idiosyncrasy reflects the prince's quirky sense of humour. Understandably, much of the correspondence highlights his interest in dogs, horses, and hawks, commonplaces of a man of his class.

Precise classification of the letters would be arduous, though certain categories are clear enough. Some concern appointments, for instance that of Robert de Parker as bailiff of Langley, or of Elias de Camera as parker and warrener there. Others provide safe conduct, as that for Aimery of the Frescobaldi house of bankers (*dilectus valletus et mercator noster*).[33] A substantial number request the justices' consideration for those for whom the prince himself or those associated with him had a particular concern: on behalf of Nicholas de Grendon at the instance of Adam de Middleton; for the prince's justice at Chester, to avoid his amercement for failure to put in an appearance before Justice Spigurnel; for John de Bordesdon (twice), and for Ralph Williamson.[34] There were similar interventions with respect to ecclesiastical jurisdiction. One letter urged the archdeacon of Northumberland not to compel Walter Reynolds, the prince's treasurer, a future archbishop of Canterbury, to build a hall before the next summer at Ingram church of which he was non-resident rector. A letter to the bishop of Ely, Robert Orford, roundly condemned Peter de Weswyk as a common thief and requested that the diocesan, if possible, prevent his purgation, which would involve the perjury of his compurgators. Weswyk, the letter claimed, had inflicted injury on the prince and his people.[35]

Common too were letters to monasteries requesting corrodies (board and lodging) – the equivalent of a modern retirement home – for those who had been in the prince's employ, for example his valet and pantler, Richard le Mareschal.[36] His advocacy of the claims of William de Rasne as provost of Wingham does not seem to have impressed Winchelsey, despite the archbishop's anxiety to oppose the papal provisor, Amadeus de St John.[37] Apart from a general regard for relatives, friends, and dependents, exemplified by intervention in the law courts and in matters of patronage, there are a few particular instances of thoughtful concern for individuals. Laurence of Bagshot, the prince's palfreyman, was to receive a gift of a tun of wine for the forthcoming marriage of his daughter, while Robert de Gayte, a valet of his household, who had been so badly wounded in the hand as to be unfit for service, was sent together with the royal surgeon, Roger Caucin, to the abbot of Chertsey, with instructions that they both be accommodated until the patient recovered. Such consideration is reminiscent of an earlier incident, the payment to Robert Bufford, a fool, on whom the prince played a trick, apparently while swimming.[38] A great many letters concern purveyance, it being difficult to provision so large a household. The Dunstable annalist complained of the denuding of the countryside while the prince's household was at Langley and St Albans. It was said that two hundred courses a day did not suffice for his kitchen. The search for provisions was peremptory and inquisitorial: allegedly scarcely a tally was left for what had been taken.[39] Other letters lay in the diplomatic field, involving the prince's relationship with pope and cardinals, a list of whom was entered for ease of reference, a practice sometimes followed by episcopal registrars.[40]

With his sisters Edward was in reasonably frequent contact. To Mary, the Amesbury nun, he wrote about an arrangement for wine to be sent to her convent, apologizing for his inability to secure a supply of sufficient quality.[41] When, with his father's permission, he was invited to pay her a visit he had to decline because of the incipient parliament of 15 September 1305, the day after the date of his letter.[42] To Elizabeth, countess of Hereford as she became with her second marriage, he wrote to ask that she approach Queen Margaret to intercede with the king on behalf of Gilbert de Clare and Piers (called Perot) Gaveston, whom together with John de Haustede and John de Weston he wished to become members of his household.[43] He also wrote at length on behalf of Maud de Mortimer of Richard's Castle, languishing in prison because her case was delayed by the diversion of justices to other tasks. On one occasion he asked Elizabeth for the services of her greyhound bitch for mating with his own dog, a fine animal. As a return favour, at her request he despatched a letter to Amanieu d'Albret, on behalf of M. James Sinibaldi, archdeacon of Winchester, who was travelling to the papal Curia, perhaps on the business of his newly acquired benefice.[44] Of John of London, the constable of Windsor, he asked that the clerk who had taught his children to sing be lent to the countess for a while so that he might instruct the children of her chapel in that art.[45] When, as we shall see, Edward I quarrelled with his son, depriving him of his income, the prince travelled for a time with the countess.[46] At that period too, Joan, by then married to Ralph Monthermer, was particularly supportive. Not only did she lend her brother certain goods, she also entrusted him with her seal, his own having been rendered of little use.[47] Many of the letters to his sisters, as to others, are commonplace enquiries as to well-being coupled with assurances of his own good health. Apart from a "tertian fever" to which both he and his sister Margaret succumbed shortly before his tenth birthday, he was little afflicted with illness in his youth or early manhood.[48]

Edward's status might give the impression that he enjoyed a degree of autonomy, but although his wardrobe and household were separate, the king determined that they should be dependent upon himself for supply and indeed for personnel. Until 1295 the Lord Edward's officials accounted to the royal wardrobe, an arrangement similar to that for Queen Eleanor and later for Queen Margaret.[49] For the regnal year November 1294-November 1295, the wardrobe officials' Book of Prests provides some limited information about the considerable sums dispersed for the king's son.[50] After that the keeper of his wardrobe, William de Bliburgh, rendered account to the exchequer, which provided the majority of the receipts, though a small amount came from the royal wardrobe and a minimal sum from amercements, gifts and fines. Some have taken this as evidence of a greater degree of independence, but even when Prince of Wales Edward's household, as Tout remarks, "was never self-sufficing";[51] a trifling sum, such as the exhibition of two scholars at Oxford for £4 4s., "is solemnly registered as paid in obedience to his father's order." Indeed, lesser sums than that had been regularly subjected to the scrutiny of the king's wardrobe officials.[52] What is more, the income of the household appears to have contracted rather than expanded.[53] When the prince was at his father's court his expenses were charged to the king, but it has been claimed that this is more a sign of the recognized custom of hospitality than further indication of dependence.[54]

The Lord Edward's curia, or court, was a microcosm of the king's. Its numbers were substantial. An account roll, apparently dating from just prior to his creation as earl of Chester, records liveries (at Christmas 1300?) granted to 140 members including nine *magistri* or tutors. At the apex of the hierarchy are four *domini*, then come six *milites*, knights, ten *pueri in custodia* or wards, fourteen *clerici*, fifty-eight *valleti et servientes*, and thirty-nine *valletti de officio* – those engaged in more servile everyday tasks. To each ward, save for Piers (Perrot) Gaveston, was attached a "tutor" responsible for his general development.[55] The curia can conveniently be glimpsed at the time of the 1304-05 roll of letters, with a supplement provided by a household account roll of 1305-06 and a scattering of other documents. Of the three *domini*, John de St John of Stanton St John in Oxfordshire, and Reginald Grey were members of baronial families, while Guy Ferre can be identified from an account of 1299 as the Lord Edward's tutor, who by 1305 was sole resident survivor of the *domini*, although the prince kept in touch with the other two by letter.[56] From among the *milites* Hugh d'Audley is addressed as "*nostre trescher bacheler*" and "*consanguineus noster*," Robert de Clifford as "*miles illustris*," while "*nostre cher bacheler*" William Inge had already embarked on a distinguished career as a lawyer, that would culminate in his appointment as a royal justice, only to be disgraced in 1341 for taking bribes. In the process he gravitated to the household of Edward's future queen, Isabella, as one of her knights.[57] There were some eight *clerici*, members of the prince's secretariat or wardrobe, many of whom were to have notable careers. William de Boudon, for example, became keeper or treasurer, later controller, of the household of Queen Isabella, as well as a royal wardrobe official and baron of the exchequer.[58] Nicholas de Hugate was destined to be keeper or treasurer of Edward II's wardrobe and likewise a baron of the exchequer.[59] Ingelard de Warley was another future keeper of the king's wardrobe, while Henry of Canterbury was to enjoy an important career in what might be termed the diplomatic service.[60]

The prince's almoner and chaplain, John de Leek or Leche, became archbishop of Dublin in 1311 and two years later was appointed treasurer of Ireland, though it would seem that he did not serve.[61] Two Dominicans, Br John de Lenham and Br John de Warfield were also attached to the household. Lenham was the prince's confessor until his death in 1317–18,[62] while Warfield was to become the first prior of Edward II's foundation at Langley and succeeded his colleague as confessor. The prince's bodily health was cared for by his physician, M. Robert de Cisterne or Sidesterne, who served in the same capacity when Edward became king.[63] Among the superior valets were various kinsfolk, such as Edmund of Cornwall, Gilbert de Clare, and Roderick of Spain, as well as John de Haustede and John de Chandos, members of rising families but with their own careers to make. The valets *de officio* occupied the base of the pyramid, men who performed such tasks as those of cook, baker, tailor, stable hand, watchman, trumpeter, fiddler, messenger, or purveyor. Thanks to his petition of 1330 we know that one "Muster Laurence Dekinham" claimed to have been Edward's barber for twenty-six years and more. His reward was a charter granting him the office of bailiff of the stewardship of the royal forest of Galtres outside York, by which he hoped to support his retirement.[64]

At the head of Prince Edward's household was the steward, in accordance with regular practice a layman of standing. A number of men held the office; at the time of the 1304-05 roll it was Miles de Stapelton, who by 1306 had been replaced by Robert de Haustede or Hallestede, a man who had earlier acted in the same capacity. The two principal officers of the wardrobe were the keeper, Walter Reynolds alias Heyne, who held that office between 1301 and 1307, and the controller, William Melton – future archbishops of Canterbury and York respectively. In the course of his duties Reynolds received a number of letters, copies of which are to be found on the 1304-05 roll.[65] Melton had seen service first as cofferer to Queen Margaret and then for four years as chamberlain or head of the local exchequer in Chester. As controller he was responsible for the supervision of the drafting, sealing and despatching of the letters under

Edward's privy seal and their enrolment – of which we have a unique example.[66] The chancellor, the man who had custody of the great seal, was the veteran William de Bliburgh (Blyborough), a former keeper of Edward's wardrobe. He seems to have journeyed widely in the service of his master and to have acted with William Inge as his attorney.[67]

Like other great men from the king downward, both lay and ecclesiastical, the prince had an advisory council, which probably did not have any precise composition. We can assume, perhaps, that the nucleus was provided by the four officers of the household, steward, keeper, controller, and chancellor, together with such other persons as were found to be necessary for the particular business in hand.[68] Though we cannot know this for certain, the prince must have attended from time to time. We have seen that Guy Ferre, in all probability the elder of that name, is the only person known to have been entitled Edward's "*magister*" or "tutor," an office at one time conferred on Walter Reynolds by the Tudor chronicler Holinshed, whom Stubbs followed. Unfortunately little is to be gleaned about the young heir's training for kingship. The apt theoretical model provided by John of Salisbury's *Policraticus* was apparently little known in England in the original, although John of Wales had made extensive use of it in his *Communiloquium*.[69] The "puer in custodia" may indeed have imbibed more of the romance world of Geoffrey of Monmouth and the chivalric ethos that came to inform the works of Jean le Bel and Jean Froissart – that is, if his father's interests are anything to go by.[70] By that route he could have become acquainted with the *De principis instructione* of Gerald of Wales, but if he did, this has not permeated to us. That he appreciated a good player on the *crwth*, a stringed instrument popular among the Welsh, is attested by the fact that a member of his household, Richard the Rhymer, travelled to Shrewsbury Abbey for instruction and subsequently returned to regale the court with his newly acquired skill.[71]

A PRINCE'S TRAINING: BAPTISM OF FIRE

Edward's literary training is uncertain. The fact that he used French rather than Latin for his coronation oath is no longer regarded as an indication of illiteracy. Latin was the language of learning: there is no evidence that the prince mastered any. It would not now be accepted that Edward, as king, was responsible for the poem attributed to him in Longleat MS 26, written in Anglo-Norman and given in English translation by Fabyan, who implies that the original was in Latin.[72] Only four books are associated with him: a work of romance, a primer, a history of the kings of England, almost certainly by Geoffrey of Monmouth, and an illustrated life of Edward the Confessor in French.[73]

His principal training was practical, going through the motions expected of him as absentee count of Ponthieu, Prince of Wales, heir to the throne, and nominal head of a large household. Although the Michaelmas Parliament of

1297 had met in his presence and he was regularly summoned between 1302 and 1307, we do not know how many such assemblies he attended. Paramount was his training for war undertaken under his father's aegis. His apparent reluctance to engage in tournaments could hardly have been looked on with favour, although the king towards the end of his reign was forced to regard them as a distraction from real warfare against the Scots.[74] As early as 1296, when the prince was twelve, an armed force scheduled to be raised from Londoners for the defence of the south coast, following the sack of Dover, was to obey his orders.[75] The second occasion on which military obligations were required of him was during his father's attempt to form a continental coalition against France. Writs were issued in October 1297 for an army to assemble at Newcastle on 6 December to accompany Edward, the king's son, against the Scots, who under the leadership of William Wallace, Andrew Murray, and William Douglas had achieved numerous successes. It was the prince who on 12 December tested the appointment of John de Warenne, earl of Surrey, as captain of the forthcoming expedition. In the event, like his grandson Edward III in comparable circumstances, the king was forced to conclude a continental truce at Tournai in January 1298, thus freeing his hands for personal conduct of Scottish affairs.[76]

Military operations brought father and son together. It has been calculated that during Edward I's regnal year November 1298-November 1299 they were in each other's company for 292 days. They were again much together in the following regnal year prior to and during the course of the Scottish campaign. Preparations for this included offerings at the shrines of the saints throughout the country and subsequently in Scotland. On 23 February 1300 Edward, in the same manner as his father, made offerings at Canterbury before the image of St Mary in the vault, at the tomb where St Thomas was first buried, at the "corona" of the saint and at the point of the sword (*punctum gladii*) by which the saint suffered martyrdom – seven shillings before each. In addition the king, his queen, and the young Edward were associated in an exceptional oblation of twelve gold florins. Further offerings to local saints punctuate the army's route to the North. Military expenditure was considerable. In round figures the fees and expenses (*vadia*) for bannerets and ordinary knights (*milites simplices*) totalled £3,077, the expenses for crossbowmen and sergeants £157, while the munitioning and provisioning of castles amounted to £17,638 and the replacement of horses and other items to £4,386. Among the bannerets was Arnold de Gaveston (Arnaldus de Gavaston), who received expenses for himself and four squires. There were also some lighter moments in Edward's military life. His chamberlain received money to enable him to indulge in a little gaming (*ad ludendum ad diversos ludos*).[77]

During the 1300 campaign the English advanced towards Galloway, took various prisoners, and laid siege to Caerlaverock Castle. But for the survival of the heraldic roll drawn up on the occasion this five-day siege might scarcely

quet of a magnificence considered not to have been witnessed since the crowning of Arthur at Caerleon. Two swans were brought into the hall upon which those present took their vows. The king's oath was that until he had avenged the wrongs done to God and the Church by Robert Bruce he would not draw his sword again, save in the cause of the Holy Land. As for the prince, he swore that he would not sleep two nights in one place until he had gone to Scotland to help in the performance of his father's vow. The chronicler Trevet confessed himself unable to recall the vows of the other knights. The version in the Westminster *Flores*, duplicated in a Canterbury-based chronicle, states that the king swore to the God of heaven and to the swans that alive or dead he would avenge the death of Comyn and enjoined the prince and others that in the event of his death his body should be regularly carried into battle in Scotland and not buried until God had given victory over the perfidious Bruce and the perjured Scots. Froissart caps the tale by claiming that the dying king made his son swear to boil his corpse so as to separate the flesh from the bones to enable the latter to be carried with the English army into Scotland. In the event, Froissart adds, the oath was disregarded by the prince.[92]

The campaign of 1306 was prefaced by Aymer de Valence's defeat of Bruce at Methven on 19 June.[93] Two fleets were raised, one from the Cinque Ports and other ports west of Dover, the other from the Thames estuary northwards. Prince Edward set forth, so Trevet says, and the identical phrase is in Rishanger, with a great band of tiros (*cum multitudine tironum*). On 13 July he informed Aymer de Valence that the garrison at Lochmaben Castle had surrendered two days previously. By the month's end he was at Forteviot close to Perth, whence he directed a demand for the urgent delivery to him at Blackness of forty tuns of wine and twenty tuns six quarters of flour. Writing again to Valence on 1 August he thanked him for the protection he had given to the abbot and convent of Cupar. By 29 August he was planning to advance beyond the Mounth (the Grampians) and ordered provisions for the army to be sent to Montrose and Aberdeen.[94] Barbour's Bruce claims that, in contrast to Valence, Edward behaved with callous brutality towards the ordinary people:

> And to the King off Inglond sone,
> Thai wrate haly as thai haid done;
> And he was blyth off that tithing,
> And for dispyte bad draw and hing
> All the prisoneris, thocht that war ma.
> But Schyr Amery did nocht sua.[95]

A similar story is in Rishanger's chronicle, though there it is the prince who was rebuked by his father for his behaviour, an idea that sits ill with the king's own well-attested actions in Scotland and his consistent contention that the Scots were not "legitimate" enemies but merely rebels, hence not entitled to the customary courtesies of war.[96] Perhaps John Barbour's condemnation is more realistic than the chivalric paeon of praise pronounced by him on Edward at a later stage.

> The eldest and apperande air
> A yhoung bachiller, stark and fair,
> Schyr Edward callit of Carnarvirnane,
> That wes the starkest man of ane
> That men fynd mycht in ony cuntre;
> Prynce off Walys that tym wes he.[97]

This panegyric was occasioned by the successful outcome of Edward's siege of Kildrummy Castle, which fell in early September with the capture of Robert's brother, Neil Bruce, who was subsequently hanged and beheaded at Berwick. Bruce's modern biographer suggests that a "brief reign of terror followed the rout at Methven and the siege of Kildrummy" and places the responsiblity "wholly with Edward I." Walter Logan and Simon Fraser, who had been with the English forces at Caerlaverock, were captured; the latter was hanged and his body together with the gallows burned in London on the king's orders. Other captives were said by the *Scotichronicon* to have been hanged at Durham in the presence of Edward of Caernarfon, the king's son. Shortly after the taking of Kildrummy the prince was told by his father to send miners and engines to Dunaverty Castle in Kintyre. Before they arrived the place had fallen.[98] These events were catastrophic for Robert Bruce, who found it prudent to leave the mainland and seek refuge in the Western Isles; possibly in Rathlin Island off the coast of Ireland, as John Barbour suggests.[99] But Edward I was afflicted by age and sickness so that, according to the Lanercost chronicler: "In all these doings the king of England was not in Scotland, but his son, with the army."[100]

Prince Edward returned to Langley, revisited Canterbury, and was at Dover in early December, presumably to greet Pedro Rodriguez, cardinal bishop of Santa Sabina, on a mission connected with the Anglo-French marriage negotiations. The cardinal is said to have treated the prince with affection, he being of Spanish descent.[101] Edward reached Northampton Castle in time to spend Christmas with his half-brothers. Meanwhile the king had issued writs for the confiscation of the lands and goods of a number of knights who had deserted the army in order to engage in a tournament. Among them were men who had been closely associated with the prince: Piers Gaveston, John Chandos, and Henry de Leyburn.[102] This may have been mere youthful exuberance but in the king's eyes it constituted irresponsible behaviour.

Parliament convened at Carlisle in January 1307: the prince was certainly nearby at Wetheral in February, although once again he is not known to have attended the sessions. Unusually perhaps, he expended a large sum in preparation for a tournament at Wark, but his father prohibited it, doubtless because of the impending Scottish campaign.[103] Bruce's fortunes revived in the early summer of 1307 when, on 10 May, he defeated Aymer of Valence at Loudon Hill. King Edward's army was to assemble yet again at Carlisle in July. He himself reached Burgh-on-Sands on 6 July, only to die there the following day, the feast of the Translation of St Thomas of Canterbury. His death was kept secret until his son's arrival twelve days later to weep for his father (*ad patrem suum deflendum*). Edward II's regnal years date (for the first time) from the day of his predecessor's death.[104]

A BRIDE FOR THE PRINCE

A regular feature of diplomacy was the dynastic marriage. Clearly the son of the renowned King Edward was an excellent match: his father had toyed with various alliances. The first of these came in 1289 when Br William de Hothum, later archbishop of Dublin, was sent to secure papal dispensation for the marriage of the four-year-old Edward with Margaret of Scotland, the "Maid of Norway," granddaughter of Alexander III of Scotland and daughter of Eric II, king of Norway. The dispensation was granted, but Margaret died at Orkney on her voyage to Scotland. According to the *Scalacronica* it had been agreed between the councillors of the two realms that during his father's lifetime Edward of Caernarfon should live in Scotland; thereafter he was to reside alternate years in Scotland and England, guided by the respective councillors of each – a somewhat impractical proposal that, had it materialized, would have altered the whole tenor of young Edward's life. The marriage settlement, the Treaty of Birgham, was concluded 18 July 1290 and confirmed by King Edward the following month.[105] The next year another arrangement was contemplated, this time with Blanche, the sister of Queen Margaret. Blanche, however, married the duke of Austria.[106] The next proposal, first mooted in 1294, involved Philippa, daughter of Count Guy of Flanders, an element in King Edward's policy of securing continental allies against France. This idea was revived early in 1297. Guy, however, was in no position to undertake an alliance unfavourable to his overlord, Philip of France. In the event the English king would leave him in the lurch.[107]

The successful proposal followed eventually from a draft treaty of 1294 that provided for the marriage of the king and Margaret of France. The immediate outcome of these negotiations was a disastrous conflict, but following Boniface VIII's preliminary arbitration of 30 June 1298, which annulled the Flemish contract, a double marriage was agreed to between the king and Margaret on the one hand, and the young Edward and Isabella, daughter of Philip IV, on the other. Pierre Dubois was advocating marriage alliances as a means of advancing Capetian power and of assimilating territory. Maybe his advice influenced Philip. Certainly there is evidence that the king viewed the duchy of Aquitaine as the inheritance of Isabella's heirs and surrendered it on that account. What he could not have anticipated was the failure of the direct Capetian male line, hence the English claim to the French throne. The arrangement made at Montreuil in June 1299 was confirmed in August by Philip. Margaret's marriage, at which Winchelsey officiated, followed on 10 September at Canterbury, accompanied by a remarkable feast, but perhaps not so remarkable as Rishanger would have us believe, for with only slight modifications he took his description straight out of Geoffrey of Monmouth's imaginative reconstruction of the Pentecostal feast at which King Arthur and his queen wore their crowns.[108]

With the peace of Paris of 20 May 1303 the way was open for the prince's marriage to Isabella. The king's envoys Amadeus, count of Savoy, and Henry Lacy, earl of Lincoln, acted as Edward's proctors for the betrothal, he having agreed on 16 May to abide by their arrangements. The ceremony took place before Isabella herself and her parents, "en le main" of the archbishop of Narbonne.[109] In November 1305 Prince Edward empowered envoys to contract a marriage on his behalf with Isabella *per verba de presenti*, that is, consent in the present rather than the future tense. Isabella did likewise, but it is clear that no marriage ensued since the process had to be recommenced two years later.[110] The couple did not meet, nor were they to do so while Edward's father lived.

In view of the advanced state of these arrangements it is surprising to learn that when Cardinal Pedro arrived at Carlisle in 1307 he is said by an anonymous newsletter to have brought with him an alternative plan for the young Edward's succession to the throne of Ferdinand IV of Castile, should that monarch die without a direct heir. This was not entirely out of the blue, since in 1303 at the time of the French treaty King Edward had written to Henry, senator of Rome, a younger brother of Alfonso X – who had died in 1284 – to thank him for his efforts with respect to a marriage between the Prince of Wales and King Sancho IV's daughter Isabella, sister of Ferdinand IV. Edward's private thoughts on this matter were said to have been delivered *viva voce*. If the newsletter is trustworthy Cardinal Pedro was playing a double game, for officially he had been sent to conclude Pope Boniface's project by arranging the second French marriage. In reply to Pedro's urgings on the latter score, Edward declared his willingness to comply provided that Philip kept his part of the bargain by restoring the whole of Gascony, in particular the impregnable castle of Mauléon.[111]

THE FUTURE KING:
THE SHADOW OF GAVESTON

Historians enjoy the benefit or disadvantage, as they choose to regard it, of hindsight. One question that demands examination without preconceived ideas is the extent to which Edward's childhood and adolescence foreshadow his subsequent conduct as king. Of course, an element in this is his relationship with Piers Gaveston as we shall call him, the son of a Bearnese knight, Arnold de Gaveston or Gavaston, who after being imprisoned as a hostage in France eventually escaped to England in 1296. It could be that his son accompanied him, as stated by the *Polistoire* in a retrospective account of his life,[112] for he first appears in the records in 1297. At that time, during the campaign in Flanders, £4 6s. was paid to "Perrot" de Gaveston; for wages covering the ninety-day period between 14 August and 11 November. In other words, he had sailed with the expedition from England.[113] An anonymous fragment of a chronicle, possibly written a generation later, tells us that "as soon as the king's son saw him he instantly fell so much in love that he forged an indissoluble bond of fraternity with him before all other mortals, which he determined to maintain." This has been interpreted less as a matter of personal infatuation than as a "technical commitment" in the tradition of the biblical David and Jonathan or Roland and Oliver (Olivier) in the *Chanson de Roland*.[114] As we have seen, Piers's name occurs in 1300 among those "pueri in custodia" of the Lord Edward's household. He was, in other words, a ward of the king.[115]

In some respects Gaveston's concerns were manifestly *not* those of the young Edward, for he was addicted to tournaments and the showmanship to which they gave rise, even to the dereliction of his purely military duties.[116] Whatever the two had in common, Gaveston was one of those whom Edward was keen to have in his entourage at a time when his irritated father was curtailing his expenditure.[117] It is conceivable that Gaveston was ordered to leave the country in 1307 because of Prince Edward's too-great dependence upon him, a closeness considered to be injurious. Thus, Hilda Johnstone argued, this was no exile following from some misconduct on Gaveston's part, such as is suggested, for instance, by the *Scalachronica,* which claims that "he was accused before the king of various crimes and vices, because of which he was not worthy to be near the king's son, and for which he was exiled and forsworn."[118] The royal mandate of 25 February 1307 – the king was then at Lanercost, where a room had been prepared for Prince Edward[119] – stipulates "certain reasons" (*acunes resons*) and there was a generous time limit for Gaveston's departure until after the tournament scheduled for the quinzaine (fifteenth day) of Easter, that is 9 April, as well as an allowance of a hundred marks from the revenues of Gascony.[120] This does not bespeak a sense of royal outrage. Hilda Johnstone therefore concluded that the king was forced "to send Peter away, not because he thinks his demerits so great that he is an unsuitable companion, but because he cannot trust the discretion of his own son. Edward, not Peter, was at this stage the prime offender."[121]

A somewhat different view of the affair is given by the Guisborough chronicler. According to him, and he supposedly gives the king's own words, the prince sent the treasurer Walter Langton to Edward with the request that he be allowed to give the county of Ponthieu to Gaveston. Angrily the king summoned his son. "You base-born son of a whore" (*Fili meretricis male generate*), he is supposed incongruously to have shouted, "do you want to give away lands now, you who have never gained any? As the Lord lives, if it were not for fear of breaking up the kingdom, you should never enjoy your inheritance." Then with both hands he proceeded to tear out as much of his son's hair as he could until, exhausted, he threw him out. As for Gaveston, he was made to swear that neither during the king's lifetime nor thereafter (*ipso vivente neque mortuo*) would he accept lands from his son. For his part the prince had to undertake, also on oath, that he would never give him any such lands.[122]

If that is in fact what happened, or something like it – as another chronicler records – it is surprising that the enraged king laid down terms so generous as to argue careful consideration. The prince was permitted to accompany his friend to the coast on a leisurely journey. He was at London on 24 April 1307, travelling from there by way of Badlesmere and Canterbury to Dover, which was reached on 5 May. There he lavished gifts of sindon (fine linen cloth) and silk on his friend who left for the small town of Crécy in Edward's county of Ponthieu, to remain there – at the prince's command – until the king's death, although by the terms of the royal decree he should have been in Gascony.[123] The prince had hoped to join an embassy to Ponthieu to conclude the French marriage negotiations. In the event this expedition, for which preparation was in train during March 1307, was countermanded in June, presumably because the king had no wish to facilitate contact between the two young men, but possibly also because he felt his own end to be approaching.[124]

There is an obvious reason for suspecting the veracity of one aspect of the story retailed by Guisborough, and that is his claim that the prince chose Treasurer Langton as his emissary. True, Langton was influential, but surely Edward had not so readily forgotten the previous occasion when he had incurred paternal wrath on that same minister's account? That was in 1305 when, the London annalist tells us, a quarrel was precipitated by Langton's breaching of his woods (*super fractione bosci sui*), presumably on some hunting expedition.[125] Apparently this gave rise to a verbal outburst on the prince's part, which he himself, in a letter to the earl of Lincoln, described as "certain words relayed to him [the king] as having taken place between himself and the bishop of Chester." The incident was alluded to subsequently in the case of William de Braose, the lord of Gower, who was guilty of much the same offence when reacting to an adverse judgment in the court of the exchequer; the king was said to have removed the prince from his household for almost half a year because of similar disrespect for his ministers.[126]

The prince's response was a submissive one. He shadowed the king at a distance of some ten or twelve leagues until such time as he should be restored to favour, a resolve that appears to have been faithfully carried out.[127] Meanwhile the king had cut off supplies of money and goods from his household and exchequer, so that he was reduced to a variety of expedients. Reynolds, his treasurer, was instructed to find money but not to let the staff of the exchequer know what he was doing. It must have been surreptitiously that the royal almoner, Henry de Blunsden, offered him a hundred marks, while his sister Joan, as we have seen, generously loaned her own seal. Only on 22 July did the king permit letters to be issued relaxing his injunctions to the sheriffs and other ministers. Henceforth the prince would be able to raise loans and to receive supplies.[128]

The apparent infatuation with Gaveston and anxiety to shower gifts upon him do indeed invite comparison with Edward's actions in the early years of his reign. On the whole, however, it is difficult to see the young prince clearly. That for his age he performed adequately in the Scottish campaigns is suggested by the lack of adverse comment; the panegyric may be conventional, but even his enemies had nothing derogatory to report about his nascent military capability. At the same time he clearly disregarded the essential training provided by knightly exercises. What is more, he was knighted somewhat late in life – his father had been dubbed at sixteen. What may be cause for comment is that we learn of no allusion to this by the king. An opposite, or at any rate more sensitive, strain is suggested by the report in the St Edmundsbury chronicle of his visit to that house with his father in 1300. He is supposed to have been made a brother in chapter, being much taken with the place. Insisting on eating the same food as the monks, he is said to have declared that he had never enjoyed anything more than the company of the fraternity.[129]

His inattention to business is suggested by a single letter sent to John de Benstead, the controller of the wardrobe, while the latter was in Ponthieu. Benstead reported that Nicholas de Gayton, one of the prince's clerks there, had complained to him that various business letters had received no response. The reply was that the prince had not received any such letters but that those sent by the seneschal of Ponthieu had been speedily answered. Hence this aspersion must be regarded as unconfirmed. Whether one can attribute the fact entirely to the prince's own decision it would be difficult to say, but it is clear that he took little interest in his own principality and likewise made no attempt to visit what were soon to become his continental possessions.[130] With respect to the latter, his father may be to blame in not providing him with opportunity. Pope Clement V, for example, had invited Edward to send his son to Lyon to witness his coronation as pope, but nothing came of this proposal.[131]

In short, while evidence is lacking for the qualities that might be looked for in a king, it would be reasonable to suggest that few shadows of what was to come appear in those records that do not have the benefit of hindsight. We might here follow the author of the *Vita Edwardi Secundi,* commenting under the year 1313: "What hopes he raised as Prince of Wales! Hopes which evaporated on his becoming king." Unless he was adopting a literary convention, this author clearly regarded subsequent developments as disappointing. If Jeremy Catto is correct in his surmise that the interpretation of Merlin's prophecy likening

Edward II to Alexander of Macedon – who would seize Scotland and all the other lands that Arthur had taken by the sword – should be ascribed to 1312–13, then the London annalist, Andrew Horn, was even slower to appreciate Edward's incapacity.[132]

2

Royal Character:
Prophesy and Retrospection

FATHER AND SON

A standard justification for what most will regard as the disappointing performance of Edward as king is the legacy of his father. This may be regarded in at
least three ways. In the first place, there is Edward I's reputation, that stood so
high that it would have necessitated a man of exceptional capacity to live up to
it. Secondly, the old king's achievements had in fact passed their apogee some
years before his death. His legacy to his son was a complex series of problems.
Lastly, and this follows as a combination of the other two, there was a high level
of expectation from an heir to so renowned a king, even one whose latter years
had been clouded by lack of success at home and abroad.

Edward I, though in most respects a practical man, was intensely interested
in his remote ancestry; more particularly in the legends, regarded as history,
that emanated from the work of Geoffrey of Monmouth. Clearly there was an
intentional demoralizing effect on the native inhabitants of Wales and Scotland.
In Wales his victory was celebrated by a jubilant ceremony derived from legend, the round table (*tabula rotunda*). This was held at Nefyn (Nevin) in the
remotest corner of Snowdonia; a corresponding "triumph" over Scotland was
commemorated in 1302 by another round table at Falkirk.[1] The concept of a
round table, which appears to have developed as something of a spectacle
attended by the ladies but was not necessarily associated with the more serious
business of the tournament, is not to be found in Geoffrey of Monmouth but in
Wace. According to the latter, Arthur established the round table for the settlement of disputes, while the actual making of the round table is described in
Laȝamon's *Brut*.[2]

Far from being carried away by fantasy, the old king made use of it for his
own purposes. Thus, he was careful to appropriate to himself the prophecies
current among the Welsh of a "British" resurgence and to despatch to London the circlet of Llywelyn – "Arthur's crown" – together with the most
sacred of Welsh relics, called in the Welsh tongue the "Croizneth."[3] Edward

I's actions in Scotland had been equally callous; they were those of a conqueror rather than of the overlord he claimed to be. In the sober words of Sir
Maurice Powicke, he did not entertain "exalted ideas about the nature of
Scottish kingship." Sir Thomas Gray reports that in 1306, when entrusting
the seal of Scotland to Sir John de Warenne, he uttered the words, presumably in jest: "A man does good business when he rids himself of a turd."[4] The
Stone of Scone was removed in 1296 to Westminster Abbey; the crown and
other Scottish regalia, together with the Black Rood of St Margaret, containing another portion of the True Cross, were likewise lodged there as gifts to
the Confessor.[5] Seven hundred years were to pass before the Stone was officially returned to Scotland.

PROPHECY IN RETROSPECT

In view of all this it is small wonder that writers turned to traditional prophecy for an outline of Prince Edward's expected accomplishments, or more
accurately, for a retrospective view of them. As it turns out, the element of
true prophecy is as rare in Edward's II's case as in most others. In his presidential address to the Royal Historical Society Sir Richard Southern demonstrated the importance of prophecy to the medieval world and beyond.
"Prophecy," he claimed, "filled the world-picture, past, present and future,
and it was the chief inspiration of all historical thinking."[6] Its interpretation
was a highly scientific matter, to which many men of intellect applied themselves. It also provided an excellent vehicle for propaganda and encouragement to its fulfilment. An appreciable proportion of late medieval English
chronicles incorporated such prophecies, usually derived from Geoffrey of
Monmouth's seventh book. They are given an important place in the *Brut*
chronicle.[7] In the case of the *Brut*, however, the prophecy of Merlin in
response to King Arthur, usually known as *The Six Last Kings*,[8] is not directly derived from Geoffrey's *Historia Regum*, for there were other prophetic
strands. Geoffrey himself was responsible for a *Libellus Merlini*, which has
not survived but is known mainly from extracts in Ordericus Vitalis, as also
for a *Vita Merlini*. Not long after his death appeared a poem entitled *The
Prophecy of Ambrosius Merlin concerning the Seven Kings*, allegedly derived
from a Welsh original, its translation into Latin being attributed to John of
Cornwall.[9] The later *Prophecy of the Six Kings to Follow King John* occurs
in English, Anglo-Norman, Welsh and Latin, and it is this particular prophecy that is incorporated in the *Brut*.[10]

The English *Brut* version of *The Six Last Kings*, in common with the others, adopts Geoffrey of Monmouth's animal imagery: the lamb represents
Henry III, the dragon Edward I, the goat Edward II, the bear his son Edward
III, while Richard II and Henry IV are symbolized respectively by the lamb
with feet of lead (elsewhere the ass) and the mole.[11] Prophecies of this kind

with their deliberate, indeed necessary occultations attracted a multitude of commentaries.[12] The author of that incorporated in the English *Brut* has no difficulty in identifying the characters of Edward's reign, particularly the earlier part. It has been cogently argued that a portion of the "prophecy" dates from 1312 – about the time of Edward of Windsor's birth, if mention of this be discountenanced as prophecy – while a revised version can be assigned to the 1330s.[13]

In this prophecy the "gote out of car" is patently Edward of Caernarfon, with "horses of silver and a berde as white as snowe" – for alas! – so runs the refrain, "Merlin speaks truth." In his time, the interpretation continues, there was great hunger among the poor and death among the rich. He lost Scotland and Gascony; there was much lechery while he was king. Also, Merlin said, this "goat" would seek out the "fleur de lys" – punningly Isabella of France. In his time, too, there would be "bridges of folk upon ditches of the sea," as was evident at Bannockburn. The stones would fall from castles and towns would be wiped out (made playn) – demonstrated by the Scots' southward march, besieging castles and burning towns. Afterwards, said Merlin, an eagle would come out of Cornwall with feathers of gold and pride without peer, who would despise lords of blood and die through a bear at "Gaversiche." This eagle is readily identifiable, from his own arms if nothing else, as Piers Gaveston, who was beheaded by connivance of the earls of Lancaster and Warwick at a place similarly named by the chroniclers. In Edward's time, Merlin prophesied, "the bear would burn and a battle be fought on an arm of the sea in a field like a shield, where many white heads should die." This, the commentator claims, refers to the battle of Myton-on-the-Swale in Yorkshire, where so many men of religion were killed that the Scots dubbed it the "white bataile." Thereafter, the bear – Thomas of Lancaster – would do the goat much harm and cause him to lose much of his land, but then, overcome by shame, the latter should don the lion's skin and recover what he had lost through a people coming out of the Northwest. And so, Edward would be able to take his revenge by the counsel of the owls, the Despensers, who had previously suffered exile. Goat and owls then come to Burton-on-Trent whence the bear "fled over the sea" together with a swine, Humphrey de Bohun (his crest was a boar). The bear subsequently would be slain at Boroughbridge, so too the swine by "an unkynde outputer" – Sir Andrew Harclay in company with the sheriff of York. The term "out-putter" is an interesting one, occurring as it does in indictments of offenders on the northern border, where it refers to those engaged in criminal offences in conjunction with the Scots. Harclay, of course, was himself to be accused of such practices.[14]

Other prophesies of Merlin were fulfilled in a similar manner. The owls would do much harm to the *fleur de lys*, reducing her "wages" to twenty shillings a day and making her travel to France to arrange peace with her brother. There follows much "straight history" because of the lack of prophetic text for interpretation. Finally, says Merlin, the "goat" would be "put into great disease" and would lead his life in much sorrow. There is, however, no mention of Edward's death in the prophecy itself.[15] In this manner Merlin's "prophecy" could be shown convincingly to have been fulfilled by the events of Edward's reign.

THE BRIDLINGTON PROPHECY

Another example of the genre is the so-called "Bridlington prophecy" which, like that interpreted by the *Brut* commentator, purports to be of ancient origin. In fact it too was written in the knowledge of the events of Edward II's reign also, to a large extent, of those of his son.[16] The truly prophetic portion is confined to the last eight of the twenty-nine chapters, which envisage the capture of Paris in 1405 by the English *gallus* (cock), the Black Prince, who would have been seventy-five years of age at that time – some ten years older than his long-senescent father at his demise in 1377.[17] Details of the discussion about authorship need not detain us here, but the earliest copies of the prophecy are anonymous. Its association with Bridlington and with John Thwenge (ob. 1379), the saintly prior of the Augustinian house there, or with the fourth twelfth-century prior, Robert of Bridlington "the scribe,"[18] are said to derive from fifteenth-century traditions, although the author of the commentary, presumably to divert suspicion from himself, suggests that it was popularly believed to have been the work of a canon regular.[19] It could even be that the compiler of the composite work of prophecy and commentary was responsible for both and that he first circulated the former and then released his commentary upon it. This idea commended itself to, among others, Thomas Wright and M.R. James. There is nothing improbable in the suggestion and much to recommend it. The most serious argument to the contrary is that other lines apparently pertaining to the prophecy are to be found elsewhere, although those incorporated in the Bridlington chronicle at the close of Edward II's reign were almost certainly added subsequently.[20]

The author of the commentary, John Ergome or Erghome, reveals his identity in a cryptogram resolved by M.R. James, although authorship was being ascribed to Ergome for this or other reasons in and before the sixteenth century.[21] He was an Augustinian friar and doctor of theology, who dedicated his work to Humphrey de Bohun, the earl of Hereford who died in 1373. It must therefore have been written shortly after Humphrey succeeded to the title – he had livery in 1363.[22] The work has been described by a modern writer as "a dense carapace of obscure verbal and meteorological symbolism." Such obfuscations Ergome proceeds to unravel for the benefit of his readers, his commentary subordinated to a sophisticated process of division and subdivision, one akin to that used in the composition of academic sermons.[23] The second chapter of the prophecy, a mere sixteen lines, is devoted to Edward II's reign. Edward is "*rex insensatus*," lacking knowledge and wisdom (*scientia et sapientia naturalis*), as Ranulf Higden demonstrates in his *Polychronicon.* Moreover, he was defeated in every war in which he engaged (*devictus in omni bello quod temptabat*), his rout at Bannockburn (not so named) having led to the subjection by the Scots of the whole of the North. "Nobilis est natus" – nobly born – he glosses as a contradiction of those who believe Edward to have been the son of a groom or swineherd (*auriga*) substituted when, owing to the negligence of his nurse, he had been savaged by a sow.[24] That he was "*infatuatus*" follows from Edward's unreasonable love for Gaveston, and here again the author relies on the *Polychronicon* to the effect that he brought opprobium to the lover, denigration to the loved one, scandal to the people, and damage to the realm (*amanti opprobrium, amasio obloquium, plebi scandalum, et regno detrimentum*).[25] His subsequent adhesion to the Despensers precipitated a confederation of the nobles and the ensuing civil war with Mortimer and the earl of Lancaster. The earl, he states, was decapitated by the Despensers' counsel and the principal men (*optimati*) of the realm were hanged and drawn.

Ergome drew three notable points from all this. In the first place, evil follows from a king who is "*fatuus et insipiens*": those speaking out for the law of the realm are killed, magnates and the wise are lost, and those who are as simple-minded as the king himself (*insipientes*) find favour. Secondly, a wise and discreet person (*sapiens et discretus*) should be the leader in war and not a foolish one under whom the people are conquered. The third noteworthy thing is that under a foolish king no one can be secure in life or wealth. Ergome goes on to suggest that a possible interpretation is that God punished the king for his misdeeds. He suffered much opprobrium during life and was then miserably killed. But Ergome posits an alternative explanation: God, following the king's contrition for his sins, crowns him in heaven. This is an interesting perspective that could indicate an awareness of the cult that developed around the dead king. At that point the expositor turns to Edward III, his birth, succession during his father's lifetime, and the death of the latter.[26] Such value as this exposition has for our purposes must be related to the perspective of the reign from the 1360s, a time when Edward III "*taurus*" was in decline and a group surrounding the Black Prince looked to him for national regeneration and a vigorous prosecution of the war against France.

ADAM DAVY'S FIVE DREAMS

Of quite another stamp is "Adam Davy's Five Dreams about Edward II."[27] This is a prophecy in dream form, bereft of the animal imagery associated with Merlin. The author identifies himself as Adam Davy, marshal of Stratford-atte-Bow, but so far he has not been satisfactorily identified despite his boast of being well known. From the information he gives the five dreams can be dated between 29

August 1307 and either 5 or 12 September 1308.[28] This precision, however, may be no more than a device to give verisimilitude to what he has to say. The actual composition could have taken place at some other time.

In the first dream Edward, armed with iron and steel, wearing a crown of gold that "became him well," stands before the shrine of Edward the Confessor. On either side is an armed knight and both proceed to smite him with their swords. He returns no stroke, yet remains unscathed. When the knights depart four streams of coloured light are emitted from his ears and spread, insofar as Davy can tell, "far and wide in the country." The second dream is prefaced by a prayer that the knight named, that is Edward, would become emperor of Christendom. In this dream Davy saw him riding on an ass as a pilgrim with a grey mantle and a cap of the same colour on his head but without hose or shoes. Yet the fact that his legs appear blood-red understandably fills the dreamer's heart with dread.

In the third of his dreams Davy finds himself in Rome with the pope and king "both of whom had a new dubbing."[29] Once again they wear grey caps but Davy can see nothing of their clothes, though the pope appears mitred, as one would expect, and the king crowned, betokening that he would be emperor of Christendom. Davy prays that the king will overcome his enemies and all wicked Saracens. On "worthing night"[30] he dreamt for the fourth time, appropriately about the Virgin Mary in whose chapel he supposedly finds himself. Christ unnailed his hands from the cross and asked his mother's permission to accompany Edward on pilgrimage, that is a crusade. This she gave since, she said, the worthy knight had served her both day and night. The dream closes with a prayer that God be with the king. In between this dream and the fifth and last a voice instructed Davy to tell the king what he had dreamt. In this last dream he thought that an angel took Edward by the hand and that the king stood before the high altar at Canterbury clothed all in red. Davy asks God – He who was on the cross on a Good Friday – to turn his dream to good. An angel bids him reveal his dream to the king; this he allegedly does. Were the predictions not to ensue, wrote Davy, he would be put in prison.[31]

It would be difficult or impossible to establish the precise purpose of the "Five Dreams." A number of associations are of interest, for instance those of the king with the shrine of St Edward at Westminster as well as with Canterbury, hence St Thomas Becket, although the latter is not actually named. Edward was to show much interest in St Thomas[32] and to seek reanointing with the oil supposedly given to the archbishop by the Virgin. The crusade was a live issue in the earlier fourteenth century, but although Edward paid it lip-service, and as we shall see took a crusading oath, he made no practical response to the challenge, for which in any case he was quite unsuited.[33] Certain particulars suggest ideas current after the king's death, for instance the wandering to Rome in the guise of a pilgrim and the possibility that the emphasis on the colour red is indicative of martyrdom. That Davy is not entirely original is suggested by similarities between aspects of his dreams and the story of the "Last King of Rome," in which it was envisaged that a king would undertake a pilgrimage to Jerusalem to defeat Antichrist and to preserve Christian rule.[34] One possible interpretation of Davy's dreams is that they constitute part of a conventional panegyric intended to welcome a new sovereign; a panegyric that looked forward to great deeds but without much sense of realism. The prophecy in Horn's London annals has a similar purpose. Another, dated as late as 1320, unrealistically envisages Edward making his son king of Scotland and he himself the emperor of France, Spain, Africa, Persia, Babylon, and the Holy Land, not to mention emperor of Constantinople and overlord of the world.[35]

Such wild exaggeration may be taken now, as doubtless it was then, with a large pinch of salt. The idea that Davy was attempting to persuade Edward II to a certain course of action by bringing favourable prophecies to his notice places too serious and precise an interpretation upon his verses – even supposing that they were truly prophetic.[36] We have already seen that by 1313 the anonymous author of the *Vita* was bemoaning Edward's lack of achievement. Side by side with this must be placed the enormous reputation that his father had built up. This is best seen, perhaps, in the *Commendatio Lamentabilis in Transitu Magni Regis Edwardi.*[37] Unfortunately the writer, like Charlemagne's biographer Einhard, was not content to use his own resources but instead adopted the model provided by Peter of Blois' description of Henry II.[38] Ostensibly the panegyric is the product of the pen of John of London, though in view of so common a name his identity is difficult to establish.[39]

THE GREAT KING EDWARD

The author of the *Commendatio,* whoever he may have been, begins with a sketch of Edward I's physical characteristics, parallel to those of Henry II. He is portrayed as a man of wisdom, faithful in friendship but implacable as an enemy, who disdained the purple and other attributes of kingship. Of excellent health, he brought a keen mind to council. He was a lover of the chase, careful in good times, constant in adverse ones. The panegyrist then proceeds to put individual lamentations into the mouths of pope, kings, the queen dowager Margaret, the bishops, the earls and barons, the knights, clergy and laity.

To the pope Edward appeared insuperable in war and glorious in peace, a great loss to the cause of the crusade. The kings regarded Edward as champion of the Church and a paragon of knighthood (*pugil ecclesiae et splendor militiae*), a lover of justice, a hater of iniquity, the captain of the whole Christian army. He had enjoyed successes in Wales and Scotland and by God's favourable disposition had received an ampler patrimony with the earldoms of Cornwall and Norfolk.[40] Naturally the widowed queen's grief is more personal, but she is also envisaged as emphasizing peace and, one supposes, the means by which such was achieved – parliaments and treaties. Surprisingly no place among the mourners is allotted to Prince Edward.

In the circumstances the bishops are made to forget the great struggles over taxation and royal encroachment on their "liberties," not to mention the wholesale confiscation of their temporalities as a coercive measure; instead they stress Edward's restoration of vacant bishoprics and abbeys. Saul defeated his thousand, David his ten thousand, but Edward his hundred thousand – Saracens, French, Scots, Welsh, and false Christians. In their turn the earls and barons are made to laud his defence of ecclesiastical liberties and his generosity in alms (which can certainly be amply substantiated), his peace, and his construction of castles and other fortifications. He had been a "*vir bellator*," both in joust and tournament, a Solomon in justice. The knights in their turn launch into an eulogy in which history is mingled with legend, for Edward had allegedly fared better than Brutus or Arthur, than Edgar, Richard I, or even Alexander. The clergy praised the tranquillity he had given to the Church and claimed his superiority to Saul. Lastly, the laity declared their salvation from every kind of peril and shipwreck. Their king had been devoted to the saints and notably to Edward the Confessor. There had been peace in the land, all had been able to pursue their own lives with safety and the people had not suffered calamity, pestilence or famine. The aged king was compared favourably with St Martin, who had frequently prayed that while the people needed him he would not refuse to undertake labour on their behalf.

Expectedly the panegyrist overlooks the king's shortcomings, claiming that in his personality, warlike capacity, and as a fosterer of the arts of peace, Edward was without peer in history – in short, an extremely hard act to follow. Yet in reality the apogee of Edward's success had passed some years previously. In his estimate of the inheritance of Edward of Caernarfon, Tout points out, as might be expected, that part of such legacy was "an admirable system of organization and administration."[41] But with it came the policy of his father that had strained the kingdom's resources to the utmost and precipitated a national crisis and widespread opposition. Wales indeed had been successfully conquered, and that country at least – as Higden thought – was not to trouble Edward II unduly. In the person of Sir Gruffydd Llwyd it was in fact to bring him support at a critical juncture, though not in his "final hour." Scotland was a different matter. There Robert Bruce was gaining support and would in time defeat a superior English army and even gain recognition of his sovereignty. Had Edward lived his only hope would have been to treat Bruce in the same manner as he had treated Wallace. The king's policies in Flanders and Gascony, and his close relationship to the French royal house which was destined shortly to peter out in the male line, were to produce elements of conflict that not only adversely affected his son's reign but largely determined the thrust of policy in the early years of that of his grandson.[42]

THE GHOST OF BECKET

There is a further prophecy to be considered, one involving Thomas Becket, a saint for whom Edward II showed much reverence, yet someone who was regularly invoked by archbishops of Canterbury when in conflict with kings. We know of this prophecy initially through a letter of Pope John XXII directed to the king, which since it mentions the presentation of credentials at the Curia in Avignon by Adam Orleton along with other ambassadors, may reasonably be ascribed to 1319 rather than 1318, the year adopted by its editor, Wickham Legg.[43] The ambassadors also delivered letters from Bishops Hothum of Ely, Salmon of Norwich, and Martival of Salisbury, which contained replies made by a Dominican friar, Nicholas, a papal penitentiary, to questions that had been put to him on a secret matter. This man, who has been reliably identified as Nicholas of Wisbech,[44] had previously visited Avignon bearing a secret proposal to the pope. The bulk of the letter is devoted to the story confided by Friar Nicholas to the pope and repeated, together with the friar's responses, so that the king would be fully aware of what had been said. This was to the effect that the Virgin Mary had appeared to St Thomas during his exile in France and told him how he would die for the Church and that the fifth king after his time would be a good man and the Church's champion, who would recover the Holy Land. For the benefit of this king and his successors she had handed over an ampulla of holy oil (*vir benignus, et ecclesie Dei pugil, pro quo suis successoribus iniungendis tradidit dicto sancto ampullam unam cum sacratissima unctione*). At the Virgin's command Thomas gave the oil to a monk of St Cyprian's monastery together with a plate of metal on which the future martyr had caused these things to be written. The monk hid them in the church of St George at Poitiers under a heavy stone. It was a copy of the information on the plate that Friar Nicholas claimed to have in his hand.

One final element in the story (the result of a conflation of legends?) is that the oil had been divinely revealed to Pope Leo, together with two gold plates, hidden at Aachen, on which the saint had written about the oil. With this oil, the friar claimed, Charlemagne had been secretly anointed by Archbishop Turpin, whose uncanonical military prowess is recorded in the *Chanson de Roland.* An attempt by a heathen soldier to secure the ampulla having failed owing to his death, it had come into the possession of the king of Germany and eventually reached Brabant. The duke of Brabant is said to have brought it to the coronation of Edward II, where the royal councillors had declined to use it in preference to the customary oil. The countess of Luxemburg, later empress, while staying with John II, duke of Brabant, and his wife Margaret, Edward II's sister,[45] had looked for a miracle from the oil and had been rewarded by being cured of a dangerous wound. As for Edward II, he purported to believe that misfortune had befallen him because of the omission of the proffered unction but that success might follow from his reanointing. He therefore asked the pope whether it would be in order for him to be anointed with the holy oil and requested him to depute someone to perform this office.

In his circumspect reply Pope John allowed that if the king truly believed the story of the Virgin Mary it would be neither sinful nor superstitious for him to be anointed with the oil. Such anointing would not detract from the initial unction, since unction did not impress anything on the soul.[46] Neither anointing nor anything else could profit Edward unless he were well disposed towards God. He was pointedly exhorted to live a virtuous life, to cultivate justice, and to preserve the liberties of the Roman church and of all the churches in his realm. On the question whether Edward ought to pursue the proposed course the pope hedged, but he declined to appoint a cardinal or other prelate to perform the function; that, in his view, should be done secretly so as to avoid scandal. Such a course would not have served Edward's purpose.

The career of Br Nicholas de Wisbech has been traced. In 1299 he visited the English court from Brabant and in February 1317 was present at a council held in the royal manor of Clarendon – together, it may be added, with the rising clerk, John de Stratford.[47] Aymer de Valence had just gone to Avignon in an attempt to persuade the pope to absolve Edward II from his oath to observe the baronial Ordinances. The friar himself departed for the Curia and in January 1318 was under instructions to visit both Avignon and Brabant, presumably in connection with the matter of the holy oil. His appointment as a papal penitentiary followed together with licence to nominate Cambridge University clerks to vacant benefices.[48] This marked the pinnacle of his achievement. Quite how the bishops of Ely, Norwich, and Salisbury came to constitute a commission of enquiry is unclear, but it is probable that both Archbishop Reynolds and the king himself were somehow involved, and conceivably the pope as well, for the matter had religious as well as secular implications. Bishop Orleton's diplomatic mission to France and Avignon, where he appears to have arrived in May 1319, certainly had other and arguably more crucial business to transact than Friar Nicholas's, though the latter's quest was far from incidental.[49]

What is clear is that Edward's hopes of a helpful outcome were dashed: there was to be no dramatic bolstering of his position by a solemn ceremony under papal aegis. In consequence the friar was disgraced, the king in April 1320 requesting that he be dismissed from his office of penitentiary as unworthy.[50] It looks very much as though Nicholas had concocted the story himself, taking advantage of the tradition of Becket's miracles and the *Prophecy of the Six Kings*. What is more, it fits in with other fabulous stories for which the friars were at least in part responsible, not least that concerned with Edward's survival after 1327. That Edward should countenance such a scheme is perhaps indicative of the man's character, he was only too anxious to clutch at a straw to save himself from the difficulties facing him in 1318 and 1319, the time of the Treaty of Leake, which was to impose a measure of restraint on his position as king. There is another facet to the story. As Marc Bloch suggested, there may have been a conscious but unsuccessful effort to emulate the French legend of the Sainte Ampoule, the oil of Clovis.[51] Nicholas's opportunist intervention, as one suspects it may have been, even if grafted on to earlier legends, was to have a revival in the time of Henry V, together with other prophecies that could be shown to have political import and hence propaganda value.[52]

That St Thomas and prophecy were very much in people's minds at the time is also suggested by a sermon preached a few years earlier in commemoration of the martyred archbishop by M. Henry de Harclay, chancellor of Oxford University and close relative of Sir Andrew Harclay.[53] During the course of his exposition Harclay quoted approvingly Joachim de Fiore's likening of the death of Becket to that of Zacharias the son of Barachias.[54] Although he forbore to linger on an interpretation of Joachim's prophecy, he did discourse at length on the retribution that according to Exodus 20: 5, would be visited on the third and fourth generation of those who hated God (*eorum qui oderunt me*). This, of course, recalls the prophecy of the kings. Harclay, for his part, claimed that retribution would follow only if the child hated God as his father had done. King John provided a case in point, for he had received punishment. Bringing this nearer home, Harclay suggested that now was the fourth generation from Henry II. The fifth person, though not named, can only be Edward II. But present retribution was not inevitable. As he tells us, in suggesting that punishment might be exacted in his own day, Harclay hoped that fear would be aroused, the right path followed, and sin rejected.[55] The preacher, then, was not prophesying inescapable evil for Edward II, but advocating the love of God whereby catastrophe might be averted. He might subsequently have argued that Edward failed to heed his warnings and so suffered the appropriate punishment, thus fulfilling the prophecy.

THE NEW KING'S CHARACTER: THE CHRONICLERS' ASSESSMENT

William Stubbs regarded Edward II as "not without some share of the chivalrous qualities that are impersonated in his son [Edward III]." He allowed him the "instinctive courage" of his line, though he was "neither an accomplished knight nor a great commander." Yet, he continued:

He has no high aims, no policy beyond the cunning of unscrupulous selfishness. He has no kingly pride or sense of duty, no industry or shame or piety. He is the first king since the Conquest who was not a man of business, well acquainted with the routine of government; he makes amusement the employment of his life; vulgar pomp, heartless extravagance, lavish improvidence, selfish indolence make him a fit centre of an intriguing court. He does no good to anyone: he bestows his favours in such a way as

to bring his favourites to destruction, and sows enmities broadcast by insult or impru-
dent neglect.[56]

Stubbs, of course, was imbued with a concept of the organic evolution of the
constitution and the role that he felt was played in it by "good" kings. The idea
of the good king was also conjured with in the fourteenth century. Edward's
name could have resounded through all the land, wrote the clerk who, it has
been hypothesized, was a somewhat elderly author of the *Vita Edwardi Secundi*. If only he had given himself to the practice of arms rather than to rustic pursuits he might have surpassed Richard I and the name of England would have
resounded throughout the earth.[57]

     The reality of Edward's behaviour was far different from anything that might
reasonably have been envisaged. A contemporary Benedictine monk from
St Werburgh's Chester, Ranulf Higden, provides the most thoroughgoing
characterization, echoes of which are discernible in a number of other chronicles. It is given here in a slightly modernized version of John Trevisa's
translation.[58]

This Edward was fair of body and great of strength, and unsteadfast of manners and of
habits, if men should believe the common tale. For he forsook the company of lords and
drew himself to harlots, to singers and to jesters, to carters and to delvers and ditchers,
to rowers, shipmen and boatmen, and to other craftsmen, and gave himself to great
drinking; he would lightly tell out privy counsel, and smite men that were about him for
but little trespass, and did more by other men's counsel than his own. He was too large
of gifts and solemnity [splendour] in making of feasts, ready to speak and variant of
deeds, unhappy against his enemies and cruel to his own household (meyne), and loved
strongly one of his familiars (queresters) and did him great reverence and worshipped
him and made him great and rich. Of this doing fell villany to the lover, evil speech and
backbiting to the love, slander to the people, harm and damage to the realm. He
advanced to states of holy church them that were unable and unworthy, that was after-
ward a stake in his eye and a spear in his side ... But in one point for this king it happened well, that Wales was never rebel against him. In other sides he misshaped himself
always. In his beginning he loved Piers of Gaveston ... because of him he was reckless
of Isabelle the queen and recked nought of the lords of the land, therefore the lords had
indignation and put out this Piers over the sea into Ireland.

Few of the other chroniclers have much good to say of Edward, although Geoffrey le Baker's *Chronicon* and its derivative, the so-called *Vita et Mors,* are
uncritical and for the king's final moments take a sympathetic view of a forlorn
Christlike figure, God's servant, whose principal grief was to be deprived of his
wife, whom he could not but love, and of the solace of his son and heir, as well
as of his other children.[59]

     The Rochester chronicler, almost certainly identifiable as William Dene, the archdeacon of Rochester, is equally uncritical of the king and even of the younger Despenser. There is a degree of pathos in his account of the last meeting between his diocesan, Hamo de Hethe, and these two men.[60] All the same, neither chronicler can bring himself to praise Edward as king. The propaganda element seems to be lacking in Dene's chronicle; indeed it is not easy to assign reasons for its composition. Perhaps the most likely suggestion is that Dene's motivation arose from a personal interest in his patron, the long-lived Bishop Hethe, and the diocese of Rochester, with which the archdeacon's day-to-day life was intimately bound up.

The most hostile chronicler is the so-called Westminster monk, Robert of Reading, who was possibly responsible for the continuation of the *Flores Historiarum* from somewhat before 1307 until February 1326, when the end of Robert's life and of his section of the chronicle is recorded in another hand.[61] His "unremitting virulence" coupled with the claim that internal evidence suggests that Robert "wrote soon after the deposition," has given rise to the hypothesis that his work, like Baker's, constitutes a piece of political propaganda written after 1326 or 1327, only this time in justification of Queen Isabella and Roger Mortimer.[62] The paramount objection to this idea is that the earliest manuscript, Chetham 6712, albeit of the latter part of the fourteenth century, declares that Robert's contribution to the chronicle came to an end with his death in 1326. To this may be added the observation that the chronicle betrays no awareness of the king's tragic end.[63]

The counter-argument that the date of Robert's death did not necessarily coincide with the end of the chronicle, since he could have left drafts for the concluding section, by itself fails to carry conviction. Even so, there is no necessity to discard the notion that it was composed after Edward II's reign, since the manuscript attribution is suspect on other grounds. Whoever appended the note of authorship must have done so in the later fourteenth century – after Murimuth's death in 1347. Secondly, only one Robert de Reading is traceable as a monk of Westminster at the appropriate time and he undeniably died in 1317.[64] Thirdly, the accompanying statement that Adam Murimuth was responsible for the chronicle between 1312–13 (6 Edward II) and 1346 is demonstrably inaccurate. Instead, it has been shown by Professor Tait that it was the Westminster continuator who made use of Murimuth's work until 1338, when he abandoned it in favour of the more concise Avesbury.[65]

On the broader topic of the chronicle's propaganda intention, certain biases correlative to the antagonism to Edward II are abundantly clear. Thus, although the author can be critical of papal policy and appointments, such as the provision of the under age Henry Burghersh to the bishopric of Lincoln, of the royal clerk Walter de Maidstone to Worcester, or of Rigaud d'Assier to Winchester, he nonetheless applauds papal action with respect to Adam Orleton's advancement to Hereford in defiance of the king. Indeed, he treats of that controversial bishop in the same exalted terms as he does the renowned Thomas de Cobham.[66] The most damaging critique of an appointment comes with the pope's alleged simoniacal dealings at the time of Reynolds's promotion to Canterbury in place of the duly elected Cobham. Reynolds, of course, was one of Edward's long-standing associates. As for Winchester, it was only to be expected that the chronicler would decry the supplanting of a fellow Benedictine, Adam of Winchester, by the papal nominee Rigaud d'Assier.[67]

To square with the notion of a propaganda document written after 1326–27, praise of Orleton would suggest composition at an early stage of the Isabella and Mortimer regime, since the bishop soon became *persona non grata*.[68] What is more, the hypothesis does not take account of the chronicler's obvious antipathy to the queen's compatriot Louis de Beaumont, the bishop of Durham, who was allegedly lame (a canonical objection?) and falsely commended to the pope but without doubt warmly championed by Isabella. Further, the provision of John Stratford to Winchester in the teeth of Edward's denunciation of the envoy is not mentioned, an odd omission in view of his subsequent nomination by Isabella as treasurer and the chronicler's bias with respect to other promotions. Here again though, Stratford, like Orleton, was soon to fall out of favour with the new government.[69]

On the whole, if Reading's chronicle is to be regarded as propaganda, it seems more likely to have been propaganda in favour of the Lancastrians than of Isabella and Mortimer, though even in that case some inconsistencies would be observable, such as an uncritical attitude towards Bartholomew Badlesmere, a prominent Kentish baron. "Reading" regards Badlesmere as a victim of Edward II's irritation rather than Lancaster's – the king's blackest hate (*odium nigerrimum*) – on account of the baron's withdrawal (dismissal?) from the office of steward of the household, an appointment claimed by Lancaster as hereditary steward of England.[70]

The *Flores* is demonstrably strongly pro-baronial and in particular eulogizes Thomas of Lancaster, decrying those who deserted or fought against him, such as Adam Banaster and Andrew Harclay, the victor of Boroughbridge.[71] Not surprisingly, therefore, the author is critical of Pembroke who, in his view, met his deserts by being overtaken by so sudden a death as to be deprived of the Church's last rites.[72] Robert Baldock, twice compared to Alchimus, one of the impious men of Israel who wished to be made a priest (1 Maccabees 7: 5), together with the Despensers, stand out as the principal malefactors. This is certainly in line with the widespread feeling at the time of Isabella's invasion in 1326.[73] The Dominican friars, Edward's favourite Order, constitute another "hate" and the detailed charges levied against them are particular to "Reading."[74]

An alternative hypothesis is that the chronicler's attitude was determined by Edward's "sacrilege" in retaining an area within the Westminster Abbey precincts called "Burgoyne" – disregarding the ancient name – and also the important London manor of Eye, as well as by his policy of decentralization. This last entailed holding parliaments away from Westminster, moving the exchequer to York, dividing it, and promoting a similar migration of the justices of King's Bench.[75] Although monastic assessments of individuals can often be shown to bear a direct relationship to patronage, this too seems to be a less than adequate explanation of the chronicler's venom. On that basis the historical Reading should have been extremely censorious of Edward I by reason of the gruelling enquiry of 1303 into the robbery of royal jewels that led to his imprisonment. The view of "Robert of Reading" is that Edward II's sloth brought disgrace rather than fame; he was forgetful of his promises, harassed the prelates of the church, was stupid and tyrannous, conspicuously avaricious, and exhibited cowardice during the Scottish campaign of 1322, barely escaping from an ambush at Byland on his return.[76] Whatever the motives behind the rhetoric of this chronicler his virulence undermines the credibility of his observations with respect to Edward's character.

That chroniclers' predispositions have corrupted their judgments of royal conduct is suggested by the contrasting accounts of Edward's behaviour at Bannockburn. The Lanercost chronicler, for whom, in common with the author of the *Vita*, Edward appears a Rehoboam to his father's Solomon, claims that together with Despenser and Henry de Beaumont he acquired everlasting shame by fleeing from the field of battle to Dunbar and then embarking on a skiff for Berwick, leaving the remnant of his army to its fate. The Peniarth version of the Welsh *Brut*, by no means sympathetic to the king, likewise alleges that he "fled disgracefully from the battle."[77] This could owe as much to prejudice as to some report of an eyewitness from the numerous Welsh contingents present at the engagement. By contrast, Barbour's *Bruce* declares that when the field was lost Aymer de Valence took the king's rein and led him away "agane his will, fra the fichting." Barbour, though, whether by chance or design detracts from this impression of royal courage by juxtaposing the heroic but fatal words of Sir Giles d'Argentan: "And I cheis heir to byde and de / Than till lif heir and schamfully fle." Argentan was at the time holding the king's rein, which he relinquished to return to the fray, where he was overcome by force of numbers. In somewhat similar vein the St Albans continuator, supposedly Trokelowe, reported that Edward "fought like a lion" (*more leonis*) and had to be forcibly dragged from the battlefield by those around him.[78] Were it not for the fact that the rest of the chronicle is noticeably unfriendly to the king, it might be maintained that this last interpretation was influenced by Edward's well-known liberality towards a monastery that lay not far from his manor of Langley. One is forced to admit that the reasons for a chronicler's bias are often elusive.

Edward's fondness for St Albans is exemplified by a story – possibly true; a story that incidentally demonstrates his fearlessness in face of the supernatural. The Ely monks, in competition with their fellow Benedictines, falsely claimed to possess the body of St Alban. On arriving at Ely in 1314 Edward ordered an examination of their relics. He found only what purported to be the cloak received by St Alban from Amphibalus in which the saint had suffered martyrdom. When the reliquary was opened this cloak miraculously appeared to be spattered with the coagulated blood of the martyr, as fresh as though it had been spilled the day before. The king, who alone was bold enough to replace the relic and to touch the shrine, expressed his pleasure that God had chosen to work miracles at Ely by virtue of the garment but pointed out that even greater miracles were to be expected at St Albans by reason of its possession of the saint's body. During the abbacy of Hugh of Eversden (1308–26), Edward gave timber and a hundred marks for the new stalls in the St Albans' quire. His head and that of his wife Isabella are carved as terminals in the hood-moulds of the "decorated" bays in the south arcade of the nave, rebuilt after the collapse of 1323. He features in the abbey's magnificently illustrated book of benefactors.[79]

Surely no partisanship could have influenced Sir Thomas Gray, who, as a Northumbrian from Heaton-on-Till, might well have had reason to be critical of Edward's failure to defend the North. Gray, a man skilled in military affairs, although admittedly writing much later, speaks well of Edward's performance at Bannockburn. The king, he claims, was only reluctantly dragged from the field as he lay about him vigorously with a mace.[80] Nonetheless, the sole occasion that Edward sustained momentum in military matters was in his campaign of 1321–22, when his forces first recaptured Leeds Castle, then subdued the Mortimers, and finally advanced beyond Burton-on-Trent, Lancaster and the earl of Hereford retreating before them. Here again, we cannot be sure of the part played by Edward on the actual battlefield.

Conway Davies declared that "in determining the policy of a government ruled from the king's household, the character of the king and his principal advisers is of the utmost importance. Hence, he continued, "the first essential of an administrator is attention to detail, Edward II was a trifler. Business of government he neglected for petty considerations." Yet some modern writers, principally Mark Buck and Natalie Fryde, have reacted strongly against some of the conclusions of Tout and Davies. In the latter part of the reign they see Edward as actively urging the exchequer officials to greater efforts to reduce the amount of debt due to the Crown, to revive old levies such as tallage and, by economy on the one hand and repressive often confiscatory measures on the other, to vastly increase the resources of the Crown.[81] Such a view presupposes a *volte face* in Edward's behaviour. Clearly such forcefulness did not extend to the affairs of Gascony: they were conducted by the younger Despenser.[82]

The popular view of Edward could have been much the same, as may be suggested by the case recorded on a Memoranda Roll of 1315–16, which Philip le Viroler of Newington brought against Robert le Messager of the same place.

Robert, he claimed, ascribed Edward's defeat at Bannockburn to the fact that he neglected to hear mass, preferring to dig ditches and dykes and to occupy himself with other "indecencia." Following the intervention of Queen Isabella Robert was released and given a corrody at Ospringe hospital in Kent. Was this outburst indicative of a common perception, a question of loose talk in a mood of exasperation, or just village rivalry?[83] There are a few indications of more robust kingly behaviour, such as Edward's confident address to the citizens of London in July 1312 requiring them to undertake the defence of the capital on his behalf, or his refusal eight years later (supposedly on his own initiative, although the overall matter had been much discussed beforehand) to accede to the additional demand of Philip V's councillors for an oath of fealty. In some quarters it has been claimed that, when he did give attention to business, his oral instructions to ministers reveal a "considerable understanding" of the workings of government. Without doubt he exhibited personal bravery of a high order when in the middle of the night his pavilion caught fire at Poissy. Immediately, nude as he was, he gathered his wife Isabella into his arms and rushed forth so that by God's grace, as the Rouen chronicler expresses it, both were saved from combustion.[84]

Perhaps with a slight element of self-contradiction, Conway Davies warns his readers of the danger that lies in "attaching too much importance to the personal character of the king in finding cause for the troubles of the reign." The "personal factor," he suggests, "may have accentuated or occasioned but did not cause them."[85] This personal factor determined that Edward would not, perhaps could not, "Take arms against a sea of troubles, And by opposing end them" (Hamlet 3.1), and led him to rely so much on Piers Gaveston and the younger Hugh le Despenser. These two men Conway Davies considers to be favourites who aroused opposition from the barons. Such opposition was the single most disruptive factor of the reign. Admittedly it was no new phenomenon, but it could have been kept in check by a monarch who knew his business and acted within the limitations revealed by his father's experience.[86]

Complementary to this dependence on favourites was Edward's determination to avenge wrongs and insults. He was, in one chronicler's words, "homme de graunt vengeance" and in consequence in 1322 was able to get his own back on Lancaster for his participation in Gaveston's destruction a decade before. Another view is provided by the admittedly suspect excusatory account incorporated by Walsingham from his St Albans source. According to this, the king was very fond of Lancaster (*intime diligebat*) and before giving orders to execute the judgment against him castigated those who had counselled the earl.[87] It is in line with recent research into Edward's reign to stress the importance of the individual, and in the present writer's view the failings of royal character remain crucial to our understanding of the disastrous denouement. Moreover, the seeds of dissolution, as will transpire from what follows, were sown in the first few years of the reign.

THE QUESTION OF EDWARD'S SEXUAL ORIENTATION

Whether or not these propensities to indulge favourites meant that Edward was a homosexual has been the subject of disagreement among modern commentators.[88] There are contemporary and near-contemporary suggestions or insinuations that he was. Bishop Orleton, for instance, was accused of having publicly declared the king to be a tyrant and a sodomite, and having advocated that it was on that account lawful to rebel against him. To this charge the bishop guardedly replied that in expounding a text from Genesis (3: 15), he applied it to [the younger] Despenser who had presumed tyrannically to dominate the queen and the realm. Later in the same document Orleton speaks of the king's immoderate and inordinate love for Despenser, while elsewhere he hints darkly at behaviour of which he forebears to speak. The much later statement of the Meaux chronicler that "Edwardus in vitio sodomitico nimium delectabat" has been generally discredited, but it clearly harks back to an assumption current in the 1320s.[89]

Froissart, though not a solitary voice, can be somewhat unreliable. That he was intensely curious about Edward's fate is demonstrated by his visit to Berkeley in 1366 in the company of the younger Despenser's descendant, Edward Despenser. His circumstantial account of the favourite's death is unrestrained in its gruesome depiction of the punishment considered appropriate to a "heretic and sodomite." These two "crimes" were regularly associated in the minds of contemporaries, as is evidenced by the accusations against the Templars.[90] Such specific details, as we shall see, can be found in earlier sources. A further consideration is that the unusual manner of the king's death as recounted by a number of chroniclers, but notably Baker, may be more symbolic than real.

At the same time, the king was clearly capable of sustained heterosexual relationships. His queen bore him four children, the first of them some five months after Gaveston's death; the last, Joan of the Tower, on 5 July 1321. In addition, Edward has been credited with a bastard, Adam, mentioned in 1322.[91] It could be significant, either of his homosexuality or of his declining relationship with Isabella, that she is not known to have been pregnant between 1321 (when her last child was born) and her departure for France in 1325. Possibly she was incapable of bearing further children, as suggested by the fact that her subsequent adulterous relationship with Mortimer is not known to have produced any. Admittedly there were unsubstantiated rumours that she did become pregnant in and before 1330; rumours apparently not voiced by English chroniclers. These derive principally from Isabella's anxiety to secure letters patent to the effect that in the event of her death her executors should have free disposal of her goods and be permitted to detain the county of Cornwall and her dower manors for a period of three years.[92]

As for Edward, could it be that he had an affair with Eleanor de Clare, the younger Despenser's wife, his own niece? The possibility stems from the evidence of gifts he showered upon her, a cryptic comment by Knighton, and a specific one by the Hainault chronicler that they were lovers. The many mentions of Eleanor in the final chamber account of the reign argue that any such relationship was a late development. She was accommodated at Sheen (Richmond) Palace during October 1325, where the king visited her, and it seems to have been in December that she was delivered of a child, which prompted an offering from Edward for grateful prayer to the Virgin.[93] All the same, a letter from Eleanor to Justice Stonor, possibly dated early in 1326, shows that she was on good terms with the queen "nostre treschere dame la Roine."[94]

The medieval connotation of "sodomite" need not concern us here, nor is it necessary to contend that the times could and did overlook homosexuality in the highest echelons of lay society. Pierre Chaplais has argued that the royal proclivity for Gaveston is explicable in terms of the ancient bond of brotherhood in arms – a compact of adoptive brotherhood (used in a technical sense) such as that between Roland and Oliver or Olivier. He considers that elements of revenge for the "brother" and performance of his appropriate burial rights, constitute recognizable elements in a compact of this kind.[95] Whether Edward was a homosexual or not is of less importance than the fact that what can certainly be interpreted as inordinate affection regularly served as the mainspring of his actions – a major factor in his deteriorating relationships with the barons and, from the earliest days of his marriage, with the queen, the source of his eventual destruction.

WAS EDWARD OF CAERNARFON A CHANGELING?

Quite apart from his sexual proclivities, it was the dichotomy between Edward's regular behaviour and that which could reasonably be expected of a king that gave credibility to the appearance of an imposter. Most chroniclers ascribe the incident to 1318. Perhaps the fullest description is the one given by the Lanercost chronicle under that year.[96] According to this source a lowly and unknown person named John de Powderham came to Oxford.[97] He made his way to the royal manor of Beaumont – still remembered by a street name – which in fulfilment of Edward's vow made on account of his escape from Bannockburn had recently been given to the Carmelite friars.[98] There he claimed to be the true heir of Edward I, denying that Edward II was of the royal blood and offering to prove it in combat either with him or a substitute. The community (*universitas*) was thrown into turmoil. Many foolish people believed the story, says one chronicler, more particularly because the king was nothing like his father, having from his youth given himself to rowing, chariot driving, ditch digging, roofing, working as a smith by night with his boon companions, engaging in other mechanical arts, as well as occupying himself with similar trifles inappropriate to the son of a monarch. Edward, who was then at

Northampton for the parliament, had the man brought before him and deri-
sively addressed him as his brother. To this the man replied that he was no
brother of his, for Edward had no drop of royal blood in his veins, a fact he
undertook to prove against him. The deranged imposter – as we must presume
him to have been – was clapped in gaol while the council deliberated on the
matter. The *Anonimalle Chronicle* states that Edward wished to allow him to
live flourishing a jester's baton or bauble but that "certain lords" determined he
should be put to death.

The Pauline annalist identifies Powderham as an Oxford "scriptor" and literate; another source states that his parents – his father was a tanner – were
brought from Exeter to testify that he was indeed their son.[99] After a few days
he was brought before the king's household steward, at that time William Montacute. On the grounds that he was attempting to usurp the realm (*jus hereditatis
regni Angliae*), he was condemned to be dragged behind horses to the gallows,
hung, and then burned. The man, disappointed of promised (supernatural?) aid,
and seeing himself to be deluded, is said to have asked leave to make a confession. In this he claimed that a certain spirit of the Lord (*quidam spiritus Domini*) appeared to him in his dreams and each time what he had promised came
true. Subsequently the spirit directed that he do homage to him, promising
to make him king and to ensure his triumph against any opposition. This done,
he was directed to go to Oxford. The story told, his barbaric punishment was
carried out.[100]

There seems little point in the chroniclers' reiteration of this tale, in several
cases at inordinate length, unless it were considered to serve some useful purpose. In part, of course, it reflects the unsatisfactory nature of Edward's kingship, for which it provides a possible explanation, and could perhaps indicate a
focus of opposition. Although by all accounts the imposter was mentally
unhinged (*fatuus*), he seems to have created a considerable stir. This might
explain why so much trouble was taken over him and why the chroniclers dilat-
ed upon the bizarre event. In the *Vita* he is said to have claimed that he was
removed from the cradle and the "king" substituted for him. Moreover, according to the same chronicler, report of the incident spread throughout the land and
was a particular irritant to the queen. Ergome, as we have seen, glossed a story
– to be found in the Meaux chronicle – that the carelessness of a nurse allowed
a sow to lacerate the infant king. To conceal the accident she substituted a
carter's son. This kind of tale has a long history.[101]

SOME OTHER ASSESSMENTS OF ROYAL CHARACTER

It is, of course, true that working from the royal itinerary one might be led to
assume that Edward's ordinary habits were just the same as those of any other
king. The trouble is that his daily doings are of little help in the absence of
appropriate commentary. If we take, for instance, his performance in parlia-

ment, the surviving records have little to say which might lead us to an estimate of his participation. There are exceptions to this. In one case, the Westminster Parliament of 1320, we do have the informed comment of an unprejudiced observer, Bishop Cobham, who conveyed his eyewitness impressions to Pope John XXII.[102]

Besides which, Holy Father, your devoted son, our lord the king, in the parliament summoned to London bore himself splendidly (*magnifice*), with prudence and discretion, contrary to his former habit rising early and presenting a nobler and pleasant countenance to prelates and lords. Present almost every day in person, he arranged what business was to be dealt with, discussed and determined. Where amendment proved necessary he ingeniously supplied what was lacking, thus giving joy to his people, ensuring their security, and providing reliable hope of an improvement in behaviour (*morum melioracionis spem firmam*).

In a corresponding letter to Cardinal Vitale Dufour the bishop wrote:[103]

Besides which, O father and chosen lord, since you are looking for favourable news about the posture and bearing of our lord the king, let me tell you that in the parliament assembled at London, where the archbishop of Canterbury, seventeen of his suffragans, and a great number of earls, barons and lords were present, he bore himself honourably, prudently and with discretion. All those wishing to speak with reasonableness he listened to patiently, assigning prelates and lords for the hearing and implementation of petitions, and in many instances supplying ingeniously of his own discernment what he felt to be lacking. On that account our people rejoice greatly, there is considerable hope of an improvement in his behaviour (*ad spem magnam morum eius melioriacionis adducitur*) and a greater possibility of unity and harmony.

The same attitude, doubtless influenced by clerical reports from England, is to be found a few years earlier in a letter sent by John XXII at the outset of his pontificate. This urged Edward to venerate churches, honour priests, hear divine offices with reverence; to listen to the cause of the orphan, the widow, or the poor; to choose fit councillors and judges who were not venal and to appoint a prudent steward of his household.[104] How are we to interpret these letters? The avuncular tone is perhaps excusable in a pope or the Canterbury metropolitan but scarcely in a diocesan bishop, particularly when it is coupled with what can only be described as marked condescension. It is the attitude of a much older father in God to an unreliable and wayward young man, not unlike the tone adopted by Archbishop Stratford in 1340–41 to the young Edward III, a far more forceful character. Even so, the implication is that in the ordinary course Edward was dilatory about his daily obligations but on this occasion he did try (untypically) to act the king and with effectiveness. One is reminded of the reported comment of the earl of Lincoln, Henry de Lacy, in response to the good intent expressed by Edward immediately after his coronation with respect to the amelioration of grievances.[105] Both bishop and earl were speedily disillusioned. It may well be that Edward had bouts of "normal" behaviour but then relapsed into his usual far from satisfactory ways.

Bearing in mind these irregularities, early in the 1900s Chalfont Robinson, under the influence of an article contributed to *La Grande Encyclopédie* by Dr. Saury, the French alienist, claimed that Edward exhibited the symptoms of a degenerate, a term applied to "individuals afflicted with hereditary taint in their physical and mental condition."[106] He argued that strength and vigour such as that exhibited by Edward could coexist with "little mentality." Characteristic of such a state of degeneracy, he thought, were the king's cruelty anger, and vicious life. These elements are certainly to be traced in Edward's behaviour as, for instance, the author of the *Vita* remarked. Others, such as Sir Thomas Gray in the *Scalachronica,* while admitting "his cruelty and the debauched life that he led" were more generous, ascribing his fall mainly to indolence and the fickleness of the English "whose diversity of spirit" (arising from a mixed population) was the "cause of their revolutions." It may be remarked that the same notion of the disadvantages of miscegenation is to be found in the *Brut* with respect to the marriages of earls into "foreign" families.[107] On that basis the king himself was a "foreigner."

Edward's fierce anger (*sevicia*), if such it was, was at least matched by his father's, which he himself had experienced, while the licentious behaviour of his son, Edward III, was to prompt comparable criticism.[108] Further, some of the examples chosen by Chalfont Robinson to bolster his thesis are no longer tenable, among them that Edward's illiteracy is demonstrated by his taking the French form of the coronation oath. Nor can it be maintained that a facility in the "mechanical arts" necessarily stems from a lack of intelligence. Centuries later, Peter the Great of Russia was to become a famous exponent of such talents.

The king's "instability of purpose" and his "transient display of real efficiency" in the campaign that began at Leeds in Kent are clear enough, but these are not in themselves indications of mental abnormality. Some of the other arguments adduced, particularly those derived from the highly coloured narrative of Geoffrey le Baker, are equally unconvincing, since no context is given for their sources, these being accepted at face value. The affirmation that Edward acted from passion in the case of his attack on Leeds Castle has to be weighed against the possibility that this was part of a preconceived plan to provoke Lord Badlesmere and to precipitate conflict with the barons. The king was indeed unforgiving and vengeful: witness the festering resentment he showed following Gaveston's "unlawful" murder and the affront to him by Lancaster in this and other matters, his harassment of certain bishops, notably Orleton, and – if the allegation be true and not just a political manoeuvre – by the threat to his wife that formed part of the justification for Edward's marital separation and confinement in 1326.[109]

In an earlier context Orleton referred to the king's "Herodiana sevicia." Although this has the appearance of a rhetorical flourish, there can be no doubt that the bishop feared the ill will of the king.[110] Here again there is no reason to suppose that Edward's reactions were any more violent than those of his father would have been in commensurate circumstances. As for his son, Edward III, his precipitate condemnation in 1340–41 of Archbishop Stratford and a host of government officials, including the justices, is well attested, so too his strong reaction against the pointed denunciations of his judicial proceedings by Bishop Thomas de Lisle. It may be, however, that by 1325 Edward II was distinctly rattled by the situation abroad; his unreasonableness to those whom he had summoned to the army, and his overall behaviour called forth this derogatory assessment from the author of the *Vita*:[111]

"The harshness (*rigor*) of the king has today increased so much that no one however great and wise dares to cross his will. Thus parliaments, colloquies and councils decide nothing these days. For the nobles of the realm, terrified by threats and the penalties inflicted on others, let the king's will have free play. Thus today will conquers reason. For whatever pleases the king, though lacking in reason, has the force of law."

Perhaps it is Edward's foolishness that was most detrimental; a foolishness that allowed himself to be manipulated by both Gaveston and Despenser and that failed to recognize the political danger inherent in alienating his wife. In short, whatever his failings, and they were many, they do not appear to amount to a pathological condition. They did, however, render him quite unsuitable for kingship. In another age the royal preoccupation with aquatic sports, swimming, and rowing, which merited incidental mention only on account of the injury they brought to his entourage or near death to himself, might have been accepted as harmless, even praiseworthy pursuits.[112] For the fourteenth-century chronicler they were an unsuitable distraction from public business the more reprehensible in that they were enjoyed in the company, not of his own social group, the earls and barons, but in that of "simple men."

As an individual Edward could be brave and decisive, as the Poissy incident demonstrates; as a king and as a military commander he was deficient. The outcome was that in the popular imagination this *roi fainéant* came to bear the blame for misfortunes that were scarcely attributable to him personally. The words of Thomas of Castleford's chronicle, now at Göttingen, provide a sorry epitaph.

þis Edwarde als anens his lede
Was wise of worde and fole in dede.
Ek he was ful ungraciouse man
Welner in alle þinges he bigan
He gaf him þof it semede no3 wele

To alkins werkes manuele.
Durande alle his daise welner
Cheping' of alkins corn was dere
Feldes failede ungre was grete
Poveraile diede for defaute of mete
Morin of men of bestes alsua
Alle Englande in contek and wa
Alle Englande in contek and strif
Na pes stabliste durande his lif
þis kyng Edwarde in þis lande here
He regnede mar than neghienteen yiere
Montance of monethes twise thre.[113]

3

Faltering Steps,
1307–1308

Successit igitur Edwardus junior seniori, sed eo modo quo
R[eh]oboam Salomoni, sicut processus et exitus ejus probant.
And so the younger Edward succeeded the elder, but in the
manner of Rehoboam to Solomon, as events were to prove.[1]

OBSEQUIES FOR A GREAT KING

Edward II was in London and Lambeth some days after his father's death.[2] As soon as he heard the news he travelled northwards and is said by the Lanercost chronicler to have reached Burgh-on-Sands on 19 July 1307, where he mourned his father. If Walter of Guisborough's report is correct, the king's death was concealed until his son's arrival and many who spoke of it prematurely were imprisoned.[3] The following day, on the feast of St. Margaret, Edward was formally proclaimed king "*par descente de heritage*" at Carlisle Castle, where he received the homage and fealty of those who had gathered for the Scottish campaign. Thereupon he joined Anthony Bek, bishop of Durham and patriarch of Jerusalem, in the funeral procession that began to make its way south. The cortège probably set out from Burgh on or about 23 July and was expected at Richmond in Yorkshire by Saturday the twenty-ninth, where Archbishop Greenfield prepared to join it from his manor of Scrooby.[4] For the young Edward it was a token journey. Before long he turned back and can be traced at Carlisle well before the end of the month. From there on 31 July he moved with his army into Scotland.[5]

The royal corpse reached Waltham just north of London on 4 August, slowed down by an enormous crowd. At the abbey the religious kept vigil two by two throughout the week and daily celebrated exequies around the corpse.[6] Chancellor Ralph Baldock professed not to have had reliable news of the king's death until 25 July, but his colleague, Treasurer Walter Langton, bishop of Coventry and Lichfield, was already travelling north and learned of it at Wentworth in Yorkshire. Brooking no delay, he set about making appropriate arrangements and was himself at Burgh by 23 July engaged on business as one of the royal executors.[7] Langton departed for Westminster to make the funeral arrangements only to be arrested and, according to some accounts, lodged in the Tower, whence he was moved to Wallingford Castle, a stronghold that had come into Gaveston's possession with the earldom of Cornwall. This would appear to be at variance with the issue of a mandate from the treasurer, dated 1 October, for the delivery of twenty thousand marks to Langton and his fellow executors for the king's exequies and the execution of his testament. In any case, it was not long before the bishop was not only imprisoned – a manifest infraction of church liberties – but, worse still, impeded from carrying out his role as executor.[8] It was logical for most of the chroniclers of the day, the author of the *Flores* providing an exception, to assume that Edward's action was prompted by Langton's behaviour in the previous reign, notably his supposed advice that Gaveston should be exiled. Furthermore, as Edward I's leading advisor he was held accountable for the dismissal of prominent men from office and was alleged to have been in possession of royal treasure.[9]

Support is given to the notion of Gaveston's complicity by the fact that his return to England immediately precedes the action against Walter Langton and that he benefited financially from the treasurer's disgrace. His influence at the time was such that he was described as the realm's principal secretary and chamberlain (*secretarium et camerarium regni summum*).[10] Winchelsey's absence from the ecclesiastical helm helps to explain why there was astonishingly little outcry against the imprisonment of a bishop. It was not until Trinity law term in 1308 that we hear of Langton's refusal to respond to charges on the grounds that being a bishop and baron by virtue of Magna Carta he was not compelled to answer while a prisoner.[11] Another ministerial casualty was Chancellor Baldock, bishop of London: retained in office from the previous reign, he was replaced during August by John Langton, the Chichester diocesan. Despite these changes, there was a strong element of continuity between Edward I's administration and that of his son. John Langton had been chancellor between 1292 and 1302, while John Benstead, a clerk of long experience in the old king's wardrobe, became keeper under Edward II, at any rate for a short time. Trusted members of the prince's household received promotion. Reynolds, former keeper of the wardrobe, assumed the treasurership on 22 August 1307, while William Melton, among others, moved from the prince's wardrobe to that of the king.[12]

Meantime, the Lanercost chronicle records, the new king advanced to Dumfries to receive the homage of such Scottish magnates as remained loyal. Then, having divided his army into three columns, he set out in fruitless pursuit of Robert Bruce.[13] Edward himself rode to Cumnock, where on 30 August at the Tinwald he deputed Aymer de Valence to act as guardian of Scotland. Valence did not long retain the position, being superseded on 13 September by Jean de Bretagne, earl of Richmond.[14] Some writers have interpreted this as a consequence of Gaveston's intervention; more recently it has been viewed as a release for other tasks.[15] Indeed, it was on 6 November that Valence, by then earl of Pembroke, was appointed with the earl of Lincoln, Henry de Lacy, in conjunction with the bishops of Durham and Norwich, to mention only the honorific members of the embassy, to travel to France to make arrangements for Edward's forthcoming marriage. At the same time, the short interval between Pembroke's appointment and release might suggest something else – possibly an anxiety on his part to leave Scotland, where the weather was notoriously inclement and military reputations more easily lost than won.[16] Indeed, Barbour does claim that Valence withdrew because of the shame of his defeat at Loudun Hill.[17]

Early September saw Edward back at Carlisle; by the ninth he was at Knaresborough, visiting Gaveston, whom he had created earl of Cornwall on 6 August while at Dumfries. The *Vita* suggests that when doubts were expressed as to whether Edward could separate the earldom from the Crown, Henry de Lacy – as elder statesman – pointed out that it had been done twice before. Apart from Lincoln five earls and Aymer de Valence, about to become one, attested the charter. On 17 August, while at Sanquhar in Dumfriesshire, Gaveston held a great feast for his royal patron who, towards the end of the month at Tibbers, received the vast sum of three hundred pounds to lavish on his favourite. Edward was entertained at the new earl's expense between 9 and 12 September, when he moved south to St Mary's York.[18] Shortly thereafter, on 13 October, the first parliament of the reign met at Northampton, where Edward is said to have confirmed his gift of the earldom.[19] The Guisborough chronicler writes that Edward promised to maintain peace in the realm and to observe the statute of Winchester (1285), designed for its better preservation. He also determined the date for his father's burial. Apart from this, the avowed purpose of the assembly was to discuss the arrangements for the royal marriage and coronation. To meet the anticipated expense a fifteenth of movables was granted by the clergy, towns, and ancient demesnes, a twentieth by the magnates and counties.[20]

Edward I's body had remained temporarily at Waltham Abbey. Guisborough provides an expansive account of proceedings on its subsequent arrival at the capital. The corpse, he says, rested the first night in Holy Trinity church, presumably Trinity Priory (Christchurch) in Aldgate, the second night at St. Paul's, and the third at the houses of the Friars Minor and of the Dominicans, whence after requiem mass had been celebrated it was conveyed to Westminster. There, on 27 October, five bishops each celebrated a mass, as in his turn did the cardinal of Spain. The final mass was celebrated by the patriarch of Jerusalem, Anthony Bek, who performed the office of burial. Ministering with him were the bishops of Winchester, Henry Woodlock, and Lincoln, John Dalderby, who respectively read the gospel and epistle. And so, the chronicler concludes, the strongest, most prudent and wisest of kings was laid to rest with his fathers in the sixty-eighth year of his life and the thirty-fifth of his reign.[21]

The funeral obsequies over, Edward, following his custom as prince, returned to his manor of Langley, where he was visited by Aymer de Valence, doubtless for instructions with respect to his mission to France.[22] On 1 December, in response to papal urging, the king ordered the arrest of the Templars, planned as a concerted move for the Wednesday after Epiphany, 10 January 1308. On the fourth Edward wrote to the kings of Portugal, Castile, Sicily and Aragon, and a week later to Pope Clement V, expressing his doubts about the Templars' guilt.[23] Possibly his reluctant compliance with Clement's wishes was intended as a conciliatory gesture towards the French monarch and the pope; equally it may be a sign of Edward's weakness.

Edward travelled to Berkhamstead for the feast of All Saints on 1 November to attend Gaveston's marriage to Margaret de Clare, the king's niece, a celebration that surely followed all too quickly upon the burial of Edward I. The following month, on Edward's advice and with his encouragement, Gaveston with conscious ostentation held a tournament at his castle of Wallingford in honour of the bride. There, in company with a group of younger knights, so we are told by the author of the *Vita*, he succeeded in discomforting his opponents, among whom were numbered the earls of Surrey, Hereford, and Arundel (Trokelowe omits Arundel but questionably adds Lancaster and Pembroke). Although the earls were left in possession of the field, the *Vita* explains that by the rules of the tournament Gaveston was adjudged the victor. The Pauline annalist claims (implausibly?) that Gaveston fraudulently brought two hundred knights to fight against an agreed sixty. We are not told whether the king witnessed this spectacle; he was certainly in the vicinity at the time. Later in the month Edward journeyed by way of Westminster to Wye in Kent, one of the Battle Abbey manors, where he spent Christmas with Gaveston, appointing him *custos* of the realm the following day, a move calculated to arouse envy and resentment.[24]

PREPARATIONS FOR CORONATION

On 18 January 1308 Edward wrote from Dover to inform the greater clergy and laity of his intended coronation a month hence, on the Sunday following St. Valentine's day. He crossed the channel to Wissant, whence he sailed to Boulogne,[25] where on 25 January he married Isabella of France in the church of Nôtre Dame.[26] The ceremony was followed by a magnificent feast.[27] While Edward was still in Boulogne a much discussed agreement was drawn up in the names of various barons – a document that we shall examine later.[28] The wedding festivities over, Edward made the return journey by way of Wissant to Dover, where he landed on 7 February. King and queen received a jubilant reception in a London bedecked like the New Jerusalem, its streets ornamented with golden hangings, but alleges Trokelowe, it was on Gaveston rather than his juvenile bride that the returned Edward heaped all his affection.[29]

Edward revealed his true self by rejecting his father's closest confidant and recalling the "brother" of his days as prince for elevation to unprecedented heights.[30] He also demonstrated a scarcely predictable anxiety for Robert Winchelsey's return from enforced exile, but a more comprehensible one for the and anti-Gaveston at the same time, since Edward would scarcely have appreciated a "protective" arrangement aimed at his favourite, however well intentioned.

While it would serve little purpose to recapitulate the arguments that have ranged around a complementary problem, the precise interpretation of the coronation oath taken by Edward II, the subject must be broached. It appears that a fourth promise was added to the traditional threefold one and that there was some overall remodelling.[59] The fourth promise runs as follows: "Sire graunte vous a tenir et garder les loys et les custumes droitureles les quiels la communaute de vostre royaume aura esleu ["*quas vulgus elegerit*" in the Latin version] et les defendrez et afforcerez al honour de Dieu a vostre poer?" To this the response was: "Jeo les graunte et promette." That is, the king was to uphold those *lawful* customs chosen (*or* which shall have been chosen) by the "commonality" of the realm.

The tense and intention of "aura esleu"[60] were under discussion in the seventeenth century when William Prynne held that it referred to future enactments, Robert Brady to retrospective ones.[61] Moreover, the fourth promise has the appearance of duplicating to some degree the intention of the introductory one requiring an affirmative answer prior to further procedure. This initial clause constitutes a request for a royal promise to preserve and confirm to the people of England the rightful laws and customs granted to them by the former (*auntiens*) kings of England; namely (*nomement*) the laws, customs and franchises granted to clergy and people by the glorious St Edward ("King Edward" ostensibly Edward II's immediate predecessor, in the liturgical Latin version).[62]

There are a number of obscurities here. For instance, we should like to know on whose authority and with what intention the oath was recast and the fourth recension of the coronation Ordo – first used in 1308 – drawn up;[63] also whether, as Richardson and Sayles suggested, the second form of the fourth recension, that is, with the prefatory rubric, is an "obvious botch", or a carefully revised document with some political purpose in mind.[64] Then there is the debatable relationship between the Latin and French versions of the oath. One of the more recent writers on the topic, R.S. Hoyt, has declared the French version of the first promise to be "clearly superior," adding that "the second and third promises of 1308 can now be said to point to the French text as the government's view of the oath as against the traditional liturgical formulas." For him the fourth promise is "straightforward and concise? in the French text, but in the Latin "awkward and ill-phrased."[65] Against the thrust of Wilkinson's argument the same author denies that from "the form of words alone" one can substantiate a theory that the oath was revolutionary.[66] Another telling point advanced by Hoyt is that it is not legitimate to attempt to establish the motives of the framers of the oath from subsequent invocations of it, whether by the king's opponents or by Edward himself.[67]

Possible political implications of the liturgical aspect of the revised Ordo have until recently been overlooked. Andrew Hughes of the University of Toronto has suggested that elements such as the introduction of the "popular" acclamation: "Fiat, fiat, vivat rex" at the beginning of the service, the setting for the antiphon *Unxerunt Salamonem*, "musically unique in the English coronation ritual" with the new triple "Vivat rex" (reintroduced after a lapse in the third Ordo) – elements that serve to remind us of Christ's ascension and of the baptism of Christ the King – are by no means fortuitous. In *Unxerunt* we also recall St. Edward, an English match for the recently canonized St. Louis. Moreover, Dr Hughes suggests, the repositioning of the antiphon *Confortare* has the effect of emphasizing the crowning. "Here we have the three pillars of the coronation; popular acclaim, divine anointing, and investiture with the symbols of temporal authority." In conclusion, he suggests, "at *Protector noster* the king enters Mass to the text used by the Pope." And so, it is argued, we have an emphasis on "popular recognition," in practice that of the assembled baronage, a strengthening of royal authority by linking the king's anointing with Christ's baptism, a conscious affirmation of the English throne as against its French counterpart, and a restatement of sovereign rights in opposition to such papal encroachment as Boniface VIII had sought to make in the bulls *Clericos laicos* (1296) and *Unam sanctam* (1302). In short, we are encouraged to see a bolstering of the "political message of the coronation." This message, however, is no mere reflection of current difficulties at home but devised with a wider perspective in mind.[68]

To return to the oath and its interpretations: according to Richardson it was framed under the tranquil circumstances of the early months of the reign. In so far as it was "proleptic," it sought to prevent the recurrence of "evils already experienced." With respect to Bishop Hethe's declaration in 1327 that "unless the king swears to maintain the laws chosen by the people he [Edward III] would not be crowned," Richardson ingeniously argued that it constituted a contract. Thereby, if a king "persisted in wrong-doing," no constraint would be possible save the knowledge that (as in the case of St Benedict's abbot) God would act as avenger, for the day would come when the offender stood before the judgment seat. In circumstances such as these Edward II would be under no more restraint than his predecessors, though he might appear to be in the wrong.[69] It was not then "revolutionary," nor, evidently, was it concerned with irritation about Gaveston.

The Pauline annalist appears to be alone in his specific statement that the earls and barons, together with the more influential men (*maiores*) from France, sought Gaveston's exile and, when Edward refused his consent, they proposed to postpone the coronation. To avoid this calamity the king promised that in the next parliament he would do anything they wanted (*se illis facturum in proximo parliamento quicquid peterent*).[70] Whatever the truth of this account, it appears that the coronation was not postponed for that reason, or surely this particular chronicler would have said so. We do know that dissension about Gaveston clouded the ceremonies: it is well attested from other sources. Doubtless it arose from his outrageous behaviour and the excessive favours bestowed upon him by the king.[71]

This Pauline chronicler goes on to state that a parliament met at Westminster at the beginning of Lent, 1308 – more precisely the first Sunday in Lent[72] –

where the king promised to accept the barons' suggestions for reform of the realm (*de statu regni*), provided that they were for the honour of God and the Church and to the profit of the king and kingdom. However, the barons were somewhat at cross purposes in that an unnamed earl naturally enough wanted to see a copy of the articles to which he was to swear, while the others responded that without the king's commission they could not ordain anything for the kingdom nor put into words what they had not yet conceived in their minds, and so the session was postponed to the quindene – fifteenth day – of Easter, 28 April. This lack of readiness must be accounted strange for those who would maintain the idea of a baronial opposition with consistent ideas.[73]

Without doubt this is the same story retailed more convincingly by Guisborough. According to him the earl of Lincoln, hearing of the king's good intentions as expressed in his mandate to the barons for the discussion of three articles concerning respectively the Church, the Crown, and the peace, exclaimed: "Blessed be God who after the wisest king has given us the promise of a good one."[74] Turning to the royal messengers he said that now the king should confirm what he had promised orally, viz. that he would accept what they ordained. This reply is said to have been acclaimed by all save the two messengers, Thomas of Lancaster and Hugh le Despenser, whereupon Lincoln asked why they declined to raise their arms in assent like the others. They responded guardedly that they would first return to the king because his will was not yet clear. The equivocal message with which they returned was that Edward had no wish to tire them further but expressed his thanks; after the quindene of Easter they could reassemble in London for parliament and treat of the matters concerned.[75]

No writs survive for a parliament in the late February of 1308, which could merely have been a meeting of those conveniently assembled for the coronation.[76] It was in response to writs of 19 January that an assembly convened at Westminster on 3 March. Apart from the barons, lay and ecclesiastical, knights may also have been summoned. Evidently it was this parliament that was "prorogued" to 28 April, the writs being dated 10 March.[77] By that time, urges the Pauline annalist, the question of Gaveston was uppermost in the minds of all. The barons came armed, though not with hostile intent, so says this favourably disposed chronicler – fearing betrayal, so the *Vita* claimed. The king remained in his palace, the earls assembled in the nearby abbey. Edward was unwilling to concede that his "brother" Gaveston should suffer exile or be diminished in honour. The earls maintained that in order effectively to conduct the business of the realm he should be deprived of his earldom and exiled. And so, from fear of the whole people, which one can interpret as meaning pressure from the earls and barons, Peter surrendered to the king his charter of enfeoffment. The charter was then handed to the earls, who allegedly burnt it. After that Gaveston hastened his departure.[78]

Supposedly it was at this Westminster Parliament of April 1308 that the earl of Lincoln, now distinctly anti-Gaveston, presented to the king a document, the much-discussed *Homage et serment* declaration, of which the Bridlington canon and the London annalist provide a version, in this context apparently alone among the chroniclers.[79] This makes a clear distinction between the person of the king and the Crown – the so-called "doctrine of capacities" – and claims that it is more to the latter than to the former that homage and allegiance are due. Should the king not be guided by reason his lieges would be bound to reinstate him in the dignity of the Crown (*coronae regem reducere et coronae statum emendare*). But how was this to be achieved? By legal means or by constraint? To have recourse to the law would not be effective, since the judges were royal judges, who could be expected, if the king's will were not in accordance with reason, to maintain and confirm the error. To preserve the oath, the argument ran, should the king fail to right a wrong and to remove something harmful to the people, as well as to the prejudice of the Crown, there must be constraint. This follows from the fact that the king is bound by oath to govern his people and his lieges to govern with him and in his support.

As for "the person spoken about", Gaveston,[80] the people should judge him as a man not to be endured, one who disinherits and impoverishes the Crown. His counsel serves to withdraw the counsel of the realm and produces discord between king and people. Moreover, he binds men to himself by an oath as stringent as that to the king, thus making himself the king's peer and enfeebling the Crown. By means of the goods (*bens*) of the Crown he has diverted to his power its authority (*la force*), thus by his misdeeds enabling him to determine whether the Crown should be destroyed and he become sovereign of the realm – treason to his liege lord, to the Crown, and contrary to his fealty. Since the lord has agreed to maintain him against every man in every respect (*en touz pointz*), without regard of reason, as behoves the king, he is unable to be judged or attainted by suit under the law; wherefore the people consider him to be attainted and judged (*le agard come home ateint e juge*) a robber of the people, traitor to his liege lord, and to the realm. They request the king, he being bound by his oath – his coronation oath that is – to maintain the laws that the people shall choose (*qe le pople eslire*), that he accept and implement the award of the people.

This is an extraordinarily well reasoned statement of political philosophy, the authorship of which is likely to remain obscure. One surmises that a clerical mind lies behind it, a mind accustomed to the problems of secular government, but whose? Winchelsey had only just returned on 24 March "cum honore magno". He was soon to enter the fray with his excommunication of the favourite. The document is a cautious one. It does not read like a petition to the king, formulated as one would expect had Lincoln presented it in parliament. What is more, it deliberately avoids names, or at any rate the best-preserved copy does. Although there is no good reason to reject the Burney manuscript's ascription of the document to Lincoln and by implication to the situation in 1308, there is also contemporary opinion that it was dated 1311 – perhaps merely reused then – and that in 1321, as we shall see, it was foisted on Despenser by a trick in order to label him a traitor.[81] Modern historians have been divided in their opinions as to its

was that early in 1310 Clement issued a mandate to Edward II for the holding of an enquiry into the credentials of the abbot-elect, who was duly confirmed in office. Whatever the merits or demerits of Kedyngton, and it would be difficult to establish them from the *ex parte* allegations, it is quite clear that Aldenham was a wily politician who cleverly exploited the "tempus congruum et acceptabile" to embarrass his opponent.[93]

Another critic of Edward's actions was Pope Clement V himself, whom he could not afford to alienate. The pope naturally leapt to the defence of bishops whom Edward II had imprisoned. To Walter Langton, bishop of Coventry and Lichfield, were added captives from the Scottish hostilities – Robert Wischard (Wishart), bishop of Glasgow, and William de Lamberton, bishop of St Andrews – incarcerated in Porchester and Winchester castles respectively. Clement directed a strongly worded letter to Edward, dated 9 April 1308 from Poitiers. He complained of the offence to God, the contempt for the Church, as well as the infringement of ecclesiastical liberty represented by Langton's incarceration. The king was exhorted to rectify the matter without further delay. Clement claimed to have ordered the archbishop of York to take the Scottish bishops into custody, whereupon Edward I had lodged them in the prison from which Edward II now refused to release them. "The most high priests (*summi sacerdotes*), that is the bishops who exercise the powers of the Apostles within the church, should be judged," he claimed, "solely by God and the vicar of God." He then launched a general complaint about the interference of the king's officers with the executors of papal bulls, the drawing up of public instruments by notaries (*tabelliones*), and the collection of annates. But was this merely bluster? The pope's biographer regards him as pursuing overall "a subservient policy in both the domestic and foreign affairs of England," a policy that "involved the papacy in difficult if not impossible situations in relation to the baronage, a large proportion of the prelates of England, and the community of the realm of Scotland as a whole."[94]

Edward was unable to resist the combined pressure of the earls,[95] the king of France, and of other English sympathizers. On 18 May 1308, bowing to *force majeure*, he issued a writ for Gaveston's banishment by the morrow of St John the Baptist, 25 June. This, he was forced to declare, accorded with the counsel of the prelates, earls, and barons of the realm which he had accepted (*par nous acordietz*).[96] The arrangement was fortified by Winchelsey's sentence of excommunication, to be incurred *ipso facto* were Gaveston to delay beyond the appointed date or to return in future. The Bridlington chronicler at this point paraphrases the *Homage et serment* declaration, stating that Edward was bound by his coronation oath to accept the people's award. However, at length the earls and barons permitted the lord king to mitigate the sentence of life and members out of respect for the earl of Gloucester whose daughter, Margaret, Gaveston had married, and so the favourite was merely banished.[97]

To sum up; the first year of Edward's reign had been packed with incident. The young king had faced no easy task, but the conflict that arose can be attributed almost entirely to his own foolishness. There remains a temptation to perceive, as did Bertie Wilkinson, a continuous thread of calculated attempts to constrain the king, from the revised coronation oath, by way of the Declaration of Boulogne and the *Homage et serment* document, to the banishment of Gaveston. Yet it was to be urged in 1321 by the barons themselves that constraint of the king was tantamount to treason, a viewpoint that has been maintained by Richardson. Although this is true, the context is a particular one, and as has been argued above, it would be unrealistic to assume that in practice there was no concept of coercing the monarch, potentially dangerous though such a course might be. The assumption that the Declaration of Boulogne was directed against Edward has been called in question, and should this be sustained it would be difficult to envisage the Declaration as complementary to the *Homage et serment* document. The latter was eventually adapted to suit differing circumstances; conceivably it is a draft and may not in fact have been brought forward by the earl of Lincoln – an honoured figure – despite the Burney manuscript, or been the the the subject of a parliamentary petition.

If we accept the contention that any coercion of the monarch was treasonable, then it is more convincing to regard the coronation oath as non-revolutionary in intent. Laws, moreover, even if "chosen by the people," had to receive the royal assent. Subsequent invocations of the oath cannot be used convincingly to determine the intentions of its framers;[98] both king and barons were to invoke it as circumstances required. Changes in the Ordo, it could be claimed, were directed towards establishing the king of England's status against his brother of France and the papacy, thus enhancing his authority rather than limiting it. If there was anything hurried about the Ordo it was the rubrics, rather than the liturgical form. The latter had been accorded considerable attention.

The barons made a series of spasmodic responses to specific situations rather than formulating a coordinated plan to constrain the monarch. Not surprisingly common elements are to be found in surviving documents, such as the Boulogne Declaration, the *Homage et serment* presentation, and Winchelsey's excommunication of Gaveston. Even so, at the time of the coronation the barons showed themselves so irresolute as to be unable to formulate a studied response to the king's offer to attend to their proposals. Constitutional historians' minute interpretation of the supposed purport of the surviving documents has lulled us into visualizing a more rational and ordered "opposition" than in fact existed. In any case, such "baronial opposition" as can be detected was not so much directed against the king as against the king's favourite, Gaveston. It was Gaveston's rash stupidity, at which the king connived, that formed the catalyst of baronial and continental resentment. Only subsequently, with the Ordinances, was "opposition" systematized to the extent of devising a scheme to ensure "right" government by the king.

4

The Last of the Gaveston Years: The Road to Bannockburn, 1308–1314

And verrily yf a Prince have wilful desire to
have about hym unwyse and yonge counseillours
or servauntz which he will gladly heare and ʒive
to them credence, it is a good and certayn
argument that thilke Prince is not wyse ne will be wyse.[1]

Sooner or later an inadequate king, by his misrule,
would provoke his magnates to insist upon
controlling his policy and administration. Granted
an hereditary monarchy in this position, constitutional
crises were inevitable and revolution not unlikely.[2]

THE GROWTH OF HOSTILITY TO GAVESTON

The six years from 1308 are given coherence by the presence of Gaveston until 1312 and by the political readjustments consequent upon his murder. The period ends on the eve of the catastrophic defeat of Edward's army at Bannockburn. Admittedly, in stressing the relationship between Gaveston and the king, there is a tendency to place less emphasis upon underlying factors, notably constitutional but also financial, social, and economic; factors that have preoccupied historians in the past and that to some degree continue to do so. Much of the struggle with Gaveston, however, while it might appear to be dominated by constitutional issues, was primarily a consequence of personal antipathy – antipathy for which Gaveston himself was mainly responsible. His flashy provocative behaviour at the coronation and subsequent banquet, his monopolizing of the king's attention – acting "quasi rex,"[3] and his notorious name calling of individual barons, all contributed to what came to be an explosive state of affairs. In all this he seems to have been aided and abetted by the ineptitude of the king, who was either oblivious to the harm which Gaveston was wreaking or more likely – blinded by his emotions – indifferent to it. Pierre Chaplais's carefully constructed thesis that Gaveston's relationship with Edward is explicable in terms of a bond of fraternity seems insufficient to account for the latter's unkingly behaviour.

Despite the closing events of his father's reign Edward II's friendship with Gaveston was not initially a focus of opposition, that is, if we discount the Pauline annalist's rumour that Edward cancelled the Stepney tournament at the time of the coronation because of Gaveston's fear that the earls planned to kill him. Indeed, the elder statesman of the day, Henry de Lacy, earl of Lincoln, put himself out to sustain the view that the earldom of Cornwall could be granted to someone outside the immediate royal family, himself heading the list of *testes*, which also included the earls of Lancaster, Surrey, Hereford, and Arundel, as well as Aymer de Valence, soon to be styled earl of Pembroke. This constituted an alienation of the royal fisc, a process the barons were shortly to repudiate. Their initial compliance seems to militate against the claim of the *Brut* chronicle that the grant of the earldom was contrary to the will of all the lords of the realm, and it does something to support Dr Maddicott's contention that despite the friction of his father's later years Edward "did not inherit an aggrieved and aggressive baronage."[4]

Lacy's attitude would be the more remarkable were we to accept another story in the *Brut* to the effect that when nearing his end Edward I called him to his deathbed, together with Guy earl of Warwick, Aymer de Valence, and Robert de Clifford, making them promise on their fealty to support his son Edward as king and not to suffer Gaveston to return to England "forto make his son use ryaute."[5] There is no clear indication of the exercise of any such guardianship role, although one historian suggests that it may not be "fanciful" to regard the association in the Boulogne document of Lincoln, Clifford – by then marshal of the royal household – and Valence as related to the former king's charge.[6] In this particular interpretation, of course, the parties to the document are viewed as acting in what they considered to be the king's best interest.

The alienation of Lacy came later as a direct result of Gaveston's intolerable behaviour – specifically his ingratitude, suggests the author of the *Vita*. The other earls soon found themselves in the same camp, though Lancaster was slow to declare himself, doubtless because he had benefited substantially from the king's goodwill and possibly because of his adolescent association with Edward. Such association, however, could equally have had a negative effect, but in Dr Maddicott's view not in this case. According to one expansive account of the coronation Lancaster served as steward (*serviebat de senescallaria*), an office that was only formally committed to him on 9 May 1309, when it was said to pertain to the earldom of Leicester and to have been formerly held by Simon de Montfort – an inauspicious precedent. Royal concessions to Lancaster seem to have continued until December 1308.[7]

It is tempting to countenance the view of the author of the *Vita* that, had Gaveston behaved prudently towards the magnates rather than regarding the king as his sole equal, he would not have had any one of them against him. There was, he admits, a secondary cause for their hatred – Gaveston's monopolizing of the royal eyes and ears. Whereas in the past it had been customary for all to have opportunity to find grace in the king's sight, when Gaveston was present Edward had a friendly mien for him alone. Ignoring any earl or baron who wished to communicate with him, Edward addressed only Gaveston.[8] A corollary to this, considered by Gaveston's latest biographer, Dr Hamilton, elaborating a point made by Maddicott, to be of greater importance than the personal conflict, is the odium that arose because of the influence exercised by the favourite on patronage, the life-blood of courtiers and not least of the earls. The Bridlington chronicler is specific about the matter: Gaveston, behind the backs of the magnates (*inconsultis regni proceribus*), was responsible for an inappropriate distribution of goods and benefits (*bonorum et beneficiorum*). The Pauline annalist goes so far as to claim that the common people (*vulgus*) dubbed Gaveston the king's idol whom, fearing to displease, Edward sought to placate as though a superior. Were any magnate to seek a special grace of the king he would send him to Piers and accept his decision. Thus the people complained that two kings ruled in one kingdom.[9] Murimuth, in common with several other chroniclers, somewhat conventionally argues that Edward eschewed his father's trusted councillors, another case of Rehoboam, whose ill fate had become proverbial. Even though it may be hard to exemplify specific use of the term "natural councillors," there is no doubt that the barons considered that they had a right to be consulted in "matters of state" and that Piers's privileged position curtailed their participation.[10]

While the chroniclers chime in unison on this topic of Gaveston's exercise of patronage and influence, it is not easy to find adequate documentary evidence in support of their contention, as his biographer makes clear. He discovered only "a few examples of Piers's control of patronage" among the royal records, while his search of the calendar of patent rolls revealed "some nine examples of favours granted at the instance of Gaveston prior to his exile in June of 1308 and seven further ones during the remaining four years of his life, hardly an excessive accumulation for one so close to the monarch."[11] Obviously this is not the whole story, and in any case, other favours would have passed by word of mouth.

As we have seen, Gaveston's intervention in the Westminster election following Abbot Walter de Wenlock's death is well attested, though ostensibly an isolated incident.[12] In contrast to Edward's later favourite, Hugh le Despenser the younger, Piers does not appear to have wielded political authority directly, preferring "to exercise his power through the king, rather than in his stead."[13] His brief period as *custos regni* from 20 December 1307 until 9 February 1308 is unremarkable and his day-to-day conduct of affairs is not thought to have provoked criticism, unless one associates the Boulogne agreement with a reaction against Gaveston's procedures.[14] If the story in the Canterbury *Polistoire* specifically refers to this period rather than to a later one, then Gaveston must already have been unpopular with the earls, for allegedly they were forced to kneel before they could present their cases to him.[15]

Another factor that rankled was Gaveston's alleged feathering of his own nest at the Crown's expense. The *Brut* chronicler alleges that he entered the royal treasury at Westminster Abbey and transferred the table of gold with the trestles of the same and many other rich jewels that at one time were the noble King Arthur's to Emery dei Frescobaldi for shipment to Gascony, whence they were never returned.[16] Guisborough suggests that in addition to Langton's treasure, Gaveston was given that of the king's father, amounting to £100,000 apart from gold and precious stones.[17] The extent of the inroads into the royal "jocalia" was supposedly brought to light in 1313 with the king's recovery from the earls of Gaveston's property. More recently, however, it has been argued by Pierre Chaplais that the jewels seized by Lancaster at Newcastle were in fact the king's property and accepted as such.[18] Prejudice, certainly exaggeration, may well have served to embroider the facts.

It is not difficult then, to accept Dr Maddicott's dismissal of Conway Davies's argument that much is to be said for "regarding the reign of Edward II as a reaction by the barons against the general tendency of Edward I's policy against their rights,"[19] or perhaps what they felt to be their rights. Having done so, we may the more readily regard the situation, one that by the Spring of 1308 threatened to deteriorate into civil war, to have been principally a consequence of Gaveston's irresponsible behaviour exacerbated by Edward's mindless connivance. It was, as the quotation from Treharne which prefaces this chapter suggests, an "inevitable" consequence of Edward's fecklessness. This is not to deny the fact that once the crisis materialized the barons would hark back to the struggles of previous reigns. The precedents lay there, the cirumstances were different.

The opposition within the country to Edward's conduct of government was formidable. It comprised all the earls save Lancaster, who at this stage took no known part in the hounding of Gaveston, Jean de Bretagne, the earl of Richmond, absent as the king's lieutenant in Scotland, possibly the earl of Gloucester, Gaveston's brother-in-law, and Robert de Vere, earl of Oxford, a political nonentity.[20] The king resorted to precautionary measures. In March 1308 he changed the custodianship of some dozen strategic strongholds including Chepstow and St Briavel's in the West, Nottingham, Rockingham and Northampton in the Midlands, Scarborough on the east coast, as well as the Tower of London. Three of these custodians, Robert de Clifford, Payn Tibetot, and John Botetourt, in charge respectively of the castles of Nottingham, Northampton and St Briavels, were signatories of the Boulogne agreement. Clifford and Tibetot were also deprived of their offices as justices of the royal forests north and south of Trent.[21] The interval between the date of the Boulogne agreement and the removal of its signatories from office is so short, well under two months in fact, that whatever interpretation we may put on their original intentions, the king soon came to regard them as other than reliable. The small band of men who remained close to the king included the elder Hugh le Despenser and a group of lesser knights such as John de Handlo, John de Hastings, Guy Ferre, John Crombwell or Cromwell, who became constable of the Tower, William Latimer, and John de Suleye.[22]

Edward withdrew from London to Gaveston's castle of Wallingford, where he spent two days, 29–30 March 1308. He then travelled back to Windsor for the Easter festival on 14 April. There he issued a prohibition to the earls and barons against the holding of a tournament at Stafford, which he doubtless feared would provide an occasion for concerting opposition. As a precaution against hostile movements he ordered the breaking down of bridges over the Thames at Kingston and Staines, a course that would not have endeared him to the local inhabitants.[23] In the event, as we saw in the previous chapter, conflict was averted by the king's submission to the demands of the barons in the parliament of April 1308. This, the *Vita* suggests, was convoked for the purpose of reconciliation, although the barons, fearing treachery, are said to have come armed. In addition to banishment – the writ is dated 18 May – Gaveston was deprived of his earldom, the lands being taken into the king's hand on 25 June 1308, the day by which he was to have left the realm.[24] The Pauline annalist states that Gaveston surrendered his charter of enfeoffment to the king, who handed it to the earls, and that they promptly burned it.[25] Hamilton, however, points out that the story is apocryphal, since the charter has survived.[26] Incongruously, though doubtless as a concession, Gaveston was permitted to retain the title for life, so he continued to be addressed as earl. To complete the process Archbishop Winchelsey detailed the reasons for his exile and inhibited him under pain of excommunication from remaining in England past the appointed date or from returning thereafter.[27]

The preliminary skirmish had been won by the barons, but the king was determined to carry on the war, having no intention of abandoning his favourite. As the *Vita* summed up the situation there was neither real love nor real peace (*nec adhuc verus amor successit, nec vera concordia*). Less than a week after he had been forced to agree to Gaveston's exile Edward pressed lands on him in Aquitaine worth three thousand marks – £2,000. This grant was subsequently vacated but replaced by a revised one of equal value.[28] There followed grants of land in England formerly held by the countess of Albermarle – again to the value of £2,000 a year,[29] and prior to his departure the king ordered that Gaveston be given 1,180 marks towards his expenses.[30] Small wonder that the *Vita* regarded the latest state to be worse than the earlier one (*sicque novissimus error priore factus est pejor*). His financial position thus secured, the favourite's prestige was further enhanced by Edward's suddenly conceived plan of making him lieutenant in Ireland in place of Richard de Burgh, the earl of Ulster, who had been appointed the previous day.[31] The magnates seem to have accepted this appointment without demur, the Bridlington chronicler alone suggesting that it was contrary to their wishes.[32]

The king was at his much-loved manor of Langley from the end of May until 11 June 1308. It is likely that Gaveston was with him for most of that time. He then proceeded by way of Windsor, Newbury, Hungerford, and Marlborough to Bristol, where on 28 June his favourite took ship for Ireland with a great company. According to the Lanercost chronicler, who is somewhat suspect at this point, he ought to have departed from Dover and the Irish venture was a private arrangement of the king's. He left with a pension of two hundred pounds, a further one hundred for his wife and, so rumour ran, many of the more precious objects from the treasury and even some blank charters under the great seal. In all these and some other matters, the Lanercost chronicler continues, only four persons of consequence openly adhered to the king: Hugh Despenser, Nicholas Segrave, William de Barford or Bereford, and William Inge.[33] Gaveston's stay in Ireland lasted just over a year, where his performance as lieutenant, insofar as it can be ascertained, seems to have been creditable.[34]

WINNING OVER THE OPPOSITION

It was to be expected that Edward would not tolerate the outcome forced upon him by a process of more than doubtful legality dependent on *force majeure*. He at once set about securing Gaveston's restoration, which had to be done by weaning the barons from their opposition, a course achieved, according to the *Vita*, by means of "gifts, promises and blandishments."[35] The youthful Gloucester was soon fully won over to the side of his brother-in-law and of the king. At Byfleet on 22 September 1308 Edward entertained Matilda, the daughter of the earl of Ulster, together with her *familia* and the earls of Warenne (Surrey) and Lancaster. A week later he was present at Waltham Abbey for the double marriage of Matilda to Gilbert de Clare, earl of Gloucester, and of her brother John to Gloucester's sister. From June 1308 Gloucester regularly witnessed royal charters, as did the earl of Richmond who on 24 May had secured the favourable release of his father's goods confiscated by Edward I.[36]

Until his lamentably early death at Bannockburn Gloucester, together with Richmond, remained loyal to the king.[37] Hereford, whose reputation for integrity stood high, not least in the mind of the chronicler Geoffrey le Baker, accommodated himself to the king early in June, if the record of his dining at the royal table is indicative. By the beginning of August 1308 he too is to be found witnessing charters.[38] The most important recruit was the ageing earl of Lincoln, who is recorded to have been with the king at Sheen Palace on 2 June. Not merely was he reconciled to Edward, but also, like many others, he assisted him with invaluable loans.[39] By June 1309 the earls of Gloucester, Hereford, Lincoln, Richmond, Ulster, and Warenne had all dined at least once with the king.[40] Even Warenne, who had borne a grudge against Gaveston since the Wallingford tournament, could now be labelled an essential friend and help (*necessarius amicus ... et fidelis adjutor*). Warwick alone, the *Vita* further claims, remained inflexible. However, "when all the others dissimulated, he could not stand alone," so that by August 1308 he too was witnessing charters and receiving what can only be interpreted as signs of royal favour.[41]

Pembroke's attitude presents a problem for his biographer. If an anonymous letter of 14 May 1308 speaks truth rather than rumour, then Pembroke and Lincoln were the leaders of baronial opposition to Gaveston; hence it is not surprising that the former's name is not recorded among those said to have dined with the king prior to the first week of July 1309. Against this it can be shown that Pembroke witnessed charters during the regnal year 1307-08 and more frequently during that of 1308-09. Furthermore, he was with the king at Byfleet on 21 November 1308, was given help to recover a debt at the exchequer and to prosecute a suit in the French court, and obtained the lordship of Haverfordwest.[42] Then, on 4 March 1309, he was associated with the earl of Richmond, the bishops of Worcester (Reynolds) and Norwich (Salmon), and others in an embassy to the French court and to the papal Curia.[43] The most likely explanation, pending more specific evidence about Pembroke's conduct at this time, would seem to be that the earl was disaffected on Gaveston's account but subsequently won over by royal favours.

No less important than the seduction of the barons was the surprising about-turn of King Philip. This is explicable on a number of counts. In the first place, even prior to the writ of 18 May 1308 for Gaveston's banishment, Edward had belatedly done justice to his dowerless wife by granting her the counties of Ponthieu and Montreuil. Other grants followed, including some £1,122 in cash from the wardrobe and exchequer. However, it seems that the dower of 10,000 *livres turnois*, the equivalent of £4,000, promised by Edward to his wife "at the church door" in accordance with Boniface VIII's arrangement, was not assigned until 5 March 1318, shortly after which she was also granted the forest of Savernake in Wiltshire.[44] It would have been unwise, not to say self-defeating, for Philip to mount a permanent vendetta against his son-in-law, a fellow monarch, so with Gaveston likely to be out of the way and the queen's settlement duly made, it was in his own interest to restore Edward's position.

Edward himself was fully aware of this situation and on 16 June 1308 he wrote to the French king from Windsor stating that Gaveston, to whom, so he claimed, the earldom of Cornwall had been granted *in absentia* and unbeknown to Piers (*absens et ignorans*), with the consent of the earls and barons, had been deprived of it when they subsequently changed their minds. He asked for Philip's help to restore peace with the baronage and informed him of his letter to the pope on the topic dated the same day. In a further letter to Clement about Winchelsey's excommunication of the earl, Edward complained that the latter had not been properly cited and had neither confessed nor been found guilty of any fault. In view of this, he requested that the sentence be relaxed *ad cautelam*.[45] Another tactic was to grant the castle and town of Blanquefort to Bertrand de Got, Clement's "nephew" (*nepos*), to the tune of "1,500 libratarum terrae Chipoten." In default this was to be made up from the customs of Bordeaux. In return Cardinal Bertrand was expected to promote the king's business at the Curia.[46]

Both Philip and Clement were quick to reorientate themselves, although as late as 13 April 1309 Edward was writing to another of the pope's *nepotes* or "nephews," Raymond de Got, cardinal deacon of Santa Maria Nuovo, thanking him for his efforts in diffusing the rancour that the king of France had formerly conceived against Gaveston. The pope may have been more immediate because Edward showed himself to be accommodating with respect to the continued imprisonment of the three bishops – Coventry and Lichfield, Glasgow and St Andrews – and to the inquisition directed against the Templars. A Gascon, Arnaud d'Aux, bishop of Poitiers, was despatched to England, and into his custody Edward delivered his "enemy" Robert Wishart, the Glasgow diocesan.[47] The ill-assorted anti-Gaveston coalition collapsed. At the beginning of November Louis, count of Evreux, the French king's brother, dined twice with Edward at Westminster,[48] and was subsequently engaged with the bishop of Soissons in negotiations for an unpopular truce with the Scots.[49] At the end of November 1308 Edward wrote a friendly letter to Philip acknowledging that he would accept what these men determined.[50] Arrangements were made for the continuation of the process of Montreuil.[51] Finally by a bull dated 25 April the pope relaxed the sentence imposed on Gaveston, thus opening the way for his return.[52] On 27 June 1309 Edward met the erstwhile exile, who had landed in Wales, by Chester.[53] The king was no strategist; the problems remained below the surface, but motivated by strong affection he had proved a wily tactician.

What, we may ask, was Thomas of Lancaster's position in the spring of 1309? Clearly it had shifted, no doubt as a direct consequence of his growing misgivings about the nature and direction of Edward's conduct. It may be, as Dr Maddicott has suggested, that he was a prominent participant in the political discussion that, it has been hypothesized, took place between 20 March and 7 April at the Dunstable tournament attended by the earls of Arundel, Gloucester, Hereford, Lancaster, and Warenne: a prelude to the grievances embodied in the eleven articles presented by the "commonality of the realm" at the parliament that met at Westminster on 27 April 1309. The king, however, does not put in an appearance there until the beginning of May.[54] In the estimation of the nineteenth century constitutional historian, William Stubbs, this was the most important assembly since that of Lincoln in 1301.[55] More recently it has been suggested that the eleven articles marked a stage midway between the *Articuli super Cartas* of 1300 and the Ordinances of 1311. At any rate there was the sort of repetition common in medieval *gravamina*.[56]

The opening general plaint was that the country was not governed according to Magna Carta, while particular grievances involved the abuses of purveyance, imposts on wine, cloth, and merchandise, the corruption of the coinage, the exercise of jurisdiction by royal stewards and marshals, the lack of machinery for the proper presentation of petitions in parliament, the misuse of writs of protection, the sale of pardons to criminals, the illegal holding of common pleas by constables of royal castles, and the unjust actions of the king's escheators in seizing the lands of tenants in chief and precluding their right of appeal to the king's court.[57] It has long been accepted that these grievances were more the concern of knights and burgesses than of magnates, though quite how and by whom the articles were formulated will doubtless remain an enigma.[58]

As in 1300 the redress of grievances was made a precondition of the grant to the king of a twenty-fifth of movables. Guisborough, who seems to be a shade confused at this point, states that the magnates conceded the twenty-fifth in return for confirmation of Magna Carta and the Charter of the Forest but would not agree to Gaveston's remaining earl of Cornwall, and so another assembly was summoned to Stamford.[59] The king had in fact sought to gain assent for Gaveston's recall and in his turn determined to bargain this for concessions with respect to the grievances.[60]

To the Stamford assembly of 27 July 1309 only the lay barons and higher clergy were summoned. To facilitate the attendance of the clerical element Edward had forbidden Archbishop Winchelsey to hold the consecration of Bishop Droxford at Canterbury earlier in the month. This assembly, says Stubbs, echoing the editor of the Parliamentary Writs, "was regarded as representing the April Parliament."[61] The king responded favourably to the petition. The "Statute of Stamford" issued on 20 August served to reinforce the law of 1300 on purveyance – the arbitrary imposition of prises or forced seizure of goods on the king's behalf constituted a perennial complaint – and the exactions on the wines, cloth, and merchandise of aliens were dropped. Six days later writs were issued for the collection of the twenty-fifth, only to be suspended on 10 December by the king, at the petition of the earls of Gloucester, Lincoln, and Cornwall, because of the non-observance of the articles.[62] The position of the bishops has been examined more fully elsewhere, but it is clear that Winchelsey was not happy with the turn of events and in particular the papal revocation of the excommunication he had pronounced.[63] As for Gaveston, according to Guisborough the mediation of the king and of Gloucester brought some of the earls to a grudging acceptance that he should remain earl of Cornwall for life.[64]

The Bridlington chronicler, who is much more detailed than Guisborough at this point, says that Gaveston by the consent of the earls, barons, and of others, was confirmed in the possession of the lands that he had formerly held in the hope that he would behave well towards the magnates in the future.[65] The *Vita* singles out the earl of Lincoln, Henry de Lacy, who had been so determined on Gaveston's exile, as the principal mediator to favour Gaveston, bringing round the earl of Warenne, who had remained hostile since the Wallingford tournament. Such, declared this chronicler, was the fickleness of the magnates.

Although, if Dr Maddicott's argument carries conviction, one must allow that at any rate some of them were uncomfortable in opposition.[66] A French version of Trevet's chronicle lends support to the *Vita*, claiming that while in Ireland Gaveston drew Lincoln to his cause (*partie*) to the great displeasure of others who made Lancaster their chieftain.[67] It is not clear which earls showed their irritation by failure to attend at Stamford, but on the basis of charter witness lists Lancaster and Arundel seem to have been absent.[68]

Gaveston proved no reformed character. Far from behaving better towards the magnates, it was at this juncture, some chroniclers suggest, that he developed his notorious habit of nicknaming the earls. In one version Gloucester is "whoreson," Lincoln "burst belly," Warwick "black hound of Arden," Pembroke "Joseph the Jew," and the "gentle" Lancaster "ceorl."[69] The dating is questionable, which is why one historian has urged that "Gloucester" refers to Ralph de Monthermer, who prior to 1307 had been addressed by that title and who lived on until 1325. However, versions of the *Brut* chronicle specifically name the earl as Robert (for Gilbert?) de Clare.[70]

In the view of his biographer, who tentatively associates him with the formulation of the demands presented in the Westminster Parliament of April 1309, Lancaster was not going to barter reform for Gaveston's rehabilitation. The royal concessions at the July Parliament at Stamford did not satisfy the earl. Indeed, Maddicott regards that assembly as marking "a real turning point" in the earl's "relations with the Crown and with his fellow magnates."[71] Hamilton remarks that all the earls save Lancaster sealed Gaveston's charter of re-enfeoffment and concludes that the restored earl deliberately altered his former practice by associating with his fellows, or at least with those of them who were willing, that is Gloucester, Lincoln, and Richmond.[72] Allegedly too, he made some attempt at curbing his ostentation. His earlier Gascon and English grants were exchanged for the lands of the earldom and other benefits were conferred upon him, though it is calculated that in total they did not exceed what the other earls might have expected. Somewhat meanly, perhaps, the royal grant of manors to Margaret, the widow of Edmund, his predecessor as earl of Cornwall, reserved an annuity to Gaveston and his wife because their value exceeded the amount due as dower.[73] There is evidence at this time, as before his exile, that Gaveston was in a position to direct the flow of royal patronage.[74]

It is a matter of individual judgment whether one accepts the chroniclers' verdict that the flamboyant Gascon continued his former provocative behaviour, or the more indulgent view of his recent apologist, Dr Hamilton. The former view seems more credible. By October 1309, Guisborough states, the earls of Arundel, Lancaster, Lincoln, Oxford, and Warwick declined "because of Peter" to attend a "Secretum Parliamentum" scheduled to meet at York on 18 October, when presumably the Scottish situation would have been the principal item on the agenda. As a result a parliament of earls, barons, and higher clergy was summoned on 26 October to the same place for 8 February 1310. The barons seem to have been unhappy about this venue and on 12 December it was changed to Westminster.[75] For the second time the barons raised objections; while their principal enemy remained on the royal couch (*regio lateret in thalamo*) they could not attend with safety. They would obey the royal writ as they were bound but intended to come armed.[76] The king, meanwhile, celebrated the Christmas festivities at Langley, compensating for Gaveston's previous absence by daily confabulations.[77] Subsequently he reluctantly agreed that Gaveston should be sent away for a time, while the earls were further mollified by assurances of their safety. The king having appointed the earls of Gloucester, Lincoln, Richmond, and Warenne to keep the peace in London, their fellow earls of Lancaster, Hereford, Pembroke, and Warwick were warned not to attend parliament in arms.[78]

The petition presented at the Westminster Parliament of February 1310 by the prelates, earls, and barons is one of the many documents incorporated in the *Annales Londonienses* as well as among the muniments of the London Guildhall. To some extent it prefigures the "Stratford Articles" of 1327 justifying Edward II's enforced abdication. The preamble warned of the grave dangers to the realm, the disinheritance and dishonour of the king and his power, and the harm to Holy Church that could not be avoided unless measures were taken by the advice of the prelates, earls, and barons and other wise men of the kingdom. The main charges were that Edward, misled by evil counsel, had wasted the lands and treasure to such an extent that he could not maintain his household. Consequently his ministers had resorted to extortion of the goods of the Church and people without making payment – contrary to Magna Carta. Squandering the inheritance of his father, Edward I, the king had lost Scotland and dismembered his lands in England and Ireland. The community of the realm had granted him a twentieth of their goods in aid of the Scottish war as well as a twenty-fourth to be rid of prises and other grievances. These sums had been frittered away, the war had not been advanced, nor had the taking of prises and other grievances been amended; on the contrary, they were increasing from day to day. In order to save the king, themselves, and the Crown, which by their allegiance they professed themselves bound to maintain, they petitioned that such perils and others be redressed by ordinance of the baronage.[79]

THE MAKING OF THE ORDINANCES

This petition has been described as "a masterly summary of the cumulative *gravamina* of the previous three years."[80] It is perhaps not so sophisticated as this eulogy might suggest but rather a down-to-earth condemnation of Edward's failure to govern that makes no allowance for the difficulties created by the barons themselves. There can be no question on at least two counts – the emphasis on evil counsel and the waste of resources – that Gaveston was the unnamed target. Undoubtedly it was to save him that the king assented to the petition on

16 March 1310, authorizing "for the honour of God, our good, and that of our realm" the election "of our free will" of a body that came to be known as the Ordainers. For their part the barons, both lay and ecclesiastical, in a declaration of 17 March promised that this would not redound to the prejudice of the king and his heirs. The authority of the elect was to last until Michaelmas and for the ensuing year, during which time they were "to ordain and establish the estate of our household and of our realm ... in accordance with law, reason and the royal coronation oath."[81]

It goes almost without saying, that despite the face-saving clause, the king acted under duress. The *Vita* is precise on the point: "unless the king conceded what they asked for, they [the barons] would not have him for their king, nor would they maintain the fealty sworn to him, especially since he did not keep the oath sworn at his coronation."[82] Here, clearly enough, is an ominous fore-shadowing of the events of 1326 at Kenilworth. The declaration of 17 March was addressed to the king in the names of the archbishop of Canterbury and ten bishops, eight earls – Gloucester, Lancaster, Lincoln, Hereford, Richmond, Pembroke, Warwick, and Arundel – and thirteen barons.

The Ordainers were elected from among those named by an involved process. First of all the bishops present elected two earls, Lincoln and Pembroke. Then the earls chose two bishops, Ralph Baldock of London and Simon of Ghent, the Salisbury diocesan. These four in their turn chose two barons, Hugh de Veer and William le Marshal. The six concluded the process by electing fifteen others, to bring the total to twenty-one. The full complement comprised Archbishop Winchelsey, four other English bishops – Chichester (John Langton) and Nor-wich (John Salmon) in addition to London and Salisbury – together with two Welsh bishops, St David's (David Martin) and Llandaff (John of Monmouth); the same eight earls mentioned above, and lastly, six barons: Hugh de Veer, William le Marshal, Robert FitzRoger, Hugh de Courtenay, William Martin, and John de Gray.[83] Following the election all swore an oath administered to the archbishop and the remainder of the Ordainers by the bishop of Chichester, whose own oath was taken by Winchelsey.

The Ordainers carried out their appointed task by producing three sets of Ordinances: the interim regulations of 1310, the "New" Ordinances of 1311, and the third Ordinances, also of 1311, confusingly called the second by con-temporary commentators, who disregard the initial set on the justifiable grounds that they were incorporated in the New Ordinances. The preliminary Ordinances were produced because speed was of the essence if the situation were not to deteriorate (*quia celeritas auxilii illud exposcebat*).[84] They are dated 19 March 1310 from the London house of the Carmelite friars. The king ordered their pub-lication by a writ of 2 August addressed to the sheriffs.[85]

These preliminary Ordinances contain six clauses, two of which might be described as conventional: the first, which provided for the maintenance of the Church's rights (*fraunchises*), and the last, which ordered the observance of

Magna Carta but added that the Ordainers might determine obscure or doubtful points during their term of authority. The second was an enabling clause. It required strict observance of the king's peace by the mayor and aldermen of the City of London so that the Ordainers could conduct their work there unmolested, with the assistance of the judges and other knowledgeable persons (*autres sages*) and in proximity to the records, particularly those of chancery and exchequer. The three substantive clauses were designed to alleviate the royal debts by prohibiting grants without the Ordainers' consent, directing that customs dues were to be received by natives rather than aliens and to be delivered to the exchequer for the maintenance of the royal household so that the king could live of his own without prises. Finally, the arrest was ordered of those foreign merchants who had collected customs since the time of Edward I's death.[86] All six clauses came to be incorporated, somewhat incongruously, in a sort of preface to the New Ordinances.[87]

The Ordainers completed their task within the eighteen months allotted to them. Quite how the resultant Ordinances were drawn up, and by whom, it would be impossible to say for certain, although the *Vita* looks upon the earl of Warwick as the guiding spirit: "consilio eius [et] ingenio ordinationes prodierunt." Apart from clause 12, designed to protect the ecclesiastical ordinaries against malicious prohibitions in purely spiritual cases, there is little evidence of clerical *gravamina*. By contrast, the long-term criticisms levelled by Lancaster and others are clearly discernible in the central group – numbered 13 to 23 – of the forty-one clauses. These constitute an interesting amalgam of principle and personality. Clause 13 demands the removal of all "evil councillors" while clause 14 requires that appointments of officers, from the chancellor and the chief justices of King's Bench and Common Pleas downwards,[88] were to be made by the counsel and assent of the baronage in parliament. If necessary, interim appointments could be made until such time as parliament met. It was laid down in clause 15 that the chief wardens of ports and of maritime castles were to be deputed in similar manner, while the following clause insisted upon the same arrangement for offices in Gascony, Ireland and Scotland – lands said to be in danger of being lost for lack of competent holders. "Suitable and sufficient" sheriffs were to be appointed by the chancellor, treasurer, and others of the council present at the time, but failing the chancellor the treasurer and barons of the exchequer and justices of the Bench were permitted to act. Clause 18 begins by lamenting the oppressions inflicted by keepers, bailiffs and other officers of the forests and for remedy ordains that their bailiwicks, even if held for life, be seized while "good and upright persons" enquire as to the truth of grievances. If found guilty such officers are to be removed. In similar fashion it is claimed in clause 19 that the chief keepers of forests this side of and beyond Trent had fined and ruined people. In future no one was to be imprisoned for vert or venison offences – damaging the forest underbrush or poaching deer – unless caught *in flagrante delicto*.

At this point a notably lengthy clause, 20, condemns Gaveston "found guilty by the examination of the prelates, earls, barons, knights and of other good and lawful men" of having badly advised the king, taken his treasure, and drawn men to himself who would stand against the "people." The author of the *Vita* did not wish to break the flow of his narrative with a recitation of the contents of the Ordinances, but this clause he gives in full as being pertinent to his theme, which concludes with the observation that in such manner Gaveston was banished by the Ordainers.[89] The following three clauses are directed respectively against the Frescobaldi, Henry de Beaumont, and his sister, the lady Isabella de Vescy. Emery dei Frescobaldi's lands were to be seized and others of that company imprisoned pending satisfactory audit of their accounts; Beaumont was to be removed from the royal council, in future to come near Edward only during sessions of parliament or at times of war, and to have his lands confiscated until compensation should be paid for the issues of those he had received contrary to the Ordinances. Isabella de Vescy who allegedly had been instrumental in procuring royal gifts for her brother to the Crown's disinheritance, was to be exiled from the court and deprived of the castle of Bamburgh. There is a strong personal element here, but more broadly these clauses constitute an attempt at restraining the king even in his closest relationships.[90]

Two clauses, 24 and 25, concern pleas of the exchequer: proper allowance was to be made in shrieval accounts for debts on production of acquittances; merchants and others were not to be permitted to make use of the court in cases of debt or trespass. The two subsequent clauses involve the royal household: people were aggrieved by stewards and marshals of the household who, it was claimed, had been hearing common pleas inappropriately. In future they were to deal solely with offences within the household. Moreover, within the "verge", that is proximity to the court, felonies had gone unpunished. To remedy this state of affairs clause 27 decreed that coroners of the districts concerned were to act in conjunction with the coroner of the household.[91]

The remainder of the Ordinances present a rather miscellaneous appearance. Some (e.g. clauses 34 and 38) seek to regulate unfairness in the courts. Of special significance in a wider sphere are clauses 9 and 29. The first of these, described by Bertie Wilkinson as "an important extension of parliamentary government,"[92] laid down that the king could not declare war or go out of the kingdom without the consent of the baronage in parliament. The second required this body to meet once a year, or twice if need be, although it should be stressed that the obligation occurs in a judicial context, being aimed at the relief of those whose cases in the royal court were impeded on the grounds that they ought not to be answered without the king. The privy seal office is criticized (clause 32) for issuing letters said to impede "the law of the land and common right" – common law, that is. Clause 31 provides for the observance of statutes made by the king's ancestors provided that they do not infringe Magna Carta or the Charter of the Forest (the interpretation of which the barons had reserved to themselves).

This insistence on keeping laws of former kings is reminiscent of the coronation oath.[93]

Certain clauses were aimed at specific long-standing abuses. Thus, prises were to be restricted to those considered "ancient, due and accustomed" (clause 10). The hue and cry was to be raised against purveyors who took them without proper payment. All new customs and maltôtes (clause 11) levied since the coronation of Edward I were to be abolished, notwithstanding the latter's charter in favour of alien merchants. Landholders had been maliciously accused of felonies in places where they held no land and had in consequence been outlawed. In future they could surrender themselves and answer where they did have land (clause 35). The coinage was to be changed (clause 30) only with the common consent of the baronage in parliament. The practice of issuing protections for those in the king's service (clause 37) had been abused by men seeking to avoid legal actions for debt or trespass. Similarly, it was alleged in clause 28 that homicide and robbery had been encouraged by the ease with which perpetrators could secure the king's peace.[94] In future no felon was to be sheltered by a charter of that kind unless in a case where the king could make such a grant in compatibility with his oath, by due process of law, and in accordance with the custom of the realm.[95]

The remaining clauses (38–41) concern themselves with the proper observance of the Ordinances. Clarification of Magna Carta and of the Charter of the Forest were to be dealt with in the next parliament (clause 38), a postponement similar to that of the household reforms which were held over until the third (or second) Ordinances (clause 13).[96] All the chief officers at the time of their assumption of responsibility were to swear to uphold the Ordinances (clause 39), while in each parliament (clause 40) a bishop, two earls, and two barons were to hear and determine cases of complaint against the king's officers.[97] Finally in clause 41, it was declared that the Ordinances, to be observed in every point, were to be issued under the great seal. The king duly accepted and confirmed them on 5 October 1311 and ordered their publication throughout the realm.

As at least one historian has pointed out, all but one of the eleven articles discussed briefly above – which themselves hark back to the *Articuli super Cartas* of 1300 – are to be found, in modified form, among the New Ordinances.[98] But the document of 1311 is both more wide ranging and more comprehensive. Stubbs considered that it provided both an indication of "the abuses and offences by which Edward had provoked the hostility of men already prejudiced against him" and a "valuable illustration of constitutional reform."[99] Of course, many of the "abuses and offences" existed in his father's reign, only to be highlighted by Edward II's patent incapacity for government. In fact, it has been argued recently that there is little in the Ordinances that cannot be traced back to Edward I; some grievances date back to the crisis of 1297, or even beyond.[100] It could also be argued that much emphasis has been placed on the concept of a clearly conceived policy of "constitutional reform;" which by implication would be for the "good" of a broad spectrum of society. Temporarily at least, the barons could foresee a wide range of business coming before parliament, where it would be monitored in their own interests or at best those of the realm as they conceived them. Stubbs, looking in vain for the "third estate," the Commons, commented that "the privileges asserted for the nation are to be exercised by the baronage."[101]

Bertie Wilkinson in a judicious chapter on the Ordinances has argued against the idea advocated by Tout and Conway Davies that the so-called reforming movement of 1310–11 was intended "to break down the system of government which has been called the household or personal system."[102] The "real aim," he suggests, "was the establishment of certain measures of reform, which aimed at the removal of certain specific grievances, but which made no attack on the system of government as a whole." The movement, he thought, was not one "of revolutionary measures and ideas," but of reaction by a baronage "confronted with the rule of an inefficient and unpopular king."[103] The detailed reform of the household was deferred in favour of that of the *status regni*, although this should not be taken to imply that there was any distinction between household and state administration. When the barons did come to treat of the household in the "Third" Ordinances it was not of its manner of functioning but of its personnel: "de familia et servis regis."[104] Hostility to the "household system," comments Wilkinson, has been detected in the insistence of the Ordinances that all issues were to be paid into the exchequer, hence to the detriment of the wardrobe.[105]

However we interpret the Ordinances, the restraints they placed on the king were substantial and varied: were he to uphold them he could no longer embark upon a Scottish campaign or even cross the sea to his Continental possessions, or those in Ireland, without first summoning a parliament and securing its permission. The personnel of his government was to be vetted as were the men or women close to his person, the latter on a basis that is not clear, except that they would have to be acceptable to the baronage. His power to distribute patronage, and hence to accumulate support, was severely curtailed. No wonder that the author of the *Vita* reported the protest of Edward and his council to the effect that "some things were to his disadvantage (*incommoda*), others fabricated out of hate (*in odium suum*)." The barons, the king claimed, had exceeded their brief which excluded "all things touching the king's sovereignty." As might be expected, the most personally distressing element was Gaveston's expulsion. The same chronicler, a convinced Montfortian, suggests that fear of civil war, the desolation of the realm, and even the king's capture and deprivation were what influenced the councillors to persuade their master to accept the Ordinances and in particular Gaveston's banishment.[106]

Edward was compelled to swear to abide by the Ordinances. He did so with the notarial protestation that he could revoke any that were to the prejudice of the king or his Crown.[107] It was a notable if short-lived victory for Lancaster, to whom the Ordinances were attributed by the highly derivative Sempringham continuation of *Le Livere de Reis de Brittanie*. As is well known, in celebration he erected a memorial tablet in St Paul's Cathedral.[108] In practice the abiding weakness of the Ordinances was that no means existed, short of civil war, for upholding them against a recalcitrant king. It was towards civil war, thanks to his vendetta against Gaveston, that Lancaster was about to move.

Edward had little intention of having his activities curbed in this manner, but Gaveston was forced to leave the country in conformity with article 20. This he did but from the Thames rather than Dover, the port prescribed. Gaveston is said by the *Vita* to have carried with him letters "testifying to his good character and loyalty," sealed both by the king and by various magnates, although the young earl of Gloucester afterwards thought better of his conduct and tore the impression of his seal from the parchment.[109] The St Albans tradition is that the exile went first to France, from which he was forced to flee.[110] It is more likely that he passed through part of France, for which safe conduct was sought, and that his destination was Flanders. Edward had written to his sister Margaret, duchess of Brabant, asking that she and her husband receive him kindly.[111] The Pauline annalist more precisely gives his place of exile as Bruges, which he is said to have left after Christmas 1311, only to claim in the following sentence that he spent the "Nativity" at York with the king. What in fact he did do was to travel to York for the February celebrations following the birth of his daughter.[112] It is probably wise to discount the rumours of his return by the end of November, when he was being sought in the Southwest by Hugh Courtenay and William Martin, erstwhile Ordainers.[113] Indeed, it is unlikely, as the London annalist claims, that he returned before Christmas and proceeded towards Windsor.[114] What is clear is that his movements were understandably shrouded in secrecy; the chroniclers were largely guessing.

Gaveston's speedy return requires a note of explanation. The most likely reason is given by the *Vita*. The king, enraged by the earls' insistence that Peter's friends should leave the court or suffer imprisonment, protested against the attempt to treat him like one who was out of his wits (*sicut providetur fatuo*) and swore on God's soul that he would exercise his own judgment and recall Gaveston.[115] This would seem to refer to the undated "Third" Ordinances. To some degree these reiterated the provisions of the New Ordinances or insisted on their implementation, but for the most part they are concerned with the enumeration of office holders and those around the king whose removal was demanded. So far as Gaveston was concerned they required the cancellation of his letters of protection and attorney, as being contrary to the Ordinances, the removal of the men, formerly in his service, who had been given custody of his confiscated lands, and the banishment of his friends and relations.[116] That these articles were promulgated in 1311 is suggested by the London annalist, who also remarked that like the earlier ones they were not obeyed.[117]

THE PURSUIT AND DEATH OF GAVESTON

King and favourite sought security at York where, on 18 January 1312, Edward issued a proclamation declaring that Gaveston had been exiled contrary to the laws and customs of the realm, which his coronation oath bound him to maintain, and that he was a good and loyal subject. The mayor and sheriffs of London were ordered to maintain the city against his enemies as were the authorities in ports and towns throughout the land.[118] Meanwhile, on 20 January, Gaveston's lands were restored to him; a week later (the twenty-sixth) the king ordered the Ordinances to be kept insofar as they were not prejudicial to himself or to the Crown.[119] But he seems to have been playing a double game. An anonymous correspondent writing from York states that Edward summoned the knights from the county before him to explain that his concessions in London were made against his will and that "he had revoked everything which the earls have done and ordained." The writer adds that the king had restored the lands of Langton, the bishop of Chester (Coventry and Lichfield), who had been sworn as treasurer and admitted as the closest confidant of the king after Gaveston, and had given the church of Cottingham to John de Hothum who, like Walter Langton, was not approved of by the Ordainers by reason of his association with Gaveston.[120]

Edward had shown his petulant hand only too readily, though he had cunningly claimed that the rehabilitation of Gaveston was in accordance with his coronation oath and that the appointment of Langton followed the letter of the Ordinances – that is, it was to last only until the next parliament. The barons were incensed. The king, after an initial show of strength when he banned gatherings of prelates and barons, played into the opposition's hands by permitting the mayor and sheriffs of London to admit the earls and barons to the city, provided they did not come armed.[121] They duly assembled at St Paul's to which place Archbishop Winchelsey had summoned the bishops for 13 March. There he is said by the *Vita* to have denounced Gaveston, who by his unscheduled return would have been *ipso facto* excommunicate.[122] One outcome of the council was the deputing of Pembroke, Hereford, and John Botetourt to prevent Langton's exercising his office at the exchequer. The barons of the exchequer duly notified the king of this interference.[123]

Winchelsey certainly had a sense of the constitutional importance of the Ordinances and we cannot deny a measure of altruism to some at least of the barons. The latter's immediate reaction was to hunt down Gaveston on the dubious assumption that if he could be silenced better government would ensue. The London annalist describes how the country was divided up into regions under the oversight of wardens: Gloucester was to be responsible for keeping the peace in Kent, Sussex, Surrey, London, and the southern parts of England; Hereford in Essex and the East; Lancaster in the West; while Robert Clifford and Henry Percy were to guard the northern March lest Edward or Gaveston should attempt to communicate with Robert Bruce, the *soi disant* king of Scots. Rumour had it that Edward would be prepared to acknowledge Bruce in return for help against his enemies.[124]

The *Vita* has a rather different story: the earls of Lancaster, Pembroke, Hereford, Arundel and Warwick bound themselves by a mutual oath and formulated a secret plan for Gaveston's capture. The earl of Gloucester, though not a party to the arrangement, is said to have promised nonetheless to abide by the earls' decision.[125] The plan, as revealed by the London annalist, was to despatch Pembroke and Warenne, less violent opponents of the favourite, to secure his person. Meanwhile, wrote the Lanercost chronicler, the barons ordered that the king should not receive a halfpenny, or even a farthing, from the exchequer.[126] During January and February the king and Gaveston remained at York, where the favourite's wife, Margaret de Clare, gave birth to a daughter, Joan. At her churching on 20 February Edward hosted an entertainment by "King Robert" and other minstrels.[127] On the tenth the custos of the castle of Wallingford had been instructed to restore it and the attached honour of St Waleric to Gaveston. At the Curia Bertrand Caillou, Gaveston's nephew, and the royal envoys were hard at work on Gaveston's behalf. It has been suggested that contingency plans were being made for the favourite's return to the Continent. We know something of the coming and going of envoys, nothing about the nature of their business.[128] The king is reported to have been at Scarborough on 28 February, perhaps in connection with Gaveston's future refuge there.[129]

The idea has been ventilated that following Gaveston's return from his third exile Queen Isabella collaborated with the "opposition," sending gifts to Hereford and Lancaster and to his countess.[130] It may be, though, that her position has been misunderstood. Edward, it has been pointed out, took the trouble to conciliate his wife with gifts, and on 31 January 1312 she was paid four hundred pounds for expenses in joining her husband in the North. Moreover, at New Year she had been careful to send him precious objects (*jocalia*) as a seasonal present.[131] Even her attitude towards Gaveston may not have been as hostile as is regularly surmised. It is at least possible that the greater security enjoyed by reason of her pregnancy and the possibility that she would bear an heir to the throne led her to be more accommodating. In any case she could scarcely throw herself on the tender mercies of her visiting uncle, Louis of Evreux, on his arrival in mid-September 1312.[132] Despite the threat of civil war the royal household had its measure of innocent enjoyment, as witnessed by the record of the Easter Monday romp in which the ladies of the queen's chamber – including the king's former nurse Alice de Leygrave – dragged Edward from his bed and were rewarded for the privilege.[133]

On 31 March 1312 the favourite was appointed custos of Carlisle and Scarborough castles.[134] A few days later, on 4 April, he swore that he would not surrender Scarborough to anyone except the king, and not to him should he be a prisoner. This unusual oath may have been occasioned by the menacing attitude of Lancaster and his reported demand that Gaveston either be handed over or sent into exile, as had been ordained. It certainly suggests Edward's fears and immediate intentions.[135] The king and Gaveston left York on 5 April and proceeded by way of Boroughbridge and Durham to Newcastle, which they probably reached on the tenth.[136] While there Gaveston was taken ill and given medical treatment.[137] Meanwhile Lancaster, who allegedly had been chosen leader of the anti-Gaveston coalition, or as Walsingham described it in the *Historia Anglicana*, "*dux electus regni nobilium*,"[138] had quietly moved northwards accompanied by Henry Percy and Robert Clifford. The baronial army, raised surreptitiously under cover of tournaments held in various parts of the country, arrived before Newcastle at the beginning of May. Lancaster's intention, so the *Historia* claims, was not to injure the king in any way but to capture Gaveston so that he could be judged in accordance with law (*secundum leges communiter editas*). The king and Gaveston were forced to flee precipitately to Tynemouth, which they reached on 3 May. The town of Newcastle, and later the castle, were surrendered, apparently without resistance. There Lancaster, after a cautious approach, captured a great quantity of treasure, armour, and horses.[139]

From Tynemouth Edward and Gaveston hurriedly set sail for Scarborough on 5 May, which they reached five days later. On 17 May the king issued an order under pain of life and limb to desist from its siege; another to the same effect was addressed to Warenne.[140] Again there is some difference of opinion about Isabella's situation. The pregnant queen is assumed by the St Albans' chroniclers Trokelowe and Walsingham to have been abandoned by her husband, whereupon Lancaster allegedly consoled her with secret messengers bearing assurances that he would not cease to pursue his quarry Gaveston until he had removed him entirely from the king's side but excused himself from meeting her personally for fear of arousing the king's indignation.[141] This has the appearance of a fictitious tale, since Isabella's own hasty departure from Tynemouth forced her to leave some of her baggage under guard at (South?) Shields (Les Sheles). On account of her pregnancy she probably did not accompany her husband to Scarborough but travelled directly to York. It could be that the St Albans' chroniclers confounded this incident with a similar one in the autumn of 1322, when Isabella was again marooned at an unnamed northern fortress by the sea and deemed it prudent to escape from the Flemings or the Scots by boat. One of her ladies died as a result and another gave premature birth. English sources overlook the incident, which has found its way into a French chronicle.[142]

The subsequent story has been told too often to require detailed repetition here.[143] The king, by retiring first to Gaveston's fortress of Knaresborough and then to York in the hope of raising the siege, allowed the baronial army to occupy a position between the besieged and a possible relieving force. This was not unfortunate in itself;[144] it became so when Edward failed to take action, possibly because he could not muster enough troops or because he preferred to persuade the barons to come to an agreement. Given time, suggests the *Vita*, he could secure the intervention of the pope and the king of France. Scarborough Castle, though a formidable defensive work with ready access to the sea, was insufficiently armed or provisioned and there was no local diversionary force to disturb Lancaster. In consequence he retired, allegedly because he did not wish to burden the neighbourhood with his foragers, leaving Pembroke and Warwick to continue the assault. This lasted for about ten days, the barons ignoring the king's command to desist. Then Gaveston, unable to escape either by land or sea, agreed to surrender under conditions. There is a distinct possibility that the king had some hand in the preliminary negotiations; the *Flores*, notably unsympathetic to the king, alleges that he offered a bribe of a thousand pounds to Pembroke.[145]

The St Albans' tradition is that Gaveston agreed to abide by the ordinance of the barons "*simpliciter, omni exceptione seclusa*," subject only to his being permitted to have discussion with the king.[146] The *Vita* records that the cornered favourite agreed to surrender to Pembroke on condition that if no agreement were reached with the earls by the first of August he should be restored to the castle and to his sister, whom he had left there.[147] The text of the document, dated at Scarborough 19 May 1312, is given by the London annalist and was also recorded among the Canterbury muniments. It is in the form of letters issued by the earls of Pembroke and Surrey, together with Henry Percy – the besiegers of Scarborough. These incorporate an agreement between them on behalf of the "community of the realm" (in practice the magnates) on the one part and Gaveston on the other, which they swore on the Lord's body to observe. They were to keep Gaveston safe until such time, prior to 1 August, as they were able to produce a proposal in consultation with the prelates, barons and other "bons gentz." This was to be presented at St Mary's Abbey, York, in the presence of Lancaster or someone appointed to act on his behalf. Should the proposal be agreeable to the king and to Gaveston, all well and good; if not, then the latter was to be allowed to return to Scarborough with the same number of men as when he surrendered it, under pain of forfeiture against the guarantors. For his part Gaveston promised not to persuade the king to alter the agreement.[148]

The St Albans' chroniclers record that discussion (a "colloquium") took place with the king at York and that Edward promised to accept all the baronial demands.[149] It is probably in connection with the anticipated debate on Gaveston's fate that writs were issued at York on 3 June for a parliament to meet at Lincoln on 23 July 1312.[150] Meanwhile, at York Pembroke was given sole custody of Gaveston; the other two guarantors fade from the picture. In accordance with some prearranged plan Pembroke took Gaveston south to Oxfordshire, apparently *en route* for Wallingford Castle, which his prisoner had held as earl of Cornwall. Gaveston being wearied by his journey, Pembroke lodged him temporarily on 9 June at Deddington, while he went to visit his wife at Bampton nearby. Deddington rectory, situated to the north of the church, was not defensible and the earl's progress was clearly known to Guy de Beauchamp, who taking advantage of the situation, surrounded the house on 10 June and took Gaveston prisoner first – so the *Anonimalle* chronicler suggests – to his seat at Elmley in Worcestershire and then to his castle at Warwick.[151]

Lancaster, Hereford, Arundel, and others, including John Botetourt, joined Warwick to map out a plan of campaign. Surviving copies of letters patent show that on the day before Gaveston's execution, which took place at Blacklow Hill on 19 June,[152] some – and probably all – agreed to stand by each other in their decision.[153] Warwick is stated to have remained in his castle while Gaveston was put to death on Lancaster's land. There was even a show of judicial propriety. Gaveston was brought before William Inge and Henry Spigurnel, justices of gaol delivery at Warwick, who on the basis of the Ordinances, which allegedly had not been officially revoked in Warwickshire,[154] pronounced that he should be hanged as a traitor to king and realm. But, as the canon of Bridlington points out, his peers were neither summoned nor present. In the event, in deference to his brother-in-law the earl of Gloucester, Gaveston was not dealt with as a traitor but run through by one Welsh footsoldier and beheaded by another.[155]

Guy de Beauchamp, the earl of Warwick, cultivated man though he was, could well have been the prime mover in this unsavoury affair. But some have followed the *Vita* in attributing the overall direction to Lancaster, the predominant baronial figure. It is possible, however, that Lancaster was overtaken by the events precipitated by Warwick. The latter has been considered intelligent and literate, but in this matter he revealed the ruffianly side of his character. Even after the deed, if the tale be true, he refused to allow four shoemakers to bury the body at Warwick but ordered that it be returned to the place of execution outside his own bailiwick. He certainly lived up to his nickname by biting its fabricator, but at the cost of his own repute. He was to die three years later, long before the full impact of his behaviour could be realized.[156]

The circumstances were such as to give rise to the rumour that Pembroke had engineered the whole affair, though this is surely unfounded. Instead he must stand accused of criminal negligence allied to an astonishing naïvety.[157] Too late he pleaded with Gloucester to vindicate the wrong done to him: "he would suffer eternal disgrace, and lose the lands he had pledged." But that young man replied that Warwick had acted with the aid and counsel of the other earls and cynically advised Pembroke to behave more circumspectly in the future.[158] Pembroke tried to gain the support of Oxford University, but neither townsmen nor clerks were anxious to be drawn into the dispute.[159] Pembroke and Warenne, angered and unhappy at their treatment, were received into the king's grace and gathered their forces in his support. Gaveston's body and severed head were taken up by the Dominican friars of Oxford, though they were unable to give his remains Christian burial because he had died excommunicate.[160]

EDWARD'S RESPONSE TO GAVESTON'S MURDER

The king, well aware of what was to be expected were Gaveston to be caught by the earls, particularly Warwick, now planned to avenge his death. We are told that Pembroke and Warenne, Despenser, Beaumont, and Edmund de Mauley, together with others of Gaveston's household, gathered round him and urged that a bold attack be made upon his enemies. Plausibly enough they stressed the unprecedented nature of the crime against the king. Pembroke's biographer, though, is anxious to mitigate the chroniclers' emphasis on his subject's bellicosity, considered to be out of character, and he seeks instead to highlight the diplomatic initiatives in which the earl was involved. At the same time, allowance must be made for the fact that the situation was charged with a good deal of emotion. Caution was by no means uppermost. Pembroke was incensed that someone placed in his custody had been killed in his despite. Edward himself, claims the *Vita*, vowed to have Warwick's head or to confiscate his goods and send him into exile. Hence he preferred to prepare for war rather than to heed the counsel of those who urged that internal strife would weaken the capacity of the English to contain the Scots.[161]

How successful had Lancaster been? Insofar as he was responsible for Gaveston's death he had made a tactical blunder. He had not merely sullied his own reputation but had also ensured that there could be no further accommodation with the king, save on a temporary basis. Hatred was the touchstone of Edward's future relationship with the earls, apart from those few whom Lancaster had alienated. It has been aptly remarked that the scene was set for the politics of the next ten years, until the *bouleversement* of 1322.[162] The attempt to determine those to whom Edward looked for everyday advice, and to coerce him by what have been termed "constitutional" means had failed; indeed, no English king at the time could have been expected to endure the straightjacket that the Ordinances attempted to force upon him. Lancaster lacked finesse, his all-or-nothing tactics coupled with the slippery tergiversations of his royal adversary ensured that only civil war could resolve the situation.

The king, anxious to receive the Londoners' support, reached the city from the North about the middle of July. Boldly addressing the citizens at Blackfriars, he complained of the barons' conduct and besought his hearers to defend the city against them. This they agreed to do.[163] From London Edward travelled to Dover, munitioned the castle there, took the fealty of the Cinque Ports, and despatched Beaumont and Pembroke to France to seek Philip IV's aid.[164] Once again he may have been playing a double game. Writs were sent to the earls of Hereford, Warwick, and Lancaster ordering them to come to London for 27 August in order to discuss the "prejudicial Ordinances" – the same day that he planned to muster his forces there, although it is possible that these were defensive rather than offensive in character.[165] For their part the magnates responsible for Gaveston's death discussed their future plans at Worcester.

Subsequently, under Lancaster's leadership, a substantial army occupied the countryside between St Albans and Ware, posing a threat to London and the future parliament.[166] Parliament, previously summoned to Lincoln, met at Westminster on 20 August 1312.[167] The papal envoy, Arnaud Nouvel, cardinal bishop of St Prisca, arrived some nine days later to act as mediator between the king and barons. He was given lodgings in the bishop of London's house by St Paul's, but the violence of the Londoners was soon brought home to him when one of his servants was killed nearby and the churchyard had to be reconciled by the bishop of St David's. Count Louis of Evreux crossed the Channel about a fortnight later, on 13 September. In the meantime the cardinal travelled to St Albans, where he stayed in the monastery, attempting to mediate with the earls, then at Wheathampstead. The barons proved belligerent, claiming that they were not versed in letters but in the practice of arms, hence they had no wish to see the documents the envoys had brought. They considered it inappropriate that educated bishops, other outsiders, or foreigners, should interfere in their affairs. This frightened the clerical negotiators, who left for London the following day.[168] Two other papal envoys, also recently arrived in England, William Testa and Arnaud d'Aux, bishop of Poitiers, were created cardinals in December.[169] The pope was clearly doing his best to bring about a settlement with men high in his confidence. Meanwhile, envoys set out for the Curia to negotiate a papal loan to tide Edward over his financial difficulties.[170]

The earls failed to arrive in London on the day appointed, but when they did appear at the beginning of September they did so fully armed.[171] Rumours of plots multiplied; some suggested that the king intended to avail himself of the occasion to capture Lancaster, others that the city was to be betrayed to the earl who would thereby ensnare Edward.[172] Despite the king's efforts Lancaster, Warwick, and Hereford entered London. They avoided an armed confrontation; instead they informed the king of their arrival and enquired the cause of his summons – something they would have learned had they attended the opening stages of the parliament. Edward by this time had been joined by the French king's brother, Louis d'Evreux, Isabella's uncle, and by Cardinal Arnaud of St Prisca, who adopted a mollifying stance.[173] There were voices in favour of attacking the earls, others were against such a course. Considering the strength of the baronial forces, the latter were the more realistic, and they gained the day.[174]

Gloucester, who as Gaveston's brother-in-law and Edward's nephew had provided a moderating influence, now stepped in as mediator, attempting to persuade Edward that in reality the barons were his friends. Not surprisingly the king would have none of it, pointing out the attacks on his property and rights, the infringements of his prerogative with respect to the recall of a subject from exile, and the cruel death inflicted on a man whom he had received into his peace. Further, he argued, Lancaster had taken his property at Newcastle, which had it been the act of a lesser man would have been accounted robbery with violence. Thus, he added ominously, such men might well be intending to seize his

Crown and to replace him with another. Rising above this peevish if justifiable complaint, Gloucester suggested that if wrongs had been done they would have to be rectified – "leniency is tried first, and if it is of no avail harsh measures may follow."[175]

Gloucester put the royal case to the barons, who after discussion among themselves, denied that they had striven to diminish the royal prerogative or contrived anything to the king's prejudice. As for the death of a certain exiled "traitor," they had acted on the authority of lawful Ordinances assented to by king and barons that "not even the king," they claimed, "by his mere will can either revoke or change." The king's peace in such case was invalid as being in contradiction of the Ordinances. Lancaster himself speciously responded that he had not stooped to plunder. Rather, having found the king's goods abandoned at Newcastle, he had first made an inventory and then retained them for Edward's use. The barons collectively disclaimed the suggestion that their coming armed to parliament was in contempt of the king or that they intended to substitute someone else. Then they counterattacked. Their labours to strengthen the realm had been misinterpreted by Edward: everything they did he construed as being to his dishonour and out of spite. They reminded him of their mutual oaths and promised to obey him if he would remit "the baseless rancour" conceived against them. This shrewd but not unexpected apologia for their actions was countered by seeming accommodation on the king's side. The barons then declared that all they wanted was a confirmation of the Ordinances and pardons for the death of Gaveston "the traitor." Edward expressed willingness to regrant the Ordinances save for the "fiscal privilege," but with dignity declined to label his former favourite a traitor. This stance, the barons pointed out, might have repercussions with respect to Gaveston's widow and heir and the regranting of the lands of the earldom. It was a temporary impasse, interpreted by the author of the *Vita* as a royal stratagem to wear down the opposition.[176]

About mid-September the king left London for Windsor. The city remained in a volatile state. Pembroke, the elder Despenser, the steward Edward de Mauley, the marshal Nicholas Segrave, and the warden of the Tower, John Crombwell (Cromwell), arrived at the Guildhall to remind the authorities of their earlier promise to safeguard the city. They were met with a series of complaints about the courts of the steward and marshal, enclosure of land outside the Tower said to belong to the city, wrongful imprisonment, and a request that they be allowed to exclude all armed men – the royal councillors had themselves arrived armed. A rumour got abroad that the latter planned to capture those citizens present in the Guildhall. The consequent riot was allayed by the arrival of Mayor John de Gisors with the aldermen and by the withdrawal of the royal emissaries.[177]

The precise chronology of the discussions between the king, the intermediaries from abroad, and the barons cannot be established.[178] Preliminary talks took place at Markyate Street and Wheathampstead, both in Hertfordshire, after which the cardinals left St Albans for London because they felt threatened (*timore perterriti*) by the barons' initial xenophobia; "foreign" clerics, they felt, knew nothing of English problems. Such an attitude was doubtless confirmed by the objections to the Ordinances advanced by two French lawyers.[179] Some of the lawyers' arguments are legalistic, concerned more with abstract principles and logical inconsistencies than with current political realities. They even impugn the complex and indirect means by which the Ordainers were chosen; an argument that could derive from the niceties of clerical elections, which at every stage take account of the will of the electors. At the same time they turn the tables on the barons by claiming certain elements to be contrary to Magna Carta or the Charter of the Forest, against law and reason as well as in derogation of the rights of the king and Crown – "contra iura et rationem in derogationem iuris regis" or in "magnum dedecus regis et sue corone." Historically they point to St Louis's rejection at the Mise of Amiens of the Provisions of Oxford and the confirmation of his verdict by Popes Urban IV and Clement IV. This inchoate document – it stops short with the critique of the eleventh ordinance – could hardly have been intended as a positional paper, modification of which might lead to an agreed text. It constitutes an outright refutation of the Ordinances. The earls' response was predictable: the realm was not governed by written law but by ancient laws and customs, approved by earlier kings. Should they prove inadequate emendations ought to be made at the request of the "vulgus" by the king, his prelates, earls, and barons and established by common consent.[180]

The *Prima Tractatio* is more to the point, but in certain respects equally one-sided. The London annalist places it before the lawyers' arguments. Surprisingly it runs in the name of eight earls, among them Gloucester, Richmond, and most unexpectedly Pembroke,[181] claiming what could hardly have been true in their particular cases that the king was "*engrossi devers eux.*" It may be, however, that the document was thrashed out by both sides. If so, it indicates the strength of the baronial lobby. True, there were major baronial concessions, a promise of assistance against the Scots with four thousand men coupled with a parliamentary aid, and the return of the goods captured at Newcastle, which in any case were theoretically (as we have seen) in custody on the king's behalf. For the rest there were demands for the restoration of lands and the release of persons seized without due process, the removal of "evil councillors," and the upholding of the Ordinances "en touz lur poinz," while Gaveston is described provocatively as "commun enemy du roi et du roiaume."[182]

The survival of a roll of seventeen membranes in the Vatican archives provides further details of the protracted process whereby the barons attempted to barter the return of the royal treasure for a pardon for Gaveston's death, a promise to maintain the Ordinances, and the satisfaction of other specific complaints.[183] It also contains a list of eighteen persons, apart from Gaveston's relatives, who were to be excluded from the king's company by virtue of the

Ordinances.[184] The situation was complicated by the demand for redress of particular grievances that had emerged meanwhile, notably the case of Gruffydd de la Pole, a Lancaster retainer who was in competition with Edward's ambitious chamberlain, John Charlton, for possession of Powys, and those of Henry Percy, one of the Scarborough guarantors, and of Edmund Darel.[185]

Eventually, on 20 December 1312, a "treaty of peace" was drawn up in the cardinal's London lodging. Named in its preamble as arbitrators are the papal envoys Cardinal Arnaud and the bishop of Poitiers (soon to become a cardinal),[186] Louis count of Evreux, and the earls of Gloucester and Richmond. The earl of Hereford, Robert de Clifford, and John Botetourt acted for the absent Warwick and Lancaster; Pembroke, Hugh Despenser the elder, and Nicholas de Segrave for the king.[187] On behalf of the earls it was promised that they would submit to the king in the great hall of Westminster Palace and that on 13 January 1313 they would restore all the goods taken at Newcastle together with the value of any horses that had died in the meantime. A parliament was to be held the following Lent and an appropriate safe conduct is incorporated in the treaty, subject to its acceptance by the earls of Warwick and Lancaster. The king was to give up all rancour on account of Gaveston's death, "non-suspect" judges were to be appointed to hear the case of Gruffydd de la Pole and the goods of the Henry Percy were to be restored. For their part the barons promised not to come to parliament in arms and to induce that body to grant an appropriate aid against the Scots. There is no mention of the Ordinances and pejorative references to Gaveston are absent.[188] In many ways this was a victory for the king and, it is suggested, for Pembroke, who was closely involved in the negotiations.[189]

The agreement had now to be implemented. The first hitch arose when the jewels and other goods were not delivered on the appointed day. It was only after the cardinals' further efforts, pointing out the danger that delay would involve, that on 27 February they were surrendered to the custody of Bishop Reynolds and a king's clerk, John Sandale, by the earl of Hereford, Robert Clifford, and John Botetourt.[190] Even that did not conclude the matter, since the earls of Warwick and Lancaster had still to give their assent to the December treaty. This they did in part and somewhat grudgingly some time after mid-March, having excused themselves from coming to the parliament that assembled on the eighteenth on the grounds that the summons (of 8 January) had not been made in the form "qui in registro cancellariae invenitur."[191] The jewels had now been restored, they pointed out, and they were ready to submit to the king on their knees and to be received into his grace by letters patent in the form that they outlined.[192] They only awaited a proper summons. While accepting the necessity of an aid and the ordinance against coming armed to parliament, they subtly cavilled at the statutory pardon offered on the grounds that it would appear as though the king had conceded it under pressure contrary to the oath made at his coronation. A statute would be required only in default of a law or

to effect amendment. Likewise there was no need for any pardon of that nature
for Gaveston's adherents, since the king could act on his own royal authority.
The "acquittance" of royal displeasure for the barons was to be entrusted to the
archbishop of Canterbury or a suffragan of his (*ou a seon suffragane*), the bishops of London and Chichester, and the earls of Gloucester, Richmond, and
Arundel. Their submission once made, copies were to be delivered to the earls
and barons.[193]

Whatever he might be constrained to concede publicly for the sake of peace,
privately Edward was determined to repudiate the Ordinances, or at least those
elements he particularly disliked. As long before as 13 October 1312 three
notaries had each been paid a mark for drawing up a public instrument in trip-
licate requiring their revocation should they prove to have been made to the prejudice of the king or Crown.[194] Much earlier in that year the pope had been asked
to send envoys and to absolve the king from his oath to maintain them.[195] This
policy had not changed, as the French lawyers' submission argues, and it was
somewhat of a royal triumph, though not trumpeted as such, that the offending
regulations had not been mentioned either in the peace proposals of December
1312 or in the response of the earls in the following May. Before the earls' submission the king was able to insist on the abrogation of the "personal" Ordinances directed against Beaumont and his sister, the lady de Vescy. This opened
the way for the submission of magnates, whom the king had been keeping at
arm's length.

Despite the Scottish threat – Bruce was allegedly in the neighbourhood of
York – and the barons' postponement of submission, the king felt confident
enough to make a journey to France with his queen. In doing so he disregarded the barons' advice and also a provision of the Ordinances. He was absent
from the realm between 23 May and mid-July 1313, during which time John
Droxford, the bishop of Bath and Wells, acted as regent.[196] The occasion was
provided by the knighting at Pentecost (3 June) of Philip IV's three sons, the
eldest being Louis, king of Navarre. The following Wednesday, in a ceremony
in Nôtre Dame, all of them, in company with the English king and many of his
entourage, assumed the Cross at the hands of the Dominican Nicholas de
Fréauville, cardinal priest of St Eusebius.[197] After these ceremonies there was
a colloquium at Pontoise from the feast of Trinity until the end of June. While
there or at Poissy to the south Edward and his queen had a narrow escape when
their pavilion caught fire. Isabella apparently suffered some injury on that
account.[198] The sequel was not so fortunate, since the queen of Navarre and the
wives of Louis's two brothers were found guilty of adultery. The queen was
condemned to be deprived of her crown; all three were imprisoned and their
lovers brutally put to death.[199]

While in France Edward took the opportunity to recruit the further help of
Louis d'Evreux and of the experienced negotiator, Enguerran de Marigny. Various matters were urgent: Gascony of course, a French summons to the English

king to give aid against Flanders, and the settlement with the English barons. This last took place on 14 October 1313 while parliament, summoned for 23 September, continued in session at Westminster. Then, on 6 November, the parties agreed that no one was to be molested on account of Gaveston's death.[200] By English custom such peacemaking was celebrated by a dinner, which Edward duly gave on the same night, the compliment being reciprocated by the earls the following evening. Credit for the outcome must be given to the French intervention, not least to Enguerran de Marigny. It is not known whether he was actually present during the September Parliament: he was certainly in England during November, engaged among other things with Gascon affairs and the transfer of the Templars' lands to the Hospitallers.[201]

And so, comments the overly sanguine author of the *Vita*, Piers's death was forgiven, the earl of Pembroke reconciled, and other friends of the king were dealt with as he wished. Philosophically he ruminates on what might have happened otherwise. The earls, he thought, would have kept the king under restraint. Had not Simon de Montfort done the same with Henry III? But in the end his fate, as in the case of others who had resisted the king, was unfortunate.[202] Various factors such as the Edward's dragging out of the proceedings, the determination and possibly the partiality of some of the arbitrators, and the lack of a common front among the baronage, had combined to secure a royal victory.[203]

While this struggle was in process a momentous event had considerably heightened the monarchy's popularity: a son had been born to Queen Isabella at Windsor on St Brice's Day (13 November 1312). Great celebrations took place in London. The Fishmongers organized a magnificent pageant in which the arms of France and England were prominently displayed. The queen was attended at Westminster and preceded on her journey to Eltham Palace.[204] It would be unwise to accept the verdict of some chroniclers, notably Trokelowe, that Gaveston's fate was thereby forgotten. It was merely eclipsed temporarily by the joyous event.[205] On the third day after the birth, the infant Edward was baptized by Cardinal Arnaud.[206]

There were other developments favourable to Edward. Winchelsey's death on 11 May 1313 had removed a troublesome thorn from the royal flesh; his replacement by a trusty servant, Walter Reynolds, may not have been in the Church's best interests, but it certainly meant that in future the ecclesiastical machine, insofar as the archbishop could manipulate it, would be more attuned to the king's wishes.[207] William Testa, newly created a cardinal, loaned the king two thousand marks – a further loan of £15,000 had been negotiated by Antonio Pessagno with Enguerran de Marigny, Philip IV's well-disposed chamberlain, while in October 1313 an agreement was made whereby the pope privately offered Edward 160,000 florins (some £25,000), to be recovered from the revenues of Gascony. [208]

At long last the Scottish "rebellion" could be given attention. Preparations were in train during December 1313 and the arrival of the constable of Stirling at the beginning of the following Lent made the situation all too clear.[209] Parliamentary permission in accordance with the Ordinances or no, the king was determined to do his duty. He proceeded to assemble an army that impressed contemporaries by its size and magnificence. The disaster of Bannockburn in June 1314 was all the more unexpected; it could only weaken the royal position so recently stabilized. Edward would have to face the consequences of having failed miserably as a military leader.

A final farewell had to be made to Gaveston; the solemnity of the occasion bespeaks the strength of the king's emotions. Edward journeyed to his manor of Langley from Windsor. In his presence on 2 January 1315 Gaveston was laid to rest in the royal chapel. Edward ordained that a hundred Dominican friars should say masses for Gaveston and his antecedents. Present was a strong contingent of bishops: apart from Archbishop Reynolds, the bishops of London (Gilbert Segrave), Winchester (Henry Woodlock), Worcester (Thomas de Cobham), and Bath and Wells (John Droxford), as well as thirteen abbots, both exempt and non-exempt, and innumerable friars. Laymen were also well represented: the earls of Norfolk and Pembroke; among the barons, the two Despensers, Henry de Beaumont, Bartholomew Badlesmere, John de Handlo; as well as some fifty knights. Among the officials were Chancellor Sandale, Treasurer Norwich, Ingelard [de Warley], until recently keeper of the royal wardrobe, William Inge (surprisingly), justice of the Common Bench,[210] and John Gisors, the mayor of London, John Abel, escheator for this side of Trent, and numerous others.[211] Such was the unhappy denouement of Edward's infatuation.

5

Descent Into the Abyss: Civil Strife, 1314–1322

Apart from the Church and her spiritual weapons, and short of rebellion, there was in the state neither man nor institution possessing the power to compel the king to rule justly. ... a weak, cowardly, foolish, or tyrannical king would certainly come to grief sooner or later, especially if he kept his barons at arm's length or fell foul of the clergy.[1]

THE RISE AND DECLINE OF LANCASTER'S INFLUENCE, 1314–16

Somewhat naïvely Lancaster attributed the Bannockburn fiasco, which prefaces this period of the reign, to the non-observance of the Ordinances – or so some would have us believe, among them the authors of the *Vita* and of the Meaux chronicle, respectively a secular clerk and a religious.[2] Had Lancaster and the other recalcitrant earls been at the battle, the result might well have been the same, since shortage of numbers was hardly a factor, but at least it would have been clear that where Scotland was concerned the most powerful earl was not on the sidelines. Pembroke had taken part and maybe fought a rearguard action, by way of protecting the king.[3] The aftermath of the disaster offered opportunity for Lancaster to show his mettle as a man more capable of directing affairs than a king who had demonstrated neither the inclination nor the energy to apply himself consistently to business. That Lancaster's period of domination – his "administration" it has been called – did not result in stable government was due to a number of complex factors, some personal, some external. There can be little doubt that weaknesses of character militated against his political success. It was antipathy towards Edward rather than cooperation with him that marked the earl's conduct. This, of course, was not one-sided, Edward certainly knew how to bottle up his resentment until opportunity enabled him to wreak revenge. Lancaster was so often absent from parliament and the court, admittedly to some degree because of the relative remoteness of his estates, that he failed to exercise consistent influence on everyday affairs.[4] It could not be otherwise. There were also, as will transpire, a number of problems that neither he nor the king could have anticipated.

One feature of Lancaster's program and that of the barons acting with him, was the demand for resumption of estates alienated by the king.[5] The third ordinance declared that lands, rents, franchises, escheats, wards, and marriages were not to be dispensed without the assent of the Ordainers. Assuredly there was a political motive here, but the declared purpose was fiscal. If alienations were made, the king's estate, or "inalienable fisc" would be diminished, so that in order to maintain his obligations he would have to resort to such illegal measures as prises. Purveyance should be paid for, otherwise it would constitute an additional tax. Prises were no novelty and would not – perhaps could not – be abandoned readily. Such expedients had been used by Edward I and were likewise to be employed by Edward III.[6] Yet they did not affect all with equal severity. Rather, it has been argued, prises bore more heavily on the peasantry, since those who were better off could bribe the royal commissioners or secure exemption or amelioration in some other way. Furthermore, their incubus fell unevenly on various parts of the country.[7]

Edward II had estranged the baronage by distributing largesse to what were termed "favourites." Not only did this diminish the "inalienable fisc," it also had the effect of limiting what the barons might consider to be their legitimate call on patronage. But what was the definition of "favourite"? Was it merely a person of whom the barons did not approve because he detracted from their own influence on political decisions? Gaveston had been made an earl and so had the elder Despenser. Their fault was not their status but its newness, and the disproportionate influence they were considered to exercise. In other circumstances the elevation of the elder Despenser could hardly have called for comment. Indeed, Edward II was in some respects abstemious in these matters. He did not elevate the younger Despenser to the earldom of Gloucester, which that favourite certainly had coveted. He chose to keep that of Kent in the family, rather than satisfying the ambition of Lord Badlesmere, to curb which the new earl, Edmund of Woodstock, was associated in a commission of 3 July 1321 for the preservation of peace in the county.[8] With these creations Edward by no means matched the generosity of his son who in 1337 was to create six earls and a duke, and to endow them appropriately, a degree of largesse that was attributed to Stratford's ill-considered counsel.[9]

Edward's promise at the York Parliament of 1314 to observe the Ordinances was reiterated at that which assembled on 20 January 1315 at Westminster. At parliament's demand the Ordinances were confirmed, as was Magna Carta, and there was to be a perambulation of the forests. Perhaps as a *quid pro quo*, grants of a twentieth by the counties and of a fifteenth by the boroughs were made for the Scottish war. Writs giving effect to the Ordinances and for the appointment of those to make perambulations were issued after the parliament had dispersed on 9 March; they have been interpreted as meaning that the king was "determined to redeem his promises." The resumption of lands continued, although some of them resulted from the reiteration of previous orders not complied with.

Naturally enough the resumptions were unpopular with beneficiaries; indeed, they were considered unfair by those who had received them for services rendered. Men such as Roger Mortimer of Chirk and Henry de Beaumont could both claim to be in that category.[10] The executors of Anthony Bek, the bishop of Durham who had died in 1311 and whose goods had been taken into the king's hand on account of his debts to the Crown from as far back as Edward I's reign were finally exonerated. A pardon had been issued by the king but this time it was by assent of the prelates, earls and barons at the Westminster parliament. Members of the council and not least Lancaster himself benefited from grants and pardons.[11]

THE GREAT FAMINE AND ITS AFTERMATH

Perhaps the most unsettling feature of this period was the exceptionally bad weather. Heavy rains during the summer of 1314, the spring of 1315, and much of 1316, brought flooding, a three-year failure of crops, scarcity of food, high prices, particularly those for grain and fuel and, as a consequence, starvation, disease, and murrain of cattle. Various parts of the country were differently affected, of course, and Cuxham in Oxfordshire seems to have been largely untouched. Indeed, its gross fiscal returns were high thanks to the level of prices.[12] But it became difficult to provision northern garrisons, and in particular Berwick. The town's keeper, Lord Berkeley, repeatedly warned the king that it would fall were the shortage of supplies and men not remedied.[13] It was even difficult to secure provisions for the royal household.[14] Exceptionally, perhaps, the chronicler Dene records that the church of Rochester suffered no shortage thanks to the foresight of those responsible.[15] If that is not an exaggeration it would suggest that the effects were less disastrous in the Southeast, but possibly it reveals an example of hoarding by those with the capacity so to do.[16] By contrast a Canterbury-based chronicler, the Gervase continuator, was under the impression that the failure of food crops was widespread and that it was followed in 1318 by an equally widespread mortality of oxen.[17] At the Cistercian abbey of Newenham in Devon about 1314 the price of wheat rose to 3s. 4d. a bushel, sometimes to as much as 4s., that is 32s. a quarter. Over many years there was considerable mortality particularly among the poor, but also among animals.[18] The king attempted to stabilize prices by an ordinance of March 1315 that was issued, comments the French *Brut*, "sans assent des grauntz de la terre" – presumably the Ordainers.[19] Inevitably this reduced the availability of supplies and in February of the following year it was repealed.[20] Other economic factors accentuated the problem. The amount of money in circulation had increased with inflationary effect, real wages lagged far behind prices. The population curve that had been upwards since the late twelfth century began to slide downwards.[21] The social background was not conducive to decisive political action with its inevitable concomitant, taxation.

THE REVOLT OF ADAM BANASTER

Lancaster's projected Scottish campaign, a campaign he was supposedly eager
"to undertake ... virtually on his own initiative," was held up both by the difficulties of collecting resources owing to their prevalent scarcity, and by the revolt
in 1315 of Adam Banaster.[22] Banaster is recorded to have been nurtured by Lancaster and by him preserved from the jaws of death: "ex latibulis latrocinii et
januis mortis."[23] From this one might conclude that he had been saved from the
consequences of a murder, rather than that he had revolted against Lancaster to
secure the king's favour, as the *Vita* – a source favourable to the earl – suggests.[24] After all, it was the very time that Lancaster would have had little difficulty in securing a royal pardon on behalf of one of his military tenants. What
seems to be nearer the mark is that this was one of those local feuds prevalent
in Lancashire at this period, in this case with Sir Robert Holland or Holand,
another Lancaster retainer, who was in his turn to revolt against his patron at a
more crucial moment. Thus the Pauline annalist may be accurate in depicting
this lawlessness as an internecine dispute between two retainers,[25] one of whom
– Holland, the earl's principal household official – was clearly in receipt of a
substantial degree of patronage and allegedly taking advantage of his position.[26]
Ironically this was just what Lancaster was reacting against at national level. A
group of disaffected knights sympathetic to Banaster met on 8 October and
entered into a sworn confederacy. After some initial successes, and the murder
of Sir Henry Bury, the confederates robbed the rectory at Wigan and proceeded
to Halton Castle, which they captured, together with a substantial number of
weapons. On 31 October they advanced to Manchester flying royal banners to
disarm opposition.[27] They then proceeded by way of Wigan to Preston. By that
time Holland had mustered his forces, as had the sheriff, Edmund de Neville.
After one or possibly two engagements, the Banaster supporters were routed
and on 11 November the ringleaders Adam Banaster and Henry de Lea, were
captured and executed at Leyland, allegedly at the behest of the earl and Robert
Holland.[28] Much of the revolt had involved wanton pillage. Holland and his
adherents now proceeded to ravage the area in their turn and to wreak vengeance
on the Banasters and their associates. Whatever might be said about the rival
factions, this incident does not reflect well on Lancaster's ability to maintain
law and order within his area of strongest influence.

THE BRISTOL DISTURBANCES

The reputed author of the *Vita*, John Walwayn senior, apparently hailed from the
West Country; hence his allotment under the year 1316 of disproportionate
space to the long-standing disturbances in Bristol and to the affairs of Wales.[29]
He paints a picture of an oligarchy of fourteen, presumably guildsmen, who
were resisting the claims of the other burgesses to enjoy equal liberties and priv-

ileges. Trusting that they would secure a favourable verdict, this close-knit group requested the royal court to appoint judges to take cognizance of the case. In May of 1315 a contingent of eight Bristollians had safe conduct to Warwick for the earl's adjudication, but apparently without result. The wider community of citizens took exception to the fact that strangers were permitted to determine matters affecting their privileges and claimed that those chosen favoured their opponents. Despite the presence of the judges in the Guildhall a riot ensued in which twenty men were said to have lost their lives. Eighty inhabitants were indicted for this affray and were condemned by the royal justices at Gloucester. As they failed to appear they were banished but preferred to hide in the town, which was put into a state of defence. The fourteen guildsmen felt it prudent to leave.

The earl of Pembroke was despatched with others to secure the townsmen's submission, but they responded with vigour, asserting that they had not started the quarrel and were not guilty of offences against the king (*in dominum regem nichil deliquimus*). Were their penalties to be remitted they would be obedient. But Edward had lost patience with the recalcitrant townsmen and was determined to enforce surrender. Pembroke ordered the investment of the town but returned to London. Thus he was not himself involved in the siege, having been sent elsewhere to bring influence to bear for the election of Chancellor Sandale as bishop of Winchester.[30] Maurice de Berkeley blockaded the approach from the sea by way of the Avon, while Badlesmere, the constable, was in overall charge of the operation, assisted by Roger Mortimer, John de Wylington, and many others. A mangonel from the castle destroyed walls and buildings and in view of the overwhelming force sent against them, not to mention the lack of provisions, the citizens deemed it best to surrender, which they did on 26 July 1316. A heavy fine was exacted, part of which was used to reimburse Badlesmere for his expenses, and some ringleaders were banished. On 18 December the liberty of the town – taken into the king's hand in 1313 – was restored to the citizens and the rebellion was at an end. In 1322 those banished were pardoned and permitted to resume such of their forfeited goods as they could.[31] Considering the length of time that the town had flouted the authority of king, justices, sheriff, and constable, Edward can be commended for his clemency, although it has to be remembered that despite Walwayn's moralizing the citizens do not appear to have been antagonistic towards Edward.[32] The whole story is more complex than the version in the *Vita*. Other constituent elements were the unpopularity of customs dues, the claim by Bartholomew Badlesmere as constable of Bristol Castle to military supplies – supplies that might well be used against the town – and the king's effort to levy a tallage, originally ordered in December 1312.[33] But the author of the *Vita* is right to emphasize the uselessness of the rebellion, particularly at a time of considerable loss of trade and a chronic shortage of the necessities of life.

LLYWELYN BREN AND GRUFFYDD DE LA POLE

Trevisa, in his English version of Higden's *Polychronicon*, quoted on page 36 of chapter 2, wrote that in one respect Edward's reign went well, Wales was "never rebel against him."[34] In practice Wales did cause problems from time to time – certainly a degree of concern. One modern author has written of continued government anxiety about the allegiance of the king's Welsh subjects, an anxiety that was particularly in evidence during 1315. Three commissioners, M. John Walwayn, Philip ap Hywel, and Rhys ap Hywel, were active in the country during November and December, making their report to the court at Clipstone.[35] Also during November Sir John de Winstone and William de Hoo, a clerk, were in North Wales surveying the readiness of the castles there.[36] Robert Bruce was attempting to stir up trouble by urging the common ancestry of the Irish, and there was a danger that, following the Scottish victories, now extended to Ireland, the Welsh might take courage to resist and make common cause with their fellow Celts.[37]

It became clear by 1316 that concern about possible unrest was not misplaced. In Glamorgan there was a revolt by Llywelyn Bren, not directed against the king as such but principally against his officers and the activities of Marcher lords. This revolt had complex causes. The Clare inheritance had come into royal hands following the death at Bannockburn, without a surviving heir, of Gilbert de Clare, earl of Gloucester. There was friction between the Welsh and those appointed to administer the lordship. Llywelyn himself had been high in Earl Gilbert's esteem and held Senghenydd as a mesne lordship. Receiving no redress in the royal court for his complaint against Sir Payn de Turbeville of Coity, the king's warden, he rebelled and with the help of some prominent local Welshmen captured the constable of Caerphilly Castle outside its walls and proceeded to burn the outer ward. The timing of the revolt was misjudged: the Marcher lords, led by the newly released earl of Hereford, lord of Brecon, and including the Mortimers of Wigmore and Chirk, William de Montacute, John Giffard of Brimpsfield, Roger d'Amory, and Henry of Lancaster, soon crushed resistance. Hereford and Roger Mortimer received Llywelyn's surrender under conditions at Ystradfellte and the rebel was kept a prisoner in the Tower for two years.[38] Subsequently, when the younger Despenser had secured Glamorgan by right of his wife, he took the captive to Cardiff and had him executed with the customary barbarities, an act that brought a charge of infringing royal authority.[39]

To the north in Powys there was continuing conflict between the ambitious parvenu John Charlton and Gruffydd de la Pole. This had its origin in the premature death in 1309 of Gruffydd de la Pole (Welshpool), junior, son of Owain and grandson of Gruffydd ap Gwenwynwyn who had claimed to be a Marcher baron (*baro domini regis de Marchia*). An inquest awarded Powys to Gruffydd's sister, Hawys the younger, who proceeded to marry John Charlton, the royal chamberlain.[40] The brother of Owain de la Pole – also named Gruffydd – hence uncle of Hawys, had in 1308 succeeded his mother, Hawys the elder, as custo-

dian of the barony and claimed it through the male line by Welsh law. With the
baronial ascendency in 1311 he sought to secure judgment as to whether Powys
was held of the English Crown or by Welshery. When Edward by writ of privy
seal ordered the chancellor to make no such enquiry save by his special order,
Gruffydd resorted to arms and laid siege to the castle of Welshpool. Mediation
of the dispute was begun in the autumn of 1312 under the auspices of Cardinal
Arnaud Nouvel, the bishop of Poitiers, and Louis of Evreux. Further attempts to
resolve the conflict followed in 1313 and pardons were issued to both sides in
November. Charlton remained in possession. Lancaster's support of his rival
had proved unavailing, but in October 1316 his influence secured a further pardon for Gruffydd.[41] Royal support of Charlton, whose younger brother Thomas
was made bishop of Hereford at the king's urging, proved to be misplaced. Following the battle of Boroughbridge and Lancaster's death Charlton, together
with his abettor Roger Mortimer of Wigmore, were named among those against
the king, but somewhat mysteriously he was soon restored to favour, being pardoned in September 1322. Four years later he joined Isabella, the insurgent
queen, and captured the earl of Arundel, who had been a supporter of his rival
for Powys. The quarrel was maintained until Gruffydd's death in 1332, to be
continued thereafter by Owain Llawgoch. Charlton did not die until 1353.[42]
Problems of such complexity could not be solved by a far away government in
Westminster.

THE LINCOLN PARLIAMENT OF 1316[43]

The necessity to keep an eye on their Welsh border interests determined that
many barons were absent from the well-reported parliament that met in the
king's presence on 27 January at Lincoln, an assembly to which Llywelyn had
been summoned prior to his armed revolt to answer for his behaviour.[44] Lancaster himself did not appear until the ninth or tenth of February and business
was held up on his account and that of the other absentees. Things seem to have
got under way on the twelfth when a "full" (plenum) parliament convened in the
dean's hall. One of the reasons for the summons was declared to be the invasion
of the Scots, but when parliament reconvened on the following day in the
chapter house Scottish incursions were not to the fore. The ordinance fixing the
maximum prices for provisions was rescinded. Another statute determined the
qualifications of sheriffs and the method of their appointment. This was to be by
the chancellor – if available – the treasurer, barons of the exchequer, and justices, an arrangement similar to that embodied in the Ordinances.[45] On the 17
February, after an interval presumably devoted to diplomatic manoeuvring
behind the scenes, John Salmon, the bishop of Norwich, was ordered by the
king to announce what had been agreed: the king wished to observe the Ordinances and, with reservations, the perambulations of the forest from the time of
Edward I. Appropriate writs of enforcement were then issued.

At that point the bishop made what has been interpreted as a memorable announcement: the king bore Lancaster sincere goodwill and wished him to be his principal councillor (*de consilio domini regis capitalis*).[46] With a show of reluctance the earl, professing his great love of the king and the common good of the realm, in view of the Ordinances, which the king had accepted, and in the hope of amending matters concerning the king's household and the estate of the realm, gave his consent, provided that were his advice not accepted he could withdraw from the council without any question of bad faith. In the words of Conway Davies: "No matter touching the king or the kingdom was to be undertaken without the assent of the earl and the other prelates, earls and barons. The king was to have no independence of action. The council with Lancaster at its head was to assent to every administrative act before it was undertaken."[47] A third condition was that if any prelate or secular noble were to give counsel to the king, or perform any act considered to be detrimental to the king or kingdom, he was to be removed at the next parliament. As the Bridlington chronicler expressed it, the earl could add or subtract from the Ordinances already made as seemed best for king and kingdom – in his view, of course. A straitjacket indeed, one from which the king could be expected to extricate himself at the earliest opportunity. It did not so much establish Lancaster's position as consolidate it. Yet it was an unsustainable position; unsustainable, that is, unless the king were to concur in permanently renouncing his right to control his council and thereby the government of the realm.[48] Recently there has been a tendency to belittle the importance of Lancaster's new status, particularly in view of the fact that a commission was set up to reform the realm and royal household, one that included the archbishop and four of his suffragans, Llandaff, Chichester, Norwich, and Salisbury; four earls, Pembroke, Hereford, Arundel, and Richmond, together with Bartholomew Badlesmere. It is arguable that even as powerful an earl as Lancaster would have found it difficult to dominate such a wide-ranging group, even were he to remain constantly at court, a course for which that earl had no stomach.

Once these matters were settled parliament took up the overdue business of the Scottish war and granted an armed man from each vill, more if the vill had a market, their expenses to be met by their respective townships until the time of the muster. Those not involved with the above grant were to pay a fifteenth of their movable goods in the usual way.[49] From the Patent and Close rolls we also learn that in response to petitions ordinances were issued for North and South Wales and that men with fifty pounds a year of land or rents were to undertake knighthood. Proclamation to that effect was to be made in the county courts.[50] We need not take too seriously the comments of the *Vita* that because of the revolt of Llywelyn the parliament dealt with few issues (*de paucis consulerat*) – no mention of the earl's new status – or that of the French chronicler to the effect that little was achieved.[51] Sometimes a degree of ennui affected such commentators, even those in attendance such as Walwayn the putative author of the *Vita*. In March 1337 Bishop Hethe, who disliked the expense and time-wasting aspect of parliament, was to spend a day with his colleagues "watching the walls" and then to leave, even though war with France was on the agenda.[52]

FROM THE LINCOLN PARLIAMENT
TO THE TREATY OF LEAKE 1318

What use did Lancaster make of his position which, if not new, had acquired the accolade of authenticity? It was a position, moreover, that might well have involved continued diminution of Pembroke's influence as well as some unfavourable reaction from other magnates. During 1315 Pembroke had been away from the centre of affairs, occupied first in France and then on the Scottish border.[53] The cornerstone of Lancaster's policy, as before, was the observance of the Ordinances. Writs of 3 March 1316 directed to the sheriffs and reissued in a more rigid form on the sixth, ordered that there should be strict compliance. According to Conway Davies the second issue "with its extended terms and strict injunctions" argues that their lukewarm observance stemmed not merely from the king's objection to them but from "lack of respect paid to them by the people generally" – the term "people" being as usual difficult either to qualify or quantify.[54] Be that as it may, there would have been ample support for the attempt to restrict capricious and unjust prises, the burden of which, as has been suggested, was particularly crushing for the lower echelons of society.[55] Other requirements of the council were the payment of customs directly into the exchequer and, once again, the resumption of royal grants. Lancaster was in evidence on the council as early as 3 March; on Lady Day, 25 March, he was present together with the treasurer, chancellor, and other councillors when the mayor and alderman of the City of London came before him to offer five hundred marks for a confirmation of their liberties. On 26 April the treasurer and barons of the exchequer were ordered to resume all grants deemed detrimental to the king made contrary to the Ordinances and to regrant them more advantageously.[56] Exceptions were made, not least in Lancaster's favour, and the executors of Anthony Bek, the bishop of Durham, were exonerated for a second time.[57]

Lancaster withdrew from the court within a couple of months. He is to be found at Kenilworth and Donington in April 1316 and thereafter at various places in the North Midlands. His prolix justification was delivered in July 1317 in response to two royal letters, the first complaining that he was holding illegal confederations, the second that he had not responded to a summons to appear at Nottingham on 21 July to give counsel.[58] This meeting, intended to precede the cardinals' arrival to negotiate with the Scots, had a wide agenda, including not only the affairs of Ireland, Scotland, and Gascony but also the disturbed state of the English realm.[59] Lancaster's presence was vital. The earl denied that any meetings had been held other than in the interests of the king's peace and, in response to the second letter, declared that the Scots had entered the kingdom and were engaging in plunder, so that his presence in the North was essential. Further, he pleaded illness: "Nous ne sumes pas en estate de travailler." His more fundamental reason was that the Ordinances were not in fact being observed, that reforming measures sent by the hands of Badlesmere and the justice, William Inge, were being ignored, and that new "favourites" had appeared.[60]

Historians have advanced their own reasons for Lancaster's withdrawal from the hub of affairs. Ill health may have had something to do with it, although objective evidence is lacking: we have merely his own self-contradictory suggestion that it had prevented his coming to Nottingham in July.[61] The incursions of the Scots – both into England and Ireland – allegedly required his attention, not to mention that of the king and of the realm as a whole. He was exasperated at the lack of progress with the reforms he consistently advocated and harped incessantly on the need to obey the Ordinances, displaying little conception of the art of the possible. More to the point is his character, in which a want of capacity was combined with a sullen disposition. He lacked determination, dedication to the everyday problems of government and was too ready to withdraw when he was not getting his way.[62] Supposedly he had a genuine desire to launch a campaign against the Scots, in which case Edward's failure to act during 1316, despite strenuous efforts at a difficult time to raise money and purveyance, may well have added to his disillusionment. In that year the king had been in the North since mid-August. After Lancaster had joined him at York shortly thereafter, they engaged in an acrimonious disagreement, possibly as a consequence of a violation of the Ordinances.[63] The earl was at Pontefract in mid-September where he received letters from the king, then at Beverley.[64] Early in November Edward moved south from Newburgh to York and had left that city by the end of the month.[65] Any Scottish campaign was by then out of the question.

Thus, by the beginning of 1317 Lancaster was isolated both from the other barons and from the court. Unable to exercise power by constitutional means, he adopted a dog-in-the-manger attitude. Only violent solutions could effect his political purpose or, indeed, his purely personal ambitions. Most of the earls were opposed to him. Warwick, his ally in the murder of Gaveston, had died in 1315, and the custody of his lands was granted two years later to the elder Despenser;[66] Warenne was soon to be instrumental in snatching Lancaster's wife. Arundel, married to Warenne's sister, had earlier been on the same side as Lancaster in the de la Pole-Charlton dispute but was now estranged from him; while both Hereford and Pembroke were close to the king. Lancaster did not attend the councils summoned to Clarendon for 9 February and to Westminster for 15 April, thus abandoning to his opponents the opportunity to influence events.[67]

Who were these men whom Lancaster despised and who filled the power vacuum by providing counsel?[68] William Montacute and the two Despensers, Roger d'Amory and Hugh d'Audley, his keenest opponents, have been derogatively dubbed "curialists" or men of the court.[69] Montacute, Amory and Audley could readily be made to appear as upstarts. The propagandist author of the pro-Lancastrian *Flores Historiarum* indicts them for preying on other men and regards them as worse than Gaveston.[70] Land meant power: the Clare inheritance was the significant factor in the rise of both Amory, and Audley, as it was to a lesser extent in that of the younger Despenser, who had married the eldest of the future Clare heiresses, Eleanor, as early as 1306. It was the same year that Edward I gave permission to Warenne to marry his granddaughter, Joan, daughter of the count of Bar.[71] The Clare marriage provided Despenser with status and eventually with substantial property, but his subsequent elevation to supreme authority under the king was principally due to Edward's close relationship with him. Following the Northampton Parliament of July 1318 the barons attempted to oust the Despensers by attributing to them various offences against the estate of the king, the realm, and the Crown, but "by common council" the younger Hugh was made king's chamberlain. On 20 October the appointment was renewed in parliament at York and Despenser was to act in that capacity until the end of the reign, apart from the brief period of his exile in 1321.[72]

In May 1317 directions were given for the division of the Gloucester inheritance, but even after the three beneficiaries received their share in November their husbands continued at court.[73] Roger d'Amory was at the time arguably the most influential of the curialists, due principally to his marriage to the coheiress, Elizabeth de Clare, which brought him both a share of the inheritance and a royal grant. Perhaps next in importance was William Montacute whose father Simon, summoned to parliament from December 1299, held extensive lands in Somerset and had been at the siege of Caerlaverock in 1300. William, a knight in the royal household, succeeded to the barony in 1316. In July he was sent from the court to Bristol to pacify the dissension between Badlesmere and the citizens. The *Vita* described him as captain of the royal forces (*militie regis*) during Llywelyn Bren's revolt. From November until the same month two years later he occupied the office of steward of the household, dying in 1319.[74]

John de Warenne, earl of Warenne or Surrey, requires separate treatment. He had earlier been one of Lancaster's retainers, possibly with Arundel, and both may have been in Lancaster's pay at the Dunstable tournament in 1309, when the barons were concerting their opposition to Gaveston.[75] Warenne was doubtless alienated by Gaveston's triumphalism at the Wallingford tournament of 2 December 1307, when he found himself on the losing side with the other earls.[76] He was not chosen as an Ordainer but acted against Gaveston in 1312, being assigned to the investiture of Scarborough Castle, where the favourite had sought refuge.[77] How he subsequently became an enemy of Lancaster is less clear, but the latter certainly had designs on some of his estates. One theory is that Lancaster had urged Bishop Langton of Chichester to take action against Warenne's violation of his matrimonial vows.[78] As we have seen, Warenne had married Joan of Bar, but by 1313 he was endeavouring to have the marriage annulled,[79] and it may be that damages for having slighted Edward of Bar's sister constituted an element in the ransom demanded for Pembroke's release when in May and June of 1317 he was kept a captive somewhere in the county of Bar. The most likely reason for penalizing Pembroke is that he could have presented a petition at Avignon on Warenne's behalf for the annulment of the latter's marriage to Joan.[80] Warenne wished to marry his mistress, Matilda, or Maud, de Neyrford, and in 1316 he surrendered his estates so that they could be regranted to him with reversion to Maud and her two sons.[81] His domestic difficulties were matched by those of Lancaster, who had married Alice de Lacy, daughter of the earl of Lincoln, in 1294. According to the continuator of Trevet, it was at the Clarendon meeting in 1317 that a plan was concocted for the abduction of the childless Alice, who so far as can be ascertained, was not averse to the arrangement. This was effected at Canford in Dorset by Warenne. In the Meaux chronicler's view the object was not to commit adultery but to demonstrate contempt for the earl. In view of Alice's later colourful marital history, her acquiescence is highly likely.[82] Warenne's attentions, as we have seen, were elsewhere: he had no designs on the countess. The question remains, why this pointless irritation of Lancaster? Was it a personal vendetta carried out with the support of the curialists?[83] In the long run it did permanent harm to Warenne.

Lancaster's response was to send envoys to Edward, expressing his fears of the machinations of his enemies, asking that such men be removed from the court so that he could put in an appearance, and suggesting that without offence to the king he should take vengeance for his injuries and secure such satisfaction as might prove possible.[84] Understandably the king regarded the proposals as those of an overmighty subject. He replied that when opportunity arose he would himself avenge the contempt the earl had suffered, but he refused to remove Lancaster's "enemies" from his household, and required the earl to seek legal remedy alone for the abduction of his wife. He put the reasons for the earl's refusal to come to parliament before his household and friends and sought their opinion. Some were for depriving him of his fief for contumacy and for capturing and exiling him. More cautious voices argued the difficulty of using force against so powerful a man, particularly someone who had the Scots and Welsh as prospective allies. It were better to come to some mutual agreement, an opinion reinforced by historical precedents for civil strife. The king and earl should meet at a love-day (*dies amoris*), thrash out their differences verbally and come to an agreement. But it was reported to the earl that Edward had sworn that should Lancaster come to a meeting, he would either have his head or imprison him. Rumour or no, Lancaster took the threat seriously.[85]

The paternal solicitude of Pope John XXII for Edward manifested itself in a series of letters reflecting some of Lancaster's concerns – to ensure prudent expenditure and wise councillors – but also the curial anxiety to bring peace to Catholic Europe so that a crusade could be launched. Important, too, was papal concern to curb the manner in which royal officials had encroached upon ecclesiastical jurisdiction.[86] With these aims Cardinals Gaucelme de Jean (d'Eauze) and Luca Fieschi had landed at Dover on 22 June 1317. Two days later they paused at Canterbury for the feast of St John the Baptist, where Cardinal Gaucelme celebrated mass and, after the gospel, preached a sermon to which his brother cardinal listened while seated upon the archiepiscopal throne in the monastic choir close to the high altar.[87] From Kent the cardinals travelled to the North and were at Nottingham in the royal presence when writs for the livery of the Hereford temporalities were issued on behalf of the newly provided bishop, Adam Orleton.[88] While there they would have been fully aware of the impasse presented by Lancaster's refusal to attend and of his excuses for not doing so. They soon had their baptism of fire, in which the problems raised by the Scots – even more urgent in view of their invasion of Ireland – and by Lancaster were seen to be closely intertwined.

Following the death of Bishop Kellaw(e) of Durham, Edward, on 19 October 1316, issued his *congé d'élire*. The monks elected one of their number, Br Henry de Stamford, but the king, urged on by Queen Isabella, wrote to Pope John on 23 November claiming that this had been done regardless of a reservation by Clement V and asking that Louis de Beaumont be provided instead. In doing so he was rescinding an earlier request on behalf of Thomas Charlton. The earls of Hereford and Lancaster both visited Durham in support of their own candidates, Hereford advocating John Walwayn, Lancaster John de Kynardesley (Kinnersley), at the time an obscure clerk. The monks' request for confirmation of Stamford's election crossed with the pope's mandate, dated 16 December, quashing it. Beaumont was duly provided by a bull of 9 February 1317 and was intending to be consecrated in his cathedral on 4 September – appropriately the feast of the translation of St Cuthbert – by one of the cardinals in whose retinue he had returned. This plan was thwarted by the action of Sir Gilbert de Middleton, a Northumbrian border reiver, who captured and despoiled the cardinals' retinue, which included the new bishop and his brother, Henry de Beaumont.[89] The atrocity, vociferously castigated by the author of the *Vita* who was himself possibly one of the candidates for the see,[90] was a plot that supposedly involved Lancaster in collaboration with the Scots.[91] Moreover, warnings had been issued both by the London clergy and the Durham prior, warnings that had been ignored, presumably on the assumption that no one would be so rash as to inflict such ignominy on papal delegates. Lancaster seemingly covered up his involvement in the attack – for which there is no direct evidence – by conducting the cardinals back to York.[92] The whole affair miscarried badly. Although it is difficult to believe, Middleton appears to have intended to attack only the Beaumonts, though how his intelligence and Lancaster's could have overlooked the likely presence of the cardinals is difficult to imagine. Lancaster wriggled out of an embarrassing situation but not without discredit, Middleton suffered a horrible death in London.[93] Lancaster's next resort to force, in direct violation of the royal command, was to avenge himself on Warenne. He attacked his Yorkshire estates, appointed a constable of Conisborough Castle, seized some of its resources and at Wakefield dispossessed Maud de Neyrford of her property. Castles held by Amory – Knaresborough in Yorkshire and Alton in Staffordshire – were captured from their custodians and held for Lancaster despite the efforts of the respective sheriffs. The siege of Knaresborough by Yorkshire knights ended in negotiation thanks to rumours of a Scottish relieving expedition under the earl of Moray and the presence of substantial forces under Lancaster's command at Pontefract: another instance of the earl's readiness to serve his own interests rather than those of the realm. This lawlessness prompted a sheaf of petitions, including one from Maud de Neyrford and several from Warenne, who complained of the "menasces" of the earl of Lancaster.[94]

Meanwhile the king was attempting to hold a muster at Newcastle on 15 September 1317, with a preliminary gathering at York.[95] Despite the Middleton débâcle Lancaster was determined not to cooperate. From the security of his castle at Pontefract he denied passage to armed men on their way to York, claiming that he did so in the interests of the realm by virtue of his office of steward of England. In his opinion the stewardship gave him the right to sanction military expeditions.[96] To break the deadlock a deputation of two archbishops, Canterbury and Dublin, five bishops, and the earls of Hereford and Pembroke was despatched to Pontefract. An undated transcript among the Dodsworth manuscripts in the Bodleian Library to which Dr Maddicott drew attention and which has subsequently been twice printed, possibly originates from Pontefract priory by way of its cell Monk Bretton.[97] It appears to incorporate the agreement made at this time between Lancaster and the prelates (*les ercevesqes et evesqes dun parte, et le count de Lancastr' daltre parte*). The earl promised on behalf of himself and his men not to conduct any armed *chevauchée* contrary to the peace, nor openly or covertly to dispossess (*ne surquerra apertement ne privement*) anyone save in accordance with the law – provided no one dispossessed him or his men. He would come to parliament in peaceable fashion as befitted his estate and would show reverence to the king as his liege lord. For the purpose he and his men would be given surety. He reserved his quarrel against Warenne until the next parliament. In their turn the bishops promised, so long as the earl kept to the above, to support him with all the sanction of Holy Church. Lancaster then swore not to encroach (*ostir*) on royal power or dignity to the king's disinheritance, or that of his heirs. With the help of God and the saints he would maintain the Ordinances agreed by the prelates, earls, and barons and affirmed by the king, and he would do his utmost to restore anything alienated from king or Crown contrary to the Ordinances, in accordance with his oath at the time the Ordinances were drawn up.

From the king's standpoint this was very far from being a success story. Lancaster concedes a modified promise to refrain from violence and another to attend parliament without an armed force at his back – in other words, to behave in a law-abiding way, except with respect to Warenne. In return he is given clerical assurance of safe conduct. But in his concluding oath he reaffirms his determination to uphold the Ordinances and to strive to prevent alienations.[98] Subsequently there was a meeting at York in the cardinals' presence, where both parties promised to do nothing to the other's disadvantage. Allegedly the cardinals found that the earl was disposed to a peaceful settlement.[99] In fact it was merely a papering over of the cracks. The underlying mood was revealed when during his return journey to London the king was jeered at from the walls of Pontefract Castle and there was some danger, had Pembroke not urged milder counsel, that the fortress would be besieged. Edward did not forget; the insult was to be one of the charges against the earl in 1322.[100] Arrived in London, Cardinal Fieschi preached in St Paul's where he published a bull calling for a two-year truce with the Scots, a move that was to prove ineffective.[101] Edward, realizing the true state of Lancaster's mind, proceeded to bind men to him by indenture. Most important of those thus retained was Pembroke, followed by Badlesmere and Hereford, as well as many lesser magnates such as John Giffard of Brimpsfield, John Mowbray, John de Somery, and William la Zouche. Collectively these men were under obligation to provide a substantial force for the king's protection.[102] More surprising perhaps is the indenture of 24 November 1317, a secret agreement made in London between Roger d'Amory on the one hand and Pembroke and Badlesmere on the other. Conway Davies thought that this was an indenture to restrain the king, but what may prove a more convincing interpretation is that Amory was consenting to be bound by the other two with respect to his dealings and those of others with the king: an agreement for mutual restraint. Pembroke and Badlesmere envisaged that they would be the close advisers of Edward yet feared that commonsense policy might be undermined by so irresponsible a character as Amory. They were to that extent in sympathy with Lancaster's view of the necessity to restrict "unsuitable" royal grants.[103]

There were some outward signs of better relations with the earls and their associates. During December a London merchant delivered a large woollen hanging woven with figures of the king and his earls, designed to be used for festivities in the royal hall. Christmas was celebrated by the royal party in Westminster palace, where Edward received sumptuous gifts of plate. Presents were distributed to the earl of Angus and a large number of lesser men, among them Bartholomew Badlesmere, Henry Tyeis (Tyeys), Thomas Gray, John de Stapelton, Richard d'Amory, Robert and Roger Wateville, and Walter Beauchamp – a number of whom were associated with Lancaster.[104] Writs for a parliament to meet at Lincoln on 27 January 1318 were issued, but following a colloquium at Westminster on 30 December this was prorogued to 12 March, then to 26 June, and eventually by writs of 8 June abandoned on account of the Scottish invasion also, no doubt, because it was feared that Lancaster, at war with Warenne and Amory, would come armed despite his oath.[105] On 2 April Berwick was captured thanks to the treachery of an Englishman and in mid-August at Nottingham sentences of excommunication were promulgated against the impervious Bruce.[106]

THE TREATY OF LEAKE AND THE PARLIAMENT AT YORK, 1318

According to the Bridlington chronicler a "parliament" met at Leicester on 12 April, the Wednesday before Palm Sunday but not in the king's presence.[107]

Archbishop Reynolds and the bishops of Norwich (Salmon), Chichester (John Langton), Winchester (Sandale), Llandaff (Monmouth), and Hereford (Orleton)[108] are said to have attended as well as the earls of Lancaster, Pembroke and Hereford, together with twenty-eight barons. They swore that the Ordinances would be observed in every article, that unsuitable councillors would be removed, and that grantees of land from the king were to be attached and made to account at the exchequer for outgoings belonging to king and Crown.[109] For this purpose they should find security to be at the next parliament to receive the judgment of their peers about such lands and other benefits received after the time of the Ordinances. All transgressions by Lancaster in his effort to force the king to rule the people better – his capture of castles and goods – were to be entirely overlooked (*relaxentur et penitus remittantur*). Both the Despensers were to be retained for life by the earl of Lancaster with two hundred knights; all the earl's men who had been taken by the king's officers were to be released and, should they wish, were to receive charters pardoning their transgressions. Not surprisingly the chronicler wondered at an arrangement by which Edward was coerced, breakers of the peace could not be punished, bits were fastened on the king's teeth, and absolution was given for those who merited the gibbet. Such things, he thought, fostered hatred.[110] What they amounted to was a reiteration of Lancaster's creed: he could coerce the king in the name of the Ordinances while his own violence was to be condoned because without his cooperation peace was impossible within the realm. The bishops' concern was to maintain the peace and they were taking an active part in so doing: in that sense they were a middle party, accepting the Ordinances as a basis for negotiation. But the king's assent to their concessions had to be secured and a settlement arrived at between the principal groups. Berwick had fallen before the Leicester meeting had assembled and this must have added a sense of urgency to the discussions.[111]

At the beginning of June 1318 the council met at Westminster under the aegis of the archbishops of Dublin and Canterbury and of the earl of Pembroke. A document, of which two draft copies are extant, was drawn up.[112] It attempted to conciliate Lancaster while at the same time threatening him with sanctions should he continue to hold armed assemblies. The dorse of one of the draft copies contains the names of nine provincial bishops. Apart from the bishop of Llandaff they comprised the five bishops (including Cobham) who took part in the Leicester agreement, with the addition of four others, Coventry and Lichfield (Walter Langton), London (Newport), Ely (Hothum), and Salisbury (Martival). Also named on the dorse are the earl of Hereford, the two Despensers, Badlesmere, Amory, and Montacute. One might interpret this as a mixed group. The ecclesiastical element was seeking accommodation under pressure from the papal legates. Among the lay barons Hereford occupied a position fairly close to that of Pembroke but was considered sympathetic to Lancaster. The remainder may be termed curialists – men who wanted to sustain as much of their own interest as they could against the antagonistic stance of Lancaster.

Forced by the urgency of the situation, on 8 June the king agreed to accept the Leicester agreement and Bishop Salmon, from the pulpit in St Paul's near the great cross of the nave, announced that the king would accept the Ordinances, take Lancaster into his peace, and govern by the counsel of earls and barons.[113] Three days later in the names of Amory, Audley, Montacute, and Charlton – the first mention of this particular favourite – the king, at the request of Cardinals Gaucelme and Luca and of the nine bishops, agreed to a safe conduct for Lancaster.[114] On 9 June Edward instructed the barons of the exchequer to resume all grants[115] made in any part of his dominions to the king's detriment since 16 March 1310, whether the original grantee were alive or dead. In the event that any such gifts had been sold or alienated, the issues were to be recovered from purchasers who had received them after the Monday before St Michael (that is, 27 September) 1311, the date when the Ordinances were published.[116] Ostensibly Lancaster had won handsomely, though at the cost of much disaffection among beneficiaries of all kinds, including his *bêtes noires*, such as Audley. But the extent of such resumption is unknown. Meanwhile it became possible to issue summonses for a muster at York on 26 July.[117]

Understandably the agreement did not dispel the hostility and distrust that festered in Lancaster's mind. His warning to Geoffrey de Villers, constable of Bolingbroke Castle to be specially alert, has been taken as an indication of his distrust, although in this instance the reason was more particular in that the castle had been part of the inheritance of the earl's estranged wife.[118] This distrust was reciprocated by the king: it is hard to believe that Edward had compromised other than under the duress of circumstances. Counter-demands for revision were not long in coming. On 23 June in a garden at Horninglow by Burton-on-Trent, Lancaster's responses to articles drawn up (*ordinatos*) in London by Archbishops Bicknor of Dublin and Reynolds of Canterbury were received in Bicknor's presence and that of Bishops Salmon of Norwich and Hothum of Ely – the chancellor. The responses dealt with points previously raised at Leicester and Tutbury. At Lancaster's request, Henry Savage, clerk of Coventry and Lichfield diocese, prepared a notarial instrument embodying his response. The notary merely identified the document by its *incipit* and *explicit*, but fortunately its contents were recorded by the chronicler Knighton.[119] They show that it was proposed to soften the sweeping nature of the Leicester agreement: the suitability of each grant should be considered separately in parliament. Further, the grantees were not to be judged by their peers in parliament, as previously laid down. While Lancaster was determined that promises made to him should be honoured, he could blithely overlook his own breach of agreements by attacking the tenants of Warenne at Bromfield and Yale, for which the council was too timid to reproach him, merely informing the belligerent that Warenne had raised the matter.[120] All the same, a compromise was eventually reached allowing repeal of all alienations "since the commission"[121] and prohibiting others save with the consent of the barons in parliament. Other penal clauses, the punishment of donees in parliament, and the resumption of issues were quietly shelved.[122]

Lancaster, while protesting his anxiety to come to the king, continued to express nervousness about his safety were he to attempt so to do. He wished to attend parliament, but he could not accept the promises of safe conduct made by "evil councillors." He appreciated the promise of the prelates to take action against any who declined to negotiate a reasonable agreement but remained adamant that he would not admit such evil councillors, his enemies, into friend-ship.[123] Various missions were sent to persuade Lancaster to meet the king. A letter of 11 July despatched from Northampton by Reynolds to the Canterbury prior, Henry Eastry, records his renewed mission to Lancaster undertaken in conjunction with Archbishop Bicknor and Bishop Hothum of Ely, together with Pembroke, Badlesmere, and the younger Despenser. It suggests that the earl was prepared to accept the idea of a permanent agreement (*finalis concordia*). That is, concluded the archbishop, unless anything untoward were to upset the arrangement – which may the Comforter of all prevent (*quod advertat omnium Consolator*).[124] A week later Reynolds, anxious to keep Eastry up to date, wrote that an agreement now seemed certain and promised to send him the details later.[125] By 21 July, when he was staying at the Cistercian abbey of Biddlesden in Buckinghamshire – M. William de Bosco's burial place – Reynolds was less sanguine.[126] He wrote of his apprehension of an increasing likelihood of civil war (*guerre horrorem invalescere non sinemus*). On 20 July the king, in his turn realizing the stalemate, postponed the muster until 25 August.[127]

Reynolds hoped that Archbishop Bicknor, the bishops of Chichester (John Langton) and Ely (Hothum), the earls Pembroke and Arundel, Roger Mortimer (of Wigmore), and Badlesmere would return with better news about the octave of St Mary Magdalen (i.e., 29 July), but the situation prompted him to suggest to the prior that he put the relics of Becket and of the other saints in safe cus-tody.[128] When news did eventually arrive it was of a final agreement to the effect that all grants in rents or money were to be restored to the king, and that those who had counselled him badly were to be removed from his side and were not to return unless they could be of service in parliament or war. For his part the earl would pardon all who had transgressed against himself except Amory and Montacute, whom, he alleged, had conspired at his death. For the regulation of the king (*de regimine status regis*) he proposed that eight bishops, four earls, and as many barons should be chosen each year to be at the king's side, two bish-ops, an earl, and a baron for each quarter of the year, so that if necessary the suc-ceeding groups could correct the earlier ones. Having explained these matters, the earl said that he would be willing to come to the king whenever he wished, even if it meant going to his enemies. By this time Edward had travelled from Woodstock to Northampton, where the envoys presented these proposals. He expressed himself satisfied (*contentum*) with them. But some of the envoys bent the king's mind to their own, suggesting that he should not stand by the proposals (*ita quod concordatis huiusmodi non staretur*). Yet the earl of Pembroke, jointly with the bishops, held to what had been agreed. An assembly, or *tractatus*, at Northampton then discussed the matter with the king. Despite considerable difference of opinion it was finally agreed that the same envoys should try to mollify the earl (*ad mitigandum Comitem et alliciendum ad vias laxiores*).[129] Finally on Monday, 7 August, in a field between Loughborough and Leicester in the presence of the cardinals, bishops, earls – except Warenne – also many barons,[130] they all came together with Lancaster and embraced to the joy of the crowd of people assembled there. Reynolds himself was absent because of sickness with which he had been afflicted on the previous night while at Leicester. But he rejoiced that thanks to his efforts and those of the other mediators a consensus had been reached and sanguinely recorded that on the Tuesday and Wednesday, and for some further days, the king and Lancaster met with others outside Nottingham to discuss how measures could be taken in the parliament to meet at Lincoln in the quindene of Michaelmas for the protection of the North against the Scots.[131] A footnote was appended to the effect that after the king and Lancaster had exchanged the kiss of peace, Edward gave a singularly fine palfrey to Lancaster in recognition of his great love (*ex habundancia amoris quem ad eum gesserat*).[132]

The way was now clear for the sealing of the formal agreement, or "treaty", at Leake, Nottinghamshire, south of Loughborough, on 9 August.[133] This was in the form of an indenture between Lancaster and an embassy consisting of Archbishop Bicknor of Dublin, the bishops of Norwich (Salmon), Ely (Hothum), and Chichester (John Langton), the earls of Pembroke and Arundel, Roger Mortimer (of Wigmore), John de Somery, Badlesmere, Ralph Basset, and John Botetourt. We may no longer describe this group as "a representative gathering of members of the middle party," but it did contain most of those who had been long engaged in the seemingly interminable negotiations and who genuinely desired an agreement. If not "a triumph of the middle party,"[134] it was at least a triumph for the bishops and their long-term aim of peace within the realm.[135] Whatever one may think of Reynolds, and from time to time he certainly appears weak, even sycophantic, he had worked tirelessly for an accommodation and was exceptionally relieved to see the favourable outcome of his efforts. It was agreed that a body of ecclesiastics and laymen should remain with Edward until the next parliament; this to consist of the bishops of Norwich (Salmon), Chichester (John Langton), Ely (Hothum), Salisbury (Martival), St David's (Martin), Carlisle (Halton), Hereford (Orleton), and Worcester (Cobham), together with the earls of Pembroke, Richmond, and Hereford, the barons Hugh de Courtenay, Roger Mortimer, John de Somery, John de Segrave, John de Gray, and a banneret of Lancaster's choosing. Of these, five persons – two bishops, an earl, a baron, and Lancaster's banneret – were to attend constantly upon the king. Lancaster was to be acquitted of all felonies and trespasses prior to 25 July 1318 and promised not to pursue those who had done him an injury, but he reserved his quarrel with Warenne.[136]

One question is likely to remain unanswerable. Why was Lancaster himself not a member of the standing council? His biographer is of the opinion that this was a concession to the court party and a "mitigation" of the earl's aims. Since he could not trust any member of the council to act for him, Lancaster had to have a reliable retainer even if he lacked the clout of his principal.[137] Pembroke's biographer, emphasizes the close relationship between those who witnessed the Leake document and the king. Hence, he argues, "the council system as a whole" constituted "a serious defeat for Lancaster."[138] Perhaps so, since he could rely on nobody but himself. Possibly he had merely profited from experience. As for the standing council of five, its effectiveness was seemingly short-lived.[139] The 1316 precedent of council leadership had not been a success and the earl, no diligent administrator, certainly not a committee man, had found it inconvenient to devote permanent attention to the minutiae of conciliar business. By reason of its size the council would put a curb on individuals: instead the earl could operate as a menacing figure in the background. Yet Lancaster's shelving of his claim to appoint the steward of the household does indicate weakness, even if this was to be of short duration.[140] It is therefore arguable that he was content to have a reliable deputy, and that this did not represent any diminution of his underlying intention. In any case, the permanent council was a notable achievement for those who wished to restrain the monarch and attention could surely now be paid to the pressing business of Scotland. It was time, thought the author of the *Vita*, for Edward to emulate Nebuchadnezzar, who did nothing before the twelfth year of his reign, but who then flourished and became a powerful monarch. It was wishful thinking.[141]

But if Reynolds and some of the chroniclers were overly sanguine, appearances were to prove deceptive. The parliament, which assembled at York on 20 October 1318 and sat until 9 December,[142] was intended to implement the agreement so painfully arrived at and to concert measures against the Scots, although on that score nothing could be done militarily because of the lateness of the season. Even so, the levies required in August from certain towns were not disbanded until the beginning of November.[143] For once Lancaster put in a lengthy appearance, from 26 October until 22 November, thereafter being represented by Roger Belers, a baron of the exchequer, and Michael de Meldon.[144] Davies thought it by far the most important parliament of the reign. The two archbishops were there and an unusually high complement of diocesan bishops, eleven in all.[145] There were seven earls, apart from Lancaster: Norfolk, the earl marshal, Richmond, Pembroke, Hereford, Arundel, Atholl, and Angus. Significant absentees were Warenne and the elder Despenser. One of the first items was a ritual recital of the Magna Carta. To the committee established at Leake were added the bishops of Winchester and Coventry and Lichfield, both of whom had considerable administrative experience, as well as a number of barons, ominously the younger Despenser, together with Badlesmere, Roger Mortimer of Wigmore, William Martin, John of Somery, Giffard of Brimpsfield, and Botetourt.[146] A committee was chosen to draw up a scheme for reform of the household with

Archbishop Melton of York at its head, and consisting of an earl (Hereford), the barons Mortimer of Wigmore, John of Somery, and Walter de Norwich, an experienced official, chief baron of the exchequer, and the bishops of Ely (Hothum, the chancellor), and Norwich (Salmon).[147] Following the appointment of the usual committees to hear petitions the articles of the Leake indenture were affirmed and enrolled. The king expressed his willingness to accept the standing quarterly committee, conceding that in view of the serious problems in Scotland and Ireland, he needed counsel, provided that such an arrangement did not interfere with the lawful established functions of his officers. Chancellor Hothum was ordered to make unconditional charters in favour of Lancaster and his adherents for all actions against his peace,[148] including – according to one chronicler – those of Gaveston and Banaster.[149] Hothum also grasped the opportunity to secure confirmation of the charters pertaining to his see of Ely.[150]

Pending the report of the parliamentary committee the position of the administrative and judicial officers was considered. On 16 November on the advice of the council (*per consilium*) Walwayn was replaced as treasurer by Sandale, the bishop of Winchester, after serving for only five months.[151] It seems remarkable that if Walwayn was the author of the *Vita* he not only fails to comment, even indirectly, on this change, but entirely omits mention *eo nomine* of this crucial parliament.[152] In 1321 the king was to claim that Walwayn's removal was not due to any demerit.[153] The chief justices of the courts of King's Bench and Common Pleas, Henry le Scrope and William de Bereford, were confirmed in their offices, as was Walter de Norwich, chief baron of the exchequer. Badlesmere, who displaced Montacute as steward of the household despite a protest from Lancaster, who claimed the right to appoint by reason of his stewardship of England, was also confirmed as constable of Bristol. Thomas Charlton, favoured by the king for a bishopric, was retained as clerk of the privy seal, while the younger Despenser was made chamberlain by the council's consent and by the request of the great men of the land (*par consail et a la requeste de grantz*). Montacute, objectionable to Lancaster, allegedly even a threat to his safety, was removed from the scene by his appointment as seneschal of Gascony. On balance it would seem that Lancaster's wishes were overruled by members of the council, more particularly with respect to the advancement of Despenser and Badlesmere. Subsequently local administration came under review and on 29 November all the sheriffs, save those for counties on the northern border, were replaced.[154] Tout considered that the committee for the reform of the household relied on its chief officers for the detailed work: the steward (Badlesmere), sole representative of the parliamentary committee, the chamberlain (Despenser), the keeper or treasurer (Northburgh), and the controller of the wardrobe (Wigton). At any rate, these men were responsible for drafting the wide-ranging Ordinance of York, completed on 6 December, so it is not surprising that the changes they advocated were not particularly drastic.[155] The Statute of York nonetheless served to improve judicial procedure.[156]

Lancaster had gained little or nothing politically from the various arrangements of Leake and York. The reconstructed council and administration were
scarcely favourable to him – far from it. There is no evidence that his representative on the council took any significant part in high-level decisions. Any
rejoicing at Montacute's removal from the stewardship must have evaporated
with Badlesmere's appointment in the face of the earl's claim. It is likely that
Lancaster's hostility towards the new appointee, a hostility that boded ill for
both parties, arose at this time. The younger Despenser was shortly to become
his latest worst enemy and even Montacute's removal to Gascony might have
been regarded as promotion. One of the principal planks in Lancaster's platform, the resumption of grants, had been whittled down. In line with the
mitigation suggested by the bishops, cases were to be decided on their merits –
theoretically a more rational solution – but Montacute, Amory, Despenser, and
Badlesmere all benefited from this change of emphasis.[157]

Lancaster's own profits and aggrandizement were another matter. Indeed it
is tempting to conclude that the earl was content to trade his reforming ideas
and his own political position for private advantage, for money, and for what
most great lords were anxious to achieve – consolidation of their estates. Lancaster's "uncharacteristic behaviour" in withdrawing from his formerly intran-
sigent position is explained by his biographer.[158] His enemies, Amory, Audley
and Montacute, were forced to acknowledge "debts" for sums collectively
totalling more than £1,700, by way of amends for unspecified injuries.[159]
According to Maddicott this was the penalty that the "middle party" – perhaps
one should say the moderate element – had exacted from the courtiers as return
for the settlement.

The accommodation with Warenne was an even more remarkable instance of
Lancaster's aggressive acquisitiveness.[160] It transpires from his petition of 1322
that Warenne, in an attempt to come to an arrangement with Lancaster, had visited him six years before, at his suggestion, but once in his power he was threatened with death unless he released his Yorkshire lands and those in North Wales,
Bromfield, Yale, and Holt Castle as well as the reversion of his Norfolk estates.
In addition he was forced to pledge himself on the security of all his lands to
pay fifty thousand pounds within a month. This was not exacted for reasons that
can only be surmised – moderates were unwilling to upset the balance by letting
the earl go so far. It would have ruined Warenne. He had to await Lancaster's
demise before he could recover his Welsh lands, but it was not until 1326 that
he regained the Yorkshire manors, and then only for life. Lancaster's part in this
enforced exchange of lands was to concede to Warenne a life interest in his
remote manors in Somerset, Dorset, and Wiltshire. Warenne had indeed paid
dearly for helping Lancaster's wife to escape from a notoriously unfaithful husband. The younger Despenser was harder to pin down. Rumour had it that he
had taken the precaution of going to Compostella on pilgrimage.[161] Jealousy
and pride lay at the base of most of Lancaster's actions, allied to greed and self-

interest. Regardless of the interests of the country – particularly the North – he was quite willing to ally with the Scots against Beaumont. It was the threat of the fall of Norham that brought the moderates to placate Lancaster with a settlement so much to his personal advantage.[162]

FROM LEAKE TO THE COLLAPSE OF POLITICAL COMPROMISE, 1318–20

The year 1319 opened more propitiously than usual. In summing up the new situation the author of the *Vita* wrote of the good omens: a miracle had occurred – during the elevation at a mass attended by Robert Bruce a dove had snatched the host from the priest's hands; God had given victory over Edward Bruce in Ireland; the dearth had given way to plenty; the king had been reconciled to his barons and his personal following (*privata familia*) had left the court. No longer need England fear her enemies. On the other hand, if we read between the lines of *Bridlington*, the accord between king and earl was more apparent than real.[163] Meanwhile, however, the clergy were asked to summon a convocation for the purpose of granting a subsidy of a third of their goods for the Scottish campaign. The convocation assembled at St Paul's on 20 April and subsequently at the house of the Carmelites, but after fifteen days the clergy had not come to an affirmative decision. What part Reynolds played in these debates does not seem to have been recorded,[164] but it was finally decided that envoys should be sent by the king to secure papal permission. The chronicler Murimuth, as he tells us himself, was despatched for the purpose. Following papal assent a tenth, the customary levy, was conceded.[165]

Parliament assembled at York for 6 May 1319 and continued until the twenty-fifth, while a muster at Newcastle was ordered for 10 June. Lancaster attended the assembly with a substantial retinue, determined to revive the business of the stewardship.[166] The previous parliament had offered to have the records examined and this time Lancaster must have pursued the matter since the exchequer was ordered to enquire about knights' fees held by Simon de Montfort and subsequent earls of Leicester on account of the stewardship.[167] Nothing further transpired at this time. Lancaster was relying partly on the imprecision of the documentary evidence, partly on an analogy between the steward's position and that of the other hereditary officials: the earl marshal (Norfolk), appointed a deputy in King's Bench and the exchequer, while the household chamberlain (Warwick) and the constable (Hereford) likewise appointed deputies in the exchequer.[168] Maddicott argues further that Montacute's stewardship had enabled him to exert influence close to the king: Lancaster would have the potential to do likewise through his nominee, even though himself excluded from the council.[169] The much debated "Tract on the Office of the Steward," possibly drawn up in 1321 at the time of the process against the Despensers, encapsulated a much more ambitious authority. After the king the office gave the steward the right to regulate the whole kingdom and all the legal officers (*supervidere et regulare sub rege et immediate post regem ... totum regnum Anglie et omnes ministros legum*), whether in peace or war, with power to remove corrupt officers and intervene against "evil councillors." The tract closes with the case of Gaveston[170] who, though outlawed by the magnates and communitas, returned without the magnates' consent. When this came to the notice of the steward and constable he was beheaded by them as public enemy of the king and kingdom. This is all very close to Lancaster's own declared aspirations and provides justification for Gaveston's brutal despatch. The association with the constable (Hereford) has been interpreted as a reflection of the opportunist nature of the document – in 1321 Hereford had only recently come over to the Lancastrian camp, but his predecessor had far less to do with Gaveston's death than the then chamberlain, Warwick.[171]

An impressive force was gathered for the Scottish expedition, the contingent provided by Lancaster forming a substantial part of it. Evidence that he was paid for his contribution to the army is lacking; it is even possible that he preferred to remain independent, free from obligation to the king.[172] In the event the single-mindedness of his participation has been brought into question. It may be some slight mitigation that Edward in an unguarded moment is said to have remarked that once the siege was over he would turn again to the wrong done to Gaveston.[173] Following the premature withdrawal of Lancaster's contingent the investiture of Berwick in the autumn of 1319 had to be abandoned: the earl was even suspected of allowing the Scots to pass unopposed through his lines. The disaster of Myton and the virtually unopposed escape of the Scottish raiders certainly serve to highlight the possible involvement of Lancaster with the Scots, and the critical state of the recently concluded agreement between king and earl.[174] The truth is hard to come by, but rumours were rife. Lancaster's alleged treachery can be supported by documentary evidence – the younger Despenser's claim in a letter to the sheriff of Glamorgan that Lancaster had invited the Scots and given them assistance so that the king was forced to withdraw.[175] This is countered by a chronicler who suggests Despenser had a hand in the Scottish raid to capture Queen Isabella, and that he then put the blame on Lancaster.[176] The *Vita* does not presume to identify the "traitor Achitophel" despite the length of its circumstantial story about a captured spy who revealed the plot, but later on it does give credence to a host of rumours including one that the earl had received forty thousand pounds from Bruce and duly moralizes about behaviour that could only tarnish his reputation.[177] The earl in an attempt to dispel the rumours purged himself before a number of his peers, but whether this was sufficient, as the *Vita* thought, to turn a thorn into a lily, or dross into gold, is another matter.[178] The author of the *Flores* takes the opportunity, after reciting how the bishop of Norwich (Salmon) had consecrated the chrism in Westminster Abbey, to lament the military incapacity of a king who had squandered much of the dignity and honour of the Crown and had failed to emulate the glorious triumphs of his ancestors.[179]

By 5 October the king and the wardrobe clerks were back in York. A council meeting eight days later discussed the necessity to provide a better defensive system for the northern counties and immediate arrangements were made for the establishment of a local militia.[180] Edward had proved ineffectual in his management of the army;[181] another campaign was for the moment unthinkable, particularly since there was urgent need for him to perform homage to Philip V of France, who had succeeded to the throne three years before.[182] As a result a two-year truce was arranged on 29 December.[183] On 6 November a parliament was summoned to York for 20 January 1320, the summonses being confined to the clergy and baronage.[184] Lancaster, perhaps irritated by the fact that the truce with the Scots had not been approved by a parliamentary assembly, is said by some chroniclers to have been absent,[185] claiming it to be improper to hold a parliament "in cameris," by which he appears to have meant one packed by the king's friends and supporters (*regem et collaterales suos sibi suspectos*), rather than one that lacked elements of the Commons.[186] Surprisingly, though, the earl is named as witnessing a royal charter on 29 January, just prior to the king's departure for Doncaster, which suggests that he was present at least for a time.[187] In any case, did the earl's non-participation arise wholly or in part from his unpopularity following the Scottish campaign and his resultant feeling of isolation?

The January 1320 parliament and the period immediately following saw major changes in the officers of state. Hothum's replacement in the chancellorship on the twenty-sixth by John Salmon, bishop of Norwich, is usually attributed to his responsibility for the Myton débâcle. Perhaps this was so only indirectly. The real complaint may be that he was responsible for moving the exchequer and other records to York, where they were endangered. Subsequently he was to be accused of disaffection and was among the bishops whose temporalities were allegedly interfered with by the Despensers.[188] More controversially, on the following day Robert Baldock became keeper of the privy seal. This was attributed to the counsel of the Despensers in the articles of their indictment in 1321.[189] Surprisingly, perhaps, Walter Stapeldon succeeded Walter Norwich as treasurer on 18 February. His appointment was not in parliament, and is said to have been at Edward's behest.[190] The biased *Flores* is content to attribute the appointments between 1318 and 1320 of Stapeldon, Salmon, Despenser junior and Badlesmere to the king.[191]

Meanwhile, Edward was concerned about the question of homage. Already in June 1318 an embassy appointed to take the oath on the king's behalf had been told at the French court to return with more appropriate documents containing the exact terms of homage.[192] Edward made the excuse that he was engaged with Scotland. This matter was overtaken by the seneschal of Gascony's reports of encroachment by Philip's officials there. May 1319 saw the reappointment of Bishop Orleton, on this occasion in association with Stapeldon, Baldock, and M. Richard Burton, to perform homage in Edward's name. Once again the matter was postponed. Orleton, who had also been engaged for many months in diplomatic negotiation at Avignon, reported to the royal council at Loughborough.[193] The envoy carried eight bulls in his baggage: two of them concerned the papal tenth, which Edward hoped to divert to his own purposes, the third recited the process against Robert Bruce, the fourth cited certain Scottish prelates to appear at the Curia, while the fifth directed English archbishops and bishops to pronounce excommunication of those who invaded the realm or who gave help and encouragement to them. Two final bulls were directed to Cardinals Gaucelme d'Eauze and Luca Fieschi for pronouncing sentences against Bruce, but as the cardinals had already left the kingdom they were entrusted to Baldock, the new keeper of the privy seal.

Towards the end of March 1320 a further embassy left England, consisting of the elder Despenser, Orleton, and Badlesmere – clearly men in whom the king had implicit trust. It reached Paris by 1 April, when arrangements were made for the no-longer-to-be-avoided meeting between Edward and Philip. In early May the envoys were in Avignon, where together with the king's half-brother, Edmund, they presented their letters of credence to the pope. The business at the Curia was varied and complex. Ostensibly the urgent task was to press the candidature of Badlesmere's young nephew, M. Henry de Burghersh – already disappointed of Winchester – to the see of Lincoln, the chapter's candidate, Anthony Bek, having gone to press his case at the Curia following Reynolds' refusal to grant confirmation.[194] To Orleton personally the question of Cantilupe's imminent canonization was of particular moment. A highly secret matter, revealed only by the chronicler Trevet, was Edmund of Woodstock's plea for Edward's absolution from his oath to observe the Ordinances – a plea that was successful.[195]

The king as duke of Gascony could no longer put off a personal appearance before his overlord. The Rochester chronicler gives some interesting details of his progress towards the coast in June 1320. He set off together with the queen and a respectable number of nobles and magnates. The steward of the household, Badlesmere, gave the king and his party a splendid reception in his castle of Chilham in Kent, and when the party left he gave presents to all in accordance with their status. Arrived at Dover the king deliberated with his men about the possibility of excusing himself from doing homage or instead sending envoys to the king of France and to Avignon.[196] In the event Edward sailed from Dover on 19 June.[197] On the return journey the envoys met the royal entourage at Amiens, where on 30 June they attended the long-postponed ceremony of homage. The whole company, about to re-embark, paused at Boulogne where Burghersh, the new bishop of Lincoln, was consecrated in the king's presence on 20 July by one of the three bishops present, Orleton, Salmon, and Stapeldon.[198]

Those in royal favour are now clearly visible. Montacute (Montagu) had died in 1319, but the younger Despenser, having secured his Gloucester inheritance, had moved particularly close to Edward. The elder Despenser was also influential, though he kept more in the background, Badlesmere seemed to be moving towards greater favours, Baldock was launched on his career, and the initially obscure Stapeldon was firmly entrenched as an official. It even appeared that Orleton, an able diplomat, might be chosen for some administrative post. The Westminster Parliament of October 1320 was well attended, Lancaster's absence in the North being all the more pointed.[199] But he was represented, and on the assembly's dispersal two recently appointed bishops, Stephen Gravesend of London and Rigaud d'Assier, were sent to the earl, apparently at papal suggestion, carrying with them an appropriate bull.[200] Assier was consecrated by Gravesend at St Albans on 16 November, but the latter fell ill at Northampton, and it is uncertain whether the mission actually reached its destination.[201]

The Rochester chronicler writes that petitions were presented lamenting the unfortunate state of the realm: jurors perjured themselves in assizes and inquisitions, whether before lay or ecclesiastical judges; it was a commonplace that men were kidnapped and taken to unknown places, whence they never reappeared; because of the deceit and cupidity of the great, and their practices of protection and maintenance, no justice could be exerted against such jurors, kidnappers and common robbers, to the endangering of the realm. Order was made that prelates should excommunicate perjurers and reserve their absolution to themselves, and that justices – termed of trailbaston – in every county should punish all kidnappers and felons. The chronicler adds that because some great persons feared that their men would be harmed, certain of them, including Badlesmere in Kent, prevented justices coming into their territory.[202] As shown in an earlier chapter, Bishop Cobham, in letters to the pope and to Cardinal Vitale Dufour, has left an eyewitness account of the king's behaviour at this time, praising his deportment, prudence, and discretion, and emphasizing his unaccustomed early rising and cheerful mien.[203] Thus it was with a good heart that the bishop took up the heavy burden laid upon him of treating with the Scots.[204] Perhaps he would have been forced to agree with a later assessment that the parliament "saw a final and unexpected victory for the forces of moderation before the débâcle brought about by the ambition of the Despensers."[205] It is possible that the king was merely being two-faced, thereby seeking to delude his former opponents. Regardless of his absolution from the oath to maintain the Ordinances, he instructed the officers of the exchequer to see that they were obeyed.[206]

THE DESPENSERS' SCHEMES AND THE BARONIAL REACTION
1320–21

Lancaster, although he was still advocating the canonization of his mentor and hero, Archbishop Winchelsey,[207] would appear to have traded a political compromise for his own aggrandizement – a compromise that relegated the Ordinances to secondary significance. At this juncture the earl was faced by the Despensers' encroachments in Wales, which served to upset the Marcher barons as well as himself. The increasing influence at court of the Despensers, Baldock, and to a lesser degree Arundel, further stimulated his anger against "favourites" and their usurpation of baronial counsel in the affairs of the realm.

The younger Despenser, as soon as his share of the Clare inheritance was released in 1317, began the process of enlarging his authority in South Wales. On 18 November in that year he obtained, with the consent of parliament, a grant for life of the castle and town of Dryslwyn and of the stewardship of Cantrefmawr – lying between Is Aeron bordering the west coast and Cantref Bychan to the east; the latter in the possession of John Giffard of Brimpsfield. The grant was made until such time as Despenser should be provided elsewhere with lands to the value of six hundred marks. By virtue of it he became constable of Dinefwr castle.[208] At the same time he was granted all royal and other liberties within his land of Glamorgan where, according to Conway Davies, he acted responsibly as an able administrator who gave his attention even to minor details and also "had definite constitutional principles."[209] What soon aroused opposition was his policy of opportunist aggrandizement. For instance, he outmanoeuvred Audley by taking the homage of the men of Gwenllwyg and Machen, so that his brother-in-law felt obliged to enfeoff him with a portion of these lands. What seems to have been a forceful exchange – not dissimilar to that imposed on Warenne by Lancaster – entailed Audley's loss of Newport town and castle.[210] More widespread irritation was caused by Despenser's interference in Gower. William de Braose or Brewosa, an impecunious baron, was contemplating selling his land, which Hereford, the Mortimers of Chirk and Wigmore, and Despenser were all prepared to purchase. But Braose's daughter had married John de Mowbray, to whom and to whose heirs Braose then granted the honour of Gower, with remainder to Hereford.[211] John Yweyn or Inge had acted as Braose's bailiff, but by 1318 he was in Despenser's service and doubtless as a consequence fell foul of his former master, who seized his Gower lands. He was appealed of murder and imprisoned in Swansea Castle, and on 4 August 1319 the king ordered an investigation.[212] Despenser tried to impede Mowbray's possession and at his suggestion the king took Gower into his hands on the grounds that it had been obtained without licence.[213] This was regarded as being contrary to the custom of the March (*legi Marchiae preiudicialem, fieri discernebat*), consequently inimical to accepted practices of inheritance, a view decried by Despenser, who allegedly argued that it smacked of treason.[214] As could have been anticipated, the king's order was resisted.[215]

Despenser's machinations soon brought a united front of Marcher lords, chief among them Hereford, but also Mowbray, Amory, Audley, Clifford,[216] and the Mortimers. Confederacies and disturbances soon followed. Rhys ap Hywel, who in 1315 had been involved in preparations against an invasion of South Wales, and who in the following year raised two thousand men for service in Scotland, had subsequently taken service with Mortimer of Wigmore and, more particularly, with Hereford. Despenser was well aware of his activities and in a letter to John Yweyn (Inge), his sheriff of Glamorgan, suggested that it might be prudent to secure a commission to apprehend Rhys.[217] There were others who remained loyal, however. Sir Rhys ap Gruffydd was consistently so, raising men during the Llywelyn Bren revolt, then for service in Scotland, and on 2 February 1322 executing the mandate for seizure of Mowbray's lordship of Gower.[218]

A dangerous state of affairs ensued with assemblies of barons allegedly plotting disturbances or interfering with matters pertaining to the Crown. These were forbidden by the king, who named known participants, headed by the earls of Hereford, Warenne and Arundel, but including a number of Yorkshire barons – an indication of the widespread nature of disaffection.[219] An anonymous informant (perhaps an overconfident Robert Baldock), in a letter of 27 February 1321 from Newcastle, wrote of Lancaster's threat to call out his retainers and to create disturbances in Wales. There was no real cause for fear, he suggested, but it would be as well were the younger Despenser to make speedy preparations. For Badlesmere ambushes were being prepared both in the North – where he had been concerned with arranging a Scottish truce[220] – and in the South, but the baron was taking countermeasures by raising a large force of men-at-arms. Once alerted, Despenser reproved Sheriff Inge for not keeping him better informed and under threat ordered him to make defensive preparations, including the taking of hostages.[221]

In short, there was imminent danger of a civil war in March 1321, as both the king and Despenser attempted to put the Welsh castles in a state of readiness. In Knighton's view, Despenser led Edward around at will for his own aggrandizement.[222] Edward had been at Westminster on 1 March, on the sixth he left Windsor and by the twenty-seventh was at Gloucester. The king's absence, that of his chief ministers and those closest to him – Pembroke, the younger Despenser and Baldock – caused difficulties for a mission newly returned with urgent news of Gascon affairs. Hereford was summoned to appear at Gloucester on 5 April but declined to come.[223] Armed confrontation was averted by wiser counsel. The confederates sent the abbot of Dore to the king requesting that he summon a parliament in which the state of the Church and realm could be discussed.[224] Edward, whether by his own cunning or acting on the advice of those close to him, resumed possession of Hereford's castle of Builth, claiming that this was done by virtue of the Ordinances. He also summoned Hereford and the younger Mortimer to Oxford for 10 May ostensibly to give counsel.[225] For their part, the Marchers even contrived some diversionary activity on the other side of the country, in Norfolk, where Robert de Walkfare, a close adherent – according to Walsingham, a relative (*affinis* and *consanguineus*) of the earl of Lancaster – as well as a friend of Hereford, urged the release of William de Somerton, the prior of Binham, whom the abbot of St Albans, the mother house, had imprisoned. Walkfare acted on the grounds that the younger Despenser was behind the abbot and was accounted a "public enemy of that region" (*reputabatur publicus inimicus regionis*). To bully the abbot was indirectly to attack the king, hence Despenser.[226]

In early May 1321 the confederates moved in force to despoil the goods of the Despensers in Wales and the March, after which they did the same to the lands they held elsewhere.[227] They did likewise to those of John de Cromwell and of John de Handlo, a supporter of the elder Despenser.[228] Arundel also suffered, thanks to the hostility of the younger Mortimer, who first occupied the town of Cardiff and took George Gorges – constable of the castle there – prisoner to Wigmore, and then proceeded to capture Arundel's castle of Clun.[229] Lancaster, who remained at Pontefract, played no personal part in this brigandage but he was assumed to be the real leader, nothing being done unless by his counsel and at his direction.[230] The Rochester chronicler declares that the devastators claimed to act in the interest of the king and kingdom and that to make the point they placed the royal banner in whatever castle or territory they captured on the basis, according to them, that they kept it for the king.[231] This lawlessness engendered a widespread feeling of unease. Bishop Cobham, who had worked conscientiously for peace both within the realm and with the Scots wrote to the pope and cardinals of the outbreak of that worst kind of strife, civil war (*familiaris hostilitas ... bellum intestinum*). Earls and barons with a considerable number of people were capturing castles, committing homicides, for what purpose he confessed he did not know. Indeed, he claimed, no one knew, save one of the participating confederates.[232]

While these activities served to concentrate the opposition, there were other reasons for baronial hostility among those who felt left out of the counsels of the realm. According to the Pauline annalist, Despenser removed persons at will from the king's household, substituting others without the consent of the magnates.[233] Baker is even more forthright. There were those, he claims, who considered Despenser to be "another king, or more accurately ruler of the king – the royal mind – in the manner of Gaveston, so presumptuous that he frequently kept certain nobles from speaking to the king. Moreover when the king, out of his magnanimity was preoccupied with many people addressing him about their affairs, Despenser threw back answers, not those asked for but to the contrary, pretending them to be to the king's advantage."[234] An anonymous chronicler, who has left a vestigial work covering only the Gaveston years and those of the younger Despenser until 1322, is even more expansive about the favourite's supposed misbehaviour.[235] The Lanercost chronicler is by contrast succinct: the younger Despenser was as the "English king's right eye" (*quasi oculus dexter regis Angliae*). In his view Despenser was anxious to reunite the whole of the Gloucester earldom, and although he does not say so, Despenser doubtless coveted the title as well.[236]

Lancaster now moves to centre stage with his endeavours to form a coalition of his own retainers, northern barons, and the Marchers, as well as to devise a political program that they could be persuaded to accept. Two quasi-parliaments were summoned by the earl. The first met in the chapter house of Pontefract Priory on 24 May 1321 and was attended, so the Bridlington chronicler informs us,[237] by the earl's own retainers (*primo cum suis*) together with fifteen named barons and bannerets, mainly men with Yorkshire connections.[238] Because of various disturbances in the realm, threatening its peace, they agreed a pact for mutual defence, so that if someone were to rise up against any of them or against the earl, they would provide aid against such malicious persons. In this way it was thought peace would be better preserved. This confederation document, written in French, was sealed by all present. But it was nonetheless felt that such business required the counsel of other great men, more particularly the prelates, so the earl of Lancaster summoned the prelates of the province and diocese of York to meet at Sherburn-in-Elmet on the Sunday after the Nativity of St John the Baptist – i.e., 28 June. On that day there assembled the archbishop of York (William Melton), and the bishops of Durham (Beaumont) and Carlisle (John Halton), the earls of Lancaster and Hereford, abbots and priors, as well as many barons, bannerets, and knights, both northerners and southerners (*australes et boriales*). At this stage those summoned included not only Hereford but also other Marchers under the term "australes," although the church representatives, whether seculars or regulars, were confined to the northern province.[239] At the earl's command Sir John Bek read out certain articles in French concerned with matters that allegedly called for correction. Rather than give the text verbatim – its meaning veiled by smooth phrases (*blandis sermonibus velabantur*) – the chronicler preferred to summarize it in Latin. The text is clearly influenced by Lancaster perhaps through the medium of clerical advisors and is itemized in the following paraphrase:

• Should any injuries, grievances or harm be experienced as the result of the king's evil councillors, or of less than competent ministers, they are to be aired before the earl so that by unanimous assent and common council (*per assensum unanimem et commune consilium*) remedy can be provided.
• It would seem that those who occupy the offices of the realm, chancellor, treasurer, chamberlain, justices, keeper of the secret seal, escheators, and others, ought to be elected (*per electionem constitui debuissent*), and that men who received their offices contrary to the Ordinances are the cause of the renewed ills and oppressions of the people.
• There should be remedy for those tenants in chief and others who have suffered forfeiture and disinheritance by royal power without the assent of the peers of the land.
• Justices appointed by royal commission, at the instigation of evil councillors make enquiry about various misdeeds (*transgressiones*), and indict magnates so that for carefully contrived reasons (*causis variis exquisitis*) they can be disinherited contrary to the established laws (*leges usitatas*) and to the oppression of the people.
• The evil councillors appoint justices itinerant for London and make the king issue the writ *Quo warranto*, thereby forcing men to respond for rents and

liberties which they and their ancestors have enjoyed, and that have been in existence since the Conquest. By such oppressions they disinherit the people and afflict them.

- It was necessary to discuss the grievances of foreign merchants who, contrary to royal charters granted to them, after the purchase of merchandise have to go to St. Omer, to conduct sales there to the great disadvantage of the people.

- They should discuss with the earl how treaties and binding agreements (*confoederationes et alligationes*) already begun should be annulled. Were they to be concluded they would be to their and our destruction and to that of the whole people of England.

- There was a question about how the king, at the instigation of councillors, retains all the advocates and legal experts (*defensores et iurisperiti*) so that when magnates or lesser men are impleaded by the king they are deprived of counsel. His progenitors only retained two sergeants for his pleas.

After the articles had been recited the earl asked the clergy to withdraw and to reply as they wished. They retired to the rectory and then sent their response to the earl. This effectively poured cold water on any bellicose intention but at the same time served as an emollient. After expressing their approval of the earl's evident love of the country the prelates stressed the urgency of dealing with the Scots, stating themselves to be eager to help the earl and other great men, though reserving the status of clergy and Church. As to the recent disturbances in the realm, there should be tolerance until agreement could be reached in the next parliament by means of peaceful discussion. At that juncture, Bridlington concludes, the assembly broke up.[240] There is no mention of any sealing of an indenture.

The indenture itself has not survived, but an inventory of Lancaster's muniments does record that a treaty (*tretiz*) concluded at Sherburn on 28 June 1321 had twenty-five seals, and it has been argued persuasively that these were principally of Lancaster's retainers.[241] Professor Wilkinson discussed the various chronicles and auxiliary manuscripts at length, in particular collections of material to be found in Register I at Canterbury Cathedral Library and Lambeth MS 1213. Register I contains *inter alia* the articles of the Sherburn assembly in the original French and a copy of the indenture itself. The Lambeth manuscript includes the indenture, but not the articles. Wilkinson tried to reconcile the conflicting evidence of the sources by advancing the hypothesis that there were two Sherburn meetings – of Marchers and northerners respectively – and that the sources in Register I and the Bridlington chronicler have a northern provenance, while the Lambeth collection is of Welsh border origin, enshrining the program of the Marcher barons. But this has rightly been regarded as unduly subtle. The reality seems to be that there was only one meeting[242] and that the detailed accounts in the *Flores* and *Bridlington* are capable of reconciliation, bearing in mind that both lacked precision in their enumeration of the participants. Another problem concerns the signatories. The indenture in the Lambeth MS seemingly presupposes that it would be sealed by all relevant groups: Lancaster's retainers, the Marchers, and the northerners, although in fact the last refused to seal it, an unfortunate portent for the earl. The Canterbury register may contain a version revised by the Marchers and presented by them, and this was sealed principally by Lancaster's retainers but also by a few others. It remains difficult to see why the Marchers did not seal it themselves even if their antagonism to the Despensers was well enough known.[243]

The chronicler Trevet records an attempt on the king's part to contact Lancaster, apparently at Sherburn. Archbishop Reynolds and Badlesmere, he reports, were sent on an unsuccessful mission to curb the persecution of the Despensers. Badlesmere is said to have stayed behind with the barons despite the fact that he was *persona non grata* with Lancaster, leaving Reynolds to return on his own.[244] However, the archbishop's itinerary gives no indication that, apart from a brief stay at Lambeth, he travelled outside Kent at this time.[245] The Rochester chronicler, whose principal subject, Bishop Hethe, was closely connected to Reynolds, also makes no mention of any such mission. The Marcher barons were already determined on the Despensers' exile and the St Albans chronicler states that a draft indictment had been drawn up at Sherburn.[246] Bishop Orleton returned from France at the end of April and attended a council summoned by the king to consider what should be done. Apparently this was intended to meet at Oxford but its venue was altered to Westminster.[247] Together with two other unnamed bishops Orleton was despatched to the west to rally supporters in the March.[248]

On 15 May 1321 parliament was summoned to Westminster for 15 July, where it continued to sit until 22 August.[249] Meanwhile, Despenser manors in Leicestershire were sacked by Robert Holland, who with William de Bredon allegedly played havoc armed *cap-à-pie* in the town of Loughborough on the morrow of the feast of the Translation of St Thomas (8 July 1321).[250] The Marchers moved towards London in great array – "*cum maxima pompa et strepitu armorum*," staying for three days round about 22 July at St Albans abbey, to the distress of the monks, for whom Edward had a particular affection. The day before, a frightened Reynolds from Lambeth issued a forty days' indulgence for the peace of the realm.[251] The bishops of London (Gravesend), Salisbury (Martival), Ely (Hothum), Hereford (Orleton), and Chichester (John Langton) were sent northwards to urge peace, in much the same way as their counterparts in the province of York had done at Sherburn.[252] According to the Rochester chronicler, the barons and their supporters, some twenty-five in number,[253] sought the assistance of John de Grey and other local men, under threat of destroying their lands. Their progress was marked by devastation and impoverishment of the countryside.[254] All were arrayed in green livery with a yellow quarter on the right arm as though they had been quartered by the Despensers, father and son.[255] The bishops and the earls of Richmond, Arundel, Warenne (Surrey), and Pembroke then met the baronial leaders at Clerkenwell on 27 July, where the earls are said to have joined them. Predictably the bishops declined to do so.[256]

The account given by the Historia Roffensis is expanded by the Pauline annalist. According to the latter, and he is very detailed for the period from 29 July until 14 August,[257] the barons, for the most part armed, arrived at London from Waltham on the twenty-ninth. They did not enter the city immediately, but stayed outside at Islington and Smithfield, divided into three contingents (*acies*). They then dispersed themselves peacefully in various lodgings, Mortimer at Clerkenwell, Hereford with the army at Holborn in Lancaster's houses, Roger d'Amory at the New Temple, and Audley at St Bartholomew's Priory, Smithfield, while others lodged in Smithfield, Holborn, and Fleet Street – some 1,500 of them. Various discussions took place with the bishops at the New Temple and at the Carmelites' house, the bishops ferrying messages between king and barons.[258]

Two knights were despatched with a petition to the king to say that their principals considered the Despensers to be enemies and traitors to both king and kingdom, with the request that they be brought into parliament to receive by the award (*agard*) of the peers what they deserved: to be exiled permanently, and themselves and their heirs disinherited.[259] Subsequently a further meeting took place at the Carmelite friary in the city where Badlesmere denounced the younger Despenser as a traitor. To substantiate the charge he produced a document (the *Homage et serment* declaration), which, with its distinction between king and Crown, was in fact a statement of the baronial position used in 1308 and against Gaveston in 1311. The version rehearsed by the Rochester chronicler is that of 1311, but, as he points out, the name of Despenser was substituted for that of Gaveston. Such an obvious device cut no ice with Bishop Hethe, who from that time forth detested the insurgent barons and regarded them as suspect.[260] There have been many attempts to explain this farcical manoeuvre, but it looks as though the barons were merely being naïve and it may be best to treat the incident in the same manner as Bishop Hethe – as a blatant piece of trickery that exploded in Badlesmere's face and that his allies were content to adopt.[261]

At this point – on 28 July – the king's half-brother was made earl of Kent, anticipation of which doubtless helped to foster the antagonism of Badlesmere to those at court, for he had been expanding his influence in the county.[262] Immediately Pembroke, acting as intermediary and as the barons' spokesman, urged the deportation of the Despensers and the disinheritance of their heirs. The king's response was that it would be unjust and contrary to his oath that anyone should be exiled without opportunity to respond and suggested that the Despensers could dwell in Ireland until such time as the magnates' hearts softened. It was, he said, to be deplored that *generosi* and noblemen should be judged in such a manner. But Pembroke interjected that the king had to choose between two courses: either war between his men or the exile of two of them – it had to be one or the other. It was preferable to pardon the mass of the people rather than two persons.[263] Edward, continues the chronicler, was not won over by the prayers of the prelates, earls, barons, and others gathered there but was compelled by force, fear, and necessity to consent unwillingly to their petitions. He withdrew with a bitter heart.

On 14 August the earls and barons assembled in the king's great hall at Westminster, the prelates meeting separately in the great chamber. The barons reiterated their demand that the Despensers be exiled as traitors and enemies of the king and kingdom, declaring that if the law of the land did not permit this, as peers of the realm they should pass a new law in full parliament (*novam edere legem et statuere in pleno parliamento*) as is the custom of the realm. In accordance with that custom they straightway determined and decreed (*statuerunt et decreverunt*) that the Despensers were judicially exiled without hope of return and perpetually disinherited together with their heirs. The earl of Hereford read the statute (*statutum*).[264] The *Anonimalle Chronicle* dates this precisely to 14 August. As soon as he heard the news the elder Despenser, who was then at Canterbury, blaming his son's behaviour (*malveis port*) for this disastrous outcome, crossed the sea from Dover, where he abandoned his familia.[265] As for the king, in great sadness he retired to his chamber.

The prelates made their farewells, according to the Rochester chronicler protesting that they would never consent to the exile.[266] As for the younger Despenser, he is said to have been accompanied by the king to Dover (shades of Gaveston?) where in the habit of the abbot of Langdon he crossed the Channel and came to Paris.[267] But fearing for his safety there, owing to the presence of the earl of Pembroke at the French court, he returned in the habit of the abbot to Westminster and threw himself at the king's feet, but received no friendly word from him (*pulcrum verbum ab eo habere non potuit*).[268] Later the king ordered the mariners of Sandwich to guard him and, according to the Rochester chronicler, sought the advice of the barons of the Cinque Ports as to how the rebels could be resisted and the realm preserved from civil war. Their suggestion was that he should collect a people's army (*collecto exercitu populari*) and sweep through the country punishing the rebels, while they would gather a fleet to sack the maritime towns of the rebels. Seizing their opportunity they attacked the port of Southampton and torched the ships there, thus allegedly striking terror into the barons.[269] Meanwhile the younger Despenser resorted to piracy, captured two well laden dromonds, despoiled them of their cargo said to have been worth sixty thousand pounds – some of it belonging to the pope – and kept the ships themselves.[270] As for the rebellious barons, they demanded a royal pardon for their own and their followers' depredations, robberies, thefts, homicides, and felonies, committed from the first week of Lent (8 March), when they began to ride with the royal banner displayed to destroy the lands of the Despensers, until 14 August – the day the king conceded their demands for the Despensers' exile – continuing, Dene adds, until 19 August, so that they could carry out further depredations. Edward replied that he could not do this in defiance of his coronation oath.[271]

Dene, the Rochester chronicler from whom the above narrative is mainly derived, was at no time sympathetic to the barons. The *Vita* is perhaps more circumspect, but certainly gives the barons' case fully. According to this account, the king prior to the Westminster parliament refused to listen to their petitions, whereupon they declared that unless he did so they would renounce their homage and choose another ruler (*alium rectorem sibi preficerent*) to do justice and to humble the guilty and the proud (*collum nocentium et superborum humiliaret*). This threat was carried to Edward by Pembroke and others, who were ostensibly acting as mediators (*qui videbantur mediatores*), although they had also taken the oath to uphold to the death the quarrels of the barons. The words put into Pembroke's mouth at this stage are different from those recorded by Dene, but the gist of the argument is much the same. Edward should realize the danger and prefer no one to himself.[272] He was to heed the power of the barons and not make the excuse that the business was begun by the barons: it was for the common good that the country should be rid of evil men. If he were to heed the barons he would reign in power and glory, otherwise he could well lose both the kingdom and all of them. At that point the archbishop was sent as an emissary to summon the barons to parliament.[273] As the chronicler then points out, no one was present to put the case for the Despensers; they were found guilty, proscribed, and disinherited in the presence of the king, prelates, earls, and barons.[274] Such judgment was to be irreversible.

Faced with this outcome, the author of the *Vita* attempts to plumb the differing opinions current at the time, injecting his own moral bias. Despenser the father, brutal and greedy (*ferus et cupidus*), had injured a great number and procured the excommunication of many. He had abused his powers as justice of the forest and extorted ransoms and unjustly taken possession of property. Since the son benefited from the wickedness of his father he should also bear guilt. But, according to some, the son's malice outweighed the harshness of the father. But there were others who, though they felt the judgment to be a just one, considered that the barons' subsequent destruction of the Despensers' manors, the seizure of their goods, and the extortion of ransoms from their retinues had turned what might have been a just cause into an unjust one (*Si iustam causam prius habuerint, ius et iniuriam modo converterunt*). This contradiction is echoed by Bridlington, who records what is apparently the later protest of the Despensers, discussed below.[275]

As we have seen, Lancaster strove to knit together, in opposition to the king, his own men, the Marchers, and, with appreciably less success, the northerners. One of the relevant documents in his strategy, it has been alleged, is the *Modus*

Tenendi Parliamentum, a text, frequently found in association with the "Tract on the Office of Steward," that claims spuriously to represent practice of great antiquity. There are two main recensions "A" and "B."[276] The earlier "B version" has some of its chapters out of sequence, the consequence, it has been suggested, of the incorrect folding of an inner bifolium while in an unbound state. A consensus of scholarly opinion has until comparatively recently associated it with the reign of Edward II, indeed more particularly with the parliament of July 1321 and the attack on the Despensers.[277] One of the elements in favour of that date, it has been argued, is that this recension "speaks of the clergy being summoned to parliament as proctors of the clergy, although the attendance of clerical proctors as a group ceased after about 1322 [1332?]."[278] However, there is no evidence for regarding either of these dates as a watershed with respect to clerical summonses.[279] Other problems connected with the *Modus* are its authorship and its political nature. Of the first nothing is known for certain, although Dr Maddicott considered that in seeking an author "it might be more profitable to search among Lancaster's own household clerks than among those of the chancery or the exchequer."[280] The tract's purpose is debatable. Could it have originated as a political pamphlet – though no violent polemic, despite the fact that it is only found in conjunction with legal or procedural texts?[281] Here again, Dr Maddicott observes striking resemblances between items of Lancaster's program and specific articles of the *Modus*.[282] A prominent position is given in the *Modus* to the steward, and in the case of disputes threatening internal peace, the steward, constable and marshal, or two of them, were to choose a committee of twenty-five, whereas in the "Tract" there is no mention of the marshal. Significantly, perhaps, the Earl Marshal, Thomas of Brotherton, only came of age in June 1321.[283] In any case, the argument runs, the *Modus* does not represent actual practice. On the contrary it is said to depict an ideal situation, indulges in a good deal of wishful thinking, and is capable of being adapted to a variety of political situations. The most recent commentators, coming from a more literary perspective, have endeavoured to show that the *Modus* had its origin in what is termed "the reformist culture in the English and Irish civil service" at the end of Edward III's reign. They would prefer to posit the authorship of an exchequer clerk They see the B text or recension emerging "in 1386 and 1388 in the hands of the appellants, justifying certain constitutional principles urged in the course of their *coup d'état*." Moreover, they suggest some parallels with *Piers Plowman*. But whether the tract was merely being adapted to a new situation remains an unsettled question. A further point made by these authors is that the Courtenay Cartulary,[284] which contains the earliest copy of the *Modus* (in French, though), also includes, adjacent to it, a recension of the articles of accusation against Roger Mortimer in 1330. Can it be more than a striking coincidence that Philip de Courtenay, nephew of Archbishop William Courtenay, was lieutenant in Ireland between 1383 and 1385, succeeding Roger Mortimer's descendant, another Roger who, as a child, was appointed lieutenant by the

English king?[285] Pending further debate the *Modus* cannot with any degree of certainty be used to illuminate the situation in Edward II's reign.

We are on more certain ground with the tournament held by the barons at Witney in the autumn, the earl of Pembroke on one side, Hereford on the other bearing the arms of Badlesmere.[286] Edward now saw his opportunity to reverse the tables on his tormentors. Badlesmere, a former supporter who in the king's view had basely deserted the court, was his first quarry. He sent knights from his chamber and many others to Dover Castle, to the discomfiture of the ambitious but disappointed baron, who promptly munitioned his castles of Leeds and Chilham, putting them in a state of defence. Edward then recalled his knights from Dover and forbade anyone to allow Badlesmere, whom he knew to be in Essex, to enter Tilbury or any place in Kent. A few days before the July Parliament, Badlesmere, contrary to the royal prohibition, entered Tilbury and then Hengham (Henham), Leeds, and Chilham castles. Finally he arrived at Canterbury where, to the consternation of the whole town, he was accompanied by nineteen knights, their armorial bearings concealed under their overtunics. The party, with the squires now openly displaying the baron's armour,[287] reached the shrine of St Thomas, where John de Crombwell (Cromwell) and his wife, surprisingly and for reasons unknown, seem to have been taking sanctuary, and where they sought Badlesmere's help and friendship. This, so far as was possible within the baron's entourage, was vouchsafed, Badlesmere promising to forward Cromwell's affairs within his area. Thereupon they all returned to Oxfordshire.[288]

In the absence of Badlesmere at Witney, Queen Isabella on 3 October arrived at the gate of Leeds Castle, a castle the king had granted to the baron in exchange for the manor of Adderley in Shropshire. She demanded entrance but was refused. This was doubly chagrining: not only was it a personal slight, but the castle, valued at fifty pounds a year, had been assigned in 1299 to Edward's stepmother Queen Margaret as dower. On her death it should have come into Isabella's possession by reversion.[289] Badlesmere hastened to give support to his wife, Margaret de Clare, who with Bartholomew Burghersh and Walter Colpeper had been left to defend the castle. He despatched knights from Witney together with a large following. Thomas de Aldone was appointed constable and ordered to defend the castle with vigour, admitting neither queen nor king. Edward, piqued by such insolence, acted with rare determination, collected a large force, and with the help of siege engines invested the castle for some fifteen days.[290] Hearing this, Badlesmere tried to persuade Hereford, the younger Mortimer, and his uncle, Mortimer of Chirk, to intervene on his behalf and to raise the siege. However, having arrived at Kingston, from which they threatened the capital, the barons, rather than moving to Kent, returned to their own lands. There was nothing for it but to surrender the castle. This was done, as we shall see, at curfew on the Eve of All Saints (31 October), under promise of mercy[291]. Edward exploited his advantage by sending two knights to receive the keys of Chilham Castle from its constable, Philip de Valognes, who duly surrendered them. On being conducted to the king he was told to hand over all the goods within the castle and those of his lord, Badlesmere, to the earl of Atholl, in whose entourage he remained, becoming steward of his household. Walter Colpeper, bailiff of the seven hundreds, who had been indentured to Badlesmere,[292] was drawn and hung outside the walls of Leeds together with six others (twelve, according to the Pauline annalist). The various prisoners were taken in chains to the castles of Canterbury, Rochester, and Tonbridge. The king himself advanced to Tonbridge Castle, in the possession of Hugh d'Audley. He found it deserted its defender, Thomas Colpeper, having wisely fled to fight another day. Once back in London the king appointed justices to travel to Kent for the trial of Badlesmere's supporters. But when the justices, sitting in the hall of Canterbury Castle, were about to pass sentence Edward relented and sent one Daniel de Bengham to order them to abandon further proceedings.[293]

Thus the king's initial move against the barons had been entirely successful. Kent, Badlesmere's base, had been subdued with relatively little bloodshed. But an important question presents itself. Why had the barons not moved to support Badlesmere? Lancaster, given to a degree of petty resentment, would certainly have continued to regard his elevation to the stewardship of the household as offensive to his own claim to make the appointment, while in his turn the king conceived a "black hatred" against the baron for having given up the office.[294] The *Vita* hints at other transgressions against the earl.[295] Possibly the baron's ridiculous use of the *Homage et serment* declaration is one of them. But at this stage, being far away in the North, Lancaster was in no position to provide any assistance, nor so far as is known was any requested – only, perhaps, his approval. The Marchers alone were able to help militarily, and having made their point about the Despensers, they had little wish to risk their forces so far from home in the interests of a recent turncoat. The Rochester chronicler casts valuable light on the attempts, short of military intervention, to reach a settlement prior to the fall of Leeds.[296] Reynolds is said to have called together the bishops of London and Rochester and to have met Hereford and others between Wimbledon and Kingston, on the route to London. Pembroke once again acted as intermediary between rebels and king.

Three days later, at the barons' camp at Kingston, the prelates resumed their attempt at compromise. Badlesmere proposed that the same prelates should go to Edward accompanied by Pembroke with the suggestion that until the next parliament Leeds should be delivered to Edward with all its contents – excepting his wife, relatives, and friends. He further claimed that the prerogative of the king in the case of refusal of entry should not be assumed to provide a legal right for the queen, who was merely his wife. Denial of entry to the king should be dealt with in parliament, not elsewhere, by the peers of the realm in accordance with Magna Carta. Before this suggestion reached Edward at Leeds a messenger arrived at Lambeth to convey the news that the siege was well advanced. The king had erected machines and was making a vigorous assault.[297] Leeds captured, the bishops resumed their discussions with Edward on All Souls day (2 November). Two of their number, Gravesend and Hethe, together with the earls of Pembroke and Richmond then approached the barons at Uxbridge with the message that the king concurred with their request, conveyed by the earl of Pembroke, that a venue should be arranged to investigate those responsible for so many of the realm's ills so that they could be punished. They arrived on the sixth and at first the barons, particularly those whom the king had promoted – so the Rochester chronicler alleged – concentrated on blaming him for many shameful acts and enumerating his defects (*regem vituperaliter contempnentes et recitantes defectus regis sicut improbi et ingrati*). Eventually, reason prevailing, they sent two knights with the bishops. Lancaster, it is suggested, was satisfied with the outcome, but the barons blamed the capture of Leeds and the subsequent hangings entirely on Pembroke and uttered threats against him, whereupon the earl joined the bishops at Bromley and on returning with them met the king.[298] The *Vita* claims that Lancaster's prohibition prevented the barons from assisting Badlesmere, but the Gervase continuator makes it clear that his ill will only became practical politics with the barons' Welsh campaign.[299] Before that Badlesmere was in full cooperation with the Marchers.

Regardless of the bishops' efforts to calm the situation, Edward determined to follow up his success at national level, but first he had to pave the way for the Despensers' recall. Reynolds was ordered to summon a provincial council for that purpose. His mandate, dated 14 November from Lambeth, required the clergy to assemble at St Paul's on 1 December. When the remoter bishops received these mandates towards the end of November there was no time to make the necessary preparations for a trek across the country in adverse weather. Apart from the archbishop only four diocesan bishops are known to have attended: Hothum of Ely, Gravesend of London, Martival of Salisbury, and Hethe of Rochester.[300] The day before the council the king issued a mandate forbidding the prelates from proceeding in matters touching the Crown. This warning mandate, however, should not be regarded as novel. It was regularly issued prior to provincial councils. Edward sent the earls of Richmond and Arundel with Robert Baldock, who had a legal training, to present the Despensers' protest against their sentence.[301] This delineates nine articles of procedural error: the accused had not been called in their defence; they had not been found guilty of criminal behaviour; nothing objected against them touched on felony or treason and therefore did not entail proscription or exile; process had been undertaken contrary to the king's record (*recordum regis*); the matter had been considered in the absence of the clergy – hence without common assent; entry had been made to parliament by armed men and in the king's presence; all those undertaking the judgment were capital enemies of the accused; the greater part of them were motivated by asperity; and lastly, the king had not agreed to the judgment, so that altogether they had acted contrary to Magna Carta and had thus incurred greater excommunication.[302] There is much truth in this, even though it is special pleading. To paraphrase Bridlington: the makers of laws had become their corruptors; the earl of Lancaster had forced the king to pardon him and some thousand others – the same earl who had sworn that certain Ordinances should be upheld, whereby the king was prevented from doing just that.[303]

THE CRUSHING OF REBELLION 1321–22

After an interval in Essex, where he may have been concerned with Badlesmere's lands there, Edward left for the West to confront the Mortimers, Giffard, the earl of Hereford, and their allies. The *Vita* states that the king's young half-brothers, Thomas of Brotherton, the earl marshal, and Edmund "of Woodstock," newly created earl of Kent, came to his aid. Despite their youth – they were barely twenty years of age – he considered them to be competent (*strenui*) soldiers. He adds that Pembroke went over to the king's side because, so it was said, Lancaster accused him of faithlessness (*infidum et varium*). There was a degree of truth in this as Pembroke, having responded to the king's command to move against his former ally Badlesmere at Leeds, was now committed not only to the king but also to the Despensers.[304] From Reading Edward journeyed through the Cotswolds by way of Cricklade, reaching Cirencester by 20 December, where he spent Christmas. About this time his men destroyed John Giffard's castle at Brimpsfield.[305] By 6 December the barons had captured Gloucester, thus obstructing the passage of the River Severn. The Canterbury-based Gervase continuator states that the barons were unwilling to oppose the king directly, even though their force was allegedly four times greater.[306] Instead, they retreated before him, leaving a trail of devastation in their wake.[307] A later indictment, of 1324, claims that as the younger Mortimer advanced – presumably from Worcester – by way of Bromyard towards Ledbury, he stopped, probably in late November, at Orleton's manor of Bosbury where he held secret conclave with the bishop, allegedly one of his adherents. On the following day the bishop was said to have sent reinforcements to Ledbury consisting of armed men and equipment, comprising his marshal and eight other men. With these reinforcements Mortimer then went back on his tracks and marched to Gloucester. It is easy to accept this indictment at face value, but some of the background is revealed in a collection of manuscripts discovered at Hereford, conveniently dubbed the bishop's "defence brief." There can be no doubting Orleton's closeness to Mortimer, his parishioner, whose secular influence was prominent in the diocese, but whether he was responsible for "sending" members of his entourage is questionable. No doubt Mortimer's intention was to insist, with threats if need be, that certain men join him. Some of those named can be shown clearly to have had affiliations other than with the bishop, for instance with Roger d'Amory and Gilbert Talbot. There is plenty of evidence for the Mortimers' use of coercion to secure compliance with their wishes.[308]

The only other bridge between Gloucester and Bridgnorth was at Worcester, towards which the royal forces now proceeded. But the Worcester crossing was also defended. The baronial forces are said to have arrived at Bridgnorth on 5 January yelling "Wesseheil" in their maternal tongue. For a time a royal contingent – an advance guard under Fulk FitzWarren sent to prepare for the king's crossing – defended the gate, but others burned it down and forced the king's men to flee.[309] Thereupon the rebels helped themselves to the king's horses and provisions and sacked the town.[310] By the time of the king's arrival Bridgnorth had been fired and the bridge in the lower town burned down. It was now evident that Edward was in earnest and likely to prevail, so the Mortimers were doubly unwilling to risk a battle without support from Lancaster, who remained stubbornly at Pontefract. There were other factors in the king's favour: the capture by Sir Gruffydd Llwyd of the castles of Welshpool, Chirk, and Clun, whose wardens had been appointed by the elder Mortimer, and the volatile Robert Ewer's ravaging of the Mortimer lands.[311] Meanwhile the barons had sent emissaries to Lancaster,[312] asking for his counsel and assistance. He is said to have replied that he wished the "statutes or Ordinances" made in Archbishop Winchelsey's time to be observed, and that the barons be given such help as he could, but he declined to accompany them until Badlesmere had been completely removed from among them. This was done and the baron was abandoned to the king's persecution.[313]

With the convergence of the royal army on Shrewsbury the Mortimers, despairing of assistance from Lancaster, their power crippled by the attacks of Gruffydd Llwyd and Robert Ewer, decided to come to an accommodation with the king rather than to dispute his passage of the Severn. A safe conduct in the names of the king's two half-brothers, and of the earls of Pembroke, Richmond, Arundel, and Warenne was issued on 13 January at nearby Newport in Shropshire. This was twice extended for further negotiation. The Wigmore chronicler states that the barons' surrender (on 23 January at Ross) was in expectation of the king's grace (*gratiam inde sperantes*) and there are suggestions in a number of chroniclers that the mediation was fraudulent.[314] Instead of being pardoned the Mortimers were attached and imprisoned in the Tower of London. Others followed their lead and submitted, for instance the elder Hugh d'Audley, Maurice de Berkeley, and Rhys ap Hywel, the first two being imprisoned at Wallingford, while Rhys was sent to Dover.[315] The king took their lands into his hands, including Berkeley Castle, and according to one account provided them with a daily subsistence allowance of two shillings (*unicuique eorum iis. quotidie precepit*). Allegedly the earl of Hereford was on the point of coming to the king, but hearing what had happened to his former allies, he fled to the north, where he acquainted the other Contrariants with what had occurred, so that they likewise despaired of gaining the king's pardon.[316] But Edward did not at once move to the North. He travelled by way of Ludlow to Hereford where he remained between 29 January and 4 February and upbraided the bishop (*acriter increpavit*) with the accusation that he had supported the barons against their natural lord.[317] In revenge he confiscated many of his goods. How unjust this action was it is difficult to say, but Edward well knew of Orleton's sympathy for Mortimer, which would have provided irritation enough. Certainly these charges were not pursued at the time and Bishops Castle was restored as early as 6 February, followed on the eighth by the grant of protection for a year.[318] From Hereford the king travelled quickly to Gloucester, arriving there by 6 February.[319] While there Sir Roger de Elmbridge, sheriff of Herefordshire, was brought before him and condemned to death for riding with the barons and wearing their livery while holding the pleas of the county. He was hanged in the same livery, doubtless as an example to others.[320] It must have been during his advance that Edward received news of the besieging of the royal castle of Tickhill.[321]

It has been argued that up to that point the king had not envisaged a full-scale campaign against the barons, merely skirmishing in the Marches, but that the siege of Tickhill, which began on 10 January, "provoked in Edward a new resolution to crush Lancaster finally" and marked the commencement of "open conflict" between king and earl – a view supposedly endorsed by the perspicacious author of the Lanercost chronicle.[322] In fact this northern chronicler asserts that the Lancastrians only acted upon hearing a report of the Despensers' recall. In his view, then, that was the underlying cause of the civil war and final showdown with the king's overmighty cousin.[323] In the opinion of the Gervase continuator the king acted on the advice of men envious of Hereford, Lancaster and the barons – that is to say, on that of the Despensers rather than of the Holy Spirit![324] One possible interpretation of Edward's actions in 1321–22 is that he demonstrated no long-term strategical objective; instead he took every tactical advantage that came his way. Faced with the Marcher threat at Kingston he capitulated to the demand for the Despensers' exile, but then discerning Badlesmere's isolation he acted with unwonted energy. Seizing upon the weakness of the barons' legal position he then forced the prelates to impugn the judgment against the Despensers. Having thus achieved the bishops' grudging support for a reconsideration of the matter in parliament, and having also disposed of the weakest and least-supported of the barons, he determined to restrain the Marchers, who had originated the attack on the Despensers' lands. When they proved unwilling to do more than impede his progress, and when Lancaster showed himself reluctant to come to their aid, those accompanying king were able to persuade the waverers to accept terms that in the event do not seem to have been observed. Even when the king's forces progressed to the north they acted with great circumspection, advancing "lente pede," as the Lanercost chronicler expressed it.[325] That eventual success lay with the king was equally due to the failure of the barons to combine against him with any sense of ordered purpose. Lancaster, defending the Ordinances to the last and heavily influenced by hatred of the Despensers on the one hand, of Badlesmere on the other, lost support in the North and even turned to the old enemy, the Scots, for aid. He too, had no strategic plan.

The end was clearly in sight and there is no need to recapitulate it in any detail. The fact that the Marchers had so readily collapsed proved a disincentive to others whom Lancaster attempted to muster in his support. From Archbishop Melton and the northern clergy he succeeded in raising two thousand marks, ostensibly for defence against the Scots. In view of the archbishop's administrative experience and his record of consistent loyalty to the king, and after his death to his name, this concession comes as somewhat of a surprise,[326] even though at about that time Andrew Harclay had told the king that there was nothing to impede the Scots' depredations given the expiry of the truce.[327] Attempts to raise recruits from the towns met with prevarication, even at Leicester; clearly townsmen were unwilling to risk their future by lending support to rebellion, unless coerced. Some of the best evidence for Lancashire is provided by the pleas held at Wigan recorded among the Coram Rege Rolls.[328]

The weather was not conducive to campaigning. According to the Historia Roffensis it began to freeze on 10 January and only ceased on 23 March.[329] But despite the difficulties of weather, scarcity, and hazardous roads,[330] the king left Gloucester on 17 February and reached Coventry by the twenty-seventh, where he awaited the arrival of further levies.[331] As he moved northwards the Despensers are said to have joined him at Lichfield.[332] From there he advanced to Burton-on-Trent, which he reached by 10 March. According to the Gervase continuator David Strathbogie, the earl of Atholl, was appointed constable, and the army advanced in three sections.[333] Meanwhile, Mowbray and Hereford had preceded him to the North. They claimed – as did Lancaster himself – that their banners were not raised against the king but rather against the enemies of king and kingdom, the Despensers. Lancaster, on hearing of the king's setting off for the north, moved south to Tutbury Castle, where the fleeing Marchers found him at table.[334] Arrived at the River Trent, an advance party from the royal army was sent to test the defences of the bridge. The resulting encounter lasted some three days before a viable ford was discovered higher up, where a crossing was effected on 10 March, compelling the baronial forces to withdraw with some losses.[335] "Why had the earl done so?" was the question posed by the sympathetic author of the *Vita*. After all, in times past Lancaster had many times resisted the king, but now he had the earl of Hereford with him and the finer part of the English chivalry.[336] One reason – despite the assumption of the *Vita* that the earl's retreat was inexplicable – was probably the size of the royal army;[337] another was the fact that Sir Robert Holland had failed to arrive with expected reinforcements of five hundred men. As soon transpired, he was in process of changing sides, together with a number of armed men – two hundred, thought the Gervase continuator, who termed him "principalis consiliarius comitis Lancastrie." This betrayal, says the *Brut*, prompted the earl to exclaim: "He hath ful evil yielded me my goodness, and the worship that I to him have done, and through my kindness have him advanced, and made him high from low; and he maketh me go from high to low; but yet shall he die in cruel death."[338] And so it proved. Holland, whatever his expectations, was not received into the king's peace, his lands had already been confiscated, and he was escorted to prison at Dover.[339] But he was a great survivor and secured the return of his lands in Edward III's reign, despite the opposition of Lancaster's brother and heir, Henry, only to be murdered in 1328, possibly at Henry's instigation or by Lancastrian sympathizers bent on avenging what they doubtless considered to have been his ingratitude and treachery.[340]

Baker's interpretation of events is that the barons, seeing the writing clearly on the wall, began to waver, some of them suggesting that it would be wiser to enter the king's peace. But this suggestion was hateful to Lancaster, foolishly secure in the belief that as a close relative of the king he had nothing to fear, having armed himself only against the traitor Hugh Despenser. As for Humphrey de Bohun, earl of Hereford, a vigorous and warlike knight, he had no intention of being reconciled to the king and the Despensers, preferring to die in battle than by the withdrawal of his knights to suffer incarceration, exile, or even the penalty of death.[341] Another source claims that he had a contingency plan to take refuge in Hainault with the count, his kinsman.[342]

The Lancastrian forces were pursued to Tutbury, where the castle had been abandoned, leaving Roger d'Amory, who had been mortally wounded in the previous action, to linger a few days longer in Tutbury Priory.[343] Warenne and Atholl were sent to pursue the fugitives to Pontefract, where the town and castle were invested, although Lancaster's constable – like the constable of Kenilworth – would not surrender until he heard of the defeat at Boroughbridge.[344] The Lancastrians during their brief stay at Pontefract were in a quandary as to their best course of action. They consulted together in the Dominican convent. The general opinion was that they should go to Lancaster's fortress of Dunstanburgh on the Northumbrian coast, but the earl argued that were they to do so they would be assumed to be associating themselves with the nearby Scots and be taken for traitors. He declared that he would go no further than Pontefract. But Sir Roger Clifford angrily drew his sword and declared that either Lancaster went or he would slay him then and there. Thereupon the earl consented to go wheresoever they chose to lead.[345] If this is an accurate reflection of the situation it points to the great earl's abject weakness at a time of supreme crisis in his affairs. Admittedly he had been severely affected by Holland's treachery, and his force had been reduced to such a degree that there was no hope of meeting the royal army in open battle.

Meanwhile, Sir Andrew Harclay had been ordered to gather a force from the counties of Cumberland and Westmorland, a process that according to the *Brut* had determined the barons to go south to prevent the king's forces crossing the Trent. While at Ripon, Harclay learned of Lancaster's approach and by night went to nearby Boroughbridge to hold the bridge over the River Ure.[346] At a preliminary parley Lancaster tried to win him over to his side by bemoaning how the king was being led by the false counsel of the Despensers, Arundel, and that "false pilede clerk" Robert Baldock. He offered him "the best part of five earldoms" and made the equally unlikely promise that he would always abide by his counsel. Harclay's response was unequivocal, nothing would tempt him to act without the king's authority for fear of being regarded evermore as a traitor. To this response the earl allegedly prophesied "that or this year be gone, that thou shall be taken and held for a traitor, and more than ye hold us now; and in worse death ye shall die, than ever did knight of England." The *Brut* makes no bones about its prejudices. Harclay was a false traitor, a forsworn man, for it was through the earl that he had taken the arms of chivalry; through him that he had been made a knight.[347] It may be added that on 11 March the rebels had already been denounced as traitors by the king and accompanying earls of Kent, Richmond, Pembroke, and Atholl.[348]

The ensuing battle was joined on 16 March for possession of the wooden bridge over the Ure, too narrow a structure to take a mounted knight equipped for battle. As a result, the dismounted Hereford, advancing boldly with Clifford "more leonum," was ungallantly pierced to death on his unprotected fundament by a Welsh pikeman hidden beneath the planking. Lancaster tried to ford the river, but Harclay protected each crossing with men-at-arms. Roger de Clifford, badly wounded, sought refuge in the town.[349] The Lanercost chronicle, knowledgeable about campaigning in the North, explains the encounter in more technical fashion. Harclay, though with a smallish force, was using Scottish tactics. He dismounted his men to defend the north side of the bridge with lances. Others, similarly equipped with lances, were arranged in a close-packed Scottish-type schiltron (*in scheltrum secundum modum Scotorum*). The archers were arranged so as to send a dense mass of arrows into the crowded knights on whom Lancaster relied. Thus the earl was forced to withdraw from his attempt to cross the river and dared not approach again. Such tactics were murderously successful.[350]

Eventually, according to among others the Lanercost chronicler and the author of the *Vita*, a truce until the following day was arranged with Harclay at Lancaster's request, the understanding being that on the morrow the earl would resume the fight or surrender. Meanwhile, each returned to his lodging, but Harclay, accustomed to the guerrilla tactics of the Scots, was careful to maintain his guard on the bridge and river crossings. That same night the sheriff of York arrived with a substantial force and with his aid Harclay entered the town early in the morning and captured the earl and most of the other knights. The Lanercost chronicler observes that following the death of Hereford his knights all slipped away, together with others attached to Lancaster and the wounded Clifford. The only option for the earl, Clifford, Mowbray, and the remainder was to surrender to Harclay. The *Vita* claims that some hundred knights were captured, another chronicler gives, more precisely, seventeen barons and eighty knights and armigers.[351] The earl was initially taken to York, but on the king's arrival at Pontefract he ordered him to be brought there, where he was incarcerated in a recently built tower, intended by the earl, rumour had it, to cage the king himself. According to the strongly pro-Lancaster *Anonimalle Chronicle* the younger Despenser took the opportunity of reviling the earl to his face.[352] The next day

he was led into the hall "bareheaded as a thief in a fair hall within his own castle that he had made therein many a fair feast both to rich and eke to poor."[353]
There seven comital judges were arrayed: Kent, Warenne, Richmond, Pembroke, Arundel, Atholl, and Angus – the most reliable list, only two of whom,
Warenne and Arundel, could justifiably be labelled Lancaster's enemies. Sir
Robert Malberthorpe, a justice of King's Bench, gave the judgment in the king's
name. "Thomas," he said, "our lord king put upon you that ye have in his land
ridden with banner displayed against his peace as a traitor."[354] To which the
"gentle Thomas" replied, "Nay lords, forsooth and by St Thomas I was never
traitor." The court condemned him to be drawn, hanged, and finally beheaded,
but on account of his royal blood this was commuted to beheading – the hanging was remitted, according to a version of the *Brut*, "for the love of Queen
Isabelle." He was not permitted to speak in his defence. He is said to have
exclaimed ironically: "This is indeed a powerful court, greater in authority,
where no response is heard nor any mitigation admitted."[355]

What had been adopted was a summary process of martial law, although it has
been claimed that the king, at the younger Despenser's specific urging – worried
by his own possible fate in case of defeat – had not in fact unfurled his banners,
so that technically no state of war had existed.[356] It was the earl's rank that produced a widespread feeling of revulsion: the Lanercost chronicler thought that
but for his abuse of Gaveston he would have been either imprisoned or exiled.[357]
On the other hand, the largely sympathetic *Vita* declared that Lancaster had disgraced the royal stock (*regalem prosapiam tuam quam infamas*), and that traitors
justly suffer the ultimate penalty (*proditores tamen iuste maxima poena plectun-
tur*).[358] After the sentence Lancaster was placed on a mule and taken to the place
of execution, a hill outside the town where on 22 March, the morrow of the feast
of St Benedict, he was beheaded like a common felon.[359] The moral could easily be drawn that Lancaster had cut off Piers Gaveston's head, with even less semblance of judicial propriety, and now he had lost his own.[360] Lancaster had been
hoisted with his own petard: the king had gained his revenge at last. The *Vita* was
not slow to cite the biblical precedents of Abner and Judah.[361] Put to death at the
same time as Lancaster, and likewise "per recordum regis," were William
Tuchet, Henry de Bradbourne – Lancaster's retainers, together with Warin de
Lisle (Insula), William FitzWilliam, William Cheyne, and Thomas Mauduit.[362]

It is not easy for us to comprehend the intensity with which Lancaster's death
was lamented – though not apparently in York;[363] a man so noble, so wealthy,
so powerful.[364] As Stubbs aptly summed up: "The cause was better than the man
or the principles on which he maintained it."[365] Lancaster felt that he was tread-
ing in the steps of Simon de Montfort, his predecessor as earl of Leicester, and
those of Robert Winchelsey, the upholder of the Ordinances. But what sort of a
reformer was he? And what sort of an influence would he have exercised had he
been able to establish his extensive claims as steward? The concept of permanently controlling even an unfortunate king – such as Edward undoubtedly was

– by a resident council of barons and prelates was scarcely a viable one for other than the shortest of terms. He had inherited a concept of "reform" but no capacity to effect it. He had himself been given the opportunity to act as leader of the council, only to prove inadequate and no better an administrator than the king. He complained of Edward's unjust actions, but he himself was capable of equal injustices, personal aggrandizement, and maladministration. On a number of occasions he sacrificed his principles to his own advancement. His part in Gaveston's summary execution, in the Middleton affair, the despoiling of Warenne, and with respect to the Despensers' exile highlight his resort to violence and illegality when thwarted. He was unable to retain the loyalty of his own men, notably Adam Banaster and Robert Holland, and permitted them and others to indulge in the kind of violence that he would have deplored in the king or his ministers. His personal hates were permitted to cloud his judgment, as is so noticeable in the cases of Gaveston and Badlesmere. He claimed to abhor traitors, but he was one himself, raising rebellion against the king, even cooperating with the Scots,[366] and appearing armed at parliament. His record as a defender of the northern parts is abysmal. Doubtless he was not a hypocrite by intention, but he was one nonetheless. Worse still, for one who held five earldoms, he was no soldier, neither a strategist nor a tactician. He failed to put in an appearance at Bannockburn, and when the baronial revolt of 1321–22 broke out he could not determine at what point, if any, he wished to join it effectively, preferring to give advice and make promises from a safe distance. When the Marchers had been defeated for lack of support, he showed an equal lack of resolution in preventing the mobilization of royal forces. His campaign was little more than a feeble response to a clearly perceived threat. At Boroughbridge itself, his performance can only be compared adversely to the professionalism of Harclay. He too could surely have made himself as aware of the distinctive tactics employed by the Scots. In normal circumstances with a reasonably competent king his death would shortly have been regarded as a benefit, but circumstances were not normal and the king was incompetent and vicious to boot.

6

The Tyrannous Years: Baldock, Stapeldon and the Despensers, 1322–1326

And when Kyng Edward of England had brought the flower of chivalry unto this death, through counsel of Sir Hugh the Spenser the father, and Sir Hugh his son, he became as wood [wild?] as a lion and whatsoever the Spensers would have done, it was done. And so well the king loved them that they might do with him all that they would. Wherefore the king gave unto Hugh the Spenser the father the earldom of Winchester, and to Sir Andrew of Harclay, the earldom of Carlisle, in prejudice and harming of his crown. And King Edward though, through counsel of the Spensers disinherited all them that had been against him in any quarrel with Thomas of Lancaster, and many others were disinherited also, for reason that the Spensers coveted forto have their lands, and so they had all they would desire, with wrong, and against all reason.[1]

AFTER BOROUGHBRIDGE: RETRIBUTION

Magna Carta had provided a scheme whereby for the reform of the realm and the better settling of the quarrel between king and barons the latter were to choose twenty-five of their number, of whom four could act to preserve peace and the liberties granted by the king. Any failure on the part of the king in such matters was to be brought to the notice of the four barons, and if they could not gain redress the grievances were to be referred to the whole twenty-five. They could then distress the king in every way, such as by seizing castles, lands, and possessions.[2] Thus Lancaster's scheme for Ordinances and a permanent council had a well-established precedent. Also permissible was armed opposition to a king who had failed to act in accordance with Magna Carta and the laws of the realm. In a celebrated clause the charter had even provided that no free man should be taken, imprisoned, disseisined, outlawed, or exiled, or in any manner destroyed, except by lawful judgment of his peers or by the law of the land.[3] This concept had been violated by the barons themselves in the cases of Gaveston and the Despensers, to mention only two, and was to be violated by the king and his representatives in the years following Boroughbridge. Stubbs, who was seeking to chart the unfolding of the constitution, and who felt that Edward was no tyrant, was not impressed with Lancaster's record: "During his tenure of power few parliaments were called, little or no legislation, except the Ordinances, had been effected; no great national act had been undertaken; he had not even attempted to arrest the decline of England in military strength and reputation, or to recover the ground lost by the incompetency of the king."[4] There is more than a degree of justice in this assessment.

Now that the turmoil of the earlier years of the reign had subsided, it became possible to usher in a period in which there was no armed threat to royal authority. It was, though, a period of lawlessness. Whether such lawlessness was appreciably greater than formerly it would be difficult to determine. The unrest was stimulated by the desire of many to act against those now being pursued for their cooperation with the rebellious barons. Many of the Contrariants, as they were described, men who had lost land and consequently income, were reduced to brigandage. Nor was it to be expected that Edward could so mend his ways as to provide firm government, government that would be seen to be fair. Instead he allowed the Despensers, particularly the younger Hugh, and Robert Baldock, with Stapeldon a willing henchman, to exercise a control that was to bring a full treasury but an inevitable backlash.

But first, catharsis. It is scarcely remarkable that the author of the *Vita* should exclaim at so monstrous a reversal of fortune: those once dressed in fine raiment were reduced to rags, bound in chains, and imprisoned. It was, he thought, by God's assistance that so small a band had overcome so many knights – a force allegedly seven times as numerous. There was a revengeful aftermath. The punishment of hanging, drawing and quartering has been considered "novel" for England, a barbarous practice confined to the Scottish and Welsh rebellions, and to which the young Prince Edward had been introduced by his father.[5] Gilbert de Middleton is said to have provided the first instance during Edward II's reign of an English nobleman being put to death in such manner. His offence was inordinately outrageous in that it involved cardinals under royal protection.[6] The *Vita* states that the castles of Badlesmere, and of the earl of Hereford, Roger d'Amory, and Audley were readily surrendered because the vengeance exacted at Leeds had terrified everyone (*vehementer terruit omnes*). But the chronicler does not give the impression that he felt such punishment to be exceptional, merely condign. Declaring that Leeds Castle contained robbers, homicides, and traitors, he concludes that the king wished to make an example to deter others. No one could build a castle without a licence, so it was equally wrong to defend castles against the king.[7] Yet a modern writer has argued that the brutality evidenced at this time not merely lacked precedent but also coincided with the Despensers' ascendancy.[8] It is equally likely that the king himself, although sporadically given to clemency, approved of these extreme measures against men who, either themselves or through their associates, had disturbed his reign since its inception and who had even raised the spectre of enforced abdication.

However that may be, further executions followed at York, where John Mowbray – whom, as we have seen, the king had bound to himself by indenture – and the wounded Roger Clifford were among the victims. All of them are said to have been first drawn and then hung in chains.[9] At Bristol, Sir Henry Wilington and Sir Henry Montfort were drawn and hung; at Gloucester, Sir John Giffard of Brimpsfield, the last of his line,[10] and the former sheriff of Hereford, Sir Roger Elmbridge; at London, Sir Henry Tyeys or Tyies; at Winchelsea, Sir Thomas Colpeper; at Windsor,[11] Sir Francis Aldham; at Canterbury,[12] Sir Bartholomew Badlesmere[12] and Sir Bartholomew Ashburnham; and at Cardiff, Sir William Fleming.[13] To these the French chronicle adds the name of Stephen Baret, drawn and hung at "Collyere" (Gower). Five persons fled abroad: John Botetourt, John de Kingston, Nicholas Percy, John Maltravers the younger, and William Trussell.[14] By such means the king could be certain that the fate of these men, consequent upon their rebellion, was firmly impressed on the areas from which they originated. According to Murimuth, among others, it was only in the Lent Parliament of 1324 that the prelates successfully petitioned at Westminster for the bodies of the nobles still hanging on the gallows to be given ecclesiastical burial.[16]

In addition to those who were killed in battle or subsequently put to death, many nobles were incarcerated indefinitely. The *Vita* suggests that after Boroughbridge there were a hundred captives, sixty-two of whom are said by the Lanercost chronicler to have been kept in prison.[17] Baker actually gives the names of ten barons who were imprisoned and adds to them sixty-two unnamed knights.[18] Another chronicler lists eighty-three.[19] The Mortimers, uncle and nephew, were consigned to the Tower. A panel of five judges on 2 August 1322 condemned them to death by drawing and hanging, but at the king's order the sentence was for the time being commuted to life imprisonment.[20] The uncle died in captivity four years later.[21] The story in the *Brut* is that hearing that sentence of death was in fact to be carried out, Roger Mortimer of Wigmore managed to escape by drugging his guards, apparently on the night of 31 July–1 August 1323 – appropriately the feast of St Peter ad Vincula – and made his way to the Continent.[22] The incident is discussed more fully below. Numerous others were kept prisoner in the Tower and are enumerated in February 1323.[23] Maurice de Berkeley and Hugh Audley senior were under a somewhat slack restraint in the royal castle of Wallingford, from which Berkeley, as we shall see, unsuccessfully attempted to escape in January 1323.[24] Not content with acting against the nobles themselves, the authorities also imprisoned their wives and children and kept them on short commons.[25]

THE PARLIAMENT AT YORK, MAY 1322

On 14 March, two days before the battle of Boroughbridge, a parliament had been summoned to York for 2 May, apparently in anticipation of the royal victory. Surprisingly, the chroniclers have little to say about it. The *Vita* at this point has a lacuna of six leaves, otherwise it might have provided an exception. Of the other chronicles, the Historia Roffensis gives the longest account, doubtless because Bishop Hethe was in attendance and complaining, as usual, about the expense – thirty-three pounds over five weeks.[26] Those summoned comprised prelates, lay magnates, knights, and burgesses, as well as barons of the Cinque Ports, and for the first time, twenty-four representatives from South Wales and an equal number from North Wales. This "full representation" sat until 19 May when the Commons were dismissed, the lords continuing until 7 July.[27] An agenda referred by the king to his council was printed by Baldwin and then Davies, who thought that it preceded the May parliament, and again by W.M. Ormrod who argues for a date between the May and November parliaments.[28] The first two items are the repeal of the Ordinances and the putting of the "bons pointz" into a statute. It was not until 19 May that the Ordinances were repealed in the Statute of York, the sheriffs throughout the realm being informed on that day by letters patent, as also were the justices. Both were instructed to publish them.[29] The statute itself has been the subject of much discussion and no little altercation, mainly because of those who found in it deep constitutional significance and who considered it to be instrumental in increasing the importance of the Commons in parliament.[30]

The statute can conveniently be considered as five separate paragraphs or clauses.[31] The first recites the fact that power had been granted to certain great men – prelates, earls, and barons – so that they could elect individuals to ordain and establish the estate of both the king's household and that of his realm; such Ordinances to be to the honour of God, the honour and profit of Holy Church, to that of the king, as well as to the profit of the people according to law and reason (*solonc droit et reson*) and the oath taken by the king at his coronation. The archbishop of Canterbury, the bishops, earls, and barons thus elected (*eslutz*) had drawn up these Ordinances, the text of which began "Sachez qe come le xvime jour de Marz" in the third year of the reign (1310)[32] and ending with the date 5 October 1311 at London. The second clause states that the parliament at York – including among the prelates, earls, and barons, the surviving Ordainers, and also the Commons (*le commun du roialme*) assembled by royal command – rehearsed and examined the Ordinances. The examination found that the fundamental power (*poair real*) of the king had been restrained in many ways that it ought not to have been (*countre devoir*), to the blemishment of his lordship and against the estate of the Crown (*seigneurie reale et countre lestat de la coronne*). Also because of Ordinances and purveyances made by subjects concerning the power (*le poair real*) of the king's ancestors, disputes and war had arisen in the realm, putting the land in jeopardy.

In consequence, the third clause states, it is agreed at the parliament by the king and by the said prelates, earls, and barons and the whole community of the realm (*et tote la commune du roialme*) there assembled that all the things ordained and contained in the Ordinances should have no effect in perpetuity (*a touz jours*) but that the statutes and arrangements (*establissements*) duly made by the king and his ancestors prior to the Ordinances were to remain in force. In future, the fourth clause continues, any ordinances or purveyances made by the king's subjects or those of his heirs, by whatsoever authority or commission (*par quele poair ou commission*), against the estate of the king or his heirs or that of the Crown, are to be null and void. The concluding clause declares that matters to be established for the estate of the king and his heirs, and for the estate of the realm and of the people, are to be treated, accorded, and established in parliament by the king, and with the assent of the prelates, earls, and barons and the community of the realm, as has been accustomed (*auxint come ad este acustume cea enarere*).

Analysis suggests that, although the terminology of the statute may present difficulties to modern commentators, it is neither as ambiguous nor as ill drafted a document as has sometimes been suggested. The king's council knew what it was doing. The Ordainers, it cogently states, were given authority, but went beyond it. The York Parliament agreed that such Ordinances had in the past infringed royal power and brought internal discord. They were therefore void. Further, any future ordinances of that kind fabricated by subjects – whatever the nature of their commission – were likewise to be null. In future matters that affected the estates of the king, and of his realm and people, were to be dealt with by prelates, earls, barons, and the commonalty of the realm – as in the past. Stubbs viewed this last element as having major constitutional implications. Just as Magna Carta had shown how the "commune consilium regni" could be arrived at, and Edward I had added the principle that what affected all should be approved by all, so "Edward II, uttering words of which he could faintly realize the importance, enunciates a still more elaborate formula of constitutional law." But the inference that this final clause gave the Commons a particular status for the future has not been sustained.[33]

The parliament also dealt with the "bons pointz" of the Ordinances.[34] This has been taken to be a sign of the king's "desire for reform," but it aroused little comment from the chroniclers.[35] For the most part the statute that emerged was a reaffirmation of earlier legislation with an eye to the more effective administration of measures taken in the time of the king's father, Edward I. The statute opened, as did Magna Carta, with a confirmation of the liberties of the Church. The king's peace was to be firmly maintained, as was the measure regulating prises and the punishment to be meted out to offenders.[36] Sheriffs and hundredmen were to be appointed in accordance with the statute made at the Lincoln Parliament of 1316 – by the chancellor if available, and by the treasurer, barons of the exchequer, and justices. Edward I's concession with respect to the forests and indictments arising from trespasses of vert and venison was to be fully upheld. There were regulations for the estate of the steward and marshals and with respect to their conduct of pleas. They were to receive advocates for both defendants and plaintiffs. Steward or marshals acting contrary to the statute were to be punished. Complainants against them could secure a writ of chancery and plead before the king. There follows a reiteration of ordinances 33, 35, and 36, concerning merchants, outlawries, and appeals. In short, there was every appearance that the king – or whoever was behind what can only be regarded as a surprisingly conciliatory measure – was intent on administrative reform with an eye to removing both confusion and abuses. The impetus for this undoubtedly had been the pressure exerted by the Ordainers and their attempts at coercion.

What caught the attention of most of the chroniclers was not the repudiation of the Ordinances but other matters: the revocation in parliament of the process against the Despensers and the restitution of all their possessions; the creation of the elder Despenser as earl of Winchester, of the victorious Andrew Harclay as earl of Carlisle, and the preparations made for a long-overdue Scottish expedition. The king is said to have expounded to the prelates, earls, and barons the injuries suffered at the hands of the Scots – reportedly favoured by domestic rebels – and to have expressed his desire to do battle with them. A tenth was granted for the purpose by the lords, a sixth was to come from ancient demesne and the same proportion from burgesses of towns. The lower clergy made a grant of five pence in the mark. It was all too late. Already the Scots, taking advantage of the dislocation caused by Lancaster and the barons, had engaged in a number of raids in the North. When they returned to Scotland on 24 July they had been in England for three weeks and three days. The king was at Newcastle by the beginning of August but after entering Scotland with a substantial army he was once again forced to retreat, his forces ravaged by hunger and dysentery. Having devastated the Northwest, Cumberland, and Westmorland, the Scots now turned their attention to Yorkshire. Their commandolike attack at Byland, where the king narrowly avoided capture, compelled him to withdraw to York. Yet again his military operations had ended in disaster.[37]

THE AFTERMATH OF CIVIL WAR

For the squire exerts himself, striving in virtually every sphere to surpass the knight, as does the knight the baron, the baron the earl, the earl the king. Moreover, should resources be lacking due to the inadequacy of inherited estates, they turn to plunder, despoiling their neighbour, pillaging those subject to them, and for such infamous business they employ God's own ministers. Hence it is that the magnates of the realm fall in battle or die without male heir, while the females divide the inheritance so that the paternal name disappears for ever.[38]

Thus does the most philosophical of the chroniclers of the reign sum up the society of his day: a society in which inferiors are disregarded or worse, equals despised, and there is perennial strife to improve one's own position. The analysis is supported by modern research. "The use of force had become commonplace at all levels of society during Edward's reign, and the minor gentry who took part in demonstrations of force on behalf of their lords in political or social disputes, did not hesitate to employ force in a like manner for their own benefit."[39] The additional hazards accruing to baronial families from both war and civil rebellion is obvious enough, but it has been argued that the lesser gentry were particularly vulnerable. At the best of times their economic position was tenuous During the period 1315–17 they were badly hit by the famine and there were renewed shortages in 1322, aggravated in some parts by the passage of the armies.[40] They could readily fall prey to the acquisitiveness of more powerful lords, yet they needed patronage and a degree of ambition – often a recipe for disorder – if they were to survive.[41]

There was much coercion at the time of the 1321–22 revolt, both on the part of the Contrariants and of the king. To take one example of baronial intimidation as recounted by the victim, Sir Roger de Chandos. Summoned to answer before a commission of justices for Herefordshire headed by Hervy de Staunton, he claimed that Roger Mortimer, the younger Hugh d'Audley, John Giffard, Henry Tyeys, and others had threatened to take his life and to burn his manors. About Easter (19 April) 1321 together with John Maltravers they came by night to his castle at Snodhill, Herefordshire, entered it by force of arms and stayed the night. Mortimer of Wigmore arrived in the morning and with the others warned him to prepare horses and arms to attend the parliament in London. Roger replied that he was the king's liegeman, but under threat of death and the burning of his castle and manors he unwillingly (so he claimed) accompanied the Contrariants to Kingston and London as if he were a prisoner (*quasi attachiatum*). As soon as he could he made his escape and returned to Hereford where he joined with the citizens and other loyal men in guarding the city and castle. The jurors of the hundred swore on oath that at the outset of the insurrection Mortimer wished Roger to remain with him (*ad commorandum secum*), offering a large fee for life, but Roger refused. They then attested the truth of his statement, with some minor variations. At which point the case was adjourned to a later date. The Chandos case epitomizes the difficulties of resisting coercion as well as the general confusion of loyalties. His good faith established, he was pricked sheriff in January 1322 as successor to the rebellious Elmbridge.[42]

As for the king, he endeavoured to raise men in accordance with the statute of Winchester (1285) but with the obligation to serve without pay.[43] There was an expected reluctance to respond, particularly while the issue remained in doubt, and writs were issued for the disobedient to be apprehended and fined forty shillings.[44] The county of Hereford was assessed at five hundred men, for ten of whom the town of Ledbury was responsible. These men, whose rations were the responsibility of the local community, were to serve for fifteen days against the rebels and Scots.[45] Clerics also were requested to provide additional monetary support. Bishop Hethe of Rochester sent twenty pounds by his steward but either it was too little, conjectured the Rochester chronicler, or the king wished to excuse a poor bishop, because the donation was returned.[46] Another inevitable feature of the campaign was the levying of purveyance. The king did not necessarily have the capacity to store grain on a regular basis, so it had to be collected in time of need. The sheriff of Gloucestershire stocked Bristol Castle with grain and beans but claimed that in July 1321 – when the Marchers were in process of gathering their forces for their expedition to London – the mayor and royal bailiffs had carried off the grain. The truth of the matter does not seem to have been established, but Bristol would barely have recovered from the siege it had endured in 1316 at the time of the previous period of scarcity.[47]

A recent historian of the post-Boroughbridge period has emphasized that the royal victory "meant a social dislocation and territorial revolution which has hitherto passed without much comment."[48] The Contrariants suffered widespread plundering and confiscation of their property, a redistribution that has yet to be examined county by county – as has been done for Herefordshire and Gloucestershire.[49] There was also the devastation inflicted by the deprived Contrariants on the loyalists. Other unrelated disturbance may be attributed to perennial lawlessness, likely to be more intense after a time of civil war or political uncertainty, a point borne out in 1326–27. Thus there was an attack by the mayor and townsmen on the University of Cambridge, in which much damage was done to the Inns or Halls and to books and other goods belonging to masters and students.[50] Then there were the incursions against the Hanseatic merchants.[51]

On 8 July 1322 the king appointed a commission consisting of the chancellor, the chief justices of King's Bench and Common Pleas, the keeper of the rolls and a king's sergeant. Their remit was to receive from those imprisoned security on oath and by bond of loyal behaviour, as well as by mainpernors or sureties under penalty. Thereafter they were to come to the king to receive their lands. Less significant prisoners were to be treated similarly, and by way of record enrolment was to be made in chancery for their loyal behaviour and payment of ransom. They were likewise to provide mainpernors under penalty and only when they had delivered such securities were their lands to be released. Persons with no resources were to be delivered "of the king's alms." The undertaking by the rebels provided that if they failed in any point with respect to their oath of loyalty they could be imprisoned at the king's will, their lands seized and their chattels forfeited. Remarkably, rebels sometimes secured mainpernors from their loyalist opponents. For instance, Sir Gruffydd Llwyd, leader of the attack on Mortimer's lands, was one of the mainpernors of John Walwayn, who was closely attached to Hereford, a beneficiary of his will and one of his executors.[52]

Some of the fines imposed were extremely burdensome – as much as two thousand marks in the case of Nicholas Stapleton, a Yorkshire knight and a member of Lancaster's retinue captured at Boroughbridge, a thousand marks in that of Adam de Swillington, who had been indentured to Lancaster in 1317.[53] Gilbert Talbot, who with his sons Richard and Gilbert rode with Mortimer's forces in 1321, lost some of his lands to the younger Despenser, and suffered a heavy fine, but how much of it he paid is uncertain. Despite his pardon he was still being harassed by the royal justices in 1324. The fine was eventually remitted in 1327 at the petition of the council, at which time he became king's chamberlain.[54] As in all civil wars, families were divided in their loyalties. Evidence is lacking for Henry of Lancaster's attitude to his brother's policy at this time, although he was later to espouse "Lancastrian tenets." What is clear is that the brothers had little to do with each other, possibly because of Thomas's difficult temperament.[55] Henry's lands were temporarily confiscated nonetheless, as were those of Richard d'Amory, who was imprisoned at Oxford, although he had remained loyal to the king. In Amory's case there was swift rehabilitation and in July 1322 he became steward of the royal household, an office he held until 5 May 1325.[56]

There were various possibilities for mitigating the penalties imposed on Contrariants. Allowing fines to be paid by instalment had the effect of making them more bearable while at the same time, from the king's point of view, they provided an assurance of continued good behaviour. Another opportunity for mitigation would be to offer to serve against the Scots. Gilbert atte Nasshe (or Ash), one of those allegedly sent by Bishop Orleton to join Mortimer but in fact one of the baron's retainers, was allowed to find mainpernors for his service in Scotland, but in the event he was appointed to oversee the lands of his fellow rebel Gilbert Talbot.[57] Again, the intercession of a loyalist lord might enable a rebel to obtain a pardon, as was the case with John Dalton, Lancaster's trusted but overzealous, not to say oppressive, bailiff of Pickering, who was also among those who had taken the precaution of receiving livery (*robas*) from Eleanor, widow of Henry Percy.[58] Sometimes, as in Bogo de Knoville's case,[59] a rebel was admitted to royal service. Very late in the day – about a month after Isabella's landing with an invasion force – half of Knoville's fine was remitted by a government that had already abandoned London.[60] It has been calculated that 158 of the larger fines amounted to fifteen thousand pounds. In addition there was a substantial income from the lands and property of the Contrariants, even allowing for what had already been plundered.[61]

Doubtless investigation into local situations will reveal many to parallel Robert de Prestbury, a man with a violent past. Among those pardoned for the death of Gaveston, in 1318 he participated in the notorious raid on the absent Pembroke's manor of Painswick.[62] Pardoned in 1321 for participation in the anti-Despenser brigandage, he soon lost his lands for involvement in the Marcher revolt. With the political *bouleversement* of 1326 he attached himself to Roger Mortimer and regained possession of his estates.[63] He had held some three hundred acres of arable in the Gloucestershire village of that name, and with the connivance of John Giffard of Boyton absorbed lands of Henry de Hatherley, at the time a prisoner of the Scots, by means of a series of "final concords" incorporating fictitious transfers of property.[64] This is only one example of what was a widespread state of disorder both at this time and somewhat later – others that have been closely examined are the Derbyshire Coterels between the late 1320s and the mid–1330s and the Leicestershire Folvilles during roughly the same period.[65] Less well known, but equally lawless, were the Irbys of the Forest of Dean in Gloucestershire.

THE IRBY CLAN AND THE PERSECUTION
OF "RECALCITRANT" BISHOPS

The Irbys or Irebys and their companions in crime were notorious in the Marcher area. In 1324 Richard Irby was accused of having ridden to London with Hereford, Amory, and Mortimer three years earlier, but he denied the charge and put himself on the country. Thereupon the jurors swore that he was an adherent of Roger d'Amory and had ridden with him from the Forest of Dean – Richard came from Ruardean[66] – to London. Thus convicted, Irby was imprisoned. Quite how he secured his release is not known, but by October 1321 he had ingratiated himself with the king's supporters and on 23 January 1322 was one of those commissioned to take the castle of St Briavel's, to arrest any Contrariants he found there, and to detain their goods for the king's use.[67] The sheriff of Gloucester subsequently returned that he had also retained goods forfeited to the king and taken oxen under the pretence that he was a royal bailiff. Moreover, he had exceeded his commission by impounding the goods of men who were not rebels. He was fined the surprisingly small sum of five marks for these offences and ordered to provide mainpernors, one of whom was his brother William.[68] In February 1325 a writ ordered the treasurer and barons of the exchequer not to trouble Richard on account of those goods he had improperly appropriated during the period between 17 October 1321 and 5 April 1322, when he was acting for the king.[69]

Meanwhile, Richard Irby had taken advantage of the chaotic situation in the West. He seems to have developed a habit of pillaging the property of the bishop of Hereford at Ross and also that of the rector there. The origin of the attacks on the bishop's property was the claim by the brothers Irby, of whom John seems to have been the eldest, and of their mother, to pannage of pigs in the episcopal woods at Ross. In 1306 John swore to abandon the suit against Bishop Swinfield on that account, in return for which his captured pigs were released, subject to payment for the pannage. Peace was short-lived, John and his brothers Richard and Walter were excommunicated for cutting down the bishop's trees near Hope Mansel and taking away the timber. In March 1307 they appeared before Swinfield in the chapel of his manor of Ross and sought absolution. This was granted subject to the penance of making an Easter pilgrimage to Hereford Cathedral to leave oblations at the images of Mary and the blessed Ethelbert, whose liberties they had infringed. Were they to reoffend they were under obligation to pay a hundred shillings towards the cathedral fabric: the oath taken by John Irby about the pannage was to remain in force.[70]

In August 1316 Richard Irby led a seven-man raid on the rectory lands at Ross, stealing horses, grain, other property allegedly worth a hundred pounds, and assaulting the servants of the rector, James de Henley, who brought an action in the king's court. Henley appears to have been a member of the bishop's *familia*: his despoilers must have incurred *ipso facto* excommunication, although of this nothing is said at the time.[71] The process was repeated on 26

January 1322, four days after the Mortimers' surrender at Shrewsbury,[72] but this time Richard had a band of twenty-five. Doubtless it was felt that following the Marcher revolt the moment was opportune. Parson Henley in the court of Common Pleas once again claimed that goods worth in excess of one hundred pounds had been carried off.[73] Still unsated, the Irbys determined to embarrass the bishop of Hereford, Adam Orleton, while he was conveniently absent at the York Parliament of April 1322. Orleton was the subject of Edward's suspicion because of his inevitable association with his overmighty parishioner, Roger Mortimer. Possibly the malefactors hoped that this fact might slow down action against them. At any rate, twenty-seven men, including Richard Irby, his brother Thomas, and Hugh Hatheway, member of a family previously involved in the Irbys' raids, were summoned to York by a writ of 3 June to answer the plea that by force of arms they had seized goods and chattels of the bishop at Ross and carried them off. A further writ naming the same three, as well as others, required them to answer for cutting down the bishop's trees there.[74] Yet another writ against Richard Irby and his associates required them to answer for the abduction from Orleton's manor of Upton of two horses, twelve oxen, and two hundred and forty sheep, to the tune of forty pounds. On his return to his manor of Sugwas the bishop on 4 June ordered the Hereford chapter and the officers of the diocese to declare the malefactors and their abettors excommunicate – the regular concomitant of violation of ecclesiastical property.[75]

In the credulous atmosphere of the aftermath of rebellion this sentence provided the opportunity for hostile petitioners to request that Robert de Aston, William Irby the prior of St Guthlac's Hereford, and Richard de Scholle – known to be no friends of the bishop – be appointed to make enquiry about clerics in the dioceses of Hereford and Worcester who were enemies or Contrariants to the king or had abetted such enemies, and to ascertain the names of those responsible for the "horrible" excommunication of men who, when the king was in the Marches of Wales, had rightly removed property from Orleton's woods and parks, he being the king's avowed enemy.[76] The petitioners indicted Walter de Nasse or Nash, constable of the Forest of Dean (Irby territory, of course) as waster of the king's substance and counsellor of Roger d'Amory and Thomas de Berkeley. Further, the petitioners alleged, John de Lynton, Howel le Waleys and the bishop's marshal, Tristram, had escaped from Boroughbridge and were harassing the royal forces in the locality. In his response, dated from York,[77] probably on 23 June 1322 – the day is not legible – the king or those acting for him, whether deliberately or because of a genuine confusion, kaleidoscoped two incidents, both of which could well have merited excommunication *ipso facto*. The first was on 27 January 1322, towards the close of the Marcher revolt and just prior to the king's rebuke to Orleton at Hereford. The king and his half-brother Edmund, earl of Kent, went hunting in the bishop's parks, no doubt in vengeful mood. The other occasion was the Irby raid just described. In the first instance, as Orleton pointed out when towards the end of November he eventually appeared before the king and his council at York, he had not fulminated any excommunication and was prepared to put himself on the country – the testimony of a local jury – to prove it. In the second case, as he had earlier explained in response to a mandate alleging that he had acted in contempt of the king, his sentence had nothing to do with his *parks* but concerned his *manors* of Ross and Upton in the Forest of Dean. It was a general excommunication, no offenders being named, certainly not anyone acting on royal authority. The bishop repudiated the implication that such excommunication was intended to comprise the earlier incident as well.[78] There is every indication that the prosecution was a malicious one and that the consequent smokescreen would enable the malefactors to get away with their depredations. In June of 1323 Orleton declared William Irby excommunicate, describing him as a wandering monk (*monachus girovagus*) – a type denounced by St Benedict.[79] At Easter (27 March) the prior, in violation of a canon of the Council of Vienne (1311–12) – an assembly attended by Orleton – had given the Eucharist to a lady who was herself excommunicate. Orleton requested his neighbour at Worcester, Bishop Cobham, to pronounce Irby excommunicate – and not for the last time.[80] Clearly some did not take this penalty too seriously.

The bishop's situation was further compromised in 1323 by the escape of Roger Mortimer of Wigmore from the Tower of London at the beginning of August. The idea that Orleton was spending his time at his Berkshire retreat at Shinfield plotting the baron's release is an erroneous conjecture, largely arising from the misconception shared by a number of chroniclers that the escape took place in 1324 and by the fact that there appears to be an error in the transcription of Baker's *Chronicon* at this point.[81] With the proper date established it becomes clear that Orleton was in his diocese at the relevant time and in no position to take part in a scheme that had to be contrived at short notice.[82] All the same, the king seized the moment to root out all those who allegedly had taken some part in the recent rebellion and who had not been dealt with.[83] Two months after Mortimer's escape a writ was issued from Skipton, Yorkshire, appointing justices to act in Lancashire, Derbyshire, Staffordshire, and elsewhere.[84] Further commissions were issued from Kenilworth (28 December) and Worcester (10 January 1324), concerning Worcestershire, Gloucestershire, and Herefordshire. The charge against Orleton has nothing to do with Mortimer's escape but harks back to the rebellion of 1321–22. Allegedly he met Mortimer at the episcopal manor of Bosbury and subsequently sent men to join the baron's forces at Ledbury. His own view of the situation was that he was perfectly entitled to discuss matters with his parishioner. As for the supply of armed men, an independent source disclaims the bishop's responsibility for the actions of most of them. Significantly, perhaps, James de Henley was also accused of sending help to the rebels.[85] Doubtless this supposed involvement was known to the king in February 1322 when he personally upbraided the bishop at Hereford, but like other charges previously aired, many of them pardoned, they were reiterated in the assize court. Orleton did not attempt to rebut the accusation, but stood on the high ground of ecclesiastical privilege: he was "bishop of Hereford by God's will and that of the pope." The content of the articles imputed to him was so weighty that he ought not to respond in that court, "nor could he do so without offense to God (*offensa divina*) and Holy Church." Orleton next appeared before Edward himself at Westminster on 24 February 1324, the day after parliament assembled. He was there termed traitor (*proditor*) while Gilbert atte Nasshe, one of those allegedly sent to Mortimer by Orleton, was reported to have been convicted, despite his plea that he had only joined Mortimer under threat of death. Orleton repeated his previous statement and was claimed for the Church by Archbishop Reynolds, under orders to bring him before the king on 19 March, the day following the dispersal of parliament. Another jury from Hereford was empanelled, this time with nine new members, and they found the bishop guilty as indicted. An order was given for the sheriff to seize his goods, chattels, and lands.[86] Blaneforde, however, makes the point, that Orleton was condemned *in absentia*, a claim supported by an entry on the Close Roll of the first year of Edward III's reign. This, as Vernon Harcourt pointed out, is a direct contradiction of the Coram Rege roll.[87] Orleton petitioned against the decision on the grounds of error in the process, but it was not until 1327 that it was reversed on those grounds.[88]

Other aspects of the case need to be noticed. Although the word "treason" was loosely bandied about – the king himself using the equivalent (*crimen laese majestatis*) in a letter of 1325 complaining to the pope about Orleton's conduct – the legal records speak only of "trespass" (*transgressio*), as does Orleton himself. Trespass was a wide-ranging term much in use at the time.[89] The impartiality of the process is questionable; some of the jurors, such as Adam Halfnaked, Richard de Scholle, and Walter de Brugge, were known enemies of the bishop.[90] Halfnaked had at one time been entrusted with the temporalities of St Guthlac's by the king, apparently in the interest of Prior William Irby, with whom he was closely associated.[91] Meanwhile, in March 1324, Prior Irby, in association with the royal escheator, John de Hampton, had been given custody of Orleton's temporalities.[92] This appointment may be connected with his violent behaviour in front of the bishop, since in May a commission of oyer and terminer was set up to try those of Orleton's friends, including his clerical brothers Thomas and John, who had driven off the stock from the episcopal manors.[93] The violent incident took place while Orleton was on visitation at Ross and celebrating pontifical high mass for the feast of St George (23 April) in the parish church of St Mary. Prior William, allegedly uttering blasphemous words, disrupted the service and the visitation. The bishop promptly excommunicated him. On 2 August 1324 Orleton ordered this sentence to be promulgated and asked the bishop of Worcester, Cobham, to do the same throughout his churches in Gloucestershire lying within the southern archdeaconry of that diocese.[94] Irby appealed for "tuition" to the Court of Canterbury, but the case was remitted to the bishop, so that Irby was forced to seek out the diocesan in London, where he agreed to accept ecclesiastical penalties. Orleton, in accordance with regular canonical practice, gave instructions to commissaries to pronounce absolution from his sentence and to impose suitable penance, while at the same time making it clear that any excommunication incurred *ipso facto* by reason of the canons would require papal absolution. In the event, some of the commissaries were unavailable, thus delaying the execution of the mandate. Irby promptly complained to the Canterbury Court on the grounds of defect of justice, whereupon the bishop was cited to explain his failure to act. On receipt of the court's mandate Orleton obediently issued a further commission for Irby's absolution.[95]

Let us return to our scarcely unprejudiced juror, Adam Halfnaked. On 17 October 1324 he was entrusted with the custodianship of the Hereford temporalities. For the period until Michaelmas 1325 he paid just over £335 into the treasury from the bishop's Herefordshire manors and was allowed ten pounds for his pains.[96] Blaneforde gives a graphic impression of the bishop's plight, his goods thrown into the highway to be looted by passers-by. The chronicler is supported by the evidence of a royal writ addressed to John Inge, William Irby, and John of Towcester, who for a time was also custodian of Shinfield, Orleton's refuge in Berkshire.[97] The writ declares that these "custodians" had exceeded their commission by removing episcopal ornaments, vestments, and other items, prohibiting the dean and chapter of Hereford from communicating with their diocesan and forbidding anyone to receive him, to provide him with provisions, or even to approach him for confession. All the items pertaining to the spirituality were to be restored and the bishop was not to impeded in the exercise of his episcopal office.[98] So difficult was it for Orleton to perform his duties in person that during 1324 he spent some months in London, and for most of 1325 and much of 1326 he remained in the Hereford dean and chapter's rectory of Shinfield, Berkshire. Hostile custodians damaged the bishopric's resources to such an extent that Orleton had subsequently to borrow in order to repair the buildings. The sympathetic pope ordered that he was not to be pursued for dilapidations incurred through no fault of his own.[99] One reason why the king and Baldock, no doubt the younger Despenser too, were so virulent in their treatment of Orleton may be that, unlike Stratford, he apparently refused to compromise his ecclesiastical status by sealing a recognizance for ten thousand pounds, or to bind himself by oath to the younger Despenser in similar manner.[100]

Other bishops received ill treatment because they were implicated in the rebellion by reason of their sympathies with individual participants, such as Droxford of Bath and Wells – whom the king sought to replace with his friend, Abbot William of the Premonstratensian house of Langdon – or Burghersh of Lincoln, whose relatives had been put to death.[101] In the case of Stratford, bishop of Winchester, and later in that of Ayrminne, bishop of Norwich, it was because of acceptance of a bishopric contrary to the king's wish.[102] With respect to Hothum, bishop of Ely, the reason is less obvious.[103] In all these instances the king encroached on the bishops' temporalities and not infrequently on their ecclesiastical patronage. It is noticeable that when the papal envoys arrived in

England in early November 1324 the bishops who went to meet them, Stratford of Winchester, Burghersh of Lincoln, Eaglescliff of Llandaff, and Cobham of Worcester, had all been provided, or in Eaglescliff's case translated, by the pope, half of them being *personae non gratae* to the king.[104] Cobham was uneasy about the king's conduct but reported to the Curia that he hoped for the amelioration of his anger, he having personally approached Edward.[105] Cobham's caution enabled him to exercise some influence and despite the unprecedented treatment of his colleagues he remained conspicuously loyal. Another bishop who showed no open hostility to the king's actions was Hamo de Hethe of Rochester, a monk. From the reporting of the local chronicler it would seem that the king was on excellent terms with Hethe; he even felt under obligation to him, an obligation that he had been unable to repay. The bishop's relationship with the younger Despenser was also a friendly one, but Hethe was not unprepared to voice his criticisms, as he once threatened to do in a sermon.[106] Other bishops, such as Norwich (Salmon) and Stapeldon (Exeter) were by the nature of their secular offices either well disposed or at least cooperative.

Edward II's reign marks an important stage in the oppression of bishops by the secular power. Under Edward I there had been struggles between king and dominant primates, Pecham and Winchelsey. During Edward II's reign the accommodating Reynolds replaced Winchelsey, and from that quarter came little resistance. But in Edward III's early years Stratford proved a match for a bullying monarch. Nonetheless, the third Edward, once well established, would brook no resistance from members of the episcopate, as Bishop Lisle of Ely was to learn to his cost.[107]

THE REGIME OF THE DESPENSERS, CHANCELLOR BALDOCK, AND TREASURER STAPELDON

The Despensers, Robert Baldock, and Walter Stapeldon were to form the bulwark of the government for the period from Boroughbridge until the end of the reign. These were the men who were to be blamed for what was considered to be the oppressive rule of the years 1322 to 1326. Pembroke, according to his biographer a moderate man who had never sought perquisites above those normally accorded to a loyal servant of the Crown, was sidelined. Unpopular with the Despensers for his support of their exile, he had in a sense compromised his position by coming out against the enemies of the Despensers in the Marches, thus helping to engineer a royal victory that was to leave the younger Despenser in control of the king and of the administration. In 1322 he was humiliated by having to take an oath of loyalty to the king, and though just before his sudden death in 1324 he was accounted one of "les plus privetz le Roi," in fact his influence had been largely overshadowed. His last years were difficult financially, largely as a consequence of the ransom that had to be paid for his release from imprisonment incurred while on royal service abroad. His widow was likewise in financial difficulties and had to complain to Edward III that debts owed to her husband by his father and grandfather remained unpaid.[108]

Already in 1320, prior to the civil war, the Despensers, Baldock and Stapeldon occupied positions of power. After 1322 "they dominated everything."[109] Baldock became keeper of the privy seal on 27 January 1320 (he was also keeper of the wardrobe from 7 July), an office he held until 7 July 1323. Shortly after this, on 20 August, he became chancellor, holding that office until the end of Edward II's personal rule. Stapeldon, who was appointed treasurer on 18 February 1320 and forced to resign under baronial pressure on 25 August in the following year, resumed the office on 10 May 1322, holding it until he was succeeded on 3 July 1325 by William Melton, an experienced administrator.[110] The chancellor, appointed on 26 January 1320, was John Salmon, the bishop of Norwich, who was said officially to have been nominated by the king in full parliament.[111] But by this time he was elderly and on 5 June 1323 he surrendered the seal, which some months later was assumed by Baldock, as stated above.[112]

The younger Hugh Despenser was predominant during the final years of Edward's reign, exercising his authority mainly through the administrative and judicial officers he had appointed. Additionally, he is credited with having taken a personal interest in his office of chamberlain.[113] At least one modern historian has claimed that he was guilty of "insatiable greed and rapacity," which provided "the mainsprings of his evil influence upon the king."[114] The chroniclers fairly unanimously concur in reporting the Despensers' malign influence. Baker, for instance, writes of them as earls of Winchester and Gloucester (*sic*) and suggests that after Boroughbridge many nobles who might have been put to death were saved by their grace. But where their lives were spared, it was only at the cost of selling some of their finest manors. So the "earls" became hateful to all, not only because the king loved them more than others but also because, moved by a spirit of pride and ambition, they impoverished knights by cruel exactions – the price of redemption – and disinherited their sons. It seemed insupportable, concluded Baker, that there should be three kings in England at one time. In Baker's view many loved King Edward, but many more out of fear hated the two King Hughs.[115] The *Vita* is condemnatory too. When, in 1325, the indecisive king failed to cross to Gascony, he left the infantrymen, who had already embarked, without pay – with predictably chaotic results. This chronicler claims that the king had much treasure, indeed he was accounted superior to all his ancestors in amassing money. Yet, he remarks, the king's meanness was ordinarily attributed to Hugh (the younger Despenser), in common with most other ills of the realm, and on that account there was a plot to kill him.[116]

The indictment of the Despensers in 1321, admittedly partisan, reflects quite clearly both their previous and subsequent *modus operandi*. They are said to have prevented the great of the land from approaching the king, save in their hearing, to have repelled the magnates and good councillors, and to have drawn royal power to themselves, thus to the king's disinheritance. To satisfy their cupidity and for the destruction and disinheritance of the people and magnates, they removed good councillors and ministers, introducing evil and false ones of their own persuasion, such as Robert Baldock, custos of the privy seal, William de Cusance, an alien, keeper of the wardrobe, and William de Cliff, like Cusance one of the younger Hugh Despenser's clerks.[117] No writ touching the Despensers was permitted to issue from the chancery, and the business of others was either impeded or promoted as they thought fit. They appointed inadequate sheriffs, escheators, constables of castles, and others to administer the king's affairs, also insufficiently knowledgeable justices. Justice itself they corrupted.[118] They were enabled to effect these policies, it has been claimed, by maintaining "a sprawling clientele of retainers, administrators and servants," men attached to them in various degrees of closeness but by no means necessarily by indenture.[119] In this respect the Despensers were not noticeably different from Pembroke and Lancaster. For instance, from the lists provided by Pembroke's biographer it is possible to determine those men who were associated with him and at what period, the strength of his retinue on various campaigns between 1297 and 1324, the grants of land they enjoyed thanks to their patron, and the official posts they held, for instance as sheriffs, justices, or constables.[120] There can be no doubt that Lancaster's retinue was even more splendid, but unfortunately it has not been itemized with comparable lucidity.[121]

Why then did this supportive "network" fail to provide a more permanent power base? Long ago Tout remarked upon the speed with which the official class deserted the king and the Despenser regime in the hour of their greatest need.[122] Their supporters among the knights and barons, where they could, made their peace with the succeeding governing clique. It was a feature of society that loyalties could migrate from one powerful, or formerly powerful lord, to another, or even, as in Edward II's case, from the king himself.[123] Lancaster, as we have seen, suffered the humiliation of the defection of Sir Adam Banaster and in his final hours of Sir Robert Holland and Sir Roger Belers. The Despensers absorbed knights who had served Pembroke, such as Sir Constantine Mortimer and Sir William Lovel,[124] or some of the 1321–22 rebels, such as John le Boteler of Llantwit, a Berkeley retainer who became the younger Despenser's steward in the counties of Worcester, Gloucester, and Stafford.[125] Fortunately the recruitment of supporters by the Despensers has been analyzed, thus providing an excellent starting point for considering this question.[126] Preliminary listings record eighteen "clients" of the elder Despenser – the term being used because of the lack of evidence for attachment by formal indentures,[127] while for the younger Despenser there are seventy-seven names. A large proportion of the latter were also in royal service.[128] Conway Davies pointed out for a slightly earlier period the weakness that arose from this "divided allegiance or divided obligation" – the serving of more than one lord simultaneously. But he regarded the "divided control between barons and the household system" as being "insufficient to endanger the permanence of the household system."

Another source of weakness Davies identified was the conflict between the administrative and executive arms of government.[129] This last was perhaps not so evident during the Despenser years, when men such as Baldock and Stapeldon seem to have been working in concert with the younger Despenser who was perceived as being responsible for injustices. On the other hand, it would be unwise, we are advised – not surprisingly – to assume that the Despensers and their clerical mentors were "deeply preoccupied with the day-to-day minutiae of household reform."[130] Further, the trend has been to argue that reforms in the exchequer and household – attributed by Tout to Melton,[131] to the keepers of the wardrobe Northburgh and Waltham,[132] to Robert Baldock, and more particularly to Stapeldon[133] – were primarily motivated by greed.[134]

Despite recent research, indeed partly because of it, it remains difficult to account for the Despensers' overriding power. Although its basis was the king's confidence, friendship, and active support, its fragility is clear enough. It has been calculated that the Despensers' immediate clientage comprised only some two to three dozen knights or landholders of comparable income, such as John Boteler, who avoided undertaking the burdens of knighthood. Worse still, the loyalty of clients could not be relied upon when fortunes changed. They readily migrated to other foci of power, as Lancaster had found to his cost; for once he adopted rebellion as a means of political coercion he readily lost support in the North and elsewhere. The recognizance was a potent weapon for ensuring loyalty since a monetary penalty was attached in the case of failure to observe its terms. Davies surmises that its use by the Despensers must have been quite general; certainly the recognizance was a useful deterrent to those of doubtful loyalty, whether lay or ecclesiastical. Davies even goes so far as to claim that "after 1322 the country seems to have been ruled largely by recognizance." Such recognizances were in general made with the king. The Fine Rolls reveal their prevalence and the fact that they were regularly forced upon reluctant parties is demonstrated by their wholesale repudiation in 1327.[135] Inevitably such recognizances bred resentment against those who imposed them.

Both Despensers, but particularly the elder Hugh, earl of Winchester, received substantial grants of lands of deceased Contrariants. Winchester, for instance, received property formerly belonging to Amory, Giffard of Brimpsfield, Badlesmere, Tyeys, Lisle, Bohun, and Kingston, thereby extending his holdings from Wiltshire and the Midlands to Surrey and Sussex, where his lands were based on the manor of Kennington close to London. His son concentrated on extending his vast lordship in South Wales and the Marcher area.[136] In 1326 the younger Hugh's estates provided some £7,150 of income – a substantial increase over the sum received by Gilbert de Clare at the time of his death in 1314 – those of his father over £3,800. As a comparison, Lancaster's estates produced some £11,000 a year. In 1324, before the decline of his fortunes, Despenser is said to have had almost £6000 deposited with the Bardi and Peruzzi and a further £1000 was discovered at Caerphilly (Caerffili) Castle in 1327. This despite considerable current expenditure.[137] The false impression has been given that Despenser was even responsible for building the great concentric fortress of Caerphilly inherited from the Clares.[138] Its builder is in fact unknown, though James of St George, who died about 1309, has been suggested as a possible candidate in view of the castle's resemblance to Harlech. What is known is that the carpenter William Hurley was at Caerphilly in 1326, together with the master mason, Thomas de la Bataille. It could well be that they were engaged in rebuilding the hall and some adjacent private chambers, the remains of which are stylistically of the fourteenth-century. But these modifications were relatively minor.[139]

The shrievalty was a potential source of control at local level, but it has been argued that both king and Despensers adopted a *laissez-faire* policy towards such appointments. Between October 1321 and October 1326, according to a recent calculation, seventy-three men were appointed sheriffs who, by the terms of the Ordinances and the Lincoln statute of 1316, were to be chosen by the chancellor – if available – the treasurer, and others of the council who were present.[140] In the circumstances of 1311 and 1316 this was intended as a measure of control or at any rate restraint, but such was not the case under the Despensers. Of those appointed, seven were the king's household knights or other members of his household. Eight, roughly a tenth, were related to the family of the Despensers, and in relationships to sheriffs the Despensers did not stand alone. In Professor Saul's view there was no attempt at control, nor were dismissals more common during the Despenser regime than at other times. In other words, the office was regarded more as an administrative than a political one, a stance that could be said to have had fatal consequences in 1326. It is remarkable that the new government replaced only nine sheriffs, as being in its view unsuitable, few of whom were Despenser associates. However, bearing in mind the small number of those in any position who continued loyal to the Despensers, it might be assumed that political affiliations would not have been maintained by sheriffs under the stress of Isabella's invasion.[141]

The practice with respect to the custodianship of castles, obviously an important element in securing the countryside, was that some were granted with the office of sheriff, while others had separate custodians. From the printed Fine Rolls Professor Saul has calculated that some sixty-seven appointments, excluding constabularies attached to shrievalties, were made between November 1321 and 16 October 1326. Of these thirty were members of the royal household, knights, valets, or clerks; five were associated with the Despensers; four were *curiales*, including two former seneschals of Gascony; two judges – Geoffrey le Scrope and John Stonor – and one exchequer baron. That is, forty-two constables can in a broad sense be categorized as *curiales*. Moreover, all but one of the constables appointed between 8 December 1325 and 16 October 1326, when the kingdom was felt to be particularly vulnerable, were somehow connected with the court. Of these only Sir John Felton, who was eventually to surrender Caerphilly Castle in 1327, put up any real resistance.[142]

Another important element of "social control", to use a modern term, was the judiciary. There does not seem to be any evidence that the courts of King's Bench and Common Pleas were "packed," certainly not after 1322. It has been said that judges were as involved in the network of corruption as were the Despensers themselves, but allegedly some were men of distinction. For instance William Herle, who has been dubbed "the greatest lawyer of his age," was renowned, it is said, for the soundness of his judgments, while Stonor was allegedly a man of integrity.[143] It could be indicative of their relative impartiality that all the judges were reappointed in the subsequent reign. Herle, a justice of Common Pleas and in 1322 one of those who had condemned the Mortimers, was made chief justice on 29 January 1327; Geoffrey le Scrope, chief justice of King's Bench since 1324, was reappointed in March of that year.[144]

A common means of perverting the course of justice was to bring malicious indictments – under the Despensers an "everyday occurrence," thought Professor Saul. One such is of particular interest because it concerns Thomas de Bishopsdon or Bishopton, a clerk of Canterbury diocese, allegedly an "adherent" of Adam Orleton.[145] The bishop did indeed have some connection with him during his diplomatic journeys. On the indictment of one Roger Lumbard, Bishopton was accused of assisting the king's enemies at the coast. He was arrested and forced to pay a hundred pounds to secure the younger Despenser's favour. In similar manner commissions of oyer and terminer might be manipulated to uphold malicious prosecutions, juries could be packed (as in Bishop Orleton's case), and judges sympathetic to one's case might be procured.[146] But to what extent these corruptions were more pronounced than usual it would be difficult, indeed impossible, to determine. Richard Kaeuper has examined the incidence of commissions of oyer and terminer for the fourteenth century. They were popular in the earlier part of Edward II's reign, reaching a peak in 1318. Thereafter there was a decline and a low point was reached in the king's last year. It is acknowledged that the Despensers' wishes may have influenced the issue of individual petitions, but activity by the King's Bench as a court of first instance in cases of indictment for trespasses and felonies may well have assisted the decline in the number of commissions of oyer and terminer.[147]

The result was no better with coastal defence. John de St John and his brother Edward were appointed to defend the south coast, but both joined Queen Isabella in 1326. Off the east coast Sir Robert de Camoys and Sir Robert Wateville were in charge of mustering the ships. Despite the fact that all sizeable vessels from the Thames mouth northwards were to assemble at Orwell by 21 September, armed and victualled for a month, this was exactly the area where the queen and Mortimer made their landfall. According to the French Chronicle the sailors refused to fight because of their dislike of Despenser and instead carried out a piratical attack on the coast of Normandy.[148]

Professor Saul's thesis is that by and large the Despensers made no effort to build up a strong political and administrative position. On the other hand, Dr

Waugh suggests that in comparing the retinues of the Despensers with those of Pembroke and Lancaster, a marked discrepancy emerges. The Despensers had far more clients in the central administration than either of the others. Only six out of twenty-five Pembroke retainers in 1321–22 could be described as being close to the court, while the figure for the Despensers is twenty out of ninety-six. At that time some sixty-nine percent of Despenser retainers were in the service of the Crown, almost double the percentage (thirty-six) for Pembroke retainers. A further point made by Waugh is that, unlike those of Pembroke and Lancaster, the retinues of the Despensers did not have a strong military flavour.[149] In any case the Despensers' acquisitiveness, more particularly that of the younger Despenser, ensured that they made numerous enemies, both lay and ecclesiastical, who were by no means merely Contrariants – either deprived of their lands or a portion of them, and anxious for their recovery. Others were bent on ridding themselves of the obligations of forced recognizance or fines kept in abeyance during good behaviour. The Despensers did not, the argument runs, build up a strong group at court to replace those who had been exiled, alienated, or killed. Unlike the "Lancastrians" they had no real policy save aggrandizement of themselves and of the king, who, having inherited a heavy deficit, had accumulated a substantial treasure by the end of his reign.[150]

The Rochester chronicler records the boast of the younger Despenser that but for the actions of the queen and the bishop of Norwich, William Ayrminne, in stirring up discord with the French king, the English monarch would have had no equal in wealth.[151] Other chroniclers support this assertion of royal affluence. The author of the *Brut* thought that thanks to the taking of "the goods that were in Holy Church" (particularly income from confiscated temporalities), forfeitures, and tallage, he was the richest English king since William the Bastard.[152] More precisely, it has been calculated that the Contrariants' lands brought in some £12,000 a year, fines imposed on those involved were nominally worth even more – insofar as they were actually collected rather than being used as a method of ensuring good behaviour, while a subsidy was assessed at £42,000, though doubtless far from being as lucrative as that figure implies. Diversion of a papal tenth for two years in 1322 was in theory worth about a further £38,000.[153] In the raising of clerical taxation the king had a ready cooperator in Archbishop Reynolds, despite the complaints of the lower clergy and some of the bishops.[154] In addition to such exceptional revenue there was a concerted effort to collect outstanding arrears and to levy feudal incidents and long outstanding debts.[155] Another source of income, with the advantage that consent did not have to be sought, was that derived from the customs, particularly the taxes on the export of wool, that Edward III was to find essential for financing the French war.[156]

One should remember that it was impossible for the Despensers, as it had been for the Lancastrians, permanently to keep a controlling hand on government at every level. It may be, as has been suggested, that suborning ministers, indulging in bribery, indeed overall corruption, flew in the face of a general assumption that such practices were understood to be morally wrong and that they ran counter to the principles elaborated by Glanvill and Bracton, principles adopted by reformers in the thirteenth and fourteenth centuries.[157] It would be reassuring to accept this theory, but perhaps of more immediate consequence was the king's own failure to govern, coupled with the dislike of men who permanently "bent the royal ear," and whose manner of control was basically egocentric and tyrannical.

BISHOP STAPELDON, ROGER BELERS, AND THE EXCHEQUER

One of the problems about the so-called years of tyranny is the extent to which the king was personally responsible: a topic touched upon in chapter 2 when discussing the king's character. Perhaps the question is insoluble. The bulk of historical opinion has concluded that Edward was no man of business. There is much contemporary support for the view, and not merely from the chroniclers. Hence, it appears unlikely, on the face of it, that he could have taken a consistent personal interest in the execution of the reforms in fiscal administration and the operation of the exchequer.[158] Recently, though, it has been claimed that the king did exercise considerable personal influence in financial matters. He is said to have expressed concern about fiscal secrecy, distrusted his officials, felt that they did not work sufficiently hard, and adopted directives "clearly contrary to the preferences and habits of his officials," his principal purpose being to increase royal revenue.[159] It has been rightly said that it was impossible – for isolated individuals, that is – to contravene the king's will: "There simply was no means short of rebellion of checking the executive authority of the king when he chose to use it."[160] Under the year 1325 the author of the *Vita*, nearing the end of his chronicle and possibly close to his deathbed, lamented that no one dared to oppose the king's will, parliaments counted for nothing, the magnates cowed by threats and by the penalties suffered by others, allowed Edward's wishes free rein. Coining an apophthegm, he concludes: "nowadays inclination overrules reason" (*Sic voluntas hodie vincit rationem*).[161]

Arguments about Edward's apparent concern for business need to be treated with caution and in appropriate context. For instance, the *Vita*'s author was not describing Edward's close attention to business but his wilful idiosyncrasy. Writs issued in the king's name, even under his secret seal, often disguise the operative personality or personalities behind them. There can be no doubt that the younger Hugh Despenser was the ultimate power behind the throne; Chancellor Baldock and Treasurer Stapeldon his willing cooperators.[162] Equally, in "foreign affairs" everyone accepted Despenser's authority, although his influence was far from being beneficial, since his vacillation in dealing with the question of homage was a major factor in facilitating the successful invasion of 1326 from Hainault.[163] Yet it is Stapeldon who has been particularly associated with financial policy and administration. At one time historians thought that the victory of Boroughbridge would enable the king to strengthen his control of government and finance through the household departments, notably the chamber and wardrobe. However, when it became necessary to administer the confiscated lands of the Contrariants this task was transferred from the temporary control of the chamber to that of the exchequer. This was done, it is convincingly argued, because the exchequer alone had the resources to cope with the situation. It also explains why the exchequer was subject to reform at this time, by means of the ordinances issued at Cowick in June 1323, at Westminster in May 1324, and in June 1326.[164] Stapeldon's name is not the only one to be connected with such measures. Roger, later Sir Roger Beler or Belers,[165] who had been closely associated with Thomas of Lancaster, was appointed in May of 1322 as one of the chief auditors, with responsibility for ensuring that proper account was made of the profits of the confiscated lands.[166] On 20 July Belers became a baron of the exchequer as a reward, according to Tout, for his betrayal of Lancaster. His appointment was closely followed by the transfer of the lands of the Contrariants to the exchequer.[167] By a privy seal writ of 16 June 1324 the exchequer, at Belers's urging, was divided into two courts. He was promoted chief baron in charge of the southern division (*en la nouvelle place*), while Walter Norwich, already chief baron, who may be described as Belers's rival, was now confined to affairs of the northern region (*en la place qe vous ore tenez*).[168] Significantly the division was abandoned, this time on Stapeldon's advice, following Belers's murder in 1326,[169] the unity of the exchequer being restored by William Melton's ordinance of 30 June in that year.[170]

One feature of the period was the calendaring of important documents, a prerequisite of informed action whether in diplomatic or financial affairs. Two notable clerks, John Hildesle and Henry de Canterbury, had been responsible for compiling respectively the Gascon Register and the Gascon Calendar. Stapeldon followed in their footsteps with his calendar, completed in 1323, about half of which involved diplomatic material.[171] The major factor in the compilation of exchequer and other financial documents was the king's anxiety and that of Despenser to amass a substantial sum of money and treasure. This was stimulated by the difficulty in securing grants whether from clergy or laity between 1323 and 1325.[172] Some of the stringent measures, amounting to corruption, employed by Stapeldon and Belers in the course of their work are detailed by Dr Buck in his explanation of Stapeldon's unpopularity. The case of John Sandale's executors, unable to provide receipts on account of the king's seizure of the bishop's effects, must have been considered particularly reprehensible, for there was an added "spiritual" dimension in unjustly taking ecclesiastical property, an offence involving excommunication *ipso facto*.[173] A combination of efficiency and greed even over such a short period was enough to seal the fate of Baldock, Stapeldon, and the Despensers, once the king's protection was removed.

THE RUMBLINGS OF DISCONTENT

The existence of the Contrariants, many of them in prison, the failure of the Scottish campaigns, and the nest of exiles abroad all served to foster elements of rebellion. Robert Ewer – called *Aquarius* from the household office, held by the family, of preparing the king's bath – was a mercurial Hampshire knight in the confidence of Edward II who entrusted him with the custody of Odiham castle. In 1320 he organized a minor revolt, apparently against the Despensers, and threatened any who attempted to capture him with death. He was pardoned and, as we have seen, took a major part in the offensive against the Marchers, being one of those entrusted with conveying the captured Mortimers to London. The author of the *Vita* gives more details of his character and miserable end than any other chronicler. Ewer he describes as an adulterer; an adventurer who indulged in murder and plunder. Despite his earlier military cooperation with the king, he took the opportunity provided by preoccupation with the Scottish expedition of 1322 to attack the property of the elder Despenser, earl of Winchester, in the southern counties. Perhaps this is explicable as a revival of his former antagonism. He then ostentatiously distributed his ill-gotten gains in alms to the poor for the benefit of the souls of Henry Tyeys and Warin de Lisle whose manors the earl had received following their condemnation and death. The clerical author considered that distribution in such circumstances could not be rightly termed "alms," but constituted a kind of theft. The earl, fearing a personal attack, fled to Windsor, where he attempted to muster forces with the aid of the earl of Kent. Once the euphoria of the raid was over, Ewer's forces melted away. Initially he is reported to have gone to Lancashire and was rumoured to be fomenting disaffection in Wales. Eventually he was captured at Southampton while attempting to flee abroad. When accused before the justices he refused to answer and so, says the *Vita*, he suffered the fate of all such men: solitary confinement on a starvation diet, his body pressed down by an iron weight. Not surprisingly, after a few days he died.[174]

Another episode, or series of episodes, could be described as the "three castles conspiracy," an organized attempt to release important Contrariants imprisoned in the royal strongholds of Wallingford, Windsor, and the Tower of London. To what extent there was overall collaboration is unknown, although a royal commission of enquiry, appointed 7 April 1323, implies as much.[175] Once again we are dependent on the *Vita* for a lengthy account of the Wallingford affair, which bears marked similarities to the escape of Mortimer from the Tower some six months later.[176] Maurice de Berkeley, the principal prisoner, was accustomed to receive visits from a faithful esquire, who on this particular occasion brought a number of friends into the castle with him, the regime for the prisoners being far from strict. The constable of the castle was invited to dine with his charges, but at an appropriate moment the keys of the fortress were demanded from him under threat. Other conspirators were promptly admitted by a postern. Before Berkeley could be spirited away a report of what was happening in the inner ward was relayed to the town and the squire's own messenger, sent to bring appropriate help, decided that his mission was too dangerous, so he revealed all to the mayor. In a short time the sheriff arrived, to be informed that the castle had been entered by royal warrant. Having verified that such was not the case, he and the earls of Winchester and Kent discovered Berkeley in his usual place of confinement, while the conspirators sought sanctuary in the chapel from which they were promptly dragged. Berkeley protested his innocence and was left to die in his prison three years later. The ready cooperation of the townsfolk with the authorities, if accurate, demonstrates a lack of sympathy for the Contrariants. In view of the widespread disaffection this seems remarkable; possibly it was a local phenomenon.

The imprisonment of the Mortimers has already been mentioned in the context of the aftermath of Boroughbridge. At the beginning of August 1323 the younger Mortimer was freed by a ruse whereby the subgaolers of the Tower's constable, Sir Stephen Segrave, were drugged. Under judicial examination Segrave claimed that he had been deluded by a squire in whom he had complete trust. In connivance with Mortimer this squire had administered an ingenious potion which had induced a heavy sleep.[177] According to the *Vita* and a subsequent inquisition at Portsmouth cited by the chronicler, it was Ralph de Boktone, a London merchant, who engineered the subsequent escape. Mortimer and his fellow escapees were taken across the Thames to the mills of John Gisors, a prominent member of the pepperers' company who had until recently been a London alderman. They mounted seven horses hidden in nearby buildings belonging to the abbot (of Westminster?) and rode to "Baselehorde" where they were picked up by an unwitting boatman from the Isle of Wight. He was subsequently compelled to transfer them to one of Boktone's vessels out of Normandy. The plan seems to have been so effective that there was no pursuit. Segrave was fortunate to escape with his life considering his manifest carelessness and the government's irritation.[178] Another escape, often overlooked, is that of the Lancastrian, Robert Walkfare, and his fellow prisoners from Corfe Castle. This was effected by killing their custodian. A corresponding feat was to be attributed to Edward of Caernarfon himself.[179]

Andrew Harclay was a member of an intelligent but unscrupulous Cumberland family that also produced Dr Henry Harclay, Oxford chancellor and preacher of the sermon prior to translation of Gaveston's body from the convent of the Oxford Black Friars for burial at Langley.[180] Andrew, who had ensured the victory of Boroughbridge and gained an earldom on that account, was another of the casualties of the post-Lancaster regime. Justifiably, he was irritated by the king's unwillingness to take any decisive action against Scottish raiders, as exemplified by his reported conversation with Edward in the *Vita*.[181] Early in February 1323, the year following his elevation, his arrest was ordered for having given assistance to the Scots. He had realized the impossibility, so far as the North of England was concerned, of continuing a struggle that, under the inept

Edward, was certain to remain unresolved. He had therefore attempted to force the king's hand by devising a permanent agreement with Bruce. It was a sad end to one of the ablest military leaders, destroyed – not untypically at this period – by the connivance of an envious rival, Sir Anthony Lucy.[182]

Geoffrey le Baker's conspiracy theory was that Bishops Orleton and Burghersh in conjunction with the queen, were engaged in a plot to overthrow not merely the Despensers but also the king.[183] There is no evidence for any such comprehensive plan; indeed, neither bishop was in a position to effect anything of the kind.[184] There is an account in the *Vita* of a suspect letter sent by Orleton to Henry of Lancaster, Thomas's brother and by then earl of Leicester,[185] asking him to say a good word to the king to ensure a reconciliation. Cautiously the earl is said to have counselled patience in tribulation, though the words attributed to him must surely have come from the pen of an ecclesiastic. This did not discourage those around the king who were anxious to smell treason on every side or at any rate to frighten potential recalcitrants.[186] The earl was further accused of adopting his condemned brother's arms and of setting up a cross outside Leicester for the benefit of his brother's soul. Henry convincingly argued that the arms he adopted were his father's, but less convincingly that the cross was not intended to offend the king but to stimulate spiritual devotion for the welfare of his brother's soul. After all, he added, the Church advocated prayers for heretics and Jews. The earl was summoned to answer the charges at the parliament held at Westminster in June 1325, but there were more important matters to consider, principally the king's projected visit to France. As a result the accusations were quietly dropped, but Lancaster's alienation had been strengthened. He only had to await an opportunity to reveal his underlying feelings.[187]

There were many other examples of discontent and lawlessness, but to what extent these were exceptional for the century must remain largely a matter of opinion. At Coventry even witchcraft was attempted to eliminate the king and the Despensers as well as more local enemies.[188] The Pauline annalist records an exceptional detail: on 21 November 1323 the gates of London were closed against those intent on ambushing the king (*insidiantes domini regis*) and other evildoers. Three years later he recounts the riot between the north and south apprentices of the Bench that left many dead.[189] The Rochester diocesan, Hamo de Hethe, anticipating the worst, was building a wall round his property at Halling, while the chronicler of his episcopate laments that the hearts of all were turned against the king, the people – as always – being seditious.[190] Even Archbishop Melton's pallium and episcopal "ornamenta," kept in his private chapel, were not safe from nocturnal robbers.[191]

QUEEN ISABELLA AND THE EXILES IN FRANCE

Edward's irredeemable error was to permit his wife and son to travel to France and to establish themselves there while he remained at home. Baker claims that

Edward's reluctance to perform his obligations in person stemmed from the Despensers' fear that, deprived of their royal protector, they might suffer at the hand of unnamed enemies.[192] The *Vita* states that the Despensers argued that the king's person would be endangered were he to go abroad, and that anyone who advocated such a course was a traitor.[193] This fear is reiterated by the Rochester chronicler, who writes of the prospect of an ambush at Wissant, but in his account there are no aspersions against the Despensers, with the younger of whom Bishop Hethe was on reasonable, even friendly, terms, albeit not uncritical.[194] At a later stage, when the disastrous outcome became clear, the *Brut* records that the younger Despenser blamed his father for counselling Isabella's employment as a go-between.[195] The perspicacious author of the *Vita*, who before the event did worry about the possible outcome, remarks that Isabella was happy to leave England for two reasons: she was pleased to visit her relatives and to leave Hugh Despenser, the man responsible for her uncle Lancaster's death and for the loss of her servants and rents.[196] If such were the case, she was careful to hide her feelings, for allegedly she had bidden Hugh an amicable farewell and subsequently sent him friendly letters which he had produced in parliament as evidence of his good faith.[197]

The commencement of Isabella's relationship with the exiled Mortimer is more difficult to establish. There is as yet no firm evidence that any intimacy existed between them prior to his flight to France, although she did show a womanly sympathy for the difficulties of Roger Mortimer's wife, her "cher cousyne" Joan.[198] In their despatch of 13 December 1323 M. John Shoredich and his co-envoys reported that Mortimer and the other English exiles had been favourably received by the count of Boulogne, and from time to time during the negotiations with the French the complaint was raised that shelter, even favour, was being shown to the "traitors." Mortimer was not initially regarded as being well disposed towards the queen. As late as February 1325 the English government expressed the fear (real or suppositious) that he and the other enemies of the English king might behave in a hostile fashion towards Isabella.[199] But by the end of the year there was reason to believe that Mortimer enjoyed an intimacy with the queen, more than an inkling of which must have been carried back by Stapeldon late in October.[200] Baker, admittedly no partisan of the queen, expressly states in the so-called *Vita et Mors* that she was in the illicit embraces of Mortimer,[201] and the baron is specifically denounced in a proclamation of February 1326.[202]

The king made desperate efforts to secure the return of his wife and son. In a letter to Isabella on 1 December 1325 he began by stating that he had often ordered her to return. For her part the queen is said to have sworn that she would not come back until the traitors to king and realm were removed from Edward's side and punished in accordance with their deserts.[203] Common report had it, so we are informed by the English *Brut*, that Isabella and her son were exiled, a rumour strongly denied by the government, although according to the Wigmore Chronicle such exile was published throughout the counties, while another chronicle tells of a similar proclamation in London.[204] When the king was in the privacy of the prior's chamber at Rochester in mid-June 1326 he pointed out to Bishop Hethe the precedent of a certain queen who, being unwilling to obey her husband, was deprived of her dignity. To this the bishop replied that the person who had told him that should have ill thanks for the suggestion. It has been hypothesized that he had in mind Eadburh, daughter of Offa of Mercia and wife of King Beorhtric of Wessex, whose story is told by Asser. She had slandered the king's councillors. So far, so good. But Eadburh's chief crime was inadvertently to kill her husband, who swallowed the poison prepared for his young favourite. Admittedly she too sought refuge in the "French" court – that of Charlemagne, who provided her with an abbacy; but later, convicted of unchastity, she died in poverty at Pavia.[205] Rumours of all kinds were being disseminated. One current in the Low Countries and supported by some English evidence, was that Edward was having an affair with the younger Despenser's wife, Eleanor de Clare,[206] another – perhaps more difficult to assess – that he was trying to secure a divorce from his wife.[207]

A London chronicle records that Isabella's letters were intercepted, that she adopted widow's weeds as though she had lost her husband, and that the "people" deplored her plight in view of her efforts for peace.[208] Orleton, in what has been called his *Apologia* – his *Responsiones* to a damning indictment – provides a copy of a letter dated 5 February 1326 from Paris. This purports to be Isabella's reply to one from Archbishop Reynolds, in which he had pressed her to return, arguing that Despenser intended her no harm. She responded that she would not have left the company of her husband without good and reasonable cause – danger to her life – knowing that Despenser, who wished her dishonour, had full control of the realm and of the king. These, she declared, were indubitable facts that she had long concealed. She could not rejoin the king without putting herself in danger of death, about which she was unable to speak.[209] In his turn Mortimer constituted a potential, even an actual threat to those advising Edward, and allegedly a plot of his was discovered for the assassination of the king, Despenser, Baldock, Arundel, and others. Action was taken against his wife and her associates.[210] In a letter to his fellow monarch Edward reminded him, as he had frequently done before, that sanctuary should not be given to Mortimer, denounced the behaviour of Isabella, refuted the allegations against the younger Despenser, and accused his wife of adultery.[211] To the pope he complained that Isabella had received Mortimer into her company (*comitiva*) and that the latter had openly flaunted the livery of the duke of Aquitaine before the populace of Paris during the festivities for the coronation of the French queen, Jeanne of Evreux, Charles's third wife, sister of the count of Evreux.[212] Another chronicler goes so far as to state that Isabella appointed Mortimer as director or tutor of the young prince.[213]

In view of Isabella's own adultery her position at the court of Charles IV was at best anomalous and her continued stay there open to cavil.[214] After all, Charles had imprisoned his wife Blanche for the same offence. However, for some time Isabella's brother *did* supplement her much-attenuated income with a loan and the Bardi also provided financial support.[215] A theory has been advanced that the chroniclers who suggested that Charles wished to rid himself of his sister – a view espoused by Perroy – were ill-informed since Philip of Valois, who was likely to succeed to the French throne if women were excluded, would have been anxious to have Isabella, the direct heir, in his debt. She is said to have shown her gratitude by renouncing her son's claim to the French throne.[216] In fact, on the morrow following Philip VI's coronation on 29 May 1328 Bishops Orleton and Northburgh – in compliance with a decision at the Northampton Parliament, certainly with Isabella's sanction – were in Paris, to press the claims of Edward III. This was a step that Archbishop John Stratford was to claim as a major cause of the war with France.[217]

Information passing to Reynolds from Prior Eastry and those travellers making their way through Kent was purveyed to the king. Charles is reported to have written to Guillaume of Hainault about a projected marriage between Prince Edward and one of the count's daughters. He also raised the question of possible assistance with an invasion of England.[218] Such an invasion had been in prospect since 1324. In October of that year the younger Despenser wrote to John Sturmy, admiral of the eastern fleet, with a report that a large number of ships had assembled off the coast of Holland and Zeeland with the agreement of the king of Bohemia and the count of Hainault. There were men-at-arms under the leadership of Roger Mortimer, whose destination was allegedly the coast of Norfolk and Suffolk. The admiral was to keep a keen lookout in those areas.[219]

The respective policies of France and Hainault favoured Isabella, but the papacy was determined, if humanly possible, to find a peaceful solution. A French invasion of England on Isabella's behalf would have been unpopular and might well have complicated subsequent relationships. Probably it was not seriously contemplated. On the other hand, Charles IV stood to gain, as in the event he did, were Isabella's invasion to be successful. The French king had continued to have problems with Flanders – Edward had taken advantage of these – but relationships with Hainault had been cemented by marriage, Count Guillaume having espoused Jeanne, sister of Philip of Valois, the future King Philip VI. The advantage to the count of an English marriage was that it would provide an additional safeguard against encroachment from the Empire and, coupled with alliances with Brabant, Juliers and other areas of the Low Countries would bring an element of security to the region. One final effort of papal diplomacy took place in the summer of 1326 when the archbishop of Vienne and the bishop of Orange arrived at Dover shortly after Pentecost (11 May). They were acting, according to Prior Eastry of Canterbury, not only on the pope's behalf but also on that of Charles IV and Isabella. The constable of Dover, who had specific orders with respect to their reception, prevented them from proceeding further for eight days. After that they travelled to Archbishop Reynolds' castle at Saltwood in Kent, where they arrived in some trepidation: in the words of the Pauline annalist, "trepidi et timorati."[220]

That personal danger was uppermost in the nuncios' minds is suggested by another local chronicler, who wrote that for fear of death they dared not produce their authority: "sed propter metum mortis potestatem suam demonstrare ausi nullatenus fuerunt."[221] The king rode down in haste to meet them[222] and seems to have dispelled their alarm by spending two days convivially in their company. But apart from bringing a number of bulls with them the nuncios appear to have accomplished little.[223] They were licensed to continue to Canterbury where on 9 June, together with the archbishop of Canterbury and some suffragans who were of the king's council, they held a discussion.[224] The king *ex motu proprio* responded with respect to the question concerning Isabella and on the tenth directed a letter to the pope. Nursing their disappointment, the nuncios left the country by way of Dover on 11 June. The younger Despenser confided to Bishop Hethe that in answer to a request to issue a safe conduct for the queen and her son, the response had been that there was no need for anything of the kind. The queen and her son could return with safety whenever they chose, the king having asked them to do so many times. In Despenser's view it was Mortimer who had dissuaded the queen under threat of death.[225] There is no reason to suppose that papal policy was favourable to Isabella, even though paternal advice was proffered to the king. That was regular practice. John XXII's intention was to mend the rupture between king and queen so as to preserve the marriage bond, and to prevent further civil war. Only if peace were established between France and England would the papal goals of a crusade and a common front against the emperor, Louis of Bavaria, be achieved. As for Isabella, papal nuncios were no more welcome to her in December 1326 than they had been to Edward the previous summer.[226]

Papal intervention did not herald a peaceful outcome: preparations for a hostile English expedition were underway. Some three hundred ships are said to have assembled at Porchester, with a substantial number of men aboard drawn from various counties. On the king's order, and under threat of substantial penalty, they were to sail to Normandy and there inflict as much damage as possible. Two knights, Nicholas de Cryel[227] and Robert de Kendale, were in command. The force was repulsed immediately on landing and many men perished. Two days later at the Downs the flotilla was instructed by the king to hasten to Yarmouth, but during the night fifteen of the ships were lost with their men. It was a great disaster and may supply one reason why in less than a fortnight there was no opposition to Isabella's invading fleet.[228]

Isabella's trump card was her custody of the young Prince Edward. During 1325 and the early months of 1326 the king continued negotiations with the courts of Castile, Aragon and Portugal for a marriage arrangement, while contending with rumours that the prince was about to be married "in partibus Francie."[229] The projected Hainault match was not novel, it had been mooted in 1319 in far different circumstances, probably as a means of preventing assistance being given to the Scots. At the time Philippa was approaching her ninth year.[230]

Her marriage now coincided with the wishes of both Mortimer and Isabella and provided the prospect of armed assistance. News of these developments was current in England by January 1326 when Edward was attempting to come to terms with Hainault.[231] The *Brut* tells the story of Arnold of Spain who was entrusted with five barrels of silver, valued at five thousand pounds, which was to be used to bribe the "Twelve Peers of France" to secure the exile of the queen and her son from France and if possible their covert demise. But Arnold was intercepted by sailors from Zeeland who escorted him to the count of Hainault, who then offered the treasure to Isabella.[232] According to one account the queen's passage from France was expedited by Charles's intention of handing over his sister to her husband, a plan said to have been revealed to her by Robert of Artois, a man who was anathema to the French monarchs and who eventually came to find refuge in Edward III's court. Isabella fled to Cambrai and was given protection by a simple knight, Eustace d'Ambrecicourt, until rescued by the chivalric Jean de Hainault, brother of the count of Hainault.[233]

Another story, related by Dene in the Rochester chronicle, is that of a plot supposedly instigated by "J. de Brittann" (Jean de Bretagne) for the abduction of Isabella. Warned by the French queen, she summoned the earl to her presence on the feast of the Nativity of Our Lady (8 September 1326) and learned that it was his intention to return home about the twenty-ninth when, so he claimed, he would have an abundance of goods – presumably by way of reward. Realizing her danger, she rode throughout the night to Hainault to avoid capture. Whatever truth lies behind this tale, Jean de Bretagne, whom the king regarded as a relative (*consanguineus*), is an unlikely candidate for the role of abductor unless he be considered to have performed a volte-face with the object of ingratiating himself with Edward. This is improbable in view of his adoption as a negotiator with France under the new regime of Isabella and Mortimer. Admittedly he had been one of the king's envoys and in that capacity is known to have dined with the queen as late as 6 October 1325 at Paris. But he had fallen out of favour. His lands had been confiscated; they were not to be restored until the following reign. In a letter of 18 June 1326, in reply to the pope's request that Richmond be rehabilitated, Edward recounted the earl's many misdeeds.[234] The story is more likely to have reference to the other Jean de Bretagne, duke of Brittany, whose merchants and sailors were exempted by Edward from the piratical attacks mounted by the English.[235]

ISABELLA'S INVASION

In a lengthy passage William de Nangiaco suggests that Queen Isabella did not wish to displease her husband by prolonging her stay in France and that she set off for England with her son, remaining for a while in Ponthieu in anticipation of hearing news of her husband. But then, learning of the measures that had been taken to apprehend her at the ports, she decided to go to the count of

Hainault.[236] This scarcely rings true, but exactly when she left France is uncertain. It is likely to have been either early or mid-August of 1326, although mandates of 12 August and 4 September in Edward's name assume that Charles IV was still detaining the queen and her son.[237] On the latter date instructions were sent to Bayonne for harrying the ships of the subjects of the king of France, excluding those of Flanders, with permission to retain any spoils.[238] Mortimer had already been making warlike preparations on the queen's behalf and in an agreement confirmed on 3 August between his associates (*les gens le dit Mortimer*) and the count of Hainault the latter promised to supply a flotilla of 140 ships, most of them small.[239] Mortimer apart, by this time there was a considerable coterie of exiles. Various sources suggest that among them were Henry de Beaumont – with Stapeldon a guardian of the young prince – Simon de Bereford, John Botetourt, John Cromwell, Thomas Engayne, John de Kingston, John Maltravers, Nicholas de Percy, John Ros, Thomas Roscelyn, William Trussell, Robert Walkfare, and the king's half-brother, the earl of Kent.[240] The total number of men in the invasion force is variably estimated: 1,700 according to the Canterbury-based Gervase continuator, over 1,500 according to the Pauline annalist. Included in the expedition, the *Brut* states, were Jean de Hainault and five hundred men-at-arms.[241] Beaumont's quarrel with the king in May 1323 during a royal council at Bishopthorpe is well known. Exasperated by the prospect of a truce with the Scots and the loss of his own lands in Scotland, he angrily declined to give counsel to the king although summoned as a member of Edward's "great and secret council" (*de magno et secreto consilio ipsius*). One chronicler alleged that he refused to take an oath to the king and Despenser "to live and die with them" (*oves enus a vivere et a morier*).[242]

To outward appearances Edward and the younger Despenser took every precaution to safeguard the realm, but the outcome was markedly different from that in 1321–22. The reasons for this are complex but must primarily be ascribed to the unpopularity of the regime, its oppressive character, and the consequent alienation of so many men of influence, who seized the opportunity to reinstate themselves or to take revenge on their oppressors. Perhaps more generally, if more debatably, it could be attributed to an awareness that Edward was incompetent to rule. The unsatisfactory nature of some of these precautionary military dispositions has been pointed out.[243] The array in the Midland counties of Warwick, Leicester, Nottingham, and Derby was assigned to the earls of Winchester and Leicester (Henry of Lancaster), but the latter, who had long existed on a knife's edge of suspicion, promptly turned on the elder Despenser and captured his military equipment and treasure. Archbishop Reynolds and Ralph Basset, together with John and Stephen de Cobham, Robert de Kendale, and William Grey, were entrusted with the defence of Kent. But the archbishop had no capacity for military organization even though both he and Bishop Hethe of Rochester appreciated the defenceless nature of the area. As for the loyal Hethe, he was not assigned a specific role.[244] What turned out to be the crucial area – Essex,

Hertfordshire, Norfolk, and Suffolk – was the responsibility of the earl marshal, with the aid of the eminently loyal bishop of London (Gravesend) in the first two counties and, surprisingly, of Bishop Hothum of Ely in the last two.

Admiral Sturmy was buying ships and supplies at Lynn in February 1326 but in August a renewed project for a Gascon expedition scheduled to depart from Portsmouth was postponed because negotiations with France were still being carried out.[245] Shortly thereafter instructions were given to the admiral responsible for the area from the Thames estuary westwards to prevent the arrival of any merchants save those of Brittany and Flanders, with whose rulers Edward was anxious to keep on good terms as a counterbalance to the French.[246] The constable of Dover was warned that under cover of mercantile activity letters had been smuggled in from Mortimer. Others were assigned to search the south coast for any such infiltration. An explanation of the current policy of peace with France was given to Archbishop Reynolds so that he could expound it to his flock. He and his suffragans were to prevent subversive preaching and to publish "the truth" about what had been happening. Pious works – sermons, masses, prayers, and almsgiving – were to be performed for the king and his realm. In corresponding terms the universities of Oxford and Cambridge were enjoined to dispel the audacity of malevolent persons by means of sermons and other meetings. In accordance with the advice of the nuncios, on 20 July Reynolds ordered a convocation to meet on 13 October at St Paul's.[247]

The government had ample intelligence of a prospective attack in the neighbourhood of Orwell haven in Suffolk. To counter this, on 23 July 1326 Robert de Wateville had been appointed captain and arrayer in Essex, Hertford, Norfolk, and Suffolk. Mandates of 2 September required the raising of five hundred armed men from Norfolk to be brought to the haven, while from Essex and Suffolk were to come a further two hundred together with thirteen hundred archers. Instructions were sent to the sheriffs and others on 3 September for the assembly of a fleet in the Orwell, precisely the area where Isabella was to land three weeks later. Ships were to be collected from the whole of the east coast from Tynemouth to the Suffolk ports and on 27 September, shortly after the landing, Wateville was directed to defend the area immediately under threat – the counties mentioned above together with Cambridge and Huntingdon, with command of the fleet to the north of the Thames. On the twenty-eighth all sheriffs were ordered to publish letters against Mortimer and to mobilize their forces to proceed against the invaders. The king's enemies were to be destroyed, but the earl of Kent, Isabella, and the young Edward were not to be harmed.[248]

There is a problem about Sir Robert de Wateville or Waterville: there were two men of that name not easily distinguishable. One, a relative by marriage of the elder Despenser, came from Orton Waterville (Huntingdonshire), the other from Hempstead and Panfield, Essex. The former allegedly remained loyal though scarcely reliable, the latter had a past as Badlesmere's retainer, joining the rebels at Bridgnorth and Boroughbridge.[249] With Lancaster's defeat he

secured a pardon. A Robert de Wateville was bound to the younger Despenser
by a recognizance of a hundred marks, subsequently being employed by him
and the earl of Kent in Gascony, where he surveyed military defences. In August
1324 he was named a commissioner of array but by the end of the year there
were those who were impugning his loyalty. Despite the earl of Kent's support
and that of others in Gascony, his arrest was ordered in April 1325 and he was
sent back to England. Soon restored to favour, in June 1325 he was at Glénan,
off the coast of Brittany, writing warmly to the king and Despenser. By a commission of 27 September 1326, described as "nostre cher et foial," he had been
given wide powers to levy royal forces. Yet the Bury St Edmunds chronicler,
who must have had reliable information since the queen was shortly to pass
through Bury "as if on pilgrimage," records that Wateville was among those who
fled from the invaders. If the identification is correct, his questionable health did
not prevent his joining the queen's supporters at Bristol.[250] The naval preparations proved futile. After the invading force had disembarked, the Pauline annalist relates, the ships reset their sails and were gone by sunset; only one, the vessel that had brought the queen herself, was sent to Edward by the royal sailors
– a dubious present – as he waited in the Tower of London.[251] In 1327 Wateville
received his reward, livery of the issues of the confiscated manor of Swaffham
in Norfolk. Two years later he was in the privileged position of witnessing
Edward III's homage at Amiens.[252]

The earl of Norfolk, the king's half-brother, was unambiguous about abandoning his responsibilities as principal defender of the invaded area. He joined
the queen with alacrity. The behaviour of those on the scene, notably Wateville
but including the readily compliant men of Norfolk and Suffolk,[253] coupled
with the waste of naval resources occasioned by the attack on Normandy,[254]
help to explain why the invaders' bridgehead was so easily established. The king
himself had been at Porchester where, according to the Castleford Chronicle, he
had an army of thirty thousand men. It has been wrongly assumed on the
hearsay of both Murimuth and the author of the *Flores* that Bishops Burghersh
and Orleton both rushed to join the queen. Orleton certainly did not, nor does
the evidence from his register point to Burghersh having done so either. But it
is quite clear that they did so once they had carried out the diocesan commitments on which they were engaged and after the queen's move to the West.[255]
In any case, the whole bench of bishops would shortly have to face the
inevitable. The triumph of the queen was to be resounding and immediate, the
"tyranny" of Edward's government was about to end with scarcely a whimper,
that of Isabella and Mortimer was about to begin.

7

The Iron Lady:
Isabella Triumphant, 1326–1330

The comparatively small band that landed with Isabella must have been astonished at the lack of hostility it encountered. Le Bel, a member of the expedition – his patron was Jean de Hainault – states that buffeted by contrary winds they had no idea where they were and spent three days disembarking.[1] The response of London was crucial but could scarcely be overt, as the king was still in his capital. Shortly after disembarkation letters were sent posthaste to the mayor and commonality requiring that they "help the queen and her son Edward in the quarrel and the cause that they had begun, that is to destroy the traitors of the realm."[2] On receiving no reply they sent further letters patent under the queen's seal from Baldock on 6 October.[3] They – the queen speaking for her son – claimed to have come for the "honour and profit of Holy Church and of our dear lord the king and all the realm." Their avowed intention was to use their power for the common profit of the realm and for the destruction of "Hugh Spenser our enemy." Should the mayor and commonality obey their "prayer and command" it would bring them "worship (worscip) and profit." Three days later, the feast of St Denys, a copy of the letter was attached at dawn to the cross in Cheap; other copies were posted throughout the city. The *Brut* is anticipating events at this point for, as we shall see, the king had left a week before. It nonetheless continues with the statement that while the king was "at meat" in the Tower a messenger arrived bearing news of the landing of Isabella and Sir Jean de Hainault "with men of arms without number." This the younger Despenser interpreted as good news, suggesting that the king make good cheer "for certainly they been all ours." Edward remained downcast and had not yet risen from table when another messenger arrived. This time it was the elder Despenser who queried the newcomer about the strength of the invaders: "but seven hundred men-at-arms" was the reply. Earl Despenser was dismayed by this response, correctly divining that so small a force could not have landed without the connivance of those on shore.[4]

Meanwhile the queen, who had received a welcome loan from the citizens of Ipswich, proceeded to Bury St Edmunds, as though on pilgrimage. She arrived on the feast of St Michael (29 September) and was able to take possession of the treasure deposited for safekeeping by Hervy de Staunton, the aged chief justice of the Common Bench. Loyal to the king, he was endangering his life in London with Justice Geoffrey le Scrope and Walter de Norwich, chief baron of the exchequer, who were attempting to carry on the business of government. The forced "loan" was used to pay the queen's followers. Everywhere the queen and her son went, says the Lichfield chronicler, they paid for their victuals and other necessaries: the people of the whole region joined her.[5] She proceeded to Cambridge, perhaps with the intention of securing academic support as she later attempted to do at Oxford, and for some days took advantage of the hospitality of the nearby nunnery of Barnwell. Moving south, she entered Baldock, where, apart from writing to the Londoners, she spitefully ransacked the property of Thomas Catel, brother of Chancellor Baldock.[6] By the time of her arrival she must have received intelligence of the situation in London. On reaching Dunstable the king's flight to the West would have been apparent, so she left the capital city to its own unruly devices and set off in pursuit, her progress between Cambridge and Bristol observed by various spies whose payments are recorded in the account book of the king's chamber.[7]

Propaganda and its ally rumour were well-understood weapons in the fourteenth century and constituted a feature of the campaign that had just begun. Isabella circularized the bishops and other notables, urging them to join her in the interests of the kingdom. For their part the king and some bishops tried to win over the Londoners or at least to secure their compliance. The bishops of London (Gravesend) and Winchester (Stratford), together with Archbishop Reynolds and the abbots of Waltham and Westminster, gathered at St Paul's on 30 September for the publication of a bull of excommunication, brought back by Orleton in 1320 as a weapon against the Scots and now pressed into service against the latest invaders. Some of the more suspicious hearers queried the bull's date, so that this desperate stratagem foundered.[8] Doubtless the king was disturbed by the outcome, but he still utterly failed to appreciate the gravity of his situation. Two could play at the game of deception, however, and if Baker is credible, the queen's followers distributed episcopal letters claiming that her forces had arrived in such enormous numbers that the countryside could scarcely sustain them. Moreover, they feigned the presence of two cardinals bearing bulls absolving all Englishmen from their oath of fealty to the king.[9]

At some stage, doubtless as a countermove to the queen's exhortatory letters, Edward summoned the burgesses to the Tower and besought their help against the insurgents. Their diplomatic response was that they did not wish to leave the town but would defend it, the king, and those with him insofar as they could. Edward is then said to have proclaimed, quite unrealistically, that the queen and her son and those in her company should be well received (*ut decet honeste reciperent*) with the exception of Mortimer, on whose head he put a price of a thousand pounds. Further, he ordered proclamation to be made in London, Canterbury, and other places, that any who wished to come to him, whether thieves, homicides, or men who had abjured the realm, would receive letters of peace (*litteras de pace*) from his chancery. It must have been obvious by this time, even to Edward, that many Londoners were so bitterly opposed to him, as well as to the Despensers that all their close associates, including bishops, justices, and some of the notable merchants, were in danger of their lives.[10] There were many reasons why London was irritated by royal policy. In 1321 Hervy de Staunton, William Herle, and Esmond de Passelee had held an Iter in the Tower. This judicial enquiry found that mayor John Gisors had received a homicide, Henry de Braundeston, whom he had permitted thereafter to enjoy the liberty of the city (*rejoier le fraunchise de Loundres après le felonie faite*). Moreover, many aldermen and others were indicted for false conspiracy (*de faus conspiracie*). As a punishment, the current mayor, Nicholas de Farndon, had been removed and Robert de Kendale appointed guardian until after the following Michaelmas when the city's liberties were restored and Hamo de Chigwell was elected mayor at the king's wish.[11]

While there is no need for detailed discussion of the actions of the Canterbury suffragans, certain incidents may usefully be examined.[12] The bishops were scheduled to meet at St Paul's on 13 October. That venue was too exposed, but a rump of bishops assembled across the river at the Augustinian priory of St Mary Overy in Southwark – where the omens proved threatening[13] – and then adjourned to the comparative safety of Lambeth Palace a little further along the south bank of the Thames, by which time their numbers had increased. Stapeldon was murdered on 15 October, just at the moment when Stratford was attempting to enlist Bishop Hethe as a companion to visit the queen on behalf of the others. As the tumult in the city intensified, Geoffrey le Scrope escaped on one of the archbishop's horses. Reynolds took fright: the generous-minded but courageous Hethe allowed him to commandeer his horses for his flight into Kent, he himself following with his entourage on foot.[14]

On the day of Stapeldon's brutal murder the king reached Tintern, Isabella and the young Edward Wallingford, where a proclamation of intent was drawn up under that date. By then Bishop Orleton had joined the insurgents. At Oxford, a little later in the month, he preached a sermon on a text from Genesis, "I shall put enmity between you and the woman, and thy seed and hers, and she shall bruise your head."[15] This citation, said the bishop some years later, concerned the first tyrant, the first devil, and the evil angels – the seed. He had applied it to Hugh Despenser who had presumed to domineer over the queen and the realm, to bruise whose head she had come, together with her seed, Edward.[16] The sermon was a prelude to the reading of the queen's proclamation, for the publication of which Orleton was responsible, presumably as a distinguished academic – a doctor of canon law who could well have studied at

Oxford.[17] The core of the proclamation remains the same as that of the letter of 6 October to the Londoners. It is directed against the younger Despenser, his adherents, and their misdeeds. Ostensibly the queen's sole purpose is one she had long nursed while in France: Despenser's removal from the king's side. Edward himself incurs no criticism at this stage; he is more of a victim. The proclamation is careful to delineate the oppressions suffered by all estates of the realm: the king, the Church, the barons, the people. The points it makes can be summarized as follows:

- It is notorious that the Church and the English realm are much damaged by Despenser's evil counsel.
- By his pride and covetousness of lordship and mastery over all others he has usurped royal power contrary to right, reason, and his allegiance.
- By the advice of Robert de Baldock and others of his adherents Holy Church is reviled and shamefully subjected, its prelates despoiled of their goods, and in other ways dishonoured.
- The Crown of England has been injured in various ways, to the disinheritance of the lord king and his heirs. Out of envy and with great cruelty the said Hugh without cause has delivered great men of the realm to shameful death. Some have been disinherited, others imprisoned, banished, and exiled, widows and orphans being deprived of their rights.
- The people have been afflicted by various tallages and too often by undue exactions, as well as grieved without mercy by various oppressions.
- By such evil misdoings (*mesprises*) Despenser shows himself to be a tyrant, an enemy of God, of Holy Church, of the king, and of all the realm.
- We and many others who have come with us and our company to remedy these defects have been long alienated from the good will of our lord the king by reason of the false suggestions and procurement of the said Hugh, Robert, and their adherents.
- For the common benefit of all and of each one, the hearers are directed and requested to give aid at such places and times and in such ways as they are able.

As yet there had been no confrontation with royal forces, so the success or failure of Isabella's invasion hung in the balance, but not for long. It soon became apparent that, despite various summonses, the king had no army with which to make a stand. The small but expanding insurgent force pressed on to Gloucester with the king's half-brothers, the earls of Kent and Norfolk, the earl marshal, as well as Archbishop Bicknor, the bishops of Ely (Hothum), Lincoln (Burghersh) and Hereford (Orleton), the lords William de Ros, Henry Percy, and many others. While at Gloucester,[18] according to Baker, the queen received Stapeldon's head as a sacrificial offering pleasing to Diana – incongruously the chaste huntress. The queen's army advanced, continues this loyalist chronicler, flying the standard of the young Edward, who though personally not at fault was badly led.[19] It continued to gather strength, being notably augmented at Gloucester by Marchers and by northerners under the leadership of Thomas Wake of Liddell and Henry Percy.[20] Castles were taken, while those imprisoned on account of the conflict between the king and the earls were freed. Isabella next stopped at Berkeley, where she restored the castle to Thomas de Berkeley, the heir of Maurice who had died in prison at Wallingford. On 22 October, according to one account, as the queen approached Bristol, the king boarded a boat for Chepstow only to be driven back by adverse winds. Baker is more specific. In his version the king made landfall at Chepstow on an unspecified date but then reboarded with the intention of taking refuge in Lundy Island in the Severn estuary. He describes it recognizably as defended by formidable cliffs, the sole approach steep and only passable by two men at a time, but well watered and provisioned. In the event storms prevented Edward and his few companions from reaching this haven.[21]

The waterborne escape of the king and his little entourage is both confirmed and accurately dated by a chamber account now in the library of the Society of Antiquaries. This shows that the the king was afloat between Chepstow and Cardiff for six days. On Sunday, 19 October, he was still at Chepstow, on the Monday he was at sea (*en la meer*), arriving at Cardiff on Saturday the twenty-fifth. A Canterbury-based account adds the information that about this time Edward sent two friars to the queen asking for the lives of those who were with him in the ship. The queen replied, but to what effect is not divulged.[22] Meanwhile her army advanced to Bristol where it prepared to invest the town and castle, defended by the elder Despenser, who had been sent to command the forces of the southwestern shires.[23] But, records Baker, although the place was well munitioned, desperation compelled Despenser to surrender himself to the mercy of that virago Isabella. On 27 October, he was given a summary "trial" before William Trussell of Peatling Magna,[24] chosen for the occasion as judge, in the presence of the earls of Lancaster, Norfolk, and Kent, and of Roger Mortimer, Thomas Wake, and others. The Gervase continuator says that he was drawn by horses through the town, then suspended on the gallows in his armour with arms reversed. His decapitated body was left there, his head being carried on a spear to Winchester.[25]

The Pauline annalist provides Earl Despenser's sentence in French to the effect that he had made a law that men could be condemned without right of reply; as a traitor he had been banished by the assent of the king and the barons and he had not been reconciled; he had accroached power and counselled the king to disinherit and to break the laws, as in the case of Thomas of Lancaster, whom he had caused to be put to death for no reason; he had been such a robber that all the people demanded vengeance; he had counselled the king to deprive the prelates of the Church, not allowing their customary franchises. For the treason he was to be drawn, for the robbery hung, and for his offences against the Church beheaded and his head taken to Winchester where – contrary to reason – he was earl. In that he had deprived men of their honour and dignity, his head was to be dishonoured; in that he had dishonoured chivalry and hung men with "quartered coats," he was to be hung with his quartered coat and his arms destroyed for all time. One of the few chroniclers to speak up on his behalf is the canon of Bridlington.[26] Thus Isabella took her revenge on one of the slightly less noxious of her enemies. While at Bristol, on 26 October, in the presence of the bishops – now with the addition of Ayrminne of Norwich – of Henry of Lancaster, and of other leaders of her army, proclamation was made to the effect that as the king was "extra regnum," the young duke of Aquitaine, with the assent of "the whole community of the realm," was appointed "custos regni." This title continued in use until 20 November, the date of the transfer of the great seal, thus providing a convenient fiction for administrative purposes.[27]

The king's precipitate departure from London on 2 October had left a vacuum. It had also sealed his fate, though that was not yet apparent. His intention had been to raise forces in Wales, but this and other elements of his strategic plan failed to materialize.[28] Hamo de Chigwell, the mayor, was one of the judges who had condemned Roger Mortimer and had been supported by Edward, so his position was a parlous one. Many of the Londoners, freed from restraint, took up arms and bound themselves to put to death any who opposed the queen or encroached on their liberties.[29] They rose in a body on 15 October, promising to maintain the queen's cause to the death and to destroy the enemies of the realm. A large crowd advanced to the Guildhall and to the house of the Friars Preachers where Geoffrey le Scrope, Walter de Norwich, Hervy de Staunton, and others had been staying.[30] Everyone in authority who could be found was made to swear to uphold the city's cause. The mayor – forced to kneel with his hands clasped in supplication, for fear of instant despatch[31] – the dean of St Paul's, the official of the Court of Canterbury, the dean of Arches, the abbots of Westminster and Stratford (Langthorne), the justices and clerks, all were received "into the protection of the city." The plaque that Thomas of Lancaster had had painted and hung in St. Paul's was replaced on its pillar, thus reversing an order given by the king some three years before. The Dominican friars, said to be unpopular for their pride and haughty behaviour, but no doubt primarily for the favour shown them by Edward II, were forced, apart from some three or four, to flee from their house at Baynard's Castle in Ludgate. The treasurer, the stubbornly loyal Archbishop Melton, was in the North, but Walter de Norwich, the chief baron, continued to attest exchequer writs in his absence, though predictably routine work was curtailed.[32]

The luckless John le Marshal, a familiar and "secretary" of the younger Despenser, hence accounted a spy, was prised from his house and beheaded in Cheap. The same day, 15 October, Walter Stapeldon, so one version of the story runs, hearing of the tumult, armed with a royal commission, required the mayor to surrender the keys of the gates.[33] This proved too much for Chigwell and for the mutinous populace. The bishop was set upon and beheaded together with

William Walle, described as his "nephew," and John de Padington, one of his squires.[34] The following day the rioters caught and killed Stapeldon's treasurer at Holywell outside the city gates. Had Stephen Gravesend,[35] the bishop of London, been found he could have been taken for a spy and forced to suffer the same fate. The whole city erupted. Robert Baldock's manor of Finsbury and the treasure he had lodged in St Paul's were pillaged, as was that of the earl of Arundel in the priory of Holy Trinity. Stapeldon's property outside Temple Bar was ransacked along with the house of the Bardi, where the younger Despenser had left deposits. The property of John de Charlton and William de Cliff suffered the same fate. William, one of Despenser's clerks, was kinsman to Henry de Cliff, keeper of the rolls of chancery, who was with the queen at Hereford by 20 November. Although, thanks to Despenser's efforts, the Tower had been left in a good state of defence it was attacked and taken. [36] The keys of the city were entrusted nominally to the king's young son John of Eltham. All the male prisoners were carried off to the sound of trumpets (*tube*). Mortimer's sons, Bartholomew Burghersh, Lady Badlesmere and her son Giles, Maurice de Berkeley (the younger) and his brother were among those freed and forced to swear the oath to the city.[37] The constable was ordered to keep safely the younger Despenser's wife and other ladies imprisoned there pending an order by the king, queen, and her son.[38]

This was indeed the season of the "Riffleres." The mayor, aldermen, and more senior citizens were in no position to curb the rumbustious excesses of the youthful element in the population, nor did they make any attempt to do so. The ecclesiastical courts ceased to function for almost a year and neither the mayor nor the sheriffs of London ventured to hold their pleas.[39] Only later was an (undated) ordinance issued for the maintenance of the king's peace. This condemned rioting and disturbance, as well as the "riffling" that had been so prevalent. Freedom for people to enter the city was insisted upon, with the exception of the John Charlton whose property had previously been ransacked. It would seem that he was unpopular because at the end of June 1326 he had been entrusted by the king with the regulation of the export of wool – none could leave the kingdom except under his letters testifying that it had been purchased in a Staple town.[40] Those coming in the queen's company were to be helped, but no one was to attack people or to take their goods, on the excuse that they were the king's enemies. The king's officers, his judges and ministers were not to be placed in peril under pain of forfeiture. Geoffrey le Scrope, who had ignominiously fled the city for fear of his life but would now be entering it on the queen's business, was not to be molested.[41]

At Hereford on 6 November, John Stratford had been made deputy treasurer since Treasurer Melton, who wished to distance himself from the distasteful political proceedings, remained in his diocese, unlikely to come south to resume his duties. Stratford's commission was issued in the king's name but under the seal of the duke of Aquitaine. Having been greeted by Mayor Chigwell and a crowd of Londoners on his arrival in London on 14 November, he commenced his duties three days later.[42] The constable, John Weston, was forced to surrender the keys of the Tower, which continued under the nominal guardianship of the juvenile John of Eltham. Another writ, of the same date as Stratford's, ordered John Gisors and Richard Betoyne to act as guardians of the city. Betoyne, Isabella's partisan, replaced Chigwell as mayor. Both appointees had been implicated in Mortimer's escape; their reward was immediate.[43]

It had become clear that no serious opposition to Isabella and Mortimer could be expected. The triumphant army crossed the Severn to Hereford. Much of November was spent in that town, where the queen lodged in the bishop's palace. Henry of Lancaster, Rhys ap Hywel, newly released from the Tower, and others, including the sons of Llywelyn Bren whose father, as we have seen, had been put to death as a traitor by Despenser in 1318, were despatched to find the king. The Welshmen knew the terrain; even so, some bribery of their fellow countrymen was apparently required, at least according to Baker. The king, who had arrived at Caerphilly (Caerffili) Castle on 26 October and remained there for several days, was to be found at Neath Abbey in Glamorgan between 5 and 10 November, when the abbot went with others to treat unsuccessfully with the queen. It appears that he was captured at Llantrissant not far away on the sixteenth, the day of a terrible storm. With him, or nearby, were captured a small band that included the knights Thomas Wyther and John Beck – both of whom were former associates of Thomas of Lancaster – John Blount, John Smale, Simon of Redyng, Chancellor Robert Baldock, Robert Holden – Edward's faithful controller of the wardrobe – and the younger Despenser.[44] Orleton was later to argue, perhaps disingenuously, that the king was a captive of Despenser and came willingly to his relative, the earl of Lancaster.[45] The bishop was certainly in a position to know what happened, for he met the returning party of prisoners at Monmouth, whither he was sent to collect the great seal. In the official account the king is said to have placed it in the custody of Sir William Blount, a member of his household, who returned with the bishop to "Martleye" (Much Marcle) on 26 November. On 30 November, the feast of St Andrew, the queen was present at Cirencester Abbey, where William Ayrminne, the bishop of Norwich, was given custody.[46]

Edmund FitzAlan, the earl of Arundel, was captured by John Charlton, a man who had previously abandoned his loyalty to Edward in order to join Mortimer, though later restored to royal favour. Charlton had a score to settle with the earl. Arundel had been in the rival de la Pole camp – the losing side – in the long-continuing struggle between these Marcher families. Arundel, moreover, had enjoyed a chequered career. Temporarily siding with the opposition barons during the revolt of 1321–22, he subsequently acted as one of Lancaster's judges. The Bridlington chronicler says he was put to death at Shrewsbury; more correctly it was at Hereford, as the Pauline annalist and others record. Baker claims that it was at the instance of Roger Mortimer that Arundel, John Daniel, and Thomas Micheldever were beheaded. Certainly Mortimer was Arundel's rival in parts of the March and in 1321 had seized his castle of Clun. Particularly damning was the fact that Arundel's son had married a daughter of the younger Despenser.[47]

Meanwhile, the victors made the most of the capture of the king and his associates. Edward himself, under the custodianship of Henry of Lancaster, was sent
from Monmouth Castle to Kenilworth, which he reached on 5 December, [48] The
others were to endure barbarous torments before their deaths mercifully
released them. There are various accounts of the ill treatment suffered by
Despenser, Redyng, and Baldock, the most circumstantial being those of the
Leicester chronicler, Knighton, the Pauline annalist, and the Gervase continuator.[49] The captives were escorted towards Hereford by Henry de Leybourn and
Robert de Stanegrave. There they were met by Thomas Wake, Jean de Hainault,
and their soldiers. The whole countryside came for the spectacle, sounding
trumpets and shouting at the "traitors" whom they dragged from their horses.
Despenser's clothes were removed and a tunic substituted with his arms
reversed, a crown of nettles was placed on his head, and on his bare shoulders –
both to the right and left (*dextera parte atque sinistra*) – was written the familiar verse from the Magnificat: "He has put down the mighty from their seat and
hath exalted the humble." In similar vein on his chest was inscribed verses from
one of the psalms beginning "Why do you glory in ill doing?" After Despenser
came his standard bearer, Simon de Redyng, carrying Despenser's banner
reversed. Baldock was likewise made to wear a tabard bearing his arms similarly reversed. Entering the city they were met by screaming women, especially
poor little things (*pauperculis*), who pelted them with rubbish. There is no
necessity to elaborate the terrible punishments meted out to Despenser and
Redyng but as these provide an indication of the brutality of the victors, the
most elaborate of contemporary accounts can be noted. Both Jean de Bel and
later Froissart were to repeat the details at great length.[50] Baldock and Prior
Irby, Orleton's *bête noire*, were claimed by the bishop as clerics. As for the tur-
bulent Irby, whom we have already encountered,[51] he was to spend much time
in episcopal prisons, being still incarcerated at Worcester in 1334. Baldock, sentenced to perpetual imprisonment, was taken to Orleton's London house, Mon-
talt, and from there snatched by a London mob, on the pretext that the right to
have a gaol belonged solely to the city. He died, horribly abused, in Newgate.[52]

The Bridlington chronicler alone finds space for a shortened Latin form of the
indictment of the younger Despenser. The more extended French version, incorporating the names of those who lost lands, possessions, or liberty as a consequence of Despenser's actions, is to be found in various manuscripts, six of
which have been collated by John Taylor.[53] It is an ingenuous document, another piece of propaganda that puts the blame for all the ills of the reign on one man
and his father, branding them and the courageous Harclay as traitors and – understandably in the circumstances – ignoring the traitorous behaviour of Lancaster,
the Marchers, and others who actually fought against the king. In the first place
Despenser, as his father had been, was condemned for his return after permanent
banishment and for the piracy he engaged in during that time by ransacking two
foreign vessels (dromonds) to the tune of sixty thousand livres esterlins. The

Despensers, it was alleged, had attracted royal power to themselves and, with Harclay, despoiled such worthy men as the earl of Hereford, William de Sully, Roger de Burfield (Berefeld), as well as others who had fallen at Boroughbridge. He had procured the death of the earl of Lancaster and those of others at Pontefract and York and had taken their goods. He had been responsible for the king's campaign against the Scots (Bannockburn), which had brought the loss of twenty-thousand men. On the return journey the queen had been abandoned at Tynemouth as the enemy flowed round her, while at Blackhow (in 1322) he had placed the king in the hands of the Scots. Thus, thanks to his counsel the queen could well have been lost, exposed as she was to the perils of the sea. The bishops of Hereford, Lincoln, Ely, and Norwich he had despoiled of their property, including horses, harness, and gold and silver vessels. He had induced the king, to his disinheritance, to grant the earldom of Winchester to his (Despenser's) father, that of Carlisle to Harclay. He had ejected the queen from the lands that her husband had given her and had sent a substantial sum of money to his accomplices in France to impede her return. When the queen and her followers had landed happily he had led the king out of the realm, to his dishonour, taking with him the seal and much treasure. One important section is not included in the Latin version. This refers to the staging of "false quarrels," regardless of the fact that such "confederations" were contrary to the estate of the king and Crown. Further, by his "royal power" he had forced into prison those, such as Henry de Beaumont, who had refused to undertake an oath to him.[54] Thus Despenser was the principal villain of the piece; for the time being the attitude towards Edward of those in authority had not been declared, perhaps not even determined.

Caerphilly Castle alone held out, besieged by William la Zouche de Mortimer with the aid of four hundred Welsh footmen. It was finally surrendered early in April 1327 by its redoubtable constable, John de Felton, who held out for a promise of the life of Hugh, the son of the younger Despenser. One wonders why Edward had not remained there rather than wandering about with scant hope of repelling those searching for him. In the castle he had abandoned a vast array of treasure, armour, and personal possessions, a welcome windfall for the new government.[55]

CONSOLIDATING THE NEW REGIME

The queen and her supporters had enjoyed astonishing and rapid success; a success that was celebrated at Wallingford in conjunction with the Christmas festival.[56] Present at the rejoicing over their achievement and for a discussion of future tactics were Archbishop Reynolds – carried along by the whirlwind of events – the two lawyer bishops, Orleton and Stratford, the keeper of the seal, Ayrminne, bishop of Norwich,[57] together with many nobles, including the earl of Lancaster, as he was now acknowledged to be, though not formally, the earl of Kent, and John of Eltham "*od bele compaignie des gentz de Londres*."[58] Various problems must have been discussed, including the future status of the king, but the most urgent was to salvage the queen's moral reputation. An excuse had to be found for her failure to return to the king in derogation of the sacrament of marriage. Orleton, he himself tells us, was given the task.[59] He did so by claiming publicly that were the queen to rejoin the king she would be in danger of physical violence, a fear she had expressed in a letter of 5 February 1326 sent from Paris, the text of which the bishop was able to produce.[60] This concern for the queen's marital status, as we shall see, was to be discussed again early in 1327. After Mortimer's fall three years later an item of the indictment against him was that it was he who had been responsible for promoting this idea of the king's violent behaviour.[61]

Now that Edward was imprisoned there was scant sign of resistance. Order was being established in the administration, if not in the country, where malefactors were eager to take advantage of the situation by pretending to act on behalf of the queen.[62] A deputy treasurer and a custodian of the great seal had been appointed, while the chancery records had been brought from Swansea Castle and entrusted to Henry de Cliff. For the time being the government of London had been settled. So speedy had the "revolution" been that, unaware of the crucial turn of events, two papal envoys, the archbishop of Vienne and M. John Grandisson, archdeacon of Nottingham but shortly to be provided to the see of Exeter, arrived at Dover on 10 December under a safe conduct issued on 30 November.[63] They had instructions to negotiate peace between England and France. While kept waiting they were able to celebrate Christmas and call vividly to mind an archbishop who had suffered at the hands of temporal authority. Grandisson was the celebrant at mass at the feretory of St Thomas the Martyr in Canterbury Cathedral, on the feast of his passion (29 December). Subsequently he celebrated at the high altar and afterwards conducted Vespers from the archbishop's seat in the presbytery. As far as the government was concerned, the nuncios were an embarrassment, but to antagonize them would have been unwise. They were kept away from London until the queen herself was installed in the capital. Isabella arrived on 4 January 1327 and processed through the city with great pomp (*magna solennitate*). The bishop of London, Stephen Gravesend, acting as dean of the province, had on 20 December issued a mandate, reciting that of Reynolds dated 20 July, for a council to be held at St Paul's on 16 January. The intention of the nuncios was to raise a subsidy for action against Louis of Bavaria, whom the pope did not wish to acknowledge as emperor. Significantly Bishop Stratford excused himself from attendance. The nuncios were told that a great rift between the barons and other difficulties meant that nothing could be offered, and so, "quasi timorati," as they were once again described by the Pauline annalist, they recrossed the channel on 26 January, by which time there had been startling political changes.[64]

It had become clear that there was remarkably little residual support for the king. Even the bishops, with few exceptions, had arrived at a measure of accommodation with Isabella. We do not know when the decision was made to replace Edward with his son, but it could well have been over Christmas at Wallingford. What is clear is that Bishops Orleton and Stratford were largely responsible for the quasi-legal aspect of the proceedings, although the precise responsibility of each of them was later disputed. In order to make the change of kingship acceptable there was some playing to the "assent of the people" and to as wide a representative section of the country as possible, but the power behind the scenes was that of Mortimer, Lancaster, and other barons, assisted by a quorum of bishops. The "Lancastrians" were in the ascendant, taking advantage of the strong tide of reaction against the death of Thomas of Lancaster. His glaring faults and his treachery were conveniently forgotten. Instead, plans were being made for his canonization. For similar reasons Edward in his turn would be a candidate for the odour of sanctity. A catastrophic fall from greatness and an unpleasant death were of considérable assistance.

One matter had been decided before the king's capture. On 28 October 1326 parliament was summoned, in the king's name, for 14 December, but on the seventh it was prorogued until 7 January in the new year. Finally it did assemble on that day in the presence of the queen and her son but in the absence of the king, for which the summons had made allowance. The problem facing those now in power was many-faceted. Were the king to be removed, a prospect previously threatened at least once by the barons, he ought in all justice to be permitted to answer the charges against him. Yet if the king did come to parliament there was the possibility that his situation might arouse sympathy. It would make the process easier and less fraught were the king in the remoteness of Kenilworth to be persuaded to agree to his replacement. The whole procedure would require consummate stage management so as to give the impression of widespread consent to a thoroughly desirable, well-justified change, endorsed however reluctantly by a king on whom it was forced. Another aspect was the queen's marital problem. This, Dene informs us, was addressed as at Wallingford by Orleton who, with the support of many bishops, declared on the very first day of the parliamentary proceedings that were she to return to the king she would be killed by him.[65] Baker, whose appraisal of this situation must be treated with caution since he regards Edward as a quasi-martyr, paints a different picture. This "servant of God" could not stop loving a wife unwilling to come to him, of whose embraces he had been deprived for more than a year, but who would not allow him to see his son or any of his children. He was as another Orpheus. Baker continues by suggesting that it was as a consequence of the queen's fear of being forced to return to her husband that Orleton advised the removal of her husband from the custody of Lancaster.[66]

There were two delegations to the imprisoned king at Kenilworth, the first to persuade Edward to attend parliament, or at least to put in a token appearance, the second to secure his renunciation of the kingship and to rupture the ties of homage.[67] Eastry, the prior of Canterbury, writes in a contemporary letter of a first mission of two bishops to secure the king's presence and advises that since the king had not responded positively another mission should be sent for the same purpose. But what actually transpired he wished to know rather than to witness and himself declined to attend parliament.[68] Four main near-contemporary chronicle accounts of the deposition have survived, those of Geoffrey le Baker, William Dene, and of the anonymous compilers of a section of the so-called Lanercost Chronicle and of the Canterbury chronicle now at Trinity College, Cambridge.[69] These accounts have been examined minutely elsewhere, with the conclusion that they are by no means fully reconcilable.[70] Both Baker and Dene were strongly loyalist. For them the whole procedure was distinctly distasteful. Baker calls the assembly the parliament of the queen regnant (*regina regnans*), but Dene remarks on the vast numbers that flocked to it, not only the prelates, earls, and barons, but also the "people" and especially the London citizens.[71] In writing of the Kenilworth delegation (or delegations) Baker considers Stratford, Orleton, and Burghersh to have been the chief negotiators (*college principales negocii tractandi*). Burghersh's name is added because Baker regarded him with Orleton as an *alumpnus Jezebel*, co-author of a deep-laid conspiracy. Elsewhere he is not ascribed any role. Dene has Hothum, bishop of Ely, instead of Burghersh.[72]

For the present purpose it will be sufficient to examine some of the relevant parliamentary proceedings and the meetings with the imprisoned king in more cursory fashion, concentrating to some extent on the political addresses of the bishops. The impression given by three of the accounts is that the bishops, notably Orleton and Stratford, were prime movers in the affair. Their function and that of Reynolds, now converted to the queen's cause and anxious to make his peace with the powers that be, was to explain in politically inspired "sermons" the necessity of replacing the king. We know the gist of what was said from the Gervase continuator, who alone gives a thumbnail sketch of each of the three addresses. According to him the first to speak was Orleton on the text "Where there is no ruler the people falls."[73] In this he explained the reason for his journey with others to Kenilworth, and how he commenced his exposition to the king by calling on him to hear the prayers of his people.[74] Edward had permitted many intolerable failings (*defectus*), adhered to evil counsel, and to a traitor. He had even destroyed the nobles of the realm, and had miserably lost Crown lands left to him by his illustrious father. Consequently it pleased the prelates and nobles to replace him with his son, if he would consent. Although the king replied that he had followed such counsel as the lords had given, he expressed sorrow for those failings about which the envoys had complained. Eventually he gave his consent and the homages were annulled. After Orleton had finished, Stratford expressed a wish to speak, and took the text "My head is sick" (*Capud meum doleo*).[75] Understanding by the "head" that of the king who is "caput regni," he alleged that if the head were bad so would be governance, and it would affect the rest, as in the poet's saying, "Where the head is weak the other members suffer" (*cui capud infirmum cetera membra dolent*). There followed an interval for Thomas Wake's theatrical appeal to the "people" but addressed, we must conclude, only to those assembled in parliament.[76] Then came the final address, that of Reynolds, which provided the climax: it is commented on below. The implication here is that the king had "resigned" prior to Orleton's arrival at parliament.

The ascription of texts to the various bishops is not consistent, nor is the order in which they delivered their addresses. The Lanercost chronicler, although he agrees with the Gervase continuator about the order of speakers, thought that delivery extended to three days, the third concluding (on 15 January 1327) with Reynolds's exposition of the explosive text "Vox populi vox Dei." The important point is that on the thirteenth, by popular acclamation, the king was deposed. The Gervase continuator, whose account is significantly different from all the others, is very precise about this. For him the active participants are only prelates and magnates, doubtless a realistic view. A unique feature of his version of events is the part said to have been played in parliament by Roger Mortimer, who is scarcely, if at all, mentioned elsewhere,[77] although doubtless assumed to be acting behind the scenes. In the great hall at Westminster, as the magnates' spokesman, Mortimer announced to the "people" what had been determined. He disclaimed any personal blame, alleging that he made the pronouncement with "the common assent of all." He then declared that the magnates had unanimously determined that the king should no longer have the governance of the realm, since he was insufficient, a destroyer of the barons, and of Holy Church against his [coronation] oath, in all of which he had acquiesced in evil counsel. His eldest son, the duke of Aquitaine, should reign in his stead if the people gave their assent. Thomas Wake, who had been in the forefront of Isabella's supporters, vociferously responded, his hands extended: "As far as I am concerned he shall no longer reign" (*dico pro me nunquam regnabit*). At that point, writes Dene, "Ave rex in excelsis" was declaimed, but Bishop Hethe of Rochester refused to shout with the others or to sing "Gloria laus et honor regi novo," and there was danger that he might be crushed to death. Doubtless the chronicler had this information directly from his diocesan. The Gervase continuator concludes his account by giving an inkling of the archbishop's address on the theme "Vox populi vox Dei." "You," he declares in French, "have for long suffered divers oppressions at the hands of the king and his evil councillors. You have therefore clamoured to God for a suitable remedy. And at this very instant your voice has been heard, as is clear, because by the unanimous consent of the magnates King Edward is deprived of the governance of the realm and his son put in his place – provided you are in unanimous agreement." When Reynolds had finished all the people gave their consent; raising their hands they clamoured "Fiat, fiat, Amen." Clearly the "people" referred to here, addressed in French and responding in Latin, were once again not the common crowd.

The Gervase continuator follows the archbishop's peroration with the text of William Trussell's renunciation of homage as proctor of the prelates, earls, barons, and others named in his proxy, details of which are lacking. This outcome was promptly proclaimed throughout London. Dene's version, on the contrary, claims that the nettle was firmly grasped at the outset with Orleton as the prime mover. On the first day of the parliament (7 January), he says, the bishop put the question "whom did they wish to rule, the king, or his son?" (*quem mallent regnare patrem regem al[ioquin] filium?*) Those present were to answer the following day after breakfasting. Some responded from the heart, some from fear, while others, frightened of the Londoners, were unwilling to reply at all. Eventually they shouted as if in unison for the son. In the great hall of Westminster homage was then performed, Edward being led in to the words "Ecce rex vester." The archbishop delivered his address on the theme "Vox Dei vox populi," Stratford following with "Cuius caput infirmus cetera membra dolent" and Orleton concluded with "Woe to the land whose king is a boy" (*Ve terre cuius rex puer est*) – not, as he was constrained to argue later, a reference to Edward III but to the puerilities of his father.[78]

For what happened at Kenilworth shortly after the opening of parliament Baker professed to have had as his authority a certain knight, Thomas de la More, to whom at one time a separate chronicle was attributed.[79] More, whose surname was Laurence, was a relative (*nepos*) of Bishop Stratford in whose suite he travelled to Kenilworth and in whose service he later reappears.[80] Baker tells us that he based this part of his chronicle on More's eyewitness account written in French. According to this the bishops of Winchester and Lincoln, in Lancaster's presence, secretly asked the king to resign his Crown to his son, guilefully promising that afterwards there would be no diminution of the honour paid to him. In the manner of Caiphas it was suggested that he would gain merit with God for thus securing peace for his subjects. This was coupled with the threat that should he not agree, the people, having repudiated him and his sons, might elevate in his stead someone not of royal blood. Whether Mortimer was ever considered for the role is unlikely. It was too dangerous, but doubtless Edward appreciated the possibility. Faced with this prospect the king, with many tears and sighs, declared that he would sooner end his life in Christ than disinherit his sons or continue to witness disturbance in the realm, knowing that a good shepherd gives his life for his sheep.[81]

This was the cue for Orleton's entrance – that monstrous ambassador (*infandus ambassiator*) who ceremoniously arranged the other members of the delegation in order of dignity.[82] Edward in his turn appeared from a private chamber clothed in a black robe. Overcome by the knowledge of the delegation's purpose, he swooned. Half dead he was raised from the floor by Lancaster and Stratford.[83] On the king's recovery Orleton explained their purpose, impudently unabashed at so afflicting the mind of the king, to whom he was of all men the most odious. He repeated the threat said to have been uttered initially by Stratford and Burghersh, that if he did not resign the Crown to his son they might choose someone more suitable. The king, says Baker, wept at the idea that the people were so exasperated with him as to reject his rule. Finally he agreed that his son should succeed.[84] The next day homage and allegiance were renounced by William Trussell, knight, on behalf of the whole realm,[85] and

Thomas le Blount, steward of his household, broke his staff of office. Edward was now merely a private person. Its task accomplished, the delegation returned to parliament. With respect to the promises supposedly made to the former king, Baker ruefully remarks that to the queen so much dower was assigned that barely a third of what pertained to the Crown remained for her son and Queen Philippa. As for Edward of Caernarfon, Isabella, the bishop of Hereford (a gratuitous addition), and Roger Mortimer allowed him a hundred marks a month from the royal fisc.[86]

Much constitutional significance has been deduced from the group sent to Kenilworth to renounce homage.[87] Its composition has been variously reported. Dene gives no precise numbers but says that it consisted of three bishops – London, Ely, and Hereford – two earls, two barons, and various envoys (*certi nuncii*) from the communities of the counties and of the Cinque ports (*de ... quinque portibus*) acting for all the realm (*vice omnium de regno*). Lanercost is more precise. There were twenty-four persons in all, rather curiously selected, viz. two each of the following: bishops (Stratford and Orleton), earls (Lancaster and Warenne), barons (Ross and Courtenay), abbots, priors, justices, Dominicans, Carmelites, knights from beyond Trent, knights from this side of Trent, London citizens, men from the [Cinque?] ports.[88] The Franciscans were not included at the queen's request, so that they would not be bearers of such displeasing information "quia Minores multum amabat."[89] Murimuth's composition of the unnamed deputation is different again: three bishops, two earls, two abbots, four barons, two knights from every county in England, and a certain number of persons from London, other cities and large towns, and from the ports.[90] This would surely have been an impossibly large body. What is clear is that the deposition was carried through by the prelates and barons, but that to bolster their decision as wide a section of the populace as possible was committed to accepting what had already been accomplished supposedly on behalf of the whole community of the realm. We have no information about how these "representatives" were chosen.

As has been shown, in the Gervase continuator's version of events Mortimer is said to have announced the reasons for the royal deposition, while Reynolds in his address declared that the king's oppressions were the reasons for the change of kingship. It so happens that a set of articles justifying Edward's deposition has been preserved. According to Bishop Orleton, John Stratford was present at their formulation, and he had them incorporated into a public instrument by his notary, William Mees. Moreover, according to a London chronicle "*plousours articles encountre le roy*," presumably these, were published on 13 January 1327 at Westminster by the archbishop before the whole of the baronage.[91] There is nothing surprising about these six articles. They are preserved in Lambeth MS 1213, from which they were edited with other material by Sir Roger Twysden, and also in the Winchester Cartulary. Firstly, the person of the king was declared to be insufficient for government, since throughout his time he had been controlled by others, who had counselled him badly, to the dishonour of the law, the destruction of the Church, and that of all his people. He had failed to remedy what was wrong when requested by the great and the wise of the land, or to permit amends to be made. In the second place, throughout his time he had not paid attention to good counsel or the government of the realm but had given himself to unsuitable occupations. In the third place, by defect of good government he had lost Scotland and other territories in Gascony and Ireland, although his father had left them in peace and been on terms of friendship with the king of France and other great persons. Fourthly, through his haughtiness, and by bad counsel, he had destroyed Holy Church and imprisoned churchmen. Others had been left in distress, while nobles had suffered death, imprisonment, exile, or disinheritance. Fifthly, although by his oath he was obliged to do right to all, he had not wished to do so, considering instead his own profit and covetousness and that of his close councillors. Nor had he kept the other elements of the oath made at his coronation. Finally, he had damaged his realm, leaving it and his people as lost. Worse still, by his cruelty and the defects of his person he is seen to be incorrigible, without hope of reform. All of this is so notorious as not to be gainsaid.[92]

Stubbs drew attention to the precedent of the deposition of Adolf of Nassau, king of the Romans, in 1298. There are striking similarities, but although this event may well have been remembered by the English barons, or at any rate by Stratford and the other bishops, that it provided any sort of a pattern for Edward's deposition is unlikely. Stubbs also commented that the sins of kings "are rather the justification than the cause of their rejection," particularly when a rival is in a position to assume the kingship.[93] More recently it has been suggested that canon law may have provided the inspiration as it is believed to have done in the case of Richard II at the close of the century.[94] Orleton was trained in canon law and regularly invoked it. In Edward's case it is easy to see a congruence between the articles given above and his conduct, so the cause was clear enough and the justification convincing. Certainly the availability of an undisputed heir made the changeover relatively simple, though to some extent, as will appear, it was complicated by the intervening "reign" of Mortimer and Isabella.

London, having played a crucial part in the queen's success, now came into its own. Oaths had been exacted from many people during the riots of October and the city by the same means saw an opportunity to take a prominent part in the change of government, with an eye to its own interest. On 12 January Mayor Betoyne and the aldermen addressed a letter to the prelates and magnates enquiring as to their willingness to swear an oath, in accord with the city, to maintain the cause of Isabella, to crown her son, and to depose Edward II for his many offences against his (coronation) oath and the Crown. On the following day, that of the proclamation of the new king, a vast crowd of people consented to take the oath. For the most part, they must have been men who were attending the parliament. There were four earls – Norfolk, Kent, Hereford, and Warenne but not Lancaster – with their retinues, twenty-four barons, headed by Roger Mortimer and including Giles de Badlesmere, John Maltravers, Thomas Wake of Liddel, and John de Charlton, a large number of knights, serjeants of the court (*servientes de curia*), and some judges, including Geoffrey le Scrope and John de Stonore, but only a handful of knights of the shire, the archbishops of Canterbury and Dublin, and twelve diocesan bishops. Melton (York), Carlisle (Ross), London (Gravesend), the as yet unconsecrated Exeter (Berkeley), and Durham (Beaumont) are missing,[95] the first three doubtless from contrary conviction. There was also a sprinkling of abbots and priors of the greater houses,[96] mainly local. There were a number of clerks, most of them *magistri*, including the official of the Court of Canterbury, no fewer than thirty men classed as barons of the Cinque ports, five from Bury St Edmunds, and thirteen burgesses of St Albans.[97] Why these burgesses were in London is not clear, although those from Bury St. Edmunds could have come in connection with the town's violent dispute with the abbey. Dene pauses to mention the depredations conducted at Abingdon and at Bury, where the abbot was abducted and kept in captivity abroad for three years.[98] Another oath is said to have been administered on the twentieth, by which time the young Edward is styled "king." This was taken by the archbishop and seven other bishops. Reynolds was unpopular in the city for many alleged offences (*obprobria et convicia multa sustinuit*), so to ameliorate the hostility he made a gift of wine as a peace-offering. It availed him little, for on leaving the hall he was badly roughed up (*male depressus fuit quod turpiter accidit sibi*).[99]

The political revolution was effectively accomplished. The king had surrendered his Crown, in the realization that there was no alternative. The young Edward, just over fourteen, was knighted by Jean de Hainault and on 1 February 1327 the coronation took place, the details of which are provided by Dene. Isabella judiciously absented herself by spending three days at Eltham Palace. Archbishop Reynolds crowned and anointed Edward. During the ceremony John de Sully posed the question to Bishop Hethe of Rochester: "Did the king wish to maintain the law that his people chose?" (*an rex legem quam populus suus elegit custodire vellet?*).[100] To this the bishop responded "that unless he had first taken the oath to keep the laws, he would not be crowned" (*Episcopus querenti respondens quod alioquin non coronabitur nisi prius prestet iuramentum de servando leges*). Bishops Gravesend and Stratford helped the king, on account of his tender age, by holding the crown above his head. He was then conducted to a seat in the monastic quire well above the crush of people. The bishops of Norwich and Rochester sang the Litany. and following the service all the bishops retired to the tents provided for their refreshment. *Et sic post multos horrores nocturnos sol ortus est anglis*: "And so, after many nocturnal horrors, the sun has risen on the English."[101]

THE NEW KING, ANOTHER ARTHUR

We read that Arthur, king of the Britons was admitted to rule the realm at fifteen years of age. As an indication of his devotion he carried a picture of Virgin painted on his shield. This young king now raised to the throne out of pure devotion reverently bears engraved on the seat of his heart the likeness of the Blessed Virgin, whose sweet-sounding name is often in his mouth.[102]

Parliament resumed its sitting on 3 February, thus constituting the first parliament of Edward III's reign. One urgent matter it dealt with was the annulment of all fines, sales, and gifts of land and recognizances made "per vim et duriciam" to the Despensers, Edmund, earl of Arundel, Robert Baldock, or Walter Stapeldon, justices being assigned to effect this.[103] The proceedings against Thomas of Lancaster were reversed, and a law passed against the alienation of lands held in chief. There was a flood of petitions, stretching according to Dene from the time of King John.[104] Everyone was clamouring to attract the favour of Isabella and Mortimer. Inevitably many were disappointed for, as the disgruntled Dene claims, all the greater and lesser offices were disposed of at the queen's nod (*ad nutum regine*). From this time, he considered, stemmed thoughts of resistance to Isabella and Mortimer but in secret for fear of the Londoners.[105] There are two versions of the petitions, that printed in the *Rolls of Parliament*, and that collated from unofficial records or their copies transcribed in the *Rotuli Parliamentorum Inediti*. The petitions from the unofficial records have been roughly divided into categories: clerical *gravamina*, encroachment on franchises pertaining to the bishopric of Durham, the liberties of London, principally entered on a roll containing forty-four articles, and the general petitions of the community of the realm, including those of many barons, their widows, and others who felt themselves wronged by the Despenser regime. Analysis of these petitions is overdue; but it is clear not only that London was taking full advantage of its position, accentuated by the fact that the crucial parliamentary assembly met at adjacent Westminster, but also that a great variety of Contrariants or their widows, and indeed bishops, were endeavouring to recoup the losses they had suffered as a consequence of actions attributed to the Despensers and Baldock. Some of the bishops had suffered from royal "custodians" of their temporalities, from the king's encroachment on presentations, or from theft of their goods.[106]

The *Brut* has it that "at the king's crowning" a council of "twelve great lords of England" was appointed "without which nothing should be done." This council consisted of the archbishops of Canterbury and York, the bishops of Winchester and Hereford, the earls of Lancaster, Norfolk (the earl marshal), Kent, and Warenne, and the barons Thomas Wake, Henry Percy, Oliver Ingham, and John Roos or Ros. Lancaster, we are told elsewhere, was made "chief guardian of the king."[107] The rolls of parliament, at the time of the 1330 judgment of Mortimer, state that this council had fourteen (unnamed) members, six of them barons. At least four members, a bishop, an earl, and two barons were to be permanently at the king's side. The composition of the "*Brut* council" deserves a comment. The four members of the episcopate were Melton, a staunch supporter of Edward II, Reynolds, a vicar of Bray character but because of his office important for the stability of the new government, as well as the masterminds behind the change of kingship, Orleton and Stratford, who once the crisis was over proved mutually incompatible. Two of the earls were uncles of the king. Lancaster could be expected to approve of a means of government advocated by his brother Thomas in different circumstances, while at the other end of the scale as it were – Warenne had suffered substantially at the hands of Thomas. Mortimer was omitted from the council, at his own wish one may suppose, but Oliver Ingham was a strong supporter of his. Wake, Lancaster's son-in-law, had been prominent as a fomenter of popular enthusiasm for abdication, Ros had been branded an enemy by the former king but was now steward of the household,[108] and Henry Percy had arrived early with northern levies in Isabella's camp. The group, not surprisingly, was far from homogeneous, it being necessary to include the various factions, as they were soon seen to be. For some reason the chancellor was not included *ex officio*, either deliberately or because he had not yet been appointed – although that would mean that the council had been agreed upon prior to the coronation. Bishop Hothum was chancellor from 26 January 1327 until superseded by Bishop Burghersh in the summer of 1328. Burghersh remained in office for the remainder of Mortimer and Isabella's hegemony.[109] Stratford, who had been acting as the treasurer's lieutenant until 28 January 1327, was succeeded by Orleton, who in turn relinquished the office in March. As the *Brut* adds, the ordinance was soon ignored "for the king and all the lords that should govern him, were governed and ruled after the king's mother, Dame Isabel, and by Sir Roger de Mortimer; and as they would all things were done, both amongst high and low. And they took unto them castles, towns, lands and rents, in great harm and loss unto the Crown, and of the king's state also, out of measure."[110]

Another indication of the composition of the ruling group is given by those named as testing the charter of liberties for the City of London on 6 March, a few days before the end of the parliamentary session. They are as follows: Archbishop Reynolds, Chancellor Hothum, Bishop Ayrminne, Treasurer Orleton, the earls of Norfolk, Kent, and Lancaster, with the barons Mortimer, Wake, and Roos or Ros. Already on 28 February the citizens had received a charter of pardon for any offences committed after the queen's landing on 24 September until the day of the coronation. This was followed on 4 March by the pardoning of all debts owing to the late king. The charter itself is an extensive document. Among the many concessions was freedom from prises by the constable of the Tower, whether on land or sea, and from providing sailors, ships, or soldiers outside the city: provisions with direct relevance to the recent civil disturbance.[111]

PROBLEMS OLD AND NEW

There were several immediate problems left over from the previous reign. Scotland was the most pressing. In this case the government's hand was forced by raids in the summer of 1327. At the Lincoln Parliament in September arrange-

ments were made for the removal of the exchequer and of the court of King's
Bench to York, the sheriffs of London being instructed to supply suitable con-
tainers for transport.[112] The campaign that ensued resulted in a near disaster to
the king at Stanhope Park. As will we shall see in the appropriate context, at the
instigation of Robert Bruce the extremely unpopular Treaty of Edinburgh was to
be ratified at the Northampton Parliament early in the following year, thus
bringing this long struggle to a temporary conclusion and relieving the North of
perennial devastation. In the case of France action was taken before parliament
dispersed. Bishops Stratford and Ayrminne, together with Jean de Bretagne,
Jean de Hainault, and Hugh d'Audley, were despatched to secure a truce. After
lengthy negotiation an agreement was sealed at Paris on 31 March. It was a cost-
ly arrangement, subsequently much criticized, but the lands in Gascony were to
be restored.[113] Respite was brief. Following the death of Charles IV on 1 February 1328 homage would once again be required. This time the English government initially adopted a belligerent pose by making a claim to the French
throne. The show of bravado was followed by a climb down with Edward's
acceptance of liege homage, at the behest of his mother and Mortimer.[114]

Another urgent problem was to explain the change of kingship to the papacy.
Bishop Orleton, Bartholomew Burghersh, and a highly respected secular clerk, M.
Thomas de Astley, were granted letters of credence on 24 March 1327. The ostensible purpose of the embassy was to secure dispensation for the king's marriage
to Philippa of Hainault, but the pope had expressed to his nuncio Hugh d'Angoulême his eagerness to be informed of the state of affairs in England so that he
could give advice. The bishop set out with an impressive entourage of seventy
men and forty-six horses and claimed expenses for the 299 days from leaving the
court at Westminster until his arrival to make his report at York on 22 January
1328.[115] While Orleton was abroad the bishop of Worcester, Thomas de Cobham,
died. He had been ill for some time, but any suggestion that Orleton had deliberately jeopardized his political future by volunteering to go to the Curia on the off-
chance of furthering his own promotion is unsubstantiated. Whatever Orleton's
wishes, there were good reasons for the pope's concern to advance a fellow
lawyer. After all, the bishop had manfully defended ecclesiastical rights against
Edward's "tyranny," or that of his ministers, and had manifestly suffered in consequence. His provision to the vacant see was only unfortunate in that it prevented the estimable Prior Bransford, the chapter's candidate, from becoming bishop
for another decade. The degree of government irritation demonstrates that neither
Mortimer nor Isabella felt a debt of gratitude to Orleton, a fact that militates
against the frequent assumption that he was a Mortimer man, or, in Baker's terms
a queen's bishop. So far as the government was concerned, Bransford, a local
man, was a nonentity; but an additional reason for opposing Orleton's candidature
could have been a dislike of papal provision without consultation.[116]

The temporary unity of purpose adopted by men of divergent ambitions, character, and goals was thus rapidly disintegrating. The philosophy in justification

of the *coup d'état* emphasized many of the ideas advocated by Thomas of Lancaster. To all intents and purposes the advisory responsibilities of prelates and barons had been a potent factor. True, there were to be frequent parliaments, but these were dominated by Mortimer and his supporters. Henry of Lancaster was being progressively cold-shouldered, while Stratford, having surrendered the treasurership and accomplished his mission abroad, was patently disillusioned by political developments. Orleton in his turn faded from the political though not from the diplomatic scene. In the ascendant was the new chancellor Bishop Burghersh, a man who had not taken a large part in the deposition process but who now became the strongest episcopal supporter of Queen Isabella and of Mortimer. One might be tempted to see in him a new Baldock, but unlike Baldock he was a survivor, as time would prove. Hothum, too, as chancellor for some thirteen months was initially at the centre of government, but if the witnessing of charters is indicative, by 1329 his appearances at court were drastically reduced.[117]

Internal tranquillity was difficult to establish. The continued existence of the king gave rise to moves for his release. Moreover, at the council held at Stamford in April of 1327 it was felt necessary to re-examine the queen's marital situation.[118] In view of these difficulties it is hardly surprising that arrangements were made for Edward's demise under conditions not calculated to see the light of day. Rumours abounded, but there can be little doubt that Mortimer was the prime mover here, possibly with the connivance of Isabella. Hotfoot from Berkeley with news of the former king's death came a messenger to the queen as she attended a parliament in session at Lincoln. With Edward dead, Isabella and Mortimer could arrange for the former king to have a suitably impressive funeral. This took place at St Peter's Abbey in Gloucester on 20 December, the delay being brought about by the Scottish campaign.[119]

The royal funeral was followed with almost indecent haste by the joyous reception in London of Philippa of Hainault. According to the Pauline annalist she arrived with her uncle, Jean, accompanied by Bishops Ayrminne and Orleton, on their way back from diplomatic missions. Murimuth sourly remarks that although Philippa was the daughter of Jeanne, the sister of Philip VI of France, this was of no benefit to the English.[120] The party travelled to York, where Orleton was coldly received and on 24 January 1328 the marriage ceremony took place.[121] Parliament opened on 7 February; before it dispersed on 5 March Burghersh had moved from the treasurership to replace Hothum as chancellor, Roger Northburgh, a long-serving administrator, had become treasurer, though only for a couple of months, and Richard Ayrminne was replaced by Adam Limber, who had been an official of the wardrobe and exchequer.[122] On the surface this looks like a concession to Lancastrian notions of appointments during sessions of parliament. Bishops William Ayrminne and Northburgh were despatched to discuss conditions for a settlement with the Scots. On the final day of the parliament another was summoned to Northampton for 24 April, where the "turpis pax" with Robert Bruce was ratified. This was all done, says Murimuth, at the order of Queen Isabella and Roger Mortimer, and of James Douglas, who had played a prominent part in so many northern raids. Baker predictably adds Orleton. After the marriage of David Bruce and Joan of the Tower, Edward III's sister, celebrated on 12 July at Berwick, Douglas went off to the Spanish frontier to meet his death fighting against the "Infidels."[123]

Murimuth was not the only one to decry this treaty. Baker, although he concedes that peace followed, states that the king was not well guided but led by traitors when he allowed the charter sealed by the community of the Scots and King John Balliol, acknowledging perpetual submission to England, to be carried on a spear and publicly burned at Berwick.[124] According to him the operative faction, Isabella, Orleton, and Mortimer, wished to secure an ally in case the death of Edward II was laid to their charge. Alternatively, should anything bring about the death of the new king, Mortimer with the Scots as allies could usurp the realm – and the queen. This, he thought, was the reason for the killing, in 1330, of the earl of Kent.[125] The *Brut* declared that the "great lords" were against confirming the peace, claiming that only Isabella, Mortimer, and Bishop Hothum of Ely were in favour. Quite apart from a widespread feeling that the efforts of the great warrior Edward I had been wasted, the exclusion of the "disinherited" foreshadowed trouble in the near future.[126] Among such potential troublemakers was Thomas Wake, whose disaffection surely permeated to his father-in-law.

During 1328 Mortimer, with Isabella an unwitting accomplice, was busy digging a pit for his own early destruction. The euphoria that greeted the new king, the terrifying punishment of "evil councillors," were all too easily forgotten, while the full coffers inherited from a grasping regime were emptied with rapidity. Much criticism had been levied by Thomas of Lancaster against those who feathered their own nests at the expense of the royal fisc and of other lords. Mortimer and Isabella proceeded to do just that, he acting as a king oblivious of the fact that his days were numbered.[127] The French chronicle of London takes much the same view: Isabella and Mortimer were encroaching on the power of the magnates of England and Wales, appropriating the treasure of the realm, and holding the young king in subjection.[128] One element in such aggrandizement was the chamber lands. Tout pointed out that following Edward II's reign there was a change of policy with respect to lands previously reserved for the king's chamber. Unpopularity of chamber administration is said to have made it easy to arrange that in future accounting was to be made to the exchequer, as holders of such lands had petitioned in the first parliament of Edward III's reign. The restoration of Contrariants' estates meant the handing back of many such chamber lands. Isabella's original dower of £4,500 was almost tripled to twenty thousand marks (£13,333 6s 8d). She received lands worth £8,800 a year, including many chamber manors. Indeed, Tout, who enumerated them, considered the evidence to suggest that Isabella had a lien on such properties and only gave them up to others in return for substantial compensation. Thus the matter was already well advanced when it was formally agreed in mid-March of 1327, during Bishop Orleton's treasurership, that all such lands were to be audited in future at the exchequer.[129] Isabella received much of the property of the younger Despenser in Glamorgan and Gloucestershire. Others who benefited from the spoils were the earls of Kent and Norfolk, Trussell, Beaumont, and Wake, as well as the countess of Pembroke and Joan de Warenne.[130].

Undoubtedly the most profligate of all was Mortimer himself. The marriages of his seven daughters created a web of family alliances. Katherine became the wife of Thomas Beauchamp, earl of Warwick, Joan of James d'Audley, Agnes of Laurence Hastings, later earl of Pembroke,[131] Margaret of Thomas the son of Maurice de Berkeley, Matilda of John son of John de Charlton, Blanche of Peter de Grandisson, and Beatrice of Edward son of Thomas de Brotherton, the earl marshal. In June 1327 the king and Isabella were present at Hereford for the marriages of Beatrice and Agnes. Great celebrations, regardless of expense, were held in Mortimer's castles of Ludlow and Wigmore, together with jousts and other entertainments. For several days he held a "round table" at his ancestral seat, Wigmore, in the manner of King Arthur; another, according to the Leicester chronicler, was celebrated in 1328 at Bedford, part of the earl marshal's estates.[132] This "counterfeiting" of King Arthur was considered a failure by the cynical, "for the noble knight Arthur was the most worthy lord of renown that was in all the world in his time."[133] Mortimer, appointed justiciar of North and South Wales on 20 February 1327, was granted that office for life on 27 August of the following year.[134] His ambitious climb reached its summit at the Salisbury Parliament in October 1328, when he was created earl of the March, an unprecedented title, as the Pauline annalist, among others, remarked. Much of Mortimer's largesse Avesbury believed to have come from the spoils of the Despensers.[135] The *Brut* suggests that the earl's extravagance extended to the flaunting of "wonder rich clothes out of all manner resoun, both of shaping and wearing," bearing himself so proudly that even his son Geoffrey dubbed him "King of Folly."[136]

The rapidity with which money and treasure was dissipated by Isabella, Mortimer, their friends and hangers-on is remarkable. When Stapeldon surrendered the keys of the treasury to William Melton, there was £69,000 in cash, as well as a horde of plate, jewelry, and relics.[137] This despite some £65,000 expended on the so-called war of Saint-Sardos.[138] It has been calculated that in November 1326 the treasure in the Tower and at Westminster amounted to just under £62,000 and with the plate and treasure from the proscribed earl of Arundel and the Despensers, together with that found at Caerphilly, the total amounted to over £78,000. By the time Orleton handed over the contents of the treasury to Burghersh in March 1327, barely more than £12,000 remained.[139] But if the new government's "generosity and mercy to its lesser enemies," showed that they had learnt the lesson not grasped by Edward and the Despensers that "followers and military support were more important than cash,"[140] it was to be demonstrated that such support soon evaporated, some major recipients of largesse proving remarkably fickle. Jean de Hainault, who had made Isabella's enterprise possible, was handsomely rewarded in the king's name. Thus, on 7 February 1327, he was given a pension of a thousand marks. Among other grants was an enormous one of £14,406 6s 9d, payable in two instalments, made on 6 March 1328 in return for twice providing military assistance – initially and for the Scottish campaign.[141] Mortimer's insouciant behaviour was certain to arouse the antagonism of Lancaster, who according to the pro-Lancastrian Leicester chronicler Knighton, was denied access to the king and certainly to the inner workings of the court.[142]

A RISING TIDE OF DISAFFECTION:
THE BEDFORD FIASCO

Meanwhile, important events had taken place, events that were to have an impact on the immediate future. Archbishop Reynolds, Edward II's protégé, died on 16 November 1327 at his palace by the Thames at Mortlake. Henry Burghersh, a strong supporter of the Isabella and Mortimer regime, would have proved useful to bolster governmental authority, but the election at Canterbury was allowed to go ahead unhindered and was even facilitated. For reasons unknown, the monks chose Simon de Mepham, a doctor of theology of Oxford, a man previously virtually unheard of, certainly unremarked. It has been thought that because of his subsequent support of Henry of Lancaster Mepham was the earl's candidate, but that seems unlikely in view of his lack of influence at court. True, he may not have been inclined to oppose someone who had played no part in politics. We know that Isabella wrote warmly to John XXII in Mepham's favour, bemoaning the recent disruptive behaviour of certain prelates. Whom had she in mind? Surely not those who had been instrumental in putting her son on the throne and her in a position of authority. Yet she might have felt that now that Stratford and Orleton were drifting away from her they could be blamed for the unpopular aspects of the late king's fall. Experience showed that the pope had adopted a strong line with his forceful provision of a number of bishops and his equally robust rejection of government candidates, so it may be that such knowledge influenced Mepham to make the journey to the Curia on his own behalf. All went well, Mepham was consecrated at Avignon on 5 June.[143] Reynolds's death came some two months after Edward II's murder, an event that seemed mysterious, bearing in mind the forty-two-year-old king's usual robust health. A finger of suspicion was certainly directed against Mortimer, but no one was prepared to speak out. However, it was calculated to influence adversely a number of important people, not least Edward III's uncles, as also some prominent clerics, including the bishop of London and the archbishop of York.

The internal political situation showed signs of deterioration during the summer of 1328. Lancaster did attend a council at Worcester in June, where he
expressed himself unwilling to agree to the sending of forces to Gascony until
the matter had been discussed in a larger assembly. Parliament duly met at York
on the last day of July, but Lancaster excused himself from attendance. There
was only a brief session and then, towards the end of August, a further parliament was summoned to meet at Salisbury on 16 October. On his way south at
Barlings near Lincoln, the king encountered Lancaster with an armed retinue.
The sixteen-year-old king is said to have demanded orally that the earl this time
put in an appearance.[144] Already in early August the Londoners, whose Lancastrian sympathies remained constant, were sending letters covertly to the earl of
Kent, John Stratford, and Thomas Wake. The citizens had long ago made their
peace with their diocesan, Stephen Gravesend, whom they had urged to return
to a London from which he had earlier been forced to flee for his life. They also
wrote to the new archbishop, Mepham, requesting him to work for peace.[145] In
September the City was informed of the letters of credence issued on the twenty-second from Horsford, north of Norwich, to Oliver Ingham and Bartholomew
Burghersh about the king's wishes, or more accurately those of the governing
clique.[146] What the Londoners heard was not very agreeable and they had it in
mind to persuade Archbishop Melton and many others, including various bishops and the earls of Warenne and Norfolk, to try to ensure that parliament met
at Westminster rather than Salisbury.[147] Responding on 27 September to letters
sent in the king's name the mayor admitted that Bishop Stratford and Thomas
Wake had come to the Guildhall on the Saturday (17 September) after the feast
of the Invention of the Holy Cross to discuss affairs of state. They had said that
the king ought to live of his own and to have treasure for use against his enemies. But he had none. The second point they made was that after the coronation it was agreed that the king should have prelates, earls, and barons of his
council to advise him. This had not been done. Lastly, they desired peace in the
land. The citizens alleged that their response had been that were these things
true then a parliament should be held at Westminster for their amendment. They
denied that they were making any conspiracies against the king. The letter closes with thanks for Edward's promise to come to London and to return the
"departments" of the exchequer and the King's Bench to Westminster from
York, to which they had been transferred on account of operations against the
Scots.[148] Protestations to the contrary notwithstanding, the writing was clearly
on the wall. The criticisms being voiced, but not specifically repudiated, were
strongly "Lancastrian" in tone. It was clear that the government could not rely
on the loyalty of the Londoners.

Mepham, who had landed at Dover on 5 September 1328, reached the king,
who was travelling slowly southwards in the direction of London, at Lynn,
where he performed fealty and on the nineteenth was granted livery of his temporalities . By that time he must have been fully aware of the gathering storm.

So too were Isabella and Mortimer, who at Cambridge towards the end of the month learned that Lancaster was mustering his forces at Higham Ferrers, Northamptonshire, where Stratford put in an appearance for discussions with the earl prior to leaving for London. Mepham himself was in the capital on 25 September, when he was met by a procession from St Paul's, where he made a small offering (*parva collatio*) at the high altar and "commended himself to the people," just at the time that the City was framing its reply to the king's demand for an explanation of the activities of Stratford and Wake.[149] Not quite three weeks later, on 15 October, the day before the opening of parliament, Sir Robert Holland, the betrayer of Thomas of Lancaster, who was believed to have escaped from Berkhamstead Castle, was intercepted on his way to London by Sir Thomas Wyther and his gang in Borehamwood, near Elstree in Hertfordshire. Having murdered him, they sent his head to Earl Henry. What made this act of lawlessness even worse is revealed by the *Brut* chronicle, according to which Holland had became "wonder privy with the queen Isabel and also with Mortimer." Consequently, after his crime Wyther, fearing the queen's anger, had to be concealed by Earl Henry . The degree of the earl's complicity cannot be established with any certainty.[150] The assassin had been a member of Thomas of Lancaster's retinue, but in 1326 a Sir Thomas "Wether" in Edward II's presence had sworn (under duress?) lifelong loyalty to the king and Despenser.[151]

Events at Salisbury were disturbing for the government as well as for those who put their faith in a parliamentary resolution of difficulties. The Rochester chronicler is probably echoing Bishop Hethe when he remarks that there was much talk but little action and that at this point Mepham, a political ignoramus, began to lean towards the Lancastrians.[152] Earl Henry declined to come and waited at Winchester with an armed force that was joined by a contingent said to be of six hundred Londoners, though responsibility for their presence was disavowed by the City authorities.[153] Thomas Wake, Norfolk the earl marshal, and Henry de Beaumont are said to have been with him.[154] Parliament was opened by a delegate, Walter Hervy, the archdeacon of Salisbury, although the king arrived later.[155] Lancaster made his excuses by proxy but many are supposed to have regarded them as unacceptable. The bishops advised that they should await the arrival of Bishop John Stratford, presumably knowing that he would act as Lancaster's mouthpiece. When he did appear he explained the reasons for the earl's absence. Lancaster, he bravely announced, had heard that the reason for Mortimer's making peace with the Scots was so that he would have his hands free to destroy him. But, he added, given an agreement between the two earls, all would be well. Thereupon Mortimer took an oath on Mepham's primatial cross to the effect that he would do no harm to Lancaster or cause any to be done to him. What he did not mention was that he had taken the precaution of bringing a strong body of armed men with him, including a contingent provided by John Maltravers. Stratford and Gravesend were despatched to Lancaster with details of Mortimer's promise. Additionally, they carried a message in the king's name to the effect that he desired Lancaster to come but on this occasion did not wish to see Sir Henry de Beaumont. This was not surprising since Beaumont must have decried the Scottish treaty, being the claimant to the earldom of Buchan through his wife, Alice, niece of John Comyn. He was not one to hide his feelings, as he had demonstrated under the previous king. One matter that did go ahead, though the precise date is uncertain, was the creation of three earls: Mortimer, as we have seen, became earl of the March, young John of Eltham earl of Cornwall, and James Butler earl of Ormond.[156]

The messengers did not persuade Lancaster to attend the parliament but they prompted a lengthy *pièce justificative*. This was an amplification of the grievances expressed in London. He was not motivated, Lancaster claimed, by a desire for personal profit but was acting in the interests of the Church, the king and the realm. The king should be able to live of his own without oppressing his people, but be in a position to defend his land and people. The queen should live from her dowry so that she did not have to grieve the people. Those peers chosen after the coronation to advise the king in his youth were to be held responsible at the ensuing parliament. Peace should be maintained in the realm. He excused himself for coming with an armed force; this was merely for protection from those notoriously intent on damaging him. He was willing to come under a safe conduct. Later, a clause in Mortimer's indictment held that he himself had come armed to parliament.

The response made in Edward's name was predictable enough. Admittedly the king was impoverished by the recent troubles, so he and his advisors would welcome information about means of increasing his resources. The queen's dowry should not provide an occasion for disturbance. This was a personal matter, between himself and the queen, but there would be no increased charge on that account. As for counselling, summonses had been sent regularly to the earl. Rather than responding he had removed himself from the king. It was not customary for monarchs to issue safe conducts in such circumstances. Nonetheless he had granted them on condition that the earl and his people answer at law. No other kind of safe conduct could be issued without contravening Magna Carta, which required him not to deny justice. In the event the earl did not accept the letters of safe conduct nor did he venture to come to parliament. At the request of the knights in the Commons, tired of the expensive stalemate, the assembly was adjourned on 31 October to Westminster.[157]

That matters were not quite as irenic as propaganda contrived to make them appear is illustrated by Bishop Stratford's action. He had lodged with the nuns of Wilton during the parliament, but his audacious defence of Lancaster put him in peril, or so he believed. Without licence he fled from parliament under cover of darkness, slept in the open fields, and eventually found refuge at his Downton manor. With Lancaster's evacuation of his cathedral city the bishop and his familiars found it prudent to retire to Bishops Waltham and to hide out in the nearby Chase. Later he was to be pursued in the courts for contempt.[158] When the royal forces reached Winchester at the beginning of November, they watched Lancaster's men withdraw without serious incident. By the end of the month an enquiry by the city authorities found that Lancaster, Thomas Wake, Hugh d'Audley, and Roger de Grey had stopped peacefully at Winchester on 30 October, supposedly unarmed. In the meantime the royal party, including Philippa of Hainault, Isabella, and the newly created earl of March moved towards London, with the intention of assuring themselves of the City's loyalty. They arrived either at the end of November or the beginning of December and stayed about a week.[159]

It must have been at this time that Ralph Basset and William de Clinton came to Westminster with the suggestion that if the council could arrange a meeting between Lancaster and Mortimer their differences might be settled.[160] The whole city is said to have turned out to welcome the royal party with gifts, thus successfully concealing their real sympathies. The departure of the court for the Mortimer estates in the West was closely followed by the arrival in their turn of Lancaster and his supporters. Already a citation had been sent in the names of the earls of Norfolk and Kent urging bishops, and doubtless others, to come to London the week before Christmas. The king was said to be riding through the countryside, devastating it as he went, in violation of Magna Carta and of his coronation oath, seizing goods, from both ecclesiastics and laymen, and destroying the nobles of the realm. The hand of Stratford is visible behind these moves, with the archbishop strong in his support. Mepham had initially sought the advice of Henry Eastry, the Canterbury prior, who wrote back on 16 December warning the archbishop to maintain a middle course in the manner of the "Mediator" himself, and to remember that after the person of the king he was principally under obligation to the "regimen regni." And, he warned, however it turned out, well or ill, the outcome would be imputed to him. To the earls Bishop Hethe pleaded indisposition, but Mepham, who according to the Pauline annalist reached London on 18 December, continued to press his somewhat vulnerable suffragan to join him. The bishop, perhaps not so unwell as he made out, proved impervious to such pressure, being wary of consorting with the "young and improvident" (*cum iuvenibus et improvidis*). He preferred, he said, to get on with preparations for Christmas, being reluctant to engage in political entanglements. What had happened to his friend, the previous king, was not readily forgotten. Other bishops may have been of the same mind, for evidence is lacking that any other than Stratford and Gravesend put in an appearance. At this point Mepham seems to have taken a leading role, delivering a sermon on the Sunday before Christmas in the nave of St Paul's. The following day prelates and magnates – comprising the earls of Kent and Norfolk with the lords Wake and Hugh d'Audley – discussed matters of state and how amends might be made.[161]

After London, the court had followed the precedent of Edward II and migrated westwards in the direction of Mortimer's strongholds in the Marches, possibly doubting the reliability of the Londoners. On this occasion, however, it went with a substantial army capable of reinforcement,[162] while the diplomatic interplay continued at a distance. From Gloucester a letter dated 16 December was sent with the object of deterring the Londoners from rendering aid to the dissidents. It impugned the assertion that the earl and his party were acting in the king's interests or, as they claimed, not against the king himself but against certain of his subjects – precisely the argument so frequently used by Thomas of Lancaster in the previous reign. Accompanying this letter was a lengthy document outlining recent events, from the government's viewpoint, with instructions that it be published. In answer to the suggestion that the earls of Lancaster and the March might meet to solve their differences, the king stated that measures taken by Lancaster constituted a trespass against him, so that to him alone should amends be made. At Northampton it had been agreed to send the bishops of Coventry and Lichfield and Worcester, Northburgh and Orleton, to assert his rightful claim to the throne of France.[163] The earl and others present had promised to assist him in this to their utmost. In that parliament, too, it had been agreed that justices (of Trailbaston) should be commissioned to deal with felonies and trespasses and that the magnates would support the measure. No one, great or small, was to go armed under penalty of forfeiture of their weapons and imprisonment. It had likewise been agreed that the king should live of his own, that chancellor, treasurer, and steward of the household should be appointed, and that Lancaster should be close to the king, with no important business transacted in his absence. It was the earl who had removed himself from the council with but one exception: when he came to Warwick and promised the king that he would attend the Worcester council. In accordance with Lancaster's wishes the sending of men to Gascony had then been deferred until parliament could meet at York. The earl did not come, so on the advice of those present it was decided to convene a parliament at Salisbury, to which the king travelled by way of Lincoln, Norfolk, and London, as we have seen.

The document continues with a detailed account of what had happened at London and then at Salisbury, elements of which have already been discussed.[164] In reply to this document the mayor and commonality of London stated that it had been publicly recited in the Guildhall on the eve of St Thomas (i.e., 20 December), when the lords Thomas Wake, William Trussell, and Thomas Roscelyn were present,[165] gave assurance that the City was loyal, and added that Lancaster would respond after consulting his peers. The Pauline annalist says that the king was so angered by these machinations that he proposed, on evil advice, to raise his standard and ride against them. Naturally this caused alarm to those in London and to the earl of Lancaster who, according to the court, had earlier been shadowing the royal forces in the neighbourhood of Kenilworth, as well as making military preparations at Northampton and Higham Ferrers. One possible explanation of Lancaster's movements is that in the face of the court's hostile actions he became more intent on coming to a peaceful accommodation. Retiring towards London where those of like mind were gathered, he spent Christmas independently at Waltham.[166]

In London Mepham now assumed a pivotal role by despatching a letter to Worcester, dated 23 December, by the hands of the archdeacon of Essex, M. John de Elham, a doctor of theology. This letter, which embodied a "petition of prelates, earls, barons and of the whole community of London," reminded the king that at the Salisbury Parliament it was agreed by common assent that no action was to be taken against the magnates until the coming parliament at Westminster. In the second place, he had promised at his coronation to maintain the laws and customs of England. Thirdly, the point was made that Magna Carta declared not only that the king should not proceed against any man save by judgment of his peers but also that contraveners were *ipso facto* excommunicate. The king, he declared, would be aware that it was laid down by various church councils that all persons (save the king, queen, and their children) who disturbed the peace of the realm were under sentence of excommunication. Having intelligence of the king's intention to advance in force against certain peers, Mepham urged him to desist until parliament met, when offenders could make amends or be punished by due process of law.[167] Another letter of similar tenor, dated 22 December, sent by the mayor, aldermen, and commonality of London, warned the king of the danger were he to persist in his hostile intentions. Although on Christmas Eve the confederates adjourned their discussion until after the festival, the situation was so urgent that Robert Flamberd, the common sergeant, left London with this letter on Christmas Day.[168]

On New Year's day Lancaster made his way to London where he joined the others at St Paul's. At the house of the Dominicans he made up his differences with the earl marshal, an estrangement that had resulted, says the Pauline annalist, from the killing of Robert Holland by the impetuous Wyther. On 2 January the confederates – Mepham, Stratford, the earls of Lancaster, Kent, and Norfolk, Lord Wake, among others[169] – bound themselves by oath to maintain certain ordinances for the benefit of the king and kingdom. In referring to this, a royal manifesto, apparently from the latter half of January, claims that Lancaster and others had sworn not to engage in a *chevauchée* "against the statute and the estate of the king," nor "to harm the estate of the king, his mother, or of any other, high or low." It was said to be notorious that this oath had been broken. However that may be, a delegation composed of Mepham, Gravesend, and Norfolk was despatched to the king for the ostensible purpose of making a peaceful settlement.[170] Stratford's attitude is difficult to fathom and must remain a matter of conjecture. Did he feel that insufficiently firm action was being taken? Was he disturbed by the dangerous turn of events? Did he, perhaps, resent the fact that the direction of affairs was passing from his hands? What is known is that he retired to his diocese, thus missing the final act of the drama.[171]

While the Lancastrians were organizing themselves in London, those in control of the king determined on an aggressive policy. The king remained in the neighbourhood of Gloucester and Worcester for much of December, doubtless while reinforcements arrived. Then, on the twenty-ninth, proclamation was made, and a copy sent to London for publication, that the king intended to advance to Warwick on New Year's Day, to act against those who were devastating the countryside, and to be at Leicester by the sixth. All who agreed to come to his obedience by the morrow of Epiphany (i.e., 7 January) would be received into his grace, with the exception of the barons Beaumont, Roscelyn, Wyther, and Trussell. There was probably a degree of disturbance in London at the news and the merchants had reason to complain about the illegal prises, contrary to city liberties, made for the provision of Windsor Castle. On his way the king passed Lancaster's castle at Kenilworth, a short distance from Warwick, where the constable, contrary to the custom of the land, refused entry for provisioning – shades of Leeds.[172] The king was as good or better than his word and, according to the Lancastrian sympathizer, Knighton, arrived at Leicester on 4 January 1329, stayed in the area for eight days, and devastated even the churches as though it were a time of war – days before the expiry of the ultimatum. He seems to have provisioned his force at Lancaster's expense and on the sixteenth the earl's lands were confiscated.[173] Burghersh temporarily relinquished the great seal at St Andrew's Priory, Northampton, on 15 January in the presence of the queen, the earls of Surrey and March, Henry de Percy, Oliver Ingham, John Darcy, and others. It was resumed in the safety of the Augustinian priory of Newnham in the eastern suburb of Bedford the following Thursday. Surprisingly, among those present this time were the young king's trusted councillors Richard de Bury and William de Montacute. The *Brut* gives a graphic picture of the royal army making a twenty-four mile advance by night to Bedford, Isabella clad in armour as a knight by the side of her son. Exactly when they reached the town is uncertain, but it was probably some days before the resumption of the seal on the nineteenth.[174]

Proceeding towards the royal force came the delegation from London slightly in advance of the Lancastrian army. The most expansive authority here is the usually trustworthy Dene. He is not partial to the archbishop's meddling in politics, nor indeed to the Lancastrian cause, but he may well have had access to a reliable source for what happened, possibly someone from Kent, perhaps even the Kentish knight mentioned below. According to him the mission's purpose was to dissuade the king from riding in hostile fashion and taking prises from Church and people. Were the king to fail to respond to this plea they would threaten armed resistance.[175] The enthusiastic Mepham, possibly feeling that he would be able to avert the conflict by personal persuasion, forged ahead of his fellows, his metropolitan cross and banner held firmly aloft. But if he were hoping to emulate Elias he was sadly mistaken,[176] Dene thought, for he was not of the same spiritual or moral calibre (*non tamen in spiritu et virtute Elye*). When he got close to the king's forces Mepham sent for Thomas de Aldon (Aledon), who appears to have been the Kentish knight who at the time of the siege of Leeds had been an adherent of Badlesmere,[177] in order to ask whether it was appropriate to go forward to greet the king. The answer was "yes," provided he took care not to reveal anything of his mission or to draw any conclusion until the following day. Rather, he should await his companions, for were he to let slip a scintilla of his purpose the council would draw out everything for which he had come. That was just what happened. He greeted the king and queen and their council, and having imbibed, worn out by his labours and by the journey, he waxed loquacious and revealed the whole purpose of his mission. Thereupon the king's council defended their viewpoint, justifying it to such an extent that Mepham, completely won over, changed sides and, so it is said, bound himself by oath. He was then directed to go back to the earls with the message that all who submitted to the king, save four persons,[178] would be received into his grace. On his return he was well received, but as soon as the facts were known the archbishop was held in derision, so that with great loss of repute he travelled back to Canterbury for his sparsely attended enthronement on the twenty-second.[179]

While Dene's is the most circumstantial narrative of the Bedford fiasco, the only one that amplifies Mepham's role, it needs to be treated with caution in view of the animus in this chronicle towards the archbishop. Knighton understandably is kinder to Mepham, whom he credits with taking part in an agreement for the rectifying of errors in the next parliament so as to avoid an insurgence of the Commons (*omnes communes*) in sympathy with the earl. For Knighton the blame belonged to the king's uncles, the earls of Norfolk and Kent, not merely for deserting Lancaster but also for incriminating him as seditious. Dene casts a different light on their conduct. The earls and their adherents, thrown into confusion by Mepham's cave-in, awaited the king's arrival at Bedford. As he rode up, they ran forward and prostrated themselves in the mud, receiving the king's grace but under harsh conditions pronounced by Bishop Burghersh. The date of this submission is uncertain, but according to the Gervase continuator it was 17 January. This is close, although the twelfth or thirteenth have also been suggested. It could well have been the sixteenth when orders were given for the taking into the king's hand of the lands of the earls of Lancaster and Atholl, as well as of Thomas Wake, Hugh Audley, Henry Beaumont, Henry de Ferrers, Thomas Roscelyn, William Trussell, Thomas Wyther, William de Bradshaw, and their adherents. Subsequently Lancaster was placed under obligation to pay thirty thousand pounds – eleven thousand according to the *Brut* – though the money was not in fact exacted. The names of the others involved and the amount of their recognizances are recorded in the Close Rolls.[180] Not long after, says Baker, the earl of Lancaster became blind and resolved to serve God with patience.[181] The fact that he is not to be found attesting charters during much of 1329 and 1330 does not necessarily indicate his alienation or that he was biding his time until a *coup* could be engineered.[182] For part of that period he was engaged in diplomatic activity, protection being granted to him on 12 September 1329 and again early in 1330. It is possible, of course, that he wished to keep a low profile during the extraordinary witch-hunt

launched by the government against those who still kept alive their loyalty to
Edward II, of which more will be said later.

The government had survived a threat to its continued existence. Faced by a
force of three earls, a number of barons, a contingent of Londoners under the
leadership of John de Bedeford and Thomas Chigwell, and according to the *Brut*
– doubtless with the customary exaggeration – a hundred or more knights, great
determination had been shown. There was some legal harassment of those
involved. Stratford was ordered to appear before the court of King's Bench, on
a charge of contempt arising from his hasty departure from Salisbury. Inevitably
he pursued much the same line of argument as Orleton had done in the previous
reign, and which he himself was to adopt once again in 1341. The case dragged
on from session to session until 1330, when it disappears from the records, presumably because the case was quietly dropped.[183] On 10 April 1329, the sheriff
of Bedfordshire was sent a schedule of those who came armed to Bedford, but
he responded that none could be found within his bailiwick, and commissioners
were appointed to hold an enquiry, details of which are to be found in the
records of King's Bench.[184] Any severe action was likely to increase a smoul-
dering resentment against a ruling group that had proved itself no better than the
one it had supplanted. This time, however, it was not felt to be the king's fault,
as is made clear by a number of sources.

There followed a vigorous attempt to bring the Londoners to heel. On 21 January 1329 Mayor Grantham and twenty-four citizens were summoned to St
Albans. They were questioned about the support given to Lancaster at Winchester and Bedford and instructed to enquire of the citizens whether they were
willing to punish such men or whether they needed royal help so to do. Having
held the enquiry, a delegation travelled, as instructed, to the king at Windsor,
where it arrived on 1 February. On their return the members gave an account of
their interview with Edward and his council. Then, on the fifth, a commission
of justices arrived. During their sessions John Coterel was found guilty of
abducting the abbot of Bury and hanged. The former mayor Hamo de Chigwell
was accused of harbouring him, but he claimed clergy and was delivered to
Bishop Gravesend. Having performed purgation at Orsett in Essex he returned
to the city amidst great rejoicing, a turn of events that is said to have irritated
the king and his mother, Isabella, who had returned with Queen Philippa on the
seventh. The following day a writ was issued for Chigwell's arrest and imprisonment, but he escaped and was given sanctuary by Gravesend. Clearly the
Londoners were not readily cowed.[185]

THE LULL BEFORE THE STORM:
DESPERATE REMEDIES

Now that the Scottish problem had been resolved to the satisfaction of those in
power, that Lancaster had been induced to submit, and that the Londoners, how-

ever reluctantly, had been made to realize that further disaffection would be counterproductive, the government was in a position to turn to other urgent matters. In 1328, when the claim to the throne of France had been made on behalf of Edward III, Philip VI was felt to be in a precarious position. At that time it was within the realm of practical politics, rather than a mere gesture. This is made abundantly clear by the detailed analysis of the succession made by Baker, probably some quarter of a century later, when he could justifiably describe Edward III as "ille gloriosus rex magnificusque triumphator." To the chronicler Philip was a usurper, the son of that Charles of Valois who, having traitorously tried to do away with his nephew Charles IV, in 1325, suffered an unpleasant death on that account.[186] But by 1329, if not before, Philip had consolidated his position and the English government could no longer afford to arouse his hostility. As will be described in context later, the young Edward was conducted to Amiens to perform homage. This was done with reservations on both sides, but it was a homage that was to constitute an argument against his claims in later years. The king is said to have hurried back on 11 June 1329, plagued by a threat that Philip VI was hatching a plot to abduct him.[187]

On the journey from Dover the royal party encountered Bishop Hethe and stayed in the neighbourhood of Rochester for some days. The bishop celebrated mass for the king on the newly established feast of Corpus Christi (22 June) and again on the feast of St John the Baptist (24 June). On each occasion Edward had a meal afterwards with Hethe. Roger Mortimer proved friendly and urged him to come to the forthcoming council at Windsor, but Hethe excused himself on the grounds that it was expensive for a poor bishop to attend councils and parliaments all over the realm, nor would the resources of his bishopric allow him to do so. It was quite enough for him to attend parliament when it came to London.[188] There was also time for the king's party to enjoy jousts at Canterbury and when they reached London in Cheap between the great cross and the conduit, where Queen Philippa and other ladies were fortunate to escape serious injury when one of the stages collapsed.[189] According to the London chronicler, no finer jousts had been seen in England. Hethe himself came to London for 18 February 1330 when Queen Philippa, by then heavy with child, was crowned by Archbishop Mepham in Westminster Abbey "with honour, solemnity and every kind of display, as is appropriate" (*cum honore et sollennitate et apparatu multifario ut decebat*). The bishops of Rochester and Hereford (Charlton) sang the Litany, but there was an undignified crush that occasioned damage to the episcopal copes and pastoral staffs. In the evening they all dined with the king in Westminster Hall.[190]

Mortimer – almost certainly Isabella as well – was keen to take the opportunity to flush out those in high places who still had a loyalty to Edward II, coupled with misgivings about the new regime. A bizarre plan was adopted, involving the deliberate spreading of a rumour that the former king was alive at Corfe and could be rescued. Reports to that effect were secretly disseminated by means of *agents provocateurs*, including real or feigned members of the Dominican Order – their strong association with Edward II prompts doubt as to their being willing members of any such conspiracy, although they could themselves have been duped.[191] Whatever the truth, these Mortimer agents, as they undoubtedly were, duly entrapped Edmund, earl of Kent, who appears to have been strangely credulous. He had been to the papal Curia in an attempt to secure the canonization of Thomas of Lancaster. While there, he apparently told the pope of his belief in his half-brother's survival.[192] Opportunity was taken at the Winchester Parliament, which assembled on 11 March 1330, concurrently with a convocation of the Canterbury province, to have Kent accused of treason and subsequently beheaded by a "ribaldus sceleratus de Marchalsia" on St. Cuthbert's eve (i.e., 19 March).[193] Having written and sealed a letter to that effect the earl was in no position to deny that he had genuinely believed Edward to be alive, and that he had hoped to release him. This was patently treasonable.[194]

The *Brut* suggests that, on being told, Isabella was furiously angry at what she took to be an attempt to replace her son. This was surely feigned, all part of the scheme of deception. If not, we are led to conclude that it was a plan concocted by Mortimer and others without her knowledge. On the face of it that is highly improbable; the more so, since earlier in the *Brut* narrative it is said to have been on the commandment of Isabella, as well as of Mortimer, that the king's person should be seen by the earl alone. The chronicler had already narrated the king's death at length, and at this point he refers back to that chapter. Whether Archbishop Melton, Bishop Gravesend, the abbot of Langdon, and a number of other known sympathizers of Edward II could really have been duped is doubtful. If they were not, the question remains, what did they hope to gain from lending their support? Was it just a prop to political dissent, or was there a genuine plan, making use of the rumour, to raise a revolt with help from outside the country? Kent's confession would suggest that there was: a combination of internal dissidents, exiles such as Henry de Beaumont and Thomas Roscelyn in Paris, and the cooperation of the Scots under the auspices of Donald, earl of Mar. The earl drops the names of a few seculars such as Fulk FitzWarren, John Peche, and Ingelram Berengar. Rhys ap Gruffydd was also implicated, but basically the alleged constituent members of the plot were clerical, hence scarcely militarily potent. The whole concept owes more to wishful thinking than to reality.[195] Little is known of the stance taken by the prelates at Winchester. Mepham, for whom the procedure against Kent would have been anathema but who had already had his fingers burned at Bedford, was absent. On the agenda were other weighty and urgent matters, in particular Gascony, threatened with invasion, for which the government required a subsidy. Without Mepham, said the assembled prelates, nothing definite could be decided, so a convocation was summoned for 16 April at Lambeth to discuss the subsidy.[196]

The Kent affair really was the last desperate throw of the government. Edward was "wonder sory" for this wanton killing of a favourite uncle,[197] although in Murimuth's view the earl was not much mourned by the people at large in view of his habit of forcible purveyance, without payment.[198] If it were intended as a warning that even the royal family's lives were unsafe, then it could only bolster the determination of those who had no wish to see Mortimer as king, particularly as Queen Philippa had given birth to a son – the future Black Prince – on 15 June 1330, thus assuring the royal succession.[199] The *Brut* chronicle once again summarizes the state of affairs with more than a touch of authenticity. Mortimer had become "so proud and so haughty that he held no lord of the realm his peer." Moreover, he was so covetous that he followed Queen Isabella's court, receiving "his pennyworth with the officers of the queen's household in the same manner as the king's officers." He did this to save his expenses, striving all the time to amass treasure. He was "wonder privy" with Isabella and had "so much lordship and retinue" that all the magnates were afraid of him. In consequence, the chronicler continues, the king and certain councillors were so aggrieved that they planned to bring him down on account of his responsibility for the murder of Edward II. Others were well disposed towards Mortimer and warned him of his danger, so that he became "angry as the devil."[200]

Although Mortimer's personal finances were in a buoyant state, those of the realm were not. Isabella and her paramour had perforce to surrender their custodies of Pontefract and Glamorgan for Philippa's marriage portion and this, Tout thought, could have been an indication of some weakness.[201] But they were soon to compensate themselves from the confiscation of Kent's lands and the queen mother benefited substantially from the sum that King David of Scotland had engaged to pay.[202] On 21 August 1328, when the long-serving Richard de Bury became keeper of the wardrobe, his predecessor Robert Woodhouse handed over less than two hundred pounds in cash. On 1 December 1330 Woodhouse, on his promotion to the treasurership, left to William Melton an even more paltry sum, just over forty-one pounds.[203] Much reliance was placed on financiers to bridge the gap, first the de la Poles, and then when they failed to make sufficient advances to the household, the Bardi. The amount borrowed had risen to over £19,400 in the fourteen months prior to Mortimer's fall. Yet Edward III was kept on short commons and William la Zouche, in his role as keeper of the great wardrobe responsible for the king's domestic household, threatened to resign unless he were granted more resources for purchasing supplies.[204]

One of the purposes of an embassy to Avignon comprising William Montacute, Bartholomew Burghersh, and others was to secure a diversion of the quadrennial crusading tenth to the king on account of the heavy expenses incurred by wars and internal disturbances, which had denuded the royal treasury. The pope, partly won over by the envoys' arguments, conceded that the tenth should be equally divided between himself and the king. Meanwhile the clergy were summoned to Lambeth for 16 April 1330 to give their assent to a subsidy for

Gascony. There the king's needs were expounded by William Everdon, a baron of the exchequer, and by Simon de Swanland, the mayor of London. The clergy argued that the grant recently made by the laity was adequate for the occasion. They had already been asked for a papal subsidy against heretics and had conceded a tenth for the Scottish war at the Leicester convocation of November 1327, under certain conditions promised in good faith by the bishops of Winchester (Stratford) and Ely (Hothum), and by the earl of Lancaster, but never implemented. War with Scotland was on the wane but, concluded the Pauline annalist, the subsidy had been collected and retained nonetheless. William Dene's account is very different. It concentrates exclusively on Bishop Hethe's contribution at the convocation, which was initially to leave it when he found himself in a minority of one, and then, when pressed, to return and by his continued refusal to give consent allegedly to scupper the whole affair. In the event Archbishop Mepham in a lengthy commission to the abbot of Faversham, dated 23 July 1330 from Mortlake, recited a papal bull authorizing the raising of a quadrennial tenth and gave instructions for its collection. The government's financial aims had been achieved with papal help, notwithstanding the resistance of the clergy .[205]

NEMESIS:
WILLIAM DE MONTACUTE'S COUP D'ÉTAT

There was continuing scepticism about the loyalty of the volatile Londoners. At the Winchester Parliament of 1330 they were asked for an aid for the defence of Gascony. Mortimer expressed his anger that they had harboured John de Charlton, whom he described as his "mortal enemy."[206] As a result an official letter was sent to the mayor, John de Grantham, who had it read out in the Guildhall. In response, two citizens were despatched to the king offering to provide a thousand marks' subsidy. A covering letter for Isabella humbly requested that she maintain her good will towards the City; corresponding petitions being sent to Chancellor Burghersh and Mortimer. Formal acknowledgment of the subsidy as a gift (*franchement et de bone volente*) was issued in the king's name, but in July the mayor and twenty-four men from the City were summoned to a royal council at Woodstock. For himself the mayor pleaded the excuse that he needed to stay because of the disturbed state of the City, but the required delegation was duly elected. After consultation at Woodstock a formal response was given to the king asserting the loyalty of the City – a not dissimilar document had been presented to Edward II in 1326. It was allegedly well received by the king and his council.[207] But no parliament or great council was to meet at Westminster for the remainder of the regime.

Mortimer's staunch supporters were well placed. Burghersh, loyal to the very end, remained as chancellor, while John Maltravers was succeeded as steward of the household by another stalwart, Hugh Turplington, destined to lose his life in defence of his master. Baker thought that the king, being in Mortimer's grip, like his father was deprived of all friends. This was not the case. He did have at least two trustworthy covert allies right at the centre of affairs: the experienced Richard de Bury, keeper of the privy seal, and the young William Montacute, both of whom clandestinely admitted others into their confidence. It is apposite to mention that on 11 January 1329 – the timing may be significant – Montacute, on his petition, was granted the manor of Wark-on-Tweed, Northumberland, as recompense in whole or part for the sum of two hundred marks to be paid to him for staying for life with the king with twenty men-at-arms.[208] Four days later both Montacute and Bury were present when, at the time of the collapse of the Bedford "insurrection," Bishop Burghersh surrendered the great seal to the king in Queen Isabella's chamber in St Andrew's Priory, Northampton, only to resume it at Newnham Priory later in the week. From this it would appear that Montacute was by no means under suspicion; hence it is not so surprising to find that he features prominently among those who witnessed charters during 1330 and that his brother Simon, future bishop of Worcester and Ely, received support for his preferment. These facts argue that Montacute's real sympathies were effectively concealed. Among other anti-government collaborators were numbered Robert Offord or Ufford, Edmund Bohun, who had remained with Edward II at Neath, John Molyns, John Neville of Hornby, and probably Thomas Garton, keeper of the wardrobe, while Lancaster remained cautiously in the wings.[209]

In 1330 Bury, as Edward's amanuensis, wrote the celebrated secret letter to Pope John XXII. In it the king stated that in future any matters directly involving his interest would include the words "Pater Sancte" written in his own hand. This, he confided, was a secret between himself, William Montacute, and none other. The letter had the two words clearly inscribed at the foot. Montacute, as we have seen, had accompanied Bartholomew Burghersh on an embassy to Avignon, during which he must have revealed this plan privately to the pope, who duly kept the secret.[210] It is worth noting, though, that the pope responded favourably to Queen Isabella's letters on behalf of Robert Wyville, a clerk of hers, and provided him to the important bishopric of Salisbury, a promotion that called forth a virulent condemnation from Murimuth.[211]

Rumours of opposition from both home and abroad were rife. A council of prelates and barons met at Osney on 9 July 1330, but this according to the Pauline annalist broke up without conclusion following the arrival of disturbing letters from the count of Hainault. The denouement came with the summoning of a great council to Nottingham Castle for 15 October 1330. Either then, or shortly before, Mortimer got wind of a conspiracy, perhaps assisted by his spies, one of whom is said to have been John Wyard. He angrily interrogated the king and various suspects, including Montacute, who replied enigmatically but with spirit that he was only doing his duty. Isabella took every precaution, having the castle gates locked at night and keeping the keys herself.[212] According to Baker,

Mortimer complained to the officer appointed to allot lodgings for the nobles that he should not have had the audacity to put the earl of Lancaster, an enemy of the queen, so close. Terrified, the constable allotted him a place a league outside the town, and John de Bohun, earl of Hereford and Essex, the constable of England, was given his place, or so I interpret this somewhat enigmatic sentence. What perhaps is surprising is that Edward himself was not within the castle, hence free to plot from without: conceivably a sign of his growing independence. In the words of the *Scalacronica*'s translator, he had begun "to grow in body and mind."[213] A rumour had circulated that Mortimer, Isabella's "amasius" (lover),[214] planned to usurp the kingdom. When this came to the ears of the king and his friends it is reported that they not unnaturally felt that it would be better for the realm if Mortimer were put to death. By great good fortune the constable of the castle, William Eland,[215] was amenable to Montacute's persuasion that he was acting for the king and permitted a small band of conspirators to enter by what must have been a sally port, or even a large drain, which led by a subterranean tunnel to the kitchen or hall (base?) of the principal tower where the queen was housed. The confederates included the Lancastrian Walkfare and the king himself, who kept in the background, armed. Once in the castle they penetrated to an unlocked room where they surprised Mortimer, together with Isabella and the bishop of Lincoln. During a brief struggle one of the defenders, Sir Hugh de Turplinton or Turplington, steward of the household, was killed by John Neville of Hornby.[216] Richard de Monmouth also died, while Mortimer was taken prisoner as he strove to don his armour. The reign of Mortimer and Isabella was over and the pleas of the "ferrea virago" – Baker's phrase – for mercy were ignored: "Beal fitz, Beal fitz, eiez pitie de gentil Mortymer."[217]

Mortimer and others were conducted by the earl of Lancaster, Walkfare, and others by way of Loughborough and Leicester – the scene of Mortimer's earlier depredations – to London, where they were lodged in the Tower. He was hung and drawn at Tyburn, Elms as it was then called, on 29 November, after being condemned by his peers but neither brought before them at any time nor permitted to respond to the charges. Thus, remarks Baker, he was treated in the same manner as were the earls of Lancaster, Winchester, Gloucester[*sic*], that is the younger Despenser – and Kent, who had perished unheard without lawful conviction. He received the same measure of punishment as he had meted to others. According to some of the chroniclers the substance of his indictment was as follows: he had consented to the suffocation of Edward II; he had received a large sum of money to warn the Scots at Stanhope Park, had been responsible for the despicable marriage (*vile matrimonium*) of Joan of the Tower and David Bruce, and counselled the burning of the charters of Scottish submission; he had wrongly used up all the money left in the treasury of the king and the Despensers, so that he and the queen enjoyed abundance while the king was kept impoverished; he had appropriated "fat" custodies and marriages to the king's detriment, and, lastly, he had instructed the juvenile king to perform homage and fealty to Philip of Valois. Other reasons, hinted Baker, were not revealed to all but reserved for the scrutiny of the Eternal Judge. The rolls of parliament include a more expansive indictment that runs to fourteen items. The first of them accused Mortimer of having ignored the council set up at the time of Edward III's coronation. Instead he had encroached upon royal power, appointed members of the royal household and other ministers of the realm, and surrounded the king with men instructed to spy on his deeds and words. [218]

In Tout's view the Mortimer-Isabella regime was administratively conservative: he saw Lancastrian influence in the repudiation of the reforms introduced by the Despensers. The system of "home staples" in assigned towns was abandoned at the Northampton Parliament of March 1328.[219] The arrangement of eight regional escheators was rejected in favour of the former practice of having one to the north and the other to the south of Trent.[220] An aspect of "constitutionalism" was maintained by summoning frequent parliaments, but although there was a show of decision by the magnates, the chroniclers' impression is that the overriding influence was Mortimer's. On the credit side it has been argued that during Isabella and Mortimer's period of power, there was a concerted effort by a variety of measures to induce a greater degree of law and order in the realm as a whole. Collectively they form a quite remarkable structure: the statute of Northampton (1328) – invoked against Henry of Lancaster a year later – the eyres of 1329–30, commissions of the King's Bench dubbed "trailbaston," and experimental commissions of the peace. Helen Cam, in her analysis of the opening speech of Chief Justice Geoffrey le Scrope at the Northampton eyre of 1329, argued in favour of a "concerted policy carried out, if not by the ill-famed Mortimer, at least under his auspices." Kaeuper, in reviewing this opinion, suggested that despite historians' lack of "approbation" for the regime of Isabella and Mortimer, "the effort at reform seems real, even if the novelty of some specific measures may have been exaggerated."[221] However, one commentator on the eyre viewed it – questionably – as marking an early phase of Edward III's attempt to establish himself.[222] The other side of this judicial picture is the decline in the issue of commissions of oyer and terminer, many of which involved spurious, not to say outrageous, allegations. There is said to have been a peak of two hundred and seventy such commissions in 1327, when many were attempting to reverse the injustice of Edward II's reign. But between that date and 1330 there was a marked decline. In all this Geoffrey le Scrope, who had a remarkable talent for survival and his own aggrandizement, played a significant part.[223]

Tout thought that Mortimer's government was "apparently solid," if so, the solidity was illusory. It was an edifice built on sand. Inevitably, unless his life were to be snuffed out, Edward III would before long demand his rightful place. Mortimer's position, dependent on his adulterous relationship with Isabella, was inherently precarious. He repeated all the mistakes of the Despensers, adding others of his own. Unlike the younger Despenser, he had himself promoted to an earldom, and one with an unprecedented title. He held the rightful king in thrall, in this case by veiled threat of force rather than by a close personal relationship. Whereas under Edward II treasure had been accumulated, under the "reign" of Mortimer and Isabella it had been dissipated with astonishing rapidity. Both "rulers" had been notorious for greed. Having come into power on a wave of what might be loosely interpreted as "pro-Lancastrianism," coupled with a general enthusiasm for what a large section of the populace thought would be government "by right and reason," they had themselves invoked the identical criticisms that had been levied against Edward II and his governing clique.[224] The designers of the process of abdication, Stratford and Orleton, had both been alienated, as had Lancaster. Burghersh, by contrast, came into his own and with remarkable dexterity established himself first in the confidence of Mortimer and Isabella and then of the liberated Edward III. Those who sympathized with the northern earl were numerous, while the contrived murder of the earl of Kent deceived few but frightened many. The Londoners, as ever, were suspicious of the new government, despite the benefits they had received at its hands. The evidence of the charter rolls confirms that derived from other sources: the government was reduced to a small caucus of active supporters. Apart from Mortimer himself and Burghersh, they were few indeed: principally John Maltravers – whose life would be at stake were the government to fall – Oliver Ingham, and Simon de Bereford.[225] It only needed a *coup* by a few determined men to topple such a regime without adverse repercussion.

8

Life After Death:
Edward the Penitent Hermit

And upon a time it befell that Sir Edmund of Woodstock, earl of Kent, spoke unto the pope John XXII at Avignon, and said that Almighty God had many times done for love of Thomas of Lancaster many great miracles to many men and women that were through diverse sickness undone as to the world and through his prayer they were brought unto their health. And so Sir Edmund prayed the pope heartily that he would grant him grace that the foresaid Thomas might be translated, but the pope said "Nay, he should not be translated, the same Thomas, earl of Lancaster, until the time that he were better certified of the clergy of England. ... " And when this Edmund saw that he might nought speed of his purpose as touching the translation, he prayed him of his counsel as touching Sir Edward of Caernarvon, his brother, and that not long gone was king of [England], what thing might best be done as touching his deliverance, since that a common fame is throughout England that he was alive, and whole and safe. When the pope heard him tell that Sir Edward was alive, he commanded the earl, upon his benison, that he should help, with all the power that he might, that he were delivered out of prison and save his body in all manner that he might, and for to bring this thing unto an end and he assoiled him and his company *a pena et a culpa*, and all those that should help towards his deliverance. Then took Edmund of Woodstock, earl of Kent, his leave of the pope and came back again into England. And when Edmund was come some of the friars preacher came and said that Sir Edward his brother yet was alive in the castle of Corfe under the keeping of Sir Thomas Gurney. Then sped him the foresaid Edmund as fast as he might, till that he came to the castle of Corfe, and acquainted him and spake him so fair with Sir John Daveril, that was constable of the aforesaid castle, and gave him rich gifts for to have acquaintance of him, and for to know of his counsel, and thus it befell that the aforesaid Sir Edmund prayed specially for to tell him privily of his brother, Sir Edward, if that he lived or were dead. If that he were alive, he prayed of him once to have a sight. And this John Daveril was a high-hearted man, and full of courage and answered shortly

that Sir Edward his brother was in health and under his keeping and dared show him unto
no man since it was defended him in the king's behalf, Edward, that was Edward son of
Caernarvon, and also through commandment of the queen Isabelle, the king's mother,
and of Sir Roger the Mortimer, that he should show his body to no man of the world,
save only unto him, upon pain of life and limb ... but the false traitor lied, for he was not
in his ward, but he was taken thence, and led to the castle of Berkeley through Sir
Thomas Gurney, through commandment of the Mortimer, till that he was dead. ... But
Sir Edmund of Woodstock wist nothing that his brother was dead. Whereupon he took a
letter unto the foresaid Sir John and prayed him heartily that he would take it to King
Edward his brother as his worthy lord.[1]

This extract from the *Brut* chronicle introduces one of the most extraordinary
appendices to Edward's history, that concerned with his "afterlife." This is a
story that needs to be unravelled, not only on its own account but because, like
prophecy, it helps our understanding of the age and serves to illustrate the subterfuges to which Isabella and Mortimer resorted during their regency.
Prophecy ostensibly looked forward; Edward's "afterlife" serves to salvage
something of an unsatisfactory reputation after the event, as well as to illustrate the unstable position of the victors of the *coup* that displaced him. To
some degree the new regime can be regarded as a continuation of Edward's
reign, plagued with the same internal discord: a regime bent on resolving,
come what may, the problems presented by Scotland and France. Edward's
survival was an embarrassment.

Whatever the government's later attempts at deception, Edward of Caernarfon, sometime king of England, died so far as is known on the night of September 21–22 1327 in Berkeley Castle and the news was carried to the court with
expedition. His obit was henceforth kept on 21 September, as is noted in Prior
Eastry's Canterbury register. That he lived long after that date to repent of his
misdeeds remains – as in the late 1320s and the 1330s – a myth to conjure with.
Thomas Lyman and the late George Cuttino who – it may fairly be said – left
the impression that there was something in the story and that the record on
which it is largely based is somehow authentic.[2] The "original" of this document, should we infer that such existed, has not been found. What we do have
is what purports to be a copy somewhat curiously interleaved in the *Cartulaire
de Maguelone* now housed in the *Archives départmentales d'Hérault* at Montpellier. This manuscript contains material concerned with the bishop's estates.
Its contents date mainly from the thirteenth century and the earlier half of the
fourteenth. At folio 86[r] there is an anomalous entry, numbered 120 in pencil, the
body of which occupies thirty-eight lines – filling the page. It concludes with
the valediction of *Manuel de Flisco*, the supposed author. Clearly it was felt to
be inappropriately entered since *vacat* is written in the margin. The entry is
sandwiched between two documents dating respectively from 1264 and 1299,
while copies of documents dated 1312 and 1317 appear on the recto of folio 87.

The latest dated entry that I noted in the manuscript is no. 300 at folio 286 (1337). This suggests that the document in question could be roughly contemporary with the later entries. If it were a subsequent interpolation, there is no obvious particularity about its appearance to suggest incompatibility. But one would have to suppose that there was a vacant leaf.

The letter purports to have been written to King Edward III by Manuele di Fieschi, a papal notary, in his own hand. The sender supposedly was revealing what he had heard from the confession of the king's father (*patris vestri*), Edward of Caernarfon. The Latin is somewhat peculiar, certainly at variance with other entries in the register, while some of the personal and place names are oddly spelled. *Con* is written for *cum* and the style lacks fluency. Professor Cuttino accepted these irregularities as "the language ... of an Italian writing medieval Latin." Roughly a century earlier, the antiquary Theodore Bent, likewise impressed by the document's seeming authenticity, asserted that elements of the orthography (such as *diresit* for *direxit* and *peresit* for *perrexit*) occur "exclusively at this period in the Latin documents of Genoa."[3] If Bent is correct, then we are faced with another problem. Was the letter merely a transcript by a Genoese of an original in more formal Latin? Surely a papal notary well versed in English protocol would not have written even an informal letter to the king of England in the local patois. On the contrary, he would have expected it to be translated by royal clerks for the king's benefit and they would certainly have laughed at language of that kind. Furthermore, Fieschi, who held various English benefices and was a confidant of the Salisbury chapter, would surely not have been guilty of idiosyncratic spelling of proper names.

The letter-writer was in possession of considerable circumstantial detail and, it has to be admitted, such detail might well have been available to Fieschi. What follows is a literal rendering in slightly modified form.[4]

·   THE FIESCHI LETTER

The former king at his wife's urging[5] left his entourage (*familia*) in the earl marshal's castle at Chepstow (gesosta). Fearful, he took a boat with Hugh Despenser (Ugone Dispenssario), the earl of Arundel, and others, and made his way to Glamorgan. There he was captured with Despenser and Master Robert Baldock (MS Baldoli misreading of copyist "li" for "k"?) by Henry of Lancaster (de Longo Castello) and brought to Kenilworth (Chilongurda) Castle, [the] others being [imprisoned] elsewhere. While there he relinquished the crown at the instance of many. The coronation [Edward III's] followed at the next feast of Candlemas [2 February 1327].[6] Finally he [the former king] was sent to Berkeley (Berchelee) Castle where the servant looking after him revealed that the knights Thomas de Gurney (Gourney) and Simon Bereford [or Barford, MS desbeford] were coming to kill him. [The servant] suggested that he should take his clothes to assist escape. At twilight Edward left prison and, not being recognized, at the final gate came upon the doorkeeper asleep. He speedily killed him, opened the door with the keys, and left with his custodian. The knights arrived to murder him; fearing the queen's anger and for their own persons, they extracted the porter's heart and put his corpse in a box, maliciously presenting the queen with the heart and body of the porter as though they were the king's. As the body of the king the porter was buried at Gloucester (Glocest[ri]a). Edward was then "received" at Corfe (Corf) Castle together with his custodian by Lord Thomas the castellan, the lord, John Maltravers (Maltraverse), being ignorant of this. There he was secretly kept for a year and a half. Afterwards, hearing that the earl of Kent had been beheaded because he had said that [his half-brother] was still alive, he took ship with his keeper and with the consent and counsel of the said Thomas crossed to Ireland (Yrelandam), where he remained for nine (viiii) months. Afraid of being recognised he adopted the habit of a hermit, returned to England and reached (applicuit) the port of Sandwich (Sandvic). In the same habit he crossed to Sluys. Then he went to Normandy and from there, as many do, to Languedoc. Arriving at Avignon, he gave a florin to a papal servant by whom he sent a document to Pope John, who summoned him and kept him secretly and with honour for fifteen days. Finally, after various discussions, with papal permission he went to Paris, thence to Brabant. From there he travelled to Cologne so that out of devotion he might see the Three Kings [the Magi]. Leaving Cologne he crossed through Germany (per Alemaniam), heading for Milan (Mediolanum) in Lombardy. From Milan he entered a hermitage of the castle of Melazzo (castri Milasci), where he stayed for two and a half years. Because of war he moved to another hermitage at the castle of Cecima (in castro Cecime) in Pavia diocese, where he remained for about two years, always a recluse, doing penance and praying God for [Edward III] and other sinners.

Your Manuel de Flisco, notary of the lord pope, your devoted servant (devotus servitor vester)

AUTHENTIC OR FORGED?

The chronology appears convincing apart from one incongruity. Edward is said to have remained secretly at Corfe for a year and a half prior to taking ship for Ireland on learning of the death of the earl of Kent. A year and a half after Edward's 'simulated death' would be about 21 March 1329, whereas Edmund was executed a year later, 19 March 1330.[7] In any case the former king would have had no difficulty in reaching Avignon before John XXII's death on 4 December 1334. The time required for the remainder of the journey is a matter of conjecture. The putative itinerary in the Cuttino-Lyman article suggests that Edward was in Lombardy by the summer of 1331.[8] The terminus ad quem for the confession, fabricated or not, would have to be the date of Fieschi's election as bishop of Vercelli, that is 25–26 June 1343, when the style he used would have changed.[9] Letters of attorney, to last for two years, were issued to Fieschi on 8 June 1335, so it has been supposed that this determines the earliest possible date for the confession to have been made abroad.[10] However, a Salisbury record shows Fieschi to have been abroad in September 1333, at which time the chapter requested his assistance at the papal Curia in Avignon. Letters of attorney were issued for a year in December of that year and there is no evidence to indicate Fieschi's return prior to their subsequent reissue.[11] Thus 1333 X 1343 might be taken as the revised time span during which confession could have been made to the future bishop of Vercelli.

Manuele di Fieschi was a scion of a prolific ecclesiastical family centred on Genoa; a family said to have produced two popes, Innocent IV and Adrian V, seventy-two cardinals, and a hundred bishops.[12] No strangers to England, or at any rate to English benefices, ten members of the family are indexed in the revised Le Neve.[13] Manuele himself, the son of Andrea di Fieschi, count of Lavania (Lavagna), was a master of arts who, like many another medieval cleric with a western European perspective, was a pluralist in possession of several English benefices. He had acquired the prebend of Ampleforth in York Minster by an exchange with one in Arras and was provided to Nottingham archdeaconry in 1329. Two years later he exchanged the archdeaconry for the prebend of Milton Manor in Lincoln Cathedral. In the 1320s he obtained the prebend of Netheravon in Salisbury Cathedral where he is named as canon in 1329. He was still holding his prebends in York, Lincoln, and Salisbury in April 1342 when his estate in them was ratified by the king.[14] A relative of his, Giovanni di Fieschi, son of Niccolino (Nicolinus), was a fellow canon at Salisbury. A Niccolino or Niccolò, the "cardinal of Genoa," made a member of Edward III's council at an annual retainer of twenty pounds along with the customary robes, was in 1336 successfully negotiating on behalf of his compatriots for compensation in respect of a plundered galley. This had been attacked off the dunes near Sandwich by the young Despenser at the time of his exile. Edward III denied his father's connivance, but because of his interest in the Genoese as shipbuilders from which his agent Nicolino was endeavouring to hire vessels, felt it prudent to come to an amicable settlement.[15] Carlo di Fieschi, a distant relative of Manuele, is described as the king's *consanguineus* in 1315 when acting as a royal councillor, while Cardinal Luca di Fieschi, nuncio to England in 1317–18, was frequently so designated.[16] With such connections Manuele was in an excellent position to have access to important events in Britain, including what could be gleaned about the fate of Edward II. It might even be suggested that a fabricator could well use Fieschi's name as likely to add authenticity to his forgery.

Independent evidence supports some of the more specific aspects of the story. As shown in the previous chapter, Edward was certainly afloat in a small boat in the Bristol Channel (*toutes fortz en la meer*) between Sunday 19 October and Saturday 25 October 1326. Embarking at Chepstow, he landed at Cardiff and travelled from there to Caerphilly, where he remained in the castle until 2 November. The only expense recorded while in the Channel was the nine pence paid to the Carmelite friar, Richard de Bliton, confessor possibly of the king and certainly of the younger Despenser, for petitioning St Anne to send a favourable wind (*qe ele nous envoiast bon vent*).[17] Whether the ship was becalmed or the victim of adverse gales is not clear from this account. However, a similar story told by Baker states that Edward embarked at Chepstow with the intention of reaching Lundy Island, only to be forced by a storm to land in Glamorgan. This was not surprising in view of the limited access to the island's rocky shoreline. The *Anonimalle* chronicler thought that Edward's purpose was to escape to Ireland (*voleit aver passe en Irlande*), though whether he had a sufficiently large or seaworthy vessel is doubtful.[18] That Henry of Lancaster was despatched to capture the principal parties – the king, Despenser, the earl of Arundel, and Robert Baldock – is well attested. Their capture was achieved by 16 November. Arundel was executed the following day, the younger Despenser a week later, while Baldock subsequently died in Newgate gaol in London.[19] Noteworthy is the fact that Isabella is not portrayed as the author of this vengeful policy, even though in the Fieschi document she is assumed to be the instigator of the king's murder.

Chroniclers, notably Murimuth and Baker, who is basically dependent on Murimuth, as well as the author of the usually reliable *Brut*, suggest that Edward was at some time or other at Corfe.[20] A letter dated 27 July 1327 sent by or on behalf of Thomas de Berkeley, one of Edward's two principal gaolers at Berkeley – the other being John Maltravers, Thomas's brother-in-law – warned the royal chancellor, John de Hothum, bishop of Ely, of a conspiracy to free Edward, involving men in Staffordshire, Warwickshire, and Gloucestershire. From members of his household he had learned of other movements further afield – in Buckinghamshire and neighbouring counties. The most immediate threat was posed by a marauding band led by the brothers Stephen and Thomas Dunheved, the latter a Dominican friar and papal chaplain who was seemingly indifferent to the disciplinary admonitions of his provincial.[21] These men, who were dubbed "rioters," have a strong ecclesiastical flavour, suggesting a measure of clerical support for the deposed king, particularly among the friars with whom he is known to have had a special relationship.[22] There were two other friars apart from Dunheved, one of them a Dominican, as well as a Cistercian monk from Hailes and an Augustinian canon of Llanthony-by-Gloucester.[23]

Despite the emergency, Lord Berkeley stuck doggedly to the letter of the law, arguing that his advisors considered his commission (of the peace) to be inadequate for dealing with those involved. On the first of the following month (August) he was specifically empowered to do so. But the most interesting detail comes from the opening passage of the letter, to the effect that the former king had been snatched from Berkeley and the castle itself ransacked (*d'avoir ravi le pere nostre seignor le roi hors de nostre garde et le dit chastel robbe felenousement encountre la pees*). Berkeley's new commission cites the plundering of the castle but judiciously, so it would seem, omits mention of the king's escape. Not so reticent is the mandate dated 20 August 1327 and directed to the sheriff of Oxfordshire. It records the indictment before Berkeley as keeper of the king's peace in that county and neighbouring Gloucestershire of one William de Aylemere – two rectors of this name are included in an earlier indictment[24] – for consenting to and abetting the abduction of the former king from Berkeley Castle and inciting the people to war against Edward III.[25]

Friar Dunheved is an intriguing character. During the late king's reign he had acted as a confidential messenger and in its final stages carried letters to the younger Despenser in Wales.[26] The Pauline annalist has an unconfirmed story, repeated in the unrelated Lanercost chronicle and possibly alluded to in the Historia Roffensis, to the effect that he was sent to the Roman Curia to secure a divorce between Edward and Isabella.[27] On his return, after this unsuccessful mission, he found the king had been imprisoned and proceeded to organize a sworn conspiracy of (allegedly) powerful laymen and ecclesiastics to secure his release. He is supposed to have been captured at Dunsmore in Warwickshire, where his brother Stephen had property, and brought before the queen. Incarcerated at Pontefract in June [1327], he attempted to escape but subsequently died in prison. His brother is stated to have been detained in London about the same time.[28] The Pauline annalist is not only inaccurate with respect to Dunheved's dates, he also admits that he is reporting hearsay (ut dicebatur).[29] It would be as well to caution that the air at the time was rife with rumours of various kinds.

Despite its "slighting" during the Civil War, the most imposing feature of Berkeley Castle remains the shell keep, which as at Farnham Castle embraces an earlier motte rather than being constructed on its summit. This is approached from the inner ward, somewhat unusually, by a rectangular forebuilding originally roofed in timber. At the top of the internal stairway a sharp left turn from a stone platform leads into the keep through a twelfth-century doorway modified in the fourteenth to provide a smaller entrance. This part of the keep, much altered internally, is now called the "king's gallery." On the left, viewed through a grill in the thickness of the keep wall is a relatively light and airy chamber, "King Edward's room," an upper guardroom lit on two sides by two-light windows with rectangular hood mouldings on the outside overlooking the inner ward. It would have been entered from the crenellated towerlike forebuilding by a narrow ledge above the stairway. The thickness of its wall and an adjoining staircase separate the king's room from the "king's gallery." It is in this gallery that we find a well-like shaft, said to be twenty-eight feet deep, within one of the semicircular bastions of the keep.[30] This shaft is thought to be identifiable as the malodorous charnel-hole referred to by Baker and subsequently by Higden in his *Polychronicon* – translated into English by John Trevisa, the late-fourteenth-century vicar of Berkeley and the then Lord Berkeley's chaplain.[31] A Berkeley account roll shows that at some time, but whether before or after Edward of Caernarfon's (temporary?) escape is not clear, a smith was paid for bolts, bars, and other ironwork for the king's chamber (*pro camera garderobe* [word lost] *patris regis*) as well as for providing four keys for the chamber door, that of the chapel in the tower for which windows were also made, and for an outer door towards *la Canonbury* (in the town) and the postern towards Alkington.[32] Additionally a lock was provided for the upper chamber of the outer gate with bars and hinges for the door. We may surmise that this chapel was for the king's use. It is presumably identifiable as the chapel dedicated to St John in a bastion of the keep, as distinct from that of St Mary adjacent to the great hall. Altogether there seems to have been considerable emphasis on security but possibly somewhat late in the day.[33]

Edward's supposed concealment at Corfe by the castellan "Thomas" unbeknown to John Maltravers, is questionable. Who was this Thomas? The then constable seems to have been Sir John Deveril, no friend of Edward of Caernarfon, who in 1330 was being sought for the part in deceiving the earl of Kent.[34] Could this be a confusion with Thomas Gurney, whom the *Brut* claims was there with Maltravers as royal gaoler?[35] John Maltravers, from Lytchett in Dorset, was by his first wife Thomas de Berkeley's brother-in-law. The Berkeley accounts show that he had indeed been at Corfe and that he was paid £258 8s. 2d. for expenses of the king's father in Dorset. Further, payments of three shillings and one penny and four shillings were made to couriers carrying letters to Maltravers in Dorset and, in the latter case, specifically to Corfe.[36] This does not suffice to refute the statement in the Fieschi letter, but it could be advanced as one of several instances in which real happenings appear to have been adapted to "authenticate" a fictional story.

THE TESTIMONY OF THE CHRONICLERS

That Edward was murdered is amply supported by the testimony of the chronicles, but inevitably in the volatile circumstances of the time – an insurgency led by Isabella and the subsequent replacement of the king, her husband, by her son – there was much partisan writing. The laconic Adam Murimuth declares that by common report (*dictum tamen fuit vulgariter*) he was killed as a precaution by order of John Maltravers and Thomas Gournay [Gurney].[37] The Lanercost chronicler did not commit himself, it was either a natural death or one inflicted by the violence of others.[38] Geoffrey le Baker of Swinbrook in Oxfordshire, a near neighbour of Murimuth's at Fifield, was content in the earlier portion of his chronicle merely to embroider the latter's text, but at certain points he waxes expansive.[39] The abbreviated version of the *Chronicon*, covering the reign of Edward II, was at one time mistakenly assumed to be a Latin translation of a French work by one Thomas de la More, an Oxfordshire knight from Northmoor, a neighbour to both Baker and Murimuth. As such it was published by Stubbs.[40] Maunde Thompson resolved the confusion in his definitive edition of Baker's *Chronicon* and *Chroniculum*.[41] More's family name was Laurence: not only was he a squire, as we saw earlier, in the entourage of John Stratford at the Kenilworth "abdication," but also a relative of the future archbishop.[42] Baker was involved in the unruliness of the time and with many other troublemakers had been released from prison in the closing stages of Edward II's reign in the forlorn hope that he might help to stem the tide of the insurgents.[43] The whole tenor of his chronicle for that reign exhibits a blatant partisanship. For him the villains of the piece were the virago Queen Isabella and her evil genius, the bishop of Hereford, Adam Orleton.[44]

Baker's account of the death of Edward of Caernarfon with all its circumstantial detail has particularly attracted the attention of historians and other writers. It is legitimate to pour scorn on his embellishments, as did Professor Cuttino. That Orleton sent a cryptic message, capable of being read as an instruction to kill the king, is a patent fabrication and not original at that.[45] Indeed it is arguable that the chronicle confined to Edward II's reign, which circulated separately, contains propaganda akin to the accusatory material bandied about at the time of Orleton's promotion to the see of Winchester in 1333.[46] Edward's ill treatment at the hands of his gaolers represents the "passion" of the king – a literary device in vogue at the time. He is depicted as a martyr, mockingly addressed as king, and crowned not with thorns but with hay.[47] The nub of the embellished account is the king's murder in a particularly brutal fashion; one that left no visible mark on the corpse. It was calculated that this would divert any suspicion of foul play. Baker was not an eyewitness of these events – no chronicler was. By his own admission he learned of the events after the Black Death from the captain of the guard placed over the king (*qui ductoribus Edwardi prefuit*), a repentant William Bishop.[48] Was he too a fiction? It has been thought so; after all the name was common enough at the time.[49] Yet he might be as real as the formerly elusive de la More. In 1321 a William Bishop was pardoned for acting against the Despensers and two years later was participating in a riot at Warwick.[50] But it would be rash to assume that he is recognizable as the sergeant-at-arms of Edward III mentioned in the patent rolls from 1338 until after the Black Death – apparently the man who accounted for expenses in 1355. In some respects this last William Bishop is a not unlikely candidate for the role of Baker's informant, though he could conceivably have been of a later generation.[51]

Speculation, stripped of the embellishments in Baker's story of the king's death, and the manner in which it was effected, is much the same as that to be found in other chronicles, the *Brut* for instance, but whereas Baker states that the king was suffocated by means of heavy bolsters (*cum pulvinatoribus magnis*) while held down by a weight heavier than that of fifteen strong men (*gravi mole amplius quam quindecim robustorum*), both the *Brut* and the Westminster chronicle specify that a table was employed for the purpose.[52] Moreover, the latter is emphatic that the means of death were revealed by the confession of those responsible.[53] When it became feasible to make some official statement the former king was said to have been suffocated and Roger Mortimer was held responsible.[54] Keen to authenticate his chronicle, Jean Froissart would come to Berkeley in September 1366 in the company of Hugh Despenser's grandson, Edward. But all that a very old squire could tell him was self evident: during the very year of his imprisonment at Berkeley Edward II either died [of natural causes] or his life had been cut short.[55]

That Edward could have escaped either from Berkeley or Corfe in the manner described is conceivable. It is known that several prisoners did likewise, including Sir Robert Walkfare, said by the chronicler Walsingham to have been a *consanguineus* of Thomas, earl of Lancaster. He broke out of Corfe Castle in 1326 and in doing so killed a porter, one William de Foulere.[56] Can this be the origin of the incident in the Fieschi letter? It is more difficult to accept the story that a porter's body was substituted for that of the king. In the first place we know that the body was embalmed sometime between the date of death, 21–22 September and 21 October, when it was delivered to Br John Toky or Thoky, abbot of the Benedictine abbey of St Peter's Gloucester.[57] A bronze plaque now commemorates the spot at which this transfer allegedly took place. Murimuth, who believed that Edward had been killed at the instance of Maltravers and Gurney, claims that many abbots, priors, knights, and townsmen of Bristol and Gloucester were invited to see the undamaged corpse (*corpus suum integrum*), but that they viewed it only superficially (*tale superficialiter conspexissent*). This public viewing must surely have taken place at Berkeley prior to embalming. Murimuth's intention is to question the likelihood that a robustly healthy man in his early forties could have died a natural death. As an annotator of the Peterborough chronicle expressed it: "*Edwardus vespere sanus in crastino mortuus est inventus.*"[58] Murimuth does not suggest that those who came – men who would certainly have been able to recognize the king – were being hoodwinked as to the corpse's identity, merely that they were not able to inspect the body minutely for signs of injury. It scarcely needs to be added that the king's face was a familiar sight in Gloucester and that his corpse could not have been mistaken for that of a common porter. As the funeral was postponed until late December a further question arises. How effective was embalming in the fourteenth century?

At this point one might question the statement in the *Historia* attributed to Walter Froucester (Frocester), abbot of St Peter's Gloucester between 1381 and 1412 – more than half a century after the event – that his predecessor, Thoky, braved the wrath of Mortimer and Isabella by giving burial to Edward's body when the neighbouring houses of St Augustine's Bristol, Kingswood, and Malmesbury had shrunk from so doing. His claim that the abbot had provided the funeral carriage at his own expense is possible, although it was Berkeley and Maltravers who received payment for custody of the body until its delivery to Gloucester. Moreover, Smyth in his *Lives of the Berkeleys* cites the account, seemingly no longer extant, of Thomas de Berkeley's receiver for the second year of Edward III to the effect that he paid for the trappings of the funeral carriage.[59] Once Edward was dead those holding the reins of government were anxious to give him honourable burial but in a place of their choosing, remote from London, where the reaction of the populace was a potential danger. Gloucester Abbey was the wealthiest and most prestigious house in the area. But there was another, more traditional claimant. The Westminster monk, Robert de Beby, had hastened to the court at Nottingham charged with the task of securing the royal corpse for burial in his monastery.[60] His mission proved fruitless; Isabella and her paramour were unwilling to risk the sympathy that might have been aroused, despite the unpopularity of Edward in his lifetime. Fresh in people's minds were the embarrassing scenes of devotion before the tablet erected in St Paul's in commemoration of the Ordinances by the future "martyr" Thomas of Lancaster.[61]

ARRANGEMENTS FOR EDWARD'S FUNERAL

Exigencies of state, the Scottish situation in particular, delayed the funeral until 20 December. On 16 November John Darcy, "the cousin," left the court at Pontefract for London, where he received twenty pounds from the wardrobe for expenses concerning the burial of Edward. He accounted for purchases of items of armour, saddles, horses and swords, as well as for a per diem allowance of four shillings for a banneret and of twelve pence for others of lesser status.[62] Another account for the expenses of the lying-in-state records the payment of eight shillings and nine pence for four great logs of oak and also the wages of carpenters employed to fabricate a barrier around the corpse to protect it from the crush of people, not, so it would seem, to prevent it from being seen clearly.[63] Could the embalmed body have been exposed thus for so long had it been other than the king's? Such deliberate openness militates against sinister deductions from another circumstance. "Significantly," states the Cuttino-Lyman article in reference to the funeral procession, "this was the first [recorded?] occasion in western European history when a wooden mannequin-effigy of the deceased was used instead of the body's being displayed."[64] Ernst Kantorowicz, in his provocative study, *The King's Two Bodies*, comments that the practice of using a mannequin dates from Edward's funeral: the royal "body natural" has become invisible, but the normally invisible body politic is displayed by the effigy, one "persona ficta" impersonating another," the royal "Dignitas." Edward's image, carved in the likeness of the former king, cost forty shillings, a further seven shillings and three pence being paid for a copper-gilt crown, as transpires from the account of Thomas de Useflete, supervisor of Edward III's wardrobe.[65] Had this mannequin survived – as has the death mask of Edward III – and had it lived up to its description, it would have served to dispel some of the wilder stories about the king's death. The fine alabaster figure surmounted by a freestone canopy in the choir at Gloucester was at one time thought to have preserved features "the exact form and model of those of Edward of Carnarvon himself."[66] A more practised eye, that of Arthur Gardner, was emphatic that "the face is of an ideal type rather than an accurate portrait" and subsequent experts have confirmed this view, arguing that portraiture was a later development.[67] But can we always be sure of this? Even allowing for artistic licence, it would be difficult to gainsay the argument that it was impossible in the circumstances to have passed off the facial characteristics of the gatekeeper for those of the king.

Some other astonishing echoes of reality in the Fieschi document remain to be examined. The Berkeley Muniments reveal that 37s. 8d. was paid for a silver "vase" (a heart-shaped vessel?) in which to place the king's heart.[68] According to the account of Hugh de Glanville, "the clerk appointed to have the body of the king's father brought from Berkeley Castle to St Peter's Abbey Gloucester," the evisceration was performed by an unnamed woman. He claimed expenses for conducting this woman, at the king's command (*precepto regis*), to the queen at Worcester, remaining there for one day, and then proceeding to York. It is unlikely that the juvenile king gave the order in person, hence that part of Moore's argument about Edward III's likely reactions is misdirected. What we have here is Isabella's mandate in official guise.[69] The question remains, what was her purpose in consulting the woman? Did she wish to ascertain the means of death, to satisfy herself that the corpse was that of the king, to give vent to remorse, or had she some other purpose? Perhaps the most likely explanation is a simple one, that she desired to know how her husband had died.

There is a final twist to the evidence. Isabella was herself buried in 1358 amidst a belated aura of near sanctity in the church of the Franciscan friars in London. A description of her alabaster tomb in the middle of the choir was given by a friar of the place shortly before the dissolution of the religious houses. Beneath the breast of her effigy, we are told, lay the heart of King Edward her husband (*sub pectore imaginis eius jacet cor regis Edwardi mariti sui*).[70] This was one of the defaced tombs noted by Stow in his *Survey of London,* who also claimed that Roger Mortimer was buried in the same church.[71] Assuming that we are here concerned with the heart that Isabella had presumably received over thirty years earlier, possibly from the hand of the eviscerator, we can argue a degree of remorse and no doubt of deathbed penitence – after all, her friar confessor in 1327, Robert Lamborn, was said to be buried beneath a plain slab a short distance away.[72] If the friar's story is true, and it would be a strange coincidence if it were not, clearly Isabella did not believe the heart to be that of the gatekeeper. But could she have been deceived in this, as the Fieschi document suggests? Ostensibly substitution of the heart would have presented little difficulty, but the body is another matter, it is scarcely conceivable that Isabella could have been deluded by that. The subsequent fate of the heart and the claim that Isabella's body "was dressed in a tunic and mantle in which she had been married over fifty years previously" must remain a stumbling block for the hypothesis that if her husband had really escaped it would have suited her to acquiesce in the deception.[73]

Where was the royal physician in all this? The month before the ex-king was removed to Berkeley the practitioner who had treated both him and his wife Isabella, and who was to be retained in the same capacity by Edward III, one Master Pancius de Controne, an Italian possibly from Lombardy, was granted one hundred pounds a year from royal revenues in Northampton as reward for his services.[74] The peculiarity, if such it be, lies in the timing. For whatever reason, the royal patient was removed from the doctor's list in the March of 1327. In the normal course we would expect Pancius to have been called in for consultation in the event of the captive's illness and maybe to have carried out a post mortem examination, presuming death to have occurred unexpectedly, but in any case to have supervised the evisceration. There is no hint of any such involvement. Was he deliberately kept from the scene? Subsequently he came to enjoy further grants, including the manor of Guiting in Gloucestershire, that must have left him a wealthy man.[75]

SOME INTRIGUING COINCIDENCES

In May 1332 Eleanor, Edward II's daughter, was married at Nijmegen to Reginald, count of Guelders. A detailed expense account of the time reveals that a "Willelmus de Cornevill," possibly the William of Cornwall whom we shall encounter later as the capturer of Thomas Gurney, but at the time Eleanor's "valet de chambre" (*valettus de camera*) was allowed expenses for a journey to Cologne to visit the shrine of the three kings – the Magi.[76] Are we to assume that he is going on his own or is he accompanying someone at the behest of his mistress? If the latter, who could this be? Edward of Caernarfon, a clandestine figure at his daughter's marriage? The date is not inappropriate, but we must avoid piling fantasy upon fantasy by making more of this incident than we should. Presumably many must have made such a pilgrimage from Brabant. We are on safer ground, however, with the fact that Manuele di Fieschi became provost of Arnhem in 1332: he could therefore have known about Cornwall's pilgrimage.

Related to the purported pilgrimage of Edward to Cologne is another striking coincidence arising from two entries in a wardrobe book of Edward III's reign. The king, in pursuance of his policy of alliance with the emperor, Louis IV, travelled to Coblenz in 1338 for his ceremonial investiture as vicar of the Empire. Whilst there a certain William le Galeys "the Welshman" – a suitable sobriquet for Edward of Caernarfon – was arrested at nearby Cologne. A royal sergeant-at-arms, Francis Lumbard, escorted him to the king. Details of their meeting are not disclosed, but what we do learn is that at Antwerp, the royal base on the Continent, a Francekins Forcet claimed expenses for Galeys's custody for three weeks of December 1338. Apparently the prisoner had been escorted there following his interview with the king. At that point he vanishes from history. possibly from life itself. The entries in the wardrobe book concerning this matter are separated. In the first Galeys is said to have claimed to be the king's father, in the second to have termed himself king of England, father of the present king.[77] Could the author of the Fieschi letter have got wind of this impersonation and once again used fact to bolster fiction? Alternatively, are we to believe that this was no impersonator but Edward of Caernarfon himself? Impersonations of kings were not rare and in 1318 a man (of unsound mind?) had been put to death for claiming to be the "real" king. Surely such an unkingly king as Edward must have been a changeling![78]

WHERE IS EDWARD BURIED?

The latter part of Cuttino and Lyman's article is concerned with the Italian "evidence." The positive identification by Anna Benedetti of the two places in

Lombardy in which the former king is supposed to have stayed as a hermit provides the starting point. The publication of the Fieschi letter gave rise to two plaques in the castle of Melazzo d'Acqui and another, which erroneously describes Isabella as the sister of King Philip IV of France, in the abbey of Sant'Alberto di Butrio.[79] This last claims additionally, without any supporting evidence, that the bones of Edward were stolen and taken to England and placed in the tomb at Gloucester by Edward III.[80] Thefts of such a kind were not so uncommon in the Middle Ages as the article's authors seem to suggest. There is a tradition, they continue, which goes back further than the publication of the Fieschi document, to the effect that the abbey contains a tomb of an English king and they cite the testimony in 1958 of a man of eighty-eight who claimed that his grandfather "had spoken of an English king who had taken refuge in the hermitage" [at Sant'Alberto].[81] It is difficult to evaluate this piece of oral testimony, even more difficult to connect it with Edward II. In the 1920s the iconography of a now lost historiated capital was imaginatively interpreted by Benedetti as symbolic of the political struggles in England during the Mortimer-Isabella period. As can be seen from the photographs in the *Speculum* article, one does not require an art historian to date the surviving historiated capital in the cloister gallery, and the gallery itself, to a period some two centuries before the 1320s. The tomb recess, the authors suggest, may be even earlier. Perhaps, then, this part of the article, interesting in itself, is stating the obvious so far as fourteenth century associations are concerned. There is nothing here in the way of hard evidence, still less anything about the tomb recess as it now exists, or indeed any part of the ancient abbey, to point to the burial there of Edward or any other English king. Once again, this does not serve to invalidate the Fieschi document: it does mean that no satisfactory corroborative evidence has been found in the sites with which Edward was supposedly connected.

The tomb of Edward II in what is now Gloucester Cathedral, was "opened" on 2 October 1855, apparently for the first time. A memorandum of this has been preserved in the account of Marshall Allen, subsacrist of the former abbey church (1835–58). It states that he was present together with Dr Jeune, canon in residence, Mr Waller the architect and a mason, Henry Clifford. This memorandum is not precise but it would seem that although by removing the floor on the south side of the tomb the wooden coffin, found to be "still very perfect," was exposed and a portion of it removed to reveal the leaden one "containing the remains of the king," the latter was not actually prised open. The tomb was resealed two hours later.[82] The purpose of the excavation is not specified, but it may have been merely to establish the coffin's existence. Removal of the thick sheet of lead shaped to conform to the body beneath would have served to confirm or deny the reburial of the royal bones. Failing further examination of the tomb there is little reason to doubt that Edward of Caernarfon's corpse has remained there undisturbed since December 1327 or thereabouts.

MORTIMER'S *AGENTS PROVOCATEURS* AND THE PURSUIT
OF THE MURDERERS

Perhaps the most bizarre circumstance in the whole affair and one that may well have provided the stimulus for the interpretation to be found in the Fieschi letter was that the government of Queen Isabella and Roger Mortimer deliberately fostered the idea that the former king was still alive, and at Corfe, in order to entrap those who might be tempted to organize political opposition with, it was suggested, assistance from the continent.[83] Chronicler Baker gives a most interesting account of the affair.[84] According to him, though as we have seen he is not above embroidering the truth, certain persons pretended that the former king, who had lately died, was living in the castle of Corfe. They illuminated the walls and towers with torches to give the locals the impression that some important king was being entertained there. Soon the rumour that Edward of Caernarfon was alive spread throughout England. On hearing it his half-brother Edmund, earl of Kent, sent a Dominican friar to investigate. This man bribed the gatekeeper, as he thought, to allow him to see Edward. He was warned to dress himself in secular garb to escape detection and at night was permitted to enter the hall where he saw the king sitting at a great feast. He hastened to inform the earl of what he had seen, whereupon Edmund solemnly swore that he would work to release his brother.

Hence, by the queen's connivance and that of Mortimer, the earl of Kent and other secular lords and religious were accused of an attempt to free the king and to reinstate him. The earl was beheaded, as we have seen, and many others were imprisoned, exiled, or fined.[85] The story is widely related, among others by the Pauline annalist, Adam Murimuth, the canon of Bridlington, and William Dene, archdeacon of Rochester.[86] One article of Mortimer's future indictment was that he was responsible for the fabrication.[87] The *Brut* chronicle goes further, as the extract at the beginning of this chapter shows. It relates how Earl Edmund visited Avignon to urge the "translation" of Thomas of Lancaster by reason of the many miracles performed on his account. When this proved fruitless, Edmund is said to have broached the topic of freeing his brother, Edward of Caernarfon, "since that a common fame is throughout England that he was alive and whole and safe."[88] Manoeuvres to secure Lancaster's canonization were certainly under way at the time.[89] Moreover, John XXII was constrained subsequently to respond to the Isabella-Mortimer government by discrediting Kent's story and claiming that he had believed no such thing of a king so publicly buried. In any case, he would not have dealt with an individual noble in such a manner. The funeral was overt; clearly no deception would have been possible.[90] For the present purpose the whole episode is significant only in so far as it provides an indication of a real plot against the regime. In fact, there is no evidence of support by notable laymen; those who fell foul of the authorities were mainly churchmen, many of them lowly. Yet this farcical affair does indicate widespread sympathy for the former king but only in a limited section of society. It may also indicate a seething dislike of the government that had replaced him.

The question of responsibility, whether direct or indirect, for the king's death does not require examination here. Some of the immediate circumstances however, are relevant to the Fieschi document's validity. Mortimer, Berkeley's father-in-law, following his capture at Nottingham Castle in 1330 was accused, as part of an all-embracing indictment, of having consented to the king's suffocation.[91] Three years earlier, when he and his paramour Isabella had been at the height of their power, the erstwhile king constituted a potential danger: so long as he remained alive the threat remained. At that time William Shalford was the deputy of Mortimer, the justice of North Wales. In 1330 Howel or Hywel ap Gruffydd appealed, that is levelled an accusation, against Shalford before Mortimer's successor as justice, Sir John Wysham. The charge was no less than that of compassing the death of the former king. Shalford, the Welshman alleged, had sent a letter (dated 14 September 1327) from Rhosfair in Anglesey warning Mortimer, then at Abergavenny,[92] of the hatching of conspiracies in both North and South Wales in collusion with important persons in England. Their purpose, he declared, was to spring Edward from his prison at Berkeley. Were they to meet with success Mortimer and his associates would be destroyed. He counselled that no one in either Wales or England should have further occasion to consider Edward's deliverance (*ne nul autre Dengleterre ne de Gales averoient matere de penser de sa deliveraunce*). Mortimer, it is said, at once showed the letter to William Ockley (or Ogle), with instructions to carry it to Berkeley. There he was to allow Edward's custodians to examine it and to charge them to respond appropriately. Ockley undertook the mission and in conjunction with the former king's guardians traitorously slew him.[93] The validity of the allegation is obfuscated by Welsh-English rivalry: Hywel had hoped to have the case settled on his home ground.[94] In the event the proceedings were examined in chancery, where in October 1331 the appeal was described as one that could not be finally decided in King's Bench, judgment being given for the defendant.[95] There the case fizzled out.

The significance for the present purpose is that Ockley plays a prominent role together with Sir Thomas Gurney (Gournay),[96] a Somersetshire knight with property in Englishcombe, Farrington and elsewhere. Gurney, a rebel in the early 1320s, had been imprisoned with the Mortimers in the Tower, but in 1324 was pardoned with restitution of his lands.[97] William Ockley was deputed by Thomas de Berkeley to oversee Edward of Caernarfon. At the Westminster Parliament of 1330 these overseers were jointly condemned to death for "traitorously murdering the king's father." During the course of his own defence Berkeley admitted to having appointed them but failed to say when, although if the Shalford letter is genuine, it must have been shortly before Edward's death.[98] Berkeley's own alibi was demolished by the biographer of his house, Smyth.[99] Gurney is associated with Simon de Bereford or Barford, a substantial Leicesterhire knight, as having been sent to despatch Edward. Both Bereford and Sir John Deveril, the deceiver of the credulous earl of Kent, were put to death with Mortimer but not specifically on account of complicity in the former king's murder.

Were we to discount the Fieschi letter the evidence would suggest that Ockley (rather than Bereford) and Gurney were the actual murderers, or at any rate the men who knew most about what happened. Ockley escaped abroad and is not heard of again. He may have died before pursuit could be organized. Berkeley, as Dugdale and Smyth affirm, protected Gurney until Mortimer's fall, when flight provided the only means of survival.[100] On 3 December 1330 writs were issued for the prevention of Gurney's passage abroad, and on 15 July in the following year a commission of enquiry was launched following a report that Cornishmen from Mousehole had assisted his escape and that of John Maltravers to the Continent.[101]

Thanks to a fortuitous survival of documents, we know much about Gurney's flight and can plot his route in detail.[102] It would seem to have been in May 1331 that the presence of Gurney and Maltravers in Spain first came to the notice of English officialdom, apparently because of their recognition by Isolda, the widow of Sir John de Belhouse, during her pilgrimage to the shrine of St James of Compostella.[103] Edward III wrote letters to Alfonso XI of Castile asking that Gurney, who had been arrested and pilloried in Burgos, should be delivered to the seneschal of Gascony, John de Haustede. In the second letter he requested that the prisoner be examined on the charges against him in the presence of Bernard Pelegrym or Pilgrim, a royal sergeant-at arms. No deposition of the kind requested is known to have survived. There was some hitch in the arrangements for Gurney's handover, as another of the king's emissaries, Giles of Spain, was to discover. Worse still, the prisoner escaped.[104]

Gurney, it was learned in England, had reached Naples and Sir William de Thweng or Tweng was sent to detain him. On his arrival he found the fugitive in the custody of a royal agent, William of Cornwall.[105] A ship was chartered to take Gurney to Aigues-Mortes, the walled town from which St Louis had set out on crusade. Arrived in Spain, the party was detained by a local family and was only released at the intervention of King Alfonso IV of Aragon. After crossing the Pyrenees the escort eventually reached Bayonne. The captive, possibly worn out by physical exertion and mental anxiety, fell ill and medical attention was summoned. This proved unavailing for Gurney died shortly afterwards. His body was embalmed and taken by ship to Tynemouth, Edward III being nearby in anticipation of the surrender of the Scots.

The seneschal of Gascony, Oliver Ingham, although he had been lumped with Bereford and Mortimer as a member of a despicable triumvirate (*principal moveours des dites besoignes*), had been rehabilitated as early as 8 December 1330 in consideration of his previous service in Gascony. Then in the summer of 1331 he replaced Haustede as seneschal. Having found the "traitor Gurney" at Bayonne, Ingham supposedly fiercely declared that the villain would never escape[?] or receive pardon; then, when the captive had confessed his assent to the king's death and described the manner of it, his head was cut off and

despatched to the king. Such an execution would have been in overt defiance of
Edward III's manifest wish and ignores the fact that the body was embalmed for
the journey. On the other hand it could be argued, perversely it might seem, that
Ingham had been deliberately sent with secret instructions.[106] One reason for
this narration of Gurney's journey is that his ship must have passed close to
Genoa even if it did not make a landfall there, while at Aigues-Mortes it was
close to Maguelone. Can there be any doubt that in these areas the story of
Edward II's death and knowledge of English affairs became widespread?

The idea has been mooted that Edward III did not pursue his father's murderers with vigour.[107] This was not the case. As we have seen, Mortimer, the
man exercising overall political authority at the time, was hanged at Tyburn,
admittedly for a variety of other crimes or alleged crimes as well. The condemned Gurney and Ockley escaped, the former being hounded with great per-
sistence. Clearly the king felt that if anyone knew the truth about his father's
death, that person was Gurney. Although some chroniclers assume his involvement, Maltravers was never formally accused of Edward's murder but of another offence – contriving the death of Edmund of Woodstock.[108] His second wife,
Agnes, presented an (unread) petition to the parliament of 1339 on the grounds
that her husband had been condemned unheard, but it was not until 1345 that the
first step towards his rehabilitation was taken. That Fieschi had become bishop
a mere two years before *pace* Cuttino and Lyman is no more than a convenient
coincidence, convenient, that is, for the theory that the king was responding to
the revelations of the Fieschi letter.[109] It is true that Thomas de Berkeley, despite
the weakness of his alibi and the fact that he was Mortimer's son-in-law, was
permitted to escape punishment for what at the very least must be accounted
criminal negligence – somewhat akin perhaps to the charge that could be levelled against the earl of Pembroke for permitting Gaveston's capture at Deddington. Where his mother, Isabella, was concerned Edward did show mercy.[110]
Whether she assented to her husband's death cannot be known with certainty, it
is just possible that Mortimer acted on the spur of the moment and without consulting her, but Isabella's previous conduct coupled with mounting disaffection
had made removal inevitable. Without Edward there was no immediate focus for
dissidents until the young Edward was in a position to assert himself.

The argument thus far has been directed towards assessing the validity of the
Fieschi letter, the possibility that Edward of Caernarfon could have survived,
and the credibility of the notion that another body was successfully substituted
for his own; furthermore that his presence abroad could have eluded the vigilance of his son's agents, exemplified by the successful pursuit of Gurney. Faced
with the unexpected phenomenon of the Fieschi letter Stubbs sought to account
for it by advancing three "theories." It could have been a political trick to discredit Edward III at the outbreak of war with France – particularly, one might
add, in view of his accommodation with the German emperor; the pretended
"confession" of one who, fearing that he would be implicated, "wished to secure

his own safety"; or the real confession of a madman.[111] To my mind none of these carries conviction.

A POSSIBLE EXPLANATION

Is there another credible hypothesis? Surely there is; one compatible with the prevailing ethos and with the nature of the letter that the present writer, unlike Cuttino and Lyman but in agreement with James Cooke,[112] does not believe was ever delivered. "Political canonization" by popular demand was a feature of life in England during the fourteenth century, the cases of Winchelsey and Lancaster being particularly well known. However incompetent he may have been, the former king's pitiable end aroused sympathy; a sympathy that was to manifest itself in the generous offerings made by pilgrims to his tomb at Gloucester, which served to transform the eastern limb of the abbey church. The Fieschi letter, I would suggest, is an element in the process of developing a cult. Edward is made to adopt the holiest of guises, that of a hermit perpetually devoted to prayer and the inner life. He can expiate his sins and make amends for the social and political disasters of his reign by assisting in that essential role of interceding for the world – a far better dénouement than the miserable death that he had in fact suffered. Breaking the bond of the confessional would not be regarded as reprehensible were it for the purpose of disclosing the lineaments of sanctity. The hermit life and revelation through the confessional are well-known ingredients of hagiography.[113]

Trevisa, in rendering a passage from Higden's *Polychronicon*, was fully aware of the tendency towards popular martyrdom. He couples the king's name with Lancaster's, pointing out the difference of opinion as to whether Edward should be accounted a martyr or not. As the anonymous writer of British Library Harleian MS 2261 expressed it: "Wherefore many men say that he died a martyr and did many miracles. Nevertheless keeping in prison, villainous and opprobrious death make not a martyr unless holiness of life before be correspondent."[114] There were those, such as the monks of St Albans, who were unequivocal in his praise. As a benefactor who had protected their house with his royal power, given them many precious articles and relics, and provided help towards the rebuilding of their choir and refectory, he was assured of a place among the saints.[115] Then there was one John Baston, "vadlet," who in 1340 told Edward III that he had built a chapel in honour of St John the Baptist and of "nostre seigneur le roy Edward de Karnervan, vostre piere, jesant a Gloucestre, qui Deiux assoile." This was situated at "wyke day market" in Nottingham where, he claimed, great miracles had long been performed by virtue of the said king. He asked for a concession of the forty foot plot of ground on which the chapel stood. His petition was duly granted by a writ of privy seal.[116] Baker's "passion of the king," the welcome flood of pilgrims to Gloucester, and the transformation of Edward's character, possibly even his idealized face, are all manifestations of the dead king's cult. It was a relatively simple task to build upon the recent rumours spread by

Mortimer as *agent provocateur* by continuing the story that had previously terminated at Corfe and denizing it in the Mediterranean region.

Although we may never know the precise local circumstances that gave rise to the Fieschi letter it was clearly informed by knowledge emanating from England. Its attribution to Fieschi is conceivably yet another carefully contrived circumstantial detail. Reasons have been given as to why such a cult could have had an offshoot in Lombardy or elsewhere in the Mediterranean. In the longer term its impact there may have been less remarkable but nonetheless dimly retained in folk memory, as Cuttino and Lyman have suggested. After all, Manuele di Fieschi himself, capitalizing upon his intimate knowledge of English affairs, by this means could have fostered Genoese piety. It is more than probable that he felt sympathy for the murdered monarch, but it is surely inconceivable that he sent a letter in the local patois to Edward III. Alternatively, and more likely, Fieschi's name may have been "borrowed" to lend authenticity to the whole affair. Whether due to his connivance or not, the letter attributed to him is clearly a competent forgery, a forgery with a purpose, the "sanctification" of a politically ineffective king who had been savagely done to death. Forgery was an art well developed in the Middle Ages and sainthood could be and was established by such means.[117]

PART TWO

The Colonial Empire

"The tide of English power over the British Isles appeared to reach its height in 1305. In the Lenten parliament of that year long lists of petitions from Ireland, Scotland and Gascony were considered by Edward I's councillors, while an equally impressive batch of petitions from north and west Wales was being simultaneously scrutinized by Prince Edward's council at Kennington. The arm of the king of England's justice seemed to stretch to the farthest part of the British Isles – be it Anglesey in Wales, Kerry in Ireland or Galloway in Scotland."

R.R. Davies, *Domination and Conquest*, p. 127

9

Scotland,

1290–1330

EDWARD I AS ARBITRATOR:
THE RISE AND FALL OF KING JOHN

The Scottish problem was the most irksome of all Edward I's legacies to his son.[1] It is sustainable, further, that the conflict originating in the late thirteenth century and culminating in 1328, ignominiously for the English – in what Geoffrey le Baker, mouthing the common view, dubbed the *turpis pax* of Northampton – was very largely of his own making.[2] But in English eyes it is the disastrous outcome of the conflict that must be attributed to his ineffective son. To do his father justice, it was chance allied to the certainly foolhardy, possibly amorous, conduct of Alexander III that precipitated the initial crisis of a leaderless northern kingdom.[3] Alexander's death in 1286 was followed four years later by that of his granddaughter, Margaret, a double twist of fate that led to Edward's invidious task of arbitration in the "Great Cause" of 1291–92.[4]

In May 1291, prior to his assumption of the role of adjudicator between the thirteen "Competitors" for the Scottish throne,[5] Edward I sought to secure an acknowledgment of his suzerainty from the temporary rulers of Scotland, the "Guardians," acting in conjunction with other notables. *Pace* Professor Barrow, the response of "la bone gent d'Escoce" – a phrase sometimes translated as "the community of the realm of Scotland, at other times as "the responsible men"[6] – reads as a consummate piece of evasion.[7] This does not detract from the contention that it was an established tenet of feudal society, lay or ecclesiastical, that those temporarily entrusted with government "in default of a lord" were not entitled to bind future officeholders. *Sede vacante*, as it were, there could be no compromising the status of a future king, rightfully appointed.[8] Ironically, the future king was to concede all that the English monarch had required of the Guardians.

Anxious for a speedy resolution of the affair, the Scots were forced to accede to Edward's basic demands for recognition of his overlordship, temporary possession of Scottish strongholds, and presidency of the tribunal chosen to judge between the claimants. Edward promised to restore the strongholds to the chosen king within two months and to require nothing other than homage at future vacancies of the Crown. To pursue their claims the Competitors were obliged to recognize Edward's suzerainty, though what legal sanction this had is questionable. They did, however, claim to act with the concurrence of the Guardians and of "la bone gent." Conscious of the value of the precedent, Edward sent copies of the documents issued by the Competitors for preservation in monastic chronicles.[9]

In mid-June 1291 the four Guardians and other notables individually swore fealty to Edward as "superior and direct" lord of Scotland. The English king then proclaimed that, now the realms of England and Scotland were joined, royal writs from the northern kingdom could be dealt with by the justices of Common Pleas at Westminster.[10] Of his conduct it has been charitably remarked that there was no "intention to subvert Scottish independence, merely a blinkered determination to insist upon every jot and tittle of the English king's rights."[11] Such insistence was to lead from one thing to another and eventually to war between his son and a Scottish king who owed nothing of his kingship to his southern counterpart. Indeed, one could argue that from the first Edward, determined to support his claim to overlordship by an appeal to history, however distorted by myth, pursued that same policy of "imperialism" he had espoused in Wales, its nakedness clothed in documentary justification and legal process. Almost inevitably, given John Balliol's alternation of defiance with capitulation, this led to the resumption of a direct authority that, having been affirmed by mutual agreement, was the more difficult for the Scots to gainsay.

The intricacies of the process lying behind Edward's judgment have been exhaustively expounded.[12] It was on 17 November 1292, at Berwick on Tweed, that he delivered his verdict in favour of John Balliol, who was declared the nearest heir of the "Maid of Norway," Margaret.[13] This judgment, it has been remarked, "was surely the triumph of law, common sense and respect for orderly procedure."[14] Technically it was, but the sequel proved galling to the Scots. Edward appointed the feast of St Edmund, king and martyr (20 November 1292), for Balliol's swearing of fealty for the realm of Scotland and 25 December for his homage *ubicumque*. Ten days after his oath, on St Andrew's day (30 November), the new monarch was enthroned at Scone with traditional ceremony.[15] In the event it was on the (inauspicious?) feast of the protomartyr Stephen, in the royal palace at Newcastle, that he performed homage to the English king "with his own mouth in French."[16]

Having secured his desired position *vis-à-vis* Scotland, the English king exploited it with scant consideration for adverse political consequences, remote though such must have appeared at the time. There now seems to be general agreement that Balliol was no puppet – a myth engendered by the Scottish clergy's declaration of 17 March 1309. Edward had merely adhered to strict legal process.[17] That was no consolation to the king of Scots, whose position was soon rendered untenable. Edward determined to uphold his earlier claim that appeals could be made from the Scottish to the English courts. When a petition was lodged against such action on the grounds that it was contrary to his promise in the Treaty of Birgham/Northampton (1290),[18] Edward responded through his mouthpiece, Justice Brabazon, that as overlord he had the right to review judgments delivered during the interregnum of the Guardians.[19] In December 1292 he went further with a personal declaration of his intention to entertain appeals from Scotland and even, should necessity arise, to summon the king of Scots himself.[20]

Early in 1293[21] formal instruments issued under pressure by King John freed Edward from any agreements with the Guardians and other notables and abrogated the Treaty of Birgham/Northampton.[22] The same year the Scottish king was summoned to answer in the appeal (one of several) before the King's Bench by Macduff, son of Earl Malcolm of Fife. The case is said to have been adjourned to the Michaelmas Parliament of that year at Westminster.[23] John appeared, either in that or some other parliament, but only to declare his incapacity to respond without consulting the *probi homines* of the realm (the Latin equivalent of "la bone gent d'Escoce"). Threatened with confiscation of three of his principal castles, Balliol capitulated. In a prepared statement, delivered personally before the English king and his council, he addressed Edward as "superior lord of the realm of Scotland," acknowledging his own status as liegeman for the realm that he held by right – himself and his heirs. He was given a day, 14 June 1294, to appear before the Easter Parliament with instruction to bring the writs directed to him from England. Although the patent rolls confirm that Balliol's proctors were there, the parliament's business was curtailed owing to Edward's military commitments. According to Andrew de Tong's roll, Balliol subsequently sent proctors to the Bury St Edmunds Parliament of November 1295. This is a confusion, since Bury was not a venue for parliament until 1296.[24] Record of the case then peters out.

Pressure on the Scots was relieved when Philip IV of France confiscated Aquitaine (19 May 1294). Edward, following an unsuccessful threefold demand for its restoration, renounced his homage and embarked on a policy of encircling alliances.[25] The Scottish king and various of his earls and barons were summoned to the English host, a feudal service for which they were unwilling to acknowledge liability. Edward was further distracted by widespread revolt among the Welsh, whose footsoldiers were equally reluctant to serve. In the north of that country the incipient fortress of Caernarfon was temporarily overrun and its combustible parts destroyed.[26] By May of 1295 the Scots had come to an understanding with France – by no means for the first or the last time. A formal treaty incorporating arrangements for a dynastic marriage was sealed on 23 October 1295, the day following the Franco-Norwegian treaty, with which Scotland was also associated.[27] Particularly alarming from Edward's perspective were the proceedings of a parliament which met 5 July 1295, possibly at

Scone, but more likely at Stirling.[28] Dissatisfied with Balliol's vacillation in face of Edward, it determined that a council of twelve, made up of an equal number of bishops, earls, and barons, should oversee the government of Scotland.[29] Under the aegis of this council the French alliance was sealed.[30]

The English king was soon apprised of the Scottish-French rapprochement. His concern is apparent as early as June 1294, when he placed an embargo on Scottish shipping to the Continent. The *Scalacronica* suggests, as does the Lanercost chronicler, that Edward's distrust of Scottish loyalty brought a demand for hostages from Berwick, Roxburgh, Edinburgh, and Stirling as security during the Anglo-French conflict. Furious at so blatant a violation of Balliol's homage and fealty, Edward summoned the Scottish king to appear before him on 1 March at Newcastle. He was to wait in vain. Already by writs of 3 January 1296 Edward had sought to mobilize a fleet and had enjoined Irish lords to present themselves at Whitehaven in Cumberland on the day appointed for Balliol's response. It has been urged, questionably perhaps, that Edward's mobilization was in train prior to his learning of the French treaty – subsequently claimed as a *casus belli* – and that military action in fact resulted solely from refusal to surrender the castles forfeited in consequence of Balliol's failure to respond to the English king's court.[31] In short, Edward was merely enforcing a judicial process.

Scottish resistance proceeded to escalate, encouraged by the defeat of Edward's Gascon commanders. War *à outrance* became inevitable when in April 1296 Balliol, condemning the wrongs he had suffered at Edward's hands, renounced for himself and his subjects the homage – allegedly extorted – that he owed "by reason of the lands which are held of you in your realm." This form of words disregarded the English king's claim to overlordship of Scotland while echoing the caveat of Alexander III in 1278.[32] Those loyal to Edward were evicted from their lands, among them the son of Robert Bruce (VI), the future King Robert's father, whose inheritance in Annandale passed to the Comyn earl of Buchan.[33] Yet two years later, in the London house of Bishop Anthony Bek, Balliol was to admit with disarming honesty that he had found in the realm of Scotland "men of such malice, deceit and treachery, arising from their malignity, wickedness and stratagems" that he had no intention of ever returning.[34]

The opening stages of the Scottish war were marked by atrocities. In the East the Scots massacred English merchants at Berwick, while thanks to the treachery of Robert de Ros, lord of Wark in Northumberland, seduced from his allegiance by what proved to be the unrequited love of a Scotswoman, large numbers of English were killed at nearby Pressen. In the West the Scots crossed the Solway and fired everything from the border to the suburbs of Carlisle but failed to take the town for lack of siege equipment.[35] Once Edward had mobilized his forces, all fell before him. Wark Castle was relieved, the king celebrating Easter there; Berwick, invested on 30 March 1296, was sacked early in the following month and its inhabitants slaughtered.[36] The Scottish response was to ravage Northumberland. Meanwhile, Edward despatched Earl Warenne to recover

Dunbar, which Earl Patrick's wife had betrayed to the Scots. Following a successful skirmish Dunbar Castle was surrendered, as were those of Roxburgh and Edinburgh, while Stirling was abandoned by its garrison. Edward's east-coast *chevauchée* as far as Elgin and beyond was largely unopposed.[37]

Further resistance would have been futile. The peace plan thought to have been fostered by Bishop Bek was rejected in favour of complete surrender.[38] In a document dated 2 July 1296 at Kincardine King John abjectly confessed to his rebellion. On the seventh he abrogated the French treaty and the following day resigned the kingdom "of his own free will." The royal arms were stripped from his tabard; heraldically he became a nobody, "Toom Tabard."[39] Balliol himself, his son, and many Scottish nobles were taken captive to England.[40] Edward adopted a plan for administration as "direct lord" and the fealty of a large number of Scots has been recorded, notably on the "Ragman Roll," dated 28 August 1296 from Berwick.[41]

Edward's victory kindled a patriotic reaction. The year 1297 saw much unrest, partly internecine, partly anti-English. William Wallace, about to emerge as a heroic leader, slew the English sheriff of Lanarkshire and together with Sir William Douglas made a daring raid on Scone, forcing the English justiciar to flee for his life. Douglas was subsequently captured and imprisoned at Berwick.[42] Owing to Edward's preoccupation in Flanders during 1297 and the year following, Wallace was in a strong enough position to invade northern England in a line from Cockermouth to Newcastle.[43] His great triumph came in September 1297 when he routed Earl Warenne, the governor of Scotland, at Stirling Bridge, which saw the brutal death of Hugh Cressingham, the treasurer. Though not a large-scale engagement, it was indicative of the strength of the resistance, largely comprised of poorer and "middling" men. Moreover, it led to the substantial "liberation" of Scotland – but not for long.[44] A determined Edward returned from the Continent in March 1298 and on 22 July won a resounding victory over Wallace at Falkirk.[45]

PRINCE EDWARD'S INITIATION: THE SHADOW OF BRUCE

At this juncture the adolescent Edward of Caernarfon appears on the Scottish scene as a trainee campaigner. As shown in chapter 1, he accompanied his father on the Galloway expedition of 1300 and played his part in the siege of Caerlaverock. Thereafter he was involved in the remaining campaigns of the reign, those of 1303-04 and 1306-07. The impression has already been formed that contemporary judgment of his performance was reserved: he looked well, responded to his father's military requirements, but achieved little discernible martial distinction.

With Balliol's removal the Scots undertook guardianship on his behalf, thus reviving the system of the interregnum following Alexander III's death. Wallace himself had briefly been Guardian until his resignation following his defeat at Falkirk.[46] As such he adopted the style of custodian of the realm of Scotland and leader of its army in the name of King John: "custos regni Scocie et ductor exercitus eiusdem nomine preclari principis domini Johannis Dei gracia regis Scocie."[47] The Scots were thrown back on papal intervention. In an attempt to make Edward I desist from his attacks, Boniface VIII, in a bull of 27 June 1299, apparently not delivered to the king by Archbishop Winchelsey until August of the following year, claimed that the realm of Scotland had anciently belonged of right to the Roman Church and that it still did so.[48] This contradicted King Alexander III's claim to hold his realm from God alone and the assertion in Gregory IX's bull that the Scottish king was bound to perform homage and fealty to the English monarch.[49] Edward was required to send his proctors to the Holy See to demonstrate such title to Scotland as he claimed.[50] William de Sarden, doctor of canon law and official of the Court of Canterbury,[51] drew up a document delineating the procedure he felt ought to be adopted to combat the thrust of the bull.[52] Both the barons and Edward I responded in 1301.[53] For his part the king reiterated the "historical" agreement, outlining the supposed descent of the British and English kings from Brutus and Arthur and – on safer ground – the events that followed the death of Alexander III, including the manifest atrocities committed by the rebellious Scots.

Faute de mieux the Scots supported the papal claim to be the true judge of all Christian people, thus admitting the "lordship of the Roman Church without any intermediary," and put forward their own interpretation of history. This included a traditional claim to prior Christianization, thanks to the efficacy of St Andrew's relics. English arguments, diligently culled from the chronicles, were brushed aside as unauthenticated, indeed outmoded, by subsequent documents of greater significance. Any homage that might have been performed for Scotland arose from coercion; fealty and homage had been rightly performed only for lands in England. As for earlier papal mandates, such as that of Gregory IX, they had been granted at the instance of English kings and had to be "interpreted according to the circumstances of the times."[54] Thanks to Boniface VIII's quarrel with Philip IV papal support for the Scots proved short-lived. No matter, the advent of Bruce rendered such an approach anachronistic.

Once in charge of the situation, Edward was not interested in reviving the system of Guardians. Balliol was by then in France where eventually he retired to his ancestral lands at Bailleul-en-Vimeu (Picardy).[55] Henceforth the English overlord was to be regarded as king. The "Ordinance made by the lord king for the good order of the land [pointedly *terra* rather than *regnum*] of Scotland" was promulgated in the Westminster Parliament of 1305 and ministers were appointed for its administration.[56] At least one historian considers that it offered "the hope of lasting peace in Scotland."[57] Perhaps, but it is difficult to envisage a Scotland that for long had known kings of its own being subordinated to the lieutenant of an English monarch.

The recent demonstration of what can be interpreted as "patriotism" in the face of enormous odds would argue that any arrangement that Edward wished to implement, albeit after consultation with the Scots, was doomed to failure, despite the capture of Wallace by the men of his compatriot John of Menteith in August 1305 and his hideous despatch – both a warning to other would-be "patriots" and a manifestation of Edward's vindictive rage.[58] In any event, the constitution was rendered nugatory by the *volte face* of Robert Bruce, grandson of the Competitor of the 1290s, and his gruesome and sacrilegious murder on 10 February 1306 of Comyn and his uncle. These acts came as an unexpected shock to Edward but dimly pointed the way to the future.[59]

The now-ailing king was forced to recuperate at Lanercost for almost six months from Michaelmas 1306, unable to comprehend how "King Hobbe" could elude the pursuit of his commanders.[60] Indeed, Bruce's life for some time was held by a thread, as exemplified by the story of the three "traitorous" bowmen intent on avenging Comyn's death who, responding with a misplaced sense of chivalry, allowed the cunning king to despatch them one by one.[61] Then Bruce, following up a successful attack by James Douglas on Sir John Mowbray, one of Aymer de Valence's lieutenants, emerged from his Galwegian hiding places of loch, marsh and glen to confront Valence himself at Loudon Hill, near Kilmarnock about 10 May 1307. Caught on a narrow front that denied him the opportunity to deploy his superior forces, Edward's governor was compelled to retire in disorder to his castle of Bothwell. Thus Bruce avenged the defeat at Methven against his opponent of almost exactly one year before.[62] Another force under Ralph de Monthermer, titular earl of Gloucester, likewise discomfited, sought the shelter of the castle at Ayr until it could be relieved.[63] These successes increased the morale of the Scots, as is shown by a letter of 15 May 1307, perhaps sent by Alexander Abernethy,[64] in which he writes of the belief – stimulated by popular preachers – in Bruce's ultimate triumph. And so, he continues: "May it please God to prolong King Edward's life, for when we lose him, which God forbid, men say openly that all must be on one side or they must die or leave the country with all those who love the king, if other counsel and aid be not sent to them."[65]

EDWARD II VERSUS ROBERT BRUCE: THE UNEQUAL STRUGGLE

Bruce had a long way to go. But for his indomitable will, coupled with a notorious streak of ruthlessness towards opponents, he could not have established himself in the manner that he did. While not detracting from his ability, it has to be admitted that a major factor in his success was the timely death of the still-formidable old king and his replacement by Edward II, a man incapable of sustained resolution or generalship. In the whole period from July 1307 until the conclusion of the thirteen-year truce in May 1323, the English forces, whether led by himself or his commanders, did not register a single notable success. The Pauline annalist, recording what purports to be a dictum of Bruce, suggests that the latter knew well enough what had ensured his success: he feared the bones of the dead king more than he did the live one, and, he claimed, it was a greater feat of war to wrest six inches of territory from Edward I than to gain a whole kingdom from his son.[66]

Admittedly the young Edward inherited an inflexible political stance from which he found it inconceivable to withdraw. He was the lord of Scotland, directly responsible for the government of the realm. Bruce was no king; worse still, he was a notorious oath breaker and murderer. Hence the English were in military conflict not with the ruler of an independent kingdom, but with the rebel earl of Carrick and his Scottish confederates. Not only did this have an effect on the actual conduct of the war, it also meant that there could be no permanent peace with King Robert until he was recognized as such. Bruce's biographer likens him to his inveterate opponent, Edward I, in that he exhibited "a jealous regard for the royal dignity and prerogatives, the use of parliament as the supreme organ of government, the definition and statutory declaration of the common law." Edward had absorbed Wales, a Celtic land to the west, Bruce did likewise with the western highlands.[67]

However, until Edward I's death only the excessively optimistic would have prophesied Bruce's military or political success, let alone compared him favourably with the renowned English monarch. Recently returned from a secret hiding place in the Western Isles or in Rathlin Island off the coast of Ulster, he was faced with a land in which the English and their Scottish supporters held a large number of well fortified strongholds, particularly in the South and East. They were to continue to do so until Bruce and his allies, notably James Douglas and Thomas Randolph (the younger), picked them off one by one. Geographically and politically, if that is the right word, Scotland was a difficult country to reduce, let alone to control. The lowlands of the South and East were separated from the North by the Mounth (Grampian Hills) – described by one writer as a waste, traversable only with the utmost difficulty and totally lacking in sources of food. To the West was a thinly populated region of islands, promontories and inlets with strong Celtic associations. To the Southwest lay Galloway, its terrain as intractable as its inhabitants.[68]

Edward's incompetence was not yet manifest, save perhaps to a few who knew him intimately. With the large army raised by his father he travelled north to Cumnock in Ayrshire, where on 26 August 1307 he issued a summons to parliament and shortly thereafter turned south by way of Tibbers, Tinwald, and Annan to Carlisle, which he reached at the beginning of September. The veteran Valence, now approaching forty, was soon replaced by Jean de Bretagne (John of Brittany), the earl of Richmond – a serious error of judgment.[69] The immediate threat from England removed, Bruce could occupy himself with the gradual reduction of Scotland to his cause. Edward's future interventions in Scotland were to be hamstrung by the non-cooperation of the English barons and the priority demanded by English internal affairs. Even when he did raise an army, it proved impossible to induce

Bruce to fight a pitched battle in which numbers would inevitably tell against him. Bannockburn was to prove the fatal exception.

Bruce had to contend with scattered opposition. Quite apart from those who maintained their fealty to the English king were others who had no wish to submit to his domination, among them men who upheld the Comyn cause or that of Balliol. Yet within about a year (1307-08) Bruce was in control of land from Ayrshire coast in the West to the neighbourhood of Jedburgh and Roxburgh in the Southeast. Between the Forth – the Scottish sea – and the Grampian Hills or Mounth, the English had been confined to fortified burghs or castles, while the Northwest was entirely lost to them.[70] The Lanercost chronicler describes how, taking advantage of the discord between Edward and his barons, Bruce's brother, Edward, Alexander Lindsay, Robert Boyd of Noddsdale, and James Douglas, in company with others he had brought from the remote islands of Scotland, invaded Galloway. Ignoring the fact that they had exacted tribute, in a single day they killed many of the *nobiliores* and placed the whole area under subjection. King Edward, the same chronicler suggests, would have liked, had he been able, to grant peace to Robert Bruce to provide opportunity for the suppression of his own earls and barons.[71] Guisborough, in a corrupt passage, even suggests that "James de Brus" – perhaps a confusion with Douglas – at this time began to make strikes into Northumberland.[72]

By mid-June 1308 Edward was ordering the Irish justiciar, John Wogan, to gather victuals for a Scottish expedition due to muster at Carlisle on 22 August. Requests of a similar nature were addressed to the English counties.[73] At this juncture Wogan was overshadowed by Gaveston's arrival, with the title of king's lieutenant.[74] In the event no such expedition materialized. About the beginning of Lent 1309, Pope Clement V and King Philip IV sent envoys to persuade Edward to cease fighting the Scots and to accept the *status quo* of 25 July 1308. Bruce was similarly approached, the outcome being a truce until 1 November. Nevertheless, urges the Lanercost chronicler, he did not surrender what he had usurped in the meantime.[75] Once this truce was due to expire Edward, anxious to resist any Scottish insurgence, sent John de Segrave to Berwick, and the earl of Hereford, Robert de Clifford, and John de Crombwell or Cromwell to the other side of the March at Carlisle. By 29 November another truce was arranged until 14 January 1310 and Louis, Count of Evreux, Philip IV's brother, and the bishop of Soissons were engaged in further negotiations. Additional extensions followed until well into the summer. They benefited the English, since otherwise there would have been insufficient fodder for their horses.[76] Such truces were also invaluable to Bruce and his allies for the consolidation of their position.

By the close of 1309 the Scottish leader had struggled back from an unenviable position. Buchan, Ross, Argyll, and Galloway were now mainly under his control, although Bruce's brother, Edward, did not in Barrow's view merit until 1313 the title of "Lord of Galloway", conferred on him in 1309. Barbour, by contrast, is oversanguine in kaleidoscoping Edward Bruce's achievements, claiming that he won "thretten castles" in a single year. Robert, meanwhile, had both gained covert recognition of his status from King Philip of France and held a parliament at St Andrews. In 1308 Philip had summoned both Edward II and Bruce to the French Parlement, addressing the latter as "very dear friend and earl of Carrick." But the following year Edward had cause to complain of the duplicity of the French envoy who had carried two sets of letters, one secret, addressed in Philip's own hand to the king of Scotland, the other open, to the earl of Carrick.[77]

The parliament that met at Stamford on 27 July 1309 saw Gaveston's temporary rehabilitation and also, according to Lanercost, which erroneously gives its venue as Northampton, the recitation of a papal bull (*nova sententia*) excommunicating Bruce.[78] Writs were sent to twelve earls – Gloucester, Lincoln, Lancaster, Warenne, Cornwall, Richmond, Hereford, Warwick, Arundel, Oxford, Pembroke, and Angus – as well as to a host of lesser men and to bishops and abbots, requiring their due service at Newcastle on Michaelmas day.[79] Further writs directed named lords to raise a total of some seven thousand footsoldiers from Wales. The relative strength of the great Marcher lords is perhaps indicated by the levy of eight hundred such footsoldiers from the earl of Hereford in Central Wales, the same number from Gilbert de Clare in the South, and five hundred from Roger Mortimer to be levied from his lands mainly in the Middle March. The English counties were expected to produce a lesser total.[80] Although some of the levies did arrive at Berwick, no expedition materialized. The Yorkshiremen, led by Sir Gerard Salveyn, were the subject of complaint; some were malingerers, absconding after payment of their wages, others had evaded service by bribing those responsible for the muster.[81]

Unperturbed, Edward is said to have been enjoying Christmas 1309 at Langley in the company of the newly returned Gaveston.[82] Having survived the struggle with the barons over his favourite and given a reluctant assent to the appointment of the Ordainers in March 1310, he was again able to give his attention to the Scots. Indeed, if we accept the account in the *Vita*, the king acted of his own accord (*de concilio suo*) in determining on military action.[83] The Scottish administration had been functioning as well as could be expected. Petitions from Scotland presented in the Westminster Parliament of Lent 1310 were sent for implementation to Robert de Clifford, the warden, William de Bevercote, the chancellor, and M. John de Weston, the chamberlain.[84] On 10 April 1310 Clifford was replaced as warden by John de Segrave, who was to have a hundred men-at-arms, sixty of them in his own pay. In mid-June John de Caunton was made "captain and governor" of the king's ships, which were ordered to provision Perth, while Alexander de Abernethy became warden of Scotland between the Forth and the highlands.[85]

By mid-June 1310 Edward, on the pretext that Robert Bruce had broken the truce, was planning a campaign. A fleet was to be raised by requiring any port of significance to provide one or more fully provisioned and equipped ships-of-war to be sent to to Dublin by 8 September. The fleet would then accompany Richard de Burgh and his troops on the voyage to Scotland, where the earl was to command the Irish contingent.[86] These demands met with widespread resistance. Many seaports claimed that for lack of ships or mariners they could do nothing, or alternatively that they had already sent all available vessels on the king's service.[87] There was a corresponding reluctance on the part of monastic houses when asked to supply food for the army. Thus, both the prior of Canterbury and the prior of St Oswald's, Gloucester, pleaded poverty, a plea that did not endear them to Edward. He ordered Christ Church to provide whatever it could under sealed indenture to be made with the sheriff, promising repayment the following Easter from the tenth or other income.[88] A draft letter to the sheriff of York expresses the king's irritation at his ministers' sloth in undertaking purveyance, though he insisted, perhaps unrealistically, that it should not provoke popular discontent.[89]

The *Vita* suggests that Edward's anxiety to go to Scotland stemmed from his concern to avoid the king of France's summons. As early as July 1309, Edward had despatched envoys to France with complaints of the Scots' violation of truces which Philip himself had been instrumental in arranging. Such Scottish perfidy would explain his inability to come to Pontoise.[90] It is equally likely that Edward was keen to remove himself from the scene of the negotiations that culminated in the Ordinances.

The barons were summoned to join Edward at Northampton in August 1310, but Lancaster, Pembroke – to whom in June and July the king had appealed in vain – Hereford, and Arundel, among others, did not vouchsafe a personal appearance, preferring to devote their energies to the reform program. Some chroniclers suggest their motivation was hatred of Gaveston. As keeper of the realm Lincoln also remained behind, but his moderating influence soon terminated with his death. Gloucester, although an Ordainer, Warenne, and Cornwall (Gaveston) were the only earls to accompany Edward.[91] The king left Westminster towards the end of July. Journeying north by way of Northampton, York, Beverley, Thirsk, and Darlington, he reached Newcastle by the first week in September. He then travelled to Wark and Roxburgh – committed earlier in the year to Henry de Beaumont's custody – and reached Biggar in Lanarkshire by the close of the month.[92]

A report sent by valets of the earl of Richmond declared the king to be in good health, as were the earls – Cornwall, Gloucester, and Warenne – who had joined him at Biggar *en route* for Glasgow. Although spies discovered that Bruce was on a moor near Stirling, he proved as elusive as ever. His men, the *Vita* remarks, concealed themselves in caves and woods. Such guerilla tactics elicited a grudging admiration for one who, though guilty of homicide and treachery, might still be likened to Aeneas. In any case, the king was attempting the impossible, chasing two hares simultaneously – the barons and the Scots. Inevitably he would lose now one, now the other – eventually both.

Qui binas lepores una sectabitur hora,
Uno quandoque, quandoque carebit utroque.

The royal force advanced unopposed to Linlithgow, but by the end of October it was on its way south again to Edinburgh and thence to Berwick. In December Edward had cause to complain to English ports that arms and victuals had been ferried to the Scots. Seemingly he remained at Berwick until the end of July 1311, without noticeable effect.[93]

During the king's stay at Berwick Henry de Lacy died on 5 February 1311, Gloucester being sent south to replace him as custos of the realm. This created a two-fold crisis. It was feared that in London "riots" might ensue between the new custos and Lancaster, while friction was anticipated from Lancaster's obligation to perform homage and fealty as inheritor of the earldom of Lincoln in the right of his wife. Lancaster in his usual petulant manner refused to cross the Tweed to perform his obligation outside the country, while Edward was equally unwilling to make the corresponding move into England. Civil war appeared imminent. It was Edward who climbed down, crossing the Tweed to receive the earl at Haggerston where the latter swore fealty, the homage being temporarily respited. Lancaster, however, refused to greet Gaveston, a refusal calculated to offend not only him but also the king.[94]

Peace feelers had been extended to Bruce. A week before Christmas Sir Robert Clifford and Sir Robert FitzPayn travelled to Selkirk for a parley. Subsequently the earls of Gloucester and Cornwall attempted to meet him near Melrose, but Bruce, warned of a possible attempt at his capture, failed to appear.[95] Gaveston, unlike his detractors who stayed at home, seems to have performed useful service as warden and lieutenant north of the Forth, where he succeeded Abernethy and allegedly deployed five hundred men-at-arms.[96] Shortly after the Purification (2 February 1311) he was sent to Perth to head off Bruce *en route* to Galloway, lest he should come from beyond the "mare Scotticanum" to raise an army. This is a significant remark of the Lanercost chronicler, for it shows that the hard core of Bruce's support was still considered to lie beyond the Mounth.[97] A letter from William Melton to Chancellor Reynolds tells how from Perth Gaveston travelled secretly with Sir Henry de Beaumont and a handful of attendants to consult with the king at Berwick. There he undertook to maintain his northern station until three weeks of Easter, setting out for Perth on the eve of the Annunciation (1311).[98] Another correspondent, Treasurer Sandale, privately deplored the king's incessant demands for supplies, adding the rumour that Bruce had meant to fight against the earl of Cornwall but hesitated to hazard his army in a pitched battle.[99] Had he done so and been defeated by Gaveston, this might have modified profoundly the political situation south of the border.

During April, while still at Berwick, Edward was preparing for further action against the Scots. Winchelsey was urged to provide a subsidy of twelve pence in the mark from the spiritualities of the southern province. Robert de Umfravill, earl of Angus, and numerous others were summoned to Roxburgh by the first of August, by which time Edward himself was turning his face to the South. Still at Durham early in August, he reached Westminster by the middle of the month.

He was in no mood for parliament, a correspondent wrote, but would be obliged to do what the earl of Gloucester and the council ordered.[100]

The English were too sanguine about their success in winning over the Scots to the king's peace and their plans for sending a fleet to the coast of Argyll, "one of the greatest movements in the Scottish war." The army's subsequent withdrawal provided Bruce with the opportunity for which he had been waiting. Knowing that Edward was far away and again in conflict with his barons over Gaveston, he mustered an army for 12 August and crossed the Solway. He then harried the whole area of Gilsland (Cumberland) and the greater part of Tynedale. The Lanercost chronicler records his three-day stay in that monastery, detaining many of the canons and committing other misdeeds. After eight days south of the border he withdrew with much booty, particularly cattle, but according to the report killed few men, save those who were determined to resist.[101] Respite was short; about the feast of the Nativity of the the Virgin (8 September) Robert returned, this time invading Northumberland where he ravaged Harbottle, Holystone, and Redesdale and burned areas by the Tyne towards Corbridge. This time many more inhabitants were killed and both North and South Tynedale were scoured for booty. After a fortnight the Scots went home. The Lanercost chronicler ruefully comments that the wardens of the March were unable to resist and that they themselves laid waste the countryside in the same fashion as the enemy, save that they did not kill the people or burn their houses.[102]

This harrying of the North constituted the dismal pattern of existence endured by its inhabitants for over a decade. Bruce's purpose has never been adequately explained and may in fact be inexplicable. The raids brought much booty in goods and cattle, large sums of money for "protection" or ransom, and played havoc with the defensive system in the North. The wanton devastation matched that which the Scots inflicted on Ireland during the invasion of 1315–17. Did it, one wonders, have a political purpose? Was it intended to force Edward into recognition of Bruce as king? Could it have been a front for bolstering the morale of the Scots, behind which the reduction of Scottish castles could proceed apace? There is no satisfactory answer to these questions. In practice the devastation did not force Edward II to recognize Bruce; that was a capitulation reserved for his politically embarrassed successors, Roger Mortimer and Queen Isabella in the name of Edward III. In the long run it did have a military purpose, a strategy that made capitulation a certainty.[103] One foreseeable consequence was that it became impossible to hold lands in both countries, as many, including the Scottish kings themselves, had done in the past.

In 1311 the Northumbrians thought it advisable to buy a truce until the Purification (2 February 1312), for which they paid no less than two thousand pounds, one of a growing number of arrangements made either with Bruce or with other Scottish marauders.[104] As for those living in Scotland, particularly Lothian, they were divided among themselves, some members of a family fighting for Bruce, others for the English king. Most, however, are said to have feigned loyalty to the English for fear of losing the lands they possessed south of the border. Their hearts and their bodies were in different places (*corda eorum, licet non corpora, semper erant cum suis*).[105] Allegiance was divided at the highest levels, as is shown by the Malise family, earls of Strathearn. The Earl Malise who succeeded his father of the same name in the 1270s was to walk a tightrope between the English and Scottish kings. His two youngest sons remained in England, where they had been taken as hostages for his good behaviour, whilst in 1313 his heir was to capture him at Perth and to hand him over to King Robert. Presumably it was only Bruce's regard for the younger Malise that saved Strathearn's head though not, it would seem, his dignity as earl.[106]

The year 1312 proved disastrous for the North. The barons were bending their energies to the capture of Gaveston. The king sought desperately to remove him from danger and, if the *Vita* is to be trusted, even contemplated a haven for him in Scotland. Supposedly Edward, not for the last time,[107] offered Bruce a permanent peace – which would have meant his recognition as king. To this Bruce is said to have replied trenchantly that he could not trust a king who did not keep faith with those who owed him fealty and homage and who had failed to honour the promises made to them under oath.[108] This was a case of the pot calling the kettle black. Bruce had perjured himself more than once, on the oath of his own soul and on the most precious relics.

For the March, where there was little or no defence against the Scots the consequences were horrendous: payment of tribute provided the only hope of avoiding devastation. Bruce, ever an opportunist, raised a large army and in 1312, about the feast of the Assumption (15 August), entered England, where he burned Hexham and Corbridge as well as the western areas, taking much booty and many captives. While he rested unmolested at Corbridge he despatched part of his force to Durham. It was market day; the Scots took everything that they could carry, burned the greater part of the town, killing those who resisted. They did not attempt to invade the precinct of the abbey or the castle which were, as they still are, isolated on a peninsula surrounded save for a narrow neck of land by the River Wear. The men of Durham offered two thousand pounds to secure a truce within the area of the bishopric until St John the Baptist, 24 June 1313. This was accepted subject to the extraordinary condition that free passage be allowed to the Scots for their raids further south. The men of Northumbria paid a similar sum, while those of the Northwest, Coupland, Cumberland, and Westmorland, likewise bought off the invader. Having insufficient money in hand – hardly surprising in view of the earlier ransacking – they gave hostages as surety for the remainder, after which Bruce withdrew to Scotland with his plunder-laden army.[109]

Gaveston's murder on 19 June 1312 solved nothing: it did make implacable Edward's thirst for revenge. The birth of the future Edward III on St Brice's day, 13 November, did something, but not much, to assuage the king's grief. Two courses were offered to him, suggests the *Vita*, the first to collect an army to attack his enemies (the barons), faithless men guilty of treason; the second, urged by wiser heads, to defend the land instead of destroying its defenders. The king is reported to have preferred the former advice, but Cardinal Arnaud Nouvel, the bishop of Poitiers, and Louis, count of Evreux, who were all present at the christening, doubtless added their voices to the cause of peace. Edward's revenge had to be postponed to a more favourable time.[110] Bruce continued to capitalize on the opportunities presented by these fratricidal struggles. On the night of St. Nicholas (6 December 1312) he launched a surprise attack on the town of Berwick. Scaling ladders were placed against a portion of the wall and but for the barking of a dog the town might have fallen. The Lanercost chronicler recalls a time-honoured precedent from St. Augustine's *City of God* when Rome was saved from the Gauls thanks to the geese whose cackling alerted the guards.[111] These scaling ladders, adds the chronicler from personal observation, were of remarkable manufacture, and he describes their construction in minute detail.[112]

In Scotland the years 1309 to 1314 were not a time of "orderly preparation" for Scottish independence. Rather they were a time of "dour and confused struggle." As was to be expected, the principal castles that continued to hold out for the English lay in the South. They were in three major lines associated respectively with the rivers Tay, Forth and Tweed. On the Forth and immediately south of it lay Stirling and Edinburgh, while Roxburgh, Wark, Norham, and Berwick were on the line of the Tweed. The castles of the Southwest, north of Solway – Loch Doon, Dumfries, Caerlaverock, and Buittle – were more defensible, being in the Galloway region where there was sustained hostility to the Bruce family.[113] Without hope of relief, these castles would inevitably fall one by one.

In default of the heavy siege equipment that the English were capable of deploying, the scaling tactics unsuccessfully adopted by the Scots at Berwick were tried out at Perth where on 10 January 1313, thanks to the negligence of the watch, the Scots ascended the walls and took the town. Bruce put to death the more important burgesses "of the Scottish nation," the English he permitted to go free, while the town itself was destroyed. William Oliphant, the courageous Scot who had long held it for the English, was bound and sent to the Western Isles.[114] Dumfries Castle was taken by Bruce a month later and Caerlaverock and Buittle fell shortly afterwards.[115]

With the expiry of the truce in June 1313 the Scots threatened to resume their regular raiding of the northern counties. As the Lanercost chronicler claims, the Marchers, without hope of aid from their king, who was considered to be unconcerned for their predicament, had no alternative but to submit to blackmail in order to prolong the truce until Michaelmas 1314.[116] The chronicler omitted to record that King Edward and his consort were abroad between 23 May and 16 July 1313 in response to an invitation from the French monarch. This journey was undertaken, says the *Vita*, against the advice of the earls, who seem to have believed that Bruce was in the neighbourhood of York and contemplating a march on London. Prior to his departure Edward had in fact attempted to negotiate a truce with the help of the French envoys.[117]

At the end of February 1314 James Douglas laid siege to Roxburgh Castle. Once again, the commando-style tactics of the Scots proved successful, thanks to one "Sim of the Ledows," described by Barbour as "a craftyman and a curious," who made hempen ladders with iron attachments for throwing over the wall. These were used by the besiegers to surprise the defenders who were 'making joy and bliss" on "Fastryn Eve" (Shrove Tuesday), traditionally a time of celebration prior to the Lenten fast.[118] Not to be outdone by his rival in military exploits, Sir Thomas Randolph decided to attempt the formidable castle of Edinburgh. Frontal assault was out of the question, so, profiting from his experience at Berwick and Roxburgh, he resorted to guile. Once again it is Barbour who tells the vivid story of one William Francis who when young had scaled the rock to visit his sweetheart with the aid of a twelve-foot ladder. On a murky night he repeated his youthful exploit by leading a party up the sheer rock-face. Then, as Sim had done at Roxburgh, he used the ladder to ascend the wall above unseen, for the defenders considered attack from that quarter to be impossible. Randolph himself clambered up immediately behind Francis and the resulting assault was successful.[119]

The investiture of Stirling Castle by Edward Bruce finally stung the English into retaliation. The castle was held by Sir Philip Mowbray, a Scot, who arranged a truce with his adversary to the effect that if no English army came within three miles of Stirling before Michaelmas 1314 it would be surrendered. He then went off to tell King Edward of the arrangement and to persuade him to send a relieving army. Barbour alleges that the king expressed his pleasure at the news, whereas Robert Bruce was furious with his brother for conceding such uncharacteristically generous terms.[120]

> That was unwisely done, perfay
> I herd never quhar so lang warnyng
> Was gevin to so mychty ane Kyng
> As is the Kyng of England.[121]

Was this response invented merely to make the hero's opponent appear far more formidable than he was?

MILITARY DISASTER

News of the fall of the Scottish strongholds is said to have so affected Edward that he was scarcely able to restrain his tears.[122] Summoning the earls and barons he sought their aid to put down the traitor, the self-made king of Scots. Their response was to the effect that in accordance with the Ordinances the matter should be discussed in parliament: without such sanction the earls declined to fight. Certain members of the king's council and of his household urged Edward to demand appropriate service and to set out with such determination that neither Bruce nor the Scots would be able to resist. The earls of Gloucester, Pembroke, and Hereford, as also Robert de Clifford, Hugh Despenser, and members of the royal household, would certainly come with their knights – as indeed they did. This counsel was adopted and Pembroke despatched to reconnoitre.[123] On 24 March 1314 he was made custos and lieutenant of Scotland.[124]

Royal preparations for the campaign were in full swing from early March. Another attempt was made to muster a fleet, to be commanded by John Sturmy and Peter Bard. This was to assemble by 24 June at Skinburness in Cumberland, a supply base on the west coast regularly used by the English. The Irish were summoned to render assistance and the earl of Ulster was appointed their commander, as he had been in 1310. Instructions were given to raise well over 21,500 footsoldiers from England and Wales who were to be at Wark-on-Tweed by 10 June. We have no means of knowing how many were in fact recruited. The numbers that actually fought at Bannockburn have been the subject of controversy. There could have been as many as fifteen thousand footsoldiers with some three thousand mounted men forming the core of the English army. The royal necessities were explained to the archbishops of Canterbury and York, who were requested to meet at Westminster and York respectively to arrange for the granting of an aid.[125]

Trokelowe records that by the end of March the king was at St Albans He celebrated Easter (7 April) at Ely where, as we have seen, he inspected the relics in the cathedral priory.[126] Meanwhile Edward Bruce, contrary to the truce says Lanercost, brought an army as far as Carlisle and remained for three consecutive days at Rose, the manor of the diocesan bishop. The army was sent south and west to burn, destroy, and capture. From Inglewood Forest, used as a sanctuary, the Scots drove off cattle in great numbers and took captives. Carlisle escaped attack because it was well defended. The excuse for the plunder, the chronicler claims, was that the Marchers had failed to pay their promised tribute. That they had given hostages was of no avail.[127]

The royal party made slow progress northwards, reaching Berwick by mid-June, whence it departed for Stirling on the eighteenth.[128] Lancaster and others of his persuasion sent only their strict service, claiming says the *Flores*, that it was not safe to be with such a king. The Meaux chronicler argues that the summons issued without the magnates' assent contravened the Ordinances. All the same, a magnificent army gathered, more impressive thought the author of the *Vita*, than any that had previously set out from England in his time. In its wake lumbered an impressive baggage train.[129] The Lanercost chronicler, unimpressed and in any case given to moralizing, thought that the army travelled with too much impedimenta (*cum pompa magna et apparatu curioso*) and criticized Edward for failing to prepare himself by visiting the shrines of the saints as his father had done. Instead of distributing alms and offerings he had actually taken the goods of those monasteries he passed *en route*. No wonder his army was to suffer confusion and perpetual shame.[130]

By 23 June, the *Vita* states, the English soldiers, then hard by Stirling, were weakened by lack of sleep and food. Seeing what looked like Scots stragglers at the edge of a wood, an overenthusiastic knight, Henry de Bohun (Boun), said to have been a nephew of the earl of Hereford, rode off in pursuit. Confronted unexpectedly by Bruce himself Bohun was struck down with an axe before he could return to the main force.[131] The Lanercost chronicler does not mention this encounter but describes how the first line of the English army under Clifford tried to surround the wood of Torres (the Torwood) so as to cut off the Scots, whom he thought were about to flee. The latter, however, allowed the English to come on but, once they had become detached from the main body, descended upon them and put them to flight. This marked a turning point in the battle, it gave the Scots confidence and discomfited the English.[132]

The *Scalacronica* at this juncture is more detailed, indeed apparently unique in its mention of the traitorous Sir Alexander Seton. The constable of Stirling, Sir Philip Mowbray, is said to have ridden three leagues from the castle to inform the king that the terms of his arrangement with Edward Bruce had been met – he was technically "relieved." The Scots, he warned, had blocked the roads within the Torwood, but the impetuous troops of the advance guard under the earl of Gloucester pressed on into the Park.[133] This column became involved in the unsuspected encounter with Bruce, although the rash knight is here named Mountforth rather than Bohun. The force that made the circuit of the wood, possibly in an attempt to reach Stirling Castle, as Barbour suggests, acted under the command of the lords Clifford and Beaumont. It was assailed by Thomas Randolph, ever concerned not to be outdone by his fellows. The English knights, including Sir Thomas Gray, the chronicler's father, unwilling to await the enemy, made an impetuous charge and suffered heavy casualties, Gray himself being taken prisoner. At this crucial point the Scots, considering that they had done well enough, were said to be about to leave the battlefield for a night march to Lennox. Seton, secretly detaching himself from King Edward's army, sought out Bruce in the Torwood and urged him to attack on the morrow, since the English were dispirited and would easily be defeated. The advice was adopted. At sunrise on the twenty-fourth the Scots advanced in three infantry columns against the English, who had remained under arms throughout the night in expectation of an attack. The mass of pikemen, arranged in schiltrons (or schiltroms), forced back the thickly packed English knights, who because of the narrowness of their front lacked room for manoeuvre. The rearguard was forced into the Bannock burn.[134]

Lanercost, the third and last of the major English chronicle sources for the battle, adds a few touches. It describes a preliminary exchange between the rival bowmen. The English archers covered the army's front line and soon put their adversaries to flight. When the two armies approached one another the Scots are said to have sunk to their knees and, reciting the *Pater Noster*, commended themselves to God. Having done so they advanced with determination. The mounted English knights of the first line of battle had their warhorses impaled on the Scottish lances; the remainder, compressed by the front line, were incapacitated.[135] The immediate consequences were catastrophic. The rash earl of Gloucester, unhorsed but prevented from rising by the weight of his armour, was killed. Had he been recognized by the bearings on his surcoat, which at the time he was not wearing, he would almost certainly have been ransomed.[136] The outcome was a rout.[137] Already we have had occasion to note the conflicting opinions about Edward's behaviour: his withdrawal, while preserving his person from death or, more likely, capture, sounded the death knell of this magnificent army that had so confidently arrived on the scene two days before.[138]

English casualties were heavy. Among the distinguished dead, apart from Gloucester, were Robert de Clifford, William le Marshal, Payn Tibetot, Giles d'Argentan, John Lovel, John Comyn, lord of Badenoch, son of Bruce's victim, and Edmund de Mauley, the king's steward, who drowned in one of the marshy "pools" of the area. Among the captives were the earl of Hereford, who was taken prisoner at Bothwell as he tried to reach Carlisle, John Giffard of Brimpsfield, John de Wylington, John de Segrave and Maurice de Berkeley. Pembroke made good his escape, *nudis pedibus* according to the London annalist; on foot with the Welshmen according to the Lanercost chronicler. His route is in doubt, but he could well have been with the king.[139]

The reasons for what in English eyes was a calamity of stunning proportions are not hard to seek. It is clear that generalship was lacking, True, there were many able war-seasoned veterans on the English side, such as Pembroke, Clifford, d'Argentan, Maurice de Berkeley, and Sir Ingram de Umfraville. What they lacked was an effective overall commander and a recognizable battle plan. There is no mention of King Edward's participation in the conflict until its conclusion in flight. The earl of Gloucester, who was twenty-three, and the earl of Hereford, who must have been almost forty, disputed their precedence in the vanguard. Hereford claimed that as hereditary constable he should command, while Gloucester urged his family's traditional right to lead the van. Edward, opting for youth rather than age, is said by the *Flores* to have appointed his nephew Gloucester to be both constable and commander of the army rather than his brother-in-law.[140] In practice, if the *Vita* is right, the two contenders for pre-eminence jointly commanded the van.[141] By contrast, the Scots had no doubts as to their overall commander: Bruce himself a warrior of long experience, who was aided by able and, up to a point, obedient lieutenants – notably his brother Edward, Thomas Randolph, and James Douglas – whose recent successful exploits ensured that their morale and that of their troops was high.

Gloucester, impetuous though he may have been once battle was joined, prior to the engagement is said to have advised postponement and to have suffered rebuke from the king on that account.[142] This was also the advice of Sir Ingram de Umfraville, a Scot, and was in line with the cautious approach of the constable of Stirling. Such counsel was ignored; in consequence it was a tired English force that faced the Scots on 24 June.[143] What is more, the tactics adopted by the English put them at a disadvantage. The Scots, who in Sir Thomas Gray's opinion had learned a lesson from the defeat of the French chivalry at Courtrai, fought on foot.[144] The English, unused to such practice, did not adapt in this respect to the military situation. Furthermore, they allowed themselves to be trapped in boggy land unsuitable for cavalry and in a position where their superior numbers could not be deployed. The Scots sought the shelter of the Torwood, where horsed knights would be at a grave disadvantage. To strengthen their position still more they had dug pits and camouflaged them with sticks and grass – an added hazard for heavy cavalry that further restricted its room for manoeuvre.[145] Worse still, the English, or at any rate some of them, must have been fully aware (*pace* Trokelowe) of this treacherous area of the "pools."[146] Once battle was joined they failed to make sufficient use of their archers, who could not be deployed laterally. Such fire would have been extremely destructive to the Scottish schiltrons as it proved to be on other occasions.[147]

Few chroniclers, apart from moralizing about the greater piety of the Scots and deprecating the excessive panoply of the English,[148] paused to analyze the reasons for the latter's defeat, seemingly against all the odds. Trokelowe does so. Philosophizing on the varying outcome of wars and the manner in which the sword indifferently demolishes now these, now those, he comments that fortune's wheel for once in its revolution had brought victory to the Scots. While admitting his inability to provide fully satisfactory answers for this outcome, he suggests that on the English side both men and horses were exhausted and hungry. The Scots knew the battlefield while, in his view, the English did not. The former had been fortified by food and sleep and with their densely packed squadrons were therefore more prepared for the fight.[149] There is no mention of the impetuosity of the English, their indifferent command structure, or even of the disabling traps dug by the Scots.

FROM BANNOCKBURN TO THE THIRTEEN-YEAR TRUCE

There were three major consequences of Bannockburn, as somewhat later the battle near Stirling came to be called. First was the wide acknowledgment of Robert Bruce as king of Scots by virtue of his military prowess, second was the perpetual disinheritance of those who died outside his peace,[150] while third was the increased vulnerability of the North to attack. Edward, on the advice of his immediate circle, left Berwick early in July for York, where he remained in the vicinity of the city until parliament assembled on 9 September. The *Vita* claims that discussion of Scottish affairs was postponed until the next parliament, since the earl of Hereford and other barons had not yet procured their freedom. Maddicott, however, has cited evidence to the effect that well before the parliament, thanks to Lancaster's dominance, truce negotiations commenced at Durham on Bruce's initiative.[151]

While the English prevaricated, Bruce followed up his advantage. At the beginning of August his brother, James Douglas, William de Soules,[152] and others entered England, where they laid waste Northumbria. The bishopric of Durham, which had bought them off, was apparently spared. As on previous occasions they took off booty and captives. They passed south to the Tees, some pressing on as far as Richmond, the population fleeing southwards before them. Turning north, they traversed Swaledale and Stainmoor and made their way back through Westmorland and Cumberland, burning the towns of Brough, Appleby, and Kirkoswald, among others. Then, skirting Lanercost priory, they re-entered Scotland. Fearing their return, the inhabitants of Coupland paid over a large sum of money. Subsequently North and South Tyndale were occupied, as well as Haltwhistle, Hexham, Corbridge, and other places in the vicinity of Newcastle. Tyndale, it is said, did homage to the king of Scots. Between December 1314 and midsummer of the following year there were further raids into Northumbria.[153]

Although in 1315 Edward Bruce and Thomas Randolph were to set off in an attempt to conquer Ireland, the terror in the North did not abate. King Robert's men ravaged Northumbria but the inhabitants of Cumberland bought them off for six hundred marks. Towards the end of June raiders entered the bishopric of Durham and pillaged Hartlepool, the inhabitants taking refuge in their boats. Apparently the Scots did not burn the seaport but on their return sacked the bishopric.[154] In mid-July Bruce brought an army to Carlisle where for ten days he laid siege to the city. He adopted classic methods, laying waste the surrounding areas, carrying off any grain to be found, burning the suburbs, and removing booty and livestock. Allendale, Coupland, and Westmorland were devastated, St Bees priory was ransacked. Each day of the siege at least one of the city's three gates was attacked, sometimes all three at once, but not with impunity. Impressed by the tenacity of the defenders, the besiegers quipped: "Do they not multiply and grow stones within the walls?" Even the stone-throwing engine erected by the attackers near Holy Trinity church had little effect. The townsmen replied with their own projectiles, there being some seven or eight similar machines within the walls as well as springalds. The Scots tried every tactic they knew. A wooden tower (berefrai) was constructed to overlook the wall. The townsmen matched it with one of their own, but the Scots' tower stuck in the sand as it was being dragged towards the defences. Scaling ladders were employed, thrown up simultaneously at a number of points. A "sow" was used to undermine the wall, and attempts were made to fill in the wet ditch on the eastern side with reeds, all to no purpose. As a final throw the Scots resorted to the scheme which had proved successful at Edinburgh. Covered by a major attack on the eastern flank of the city near the house of the Friars Minor, James Douglas, supported by the more audacious and agile, attempted to scale the southwestern wall by the Dominican friary where, owing to its height and inaccessibility, no attack was to be expected. As a further precaution archers were deployed to pick off any

defender who showed his head above the level of the wall. Even this proved ineffective; the ladders were thrown down and many attackers killed. On the eleventh
day, 1 August, the siege was raised and in their pursuit of the retiring Scots the English captured a number of prisoners, including John Moray and Robert Bard.[155]
This was a rare defeat for the Scots and a credit to Sir Andrew Harclay, the sheriff
of Cumberland, who had conducted the defence. Unfortunately he was himself
captured in November 1316 and only ransomed with difficulty. For the time being,
however, the successful defence of Carlisle showed what the northerners could do
in the absence of the English army. The city's initial reward was a two-edged
sword, the right to account at the exchequer for its revenues, not the fee-farm for
which the citizens had earlier petitioned. But a charter of 12 May 1316, was to remedy this omission, signalling Edward's belated generosity.[156] Despite the fact that
by early July 1315 Pembroke, together with Badlesmere appointed warden of the
area between the Trent and Roxburgh, had gathered a large force for the protection
of the Marches, this achieved little more – at the expense of considerable losses –
than a temporary Scottish withdrawal. At this stage Lancaster was made *superior
capitaneus*, but his prospective campaign came to nothing.[157]

One of the features of Scottish campaigning was its continuance during the
winter months. In mid-January 1316 Bruce arrived at Berwick by moonlight,
attacking simultaneously from land and sea. The Scots hoped to enter the town
between "Bridgehouse" and the castle, where no wall had yet been built. They
were foiled by the vigilance of the guards; John de Laundels was killed, while
Douglas himself barely escaped by boat.[158] By St John the Baptist (24 June) the
marauders were back, destroying everything in their path until they reached
Richmond, where the local landholders received them in the castle and paid a
vast sum to prevent the burning of town or countryside. Carrying their protection
money the Scots proceeded north-westwards to Furness. There they wreaked further destruction and were elated to find an abundance of iron, a commodity
somewhat scarce in Scotland. The effects of this scorched-earth policy were
aggravated by famine and pestilence. In the North grain rose to an unprecedented price. The Meaux chronicler declared that Northumbria lay derelict for fifteen
years, bereft of men and animals alike.[159] During August Edward, who moved
from Lincoln to York and Beverley, was sending messengers to Pembroke and
urging the Mortimers to join him with men-at-arms. By November Pembroke
and Hereford were at Newcastle on Tyne where they received letters about a
forthcoming campaign presumably scheduled for 1317.[160] Negotiations for a
truce were continuing simultaneously: Robert Hastings, a banneret, was sent
with Robert Baldock to "Jedworth" in the same month for that purpose.[161]

Robert Bruce's absence in Ireland relieved pressure on the North for the time
being, but the English nonetheless suffered a number of minor defeats, thanks
to the activities of Douglas, who acted as lieutenant of Scotland. A raiding party
from Berwick that had been scavenging in Teviotdale was cut off and most of
the knights including a Gascon, Raymond de Calhau or Caillou, said to have

been Gaveston's nephew, were killed.[162] Another party sent out by Sir Thomas Richmond, acting for the earl of Arundel now warden between Trent and Roxburgh, was set upon near Jedburgh,[163] while Robert Neville of Raby, the "peacock of the North," was killed by Douglas thanks to the "false traitors of the Marches."[164] Doubtless irritated by the lack of action at national level, the men of Humberside attempted a retaliatory raid of their own on Fife, probably in 1317. At first the inhabitants fled but the bishop of Dunkeld, William Sinclair, donned armour and thanks to his example the English were driven back to their boats with heavy losses.[165]

Bruce arrived back from his abortive Irish campaign in May 1317, but any concerted action against him was prevented by Lancaster's behaviour. The disaffected earl was making potentially threatening indentures with a number of men, including the Northumbrian John de Eure,[166] attacking barons favourable to Edward II and convening armed assemblies.[167] An opportunity arose for embarrassing the government, which, in association with Cardinals Luca Fieschi and Gaucelme de Jean, sent by Pope John XXII in response to an English embassy, was endeavouring to make peace overtures to Bruce.[168] A complicating factor, examined in another context in chapter 5, was the election of a bishop of Durham in succession to Richard Kellaw. The king's candidate was initially Thomas de Charlton, the earl of Hereford's was said to be John Walwayn, while Lancaster's man was John of Kinnersley or Kinardesley, one of his clerks who does not appear to have made much of a mark.[169] The monks, as was not unusual, elected a member of their community, Henry de Stamford, prior of Finchale. In the event it was Henry de Beaumont's brother, Louis, who was provided on 9 February 1317 by the pope at Queen Isabella's urging. Since the chronicler Graystanes tells us that Lancaster, Hereford, and Pembroke, among others, were in the cathedral priory at the time, there is a *prima facie* case for their putting substantial pressure on the monks in opposition to the royal wishes.[170]

An indenture of April 1317 bears witness to an unprecedented conspiracy between Sir John de Eure, Sir Robert de Sapy, guardian of the temporalities, and the prior of Durham to impede Beaumont's consecration.[171] Louis was travelling northwards in the company of the cardinals and his brother Henry, St Cuthbert's translation on 4 September being the day chosen for his consecration and enthronement in the cathedral church. The London clergy had in vain warned the cardinals of the dangers of proceeding beyond York.[172] On 1 September the travellers were intercepted and robbed south of Ferryhill, some nine miles short of Durham, by Sir Gilbert Middleton, leader of a contingent of relatives, members of local county families, and supposedly of Scots under Thomas Randolph and James Douglas.[173] Middleton, a former knight of the royal household,[174] had been notorious for his unsavoury activities in Northumbria, but a case has been made by Sir Arthur Middleton that he was no mere "schavaldore" or marauder, but a patriotic northerner. His action, it is claimed, was in the nature of a northern rebellion, inflamed by the unpopular elevation of an alien to the see of Durham. He further suggests, with a degree of plausibility, that Lancaster – even Pembroke, though this is doubtful[175] – were involved behind the scenes but that interference with the cardinals was more than they were prepared to warrant. That Lancaster acted in collusion with Middleton and with the Scots is affirmed by Maddicott. The earl was angry because of the rejection of his candidate, Kinnersley, and the promotion of Louis de Beaumont, whose brother Henry he had tried to exclude from the court.[176] The cardinals were robbed and the Beaumonts imprisoned in Mitford Castle.[177] Middleton, despite an attempted accommodation with the cardinals, was left to his fate, being condemned at Westminster and put to death with the usual barbarities on 26 January 1318.[178]

Understandably the cardinals' mission proved abortive. Bruce would not accept the bulls sent to Scotland on the pretext that they were not addressed to him as king. Their contents were discovered by a subterfuge, for the bearer, Adam Newton, a Minorite friar, was set upon and stripped "ad carnem."[179] The Pauline annalist records that on 27 November 1317 Cardinal Luca dei Fieschi celebrated mass in St Paul's and published a bull (of 1 May 1317) calling for a two-year truce between the king of England and Robert Bruce. On the following day Archbishop Reynolds declared that any who impeded it would be *ipso facto* excommunicate. The English are said to have received the bull with joy; the Scots would have none of it. Not surprisingly: up to that point they were doing very well both in Ireland and nearer home. These efforts were to no avail: at Nottingham on 19 August 1318 the cardinals fulminated the sentences against Bruce and ordered their publication throughout England, Scotland, Ireland, and Wales. Bruce, however, had no intention of breaking off hostilities while Berwick remained in English hands. Consequently, on 3 September the contumacious "rebel" was excommunicated and the realm of Scotland placed under an interdict by Cardinal Luca and his colleague Gaucelme de Jean. After the cardinals' departure the process was published on the twenty-fourth in St Paul's by the archbishops of Canterbury and Dublin sitting with three other bishops.[180]

Awkward though it might be, the Scots were now obliged to put up with papal censure, though they continued to work for its amelioration. Edward learned of the Scottish envoys' activity at the Curia from letters intercepted in January 1319. He asked for their incarceration at Avignon, yet in March, when thanking Pope John for doing so, he was incongruously forced to seek permission to open negotiations with the excommunicated rebels. Bruce himself, although accounted a man of genuine if eccentric and certainly intermittent piety, had earlier been excommunicated by reason of his sacrilegious murder of John Comyn and his uncle. Allegedly he was absolved on 12 February 1306 by his none-too-scrupulous supporter Robert Wishart, bishop of Glasgow, the excuse being that at the time Bruce could not approach his own diocesan.[181] But the crime was perpetrated within an exempt jurisdiction, a Franciscan friary, and so heinous an offence in so sacred a precinct would certainly have been a matter for the conservator of the friars' privileges, and so far as Bruce himself was concerned, for the papal penitentiary. Conditional absolution may indeed have been granted pending a visit to the Holy See. This might explain why an entry in a Trinity College Cambridge manuscript dated 23 July "pont. Clem. III [*sic*] a[nno] quinto" – 5 Clement V, i.e. 1309–10? – purports to be a copy of Bruce's absolution by Cardinal Berenger (Frédol?), then a papal penitentiary. But this is somewhat eccentric, since by a bull of 6 January 1320 the excommunication of Robert "earl of Carrick" for the Comyns' murder was renewed. Clement's successor did not regard Bruce's record as other than unfortunate. By another bull of 8 January 1320 Bruce and the bishops of St Andrews, Dunkeld, Aberdeen, and Moray were summoned to appear at the Curia and provided with an impressive safe conduct. Needless to say, they did not avail themselves of the opportunity and for their contumacy were excommunicated in June.[182]

The years 1317 and 1318 brought fresh disasters for the English. The Isle of Man was of crucial strategic importance to both England and Scotland, as well as to the English in Ireland. Since Alexander III had acquired it from Norway in 1266 it had enjoyed a chequered career. Seized by Edward I, who later restored it to John Balliol, it was supposedly for a time in Gaveston's possession and was certainly in that of Henry de Beaumont by 1311. Bruce landed at Ramsey in 1313, but the island was later wrested from the Scots. Thomas Randolph was rumoured in mid-July 1317 to be preparing to recover it and may well have done so. It remained under Scottish control from about that time until 1333, the English Parliament acknowledging the fact in 1328.[183] Then on 2 April 1318 – despite the fact that envoys were in the March of Scotland actively seeking a truce[184] – the town of Berwick was captured in a nocturnal onslaught. This, according to the Lanercost chronicler, resulted from the treachery of an Englishman, Peter of Spalding, who, other sources suggest, was not alone. In return for the promise of money and land he allowed the Scots to scale that part of the wall over which he was keeping watch. The castle held out for some eleven weeks, before capitulating for lack of provisions. Wark and Harbottle castles also surrendered when relief was not forthcoming by the appointed times. Thus the Scots gained control of the whole of Northumbria to Newcastle, apart from the sprinkling of castles that still held out. May saw the burning of Northallerton and Boroughbridge and the despoiling of Ripon. The church there had to be used for defence and the Scots were given a thousand marks to preserve the town from burning. The invaders passed to Knaresborough, which they burned, and then searched the neighbouring woods in which the inhabitants had concealed themselves and their herds. After sacking and burning Skipton-in-Craven the surfeited Scots returned home with their spoils. All resistance was at an end. There was one crumb of comfort: the defeat and death of Edward Bruce at Faughart on 14 October 1318 terminated the Irish adventure, although *ipso facto* it meant that the Scottish military effort would no longer be divided. On 3 December Robert Bruce, who still lacked a male heir, in default of such settled the succession of the Scottish throne on Robert Stewart.[185]

An outward peace being established between Edward and Lancaster, the way lay open for the siege of Berwick. This began on 7 September 1319 "with the assent of the magnates."[186] Barbour, perhaps to emphasize the tenacity of the Scots under their commander Walter the Steward, suggests that the place was ill fortified.[187] He also writes of an assault from the sea and of a ship that was prevented from reaching the walls and subsequently left stranded by the ebb tide. Clearly the siege was for a while pressed home with vigour. We hear of a "sow," later destroyed under direction of the ingenious John Crabbe, and of a "crane" capable of being wheeled by the defenders to any portion of the wall under threat.[188] Engines were shipped from York Castle and, according to the *Anonimalle Chronicle*, from Northampton and Bamburgh, while Chancellor Hothum was ordered to bring a hundred ditchers from Holderness and to lead the whole array of the County of York. All this, wrote Edward to his chancellor, was to pre-empt Robert Bruce and his allies, who were bound by oath to bring relief on a certain day. Br William de Gretham with his grooms and three horses was in attendance on the king with the banner of St Cuthbert for fifty-eight days from 1 August until 28 September at a cost of twelve pence a day.[189]

The Scots, however, being unwilling to attack the English army of over eight thousand men,[190] created a diversion in force under Thomas Randolph and James Douglas. Entering England, they left the usual trail of devastation and proceeded yet again to burn Boroughbridge. A captured spy revealed that Douglas and his accomplices intended to kidnap the queen, who was in the neighbourhood of York. She was hastily removed by water to Nottingham. The rumour, passed on by a single chronicler, that Despenser had sold the queen to the Scots must surely be discounted as a tale designed to discredit the unpopular favourite.[191] The citizens of York with a gathering of men of little substance from the neighbouring countryside (*ignoti sibi hominibus de patria*) were joined by a motley crowd of secular and religious clergy.[192] As Barbour described them:[193]

Thai gaderit, in-till full gret hy
Archeris, burges, with yhemenry,
Prestis, clerkis, monkis, and freris,
Husbandis, and men of all mysteris,
Quhill at thai sammyn assemmyllit war
Weill tuenty thousand men and mair.

On 12 September (Trokelowe wrongly gives the date as the twentieth) this motley, ill-equipped force set out under the captaincy of Archbishop Melton and Chancellor Hothum, the bishop of Ely. Inexperienced in war, they had no concept of battle formation. As was their practice, the Scots formed a schiltron, waited until three spear lengths divided the forces, and then raised a great shout, which so terrorized their opponents that they fled. Mounting their horses the Scots pursued the rabble and allegedly killed some four thousand, among them the mayor of York. Others, some thousand the Lanercost chronicler thought, were drowned in the Swale. This clerical rout was dubbed the "Chapter of Myton" or, by the Scots, the "White Battle."[194]

On learning two days later of the catastrophe Berwick's besiegers proffered divergent counsel. The king is said to have wished to send a detachment from the army to cut off the Scottish retreat, whereas the magnates who, in the Lanercost chronicler's opinion, neither wished to divide their forces nor to fight the Scots, were for raising the siege and bringing their army back to England in order to meet the enemy there.[195] Barbour claimed to see a discrepancy between the views of southerners and northerners. The former wished to remain until town and castle were won, while the latter, for fear of losing friends and goods, preferred to raise the siege and concentrate on rescuing the country. The earl of Lancaster, whom the author of the *Vita* felt had betrayed the king, was one of those who, Barbour thought, counselled Edward to withdraw. He did so on 17 September 1319.[196] The St Albans chronicler, in an attempt to explain Lancaster's departure, puts words into Edward's mouth to the effect that he intended to make the younger Despenser captain of the castle of Berwick, Roger d'Amory of the town. For his part Despenser blamed Lancaster for the abandonment of the siege and claimed that the earl was in collusion with the Scots.[197]

The outcome was that the Scottish withdrawal by way of Stainmoor and Gilsland went unmolested. Worse still, those "excommunicates," the Scots under Randolph and Douglas, returned about All Saints (1 November), when the harvest was in, and set the whole of Gilsland alight, the grain crop on which the inhabitants depended for the following year as well as the barns in which it was stored. They went on to Brough and then ravaged Westmorland and Cumberland, finally re-entering Scotland laden with booty and captives.[198] It was one of the most heartless and senseless of a lengthening series of raids against a defenceless population. This occurred about the time when the murrain that had afflicted cattle in the South spread to the North to aggravate an already insupportable situation.[199] The Castleford chronicler lamented:[200]

Durande þis Edwarde dais, þe kyng
Of alle þase tides neuer hade turnyng;
So ofte Englandes pes þai brak,
Englandes stren3 never them put bak.

Mercifully the slaughter was cut short by a truce arranged by the *sapientes* on both sides, among whom Pembroke was prominent. It was to be in force for two years from 29 December 1319 and, according to Lanercost, was proclaimed in the March on 1 January. By its terms the castle of Harbottle was to be handed over to the English ambassadors as private persons on condition that if no peace were to be concluded by Michaelmas 1321 it would either be returned to Bruce or destroyed. On 25 August orders were in fact given by

Edward for its destruction.[201] A letter from Robert Bruce to Edward II has been assigned to April or May 1320. Its rhetoric, requesting the cessation "a persecutione nostra et inquietudine populi regni nostri," recalls that of the so-called Declaration of Arbroath.[202]

This celebrated document, dated 6 April 1320, has been dubbed "The Palladian of Scottish nationality for those who require it."[203] Addressed to Pope John XXII by named Scottish barons and "the whole community of the realm of Scotland," it bemoans the wrongs suffered by the Scots at the hands of Edward I, from which they had been set free by King Robert, and requests the pope to persuade the English king to be satisfied with what he has. Here indeed lay the nub of the matter: Edward II's refusal to abandon the English claim to lordship and to recognize Bruce as king. The Declaration contains the rousing claim: "We fight not for glory, nor riches, nor honours, but for freedom alone, which no good man gives up except with his life." This neither reflects the situation then current nor, understandably, takes account of the misery inflicted for many years on the whole of the North of England by the buccaneering Scots. The document closes with the commonplace that peace among Christians would enable the pope to go to the assistance of the Holy Land – Edward III was to say as much when engaged with both the Scots and the French. But the argument has been advanced that Bruce intended, were the "holy war" against England to be resolved, to undertake a Crusade. We know that he entrusted James Douglas with this vicarious task, although in the event the latter got no further than Spain. Whatever the validity of its argument, the Declaration remains a skilful piece of diplomatic special pleading, the timing of which has not been fully appreciated. In February 1320 Bishop Orleton had returned from the papal Curia with a clutch of "anti-Scottish" bulls: one contained the cardinals' process against Bruce, another a citation of Bruce and certain Scottish prelates to Avignon, yet another invoked sentence of excommunication against invaders of the English realm and their abettors, two more were directed to the cardinals (no longer in England) for proceeding with their sentence against Bruce, while a sixth bull, addressed to the archbishop of York (Melton) and the bishops of Durham (Beaumont) and Carlisle (Halton), authorized the publication of Bruce's excommunication as the murderer of the Comyns. It was this withering blast that Scottish diplomacy was endeavouring to counteract: there could be no "holy war" under papal condemnation. Initially the propaganda failed, the pope responded to the Scottish lords – that is to the Declaration of Arbroath – by enjoining them to seize the opportunity for peace, adding that he had exhorted Edward II to do likewise. On 7 June 1320 near Corbeil the cardinals published the lengthy process against Bruce that occupies five folios of Melton's archiepiscopal register and inflicted aggravated sentences on the contumacious Scot and his supporters.[204]

Negotiations proposed for August 1320 were repeatedly postponed until March of the following year. Edward on 19 January 1321 deputed envoys to arrange either a permanent peace or at least a prolongation of the truce. The bishops of Worcester and Carlisle, Thomas de Cobham and John de Halton,[205] together with Bartholomew Badlesmere and others were sent to Newcastle-on-Tyne for the purpose. Their deliberations were delayed pending the arrival of the papal envoys Rigaud d'Assier, bishop of Winchester, and William de Laudon, those of the king of France, and the earl of Pembroke – then engaged in marriage negotiations on the Continent. Later the king wrote to say that Pembroke was still detained in France and that the earl of Hereford, previously ordered to attend, would be replaced by the earl of Richmond.

At long last the English and Scottish envoys got down to serious talking at Bamburgh. A report of the ambassadors to Edward II dated 8 April 1321 complained that, despite their declarations in favour of peace, the Scots could only be persuaded to accept a lengthy truce, for instance one of twenty-six years. This was hardly surprising in view of the fact that the so-called "Process of Scotland," incorporating the English king's claims to that country, had been delivered to the earl of Richmond so that reference might be made to it during the negotiations. On 5 May these rolls were restored to the exchequer for safekeeping in the royal treasury. A further meeting planned for September 1321 did not materialize, since by that time Edward was preparing for an incipient civil war.[206]

Edward's principal opponent, Lancaster, now turned to the Scots as prospective allies against Edward and the Despensers. His biographer, despite earlier rumours retailed with some force in the *Vita*, believes that this was an innovative move.[207] The first wind of these overtures is provided by a safe conduct dated 6 December 1321, issued by James Douglas to enable two emissaries of the earl to travel to Jedburgh. A number of other documents, or rather copies of documents, reveal a conspiracy in which Lancaster, under the incongruous sobriquet "King Arthur," is supposed to have been at Pontefract with the earl of Hereford, Roger d'Amory, Hugh d'Audley, Bartholomew Badlesmere, Roger de Clifford, and others, awaiting Scottish assistance for a sweep through England and Wales. A reciprocal agreement provided that the earl and his supporters would not join Edward against the Scots but would work for peace between the two countries. The Pauline annalist sensed a convenient forgery dutifully published by Archbishop Reynolds. The Bridlington chronicler felt that God alone knew the truth of the matter, but an indenture was (conveniently?) found on Hereford's body after Boroughbridge. It was to form part of the indictment against Lancaster.[208]

After Epiphany (6 January) 1322, with the expiry of the truce, a Scottish army again entered the bishopric of Durham, the earl of Moray taking up quarters in Darlington. James Douglas and the Steward of Scotland made depredations on every side, one of them advancing towards Hartlepool and Cleveland, the other towards Richmond, where the inhabitants, lacking means of defence or hope of relief, once again bought off the invaders. After about a fortnight the intruders returned home. Lancaster was at his castle of Pontefract, but when the northern knights came to him, in readiness to fight against the Scots, he dissimulated. He had, said the chronicler, no inclination to fight for the realm of one who wished to fight against him.[209] Andrew Harclay hastened south to warn the king that none could resist the savagery of the Scots and to seek help. Edward, preoccupied with the Marcher rebellion, is said to have responded that faced with two such enemies, he would attack the traitors and leave Bruce alone. Harclay, he advised, should return and defend the places entrusted to him. On 9 February 1322 the northerner was empowered to treat with Bruce for peace or a further truce. Boroughbridge (16 March 1322) saw the defeat of the earls of Lancaster and Hereford thanks to Harclay's intervention. This opened up the possibility that at long last Edward would be able to lead a united English army against the Scots.[210] In April orders were despatched to Ireland for the supply of a substantial force: three hundred men-at-arms, a thousand lightly armed horsemen, or hobelars, and six thousand horsemen, to be paid for out of the exiguous balance in the Irish treasury.[211]

Bruce wasted no time. Between 17 June and 24 July another ambitious raid took place. Entering England by Carlisle, he burned the bishop's manor of Rose as well as Allendale, then despoiled the Cistercian abbey of Holmcultram despite the fact that it had been colonized from Melrose and that his own father was buried there.[212] After laying waste Coupland he crossed the Duddon sands to Furness, where the Cistercian abbot met him and redeemed his land from further depredation. Notwithstanding the payment, says the Lanercost chronicler, the Scots fired various places and carried off spoil. Moving south across the Leven sands they reached Cartmel. There they burned the surrounding countryside but spared the Augustinian priory, though they drove off its flocks. They then crossed the Kent sands to Lancaster, where everything was incinerated except the small Benedictine priory and the house of the Dominican friars. The earl of Moray and James Douglas, with what is described as a large army, joined Bruce for a foray as far as Preston in Amounderness. This they also burned, save for the Franciscan house. Some of the raiders went on for a further five miles, thus penetrating eighty miles into England. At that point they turned back and on reaching Carlisle (12 July) pitched their tents round the city for five days, taking all the grain and animals they could find.[213]

Edward spent much of the summer at York making his preparations, including the arming of his youthful bastard, Adam.[214] Admirals of eastern and western fleets were appointed; the western admiral, Sir Robert de Leyburn, being optimistically empowered to appoint bailiffs of all the lands he might occupy in Scotland and the Isles.[215] The king was at Darlington on 26 July 1322 and at the beginning of August at Newcastle, where his army assembled.[216] Harclay was ordered to levy forces in Cumberland, Westmorland, and Lancaster. Cattle from those areas were to be driven south to avoid capture by the Scots.[217] There is general agreement among the chroniclers that the expedition was bedevilled by a mixture of poor organization and adverse circumstances. The author of the

Flores put the blame on the younger Despenser. The substantial army went by way of Melrose to Leith, but in anticipation the Scots had removed everything transportable beyond the Forth. The English soldiers suffered from hunger and dysentery; many died, while others sold their arms and deserted. Fordun is unusually expansive: he describes how the English sacked the monasteries of Holyrood (Edinburgh) and Melrose, at which place, Barbour states, Douglas ambushed an English column. At Melrose on the return journey, Fordun claims, the prior, a sick monk, and two lay brethren were killed in the dormitory and other monks were severely wounded. The "Lord's Body" was removed from the pyx and cast on the high altar, the pyx itself being carried off. Dryburgh Abbey was fired and reduced to rubble. It comes as no surprise that such atrocities were not recorded by the English chroniclers. Early September saw the king back at Newcastle.[218] His last expedition had failed to bring Bruce to battle; worse still, it had fizzled out in ignominious failure.[219]

Now it was the turn of the Scots. Bruce, having collected an army from both sides of the Forth, crossed by the Solway into England and for five days lay at Beaumont just north-west of Carlisle. After the by-now conventional laying waste of the countryside he moved south to "Blackemoor," identified by Professor Barrow as Sutton Bank, an area that had previously escaped destruction. Edward meanwhile lay unsuspecting at Rievaulx Abbey, or, as some accounts say, at that of Byland not far off.[220] In a rapid move to prevent the king's escape the Scots scaled the heights to scatter the earl of Richmond's troops. Both Richmond and Henry de Suly, butler of France, were captured. Rievaulx was sacked and much royal treasure taken. Bruce's main quarry, Edward himself, escaped to Bridlington and thence to York. His adversary retired to Beverley, where he mulcted the citizens, and then proceeded north to Malton, where the canons of Bridlington also bought him off, for which excommunicable offence they sought, and on 15 December received, absolution from the archbishop of York. Already, prior to the Scots' arrival, they had taken the precaution of carting all their muniments, relics, and other precious articles, accompanied by the greater part of the convent, to their church of Goxhill south of the Humber. The Scots had no need to hurry back laden as they were with booty. By the time they re-entered Scotland on 2 November they had been in England for over a month and the English king had been a fugitive in his own country.[221] The author of the *Brut* put the blame on Harclay for not having brought his forces to Byland. According to his unconfirmed account Harclay facilitated the Scots' withdrawal through Coupland and was handsomely bribed by Sir James Douglas.[222]

While the king was at York, Andrew Harclay, who on 25 March 1322 had been made earl of Carlisle on account of his services against Lancaster, and who on the following 15 September had become chief warden of the Marches, was poised with his army to join forces against the Scots, or so the Lanercost chronicler alleges. What he found was a disoriented Edward who had done nothing about gathering a force. Seeing this, he disbanded his own troops.[223] It was

borne in upon him that the king of England knew neither how to rule his kingdom nor how to defend it against the Scots, who were free to carry out their dev-
astations from year to year. It would be preferable for the community of both
realms, he thought, if each king were to possess his kingdom peacefully, without the rendering of homage, rather than for such depredations to continue. Possibly Harclay's negotiations with the Scots had resulted in a basic agreement by
Christmas 1322, allowing the formal document to be drawn up on 3 January
1323. But, comments the Lancaster chronicler, the earl made the agreement
without the knowledge or consent of the king or of the realm in parliament. He
was only an individual, who had no authority to ordain such things.[224] Nothing
could be more indicative of the ineffectiveness of Edward's rule than the fact
that both Lancaster and Harclay had independently sought to conclude private
arrangements with one who, though generally held to be a rebel, nonetheless
constituted a stable political force.

It is true that Harclay had been empowered in February 1322 to treat about a
final peace, "forma finalis pacis et concordiae," between the English king and
Bruce, but this is nowhere mentioned as the authority for his agreement of 1323.
However, it would seem that Harclay persuaded certain men of the Marches to
swear to the accord by persuading them that it had the royal assent.[225] The agreement has survived in various forms, one of which, presumed to be a copy of the
text sealed by Harclay, comes from an eighteenth-century Latin transcript, now
destroyed, of a Bergen cathedral register.[226] Another text, in French and clearly
abbreviated, was sent to Edward's council at York, with a warning that it appeared
to be the beginning of a great evil, "commencement de grant mal."[227] The essence
of the agreement was that aid should be given to Bruce so that the realm of Scotland could be held freely, "franchement, entierement, et quitement," or, as the
Bergen copy has it, entirely immune from any obligation to the English king,
"pleno iure, liberum et immune ab omni servicio exaccione vel demanda regis
Anglie."[228] The twelve arbitrators, six appointed by Bruce and six by Harclay, are
in the latter version intended to decide cases where those two disagree but in other
versions are to constitute a council – a concept familiar to the Ordainers – to order
and determine appropriately all matters concerning the good order of the two
realms, "que predictorum regnorum tangunt commodum et quietem."[229] The
agreement provided for protection for those accepting it, hostility towards those
opposing it. The Bergen version specifically stated that were the Scottish king to
bring an army into England he would not harm the lands of the earl, and vice versa.
If the earl were to ride into Scotland he would not harm those of the Scottish king.
The king of England was given a year to consent. If he did so Bruce promised to
endow an abbey in Scotland for those killed in the war, to pay forty thousand marks
sterling to Edward at the rate of four thousand a year, and to give him the marriage
of his male heir, should the council of twelve approve.[230] Were the king of England
not to consent, then the king of Scotland would not be bound further. Neither party
was to be under obligation to receive those who had opposed him.[231]

Edward wrote angrily to Harclay on 8 January 1323 – five days after the date of the agreement – deprecating the fact that the earl had permitted it and demanding details. On the thirteenth he issued an order to William Ayrminne, keeper of the rolls, to search them for the terms of Harclay's commission. Then, on 1 February, Harclay's arrest was ordered as one who adhered to the Scots – the king's rebels and enemies – in violation of his allegiance and homage.[232] Sir Anthony Lucy, a rival of Harclay's in the Northwest, who some years before had complained about his behaviour,[233] was sent to apprehend him. This was accomplished without difficulty at Carlisle Castle, the earl unaccountably having taken no precautions against the inevitable. Geoffrey le Scrope arrived at the castle on the feast of St Chad (2 March). The following day, sitting judicially, he pronounced sentence as though from the king's own mouth and by his record (*tanquam ex ore regis et recordatione regis*). Harclay was first degraded from his dignity of earl by the removal of the sword with which he had been invested by the king, and then deprived of his honour as a knight by the cutting off of his spurs. Next he was drawn to the gallows, hanged, and his head sent to London, his four quarters being displayed respectively at Carlisle, Newcastle, Bristol and Dover.[234] The condemnation of one who, despite his faults, had shown a competence rare in the military annals of Edward II's reign speaks for itself. In his country's interests, particularly its northern regions, he had assumed responsibilities that were not his, but this more out of common sense and patriotism than naked ambition. Certainly he was ambitious – his origins were modest – and like so many others of his time acquisitive and unscrupulous, yet his treason stemmed from the dichotomy between his own military capacity and the incompetence of a king who failed to protect his subjects.

Well before Harclay's death fresh approaches to the Scots were under way. Bruce used the Frenchman Henry de Suly as a go-between. He was, he said, willing to accept the proposal to extend the truce until Trinity (22 May) but objected to what must have been a draft or summary copy of Edward's letter forwarded by Suly, on the grounds that it made no mention of himself as principal, but merely of the "gentz d'Escoce." What appear to be the letters themselves, dated 14 march 1323 from Knaresborough, are addressed to "Sir Robert Bruce and his adherents."[235] A mutual exchange of letters was to be effected with Bruce through the constable of Bamburgh, who would then publish the truce.[236] William Herle and Geoffrey le Scrope left Westminster for Newcastle on 5 April and did not return until the temporary truce expired on 22 May. In the meantime an extension had been arranged until 12 June.[237] There was some delay in the arrival of the Scottish envoys, the earl of Moray, the bishop of St Andrews and others, partly because of doubts about appropriate safeguards for Moray and partly, perhaps, because of the problems arising from the conduct of business with excommunicates. But by the beginning of May they were at Newcastle, as were the earl of Pembroke, the younger Despenser, and other English representatives.[238] Finally, on 30 May at Bishopthorpe just outside York, the two sides concluded a thirteen-year truce from 12 June 1323, in the hope that during that time a permanent peace might be agreed upon.[239] The arrangements were confirmed by Bruce at Berwick on 7 June.[240] There had been a jarring note in the proceedings, an indication of their unpopularity with some who had lost lands north of the border. Henry de Beaumont, described as being of the great and secret council of the king, refused to answer when his opinion was solicited. Ordered by Edward to leave the council, he responded by saying that he preferred to be absent.[241]

The truce did not solve fundamental questions, since it failed to acknowledge Bruce's sovereignty. No new fortifications were to be built, wardens were to be appointed to settle border disputes, and ships trading with Scotland were not to be molested: all provisions that served to remove potential sources of tension. What has been identified as an earlier text permitted "Sire Robert de Brus" to seek papal absolution while the truce remained in force, but if peace were not made the sentence was to be reinstated. The intention of this clause was that the English would not oppose Scottish efforts at the Curia to secure the withdrawal of the sentences. If a permanent peace did not materialize Edward reserved the right to press for their reimposition. In the past, of course, sentences had been pronounced as a consequence of the diplomatic lobbying of the English.[242] Another clause was to the effect that neither side would assist anyone to make war on the other party. Only the "earlier" (E) text has the qualification "sauve l'alliance entre le roi de France et nous," possibly a reference to the Anglo-French treaty of 1303. At that stage Edward may have banked on having a seemingly accommodating Charles IV as an ally.[243]

Relations with France soon threatened to deteriorate and in doing so to complicate the Scottish situation. With Charles IV's accession following the death of Philip V le Long (3 January 1322), Edward once again became liable to perform homage for his French possessions. In view of Edward's Scottish preoccupations the French king did not press the matter, yet two months after the truce with Scotland Edward was summoned to Amiens for the Easter of 1324.[244] An embassy consisting of Robert de Wells, Richard of Gloucester and John Shoredich (Shoreditch) left London for Paris at the end of November and among other excuses for delaying the homage alleged that a large force of Scots had entered the realm and perpetrated many evil deeds contrary to the truce (*molt de malx contre le trewe*).[245] Confirmation of any such raid is lacking. By the time the embassy had arrived in Paris, news of the burning by the lord of Montpezat of the French king's new bastide at Saint-Sardos had reached the capital. Edward's denial of responsibility seems to have been accepted, but the subsequent proceedings in the French court and continued neglect of the obligation of homage were to lead to a confiscation of his Continental fiefs and to the War of Saint-Sardos, as it has been named.[246]

Meanwhile there had also been a deterioration in the hitherto fairly cooperative relationship between Edward and the pope. Rigaud d'Assier, the bishop of

Winchester, died at the Curia on 12 April 1323 and Edward saw an opportunity for the promotion of Robert Baldock to that wealthy see. Instead the pope provided John Stratford on 20 June and had him consecrated six days later. Edward was furious. He felt that his envoy had taken advantage of his position to feather his own nest. The attempted arraignment of Stratford covered a wide area of conflict between pope and king but is of particular interest here for Scottish affairs. Stratford and his former colleague Rigaud d'Assier had been bound by indenture to pursue certain matters, among them the resumption of the processes against the Scots and their "aggravation" if necessary; the exclusion of Scotsmen from bishoprics in Scotland, because such men were involved in the misdeeds complained of; protest against the transfer outside Scotland (where he had never been recognized) of the bishop of Glasgow, John de Eaglescliff; and insistence that to avoid prejudice to Edward he should be written to for the temporalities of Scottish bishoprics, as was allegedly the custom.[247]

Stratford's defence detailed the achievements of his mission. In response to the first point, the pope had given the necessary instructions to Cardinals Frédol and Montfavèz to intensify the sentences against the Scots, who had been adjudged rebellious towards the apostolic see. But when the king's letters brought news of the truce this policy had been abandoned. Peace became the order of the day. In the circumstances the pope felt that he ought not to intervene. Stratford pointed out that the truce included an article permitting relaxation of the sentences, provided Edward gave his consent. This would seem to demonstrate that the final form of the document did contain such a clause. He had urged nonetheless that should absolution be granted two things ought to be considered: the king's right and the infinite damage done by the Scots to the English church, the king, and to his lands. As for the Scottish bishops, the pope was not to be swayed. No Englishman could go into Scotland, so that if the king's request were granted souls would lack pastors; that was why Eaglescliff – an Englishman – had been translated. With respect to the temporalities of the Scottish bishoprics, the pope claimed that he had many times written to the king for their livery.[248]

It was against this background of difficulties in both Anglo-French and Anglo-papal relations that the negotiations for a peace with the Scots were undertaken. In January 1324, on the grounds that it would bring peace nearer, Pope John had agreed to address Bruce as king but without prejudice to the *de iure* situation. However, when on 22 May 1324 the papal envoy Hugh d'Angoulême wrote from London, he reported that "he who acts as king of Scotland" had held a council at Berwick and it was believed that were war to break out with France Bruce would come to the aid of Charles IV.[249] At Porchester some two months later, 15 July, Edward was on the one hand proposing to send forces to Aquitaine, on the other appointing negotiators for a "final peace" with Bruce.[250] Safe conduct was given to Sir Alexander Seton, Bruce's envoy, to journey to Scotland, doubtless to report to his master, and then to return to the king. Under the same date safe conducts were issued for the bishop of St Andrews and the earl of Moray together with fifty men apiece. On 23 September protection was extended to a further six negotiators. Matters came to a head in November. According to the *Vita* this was on the initiative of Robert Bruce, who claimed that only with difficulty had his men agreed to the many truces.[251] On the third Bishop Lamberton and Moray with six others were given safe conducts to York and five days later an impressive body of English negotiators was appointed: William Melton, archbishop of York; John Hothum, bishop of Ely and a former chancellor; Roger Northburgh, bishop of Coventry and Lichfield, an experienced administrator; the Despensers; Chancellor Baldock; and William Ayrminne.[252]

The *Vita* is the only chronicle to detail the negotiations. The agenda was provided by the Scots. Allegedly they required that Scotland should be free of every exaction; that by right of conquest the land to the gates of York should be free; that Bruce should have his forfeited barony of Essex; and that the Stone of Scone, supposedly brought by Scota daughter of Pharaoh, should be restored. The peace was to be sealed by the marriage of Bruce's daughter with the young Edward and the treaty confirmed by both the king of France and the pope. Edward understandably contemned these draft proposals, considering them to provide excuse for further breaches of the truce. Without prejudice to the Crown, he argued, he could not surrender his right to a long-subject Scotland. Certainly the Scots had no right to the March and the claim by virtue of perambulation could equally be turned against Scotland. It was not fitting that he should restore land to Bruce that his father, Edward I, had confiscated for manifest crime. He conceded that there would have been little difficulty in returning the Stone had the other demands been reasonable. Any peace treaty he would be only too glad to publish before any prince in the world. This was an impasse, but both sides agreed to maintain the truce.[253]

Infractions of the truce occurred early in 1326. On 12 April Edward was attempting to munition Carlisle following a surprise attempt to take the place by night. On the eastern side of the country Bishop Beaumont was instructed to fortify the castles of Norham, Alnwick, Dunstanburgh, and Wark following attempts to capture them.[254] In the same month the Scots concluded a treaty with France at Corbeil. In providing for mutual military aid against the king of England it was clearly against the spirit of the 1323 truce.[255] But in September 1326 the invasion of Queen Isabella and Roger Mortimer brought the immediate collapse of Edward's government. In this extremity, Lanercost claims, the desperate king wrote to the Scots, freely granting them the realm of Scotland and, what was worse, a great part of northern England, on condition that they helped him against the invaders. Allegedly the queen feared that her husband would attempt to reach Ireland, raise an army there, and cross to Scotland, whence with the help of the Scots and Irish he would invade England.[256] The truth or falsehood of this story is unlikely to be established.

ISABELLA AND MORTIMER: THE "SHAMEFUL PEACE"

Edward III's coronation was marked by a nocturnal raid on Norham, foiled by the castellan's vigilance. The new regime, reluctant to be provoked, gave orders (15 February 1327) for the observance of the truce which it officially confirmed on 6 March. Commissioners, headed by Archbishop Melton, were appointed on 30 April with power to negotiate and to ratify a final peace. Safe conduct was issued to them and to Robert Bruce and his retinue on 7 May. On the twenty-third all mariners were warned against impeding the negotiators. Further commissioners – Sir Henry Percy, Henry de Beaumont, the abbot of Rievaulx, Geoffrey le Scrope, William de Herle and the experienced clerk, William de Denum – were appointed on 29 May and their commission renewed as late as 10 June. These plans proved nugatory, however. Most of the relevant documents are marked "vacat." Scottish preparations necessitated countermeasures and early in April forces were summoned to York for 18 May, followed on 17 June by an order for the mobilization at York of men between sixteen and sixty. Bruce was resuming his opportunist tactics, though ill health meant that he would have to leave active campaigning to others. But he did cross to Antrim where he forced the seneschal of Ulster to send provisions to Larne, thereby appropriating a traditional English source of supply.[257]

Barbour's scarcely convincing explanation of his hero's renewed belligerence is that it was in response to attacks on Scottish shipping. Another provocation, if and when it came to his notice, would have been the safe conduct issued to Edward Balliol.[258] *Lanercost* records that on 20 July – the date is questionable – three Scottish "armies" crossed the border led by the earl of Moray, James Douglas, and the earl of Mar who, though nurtured at the English court, had returned to Scotland after Edward's capture. Barbour adds Archibald Douglas and James Stewart.[259] Whether, as *Lanercost* suggests, Mar had any serious plan for releasing the imprisoned Edward with the aid of others in England it is difficult to say, although former associates of his were being sought in the Welsh Marches.[260] A hastily raised English army, which included Hainaulters led by Jean de Hainault, as well as the chronicler Jean le Bel, travelled north to York, where there was a riot between the Hainaulters and the citizens in the course of which part of the city was burned down. Interestingly enough the prior of Canterbury had envisaged trouble of this kind. Among other objections to the use of Hainaulters he felt that as it had been declared that any who captured land would be permitted to keep it as tenants in chief, it would be dangerous for the king to have such men as tenants.[261]

After peace had been restored the army moved on to a position between Barnard Castle and Stanhope Park. The Scots kept under cover of woods, not risking a pitched battle: the king is said to have diverted to Haydon Bridge on the South Tyne in an attempt to cut off their retreat. When they remained stationary he returned. Had he rushed them he would have won the day – or such was the common opinion. The Scots were at a disadvantage, for they lacked food for themselves and fodder for their horses. But, says the Lanercost chronicler, certain magnates delayed this course of action for the eight days during which the Scots lay between them and the king's force. Then one night the Scots, allegedly warned by someone in the English army of a coming attack, left the woods, circled the king's army, and so escaped to Scotland. However, James Douglas with a handful of men (Le Bel suggests some two hundred) infiltrated the royal army, inflicted heavy casualties, and even reached the young Edward's tent – cutting two or three of the guy ropes, so Le Bel who was on the campaign would have us believe – before withdrawing unharmed. The youthful warrior was so upset by the Scots' evasion that he burst into tears.[262] It was to be a useful lesson nonetheless.[263] Various chroniclers concurred in the notion that this had been achieved by English connivance. Baker suggested darkly that "certain magnates" were responsible, while the *Brut* is clear that Mortimer was the culprit and the charge was to figure with many others in his indictment.[264]

So much for one chronicler's somewhat sketchy account (with minor additions from elsewhere) of the "Weardale campaign." Overall the chroniclers give slightly confusing versions of the affair, but Bruce's biographer has compiled a convincing, if tentative reconstruction that will be largely followed here. The Scots crossed the border as early as 15 June – the day English envoys were charged with securing an armistice – and travelled south by way of the valley of the South Tyne.[265] They pillaged and burned Weardale and what Barbour calls "Cockdaill" which, as suggested, could well be the area round Cockfield in the Gaunless valley, to the Northeast of Barnard Castle. Allegedly the English army at Durham, which lies in somewhat of a hollow, could see the fires raised by the invaders, but they failed to make contact. False intelligence that the Scots were in flight, claims the *Scalacronica*, caused the English to hasten north to Haydon Bridge. Learning of their error they turned south to Blanchland and were probably in Allendale, wrongly assumed by Maxwell in his edition of the *Scalacronica* to be Annandale, when, on 31 July, the Scots were sighted by one Thomas Rokeby. Rokeby, though captured by the Scots, was released with a message from Douglas and Moray boasting that they were only too ready to fight. The Scots, it appears, had remained all the time at Stanhope. Adopting a strong position on the south bank of the Wear (rather than the north as suggested by Barbour's editor), which they declined to relinquish, they found that the English, not unwisely, were reluctant to attack them. Later, on 3 August, they secretly crossed the river to Stanhope Park, a hunting lodge of the bishops of Durham, where they were in danger of being surrounded. About the middle of the following night Douglas launched his audacious raid killing, says Le Bel, more than three hundred Englishmen. After a long-drawn-out confrontation the main body of Scots, thanks to the defective intelligence work of the English, slipped away unnoticed under cover of darkness. Meanwhile Archibald Douglas, who had foraged throughout the bishopric of Durham, encountered local levies at Darlington where, according to the *Scalacronica*, he massacred them.[266]

After this chastening fiasco accommodation became even more urgent for the English. The Isabella-Mortimer regime could not hope to defeat the Scots, nor could it afford to squander resources on border warfare. Already there was an internal rift between Henry of Lancaster and Mortimer. As for the ailing Bruce, he was anxious to be fully recognized as king and to ensure a peaceful succession for his son. The youthful Edward was not in a position to implement whatever opinion he may have had, but his dislike of the solution arrived at was to become abundantly clear when he came of age.[267] There was another factor: the death of Charles le Bel on 1 February 1328 and the ensuing coronation of Philip VI of Valois brought a protest from an English delegation to Paris, which asserted Edward III's right to the French Crown. The Lanercost chronicler pointed out that unless peace were made with the Scots any conflict with the French, the disinheritors of Edward, would bring an invasion from the North.[268]

In a document dated 18 October (1327) from Berwick Bruce presented a series of peace proposals. The first and most important was that he should have the realm of Scotland free, without any form of subjection. There would be a marriage between Robert's infant son, David, and Edward III's sister,[269] with appropriate dower to be agreed. There was to be no automatic restoration of lands claimed by the disinherited on either side. Mutual aid was to be given against enemies, saving the treaty (of Corbeil) between Robert and the king of France. Bruce promised twenty thousand pounds within three years after the confirmation of peace, payable in instalments. The king of England was to help in the removal of papal sentences against Robert. If Edward were prepared to negotiate on these premises, Robert would send envoys to Newcastle-on-Tyne. In a document issued from Nottingham on 30 October Edward, or more realistically Isabella and Mortimer, agreed to the terms as a basis for negotiation, holding out assurance that he would allow Robert to hold Scotland freely for himself and his heirs and would urge the pope to repeal the sentences.[270]

In December of 1327 a parliament was summoned to York for February. It did not disperse until 5 March. Scottish affairs must have been high on the agenda, Bishops Ayrminne of Norwich and Burghersh of Lincoln being sent to discuss "certain articles" with the Scots. On 1 March Edward III formally conceded that Scotland, as defined by the boundaries in Alexander III's time, "should remain for ever to the eminent prince Lord Robert, by the grace of God the illustrious king of Scots, our ally and dearest friend," quit of any subjection or demand. Any right in the realm of Scotland claimed by his ancestors or confirmed by any treaties he utterly renounced. All instruments embodying obligations of the kind were to be null. Henry Percy and William la Zouche of Ashby were to take an oath to this effect upon the king's soul. Under the same date credentials were issued for the treasurer, Henry Burghersh, bishop of Lincoln, Henry Percy, William la Zouche, and Geoffrey le Scrope – by a stroke of irony the man who had condemned Harclay – to negotiate a final peace with Robert Bruce.[271] The treaty was concluded at

Edinburgh on the seventeenth and ratified by the Northampton Parliament, which assembled on 24 April 1328.[272]

To ensure permanent peace the marriage sought by King Robert between David, his son and heir, who celebrated his fourth birthday on 5 March 1324, and Joan, Edward's sister, was to be arranged. As dower she would receive three thousand pounds of annual rent. Were Joan to die then David would marry another close relative of the English king, and if David were to do so then Edward would have the marriage of the next male heir of the king of Scotland. The kings of England and Scotland were to be allies bound to assist each other, saving the latter's alliance with the king of France. Should the king of Scotland by virtue of that alliance or for any other reason make war on the king of England, then the latter could reciprocate, despite the peace. The king of Scotland was not to aid enemies of the king of England in Ireland; likewise the latter was not to assist those waging war in the Isle of Man or other Scottish Isles. All documents concerning the subjection of Scotland were to be surrendered and an indenture made to record their delivery.[273] But should the letter of the king of England annulling such documents have to be cancelled, they were to be restored. This was merely a caveat in case the treaty should not be confirmed. The English king was to further the withdrawal of lawsuits brought in the Curia against the king of Scotland or his subjects. Furthermore, he was precluded from securing condemnation in that court for any unpaid instalment of the twenty thousand pounds promised by the Scottish king "pro pace" until two months had elapsed from the due date of payment. The "laws of the Marches" were to be kept, and defects in them or disputes were to be submitted to the kings and amended by their councils. Ratification by the English was to be made before the Ascension (12 May 1328) and no prejudice was to arise from the agreement to the right of the Church in either realm. The treaty document then concludes with the oaths taken for the king of Scotland with respect to its observance and by the English envoy, Henry Percy, with respect to the performance of the marriage.[274]

As will be seen from the above, three of the basic provisions of the treaty – acknowledgment of Bruce's right to hold the kingdom freely, a dynastic marriage, and a monetary payment, albeit on a smaller scale – reflect arrangements made by Harclay five years previously. The notion of a supervisory council, akin to that of the Ordainers, was no longer current politics. If we compare the terms with Bruce's reported scheme of 1324, there is no mention of restoration of the ancestral lands in England, claims arising from Scottish perambulation of the northern counties, or of the Stone of Scone. All the same, the English government did intend to surrender the Stone and the "Black Rood," believed to be a portion of Christ's cross, seemingly as a consequence of discussion at the Northampton Parliament. A writ was issued for the Stone's delivery by the abbot and convent of Westminster to the sheriffs of London so that it could be transported to Berwick by Queen Isabella when she attended her daughter's wedding. The Londoners frustrated the move.[275] The treaty did not provide for any mutual restoration of confiscated lands, hence many persons were disinherited. In practice both kings did reinstate individuals "of special grace." Prior to her journey north Isabella received letters patent under the great seal empowering her to negotiate for mutual restitution but to what effect can only be surmised.[276]

The terms of the treaty appear generous in view of Bruce's long run of military successes, but they were certain to prove unpopular in England, save in parts of the North. It has been argued that thanks to Scrope in particular but also to William Ayrminne, the principal English negotiators, the bulk of the settlement "was most skilfully drafted in the interests of England." Perhaps, but not by the standards of the time. Even Joan of the Tower could be regarded as disparaged.[277] The loss of Scotland was something of which Edward II stood accused. Baker, notoriously prejudiced, declared that the 1328 treaty was made by the young king under the influence of traitors, "non regens nec bene rectus set per proditores ductus." He explains that the terms were made favourable to the Scots by the connivance of Isabella, Bishop Orleton, and Roger Mortimer. A version of the *Brut* claims that the treaty was devised while the king was of tender age, without good counsel or the assent of the peers of the realm, so that the Crown was disinherited for all time. Because it was by his advice, Roger Mortimer was seized at Nottingham together with his associate, Simon Bereford.[278] So far as Orleton is concerned any attribution of responsibility is baseless, Isabella and Mortimer were undoubtedly the moving spirits.[279] They were afraid, Baker suggested, of what might happen as a consequence of Edward II's death. Moreover, if the new king were to die, Roger Mortimer with the help of the Scots would usurp the kingdom and take over the queen (*auxilio Scotorum regnum et matrem regis Isabellam usurparet*). Another idea was that the treaty would clear the decks for a show-down between Mortimer and Henry of Lancaster.[280] Isabella herself benefited from the money paid by the Scots. From Bruce's viewpoint the peace was achieved in the nick of time. The children's marriage took place on 17 July 1328, he died on 7 June in the following year, which marked the beginning of the ill-fated reign of his son, David II. An early act of the emancipated Edward III was to grant a year's protection for Edward Balliol to visit England and he pressed King David for the restoration of the lands of Thomas Wake, "Lord of Liddell," and of Henry de Beaumont, "earl of Buchan." David's part of the bargain, payment of the remainder of the twenty thousand pounds, was promptly fulfilled.[281]

As was to be expected, there followed a crop of border problems. The bishop of Durham claimed that Upsettlington, near Norham, had "from time out of mind" been a part of England in which his writs ran. The Scots held that, being on the north side of the Tweed, it belonged to them. The bishop was summoned to the Scottish Parliament and complained of this to the English king. The difficulty arose, argued the Scots, because their kings had made over the land to St Cuthbert. At Tweedmouth, where a ferry to Berwick had regularly operated, the men of Berwick alleged that the whole of that water belonged to them and would not permit any English boat to touch land on the Scottish side.[282] In the event the fate of the hard-won treaty was not to be decided by peccadilloes of that kind but by other factors. Those of the disinherited, who like Henry de Beaumont had never willingly accepted arrangements with the Scots that over-looked their land claims, were clamouring for reinstatement, while the emanci-pated Edward III was determined to recover his "rights," alienated during his minority. By 1332 the whole matter had been reopened; the disinherited were about to invade Scotland, Edward Balliol was claiming to be king as heir to his father, John, while Edward himself was raising troops for the defence of the Scottish March and even putting forward English candidates for the vacant bish-opric of St Andrews.[283] The combination of "Countesse Makepees" and David "drite on auter" could provide no assurance of the peace that had for so long proved elusive.[284]

10

Ireland,

1295–1330

Nowe here beware and hertly take entente,
As ye woll answere at the laste jugemente,
That, but for sloughe and for recheleshede [recklessness],
Ye remembere and wyth all your myghte take hede
To kepen Yrelond that it be not loste,
For it is a boterasse and a poste,
Undre England, and Wales is another.[1]

THE ENGLISH COLONIES[2]

A recent biography of Edward I devotes comparatively little attention to Ireland. For that king Scotland, Wales, and Gascony were far more important: the only partially settled Ireland was scarcely a source of strength, although it did provide resources for royal campaigns and fortifications elsewhere well into Edward II's reign.[3] Yet the history of Ireland has something in common with that of both Scotland and Wales: all three experienced a Norman invasion followed by what might be termed "colonial government." In Scotland this principally affected the Lowlands, some of the most attractive land from the point of view of accessibility and productivity, hence of settlement, as the Romans had found. That country, despite William the Lion's defeat and imprisonment at Falaise in 1174, followed by his offering of his helmet, lance, and saddle on the altar of York Minster *in signum subieccionis*, was to enjoy a succession of kings who managed to build some semblance of a unitary realm. This was achieved in the face of the fissiparous tendencies of such areas as the Western Isles and Galloway – tendencies that still confronted Robert Bruce in the fourteenth century.[4] Neither Wales nor Ireland exhibited a comparable development. In the case of Wales, this was despite the efforts of Llywelyn "the last." North Wales was conquered in 1282–83, while in the South royal encroachment was made piecemeal. By the turn of the century Edward I's task of conquest had been accomplished. Only the occasional revolt was to disturb the country.[5]

As for Ireland, the English pope Adrian IV (1154–59) had claimed in the bull *Laudabiliter* – in accordance with the Donation of Constantine – that it pertained, like all islands, to the "ius Sancti Petri."[6] Henry II, though, was cautious about the use he made of this bull in view of his unwillingness to be regarded as a papal vassal.[7] Over half a century later King John, in order to extricate himself from a tight corner, was forced to receive back his kingdoms, including Ireland, from Pope Innocent III as a feudatory vassal. A charter of 1254 declared the lordship of Ireland to be inalienable from the English Crown. Thereafter the country was linked to England by the person of the king.[8] It has been suggested, though, that Pope John XXII threatened that unless Edward II responded to the grievances of the Irish church the lordship earlier conferred by the papacy might be transferred. But this threat was scarcely realistic in view of John's overall fiscal policy.[9]

Naturally enough, in those parts of the "colonies" occupied by Anglo-Norman lords their brand of feudalism was established, though with modifications suited to Irish conditions.[10] In practice this meant that those with holdings in Scotland, Wales, or Ireland also regularly held fiefs in England; men such as Roger Mortimer, Henry de Lacy, earl of Lincoln, and Gilbert de Clare, earl of Gloucester. The last two died respectively in 1311 and 1314, each without leaving a male heir. By the beginning of the fourteenth century apart from numerous "liberties" there were five earldoms: Ulster (the de Burghs), Kildare (the Offaly Geraldines), Louth (John de Bermingham, 1319–29, bestowed as a reward for the defeat of Edward Bruce at Faughart), Desmond (the Munster Geraldines), and Ormond (the Butlers). These stretched from north to south of the island on its eastern side. The seat of government was of course Dublin, surrounded by an area under its control termed the Pale, while distinction was regularly drawn between the "land of peace" and the "land of war," terms coined during the thirteenth century.[11] The former dwindled with the resurgence of the Irish in the latter part of the thirteenth century and during the fourteenth.

ANGLO-NORMAN IRELAND[12]

First of all a little needs to be said about the peculiar state of affairs in the island. There could be said to have been a threefold division, about which much has been written. The native Irish, the Gaels, were distinctive by reason of their language, laws, customs, dress, and even their hair styling (the Cúlin) and shaving preferences.[13] They were very much family or clan oriented and boasted a considerable number of petty kings, or reguli. The Irish had no real towns, apart from a few established by the Norsemen. Unlike the settlers they preferred the countryside. With the invasion towns grew up, particularly in the vicinity of castles, an essential element of Anglo-Norman domination. The lands of the native Irish continued to be encroached upon by settlers, the "Anglo-Normans" or

"Anglo-Irish," whom some historians prefer to term the "English of Ireland." These men brought with them, in addition to feudal customs, their methods of warfare, together with the administrative and judicial systems they had developed in England. Naturally enough, in the course of time there was a tendency for these long-established Galls, as they were called by the Irish annalists, to degenerate – from the English point of view – by adopting many facets of Irish culture and by intermarrying with their neighbours. They became "Hiberniores ipsis Hibernis," to repeat a well-worn cliché, perhaps misleading, perhaps indicative – in view of the fact that it implies that the origin of such elements of the population continued to be identifiable. In any case there were great variations in the "Irishness" of the settlers.[14] Then there were the born Englishmen, accounted foreigners, as from time to time were the "Anglo-Irish"; "foreigner" being an epithet applied to the controversial bishop of Ossory, Richard Ledred or Ledrede (Leatherhead), whose devotional works are perhaps hard to reconcile with his political involvement.[15] It is not to be concluded, however, that Gall and Gael were necessarily to be found on opposite sides in the many fratricidal struggles that plagued Irish history. The problem of "ethnicity" or "race," to use terminology much in vogue at the present time, is difficult in the context of medieval Ireland. The chroniclers and others regularly use the word "nacio," which has sometimes been translated (misleadingly?) as "race." Then again, the description "English" is hardly a satisfactory one for settlers who were of decidedly mixed origin. Legal distinctions, it has been argued, are more reliable than those of "nationality."[16]

In Scotland the loyalty of native bishops, as distinct from those who could be described as English, was a source of concern both to Edward II and Edward III, but in Ireland this does not seem to have been so pronounced save in exceptional times, notably during the Bruce invasion. The Church was by definition a "supra-national" organization, but this does not mean that individual bishops did not side with what might be termed nationalist movements, as was the case in Scotland. In Ireland, however, it has been claimed that "the medieval Irish bishop, whatever his racial origins, was normally prepared to cooperate with the state so long as the rights of his see were respected."[17] Be that as it may, Edward II was anxious to secure the election of English bishops to Irish sees, men whom he thought he could trust. With the Scottish invasion this became particularly important, and in letters to Avignon he denounced the treasonable activities of some Irish bishops.[18] Yet even in England the bishops initially promoted at Edward's behest turned out to be politically incompatible.

The settlers also founded monastic houses, as they had done elsewhere, particularly Benedictine and Cistercian ones. Unlike the Norman settlers in England following the victory of Hastings, they appear to have adopted the cults of Celtic saints. Church organization, which had been well advanced before their coming, was by the thirteenth century comparable to that in other parts of Western Europe. In line with developments elsewhere monastic chapters in cathedral churches were replaced by secular ones and in Henry III's time complaint was made to the papacy that Irish bishops appointed Irishmen to their churches. The validity of this complaint has not been established: there have not yet been sufficient studies of the composition of cathedral chapters, as to some degree is also the case with respect to English cathedrals.[19] But there is plenty of evidence of what nowadays would be denounced as "racialism" in the conduct of the local Cistercians, daughter houses of the abbey of Mellifont. Despite the efforts of the mother house of the Order, Cîteaux, there was a concerted attempt to exclude Englishmen.[20]

The nature of Edward II's dissatisfaction with the conduct of the Irish church is exemplified by the articles sent to Pope John XXII, to which the pontiff responded in 1325. The first of the articles declared that the "people of the Irish nation" (*gentes Hybernie nationis*) did not consider Edward to be the true lord of Ireland but a usurper. The king suggested to the pope that the remedy for this was for him to instruct the archbishops, bishops, and the religious to affirm the contrary position in their preaching and at confession. Further, they should declare that all who upheld other opinions were *ipso facto* excommunicate. Such proclamations were to be published at least four times a year in all cathedral, collegiate, and parochial churches – a time-honoured way of disseminating information. The second article emphasized the king's concern that peace was being disturbed by Irish bishops, particularly those who were neighbours of English ones, and that they assisted their "nation" by favouring and fomenting wars against the king of England and his subjects. The suggested remedy here was to amalgamate many of the superfluous and needy Irish bishoprics to neighbouring sees, particularly to places where there was a royal town. Lastly, and justifiably in ecclesiastical terms, the king claimed that many religious and canons regular who had large estates among the English admitted only Irishmen, whereas in English monasteries English and Irish were admitted indifferently. The king suggested that this policy be adopted in the interests of establishing peace and concord between the nations. The mendicants who were purely Irish (mere Hybernici), he argued, should likewise not show partiality towards their "nation."[21]

The history of Ireland at this period is characterized by internecine conflict between the Irish and settlers separately, as well as between the two, and more particularly by a series of barbaric killings, one of the most notorious of which was the massacre on Trinity Sunday 1305 of the O'Connors by the perfidious Piers Bermingham, that "nobilis debellator Hibernicorum." Allegedly this action of the "foreigners" merely pre-empted the plan of the O'Connors to kill Bermingham and other settlers.[22] Then in June 1329 John de Bermingham, who had continued the war to the west of Dublin against the Irish of Offaly, was attacked by a substantial number of English tenants who, it is suggested, may have been acting as the *posse comitatus* in response to the Berminghams' oppressions. He was killed together with his two brothers and a large number of

others, some 160 according to the chronicler Clyn, thus extinguishing the earldom of Louth.[23] In the Southwest of Ireland the Geraldine Maurice FitzThomas,
who succeeded to his lands in 1314 and fifteen years later became the first earl
of Desmond, is described as having precluded the establishment of orderly government in the region for a quarter of a century. Allied with the Irish he effectively united the Anglo-Irish lords against him, committing numerous treasonable offences and incurring a whole series of indictments, both before the
justiciar and before the sheriffs in the county courts. At long last he surrendered
to Roger Darcy the justiciar and was sent to England. Incredibly he later
returned, by then no longer "rebellious," to act as justiciar between 17 August
1355 and his death on 25 January 1356.[24] All the same, it has been claimed, in
a provocatively challenging remark, that Desmond was no more a violator of the
peace than Lancaster; the difference lay in the fact that insurrection in Ireland
appeared less dangerous – certainly less immediately so.[25]

In the Northeast the earldom of Ulster was handed down in the powerful de
Burgh family. Richard de Burgh received livery of his lands in 1280 and died in
1326, thus providing a constant for much of Edward II's reign. He followed an
expansionist policy in neighbouring Connacht, where Aedh O'Connor, who had
been made king by the justiciar, was briefly taken prisoner in 1293 by the Geraldine Thomas FitzThomas. Shortly thereafter the earl himself was captured by
the Fitzgeralds, and was only liberated by the council at the parliament of
Kilkenny in March 1295. These Anglo-Norman struggles were put to rest by a
Pax Normannica – the marriage alliances of the Desmond and Offaly Fitzgeralds with the daughters of Richard de Burgh.[26]

When in 1295 – the starting point chosen for this chapter – John Wogan was
appointed justiciar or chief governor, the prospect for the colony looked reasonably promising. Certainly the length of time he remained in office – until
August 1312, apart from an interval between 30 September 1308 and 16 May
1309 – provided a degree of continuity. Thereafter, for the rest of the reign of
Edward II and indeed beyond, with only one or two exceptions king's lieutenants, justiciars, or chief governors, as they were variously termed, held
office for brief periods of a year or so.[27] Even so, Wogan's justiciarship was
fraught with considerable unrest. He was pressed for money by the English
government. The situation was revolutionized in 1311, when the Ordainers
(clauses four and five of the Ordinances) declared that the customs were not to
be farmed by aliens but were to come directly to the exchequer: foreign merchants were to be arrested and forced to render their accounts. Orders were
issued in March 1312 for the arrest of Piero dei Frescobaldi, other members of
the society, and their goods. Justiciar Wogan and Treasurer Bicknor were
ordered to see that all such revenues in the colony passed to the Dublin exchequer. The effect on Irish revenues was slight, since collection was notoriously
difficult: the king soon reverted to the customary practice of demanding supplies and troops for the Scottish campaigns.[28] A particular threat to the land of

peace at this time was the presence of marauding bands of Irish erupting from the mountainous terrain of Leinster to the Southwest of Dublin, against whom Wogan had to wage a sustained campaign. He could not claim to have been a military leader, certainly not a successful one: in 1308 he suffered a heavy defeat at Glenmalure, which was followed by the burning of Dunlavin and other towns. Even the exchequer outside Dublin's town walls was felt to be insecure.[29]

PIERS GAVESTON IN IRELAND

There was a temporary improvement in the fortunes of the Dublin government with Gaveston's brief spell in Ireland. This began towards the end of June 1308 and lasted for almost exactly a year. It would seem that despite the ill repute in which he was held by many of the barons in England and his denigration by the chroniclers, his performance in Ireland was commendable; after all, as Baker concedes, he was adequately versed in military affairs.[30] Interestingly, this was a last minute decision by the king. The powerful Richard de Burgh, earl of Ulster, had been appointed governor on 15 June in general terms. The patent of Gaves-ton's appointment, dated the following day, gave him extensive quasi-regal authority. He was empowered to remove and appoint all officials – a power of which he made little use – and to exercise royal rights of ecclesiastical patronage. The earl of Ulster was ordered to render him every assistance and seemingly he did so with a good grace. Until the end of September, though, Wogan continued as justiciar.[31] Unlike their Irish counterparts the English chroniclers were purely negative, anxious to sustain the view of the favourite as being a lavish spendthrift; making no mention of the measures he took to deal with the parlous situation with which he was confronted. Clearly in one respect they were accurate: in contrast to the customary parsimony in Ireland, the king's lieutenant had money to spend.[32]

The Irish chroniclers were more impressed with Gaveston's achievements than with his richesse. The overdue promulgation of the statute of Winchester (1285) was probably designed to assist the Gaveston regime.[33] The newly arrived lieutenant, thanks to the availability of funds, made prests to a long list of Anglo-Norman barons, including one of a thousand pounds to Richard de Burgh, as well as to various Dublin sailors, no less than £3,242 1s. 2d. being expended on military preparations.[34] One problem that gave rise to a farcical dispute with the Dublin bailiffs and citizens was the royal grant of murage to Geoffrey de Morton, a Dublin merchant and sometime mayor. He seems to have been an unscrupulous character who received the grant ostensibly for the repair of the city walls and of Isolde's Tower adjacent to the bridge over the Liffey. The case was decided before the council – and against its wishes – in Morton's favour, in accordance with the requirement of Gaveston and the king. Some years later the dwelling that the incorrigible Morton had erected to the detriment of the defensive wall was ordered to be pulled down.[35] This strange incident apart, Gaveston was remarkably efficient. Having suppressed the O'Tooles of Wicklow, he rebuilt the royal fortress at Newcastle McKynegan, which guarded the road that led south through O'Byrne territory from Dublin to Wicklow. He also rebuilt Castlekevin to the Southwest of Newcastle – held by the archbishop of Dublin – and repaired the road that led westwards through a pass in the Wicklow mountains to Glendalough.[36] Even if much of this regaining of the initiative in the vicinity of Dublin was to prove temporary, it did something to reverse a downward trend in English affairs in the area. It has to be confessed that it is difficult to square the approval of Gaveston's behaviour in Ireland with his actions in England, to which he returned all too soon.

THE BRUCE INVASION 1315–18[37]

Various theories have been advanced about the reasons for the Bruces' involvement in Ireland at this juncture. As will be seen from what follows, Robert Bruce was no liberator of subject Celtic peoples, nor does the old suggestion hold water that he wished to remove an ambitious younger brother from under his feet.[38] More relevant is the strategic concept of a Scottish invasion of an Ireland from which had come so much of the support for English campaigns in Scotland. After Bruce's overwhelming victory at Stirling (Bannockburn) it became feasible to divert resources for the purpose. The Scots were no strangers to Ireland: Hebridean mercenaries, galloglasses (gallóglach), had been employed in the country since the end of the thirteenth century.[39] Pre-existing connections with Ulster nobles were numerous. Egidia, sister of Richard de Burgh, the earl of Ulster, the "Red earl," married James the Steward of Scotland, whose son, John, was to take part in the Bruce invasion, while in 1302 Robert Bruce had himself married as his second wife Elizabeth, one of Richard's daughters. Moreover, the earldom of Carrick, which Robert inherited from his mother, had long-standing claims to land in Antrim. The marriage to Elizabeth connected him to a wide range of Irish families, including the Geraldines of Desmond and Offaly as well as John de Bermingham. In 1306 after his defeat at Methven Bruce is believed to have sought refuge in the island of Rathlin off the Irish coast, by connivance of the Anglo-Norman Bissets – John Bisset was to accompany Edward Bruce in 1315. An undated letter addressed by Robert Bruce to the kings of Ireland, the Irish clergy, and the inhabitants of Ireland is a propagandist document pointing to the likelihood of an invasion It makes a bid for friendship, while holding out opportunity for the recovery of the Scottish nation's (*nostra nacio*) "ancient liberty."[40] Bruce is recorded to have landed in Ulster in May 1313 for the purpose of raising tribute, but to have been forced to retire by the Ulstermen.[41] There is even some suspicion, arising from rumours of his association with Bruce, that the earl connived at the landing.

Irish tradition insists that the Scots were invited by Domnall O'Neill, king of Tyrone (Tír Eoghain), who laid claim to the high-kingship of Ireland, a position he subsequently abdicated in favour of Edward Bruce. His policy, it has been suggested, was based on self-interest: to relieve the pressure on his own situation, threatened as he was both by rival Irishmen and by the earl of Ulster.[42] If such were the case, it was an extremely ill-considered move, since he unleashed far more than he bargained for, to the detriment not only of the Anglo-Irish but of the native Irish as well. It was no mere expansion of the established policy of inviting galloglasses to participate in internal conflicts. If the Scots hoped for a friendly Ireland in the wake of their landing, the manner of their operations, reminiscent of the harrowing of the North of England, was not calculated to endear them to anyone. Their behaviour in "enemy territory" might have passed for strategy,[43] but it seems to have been indiscriminate and savage, hardly conducive to mounting a coordinated "second front" against the English. Between them the warring "men of Alba" and the English "foreigners" are said to have reduced large portions of Ireland to desolation. This cannot be convincingly played down as no more than the usual devastation commonly encountered in the fourteenth century – and not only in Ireland.[44] Worse still, both as regards invaders and inhabitants, the campaign coincided with the famine years that also affected many parts of England, indeed of western Europe: an unfortunate time for the commissariat of the army; disastrous for the inhabitants of any territory through which it passed. Yet it has to be admitted that in the long run the whole affair effectively weakened the rule of the English in Ireland.[45] This was in Bruce's interest, and that of Scotland. Yet any idea of uniting the "Crowns" of Scotland and Ireland was almost certain to fail and in any case was unlikely to be welcomed by the Scottish nobles. The Irish were far from being united in support of the Scots: few Anglo-Irish, save those in Meath, changed their allegiance. In the unlikely event of a conquest of the whole island the Scottish kings would not have been able to hold on to it with their limited resources.[46] It could only have been an encumbrance, as it was to prove for the English. After all, Scotland itself was not fully united. Hindsight reveals that it placed in needless jeopardy the heir to the Scottish throne. David Bruce was not born until 1324.[47] The notion of a yet grander strategy, an Ireland to be used as a base for an expedition to Wales, is even harder to credit. Not, of course, that the Welsh were disinclined to take advantage of English difficulties elsewhere. After all, 1316 was the year of Llywelyn Bren's revolt and the Welsh castles were being put into a state of readiness.[48]

The "rash and arrogant" Edward Bruce landed,[49] probably at or near Larne, either on 25 May or, as the Annals of Ireland suggest, "not content with their own land," on the feast of St Augustine, the twenty-sixth, near Carrickfergus.[50] According to one account he brought with him six thousand seasoned troops in three hundred ships. This number may well have been exaggerated, but the force was substantial enough for the easy subjugation of Ulster. Apart from O'Neill various other native chiefs, though by no means all of them, hastened to join Bruce, anxious to escape from the grip of the earl. Some of the English, notably the Bissets and the Logans, did the same, as Edward II was informed by the unknown writer of a letter dated 18 October 1315.[51] Thomas de Mandeville and other "faithful men" were expelled from their lands.[52] Many of the English took refuge at Carrickfergus, while the earl of Ulster," a wanderer throughout Erinn," fled first to Connacht to rustle up his English and Irish allies and then south-westward to Roscommon, where he was joined by Felim O'Connor, who had been inaugurated king of Connacht in 1310, at what was said to have been "the most celebrated kingship marriage" to that time in Connacht.[53] Felim had been forced by the successes of his relative and rival for the kingship, Rori O'Connor, to abandon Connacht.[54] Bruce further secured his by-then impregnable position in Ulster with the capture of the town of Carrickfergus: the castle, which could be munitioned and its food stocks replenished from the sea, was invested in September 1315 but refused to surrender.[55] His rear secured, Bruce advanced southwards through the modern County Down, ravaging the settlers' lands. It was probably about 1 May that he was formally inaugurated as king of Ireland in the neighbourhood of Faughart. Greencastle was captured but subsequently recaptured by the "Dubliners," the custodian of the castle, Sir Robert de Coulrath, being taken back to Dublin for incarceration and trial. On 29 June with considerable brutality Bruce captured Dundalk, which he burnt.[56] He then proceeded by way of Louth to Ardee, where the Scots and their Irish allies are said to have set alight the Church of Our Lady in which men, women and children were seeking sanctuary.[57]

Meanwhile the justiciar, Edmund Butler, met the forces of the earl of Ulster and Felim on 22 July to the south of Ardee. It was decided, possibly at the earl's insistence, but with the consent of the justiciar and members of the council, that he should advance alone against Bruce, who was to be taken alive or dead.[58] De Burgh reached Coleraine and faced the Scottish forces across the River Bann, the bridge having been destroyed. Felim O'Connor was insidiously approached by Edward Bruce with the suggestion that he leave the earl to attend to his own position in Connacht. For a time he concurred with this plan. Rori O'Connor took advantage of the situation to secure his own agreement with Bruce at Coleraine and then had himself recognized as king of Connacht, where he wreaked havoc against those who opposed him.

The defection of Felim to defend his own interests forced the seriously weakened forces of the earl to retire to Connor, where a battle was fought on 10 September. This, the first major encounter with the Scots, brought defeat with heavy loss of life and the capture of the earl's cousin, William de Burgo, who was later taken to Scotland by the earl of Moray.[59] Ulster secured, Bruce left Carrickfergus and moved southwards to Meath. He passed by Dundalk and Nobber to Kells, which he burned. At Granard he ransacked the abbey, fired the new castle at Finnea, then moved on to Loughsewdy where he spent Christmas, subsequently putting the town to the torch. Passing through settler lands Bruce went as far as Castledermot, the most southerly point of his march. From there the

Scottish army turned northwards to Athy and Raban but not without some losses.[60] At Kells in the first week of December Bruce encountered Roger Mortimer, the lord of Trim, who is said to have had a large force, much of it untrustworthy.[61] Though this was easily defeated, the castle of Trim continued to hold out. Mortimer and a few followers escaped to Dublin; his tenants, the disgruntled de Lacys, joined the Scots who proceeded under their guidance through Tethmoy to Rathangan and Kildare,[62] where the castle was well defended and they were beaten off. These encounters constituted a heavy defeat for the settlers and presumably prompted the urgent repair of Dublin's defences.[63]

The English government, concerned at the outset with possible repercussions in Wales,[64] had become further alarmed at the deteriorating situation, including the questionable loyalty of the Irish magnates. A royal letter sent to the justiciar, Edmund Butler, the earl of Ulster, and twenty-eight Anglo-Irish magnates prompted a flurry of responses that provide details of the situation. The extant replies reveal a degree of collusion. In essence the magnates asserted their loyalty and pointed out the difficulties that beset them.[65] At the beginning of September 1315 the archbishops, prelates, and certain nobles met for a royal council at Lincoln. Prominent on the agenda was Scotland, but also the invasion of Ireland. It was decided to send John de Hothum as an envoy to Dublin.[66] Hothum, one of that band of Yorkshireman who served as royal clerks in Edward II's administration, was nephew of a former archbishop of Dublin, the Dominican William de Hothum.[67] He himself was to become bishop of Ely in 1316. Hothum was well qualified to assess the Irish situation: he had been a baron of the Irish exchequer since 1305, had acquired various benefices in the country, and although absent during Gaveston's lord-lieutenancy was responsible for paying his troops in Leinster. On 14 May 1309 he was appointed chancellor of the Irish exchequer, an office he retained until the end of January in the following year. He was to hold no further active appointment there. Like many other clerks he contrived to continue in employment in England after Gaveston's demise. In the autumn of 1314 he had paid a three-month visit to Ireland, charged with discovering the state of Irish finances and the possibility of financial support for the English government – apparently oblivious of any Scottish invasion plans.[68] Hothum was clearly the man for the threatened crisis. Urgency is suggested by the fact that he set out for the Welsh coast the very day of his appointment, 1 September 1315, though he was delayed at Chester by intelligence of a possible attack by the pirate Thomas Dun.[69] He had to organize an escort of armed vessels, thus delaying his arrival in Dublin until 5 November. Hothum's authority was wide-ranging, but there is no evidence that he reformed the Irish administration, changed its personnel, or managed to speed up the payment of debts to the Irish exchequer. In the circumstances this is hardly surprising; military problems were more immediate. What he did do was order the demolition of the tower of St Mary's del Dam so that the stone could be used to strengthen Dublin castle, there being a likelihood that the town would be attacked.[70]

The largely unhindered progress of Bruce as he changed direction for the North was threatened by a newly raised army on 26 January 1316 at Skerries, near Ardscull in County Kildare. This force included John and Maurice FitzThomas,[71] Thomas FitzJohn, John and Arnold Poer, Maurice de Rocheford, Miles and David de la Roche, all men who are said to have willingly answered the justiciar's summons. In the chronicler's view any one of them had forces enough to defeat Bruce, had not discord broken out, with the inevitable result that a realm divided against itself must fall. The Scots, though mauled, were left in possession of the field – effectively they were victorious.[72] Subsequently they withdrew to Leix, a place not vulnerable to mounted men-at-arms. The Anglo-Irish force kept them under observation from the vicinity of Castledermot while its leaders went to Dublin. Hothum's own account of the battle does not reveal any disagreement between the magnates, but he remarks that the terrain was difficult (*en dur champ*), perhaps unsuitable for heavily armed mounted men, and attributes the outcome to bad luck (*par mescheance*). Clearly he is masking the real state of affairs. On the credit side he alleged that the Scots suffered casualties among their best men and that only one man was lost on the English side.[73] Following this battle, on 4 February, at Hothum's request all the above magnates, with the addition of Richard de Clare who had recently arrived from Munster, came before him in Dublin and swore an oath to maintain the king's rights against all men "qui porront vivre ou morir," and without any dissimulation to attack the king's enemies. As security for their honouring this pledge they gave hostages.[74] Hothum in his turn seems to have sworn to the magnates that he would not leave Ireland until some successful action had been achieved, though it is difficult to comprehend how even a trusted envoy, liable to be recalled at any time, could take such an oath. In any case he had left Ireland by early May 1316, long before any favourable change in the military situation.[75] Nonetheless, this was clearly a *quid pro quo* to reassure the magnates that the English government would not leave them to their own devices.[76] That the magnates should have been pressed to take such an oath and to give hostages, argues that Hothum may have doubted their determination to combine to defeat the enemy. The oath makes it clear that not only did they make a pledge to the king, they also bound themselves to one another. However one interprets the Ardscull encounter – for instance as a defensive action to ensure Dublin's safety – it was a lost opportunity. After all, the Scots were impossibly remote from their Ulster base, while the Anglo-Irish had shorter lines of communication. There can be no doubt what interpretation the native Irish put on this engagement, they chose the opportunity to revolt. The O'Tooles, the O'Byrnes, the Haralds, and the Archibauds rose, devastating Wicklow and the whole countryside, territory so recently subdued by Gaveston.[77] In their own time but doubtless also constrained by famine in the countryside, the Scots withdrew to Ulster, leaving a frightened but doubtless relieved Dublin behind them.

For about a year after his successful exploratory *chevauchée*, Edward Bruce was engaged in his Ulster base. The castles of Northburgh and Greencastle fell to him, although they were subsequently recaptured; Carrickfergus was the last surviving stronghold. In April 1316 a convoy under the command of Sir Thomas Mandeville had reached the beleaguered castle. A sortie was made against the Scots in the course of which Mandeville was killed. In July another fleet of eight supply vessels left Drogheda, but it appears that the earl of Ulster used them as a means of securing the release of his relative, William de Burgo. The castle continued to be bravely defended, its garrison reduced to starvation level. Much of the credit for its eventual surrender in September 1316, subject to preservation of "life and limb," must go to the piratical Scot, Thomas Dun, who seems to have worked in close conjunction with Bruce.

Failure of the senile naval commander, John of Argyle, to harry the Scots both at the time of Edward Bruce's landing and subsequently, coupled with the loss of the Isle of Man, were major factors in the invaders' success. Only with John de Athy's appointment as admiral in June 1317 did the situation improve. At the beginning of the following month Athy attacked and killed Dun, "fortissimus latro," as well as forty of his companions. The pirate's head was despatched to Dublin.[78] Affairs on the ground in Ulster were likewise far from being entirely in Bruce's favour. Towards the end of October there is said to have been great slaughter of Scotsmen there by John Logan and Hugh Bisset, while on 5 December Logan captured John Steward and sent him to Dublin Castle.[79] Yet the Scots had not been defeated in a major engagement, so the prospect for a further campaign appeared rosy. Edward returned to Scotland to persuade his brother to join him in what he hoped would be a successful enterprise, even in the remoter regions of Leinster and Munster. Possibly the O'Briens of Thomond in the far west had suggested that if the Scots' army put in an appearance a general rising would ensue.[80] Robert Bruce was a practical man, so it is difficult to determine what, if anything, he hoped to gain on a permanent basis. It would have been quite out of character for Irishmen to unite in support of the Scots: the notion of independence, theoretically attractive, would not have sublimated the internal struggles endemic in Irish society. Nor, indeed, was there the slightest hope that despite the appeal to brotherhood, the rule of Edward Bruce would be welcome even in the short term. It had become apparent that the Irish would adopt one side or the other for their own advantage. Some of the English did likewise, but only a few of the more disgruntled – the Lacys in particular – wished to aid the Scots in the longer term. In consequence, the enterprise was a risky one from the start. Had "King Edward Bruce" been content with an appanage in Ulster, things might have been different. As for Robert Bruce, it was by no means his first interference in Irish affairs, nor was it to be his last.[81]

Robert Bruce was in Ireland by the end of January or early February 1317, together with a band of galloglasses. One factor in his calculations must have been the ease of access now that Carrickfergus could be freely used as a port of entry. The invading force traversed much-ravaged Meath, arriving at Slane with twenty thousand armed men, says a chronicler with wonted exaggeration.[82] There seems to have been near panic in Dublin. On 21 February the earl of Ulster was arrested in St Mary's Abbey, Dublin, and lodged in the castle. Later he was permitted to cross to England. He had all along been suspected of having relations with the Scots: it was now feared that he might betray the Dubliners. The Bruces arrived shortly afterwards and on hearing of the earl's fate diverted to Castleknock across the River Liffey,[83] where they ransomed the lord and his wife. To clear the ground for the defence of the walls the suburb of St Thomas was burned by the citizens. Unfortunately the fire, getting out of hand, destroyed St John's church and its chapel, as well as the exchequer building. The Scots, now that Dublin was forewarned, pitched their tents nearby at Salmon-Leap. Making no attempt to invest the city, ill prepared though it probably was, they moved south towards Leixlip and Naas, skirting the mountainous area to the east, and secretly guided by the de Lacys. Naas they plundered for two days in the usual fashion. No place however sacrosanct was spared; the looters are said even to have opened the tombs in search of treasure. In the second week of Lent the Scots reached Castledermot, where they destroyed the house of the Franciscans: the books, vestments, and other ornaments they carried off. Moving south across the river they reached Gowran. Then, passing Kilkenny without attacking it, they reached Callan about the feast of St Gregory (12 March).

The justiciar, together with Richard de Clare and other magnates, initiated moves to release the earl of Ulster. Although nothing came of it at that time an army of Ulstermen, said to have been two thousand strong, sought permission to display the king's standard. This was granted, although the army's operations are said to have caused even more damage than the Scots. About Palm Sunday news reached Dublin that the invaders had reached Kells in Ossory. The magnates gathered at Kilkenny to organize pursuit. Mortimer, created King's Lieutenant on 7 April, landed at Wexford to the Southeast, bringing with him a small force and a promise of the payment of his expenses by the English wardrobe. Arrangements were also made with Edward II's financial aide, Antonio de Pessagno, to provide Genoese mercenaries. The Ulstermen under the command of the earl of Kildare, Thomas FitzJohn (FitzGerald), were directed by the justiciar to hasten in pursuit, but they appear to have kept their distance. Bruce now moved northwestwards in the direction of the mouth of the Shannon. The Bruces had hoped to join with the native Irish of Thomond near Limerick; instead they were met not by the reputedly well disposed Donnchaid O'Brian but by the hostile forces of his opponent Murrough (Muirchertach) O'Brian. Arriving at Nenagh, they paused to devastate the Butler lands. Mortimer, meanwhile, appears to have sailed along the coast, since he is reported to have landed at Youghal on 7 April. From there, bearing his letters of appointment, he hastened to meet the justiciar – whom he ordered to await his arrival before taking action against the Scots. John of Patrickchurch's account of payments for the justiciar's troops shows that from February he had been raising men in Munster and in April took the opportunity of assaulting the Scots, while avoiding a major engagement.[84] In fact the Anglo-Irish army, despite its size, consistently failed to do more than harry the fast-disappearing Scots who, after reaching the Shannon at Castleconnell, turned northwards on their return journey to Ulster by way of Kildare and Trim. What precisely determined these tactics may never be known, although the policy of attrition was certainly defensible in view of the lack of food and of local support for the enemy. Apparently the invaders reached Trim about Easter (3 April), where they rested for a week or so, their army decimated by famine and fatigue. By the beginning of May they were back in Ulster and Robert Bruce shortly afterwards left the country. If he had planned to establish a kingdom for his brother it had proved a dismal failure. Mortimer went to Dublin and held a parliament at nearby Kilmainham, where those assembled are said to have done no more than to debate the case of the earl of Ulster, in whose cause envoys had earlier been sent to England.[85]

After much internecine fighting between the Irish in Connacht, Cathal O'Connor emerged as king. To maintain his position he sought the aid of William de Burgo and "all the foreigners."[86] Various lands were granted to him after discussion between Mortimer, Richard de Bermingham of Athenry, and others of the council. But, it has been remarked, though this settled the disturbances for the time being, it meant the "virtual abandonment of the royal county of Roscommon."[87] Mortimer was recalled to England shortly afterwards and so missed the dénouement of the Scottish invasion. Edward Bruce's activities in Ulster for the following year or so after his return from Limerick remain obscure. It was not until 14 October 1318, the feast of Pope St Calixtus, that war reopened between what the Dublin chronicler termed the Scots and the English of Ireland.[88] The precipitating factors are equally obscure. Was Bruce, emboldened by recent reinforcement from Scotland – indicated by the subsequent deaths on the field of battle of MacRhuardri and MacDomnaill, "kings" of the Hebrides and of Argyll respectively – intent on resuming his earlier plans? How was it that so strong a force, for the first time vigorously led, so confidently engaged the Scots between Dundalk and Faughart?[89] On the Scottish side the Lacys were present in strength.[90] The Anglo-Irish army included the archbishop of Armagh, the Dominican Roland Jorz, who absolved those about to engage in the conflict, as well as Milo de Verdon, and, as the chronicler Knighton tells us, Hugh de Turplington (Tryplynton), who was to die in 1330 at Nottingham in fending off Mortimer's attackers. It also included men from Drogheda, among them John Maupas or Malpas, who is recorded to have killed Edward Bruce and – hacked to pieces – to have himself fallen dead over the corpse. Almost all the Scots were said to have been killed (*omnes Scoti fere*). Few of the English in the

Scottish army escaped, among them the Lacys, Hugh and Walter, but only with difficulty. John de Bermingham led the victorious army with verve. He sent Bruce's head to Edward II, who rewarded him with the earldom of Louth, and as one source claims, his son Thomas with the barony of Ardee.[91]

Ireland by and large was now able to breathe a sigh of relief. The Loch Cé chronicler is uninhibited in his condemnation of the effect of the Scottish invasion.

Edward Bruce, the destoyer of all Erinn in general, both Foreigners and Gaeidhel, was slain by the Foreigners of Erinn, through the power of battle and bravery, at Dun-Delgan; and Mac Ruaidhri, king of Insi-Gall, and Mac Domhnaill, king of Airer-Gaeidhel, together with the men of Alba, were slain there along with him; and no better deed for the men of all Erinn was performed since the beginning of the world, since the Fomori-an race was expelled from Erinn, than this deed; for theft, and famine, and destruction of men occurred throughout Erinn during his time, for the space of three years and a half; and people used to eat one another, without doubt, throughout Erinn.[92]

THE AFTERMATH OF THE SCOTTISH INVASION

Opinions are divided as to the permanent effects of the Scottish depredations.[93] On the one hand it is possible to argue that there were fairly immediate signs of recovery. M. Maurice Jak, canon of Kildare Cathedral, is said to have built a stone bridge across the Liffey at Kilkullen and another at Leighlin (Leighlin-bridge) spanning the Barrow in Carlow, thus facilitating routes north-south and east-west respectively.[94] Even more ambitious was the attempt in 1320 under the auspices of Archbishop Bicknor to found a university at Dublin, with the consent of his chapters of Holy Trinity (Christ Church) and St Patrick, Dublin. The first chancellor was William de Rodyard, dean of St Patrick's, Dublin, who took the degree of doctor of Canon Law. It should be remembered, though, that it was Archbishop John Lech who in 1311 had petitioned Clement V for a *studium generale*, arguing that no such institution existed in Scotland, the Isle of Man, or Norway. England was the nearest recourse for Irishmen, but the dangers of the Irish Channel were notorious. A bull was duly issued in 1312. In Bicknor's time a body of statutes was drawn up, framed on the Oxford model but with some reservations in favour of the archbishop. The chronicler Clyn was sadly disappointed at the outcome; it proved to be a university in name only. This was subsequently said to have been due to lack of financial resources; doubtless an indication of inopportune timing.[95] Despite Edward III's attempts to protect Irish scholars it petered out, even in a minimal form, well before the Reformation,[96] That Ireland could produce substantial supplies of grain for the Scottish expedition of 1322 does point to some recovery in agriculture.[97]

On the other hand, there followed the inevitable unsettling enquiries as to those who had supported Bruce, a commission for that purpose being issued on

3 February 1320 to the earls of Kildare and Louth, to Arnold le Poer and John
Wogan. The statutes of that year give a dismal picture of a country devastated
by the armies of the magnates, at the mercy of corrupt officials, and of those
who enjoyed the protection of the great. Although these are common complaints
elsewhere, there is no reason to doubt their special validity in Ireland at this
time. In the parliament of 1324 is heard the familiar plaint of felons related to
great men, coupled with the remedy of trusting the latter with the apprehension
and punishment of their kin. The "great" could readily abuse their power and
terrorize the neighbourhood, or places further afield, with their armed retainers.[98] The most notorious example is provided by the first earl of Desmond,
Maurice FitzThomas, who has already been mentioned.[99] He developed an old
Irish custom of "cain," or later "coyne," akin to the repeatedly condemned prises exacted by English kings, among others. Another aspect was the exaction of
protection money, under the guise of *feoda*. Many took the line of least resistance and accepted him as their lord, a position he formally acknowledged by
letters patent. The system was extended far beyond FitzThomas's own territories; in fact his retainers became notorious throughout Ireland as "MacThomas's
rout." He derived support for his lawless plunderings from native Irish as well
as from Anglo-Irish families, Barrys, Cogans, and Roches, said to be "fideles
homines" of the king. These disturbances, which, as we shall see, extended well
into the next reign, were seemingly confined to the six counties of the South and
West of Ireland.

Events in England inevitably spilled over into Ireland. The Despensers had
re-established themselves after the battle of Boroughbridge and in the following
month, April 1322, demands were sent to Ireland for the usual preparations of
armed men at the expense of the Irish treasury. The earl of Ulster was required
to serve at his own cost. But all such preparations proved useless, the expedition
was abandoned.[100] During and after this time the personnel involved changed
radically. Mortimer, despite his defeat in Meath, had taken his part in repelling
the Scots, but on his surrender in 1322 following the unsuccessful rebellion in
the Marches of Wales, he was sent to the Tower, and the lands he held in Leix
and in Trim – by right of his wife – were taken into the king's hand. An eyre was
held at Drogheda in 1322 at which, since a suit of *De quo warranto* went undefended, the liberties of Trim were forfeited.[101] Inevitably a Despenser-versus-
Mortimer faction emerged on the Irish scene, of which more will be said below.

Another disintegrating factor was the widespread mortality among the Anglo-
Irish nobility. Richard de Clare was killed 10 May 1318, apparently by the
O'Briens and MacCarthys. His heir, Thomas, died three years later, leaving the
inheritance to be divided between his aunts, one of whom, Margaret, was the
widow of Bartholomew Badlesmere. Thereafter the English were able to exercise very little influence in this far-western lordship.[102] Edmund Butler, who
had been granted the earldom of Carrick in 1315, but who was never formally
created, died in 1321, Richard de Bermingham of Athenry in the following year,

William de Burgo and Aymer de Valence, the earl of Pembroke, in 1324, and in 1326 Richard de Burgh, earl of Ulster, who left as his heir a young grandson William, who succeeded him four years later.[103]

The fluid situation in the England of mid–1326 – anxious expectation of Queen Isabella's invasion – allegedly gave rise to Maurice FitzThomas's most ambitious scheme. For details one has mainly to rely on the enquiry conducted in 1332 at Clonmel by the Irish justiciar, Anthony de Lucy.[104] According to its findings, a plot had been hatched at Kilkenny on 7 July 1326.[105] The alleged participants were Thomas FitzJohn, earl of Kildare, John Bermingham, earl of Louth (both of whom had acted against the Scots and in the early 1320s had been justiciars),[106] Maurice FitzThomas, James Butler (created earls of Ormond and Desmond respectively in 1328 and 1329 during the Isabella-Mortimer regime),[107] Bishop Richard Ledred, Thomas Butler, William Bermingham, Thomas FitzGilbert, Maurice FitzPhilip, Robert de Caunton, and Brian O'Brien. The jury found that these men had sworn to support FitzThomas in the plan to make him king of Ireland; as their reward the others were to share the territories of the Crown. Slightly earlier a Limerick jury had declared that FitzThomas had indeed been anxious to acquire Ireland for himself, at which point he was arrested. Not only that, he had supposedly contemplated the murder of the justiciar, chancellor, treasurer, and other members of the king's council.[108] According to the Dublin annalist, as a consequence of Walter de Burgh's attack during 1330 on the lands of the earl of Desmond, as FitzThomas had recently become, both were placed in the custody of the marshal by the acting justiciar, Roger Outlaw.[109] When in June 1331 Anthony de Lucy, the new justiciar, summoned a parliament to Dublin many magnates, clearly including Maurice FitzThomas and his gang, did not attend. They did so at Kilkenny on 1 August when they submitted themselves to the king's grace, and so far as their evil deeds concerned the king they were remitted.[110]

Clearly there is a problem with respect to the "conspiracy." Was it a genuine plot, or could it have been a mere fabrication by political opponents? Alternatively, was it merely FitzThomas's fantasy, fed by his overblown ambition? It was not to be the last time that his alleged ambition to be king of Ireland surfaced.[111] It would be worthwhile to bear in mind the various fabrications that had dogged Orleton, indeed those that were to surround the person of Edward II himself. Was this another example of imputing political blame? Juries were not reliable in such cases as is exemplified by Thomas de Berkeley's acquittal and Bishop Orleton's conviction. Not infrequently they were subjected to pressures of which we can know little or nothing. Ireland was no exception. In that case a clue is provided by the fact that the juryman heading the list is John son of Robert le Poer, knight. In short, it would be wise to suspend judgment as to the veracity of the story until its context has been examined. What is clear is that there were Mortimer and Despenser factions in Ireland: factions that adopted an Irish complexion. Some of the conspirators were clearly Mortimer supporters, at any rate so far as can be judged from subsequent favours. Thus, according to Tout, FitzThomas, like many in England, had been caught up in the furore of accusation that followed Mortimer's escape from the Tower in 1323.[112] In the year previous to 1331 Mortimer had been condemned and declared largely responsible for Edward II's death, so it became possible to denigrate opponents by claiming that in 1326 they had acted against the king. FitzThomas was no longer alive to counter the charge, nor was John Bermingham who, as we have seen, had been massacred in 1329 with his two brothers, nine of his name, and many others: a horrible blood bath even by Ireland's standards.[113]

Numbered among the supposed conspirators we have noted that difficult character Bishop Richard Ledred, an English Franciscan friar. His terrier-like pursuit of iniquity plus aspects of his religiosity prompted G.O. Sayles to impute to him eccentricity, even mental disorder.[114] This elicited a vigorous defence by the editor of his poems, Edmund Colledge.[115] The bishop's determination, come what may, to suppress heresy, particularly in his bishopric of Ossory, need not detain us here, except to say that in the course of these concerns he was engaged in conflict with Arnold Poer, seneschal or steward of the liberty of Kilkenny, and then with a wealthy Kilkenny woman, Alice Kyteler. Poer, according to Colledge, was "a leader of the Despenser faction in Ireland." That may well have been the case; he was certainly in league with the Connacht and Ulster de Burghs and hostile to the Butlers, Geraldines, and Berminghams. It is recorded that the two sides were ordered to desist from molesting each other, but that in 1327 they were engaged in mutual hostilities on a large scale. Poer was worsted and sought to press his case in England.[116] This party strife would make sense of the composition of the conspiratorial body, many of whose number are known to have benefited, as we have seen, from the advent of the Isabella-Mortimer regime. Arnold Poer, thanks to Ledred had been imprisoned for a time; by 1329 he had died in confinement in Dublin Castle. There is even the possibility that the de Poer faction, in declining to obey the justiciar in 1327, was holding out – as were others in England – on behalf of the imprisoned Edward II.[117] With Edward III's majority the Poer clan and their supporters could attempt to get their own back without fear of reprisal. As for Ledred, he can be shown to have made an approach to the queen mother prior to the *coup d'état*.[118] Thereafter his appeals to the Curia and for royal support produced mixed reaction. In any case, due to the hostility of Alexander Bicknor, he was only able to reinstall himself in his diocese after that archbishop's death in 1349.[119] Bicknor, though, had become *persona non grata* to Edward II – the reason for his antagonism to the bishop of Ossory lay closer to home. It may be no more than coincidence that during the 1340s the refugee Ledred served as suffragan in the ageing Orleton's Winchester diocese. They had both suffered from a similar form of persecution.[120]

Another area of "English" Ireland that in the late 1320s suffered from disorder was Ulster. The death of Richard de Burgh, the earl, in the early summer of

1326 provided the occasion for the justiciar, John Darcy, to attempt to take the earldom into the king's hands during the minority of William, the heir. Bruce took advantage of the opportunity and the concomitant embarrassment of the English government to land at Larne. Rumour had it that he planned to invade England through Wales. Nothing came of this idea, since Bruce withdrew. Henry de Mandeville, the seneschal of Ulster, apparently bought him off by arranging a year's truce in return for supplies. In July a letter was sent to England by the Irish government with the alarming news that Bruce was preparing to conquer Ireland. Henry's part in the affair is obviously open to question – though such bribes had become a commonplace in Northern England – and his association with the earl of Desmond demonstrates his lawlessness and, worse still, his treason.[121]

Anglo-Irish conflict provided the opportunity for the Gaelic lords; much of Ireland dissolved into a state of anarchy. In 1328 the Leinster Irish chose Art MacMurrough's son, Donnell, as their king. MacMurrough was caught and imprisoned, only to escape two years later; the leader of the O'Toole clan was executed. Further south, in Kilkenny, the MacGilpatricks and the O'Brennans ransacked Athassel and Tipperary. In Carlow county, south of Leinster, the brother of James Butler, the newly elected earl of Ormond, was taken prisoner by the O'Nolans. Inevitably this brought reprisals on their lands at the hands of the earl. The O'Briens of Thomond committed mayhem under the protection of the earl of Desmond. Brian O'Brien in 1330 killed James de Beaufor, the sheriff of Limerick, but despite the efforts of the justiciar who raised a scutage for the "army of Athissel," this brought little more than the temporary arrest of the earl of Desmond as an abettor.[122]

As was to be expected, Mortimer's fall brought a reappraisal of the situation in Ireland and some radical changes. The Westminster Parliament of March 1331 was responsible for a series of ordinances for the regulation of Irish affairs and there was a resumption of grants made during Mortimer's hegemony. There was even a plan for Edward III to pay a visit to the country, though this did not materialize. Not surprisingly, such good intentions did not bring an immediate improvement in the state of affairs, although serious efforts were made to bring the earl of Desmond to heel.[123] The partition of the de Verdon lands, necessitated by the death in 1316 of Theobald leaving four daughters, was finally made in 1332. This was seriously to weaken the situation in Meath and Louth, since all the heirs were absentees.[124] But these events lie beyond our chronological limitations.

Lastly, it may be informative to note the changes of emphasis adopted by historians. In 1979 (and earlier) Jocelyn Otway-Ruthven referred to the period 1245–1315 as "the colony at its peak," while James Lydon in the *New History* of 1987 considers virtually the same period (1254–1315) as constituting "years of crisis." There seems to be little doubt about a measure of decline during the subsequent period. Commencing with the murder of the earl of Ulster, William de

Burgh, in 1333 and ending with the Black Death, the former writes of "the ebbing tide," while in the *New History* J.A. Watt is more cautious. For him the colony is "under strain" for the remainder of the century (1327–99).[125] From what has been said in this chapter, it is clear that Ireland had become a problem rather than an asset to the English government, largely for reasons beyond its control. Irish revenues were dwindling; from 1315 they were no longer a source of profit for the English Crown; in fact they had to be supplemented by finance from England.[126] Not only did the invasion of the Scots permanently weaken the colony, the squabbles of the Anglo-Irish lords served to strengthen the native Irish and to diminish the influence of the government in Dublin. The factional strife in England had its Irish counterpart. Edward III inherited a far more intractable situation than that left by his grandfather to Edward II, but in this instance the outcome was not principally the fault of Edward of Caernarfon.

11

Gascony and England's Relations with France, 1259–1330

> English policy changed from an attempt to work within the terms of the treaty of 1259 and within the legal limits of the feudal relationship to a conscious effort to achieve unchallenged sovereignty over Gascony by assuming the title, King of France, and by going to war.[1]

> Si la Gascogne a tenu dans la vie personnnelle d'Edouard II une place minuscule, les problèmes gascons se sont néanmoins posés sous son règne, en raison des faiblesses du roi, avec une acuité particulière et qu'ils ont finalement pesé très lourd sur l'histoire du règne tout entier.[2]

THE TREATY OF PARIS, 1259, AND ITS AFTERMATH

A natural starting point for a study of the recurring and complex question of Gascony and the English monarch's relationship with France is the Treaty of Paris between Henry III, much beset by problems with the barons at home, and Louis IX, who was anxious to embark on a crusade. It ended Henry's hopes that one day he could recover the Continental lands lost since the condemnation of his father, King John, in the court of Paris in 1202. Despite protestations of friendship for his fellow king and his reputation for impartial justice, St Louis was following the practice of Philip Augustus and Louis VIII in absorbing English fiefs for the Crown's benefit.[3] After many preliminary difficulties, including the reluctance of Henry's sister Eleanor, countess of Leicester, to renounce her rights, the treaty was concluded in October 1259. Thereby the English king abandoned his titles of duke of Normandy and count of Anjou and had to rest content with those of lord of Ireland and duke of Aquitaine.[4] Moreover, for the first time Henry *vis à vis* Gascony[5] entered the feudal relationship with the king of France by taking the oath of homage and fealty, that is to say, liege homage.

Louis thus established a feudal relationship with his vassal as duke of Aquitaine, a relationship that exacerbated by the numerous changes of French monarch in the initial decades of the fourteenth century, was to bring recurrent friction. It was felt both by the kings of France and those of England that the ceremony of personal homage was an abasement repugnant to a monarch.[6] There were other difficulties. As a peer of France the duke of Guienne was under obligation to perform service at court or in the feudal host. His presence was required for the anointing of a French king and he could be summoned to take his seat in the court of peers. A further problem was that raised by judicial process consequent upon the change of Gascony's status. The king of France possessed the right to hear appeals from sentences imposed by the officers in Guienne.[7] In short, the Treaty of Paris provided ample opportunity for future disagreements.

War between Edward I and Philip IV "le Bel" broke out in 1294, following Edward I's renunciation of homage on the grounds that the French king had not implemented the terms of the Treaty of Paris.[8] His homage of 1286 was held to be conditional, and having renounced it Edward made haste to secure Continental allies, while for his part Philip made overtures to the king of Scots. Pope Boniface VIII delivered his arbitration, to be sealed by the double marriage of Edward I to Margaret, sister of King Philip, and of Prince Edward to Isabella. Negotiations were hastened by Boniface VIII's action in excommunicating the French king and imposing an interdict (13 April 1303). By the time the war came to its official end in 1303 with the second Treaty of Paris, Gascony, apart from an area around Bayonne, was in the hands of the French.[9] The treaty was ratified by Edward on 10 July at Perth and by Philip on 23 August. King Edward had already married Margaret (Marguerite) in 1299 and the marriage of his son to the young Isabella (Isabelle) was to take place at an appropriate time.[10] From Edward's point of view a prominent disadvantage was that he had to sacrifice his newly cultivated Continental allies, a precedent that was remembered when Edward III adopted the same policy in the 1340s.

The 1303 treaty required a return to the situation of 1294 prior to the war, but the attempt to re-establish the authority of Edward's officers, "continuellement menacé dès avant 1294 par les officiers français des sénéchaussées," proved a slow process.[11] With minor exceptions lands occupied by the French were restored. It was arranged that Edward should perform homage, understood to be liege homage, at Amiens on 8 September 1303, unless prevented by illness or other significant impediment. In the event, Edward was involved with the Scottish war. Envoys from the French king found him at St Andrews where he declared himself unable to be at Amiens but, subject to certain conditions, willing to send his son instead, whom on 27 September 1304 he empowered to act on his behalf. To a further request for assistance against Flanders Edward offered a fleet of twenty ships, on the understanding that such assistance did not create a precedent of feudal obligation. He would, he said, expel the Flemish from England if the French acted reciprocally with respect to the Scots. The French failed to meet the English conditions and so the plan fell through.[12] Matters rested there until July 1305 when French envoys arrived at Canterbury with a further request that Edward do homage or send his son for the purpose. They were received coldly by Edward who refused to comply if other matters were to be raised at the projected meeting. All such, he declared, should be discussed beforehand between the English king and appropriately empowered ambassadors from France. He also pressed the question of the restoration of the castle of Mauléon in accordance with the treaty of 1303.

The situation took on a different aspect with the election of Pope Clement V on 5 June 1305. Anxious to secure peace in western Europe so that a crusading expedition could be launched, he sent two envoys, one of them William Testa, to persuade Edward to come to his coronation or to send his son. It would provide an excellent opportunity, thought Clement, to put the 1303 treaty into effect and to celebrate the marriage of Prince Edward and Isabella. Edward responded that neither he nor his son could come, but he promised to send a suitably prestigious embassy, choosing for the purpose Henry de Lacy, the earl of Lincoln, Hugh Despenser the elder, and among many others his expert legal negotiator Philip Martel, a royal clerk and professor of civil law. They arrived at Lyon in November to join Philip "le Bel," who remained there until early January of the following year. On 3 December the counts of Evreux, St. Pol, and Dreux were empowered in Isabella's name to contract a marriage "per verba de presenti" with Prince Edward.[13]

During the discussions between the French and English delegations Martel argued that his master was not under obligation to perform homage until all the provisions of the treaty had been implemented. Eventually it was agreed that the castle of Mauléon would be restored and within the ensuing three months homage performed. A committee of four was to assess the damages incurred by each side during the period of truce. Martel, the first keeper of the processes (*custos processuum*)[14] and Sir John de Bakewell had already been deputed to present the English case, and having taken an oath to the pope to perform their duties faithfully, they persuaded Clement to issue the bull *Ex parte tua* requiring Philip to depute his two commissaries by the end of February 1306.[15] Another bull of the same date, 13 February, appointed the prior of the Dominican house in Paris and the warden of the Franciscans there to receive the corresponding oaths of the French commissaries. Martel reached Philip and his councillors at La-Croix-Saint-Leufroy on 27 February, and the following day at Vernon he had an audience with the French chancellor who claimed that Martel had obtained the bull by fraud – a claim not infrequently made in the case of inconvenient bulls. The chancellor argued that the text made no reference to those matters of special concern to the French king. Before anything else the English king, by performing homage, should show his obedience so as to gain Philip's favour. Martel reverted to his earlier argument that first the treaty must be fully implemented. On receipt of the lands to which he was entitled by the treaty, King Edward would perform his obligations. Even if the treaty of 1303 did not allow Edward to refuse homage for the reasons advanced, that of 1259, by which the kings of France had acquired the right to exact homage, was a bilateral agreement. In any event, Philip had no right to demand feudal services. The 1259 treaty implied an enquiry to determine what were appropriate services. Thanks to French subterfuges no such inquest had taken place. Were there to be a request for military aid, urged Martel, his master would insist that any such was granted "of grace," without prejudice.

In May and June 1306 the negotiations continued at Montreuil-sur-Mer in the Pas-de-Calais. The "process" that ensued was designed to provide a means of judicial examination and decision with respect to claims for losses incurred by breaking the truce. In the main such losses were incurred by merchants, but there were also some general claims made by the English, the first for damage inflicted by the Scots as allies of the French, the second – based on England's "acknowledged" sovereignty of the sea – was aimed at what were considered to be piratical acts of the French admiral, Reyner Grimaud.[16] By mid-June the process had ground to a halt but with an agreement to resume it on 15 October. However, when Bakewell attempted to meet his counterparts in Paris for that purpose – Martel having died on 21 September at Bordeaux – no one could be found to continue the negotiations. Frustrated, he returned to England. The process was to linger on in name well into the 1330s, but for all practical purposes it had become a dead letter, though revived from time to time as an element in diplomatic negotiation.[17]

THE INHERITANCE OF EDWARD II
AND HIS EFFORTS AT COMPROMISE

It might be thought that since he had married Isabella, the only daughter of Philip IV, and his stepmother, Margaret, was also a member of the French royal family, Edward would have had less problems with France than his father. This proved not to be the case. First of all, he faced the prospect of no fewer than five successive kings: his father-in-law Philip "le Bel" (1285–1314), his brothers-in-law Louis X "Le Hutin" (1314–16), Philip V "Le Long" (1316–22), and Charles IV (1322–28), together with Isabella's nephew, John (Jean) I (1316) – the posthumous son of Louis X, who reigned for only five days. Each successive king, John excepted, required the performance of homage. A further complications arose from the claim through Isabella, following John's demise, to a portion of the kingdom of France, while the problem of Edward's deteriorating relationship with the queen, complicated by his affection for Gaveston and his close relationship with the younger Despenser, precipitated Isabella's withdrawal to France in company with the English exiles. With hindsight one might indeed claim that "All the scenery was in place for the Hundred Years' War; only the curtain needed to be rung up."[18]

The first contretemps reportedly arose at the time of the coronation when the queen's uncles, the counts of Valois and Evreux, irritated by Edward's conduct towards Gaveston, departed in high dudgeon because of the excessive attention paid to the favourite.[19] It was, of course, Gaveston and then Despenser who became thorns in the side of the young queen and who effectively diminished her influence over her husband. More immediately significant, perhaps, was the relationship of Gascony to the French Crown – a recurring source of friction on account of alleged usurpations and of damage incurred by merchants. In an attempt to provide a *modus vivendi* Clement V, about the time of Edward I's death, had been urging the king to send his son to Poitiers without delay. The question of fealty was raised early in the succeeding reign when envoys were sent to arrange a meeting between the kings. Although Philip proposed 8 or 15 July 1309 with Pontoise as the venue, Edward II responded that the notice was too short.[20] In 1310 he proposed that plenipotentiaries should deal with the underlying problems. On 2 August from Northampton the English commissioners were appointed: John Salmon, bishop of Norwich, Jean de Bretagne, earl of Richmond, Guy Ferre, and William Inge, or any two of them. They arrived in France in November, but on the twenty-second of that month Edward informed them that affairs of Scotland and the remoteness of his council meant that he could not give attention to this business but promised to send instructions after Christmas. Further writs were sent in December and on 1 January 1311 Treasurer Sandale was instructed to send additional letters to Gascony by some reliable messenger, to be followed on 6 February by others for the settlement of disputes at Abbeville, in Ponthieu.[21] A source of particular irritation was the escalation of appeals to the Parlement of Paris. In January 1311 the French proctor was arguing that Philip IV exercised sovereignty (*superioritas*) and resort (*resortum*) within the duchy of Guienne. Such a quantity of appeals, real or frivolous, threatened to absorb much of the ducal revenue. Despite ordinances designed to uphold the court of Gascony as one of both first instance and appeal, the number of appeals to Paris became higher than ever, so much so that the situation was soon regarded as desperate.[22]

The Process of Périgueux did not get under way until 27 April. The English submission comprised twenty articles derived from the previous treaties between 1259 and 1303. The principal one was that the English should receive possession of all rights and jurisdiction within the cities and dioceses of Limoges, Cahors, and Périgueux. Others included those demesnial and feudal rights in Saintonge formerly pertaining to the count of Ponthieu but that King Philip had appropriated on the count's death, a part of the Agenais that should have been returned to Guienne, as well as substantial sums of money.[23] Additionally there were complaints about the actions of the seneschal of Périgord and Quercy, who had allegedly encouraged appeals to the French court, protected appellants – who then took the opportunity to commit crimes – and devised pretexts to banish men of Guienne. The French nursed their own extensive grievances

and claims, details of which were sent by the envoys to England for consideration by the king's council. Among them were demands for damages of 926,000
livres turnois estimated to have been incurred in the last Gascon war, compensation for losses allegedly inflicted on the abbey of La Réole, and 100,000 livres
for the property of Jews in the Agenais taken by the English king. Philip also
claimed rights in the church of Bordeaux and other abbeys and churches, in
addition to islands adjacent to Normandy and various parts of the French coast,
together with a group of bastides, or fortified towns, in the Agenais.[24] Differences of this order were irreconcilable in the long term; in the short term there
was scant common ground. The conference ended on 2 June 1311 when the
English participants withdrew. In the French view the king of France was sovereign, the English king his vassal, so that every wrongdoing in Gascony was
subject to the jurisdiction of the French overlord.[25]

The early summer of 1311 saw the despatch to France of three *nuncii*: Bishop Thomas de Cobham, Sir Gilbert Peche, who was to become seneschal of
Gascony, and a lawyer, Adam de Orleton or "de Hereford," a man rapidly coming to the fore as a diplomatic envoy. Orleton subsequently directed his efforts
to preparations for the Council of Vienne where Edward was determined to
make his voice heard at a time when Pope Clement, for purposes of his own,
was bent on securing an accommodation between the English and French kings.
The responses of the French king are dated 13 August from St Ouen near St
Denis, Paris.[26] At the end of September Cobham was associated with Gilbert de
Middleton and John de Cromwell, knight, in commissions to resume the
processes of Montreuil and Périgueux.[27] Early in February of the following year
Cobham was associated with Bishop Stapeldon and the earl of Pembroke as
proctors at Paris with full powers to determine business affecting Gascony and
even to revoke any actions taken by the seneschal, Etienne Ferol, that were considered detrimental to Edward's interests. They were assisted by Masters Henry
of Canterbury, Richard de Burton, and William de Weston a doctor of civil
law,[28] experts in diplomatic and particularly Gascon affairs. A crucial problem
was the successful appeal of Amanieu d'Albret to Philip IV's court against the
overzealous former seneschal of Gascony, John Ferrers, who on the pretext that
d'Albret had usurped royal rights of pannage at Nérac had devastated his lands.
Edward was condemned to pay 20,000 *livres turnois* as compensation.[29]

At home Edward had cause to be grateful to the pope and King Philip. To the
latter he was indebted for the services as mediator of his brother, the count of
Evreux. Moreover, four of Philip's clerks contributed to the settlement of 20
December 1312, two of whom tabled arguments against the validity of the Ordinances. It is unlikely that the French king himself, although favouring compromise, would have had much sympathy with the attempted enforcement of baronial restrictions.[30] The time was propitious for a *rapprochement*. The earl of
Pembroke, Walter Stapeldon, and Thomas de Cobham were appointed on 4 February 1313 to deal with Gascon affairs, while discussions about a meeting of the

two monarchs were entrusted to the earl and to Stapeldon. The envoys set out on 10 February 1313. Pembroke had to hurry back well before the end of March, but not before an agreement had been made for a meeting with Philip at Amiens for 20 May. Stapeldon did not return until the first week of that month.[31] By that time Edward, despite the problems with which he was faced at home, not least the threat to York from the Scots, decided – without consulting parliament as required by the Ordinances and in the face of baronial disapproval[32] – that he would go to France with his queen, with whom he was arguably on better terms now that Gaveston was no longer present to monopolize her husband's attention, and that she had borne him a son, the heir to the throne.[33]

On 23 May 1313 king and queen crossed the Channel from Dover to Wissant. Travelling by way of Amiens they arrived at Paris on the sixteenth.[34] At Whitsun (3 June) they attended the ceremonies surrounding the assumption of knighthood by Philip's eldest son, Louis, the king of Navarre (1305–16), and by his other two sons, Philip and Charles.[35] Thereafter the principal business was the assumption of the Cross by both kings at Nôtre Dame on 6 June in the presence of Nicholas, cardinal of St Eusebius – together with the customary crusading vows.[36] Isabella in her turn promised to accompany her husband. Magnificent banquets set the scene for the resolution of outstanding problems in Gascony. Negotiations concluded on 2 July. Philip graciously remitted the penalties incurred by Edward's Gascon subjects and reiterated his letters of 1286 regulating appeals to the Parlement of Paris by inhabitants of the duchy. D'Albret was compensated by Edward for his losses as assessed by the French court.[37] In these and in some other ways, such as assisting with Scottish affairs, ordering Montreuil to take the oath of loyalty to the English king, and pardoning alleged offences by English officers, the French king sought to appease his vassal.[38] While in France Edward, through his financial agent, Antonio de Pessagno, borrowed a sum of £15,000,[39] but expensive though it was, the visit brought a marked improvement in the relationship between the two sovereigns, due in no small part to the cooperation of Isabella and her enhanced position. A manuscript presented to Philip IV about this time contains six miniatures in commemoration of Edward's coming, in one of which the two kings are depicted sitting together.[40] In short, the English could be credited with a diplomatic success, though a short-lived one.

Edward disembarked at Dover on 15 July but reached parliament at Westminster only in time to prorogue it to September.[41] The success of the personal approach persuaded him to repeat the experiment by making a secret journey to the Continent. He is described as being "in peregrinatione" – on pilgrimage – between 12 and 20 December 1313.[42] After sailing from Dover to Boulogne, he spent some time at Montreuil-sur-Mer.[43] The purpose of this visit is obscure. Perhaps it was once again the affairs of Gascony, alternatively something to do with Philip's summons to the host being sent into Flanders, or then again it could have concerned the projected visit of the Queen to plead the English case concerning Aquitaine in the parlement, or even the possibility that Philip could be persuaded to help with Scotland. Immediately on his return Edward issued writs for an army to assemble at Berwick the following June.[44] The cases likely to be raised in the Parlement of Paris were giving anxiety. Early in February a letter to Amaury de Craon, the seneschal of Gascony, urged him to resist the injuries inflicted by "Gallici" on citizens of Bayonne. Late in that month Edward was urging Philip to reconsider the case of Bernard Peleti, doctor of canon and civil law and a member of Edward's Gascon council. He wrote again to the seneschal of Gascony to say that he was sending M. Elias de Jonestone, a lawyer with long experience in Gascon affairs and keeper of the processes (*custos processuum*), who was to accompany Gilbert de Clare, Henry de Beaumont, and William Inge for discussion with King Philip.[45]

Queen Isabella seems to have delayed her return to the Continent by attending the enthronement at Canterbury of Walter Reynolds, one of Edward's longest-serving clerks. This took place on Sunday 17 February and, as one chronicler with strong Canterbury connections tells us, in the presence of the earls of Gloucester and Pembroke, and of the lord of Chilham (Bartholomew Badlesmere). Isabella then left for France ostensibly to perform a pilgrimage to St Mary's, Vézelay (Verdeley),[46] but she also carried petitions concerning Gascony, details of which have survived. Accompanied by the earls of Gloucester and Richmond and the Ladies Vescy, Warenne, and Despenser, she set sail from Dover with a small flotilla organized by Antonio de Pessagno. She journeyed by way of Boulogne, Amiens, and Chartres.[47] While at the French court the adulterous affairs of the three daughters-in-law of Philip with certain knights produced a scandal. Sir Thomas Gray, author of the *Scalacronica*, states that rumour pointed to Isabella as the informant. In this he is supported by a Rouen chronicle and by the circumstantial account in a Flemish source that describes how the silk purses she had given to her sisters-in-law were subsequently displayed by their enamoured knights.[48] The Gervase continuator says that Philip had the knights flayed and wickedly (*turpiter*) put to death, but that Margaret, queen of Navarre – daughter of the count of Burgundy – and the other ladies in the royal household were imprisoned. Murimuth adds that Queen Margaret was suffocated and that in the same year Louis married as his second wife Clémence, daughter of the king of Hungary.[49] The incident constitutes an ironic precedent for Isabella's own behaviour with Mortimer. Conceivably her future adultery would make a return to England as the king's consort risky, even untenable. Perhaps, too, it would have the effect of making rumours of movements for divorce more credible.[50]

NEGOTIATIONS WITH LOUIS X (1314–16)

Philip "le Bel" died on 29 November 1314, or, as the Pauline annalist thought, on the next day, the feast of St Andrew. At the behest of Edward and his queen requiem masses were said in all the churches of the city of London on the Sunday after St. Thomas the Apostle (i.e., 22 December).[51] He was succeeded by his eldest son, Louis X. In mid-May, prior to Louis's coronation in August of 1315, it was decided that the earl of Pemboke and Bishop Stapeldon should travel to the French court with further petitions concerning Gascony, also possibly to seek confirmation of agreements about that fief reached in 1313.[52] The envoys, who were joined by Antonio de Pessagno and Henry of Canterbury, received an audience before the French king and his council at Vincennes where they heard the response to the English petitions pronounced by the bishop of St Malo. By January 1316, when the Lincoln Parliament was in session, Edward II had received two citations to renew his homage. The assembly discussed various exceptions that could be made. Three had previously been advanced: insistence on the restitution of all territories promised in 1303, full implementation of clauses of the 1259 treaty, and the expulsion of Scots from France. Two additional exceptions were suggested: one, the implementation of a clause in the arbitration (1298) of Boniface VIII whereby Edward I would hold his lands on the Continent under the same conditions of homage and fealty as Henry III; the other invoked the ordinance of Louis X (1315), in which the king promised that he would not acquire any new right with respect to the fiefs of his vassals. These questions were delegated to a commission of experts, among whom was the dean of York, Robert de Pickering, DCL, a man renowned for his wisdom as a Civilian on both sides of the Channel.[53] The commission came out in favour of the performance of homage and on 15 May 1316, the earl of Richmond and Walter Stapeldon were sent to France with the intention of fixing a date for the ceremony. When they arrived at Vincennes they found Louis ill with a fever that brought his death on 5 June. They concerned themselves with other matters, a case of piracy and a dispute between Edward's officials and the citizens of Abbeville, and were back in England at the beginning of July.[54] Thus, the by-now customary reluctance to perform homage was assisted by the unexpected change of circumstances. On the envoys' return there must have been consultation with Elias Jonestone, keeper of the processes relating to Aquitaine. He was retained for 146 days, twenty-two of which were spent during August in France to seek restitution at the council's direction for the plundering of a dromond from Genoa.[55]

Louis died leaving only a daughter of four years from his first marriage. His widow Clémence was *enceinte*. Should she bear a son, the matter would be readily resolved – he would be king. But were she to give birth to a daughter a council of nobles determined that the regent, Philip, would become king, he being the next collateral heir. In the event Clémence bore a son, John (Jean), who, as mentioned earlier, lived and reigned for a mere few days. At this point, strictly speaking, an arrangement of 17 July 1316 should have come into effect whereby the count of la Marche, Philip's younger brother Charles, would have been permitted a share of the kingdom. Once he was apprised of this news Edward summoned a council to Clarendon for February 1317 to discuss the concomitant claim that he might make through his wife Isabella. To this council came M. Richard de Burton, who in early December had arrived back from a mission to the Curia, where possibly the matter was raised. These unrealistic schemes for partition came to nothing, but the disgruntled Charles departed ostentatiously from Rheims on the morning of the coronation.[56]

HOMAGE DEMANDED ANEW BY PHILIP V (1316–22)

On 25 November 1316 the new king, Philip V "le Long," summoned Edward to his coronation at Rheims scheduled for 9 January 1317. As was by now predictable, excuses were made about difficulties at home.[57] Two of Philip's clerks were sent with his demand to Gilbert Peche, seneschal of Gascony, whom they found at La Réole. He replied that the duke was not in his duchy but that he would deliver the mandate. It was not until 16 February 1318 that John Abel, knight, and M. Richard Burton were instructed to present Edward's excuses for failure to do homage.[58] On 15 April they received Philip's letters patent declaring the receipt of the excuses, permitting Edward to appoint proctors to undertake fealty on his behalf, on the understanding that they brought with them letters acknowledging that a postponement of homage had been conceded.[59] Burton continued his diplomatic efforts, for which he claimed expenses between 8 March and 9 May. Some weeks later, on 16 June 1318, Abel and Burton were joined by the new bishop of Hereford, Adam Orleton, in a commission for taking the oath of fealty. They received letters of protection until 1 August.[60] Abel accounted for the period from 18 June, when he left London, until 20 July, when he returned there, while Burton's account ran until 15 August when he arrived at Nottingham,[61] but he spent only twenty-seven of those fifty-nine days abroad.[62] Orleton's movements are not known, but he was at Rue, near Abbeville, on 29 July, apparently on his way back to England, where he appended his seal to the Treaty of Leake.[63] These journeys were to no purpose. Philip refused to accept the proffered oath of fealty on the grounds that the proctors had neglected to bring letters admitting that it was a postponement of homage. This might seem a small point but not to the French king, who was anxious to maintain this right to grant a deferral in appropriate circumstances. The envoys were requested to return with the requisite documents by 8 September. In his turn Edward responded on 12 August that in view of the unusual nature of the demand he would have to put the matter before parliament, which in the event met at York on 20 October.[64]

By this time the homage issue was complicated by problems about Ponthieu and the continued encroachments of the king of France's officials in Gascony. Orleton, Abel, and Burton were instructed at the end of August to air these concerns, although little or nothing is known of their activities.[65] On 17 December Edward issued letters of credence and empowered John de Botetourt, Abel, and Burton to agree with Philip the date of a meeting so that Edward could perform homage. Two French envoys arrived in March 1319 empowered to accept a further postponement of homage until mid-Lent 1320.[66] Edward once again used parliament as an excuse for procrastination. He would give Philip a definitive reply after the assembly scheduled to meet at York on 6 May.[67] It was there, on 24 May, that a new embassy was empowered to perform homage. Various alternative letters were carried, to be used as circumstances dictated. In addition, the envoys were to schedule the long-promised interview.[68] The proctors were Orleton, Stapeldon, Baldock, and Burton. The first of these, Orleton, was already abroad on other business. He had been at Dover on 28 February 1319 and is next encountered at the beginning of May at Avignon. He was still there when the commission for homage was issued. What precisely occurred at the French court is not revealed, although the mission of Stapeldon and Baldock lasted from 4 July until 7 August, that of Burton from 2 July until 9 August.[69] It is suggested that the question of Flanders could have been on the agenda,[70] but homage was once again postponed.[71]

Negotiations were fast becoming farcical, but worse was to come.[72] At long last on 12 January 1320 Philip agreed to accept the proposal, put forward by Abel and Burton and earlier advanced by French envoys, that the meeting should be on mid-Lent Sunday, 9 March. On 19 February Edward replied that he would be at Dover the Wednesday before, 5 March, which would enable him to reach Amiens by the twelfth. Envoys were despatched to make the preparations at Wissant for the king's arrival and to secure safe conducts, but by 2 March the latter were still awaited.[73] The fifth saw the king at Canterbury, and, although he lingered for many days at nearby Sturry, he was back at his palace of Eltham well before the end of the month. A fresh embassy was mounted on 15 March, consisting of Bishop Orleton, the elder Hugh Despenser, and Bartholomew Badlesmere. Their instructions were to determine a revised date and to obtain safe conducts. With the addition of Edmund of Woodstock, the king's half brother, they were also given letters of credence to the pope, the Bardi advancing money for expenses at the Curia. Henry of Canterbury also carried with him material relating to Aquitaine, an indication that there remained some differences to be cleared up with the French king.[74] It is probable that a date was fixed for April but once again it had to be postponed, since on the twenty-eighth Robert de Kendale and M. Andrew Brugg were despatched to negotiate an alternative time. Finally, the Nativity of St John the Baptist (24 June) was determined upon, and on 11 June a safe conduct was reissued. Edward and his queen were at Dover on 17 June and embarked two days later. They reached Amiens on the twenty-seventh where, on the last day of the month, Edward performed homage as duke of Aquitaine and count of Ponthieu.[75] The form of the oath was the same as that adopted in 1286 by Edward I. It was prefaced by a statement deploring the failure of the French king to perform his treaty obligations but conceding that by reason of his alliance with Philip Edward was prepared to perform the oath in the same form as he had done in 1308. Conscious of the extensive preliminary discussion as to the oath's precise form, the scribe of the Winchester Cartulary meticulously recorded the texts of the five acts of homage from that of Henry III in 1259 to that of Edward II in 1320.[76]

The question of fealty remained. Thanks to the earlier confusion when fealty by proxy had been declined on technical grounds, it had still not been performed. Philip V now demanded it. Edward refused, declaring that he had not sworn fealty in 1308 at Boulogne. In any case, it was urged, Philip had made no earlier complaint on this matter. Thwarted in this demand, the French king insisted instead that the "perpetual alliance" of 1303 be renewed. Edward concurred and sent the elder Despenser as proxy to take the oath. Even then concern was expressed by the English negotiators at the contents of the letters drawn up in the French chancery.[77] Despite a degree of mutual dissatisfaction, homage had at last been performed and the royal party sailed back to England on 22 July.[78] All this was to little purpose: Philip died early in 1322, on 3 January.

Homage had by no means been the sole problem. In February 1321 Bishop Orleton was associated with the seneschal of Gascony, Amaury de Craon, and his colleague on earlier occasions, M. Richard Burton, in a commission to the French court. Orleton was engaged on this diplomatic errand for two months – from 21 February until 24 April. One of the matters requiring solution was the petition of Guy de Rochefort for settlement of a long-standing dispute with Geoffroi, lord of Montagne-sur-Dordogne, about land for which fealty was owed to Edward as duke. Another concerned a dispute involving the castle of Blanquefort in the Gironde. On their return, anxious to report on the outcome of their mission, the envoys found that disturbances had broken out in the West and those closest to the king – Pembroke, the younger Despenser and Baldock – were all absent from London. Nothing could be done for the time being.[79]

THE FINAL PHASE OF EDWARD II'S NEGOTIATIONS (1322–26): THE POLITICS OF DISASTER

The question of homage arose yet again with the coronation of Charles IV on 21 February 1322. He was to survive for the rest of Edward's reign. His first approach came in September 1323, following the conclusion of Edward's truce with the Scots. He despatched two envoys to Edward, then at Pickering in Yorkshire.[80] They carried letters couched in extremely amiable terms, with no mention of homage *eo nomine*. Without prejudice to himself or his successors, Edward was invited to come to Amiens at his convenience, either about Candlemas (2 February) or Easter of the following year, to assume his fiefs as had been done in the past. Edward responded in similarly amiable vein, rejoicing to hear of Charles's good health, promising to convoke his council as soon as possible, and thereafter to send his messengers with a response. Simultaneously he strove to disabuse the French king of the notion that all was quiet in the English realm by urging several reasons why he could not leave it safely at that time. It was beset by manifest troubles: disturbances in Lancashire, problems in Ireland, on the northern border – despite the truce – and various confederations in Wales. He concluded with a request that the French king restrain his officers from "novelties" in the duchy of Guienne, specifically with respect to the island of Oléron, the new bastide of Saint-Sardos in the Agenais, that of Créon in the Gironde, and the action against Arnaud de Caillou.

No sooner had the messengers, Robert of Wells, knight, and Masters Richard of Gloucester and John Shoredich, left for France[81] than Edward learned of the "riot" at Saint-Sardos, on the site of a projected *bastide*, during which a French official was hanged.[82] Raymond Bernard of Montpezat was behind the affair but Ralph Basset, the seneschal of Gascony, was felt by French officials to be implicated on account of his recent association with Raymond.[83] The seneschal of Périgord courteously summoned Basset to appear before him at Bergerac at the beginning of December, but on his making the excuse that business of the duchy prevented him from complying a peremptory summons was issued. Further failure to comply led to the arrest of Edward's proctor at the parlement. Charles himself was proceeding to the South via Tours – in itself a source of some anxiety for the Gascons – and on 1 January 1324 he summoned Basset, Bernard de Montpezat, and other English officials to appear before him on the twenty-third. Neither Basset nor Montpezat put in an appearance, the seneschal claiming that as the duke of Guienne was a peer of France, trial could only take place in the Great Chamber before the Parlement of Paris. A further summons, on 9 February, was disregarded and judgment was given against the defaulters. They were sentenced to banishment and the confiscation of their possessions.[84] The situation had arisen because of the disputed status of Saint-Sardos. According to the abbot of Sarlat his dependencies were *privilegati*, incapable of being detached from the French Crown. But the Saint-Sardos house, being in the Agenais, had supposedly passed into the jurisdiction of the duke of Guienne. The abbot, though, had entered into an arrangement (*paragium*) with the French king on condition that he build a *bastide* at Saint-Sardos on land forming part of the abbey's temporalities. Despite the objections of the lord of Montpezat and the duke of Guienne – to whom petitions had been directed urging the damage certain to be incurred were such a privileged *bastide* to be built – in December 1324 an *arrêt* of the Parlement of Paris declared it lawful.[85]

The request for postponement of homage was thus rendered particularly inopportune, but neither it nor the Saint-Sardos incident precipitated an immediate rupture with the French king.[86] Edward ordered his seneschal of Gascony and the constable of Bordeaux, Adam Lymbergh, to hold an enquiry and on 30 March 1324 Edmund, earl of Kent, and Alexander Bicknor, the archbishop of Dublin, received a similar commission.[87] Meanwhile on 29 December 1323 Charles wrote from Limoges in reply to the messages carried by Edward's envoys. On account of the war with Scotland he had not pressed the king to perform homage, but now he felt that the impediments advanced were not so great as to prevent his doing so. Further delay would be unwelcome both to himself and to Edward. He suggested that homage be performed within the octave of the Nativity of St John (i.e., 1 July 1324). As for the affair of Saint-Sardos, he accepted that it had not been by the wish or command of Edward, indeed he believed that the English king had at no time wished to act to his prejudice. With respect to the process against Arnaud de Caillou, neither he nor his council could consent to abandon it until the two monarchs met – as had been suggested by the envoys – but out of love for Edward he agreed to reverse the banishment, provided Caillou accepted the judgment of his court. He trusted that no persons banished from his realm would be received in that of Edward, and in his turn, as requested by the envoys, he would renew the order to expel all those banished from the realm of England.[88] In this connection the English envoys had specifically mentioned Roger Mortimer, who had escaped to France early in August 1323. It is an indication of the bad faith of King Charles that hostile English exiles were permitted to live openly in Paris and elsewhere until they migrated to Hainault.[89] As early as November Mortimer was rumoured to have sent agents to murder the king and the Despensers.[90]

A high-level embassy was organized in the spring of 1324, designed to bring to the fore the many difficulties that threatened to disrupt the peace with France. This comprised Archbishop Bicknor, Edmund earl of Kent, Richard de Grey, and M. William de Weston. Letters of safe conduct were issued by Charles at Mehun-sur-Yèvre on 25 March. As we shall see, the archbishop was not to return to make his report until January of 1325. Already, however, the situation was deteriorating. In pursuance of the *arrêt* given at Toulouse the seneschals of Toulouse and Périgord were directed to arrest those banished, to confiscate their goods, and to take possession of the castle of Montpezat. For that purpose the local districts were summoned to appear in arms on 15 March. The seneschal of Périgord had reported that the people would be willing to obey the king of France and to surrender, but that the fortress itself was held by the men of the English king who would guard it at the direction of the seneschal of Guienne. Other information from the seneschal of Périgord was to the effect that the seneschals of Guienne and the Agenais were putting their men on a war footing. In mid-March 1324 a series of documents was drawn up in protest against the anticipated seizure of Montpezat.[91] On the twenty-third King Charles respited a substantial number of cases concerning the duchy then pending in the Parlement of Paris.[92] But on the last day of April he issued an ultimatum, demanding that Montpezat cease to resist, and that "rebels" there and from Saint-Sardos should be handed over to the French. A ridiculously short term was imposed for acceptance. The English envoys, faced with imminent war, by 5 May had agreed to the conditions "comme à nous appertient," though Archbishop Bicknor of Dublin and M. William de Weston protested that as clerics they could not accept penalties involving the shedding of blood. Yet when King Charles's messengers arrived to take possession the earl and archbishop reneged on their agreement. King Charles thereupon informed the people of the duchy that he had taken it into his hand. The position of the earl of Kent and his fellow envoys was an awkward one. Edward was later to explain to Pope John that they had not possessed authority to act as they had done, being circumscribed by their indented credence.[93] A draft letter of April 1324 suggests to Queen Isabella what she might usefully say to a French knight returning to King Charles. She should emphasize the fact that Edward had no knowledge of the murders and other wrongdoing at Saint-Sardos; point out the prejudice to the duke of Guienne engendered by the summoning of a host to Montpezat; and express considerable surprise that the summons should be for Pentecost (3 June) when her brother had expected the English king to be at Amiens in the octave of the Nativity of St John, some four weeks later. She could also urge that the intention of her marriage had been to bring peace and love.[94]

In June 1324 Edward, who had not yet fully appreciated these developments, sent M. Richard de Eryom, a canon of York,[95] the by-now experienced John de Shoredich, and M. Richard de Gloucester to apologize for his failure to do homage.[96] The importance attached to the negotiations is perhaps indicated by the dispatch of the earl of Pembroke, who with the younger Despenser was closest to the king.[97] Pembroke left London somewhat before 13 June but died unexpectedly ten days later before he had a chance to reach Paris.[98] The other envoys arrived at Amiens in accordance with their instructions to excuse Edward for his failure to do homage. Not finding him there they proceeded to Annet-sur-Marne, where Charles of Valois was in process of marrying Jeanne d'Evreux. The king brusquely told them that Edward had made alliances, held castles and towns against him, and received those whom he had banished in England and elsewhere. He could "find no man" (*qil ne trouve homme*) for the duchy of Guienne and the county of Ponthieu, so he was compelled to take them into his hands. In their letter dated 10 July from Abbeville recounting these proceedings the envoys warned Edward that the French were blocking the ports, but if he did not send men Gascony would be lost to him. Indeed Charles had summoned his vassals in arms to Moissac for 8 July but postponed the levy until 5 August. The force was being led by Charles, count of Valois, no friend of England's,[99] or as Baker expressed it: "vir habens Anglicos maxime odiosos."[100] The count was expected to be in Gascony by early August.[101] Edward was at Porchester in July 1324 deciding on counter-measures. John de Cromwell was appointed admiral of a fleet preparing to set out for Gascony while John de Segrave senior and Fulk Fitzwarin were ordered to assemble forces at Plymouth until such time as they could sail to reinforce Earl Edmund who, on 20 July, was appointed lieutenant in Aquitaine.[102]

Negotiations about the surrender of Montpezat continued through June and July 1324. Prior to 8 July John Salmon, the bishop of Norwich, Henry de Suly, Richard Eryom, John de Shoredich, and Richard de Gloucester agreed to surrender it to King Charles on terms – it was shortly to be handed back – for which purpose special proctors were appointed. On the eighth John Stonore was appointed constable with instructions to effect the surrender to the French king. Before this could be done the castle of Montpezat was razed to the ground.[103] Edward retaliated on the twenty-first by ordering the arrest of all French subjects in England and confiscation of their goods. Benefices held by foreigners were included, although for diplomatic reasons exceptions were soon made for cardinals.[104] On 18 September Isabella's lands were taken into the king's hand. Ostensibly this was on account of a possible threat from the French, but the evidence suggests that it was principally a punitive measure, as the author of the *Vita*, among other chroniclers, thought. It was certainly to the queen's displeasure and was subsequently attributed to the malice of the Despensers and Baldock or to Treasurer Stapeldon, in whose diocese most of her lands lay and whose responsibility it was to carry out the administrative details. However, she was given an allowance of a thousand marks a year for her household and eight marks a day – or, according to a version of the English *Brut*, only one pound – for sustenance.[105] Twenty-seven members of her retinue, including two chaplains and her doctor, were sent back to France.[106] Bishop Hethe, while on his way towards Stone in Kent for celebration of his diocese's patronal festival of St Andrew (30 November), encountered others returning from the continent near Greenwich, lamenting the discord that had arisen between queen and king.[107] Possibly this indicated a deliberate economy or, more likely, a division of loyalty (on national lines) forced upon the queen's household. Some Englishmen who returned had their expenses reimbursed by the king.[108]

Edward's irritation at the conduct of the queen's French relatives was understandable, even though it was his own procrastination in the matter of homage that had been largely responsible for the immediate crisis. By the beginning of September the Agenais had been overrun, apart from a few pockets of resistance. Elsewhere little more than La Réole in the Gironde held out with the earl of Kent and Archbishop Bicknor. A truce was concluded there on 22 September; shortly thereafter it was surrendered to Charles of Valois.[109] Complaints were subsequently to be made to Pope John about the treacherous action of Bicknor in surrendering La Réole. These were rightly disregarded, but significantly this accusation is coupled with another to the effect that the archbishop criticized the younger Despenser, who was almost entirely responsible for Gascon policy, as his many letters clearly demonstrate. It is in fact known that Bicknor and M. William Weston complained to Despenser of the lack of attention to their despatches and calls for assistance. Despenser repudiated the suggestion that it was any fault of his and blamed the difficulties of communication with Gascony.[110] His excuses for failing to render due support are more fully expressed in a letter to the seneschal, Ralph Basset, about the same time.[111] That there was considerable delay in sending substantial forces is evident. A fleet initially summoned to assemble at Portsmouth on 27 August did not sail under Admiral Robert Bendin until 18 September. Contrary winds drove it back from the coast of Brittany into Falmouth haven, whence it again set sail on 22 September, by which time a truce had been arranged at La Réole. The eastern fleet under Admiral Sturmy was diverted from the Gascon expedition to guard the English coast in view of the appearance of a hostile fleet of some hundred and eighty ships off Zeeland. This information was sent by Archbishop Reynolds who thought that the ships assembled by the count of Hainault contained a vast array of armed men from Hainault, Germany, and France, together with those banished from England, a sure indication that the French king did not want peace. He expressed concern that Sandwich and other parts of the Kent coast were virtually undefended and open to any raiding party.[112] Further convoys under Admirals Robert

Bendin and Robert Bataille sailed in early November from Portsmouth and Winchelsea respectively with supplies and money for Bordeaux.[113]

The full nature of the débâcle had been revealed to Despenser and the king towards the beginning of October 1324 with the arrival at Porchester of two pinnaces, respectively from Bordeaux and Bayonne. They were carrying John de Aspale, a valet of the earl of Kent, and M. Robert de Redmere, a clerk of Adam de Lymbergh, the constable of Bordeaux.[114] In December 1324 the seneschal, Ralph Basset, despatched an interesting letter to Despenser in which he argued that Edward was under no obligation to perform homage in view of the fact that the king of France had disrupted the peace guaranteed under established agreements. He suggested that documents be searched for the claim of the king of Spain to receive homage from the area up to the River Dordogne. In such case Edward would be able to seek his aid for any war against France. This was not, it has to be admitted, practical politics.[115]

The English government sought to restore its position by advancing on numerous fronts: sending forces to Guienne, proposing a marriage alliance with Castile and/or Aragon, sounding out a rapprochement with the papacy, reopening the question of an interview between the French and English monarchs, sending Isabella as an emissary to France, and ultimately the young Prince Edward to perform homage. There had been a number of disagreements with the Curia; for instance, the dispute over the Aylesbury prebend; the seizure of benefices held by aliens; the rejection by the pope of Baldock's candidature for a bishopric; and most recently the bitter attack on John Stratford and other bishops. Stratford was hurriedly rehabilitated, although subject to a heavy penalty in case of "misbehaviour." He was too valuable a diplomat, particularly with respect to the papacy, for his services to be disregarded. Towards the end of September 1324 it was proposed that the English position should be placed before the papal Curia in the same manner as in the time of Boniface VIII and Clement V, and that Stratford, with some expert clerks from the royal council to assist him, should review the arrangements made in the time of Edward I and subsequently. The idea was that this would establish that the English king had not infringed agreements, notably those entered into by the earl of Pembroke and Bishop Stapeldon of Exeter. Further, it would show that the French *arrêts* had been in violation of peace and in contravention of franchises previously confirmed.[116]

Parliament met in London on 20 October 1324 and dispersed on 10 November.[117] It seems to have held some sessions at Mortlake in late October and early November, presumably in the archbishop's palace, and others subsequently at Westminster.[118] Apparently it is for this parliament that there survive both an address by Edward himself and vestigial answers to the thirteen points scheduled for discussion about Gascon affairs.[119] Edward claims to have done all that pertained to him, yet he requires to know the opinion of all, both individually and collectively, on the business in question. Between himself and those present he wishes to have no dissimulation, but clear and overt responses. The "points" discussed are merely alluded to, not detailed, but clearly they were concerned with reasons for the surrender of La Réole, the attitudes of those who were present at the siege – some of them being in league with the French, the capacity of the English to send help, the possibility of alliances, and what could be done in the case of the war's continuance. Another document, dated 1 November from Mortlake, details the advice given by the prelates and magnates regarding a possible expedition to Gascony in which the king himself might take part.[120] It was estimated that a Gascon force would require at least a thousand men-at-arms and ten thousand troops (*gentz a pee*), six thousand of them English, the rest Welsh. Prince Edward as the king's lieutenant in England should have assigned to him two archbishops, four bishops, two earls and four barons – chosen by the king – to attend him, together with the king's ministers, as well as others required for particular business. Fealty should be sworn to the young Edward in the same manner as was done when Edward I went to Flanders. Sufficient forces were to be left for the defence of the realm and arrangements were to be made, as formerly, with the Scots and Flemings.

Just as the session of parliament drew to a close Pope John's emissaries, Guillaume de Laudun, the archbishop of Vienne, and Hughes, the bishop of Orange, arrived. They are said to have reached England on 8 November 1324, to have left for Paris on the twenty-first,[121] and meanwhile to have dined on both the eleventh and the twentieth with Edward at the Tower.[122] But some of their agenda was unwelcome. They sought payment of arrears of tribute, of a portion of the biennial tenth, and an amelioration of the royal displeasure against a number of bishops who had been provided by the papacy. Four of these, Stratford, Burghersh, Eaglescliff, and Cobham, escorted the papal envoys to their lodgings and on the following day to the royal palace of Westminster.[123] Bishop Orleton would appear to have been deliberately prevented from meeting them, allegedly by threats of violence.[124] Despite these awkwardnesses the main outcome of the visit was Edward's decision to send another embassy to King Charles. Papal influence is discernible in the emphasis on the necessity for peace in Christendom so that attention could be given to the Holy Land. The ambassadors were two bishops, Salmon of Norwich and Stratford – his first mission since elevation – and two laymen, Jean de Bretagne and Henry de Beaumont. The ambassadors were to excuse the king from not having performed homage – he had not, they were to suggest, been duly summoned. They were to ask for restitution of what had been seized by the French king and to propose that Edward be given sufficient safe conduct to undertake homage. Should the question of marriage be raised, they were to enquire into what union was proposed and under what conditions and to inform King Edward. Other questions likely to be on the agenda of the talks were the three bishoprics of Limoges, Cahors, and Périgord, which the English wished to have restored to them in accordance with the agreement with Louis IX; the question of a possible French claim to the castle of Montpezat and to the *bastide* at Saint-Sardos; and the matter of Ralph Basset's banishment. The suggestion was to be mooted that the king of England might give the duchy of Guienne and his other Continental lands to his eldest son so that he could undertake homage for them. Should this proposal be accepted the ambassadors were to arrange details of time and place. Other questions concerned the prolongation to the octave of Easter and possible amendment of the terms of the truce arranged in Guienne with the earl of Kent. Finally, the ambassadors were to express the wish of the English king for the observance of all treaties and expressly for the removal of Roger Mortimer and others banished from England. Were the confiscated lands to be restored, Edward would be prepared to pay the expenses incurred on account of his default.[125]

Meanwhile Archbishop Bicknor and his fellow envoys had been traversing France on their diplomatic mission. The archbishop's expenses were calculated at 286 days, from 2 April 1324 when he was at Tilbury *en route* for Dover, until 12 January of the following year. He crossed the Channel on the 8 April and reached the French king at Berchères l'Evêque near Chartres, paid him another visit at Bois-de-Vincennes, and then went to various parts of Gascony. He returned by way of Gravelines, recrossing the Channel on 6 January 1325, slightly in advance of Bishop Stratford. In his expense account he claimed to have reported to the king at Langley,[126] and to have remained there for six days.[127] After these discussions the envoys returned to France at the beginning of March.[128] The earl and his companions were instructed to proceed amicably and to offer to redress all wrongs perpetrated against the king of France. Should they be met by other suggestions about the meeting of the kings the envoys were to say that Edward had every intention of coming by the octave of St John unless prevented by urgent necessity, in which case he would inform his fellow monarch without delay. King Charles was to be thanked for delaying the business in the Parlement of Paris and for freeing M. Pons Tournemire, Edward's proctor in that assembly.[129] There was to be no discussion of legal right (*du droit*); to questions of that kind they were to respond that their power only extended to securing delays and respites. The items of complaint to be raised by the embassy were numerous. The island of Oléron, they were to argue, had previously been held by the English kings without interference from French officials; as a consequence of a novel agreement made by the prior of St Eutrope in Saintes with the king of France, the officers of the English king have likewise been impeded; Arnaud de Caillou, a subject of the king within the duchy has been summoned to appear in Paris and because he has not appeared has been condemned to pay a thousand livres and banished; the abbess of Saintes has newly agreed to hold lands in Saintonge from the king of France, thus excluding the English king's jurisdiction. In addition there was a secret schedule of further instructions. The envoys were to try by friendly persuasion to secure the reversal of the offending processes. Should this not be achieved then they were to argue for a moratorium on all those affecting the English king until such time as the two monarchs could meet. Such interview could take place at Boulogne on 1 May 1325 or as late as the octave of St Michael. Should respite not be granted by Charles then no date was to be arranged.[130]

About 17 January 1325 Stratford in his turn reached London with the initial responses of King Charles. These had been thrashed out with the help of the papal envoys, who after leaving England had held discussions in Paris. They were not very palatable. If the king of England were to remove all impediments, Charles would be pleased to do him speedy justice. There were three suggestions made by the papal envoys on the basis of information from the council of the French king. First, were Edward to grant the Agenais and the county of Ponthieu to Charles and his heirs, the duchy of Guienne would be restored after homage. Secondly, if the Agenais were so granted the duchy and county would be restored and held from Charles, for which homage would be performed as formerly. Thirdly, were the Agenais to be given, then the French king would grant other lands and remove his hand from the duchy and county.[131]

Diplomacy had achieved little or nothing, the French were preparing an expedition to Gascony. As a result military and naval action was undertaken in April and early May 1325 when two fleets set sail, one from Portsmouth the other from Harwich, with some four thousand soldiers aboard. Warenne, earl of Surrey, had been appointed captain of those collected at Portsmouth on 1 April. The *Vita* expresses astonishment that the king should have neglected to pay the footsoldiers whom he kept waiting about, for he was known to have plenty of treasure. The Gervase continuator, without giving a date, says that Edward, unwilling to do homage, despatched the earls of Warenne and Atholl (Batheles) – David de Strathbogie – and John Segrave the elder, with the flower of the English army, as well as footsoldiers raised from every hundred in the land. In response the French force under the count of Valois was said, doubtless with much exaggeration, to have consisted of four dukes, twenty counts, five thousand men-at-arms and sixty thousand footsoldiers.[132]

Despite the activities of so many royal ambassadors, letters from Bordeaux and Bayonne written in May 1325 suggest on the one hand that the government in England was not making its wishes known, responding to information sent, or making money available for defence, and on the other, that the activities of the French were by no means popular. Gentlemen of the Agenais, it was thought, would be willing to serve Edward's cause in arms were there to be suitable men of the king's council to give advice, as well as wardens of his treasure. Also, the occupied towns might well turn back to him. The French were said to be introducing new customs and practices; a number of those aggrieved would return to the duke's allegiance were they to be granted pardon.[133]

Concurrently the question of marriage alliances had been actively pursued, a revival of the policy of Edward I.[134] Included in the account of the negotiations with France, prepared for delivery by Bishop Stratford to the king on his return in January 1325, is Charles IV's complaint that the English were procuring or attempting to procure conventions with Spain, Aragon, Hainault, and elsewhere against the French Crown, which he held to be treacherous conduct (*come crime de lese majeste*).[135] Castile was a potential ally against the French, and late in 1324 information from Edmund of Woodstock suggested that Don Juan, the infante of Castile, would be willing to ally with his relative, Edward, even against France, provided that the English king took part and provided the resources.[136] Following up this suggestion, on 18 January 1325 Edward sealed letters of credence addressed to Alfonso XI, a minor, to his tutors, and to the bishop of Burgos. The ambassadors were empowered to negotiate a marriage contract between the sister of Alfonso, Leonor, and Prince Edward, and a second between Alfonso himself and Edward II's daughter, Eleanor of Woodstock, who was not quite seven years of age. The English negotiators initially sought the re-establishment of an agreement for mutual aid against all comers, saving the faith of the Roman church, made between Alfonso X "the Wise" of Castile and Henry III of England. They sought a promise of three thousand men-at-arms for defence of the duchy of Aquitaine and other territories, but to this the Castilian negotiators replied that they might manage as many as two thousand, provided the English king paid their expenses, but that they were already committed to find forces against other enemies, particularly the Saracens.[137]

Another group of negotiators was actively engaged at the court of Aragon, where earlier schemes for marriage alliances had fallen through.[138] A proposal that Prince Edward should marry the infanta was rejected as inappropriate (*nullatenus complacere*). Another was for the marriage of Eleanor of Woodstock's younger sister, Joan "of the Tower," to the eldest son of the infante, Alfonso.[139] Two of the negotiators, John de Hildesley and Bernard Pélerin, wrote on 6 June 1325 from Glénan off the coast of Brittany to report on the state of negotiations. Alfonso, the eldest son of James (Jaime) II, together with other great men of the royal council were favourably inclined (*le desirent sovereinement*), and there was an offer of armed men, but the envoys' feeling was that too much was being demanded of the English king (*il demandent trop grossement du vostre*). During their return journey, one of the envoys, Robert de Thorp, was captured by the lord of Cazeneuve on 11 May as he approached Bordeaux. He was not released until February of the following year. Despite all the diplomatic niceties, it should have been clear from the start that the aged king of Aragon had no desire to fall out with his neighbour, Charles IV. Already in 1324 James II had repudiated the notion that at the time of the siege of La Réole he intended to form an alliance against the French king. He remembered all too well the lengthy campaigns against Charles of Valois for possession of Sicily. In letters of April 1325 written to Edward II and Charles IV, the king of Aragon declared that he had no intention of entering into such alliances as had been proposed, but that he would be willing to act as an intermediary for securing peace between the parties.[140] In a letter of January 1325 from Bordeaux, Raymond Durand, Ralph Basset's lieutenant, wrote of the advantage of alliances with Spain, Aragon, and Portugal. At the time Edward was attempting to gain the support of the Portuguese monarch,

Dionigi (Diniz), who had married a daughter of Peter III of Aragon, against Antonio de Pessagno, whose brother, Manuele, was admiral of the Portuguese fleet of Genoa. Pessagno had been declared a traitor for deserting the English cause for that of Charles IV, from whom he had received a substantial loan.[141]

These diplomatic efforts were both expensive and unproductive. In a letter to Pope John, Edward claimed that he had been prepared to make peace but that the French were procrastinating and had kept his ambassadors waiting around. Having heard, both on his own account and from the papal envoys, that were Isabella to be sent to her brother, the latter would consent to a firm peace, he has decided to do this. But with whom had the idea of sending the queen originated? Chroniclers have been anxious, thanks to the benefit of hindsight, to find a scapegoat. Murimuth merely states that the queen crossed the sea. Geoffrey le Baker, expanding in his somewhat convoluted style on so exiguous a text, provides his own explanation, accompanied by vituperation. His imaginative thesis runs as follows. The realm was ruled by three kings, the Despensers being two of them. The Despensers were hated but also feared. Orleton, deprived of his temporalities, hated them, Bishop Burghersh of Lincoln feared them and on that account hated them also. The Despensers provoked the queen's anger by meanly counselling the cutting down of her familia and substantially reducing her income. Insatiable feminine avarice being thus frustrated, in the manner of her sex not only did she explode in anger against the Despensers but also against her husband. The king of France bemoaned the fact that a daughter of one king and a sister of several more should be married to so miserly a king and treated like a bondwoman, a mere stipendiary of the Despensers. As for Isabella, she supposedly wished there were no Channel dividing France (Neustria) from England; either it should be dried up or a broad bridge (*pontem latum securum*) built so that her frequent letters could be conveyed to her brother. Who, asks Baker, was available to console her? Only the bishop of Hereford, it seems, who allegedly proceeded to stoke that virago's indignation. The bishop of Lincoln was privy to both their secrets and, knowing where the wolf's lair was to be found (*sciens qua cavea wlpem reperiret*), worked his blandishments on the queen, while Orleton fomented a fresh civil disturbance by urging that if the queen went to France she could implore aid against the Despensers. Isabella, applauding such a goal, sought occasion to make the journey.[142]

It so happened, Baker continues, that it became necessary to send an embassy to France. For such an important matter the king wished to cross the Channel, but the Despensers,[143] fearing that if he did so they might fall into their enemies' hands, were against his doing so. Yet they did not wish to accompany him because the king of France, with the queen's faction and that of Roger Mortimer, hated them.[144] All fell into place. Isabella persuaded her husband, the magnates came to the opinion that a prudent and conciliatory queen would provide no small opportunity for securing peace, the Despensers felt that the plan would obviate the king's departure, while Bishops Orleton and Burghersh secretly encouraged the king's councillors to accept the scheme. As can be seen from the above, there is no mention of the pope, merely a conspiracy begun by Orleton, later joined by Burghersh and then entered into by an angry queen – all of whom Baker detested What is not made clear is how either Orleton or Burghersh, who were in such bad odour with the government, could possibly have exercised the influence suggested. Baker has conceived a pattern of events for the latter part of the reign; a pattern involving a preconcerted plan, principally of Orleton's conception, to displace the Despensers but also the king – for whom the chronicler demonstrates much sympathy throughout.[145]

The author of the *Vita* did not have the benefit of hindsight. His chronicle finishes in 1325, very possibly shortly before his demise. Even so, he suggested, many considered that Isabella would not return unless the younger Despenser were removed from Edward's side. At the end of his chronicle he tells us that the queen did indeed refuse to return with her son – but no more than that. For him it was the king who, thinking that nothing could be achieved by sending further embassies, proposed to send his queen, she being a blood relation of the French king. But, he concluded, apart from a temporary extension of the truce, Isabella was no more successful than anyone else, an appraisal that has been generally accepted.[146] The Gervase continuator likewise imputes no blame: the king acted with the consent of the prelates, earls, and barons, in the belief that peace could not be brought about except by the queen.[147] The author of the Lanercost Chronicle devotes considerable space to the supposed reasons for the queen's departure. In agreement with the *Vita* he argues that the king sent his consort thinking that, as she promised, she would bring peace between himself and the French king. But he advanced a second reason for queen's desire to undertake the journey. Allegedly the younger Despenser was attempting to procure in the Curia a divorce between the king and Isabella and for that purpose had despatched a Dominican friar, Thomas Dunheved,[148] together with a companion and a secular clerk – none other than Robert Baldock. It was at their[149] instigation that the king took lands and rents granted to the queen into his hand, giving her twenty shillings a day for herself and her whole retinue, removing her own special servants (*ministros*) and appointing Despenser's wife as custodian, without whose knowledge Isabella could not write anything. It was to remedy that situation that the queen wished to visit her brother.[150]

Whatever the chroniclers surmised or stated as fact, it is unlikely that at the time King Charles, the pope – who designated Isabella an "angel of peace" – Orleton, Burghersh, or even the queen herself had any idea of what the outcome of the journey would be. Nor is it possible to divine quite when Isabella decided not to return. We do know that the confiscation of her lands and the short commons permitted for her stay in France irritated her. The many surviving documents point to Baker's story being pure invention. Isabella's mission was undertaken because King Charles let it be known that he was agreeable, since the scheme was favoured by the papal envoys, advocated by the king's ambassadors to the court of France, and subsequently approved by councillors at home. All, including Edward, who more than anyone else should have been alive to the danger, appear to have been blind to the fact that Isabella might seize the opportunity to impose conditions for her return.

The bishop of Winchester returned with a series of *pourparlers* scheduled for discussion at a council hastily summoned to Westminster, where those present counselled against allowing the young Prince Edward to go to France but supported the idea that the queen should make the journey.[151] In letters of 5 March 1325 the king thanked his envoys, Bishops Salmon and Stratford and Jean de Bretagne, who had since returned to Paris, both for their counsel and their specific request that his queen be permitted to go to France. He was sending William Ayrminne to join them.[152] Isabella landed at Wissant four days later, made a leisurely progress in the direction of Paris and on the twenty-first arrived at her brother's palace at Poissy, where she had discussions with the English envoys.[153] By the end of the month it was clear that the negotiations, despite the queen's efforts in cooperation with those of the papal envoys, the bishop of Orange and the archbishop of Vienne,[154] were making little progress. The sole agreement was to extend the truce from 14 April until 9 June.[155] William Dene in the *Historia Roffensis*, doubtless influenced by rumour, felt that the failure was due to Roger Mortimer's machinations, persuading the queen *not* to make peace.[156]

Bishop Stratford and William Ayrminne were sent back to Edward, then at Beaulieu, in Hampshire,[157] with the queen's letters and the various despatches of the negotiators. King Charles expressed himself willing to restore Guienne and Ponthieu after due performance of homage and payment of the expenses incurred. On 3 May 1325 Edward's answer was sent. He excused his former behaviour by declaring that he had duly sent envoys requesting postponement of homage for lawful reasons. But when the French king demanded that he perform homage at Amiens in the octave of St John the Baptist (i.e., 1 July), Edward responded that it was not possible to come without bodily danger because Charles had summoned his host to occupy Gascony and would not withdraw. Nonetheless he expressed willingness to carry out his obligation of homage but only if the king of France were to dispense speedy justice with respect to his occupation of Gascony. At the beginning of May the envoys, Stratford and Ayrminne, returned to France with Edward's response.[158] In a letter of 14 May to the pope the king complained of the unfairness of the French demands. No peace had been concluded and he was expected to surrender his possessions to the king of France, to perform homage, and then have them restored, apart from those awaiting judgment in the French court. Furthermore, the term allowed for the envoys to convey his decision on such proposals was too brief. His councillors were in no position to decide between such opposites: acceptance of terms that might entail disinheritance followed by war, or rejection that would trigger immediate conflict.[159]

On 30 May 1325 Isabella was in the royal palace at Paris in the presence of the council of the French king. The following day, with Bishop Salmon, Jean de

Bretagne, and William Ayrminne acting as Edward's "messages et procureurs," an agreement was reached. During June the details were thrashed out and the truce was prolonged.[160] Despite his dissatisfaction with the terms, Edward was constrained to reply on 13 June accepting the proposals. These included King Charles's provisional right to appoint a seneschal in the Agenais. Edward would be allowed to retain control of the castles, but their constables were to be restricted in that they could not raise additional troops without permission of the seneschal. The English king was to perform homage at Beauvais on 15 August, a date later postponed to 29 August. This would bring the restoration of territory in France with the exception of the Agenais, the right to which was to be settled by the French court.[161]

Parliament assembled at Westminster on 25 June 1325 to review the agreement. The Rochester chronicler provides unusually lengthy treatment. He records that the king's plenipotentiary, William Ayrminne,[162] had agreed that the king of France should hold the duchy of Aquitaine, seized for non-performance of homage, by such right as he presently possessed, which he considered to be sufficient (*quod ius sufficiens reputavit*). Should the English king wish to have his right determined by the peers of the realm he could prosecute his case in the court of France where he would receive justice. King Charles wished this arrangement to be confirmed by the king's letters. The question arose whether Edward ought to repudiate his proxy, which he could not, or confirm the arrangement and cross to France. It was finally agreed that he should make the journey.[163] This opinion delivered, the king turned to other business – the removal of the treasurer from his office.[164] But though the principle had been conceded Edward was quite unable to make up his mind, and it was his dilatory behaviour that precipitated the subsequent crisis, indeed his eventual fall. During the latter part of August 1325 he was hovering uncertainly at Sturry near Canterbury, at Wingham where the archbishop had a palace, and subsequently at Langdon, near Dover, with his friend the abbot of the Premonstratensian house there. Ostensibly this was to keep in the closest possible touch with his agents on the Continent. At Wingham Archbishop Reynolds, the bishops of London, Ely, Exeter, Chichester, and Carlisle, assembled with many others to discuss whether or not the king should cross the Channel. When Bishop Hethe of Rochester – a man well disposed towards Edward – arrived to conduct Edward to the shore, he was given instructions to await the outcome of the matter. Debate continued at Langdon, where the more nervous suggested that were Edward to travel by way of Wissant he might be ambushed. Even if he did go to the French king he might find those prepared to subject him to war. Thus a mixture of persuasion and fear served to prohibit Edward from going at all.[165] It was at Langdon on 24 August, less than a week before Edward was supposed to be at Beauvais, that the king wrote to excuse himself on the grounds of a sudden illness, a condition more likely to have been feigned than real. But to swear to the validity of his condition he deputed Bishop Stratford and M. John de Bruton, a canon of Exeter.[166]

Already, some months before, it had been decided to seek the French king's approval for a transfer of Aquitaine to the king's son. Bishop Stratford, Ayrminne (shortly to become bishop of Norwich) and the earl of Richmond were on 5 July 1325 appointed for that purpose.[167] The two secular clerks were then authorized to act by themselves, or Stratford alone.[168] All three ambassadors were entrusted with a further proposal: the marriage of Joan "of the Tower" to the son of Charles of Valois.[169] Stratford, who took a particularly prominent part in all these negotiations, was commissioned to promise money to those who gave assistance to Edward, with authority to borrow on the king's behalf.[170] On 2 September 1325 by royal charter the young Edward, earl of Chester, was invested with the county of Ponthieu and that of Montreuil in the Pas de Calais and, just over a week later, on the tenth, with the duchy of Aquitaine.[171] Signification of the grant was sent to King Charles under the latter date. Edward explained that for reasons he had already given, he was sending his eldest son, the French king's nephew, to him so that he could perform homage. He had learned from the queen and other envoys that this was agreeable. He asked his brother-in-law to receive Edward graciously, to accompany whom he had assigned Bishop Stapeldon of Exeter and Henry de Beaumont.[172]

The duke of Guienne sailed from Dover on 12 September, the king being there to see him off, having extracted a promise, as he was later to remind him, not to marry or to act with respect to the duchy contrary to his instructions.[173] On the twenty-fourth at Vincennes Charles issued letters of dispensation to the duke, so that although he had not quite completed his thirteenth year, "he was freed from paternal authority and made as of superior years and capable of ruling."[174] On the same day, in the presence of his mother and of three English bishops, Stratford, Stapeldon, and Ayrminne, the recently consecrated Norwich diocesan,[175] as well as of the earl of Richmond, Henry de Beaumont, John Cromwell, and Gilbert Talbot, acting as councillors, Edward performed the homage that his father had neglected to perform and promised to maintain the peace now established. He also engaged himself to pay to his suzerain a relief of sixty thousand livres *parisis*.[176] By his letters patent dated 7 October 1325 from Paris, under the titles duke of Aquitaine, "comes" of Chester, Ponthieu, and Montreuil, Edward appointed Oliver de Ingham seneschal of the duchy.[177] Back in England Archbishop Reynolds, in a circular of 22 September to his province, explained that by the advice of the queen, the papal nuncios, of Stratford and the earl of Richmond, it was better for the king to remain at home engaged in the affairs of the kingdom and to send his son to perform homage instead. He issued a forty days' indulgence for those who prayed for the safe return of the queen and her son and urged his comprovincial bishops to add to his indulgence one of their own.[178]

The affair was no sooner concluded than doubts arose in Edward's mind. The arrangement had been to the advantage of Charles IV, who held on to the Agenais and other lands captured by Charles of Valois. Already early in March

1326, Ayrminne, Edward's plenipotentiary, though still in France, was summoned before the King's Bench for falsely, maliciously and treacherously acting *ultra vires* by agreeing, contrary to the royal desire and intention, that the king of France should continue to hold certain lands to the king's manifest disinheritance.[179] He was doubly unpopular with the government on that account and because, in its view, he had feathered his own nest while abroad, to Chancellor Baldock's detriment, by accepting provision to the see of Norwich. Even worse, his promotion was said to have been at the urging of the French king and of Queen Isabella.[180] The Rochester chronicler records the younger Despenser's passionate plaint in the sympathetic ear of Bishop Hethe that Ayrminne had betrayed the English king, for which misdeed he had been rewarded with a bishopric. But for the queen and bishop, he averred, the king of England would have brooked no equal in wealth, but in conjunction with their accomplices they had stirred up discord between the kings.[181] This less-than-satisfactory outcome helped to precipitate a further conflict in 1326, when King Edward, on the grounds that the young duke was under the direction of others, tried to resume his control over his Continental possessions under the guise of being their "governor and administrator." In this capacity he sent a copy of the convention agreed between King Charles and himself and sealed by John Stratford concerning the disputed Mauléon in the Basses Pyrénées. This place, according to the seneschal of Gascony, was well disposed to the English king. Charles promptly reoccupied parts of the duchy from which he was in process of withdrawing.[182] The renewed hostilities were brought to an end on 31 March 1327 by the Treaty of Paris, which was ratified in the name of the young Edward III on 11 April.[183]

THE FINAL PHASE:
THE ACCEPTANCE OF LIEGE HOMAGE (1327–31)

The French nettle had to be grasped by the new administration. The keeper of the processes, Elias Jonestone, was kept busy for the first year of the new reign carrying transcripts of the various processes to the 1328 parliaments of Westminster, Lincoln, and York, as well as the councils at Stamford, York, Nottingham, Worcester, and Lichfield.[184] From the Rochester chronicle it would appear that it was at the Lenten Parliament of 1329 at Westminster that Ayrminne's former conduct attracted further hostile scrutiny.[185] The question of homage had again became a burning issue following the crowning on 29 May 1328 of Philip VI of Valois at Rheims, whose position at the time appeared tenuous.[186] On the morrow of the coronation ceremony, Bishops Orleton and Northburgh arrived at Paris to press the claims of Edward III through his mother Isabella.[187] Shortly afterwards, perhaps in June 1328, the burgomaster of Bruges, Guillaume le Doyen (le Deken), travelled to England where, according to the accusation later levelled against him, he sought to recognize Edward III as king of France: an ill-timed venture, shortly followed by the disastrous defeat of the Flamands at Cassel.[188]

Philip responded in November by sending Pierre Roger, the abbot of Fécamp, and Bouchard de Montmorency, with a summons for Edward to perform his feudal obligations. The French chroniclers disagree on the envoys' reception. One account records a friendly welcome and favourable response by the earl of Kent, another evasiveness, followed eventually by an interview with Isabella, who remarked astringently that the son of a king could not perform homage to the son of a count, a rejoinder that has a characteristic ring. Reprisals followed. Philip gave instructions for the revenues of Gascony to be seized.[189] A further embassy visited Edward and the court at Windsor between 28 January and 5 February 1329 and then proceeded to London where parliament was in session from the ninth. During the proceedings Ayrminne was supposedly forced to counter the allegation of misusing the authority given him and involving the former king in a dispute. Allegedly he did so by placing the onus for what was agreed on Queen Isabella. She is said to have responded with vigour: "I am a woman and did what I could with such knowledge as I had, being ignorant of the law. You, a clerk and royal ambassador, ought to have acted with more circumspection, the [fault] is to be imputed to you not to me. That evil you have sown you must now reap." At that point, so the chronicler concludes, it was decided to send Ayrminne with Orleton to France to salve the wound.[190] In fact they did not go until a year later, February 1330. In any case, it is difficult to imagine that Ayrminne would have had the temerity to provoke Isabella in this way when she was at the height of her power, having settled the Scottish question to her satisfaction and stifled the Lancastrian "rebellion." That Ayrminne is likely to have been blamed for an unsatisfactory outcome to the earlier agreement is highly likely. We are reliably told that it was during the parliamentary session that the Bishop of London, Stephen Gravesend, informed the ambassadors that Edward had agreed to go to France to perform his duty.[191]

The popularity of the government of Isabella and Mortimer was in rapid decline. It may well be that on reflection the queen, anxious not to precipitate another expensive war over Gascony, was willing to overlook the claims she had previously made for her son. Thomas Charlton, bishop of Hereford, and Bartholomew Burghersh were sent to France to excuse his failure to perform homage and to make arrangements for his coming. Their embassy lasted almost a month. A fortnight after their return, on 26 May 1329, the 16-year-old Edward took ship and performed homage to Philip on 6 June in the choir of Amiens Cathedral. The form of words used on this occasion was the same as had been pronounced in 1286 by his grandfather and in 1320 by his father. Both sides made exceptions: the French king did not accept homage for the lands occupied during the war of Saint-Sardos, while on behalf of the English king, Bishop Burghersh of Lincoln declared that Edward, in taking the oath, had no intention of abandoning any of his rights in the duchy.[192]

Such homage did not satisfy King Philip for long, and in 1330 Edward was summoned to appear before the French Parlement on 28 July, both to declare that the homage undertaken in 1329 was liege homage and to swear fealty. In the meantime, on 5 February at Eltham, a prestigious English embassy was briefed. At its head were the veteran negotiators Orleton and Ayrminne, together with Henry, earl of Leicester, and William lord Ros of Hamlake, accompanied by two specialist clerks, John Walwayn the younger and John de Schordich.[193] Their purpose was twofold. Firstly, to arrange a double marriage uniting the English and French royal houses, between, on the one hand, John, eldest son of Philip with Edward's sister, Eleanor; on the other, John of Eltham, younger brother of the English king, with Marie, Philip's daughter.[194] Secondly, the envoys were to clarify the oath taken at Amiens in 1329, and to continue the interminable quasi-legal processes of Montreuil and Périgueux. A report of the negotiations was delivered to the king at Reading on 25 March 1330. It was not reassuring. At Woodstock on 10 April Bishops Orleton and Ayrminne, together with Walwayn and Shoredich, were given further instructions, in particular to press the marriage of Eleanor and John. The marriage schemes foundered, but at Bois-de-Vincennes a convention was sealed on 8 May by Orleton, Ayrminne, and Shoredich, that provided a settlement, even if temporary, of some Gascon issues. On 8 July at Woodstock Edward agreed to accept the arrangements for mutual compensation to be made by his envoys.[195]

A temporary respite ensued. Edward was summoned on 1 September 1330 to appear before his peers of the court of France on 14 December. He made his excuses, or rather they were made for him. At the time there was a growing antipathy to the rule of Isabella and Mortimer and a restiveness on the young Edward's part, which terminated, as we have seen, in the *coup d'état* of October, Mortimer's capture, and subsequent execution. But before Edward III had time to settle himself firmly at the head of government he was forced to face the question yet again. The former negotiators Orleton, Ayrminne, and Shoredich were deputed, together with Thomas Sampson, a secular clerk – who with Shoredich had been studying the Gascon documents so that parliament could be briefed, and two laymen, Henry Percy and Hugh d'Audley, to continue the discussions of the previous year. Orleton claimed expenses from 23 January – he crossed from Dover on the twenty-eighth – until 25 March 1331, when he returned to Edward at Westminster to make his report. The outcome was the Paris agreement of 9 March 1331, in which Edward conceded that liege homage should be performed, the precise formula to be used on future occasions being published in letters patent of 30 March. It followed the wording of the 1329 oath but with the addition of the important word "liege."[196] According to Déprez Edward conceded the point out of duplicity; he needed to play for time even at the cost of temporary humiliation.[197] In consequence the king with a few companions, Montacute and Stratford among them, made a secret and potentially hazardous journey to France at the beginning of April. Between the twelfth and sixteenth of that month he remained at Pont-Sainte-Maxence, with King Philip close by at Saint-Christophe.[198] There does not seem to have been any repetition of homage, which would have been unprecedented. Instead the formal act sealed by the vassal was considered sufficient to establish retrospectively the nature of the homage performed at Amiens.[199] The arrangements were endorsed at the Westminster Parliament of September 1331 at Chancellor Stratford's urging. This act, according to the papal Curia, was to constitute one of three reasons why in the 1340s Edward III could not rightly claim the throne of France.[200]

Since on 28 November 1330 Bishop Stratford had replaced Bishop Burghersh as chancellor, it was principally to him that this irenic policy was to be attributed. When, as archbishop, he was under attack in 1340, the taking of the oath of liege homage was a charge laid against him. The chronicler Baker, who regarded Stratford in a friendly light, defended him: he had not acted to the king's prejudice or to appease the tyrant Philip, but solely in the interests of the English realm.[201] Already in 1331 the scene was set for a decline in the relationship with France and a drift towards war as the only solution to the festering problem of Gascony. More to the point, a martial king had succeeded a militarily inept one.

Summing Up

It would have taken a man far more able and politically astute than Edward II to cope successfully with the many-faceted situation inherited from his father.[1] Gascony and relations with the French monarchy were to pose gnawing problems throughout the reign and far beyond. The twin marriages of Edward I and Edward II, designed to provide a dynastic solution, lamentably failed so to do. At a pragmatic level Edward II might well have felt cheated by Isabella's inability to win over her royal brothers. But it is arguable that in large measure his marriage failed, not for that reason but because of his infatuation first with Gaveston and then with the younger Despenser. As the spurned Isabella was to demonstrate, she was both determined and ruthless in pursuing a course of action, her consort by and large was not. During the latter part of the reign the younger Despenser was the mainspring of royal government and policy. Edward's fear – stimulated by that of the Despensers – to perform his obligations of homage in person, determined the fatal plan to send first his wife and then his son to France.[2] He was a procrastinator; someone who shunned unpleasant duties whether administrative, political or military.

The Bridlington chronicler commented that the young Edward's marriage was made "in the hope of peace and the recovery of lands on the continent," yet once the marriage had been undertaken the occupation nonetheless continued.[3] Quite so, but the author of the *Vita* could also put these words into Isabella's mouth: "I feel that marriage is the joining of a woman with a man, the maintaining of a seamless manner of life, but there is someone who is trying to break this bond between my husband and myself. I declare that I am unwilling to return until this interloper has been removed." And so, Edward's queen allegedly proposed to wear widow's weeds until she should be "avenged of this Pharisee." In response Edward suggested that some unknown person must have put the idea into her head.[4] This may well have been so. Mortimer emerged as that "unknown person." When the younger Despenser was eventually removed the selfsame argument was used, but by this time what supposedly came between Isabella and her husband was her fear, either simulated or conveniently magnified, of her husband's violence, coupled with the unstated fact that she no longer wished to be his consort.

These personal and matrimonial difficulties were exacerbated by others over which Edward exercised equally little control. During their sway the remaining Capetians, despite weaknesses of their own, effectively whittled away the power of the English kings in France, in part consciously, in part through the deliberate actions of their local officials. The removal of Edward I's formidable presence left a whole range of Gascon problems unresolved.[5] Over the next twenty years the frequent mortality of the French kings accentuated the demands upon a duke of Gascony who, though king of England, yet had much Continental ancestry in his blood – from Anjou, Aquitaine, Angoulême, Provence and Castile.[6] Even Edward II's grant of Aquitaine to his son was not unprecedented. In somewhat different circumstances Edward I had conceded the duchy, but not the title of duke, to the young Edward of Caernarfon, and may have had the intention of permitting his son to perform homage in his stead. He died before these plans could be effected.[7]

Whereas Edward II was losing his Continental possessions by erosion and inactivity, the case of Scotland was very different. Robert Bruce and his aides decisively removed any prospect of restoring English hegemony. The defeat of Bannockburn and the ridicule it engendered proved irreversible. Internal strife precluded a united front against the Scots who carried the conflict south of the border. The northern part of England was condemned to repeated devastation, being reduced to buying off the invaders as the sole available remedy. For lack of royal action an army of clerics and hastily assembled levies was disastrously routed at Myton. The earls of Lancaster and Carlisle came to be stigmatized as traitors for their dealings with the enemy. In the latter case it was a policy of desperation, precipitated by Edward's military incapacity. Worse still, the Scottish "rebels" spilled over into Ireland, a land that had provided troops and supplies for Edwardian Scottish campaigns. In so doing they overstretched themselves: they either failed to appreciate the complexity of the Irish situation, or chose to ignore it. Their scorched earth policy did nothing to endear them to their fellow Celts – as they felt themselves to be – or to those few English settlers who joined them. Given their overall strategy, if it can be so dignified, their victories could only be ephemeral. Edward did nothing in person to bolster the military operations in Ireland, but at least the parlous state of the English there was not solely a consequence of his inadequacy. There was an embarrassing degree of "Celtic resurgence," coupled with a whole series of deaths among the Anglo-Irish that paralyzed large sections of the baronage.

As has been suggested, it is a slight exaggeration to say with the Chester chronicler that Wales caused no trouble to Edward, even after the rising of Llywelyn Bren in 1316, but on the whole such trouble did not inconvenience him to any great extent, despite many rumours of projected insurrection, even of a second front to be launched from a Scottish kingship of Ireland. The trouble was more with the unruly Marcher barons than with the indigenous Welsh. Edward counted on support in Wales and did receive some, notably from Sir Gruffydd Llwyd. In any case there were considerable differences between North and South Wales. In the North there was some attachment to English law, whereas in the South Welsh legal methods were preferred. Above all, the Welsh disliked the aggrandizement of the Roger Mortimers of Chirk and Wigmore, the former being made justice of North and South Wales in 1308, the latter in 1327.[8] Though Edward could do little to prevent the internecine conflict in the Marches, his support of the younger Despenser acted as a stimulant. The *bouleversement* of the rebels in 1321–22, men who for the most part had no wish to be regarded as such, was effective in producing a reasonable degree of internal peace for the remainder of the reign. Yet when Edward retired to Wales in 1326 he did not receive the support for which he had hoped, certainly expected. His capture was effected by, among others, Rhys ap Hywel, whose lands had been confiscated by the king and who had only recently been released from a lengthy imprisonment at Dover and the Tower of London.[9] Yet, following Edward's incarceration, rumours percolated to the government of plots in Wales to set him free. In his turn, Mortimer, fearing that his regime and that of Isabella might be overthrown by Henry of Lancaster, travelled with the queen mother, the king, and the court.to the comparative security of his Welsh border patrimony, abandoning London for the time being. In view of the capital's crucial part in the *coup* of 1326 this was a dangerous strategy.

Within England itself, the notion of a concerted "baronial opposition" bent on commanding the machinery of government has been dealt a blow. What we see is a less coherent structure: individual barons pursuing their own agendas but from time to time drawing together under the convenient umbrella of the Ordinances. The "middle party" between courtiers and opposing barons has likewise been largely relegated to limbo, in favour of a more subtle hypothesis of individual fluctuating loyalties. Thus, even if from time to time we can discern a group poised somewhere between the king and those in blatant opposition, its composition varied. The episcopate, by and large, was anxious to bring accommodation between the king, his favourite councillors, and those elements of the baronage that sought to get their way by force. Lancaster was no more fit to rule than Edward himself and amply demonstrated the fact. Nor was he capable of constructive criticism, it was the Ordinances or nothing: no medieval king could allow himself to be hamstrung in that manner. The earl's character, despite the popular outcry in favour of his "sainthood," was not attractive.[10] Of his own habit of aggrandizement his biographer has written: "Chicanery and extortion were characteristic of Lancaster's dealings in land." His private life was no better. Despite his five earldoms he was as greedy and acquisitive as those whom he sought to restrain. In this cause Sir Robert Holland was his unscrupulous agent.[11] Lancaster lacked any sense of military strategy or of tactical initiative. His abandonment of Badlesmere was hardly commendable from the point of view of the other barons under arms, nor was it defensible from his own longer-term interests. It encouraged the king to make a uniquely determined effort to crush rebellion. Yet Lancaster's death – despite his conniving with the Scots he avoided the excruciating fate of a traitor – was mourned in a country where great men were held in awe. His fall seemed so catastrophic, his end so pitiful. The same reaction was to follow Edward's somewhat different death.

There is a strange dichotomy between the barons' and particularly Lancaster's behaviour within their own domains, indeed beyond them too, and the "constitutionalism" invoked in the Ordinances to restrain the king supposedly in the interests of the "people." The episcopate was anxious to support measures which prevented the king from acting in an arbitrary fashion, but when Winchelsey was succeeded by Reynolds there was no individual with sufficient moral authority to stand up to the king. The concept of imposing the Ordinances on a reluctant monarch was shown not to be viable, while the barons were for the most part selfish and greedy even while they advocated "constitutional ideas." There were exceptions, even here, Pembroke unquestionably being one. His unexpectedly early death removed an influence that has been regarded as generally beneficial.

Lancaster's death ushered in a period of opportunity for concerted action, and for responsible rule. Neither of these desiderata was obtained. This was hardly surprising in view of Edward's previous behaviour. The rigour of the king's measures to suppress the rebels has often been criticized. Contrariants, it has been argued somewhat questionably, had been forced into revolt, while, more justifiably, bishops resisted what they felt to be severe encroachments on the liberties of the Church. Against this view it may be observed that open rebellion was one that merited condign punishment rather than temporary imprisonment with subsequent pardon. Erstwhile rebels who were allowed to live to fight another day, such as Roger Mortimer, Robert de Wateville, Thomas Gurney, and a host of others, were to be the instruments of Edward of Caernarfon's downfall or death.[12]

The king faltered in unkingly fashion when it came to his obligation of homage in France, failed abysmally to mount a single successful Scottish expedition, and allowed a small caucus to direct his administration. In view of the manifest threats to his kingdom to the modern observer it must appear feckless of Edward to spend the spring months of 1326 at Kenilworth donating articles of silver to the Despensers and, in June, to be distributing valuable velvet cloth to the earl of Arundel, the younger Despenser, and Bishop Stapeldon.[13] There was much lawlessness, though this is difficult to quantify, nor can one make reliable comparisons with other periods. Money was amassed, but put to no good purpose, and when Isabella's invasion came few could be found to defend the king. He considered it prudent to desert a capital that exploded into violent reaction against his ministers. His abandonment of London and subsequent failure to remain in a well-provisioned and eminently defensible Caerphilly Castle, in the hope of a more favourable turn of events, were his final mistakes. He became no more than a *roi fainéant* meandering aimlessly with a minuscule band of fugitives. Lacking any plan, his will to survive evaporated: an unexpected denouement that initially took his queen by surprise. From that moment his ultimate fate was sealed.

Personal factors have been considered an important, even an overriding element in the downfall of Edward. His style of kingship was not calculated to attract a following any more than that of Richard II. Faced with many similar difficulties Richard was to develop a "vigorous new kingship" intended to enhance the "prestige and authority" of monarchy. Although Edward had a corresponding anxiety to set himself apart with the aid of the holy oil of St. Thomas, his reputation was of a man with unkingly pursuits. Richard's attempts to bolster his position were unavailing. In the same manner as his great-grandfather his kingdom fell away before a determined opponent.[14] Admittedly Edward faced military, social, economic and climatic problems in abundance, but it was the character of the king himself that proved the crucial factor in the collapse of his rule. His failings were matched not merely by the selfishness of most of the barons but also by their lack of statesmanship. As for the Church, Archbishop Reynolds, whose role should have been that of principal councillor, with a responsibility for Edward's spiritual and temporal welfare, acted throughout the reign with excessive caution, anxious above all not to cross the king or his government. Thus, except on rare occasions the bishops manifestly lacked leadership. Some acted individually and suffered in consequence.

Without question Edward faced difficulties not of his own making, but he dealt with them inadequately, sporadically and with vacillation. He could inspire little military confidence, despite earlier somewhat romantic hopes, and only occasionally did his attention to business merit favourable comment, in itself an indication of his usual demeanour. His excessive reliance on a small caucus, notably on his "favourites," Piers Gaveston and the younger Hugh Despenser, quite apart from the question of any sexual relationship, were certain to cause problems with those who felt that they had a right to share in counselling the king, or who were held in thrall by recognizances – a system institutionalized by the younger Despenser.

In certain spheres the government of Edward had a measure of success, or partial success. Financially Edward I left his son a heavy debt. During the course of the reign this was transformed into a substantial surplus – despite the loss of income from the northern counties. What is not so clear is the purpose of such accumulation of wealth. The reverse side of the coin was disregarded. Some of this wealth was acquired by means calculated to brand as public enemies those ministers who were entrusted with its gathering. The outcome was that it was left in various safe deposits to be squandered by Isabella and Mortimer. As for administrative reform – the work of such dedicated civil servants as Stapeldon, Belers, and others – much of it was devoted to a pointless accretion rather than to ensuring the long-term solvency of the nation's finances or permitting the king to live adequately of his own, a course frequently enjoined upon him and other monarchs, but seldom if ever heeded.

The "reign", or regency, of Isabella and Mortimer began with a mixture of euphoria and foreboding. Once those men who had angered the queen – and doubtless Mortimer – had suffered vengeful punishment, no pogrom followed. The change of king was achieved with an outward semblance of legality, or quasi-legality. Yet, while Edward of Caernarfon remained alive, there was always the possibility that he might escape. Various incidents bear witness to the fact that there were still men willing to risk their lives for him, even though they were neither great in number nor politically powerful. His temporary release from Berkeley was achieved by a strangely heterogeneous and unremarkable band of sympathizers. The incident is more a reflection of the weakness of security at Berkeley than of the strength of his supporters. Mortimer kept very much in the background, concealing his hand, but in the nature of things he could not permanently control the young king, as he for the most part seems to have controlled Isabella, unless he were to resort to physical constraint. His relationship with the queen was not one that could be overlooked by churchmen, though few hints of their unfavourable reaction are to be found, fewer perhaps than those against Edward's alleged homosexual practices.

The unity of those who assisted in Edward's overthrow was soon fractured. The idea of a council of twelve (or of fourteen) became a dead letter. Henry of Lancaster, effectively isolated, was propelled into an ill-advised quasi-rebellion that fizzled out, fortunately without bloodshed. John Stratford, one of the able men who had master-minded the process of Edward II's dispossession, felt his life to be threatened, while the indefatigable Orleton, after a brief period of office and some diplomatic activity to interpret events for the papacy, retired to his diocese. Henry Burghersh, the Lincoln diocesan, rose to fill the clerical vacuum. The government sought to disencumber itself by concluding a disadvantageous treaty with the French and securing at last a "permanent peace" with the Scots, which left a substantial number of disinherited, a source of future trouble. However sensible it may appear to modern eyes, this was prodigiously unpopular at the time – decades of effort had been dissipated at a stroke. At home would-be supporters of Edward of Caernarfon were flushed out by trickery, a process which brought about the callous and needless death of the new king's uncle, the earl of Kent. The nature of Mortimer's long-term intentions must remain a mystery, though there were rumours that he had designs on the Crown. Despite its efforts at conciliating the country's old foes, the regime that he dominated was neither successful overall nor able to command a strong following. It fell unrepented as a result of a *coup d'état* carried out by a small group pledged to release Edward III from tutelage. The new and militarily glorious reign of Edward III could begin.

As for Edward of Caernarfon – flawed king that he was – he continued to inspire spiritual devotion, a devotion fostered by St Peter's Abbey for the increased financial advantages that the performance of miracles and consequent canonization could be expected to bring. Richard II visited the tomb of his ancestor in August 1386 and Br William Brut, a Gloucester monk, was for many years engaged in forwarding the process at the Curia. Yet even the efforts of the archbishop of York, Richard Scrope, destined to suffer execution as a traitor to Richard's supplanter, Henry IV, failed to prevail upon Pope Urban VI. There was to be no successful outcome for Edward even in death.[15]

Appendices

Two Accounts of the Deposition of Edward II

Gervase continuator (Canterbury based?)
TCC R.5 41 fos. 125^r (124)–6^r
Parliamentum London. rege absente [marginal rubric]
Eodem tempore vii^o Idus Januarii [4 January 1327] incepit parliamentum London. absente Rege in presencia Regine et filii sui, ubi Londonienses fecerunt sibi iurare episcopos, comites et barones similiter et milites et quotquot ibi erant. Et archiepiscopus Cant. antequam voluerunt ipsum in amiciciam recipere optulit eis .l. dolia vini et postea iuramentum fecit. In isto parliamento ex unanimi assensu episcoporum et procerum et tocius populi depositus est dominus Edwardus Rex Anglie secundus [MS ii^{us}] a gubernacione terre sue, et filius suus primogenitus Edwardus dux Acquitann. subrogatus est, ut sequitur.

Deposicio Regis Edwardi secundi [marginal rubric]
Forma deposicionis Regis Edwardi Anglie post conquestum secundi
Memorandum quod die Sancti Hillarii episcopi et confessoris [13 January] anno dominice Incarnacionis M^l CCCXXVI^o in parliamento apud Westmonasterium prelatorum et procerum fere tocius regni mutuo tractatu prehabito in palacio regio in aula magna Westm. acta sunt hec subscripta coram prelatis et magnatibus regni in communi aula convenientibus prelibata. Primo, dominus Rogerus Mortimer, cui dictum fuerat ex parte magnatum quod illud quod ordinatum fuerat populo pronunciaret, se excusavit dicendo se non debere culpari de iure super huiusmodi pronunciacione pro eo quod communi omnium assensu sibi fuerat hoc iniunctum. Retulit igitur coram populo quod inter magnates ita fuerat unanimiter concordatum quod Rex regni gubernaculum amodo non haberet quia insufficiens et procerum regni destructor et ecclesie sancte contra iuramentum suum et coronam malo consilio adquiescens fuit. Et ideo primogenitus eius dux Acquitann. pro eo regnaret si populus preberet assensum. Et respondit dominus T[homas] de Wak. sursum manus extendens, *dico pro me nunquam regnabit*. Et dominus episcopus Herefordie accepit pro themate illud Proverbiorum xiii^o capitulo [Proverbs 11:13] *Ubi non est gubernator populus corruet*. Quo proposito causam destina-

cionis sue et aliorum magnatum ad Regem apud castrum de <124ᵛ> Kenyng-
worth et qualiter Regem alloquebatur evidenter exposuit. Premisso enim sue
locucionis exordio, videlicet *Audi preces populi tui* Paralipom. iio capitulo viᵒ [2
Paralipomenon 6:21], Regi multos et magnos defectus et intollerabiles in suo
regimine patefecit, videlicet quod malo consilio et proditorio adhesit, quod eciam
proceres regni destruxit et terras corone sue, quas ei pater suus rex Anglie illustris Edwardus integras reliquerat, miserabiliter amiserat. Unde placuit prelatis et
proceribus regni filium suum in regni gubernaculo substituere loco sui si ipse
suum preberet assensum. Qui licet respondebat quod tali consilio quale ei magnates ordinaverant utebatur, tamen factorum suorum penitens, hiis que nuncii ipsi
postulaverant suum assensum exhibebat, et homagia magnatum sibi prius facta et
tunc ei reexhibita adnullabantur. Subsequenter dominus Wynton. episcopus cupi-
ens alloqui populum sic exorsus est, *Capud meum doleo*, iiiio Regum capitulo
iiiiᵒ [4 Kings 4:19], et protractando per caput ipsum regem qui est caput regni
intelligens, pro malo illius capitis gubernaculo se dolere affirmabat et infirmi-
tatem capitis huius in sui dolore retorquebat, iuxta illud poeticum *Cui capud
infirmum cetera membra dolent*, et alia multa indecencia et mala ecclesie Dei et
regno illata aperte repetens, filium suum primogenitum unanimi procerum assensu in regni gubernaculo fore substituendum concludebat, si populus huic prelatorum et procerum ordinacioni conniveret. Quo facto dominus T[homas] de Wak.
extensis brachiis et vibratis manibus a populo quesivit si huic ordinacioni con-
sentiret. et idem voce clamosa pariter acclamabat. Tandem dominus archiepiscopus Cantuarensis sic incepit alloquendo populum *Vox populi vox Dei*, hec verba
in gallico exponendo coram omni populo inquit: *Dilectissimi, bene noscis quod
variis oppressionibus iam per Regem et suos malos consiliarios tempore diuturno
afflicti estis. Et iccirco ad Deum pro remedio habendo sedulo acclamastis. Unde
instanti ipse vox vestra exaudita est ut patet quia ex omni[um] mag <125ʳ> natum
unanimi consensu dominus Rex Edwardus a gubernaculo regni privatus est et filius ipsius in loco eius subrogatus si unanimiter consentitis, ita tamen quod sano
consilio sapientum virorum regni sui adherat expositaque Regis insufficiencia ut
prius et gravaminibus ecclesie Dei et regni per ipsum illatis.* Quod audiens, populus universus unanimi consensu rursus manus ut prius extendentes clamabat,
Fiat, fiat, amen.
Homagia Regi Edwardo secundo reexhibita.
[The text of the renunciation, printed in Fryde, *Tyranny and Fall*, pp. 234-5, is
close, apart from orthographical variations, to the marginally better text printed
in *Rot. Parl. Inediti*, p. 101.]

Historia Roffensis, fos. 49ʳ-50ʳ
BL Cotton MS Faustina B. V

In crastino Epiphanie videlicet die Mercurii [7 January 1327] apud Westmonasterium omnes prelati, comites, barones atque populus in multitudine magna et

precipue cives London. cum magno strepitu ad parliamentum Regine regnantis convenerunt. In quo per Her[e]fo[r]d. episcopum adherentibus sibi multis aliis episcopis propositum fuit quod si regina regi adhereret occideretur ab eo, et tandem quesitum fuit quem mallent regnare, patrem regem al[iter] filium, et hoc primo die parliamenti. Et congregatis in parliamento <49ᵛ> per eundem episopum iniunctum fuit quod quilibet ad suum hospicium iret et in crastino post sumpcionem cibi et potus omnes potati redirent et questioni episcopi responderent, hora tercia. Quibus redeuntibus iterato proposita eadem questione quidam ex habundancia cordis, quidam metu ducti, nonnulli tacite propter metum London[iensium] questioni respondere nolentes, tandem una voce omnium filius in Regem sublimatur, factis sibi homagiis in magnam aulam novum Regem duxerunt, dicentes *Ecce rex vester*. Archiepiscopus Cantuarensis W[alterus] puplice predicavit *Vox populi vox Dei*. Wynton. episcopus addidit *Cuius capud infirmum cetera membra dolent*, Her[e]ford. subdidit *Ve terre cuius rex puer est*. Et pace facta in populo per T[homam] Wake et London[ienses] sibi adherentes *Ave rex in excelsis* proclamatur. In qua proclamacione episcopus Roffensis stans in excelsis cum aliis prelatis et maioribus regni, quia non cecinit cum aliis nec consentit canere *Gloria laus et honor* Regi novo male est depressus et comminatus ad mortem. Episcopus Roffensis licet a iusticiariis ad faciendum fidelitatem Regi sicut ceteri prelati, nullam tamen fecit, sed misit archiepiscopum ad respondendum pro eo. Archiepiscopus Eboracensis, episcopi Londoniensis, Roffensis et Carliolensis cum aliis non consenserunt. Hiis itaque peractis missi sunt ad patrem qui fuit Rex, Londonensis, Eliensis et Herefordensis episcopi, duo comites, duo barones, de commitatibus civitatibus et quinque portibus certi nuncii vice omnium de regno apud Kelyngworth ubi Rex qui fuit in carcere et custodia comitis Lancastrie detentus fuit, ad reddendum sursum homagia, et reddiderunt, ubi rex qui fuit genibus provolutis manibus levatis peciit veniam de commissis et ut eum vivere sinerent et non occiderent humiliter peciit. Cui Herefordensis penitenti et veniam petenti severum durum et crudelem inrespondendo se ostendit. Homagiis sursum redditis Regi in custodia detento ad parliamentum London., nuncii redierunt. <50ʳ> Mox ad coronandum novum regem dies Dominicus in vigilia Purificacionis [1 February 1327] statuit.

A Summary of the Charges Against Mortimer Incorporated in the Rolls of Parliament

From Rot. Parl. 2, pp. 52–3.

1 At the Westminster Parliament held after the coronation it had been ordained that four bishops, four earls and six barons should remain near the king to counsel him. At all times there should be four of them in attendance: a bishop, an earl, and two barons at least. After the parliament Mortimer had accroached royal power and the government of the realm, and at his will had removed ministers in the king's household and elsewhere in the realm, and appointed instead men in agreement with him. He had placed John Wyard and others around the king to spy out his deeds and words. To such an extent was the king surrounded by his enemies that he could do nothing of his own will without being under surveillance.

2 When the father of the present king was at Kenilworth by ordinance of the peers, to live there in such a manner as appropriate, by accroachment to himself of royal power Mortimer had ordered that he should be removed to Berkeley Castle where by him and his men he was traitorously, feloniously and falsely murdered.

3 By writ under the great seal, he forbade any to come in arms to the parliament at Salisbury; in contravention of which ordinance he and his supporters (covyne) themselves arrived armed. On that account the earl of Lancaster and others did not come. Also, when the prelates were assembled for parliament in a house, Mortimer with armed men broke in and threatened them on peril of life and limb should any say or do anything against his will. In the parliament, by accroachment of royal power, he made the king create him earl of the March with many lands, in disinheritance of the king and crown. Subsequently he and his coven led the king to Winchester, where Lancaster and other peers had come towards the Salisbury parliament; whereupon the latter, to avoid anything contrary to the reverence due to the king, had returned to their own lands, regretting the fact that they could not speak to or counsel the king as they ought.

4 Mortimer by the same royal power made the king conduct a chevauche against the earl of Lancaster and other peers, who were required to be near the

king to counsel him. They used such force that the said earl and others of his company who desired the profit of king and kingdom, submitted to the king's grace, saving life and limb, and their inheritance. They were committed to so high a ransom as to extend to half the value of their lands; others were forced to leave the realm, their lands seized, contrary to Magna Carta and the law of the land.

5 Mortimer, knowing that the father of the king was dead and buried, with others deceived the earl of Kent, who desired to know the truth, into thinking he was still alive. And by every way he knew, by means of royal power he apprehended the said earl at the parliament of Winchester and had him put to death.

6 He made the king give him, his children, and his supporters, castles, towns, manors, franchises in England, Ireland and Wales to the detriment of the crown.

7 By letters under seal sent to many great knights and others, he ordered them to come to the king and then charged them to go to Gascony, where they were to seize fines and ransoms to his profit and those of his followers.

8 He maliciously brought discord between the former king and the queen mother by suggesting that were she to come to him she would be killed by a knife or murdered in some other way. By this and other subtleties he prevented the queen from coming to her husband to the great dishonour of the king's father and the queen mother, thus threatening great future harm to the realm, which God forbid.

9 He had taken for himself and his companions limitless royal treasure, in money and jewels, to the king's destruction, since he had nothing with which to pay or on which to live.

10 He had taken for himself and his supporters (de sa alliance) the twenty thousand marks from Scotland paid for peace, nothing of which came to the king's profit.

11 He exacted prises in the realm as if he were king, and with his company doubled the number of those in the household of the king and the queen, to the destruction of the people, and without making any payment other than as they thought fit.

12 He made the king grant upwards of two hundred charters to those in Ireland who had killed the magnates (grantz) and others of that land, who were of the king's allegiance (foi). The king should rather in reason have avenged their deaths than pardoned them contrary to the statute and the agreement of parliament.

13 He compassed to destroy those who succoured the king and who were most secret with him. In the presence of the queen mother, the bishops of Lincoln (Burghersh) and Salisbury (Wyville) and others of the council, the very Friday before he was taken in the middle of the night, he had asserted that these confidants were his foes intent on the destruction of the queen mother and of himself, and that the word of the king should not be believed before his own (la parole le roi ne poeit estre creu a contraire de son dit).

Maps
and
Genealogical Tables

ORKNEY

• Elgin

KILDRUMMY
• Aberdeen

The Mounth
METHVEN
Scone • St. Andrews

Stirling
• Bothwell
LOUDOUN
HILL
Ayr
GALLOWAY
Edinburgh
Dunbar
Berwick
River Tweed
Roxburgh
The Forest

Rathlin Island

Caerlaverock
Lanercost Pr.
Carlisle
Newcastle-
upon-Tyne
Solway Firth
Skinburness

MAN

SCOTLAND IN THE FOURTEENTH CENTURY

Rathlin Island

• Coleraine

• Larne

Carrickfergus

ULSTER

• Faughert
• Dundalk
• Louth
• Ardee
Kells • • Drogheda
CONNACHT
Roscommon •
Loughsewdy •
• Trim

• Dublin

Athenry •

LEINSTER

• Kildare
• Newcastle
• Castlekevin
• Wicklow

Castledermot

• Limerick
• Kilkenny

River Shannon

• Tipperary

• Wexford

MUNSTER

Youghal •

IRELAND IN THE FOURTEENTH CENTURY

THE PURSUIT AND CAPTURE OF SIR THOMAS GURNEY

KEY Sir Thomas Gurney's escape route from Berkeley   ···->···->
     Route taken by Sir William Thweng and the captive Gurney   ·······>·······>
  1 Gurney imprisoned at Burgos.
  2 Arrest of Gurney at Naples.
  3 Gurney dies at Bayonne after illness unsuccessfully treated by his captors.
  4 His body embalmed prior to shipment from Bordeaux to Sandwich.
  5 Thweng makes landfall at Tynemouth and report to Edward III at Berwick.

THE SUPPOSED JOURNEYINGS OF EDWARD OF CAERNARFON

KEY Edward of Caernarfon's supposed route   ·······>·······>·······>·······>

1 Burial of the body of King Edward II at St. Peter's Abbey, Gloucester.
2 The route adopted assumes that Edward of Caernarfon would have travelled from Ireland to Sandwich by sea rather than landing on the west coast and following the more dangerous overland route. The Fieschi letter merely states that he returned (redivit) to England and touched (applicuit) at Sandwich before crossing to Sluys.
3 Edward meets Pope John XXII at Avignon.
4 Edward makes a pilgrimage to the shrine of the Three Kings at Cologne. Interestingly the sole dedication to the Magi in England appears to have been the chapel, founded in 1504 and still surviving, attached to John Foster's hospital in Bristol.
5 Edward III made vicar of the Empire by Louis IV in September 1338.
6 Manuele de Fieschi promoted bishop of Vercelli in 1343.

ENGLAND

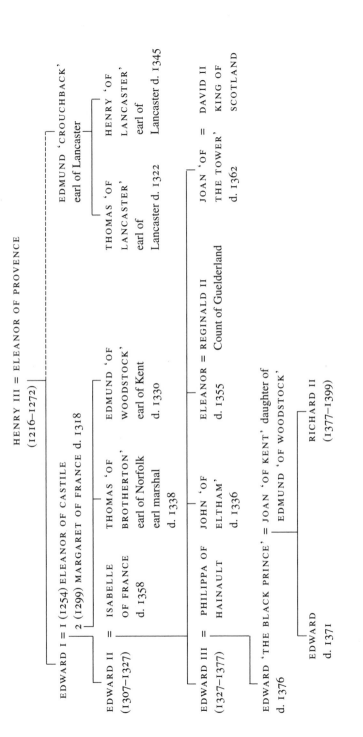

HENRY III = ELEANOR OF PROVENCE
(1216–1272)

EDWARD I = 1 (1254) ELEANOR OF CASTILE
2 (1299) MARGARET OF FRANCE d. 1318

EDMUND 'CROUCHBACK'
earl of Lancaster

EDWARD II
(1307–1327)

ISABELLE
OF FRANCE
d. 1358

THOMAS 'OF
BROTHERTON'
earl of Norfolk
earl marshal
d. 1338

EDMUND 'OF
WOODSTOCK'
earl of Kent
d. 1330

THOMAS 'OF
LANCASTER'
earl of
Lancaster d. 1322

HENRY 'OF
LANCASTER'
earl of
Lancaster d. 1345

EDWARD III
(1327–1377)

PHILIPPA OF
HAINAULT

JOHN 'OF
ELTHAM'
d. 1336

ELEANOR = REGINALD II
d. 1355   Count of Guelderland

JOAN 'OF   =   DAVID II
THE TOWER'   KING OF
d. 1362   SCOTLAND

EDWARD 'THE BLACK PRINCE' = JOAN 'OF KENT' daughter of
d. 1376   EDMUND 'OF WOODSTOCK'

EDWARD
d. 1371

RICHARD II
(1377–1399)

FRANCE

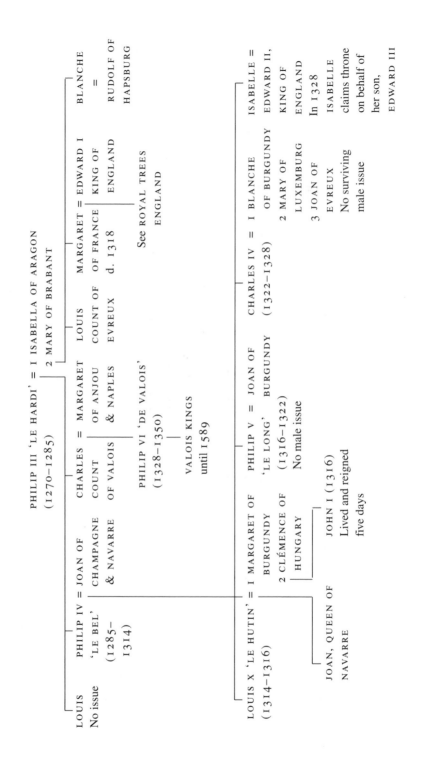

PHILIP III 'LE HARDI' = 1 ISABELLA OF ARAGON
(1270–1285) 2 MARY OF BRABANT

LOUIS
No issue

PHILIP IV = JOAN OF
'LE BEL' CHAMPAGNE
(1285– & NAVARRE
1314)

CHARLES = MARGARET
COUNT OF ANJOU
OF VALOIS & NAPLES

PHILIP VI 'DE VALOIS'
(1328–1350)

VALOIS KINGS
until 1589

LOUIS
COUNT OF
EVREUX

MARGARET = EDWARD I
OF FRANCE KING OF
d. 1318 ENGLAND

See ROYAL TREES
ENGLAND

BLANCHE
=
RUDOLF OF
HAPSBURG

LOUIS X 'LE HUTIN' = 1 MARGARET OF
(1314–1316) BURGUNDY
2 CLÉMENCE OF
HUNGARY

JOAN, QUEEN OF
NAVARRE

JOHN I (1316)
Lived and reigned
five days

PHILIP V = JOAN OF
'LE LONG' BURGUNDY
(1316–1322)
No male issue

CHARLES IV = 1 BLANCHE
(1322–1328) OF BURGUNDY
2 MARY OF
LUXEMBURG
3 JOAN OF
EVREUX
No surviving
male issue

ISABELLE = EDWARD II,
KING OF
ENGLAND

In 1328
ISABELLE
claims throne
on behalf of
her son,
EDWARD III

Notes

CHAPTER ONE

1 *Ann. Waverley*, p. 401; *Ann. Wigorn.*, p. 490; *Ann. Osney/Wykes*, pp. 295–6; *Flores* 3, p. 64; *Scalacronica*, ed. Stevenson, p. 109; *Lanercost*, pp. 113–14, *Guisborough*, p. 222. Payments to the poor of nine pounds at birth and of ten pounds at baptism are recorded in PRO E101/351/15.

2 Edwards, "Castle Building," pp. 43–5; Taylor, "Birth of Edward of Caernarvon," pp. 256–61; "Caernarvon Castle," pp. 9–10; *Studies* ("The Date of Caernarvon Castle"), pp. 129–38. Accounts for the new work from 24 June 1283 until after Queen Eleanor's departure on 20 August 1283 are in two rolls: PRO E101/3/29. /351/9.

3 *Flores* 3, p. 59 (s.a. 1283), cited Taylor, *Studies* ("The Castle of St. Georges d'Esperanche"), p. 38. Cf. *Ann. Waverley*, p. 401, which claims that it was the body "magni imperatoris nobilis Constantini." It was Constantine Chlorus, father of Constantine the Great whose body was reputedly found at Segontium. But see *William Worcestre Itineraries*, pp. 44–5 and nn.; also Dumville, "Sub-Roman Britain," pp. 173–92.

4 The king's genealogical tree, concocted for his claim to Scottish overlordship, is in Bodl. Lib. MS Bodl. Rolls 3, apart from two final membranes in BL Cotton MS Galba Ch. XIV 4. There was much borrowing from Geoffrey of Monmouth.

5 *Glastoniensis Cronica*, pp. 246–9; *Chronicle of Glastonbury*, pp. 242–7 (cap. 129); *Giraldus Cambrensis* 4, pp. 47–51; 8, pp. 126–9 (in greater detail). According to *Coggeshall*, p. 35, the tombs had already been opened in 1291. Treharne, *Glastonbury Legends*, is critical of the finds.

6 Taylor, *Studies*, p. 26 ("Castle-Building in Thirteenth-Century Wales and Savoy"); *King's Works* (ed. Colvin) 1, pp. 370–1. The walls of Caernarfon and Constantinople are illustrated side by side in plates 18a and b, c, d, in *Studies*, and plate 15 in *King's Works* (ed. Colvin).

7 Powel, *Princes of Wales*, pp. 376–7; Stow, *Annales* (1601), pp. 309–10.

8 Powicke, *Thirteenth Century*, pp. 400–6; EC, p. 60; *Littere Wallie* (text of the

treaty of Montgomery), pp. 1–4; Edwards, *Principality of Wales*, pp. 5–8; Walker, "The Welsh War of 1294–5," in *Book of Prests*, pp. xxvi–liii, App. D, pp. 226–7.

9 *Ann. Dunst.*, p. 313. The "Alfonso psalter," BL Add. MS 24686, was exhibit no. 357 in the Age of Chivalry Exhibition (*Catalogue*, p. 355); also Parsons, *Court of Eleanor*, pp. 36–7.

10 *EC*, p. 8, citing BL Add. MS 7965, fo. 3r, and *Liber Quotidianus*, p. 20 (SA MS 119, p. 25). Many other examples of royal offerings at home and abroad on Edward's behalf are in *RWH* 1 and 2, index s.v. "Edward of Carnarvon."

11 *EC*, p. 9, with details of the prince's journey from Caernarfon to his father at Chester and for the repairs of the young Edward's carriage and those of his sisters, from PRO E101/351/12 m.2 (E372/130/m.6), SC6/1170/12/m.5.

12 *EC*, p. 9; *CCR 1307–1313*, pp. 264, 341, 510, 581–2; *Letters*, pp. 46–7; Bodl. Lib. Tanner MS 197, fo. 54ʳ (1312). She is apparently the "Alicia de la Grave" mentioned as "berceresse" or "rocker" in Johnstone, "Wardrobe and Household of Henry," p. 390 and n. 4. See also Parsons, *Court of Eleanor*, p. 107 and n. Later she was attached to Queen Isabella's chamber: Blackley and Hermansen, *Household Book*, index s.v. "Legrave."

13 *EC*, p. 23: PRO E101/352/8, /16, now in *RWH* 2, pp. 414–16, 419–22, especially nos. 3432, 3455 (E372/144 m. 18); Green, *Princesses* 2, p. 201.

14 *Age of Chivalry*, pp. 361–6 nos. 368–79; Galloway, *Eleanor of Castile and Her Monuments*; *King's Works* (ed. Colvin) 1, plate 35; RCHM *Westminster*, plate 186; Parsons, *Court of Eleanor*, pp. 23–7, 132–3.

15 *EC*, p. 24 (from PRO SC8/16/170). This is dated from Ludgershall 1 September [1286–91] in *L&I* 15.

16 PRO E101/355/30 (single membrane), expenses of Queen Margaret and the Lord Edward 3–26 November 1299. Listed in Johnstone, "Household and Wardrobe Accounts," p. 41.

17 *Letters*, p. 70 (no. 285). Agnes "dame de Offali et Bailluel" married firstly Hugh of Balliol.

18 The significance of Lancaster's appointment (he had lost the county of Champagne as a consequence of Philip IV's marriage to the heiress) is emphasized by Johnstone, "Ponthieu," pp. 447–8, who provides a description of the county and of its administration from original records.

19 Johnstone, "Ponthieu," pp. 448–9. These accounts are among the "Ancient Miscellanea" of the King's Remembrancer: PRO E101/156/1ff. *Guide*, p. 50.

20 Johnstone, "Ponthieu," pp. 449–52.

21 Stubbs, *Charters*, p. 432, citing *Hemingburgh* 2, p. 121 (as *Guisborough*, pp. 289–90). *Langtoft*, pp. 287–93, also describes the incident. Denton, *Winchelsey*, chapters 3–4, deals with the archbishop's activities between 1294 and 1297, and denies that he was in any real sense the leader of a lay opposition.

22 *EC*, p. 35, *Guisborough*, p. 291. Cf. *Cotton*, pp. 325–7.

23 *HBC*, p. 38.

24 *EC*, p. 36; *Canterbury Register Winchelsey*, pp,. 203–4; *Rishanger*, p. 179,
    in common with *Nicholai Trevet Annales*, p. 365, provides only five names.
25 *EC*, pp. 36–42; *Cotton*, pp. 337–9; *Guisborough*, pp. 290–4, 308–13. Stubbs,
    Charters, pp. 482–94, for the *Confirmatio Cartarum* and the much disputed *De
    Tallagio non concedendo*. Graves, *Bibliography*, p. 508, lists the material on this
    topic up to about 1974. The fullest account of the 1297–98 crisis is that of Prest-
    wich in his introduction to *Documents*.
26 These lands are enumerated by Johnstone, *EC*, pp. 55–63, by Edwards,
    Principality of Wales, pp. 11–16, by Tout, *Chapters* 2, 169–70, more recently by
    Jones, "Princes and Principality of Wales," pp. 61–3 (with map). For West Wales
    see Lloyd, *Story of Ceredigion*. The list of those who performed homage and fealty
    (PRO E313/8/31) is in *CPR 1343–1345*, pp. 227–34. Johnstone, *EC*, p. 60, suggests
    by analogy with the events of 1343 that Edward was invested with the sword of the
    Chester earldom, and for the principality, a circlet – possibly that taken from Lly-
    welyn ap Gruffydd ("Arthur's crown"?) – a ring, and a silver rod. *HBC*, p. 486; R.
    H. Morris, "The Investiture of the Prince of Wales," pp. 220, 232–3 (1301 charter).
27 PRO E101/353/18, described in *EC*, pp. 25–30.
28 EC, p. 65; PRO SC11/729, which provides an extent of the manor. RCHM *Hert-
    fordshire*, pp. 133–5. Remains of the house are now vestigial.
29 *EC*, p. 26, provides an itinerary from PRO E101/353/18.
30 Ibid.; Du Boulay, "Pipe Roll Account during Pecham Vacancy." For the principal
    royal residences see *King's Works* (ed. Colvin).
31 Barrow, *Bruce*, p. 143, states that Edward Bruce was a member of the prince's
    household (citing "ibid." [*Documents* 2, ed. Stevenson] no. 394[?], but see no.
    491). More precisely he was a prisoner. For the shifting allegiance of the Earls
    Malise of Strathearn at this time see Neville, "The Political Allegiance of the earls
    of Strathearn," pp. 134–43.
32 *Letters*, pp. xxxvii–xxxviii, 11 (no. 45), and see n. 17 above. Their editor consid-
    ered that there were between six and seven hundred letters: ibid., p. xi. I have
    numbered them to 741 in accordance with the rubrics.
33 Ibid., p. 162 (nos. 728–30).
34 Ibid., pp. 36, 157 (nos. 135, 705). One of the justices approached was Ralph de
    Hengham. An Oliver Hengham is said to have been brought up with the prince.
    Parsons, *Court of Eleanor*, p. 155 n. 3.
35 Ibid., pp. 150, 156 (nos. 679, 700) and the editor's comments, p. xxvi. For
    Reynolds's holding of Ingram church see Wright, *Reynolds*, p. 362.
36 Ibid., p. 148 (no. 664).
37 Ibid., pp. 86–7 (no. 354) 142 (no. 640). *Canterbury Register Winchelsey*, pp.
    587–92, 897–8.
38 *Letters*, pp. 105 (no 436), 7 (no. 23); *CDS* 2, no. 1413, p. 369. Another example of
    Edward's aquatic activity occurs in SA MS 121, p. 62, when a "garcio" of the
    archbishop of Canterbury (Reynolds) arrived bearing a belt that Edward (then
    king) had lost in the Thames.

39 *Ann. Dunst.*, pp. 392–3. Purveyance was, of course, a perennial grievance against the great from the king downward.

40 *Letters*, p. 151 (no. 682).

41 Ibid., p. 124 (no. 544). She may have been professed 15 August 1286 with the infant Lord Edward present. Green, *Princesses* 2, p. 409.

42 *Letters*, p. 115 (no. 493); *HBC*, p. 551.

43 Ibid., p. 70 (no. 286). John de Weston (the younger) seems to be identifiable as the marshal of Edward II's household in the 1320s. He had been maimed in royal service. A John de Haustede was appointed seneschal of Gascony in November 1327 temp. Edward III (he died 1336); Chaplais, *War of Saint-Sardos*, p. 257 n. 1; Tout, *Chapters* 2, p. 252 n. 1, 6 index s.v. "Weston"; Parsons, *Court of Eleanor*, pp. 35–8.

44 *Letters*, pp. 75, 116, 120 (nos. 304, 494, 517). *Le Neve* 4, p. 50 gives the date of Sinibaldi's collation as 31 July 1304.

45 *Letters*, p. 133 (no. 589).

46 Johnstone, "Wardrobe and Household Accounts," p. 42; PRO E101/370/30.

47 *Letters*, p. 61 (no. 240). For Joan's runaway marriage to the "unknown" Monthermer and the latter's subsequent career see Green, *Princesses* 2, pp. 342–59. That he was illegitimate is suggested by *Ann. Lond.*, p. 133.

48 *EC*, pp. 12–13; Johnstone, "Wardrobe and Household of Henry," p. 397 n. 3.

49 Tout, *Chapters* 2, pp. 42–3; Johnstone, "Wardrobe and Household of Henry," p. 393. For the last year there is a useful additional source, the *Book of Prests*. Parsons, *Court of Eleanor*, points out (pp. 10 n. 29, 154) that five of that queen's household knights, John Besilles, Robert de Crévequer, Simon de Creye, Eustace de Hache (Hatch), and John de Hengham, appear in that of Edward in 1289.

50 Since the index to the *Book of Prests* is defective, it may be worth adding that I found expenses connected with the Lord Edward on pp. 63, 72, 74, 88, 97, 99, 103–5, 113, 127–8, 130, 135, 143, 158, 193, 205–8, 216 (from Walter Langton's enrolled account). William, the hunter of the king's son, going "extra curia" to Maresfield, Sussex, with twelve dogs, was paid at one shilling a day for eight days (p. 193). William de Bliburgh received £850 18s. 5d. (p. 135) for Edward's expenses according to twenty-seven schedules (*particulis*); for the twenty-second regnal year (1293–4) £799 14s. 41/2d.; for his trip to Paris that year, £23 19s. 8d.; and for the twenty-third regnal year, £1,919 6s. 11/2d. – a total of £2,473 2d. (pp. 205–6). Johnstone, *EC*, p. 69, gives the everyday expenses of Edward's household as £1,740 for 1302-03, while more than £3,900 was spent on "alms, necessaries, wages, and purchases of cloth, furs and jewels."

51 Tout, *Chapters* 2, pp. 167 and nn. 1–2; 174. At p. 169 n. 2 he lists the extant accounts (1301-07) of the "glorified wardrobe" of the prince.

52 Ibid., pp. 174 n. 1, 175–6.

53 *EC*, pp. 11–12.

54 Tout, *Chapters* 2, p. 175. Cf. *EC*, p. 71 n. 2. The same practice was followed when the Lord Edward was on campaign in 1299–1300, for which see SA MS 119.

55 Johnstone, "Wardrobe and Household Accounts," p. 42 and n. 2, from PRO
    E101/360/17; *EC*, pp. 75–6.

56 *EC*, pp. 13–17. The sole record so far discovered of Ferre as "magister" is in PRO
    E101/355/17. See also *Letters*, p. 36 (no.134), 117 (no. 504); Holinshed, *Chroni-
    cles* 2, p. 547, spread the sixteenth-century notion that Reynolds was Edward's
    tutor. Cf. Wright, *Reynolds*, p. 250 and n. 35. For the Ferre family see Parsons,
    Court of Eleanor, pp. 32–5 and index s.v.

57 New DNB, s.v.; Tout, *Chapters* 5, p. 242 n. 4; Putnam, *Shareshull*, pp. 138–9.

58 *Letters,* pp. xiii–xv. For Boudon: Tout, *Chapters* 6, index s.v.; Blackley and Her-
    mansen, *Household Book,* pp. xii–xiii and index s.v. In 1300 Boudon occurs as
    "ostiarius" of Edward's wardrobe arranging for its carriage from Stamford to York.
    SA MS 119, p. 56 (bis).

59 Tout, *Chapters* 6, index s.v.

60 Ibid., index s.v.; Cuttino, "Henry of Canterbury."

61 *Letters*, p. xiv; *HBC*, p. 351. Leek is mentioned in SA MS 119, p. 34, as being
    entrusted with offerings on the prince's behalf at a penny a day for 133 days from
    20 November 1299.

62 At which time the king paid four pounds for Lenham, who lay *in extremis*, SA MS
    120, p. 14.

63 *Letters*, p. xv; *CDS* 2, nos. 1249, 1413. For a biography of this clerk-physician see
    Emden, *Biog. Oxon,*, s.v. Sidesterne. He had been at the deathbed of Archbishop
    Pecham and is mentioned as the king's physician in 1310. *CPR 1307–1313*, pp.
    220, 268. In a letter of 1313 to the pope he is termed one: "qui complexionem nos-
    tram, ac corporis nostri statum prae omnibus aliis novit diligenter." *Foedera* 2 i, p.
    215.

64 Ibid. At the time of the king's attempt to cut down the prince's entourage Haustede
    and a John de Weston (a man of this name was one of the knights in the prince's
    household), designated "yeomen," were permitted to remain in his company. *EC*,
    p. 100 and see nn. 43 above, 65 below. For Dekinham's petition in parliament for
    the implementation of his charter: *Rot. Parl.* 2, p. 33.

65 *Letters*, pp.xix–xxiii; SA MS 119, p. 49; Tout, *Chapters* 6, index s.v. "Melton."
    Wright, *Reynolds*, seemingly was unaware of the alias Heyne, to be found in the
    Book of Prests, pp. 87, 104, and in *Ann. Lond.*, p. 229. There were two Robert de
    Haustedes (sometimes written Hallestede), the elder of whom died 1321–22. The
    younger, a man closely associated with Edward when king, died about 1330. He
    may be indicated here, though only in his early twenties. Cf. Parsons, *Court of
    Eleanor*, pp. 36–8. "Robert de Hallestede" is described as the prince's steward in a
    document of 1302 X 1304; *CDS* 5, no. 392 p.187; PRO SC1/28/78.

66 *Letters*, p. xxii.

67 Ibid., pp. xxiii–xxiv. For Bliburgh as keeper of the Lord Edward's wardrobe in
    1294–5, see *Book of Prests*, index s.v. A full account of his career is to be found in
    Tout, *Chapters*, especially 2, pp. 166–8, 178–80, and 6, index s.v. "Blyborough."

68· *Letters*, pp. xxiv–xxv.

69 Ullmann, "John of Salisbury's *Policraticus*," p. 522: "Despite the comprehensive-
ness of his doctrine John of Salisbury left but few traces of influence in his own
country." On the other hand, as a theorist he ranks high among those who study the
role of the monarch in the later Middle Ages. E.g. Myers, *Medieval Kingship*,
especially chapter 6.

70 Griscom's edition of *The Historia Regum* of Geoffrey of Monmouth also includes
a literal translation by R.E. Jones of a Welsh MS from Jesus College, Oxford, and
provides in Part 1 a valuable introduction which emphasizes (contrary to the common conception of scholars) the historical as well as the literary importance of
Geoffrey's work.

71 *EC*, pp. 64–5 and n. 5; *Letters*, pp. xlv–xlvi, 114 no. 490. Cf. BL Add. MS 22923,
fo. 5^r, for a record of the payment of twenty shillings to Roger de Croudere (his
sister Elizabeth's minstrel) for playing before Edward at Wetheral, 3 April 1307.
She had by then married (secondly) Humphrey de Bohun, earl of Hereford (ob.
1322).

72 See Studer, "An Anglo-Norman Poem by Edward II"; Smallwood, "Lament of
Edward II" (using also BL Royal MS 20 A III as a parallel text), and most recently
Valente, "The Lament of Edward II." Fabyan, *Chronicles*, pp. 430–2.

73 *EC*, p. 18, has detailed references. The primer, bought from William the book-
binder "ad opus domini Edwardi filii," cost two pounds. SA MS 119, p. 48. The
"book of romance" had belonged to Eleanor of Provence. Others are mentioned in
wardrobe accounts. Named by Green, *Princesses* 2, p. 284, they include *Roman de
Guillaume le Conquerant*, a chronicle, and Palladius Rutilius's *De re rustica* (SA
MS 119, p. 281) which, from what we know of his proclivities, would have interested Edward. Cavenaugh, "Royal Books," pp. 307–8, is dependent on *EC*.
Edward,when king, gave *Tristrem* (*Tristan*), a large book kept in the exchequer, to
the younger Despenser. SA MS 122, p. 92. Cf. *Canterbury Register Chichele* 2,
p.lvi and n. 8.

74 *EC*, p. 17 and n. 5, where his seeming attitude conflicts with the youthful addiction
to tournaments of Thomas and Henry of Lancaster (PRO E101/153/4; /353/18 mm.
3, 6). Contrary to the opinion of some scholars, tournaments were felt to be a useful form of practice for war. Pierre Dubois, when instructed by Philip IV to protest
against a papal bull condemning them, declared "que tout le monde se plaignait de
la bulle, et qu'il n'y avait pas de meilleure préparation à la croisade, dont le pape
invoqua les intérêts, que les turnois." See Petit, *Charles de Valois*, p. 229 (citing
Ch-V Langlois, *Revue historique* 41 [1889], pp. 84–91).

75 *EC*, p. 33; *Calendar of Letter-Book C*, pp. iii–v, 22–4; *Liber Custumarum* 1, pp.
71–7; *Parl. Writs* 1, pp. 278–9 nos. 13–17. Men from London were resident with
the Lord Edward for some time (PRO E372/147 m. 28).The *Book of Prests*, p. 97,
reveals that on an earlier occasion in 1294–95 while at Canterbury, Walter
Reynolds alias Heyne was allowed £20 10s. 8d. for the expenses of fifty crossbowmen and fifty archers in Edward's company for sixteen days from 7 October
(1294).

76 *EC*, pp. 41–2; *Documents*, ed. Prestwich, pp. 36–7; *Documents*, ed. Stevenson, 2
no. 489; Powicke, *Thirteenth Century*, p. 649; Haines, *John Stratford*, pp. 278–80.
For Tournai (1298): *Treaty Rolls* 1, pp. 143–5; *Foedera* 1 ii, pp. 885–6.

77 EC, p. 44; SA MS 119, pp. 33, 121, 126–7, 144, 169–70, 176.

78 SA MS 119, p. 60 (named prisoners); *Rishanger*, p. 440; *Langtoft*, p. 327;
Scalacronica, ed. Stevenson, pp. 112–13 and p. 111, map. 6 for the 1300-01 campaigns; ed. Maxwell, p. 23. Gaveston was in the field at this time. He was paid
forty marks for replacing his bay horse killed in the war, while the young Edward
received sixty shillings for the loss of a rouncey, or nag (SA MS 119, p. 138). See
Watson, *Under the Hammer*, pp. 107–8, and in general ibid., chapter 4.

79 *EC*, pp. 48–54; *Caerlaverock* (ed. Wright), pp. 17–18. Edward is not called Prince
of Wales, but his father is (ibid., p. 8), He bore his father's arms with a *bleu label*.
John de St John is addressed as "King's lieutenant and captain in Cumberland,
Westmorland, Lancashire and Annandale" in *CPR 1292–1301*, pp. 490–1, and in
SA MS 119, p. 140, he is termed captain of the March of Cumbria and Wales. For
his death: *CDS* 5, no. 292, pp.173–4.

80 *EC*, p. 54; Powicke, *Thirteenth Century*, p. 593: "on 30 October at Dumfries he
[Edward] had agreed to a truce with the Scots to last until Pentecost 1301."

81 Ashridge was originally a house of seven priest-brothers, re-endowed by the Black
Prince as a house of Bonshommes. Knowles and Hadcock, *Religious Houses*, p.
179; *EC*, p. 54; Midgley, *Ministers' Accounts*. For the topic of division of the body
see: Brown, "Death and the Human Body"; Bradford, *Heart Burial*. Eleanor of
Castile's viscera were buried in Lincoln Cathedral, her heart in a chapel of the
Dominicans' church in London, her body in Westminster Abbey. See *Lanercost*,
pp. 137–8 (incorporating an epitaph); Parsons, *Court of Eleanor*, pp. 16–17 and n.

82 *Lanercost*, p. 200; Barrow, *Bruce*, pp. 120–1; *CDS* 2, nos. 1191 – the source of the
"taming of the pride of the Scots" quotation, 1284. For the St Ninian incident see
CDS 2, no. 1225 p. 535 (transcript); also ibid. 5, p. 65, correcting the date to 25
September.

83 *EC*, pp. 87–8; Powicke, *Thirteenth Century*, pp. 653–4, describes the 1303 treaty
as "a breathing space in the interminable wrangle which the treaty of 1259 had
produced." Chaplais, after discussing Henry III's permitting an independent allod
(Gascony) to be transformed into a feudal fief, concludes: "Saint Louis pourait
bien se flatter d'avoir fait bon emploi des concessions territoriales faites a son
ancien adversaire." *Essays* II, "Le Traité de Paris de 1259," pp. 121–37; V, "La
Souveraineté du Roi de France en Guyenne," pp. 449–69. For the lengthy legal
negotiations, the processes of Montreuil, Périgueux and Agen, which followed
from the treaty of 1303 and from earlier ones, see Cuttino, *Diplomatic Administration*, chapter 3; Chaplais, *Essays* I, "Making of the Treaty of Paris."

84 *CDS* 2, nos. 1413 (PRO E101/363/18: account book of the controller of Prince
Edward's wardrobe 20 November 1302–20 November 1303), 1462, 1470, 1504;
Documents, ed. Stevenson, 2 nos. 631, 634, 640.

85 *Langtoft* 2, p. 348, writes of a two-pronged thrust. Barrow, *Bruce,* pp. 126–7, gives

an account of the campaigning and the king's itinerary for 1303-04, ibid., p. 125
map. 7. See also Watson, *Under the Hammer*, chapter 6; Fordun, *Chronica* 1, pp.
336–7; 2, p. 329, *CDS* 2, nos. 1396 (*Documents*, ed. Stevenson, 2 no. 625: transcript of the Elgin document), 1509, 1516 (PRO E101/365/12, the prince's household roll 20 November 1303–19 April 1304). See also Lydon, "Edward I, Ireland
and Scotland," pp. 43–61; chapters 9–10 below.

86 *CDS* 2, nos. 1413, 1516; Barrow, *Bruce*, pp. 128–30, 136–8; the citation in the text
is from p. 130. For the notarial instrument dated 24 July recording the surrender:
Foedera I ii, p. 966.

87 *EC,* pp. 94–5; Chaplais, *Essays* IV, "Le Duché-Pairie de Guyenne," pp. 135–8.
PRO C47/27/5 is the report of envoys sent to France to excuse the king's absence
and to express his regrets. This is published with brief commentary by Johnson,
"The homage for Guienne in 1304," pp. 728–9. See also *CDS* 5, no. 381 p. 186.
Edward I's response of 10 April 1204 and another letter of September of that year
are printed by Cuttino, "Memorandum Book," pp. 82–5.

88 *EC*, p. 94; *CCR 1302–1307*, p. 174; *CPR 1301–1307*, pp. 263–4; *Foedera* I ii, pp.
966–7.

89 Chaplais, *Essays* IV, "Le Duché-Pairie de Guyenne," pp. 137–8 and n. 12; Johnson, "The Homage for Guienne in 1304," pp. 728–9. See also n. 87 above.

90 *Foedera* I ii, p. 983; *CPR 1301–1307*, p. 424; *CDS* 2, nos. 1773, 1777, 1780 et
seq. For Comyn's murder *inter alia* : *Scalacronica*, ed. Stevenson, pp. 129–30 (in
detail), ed. Maxwell, pp. 28–30; Barbour, *Bruce* 2, ll. 31–6 (pp. 19, 388–9 nn.);
Guisborough, pp. 366–7; Smallwood, "An unpublished account." For the ceremonies at Scone on 25 and 27 March: Barrow, *Bruce*, pp. 150–2. *Ann. Lond.,* pp.
139–42, details the fate of Wallace at Westminster. Details of taxation at this time
are to be found in Harriss, *King, Parliament, and Public Finance*, chapters 1–5,
and Mitchell, *Taxation in Medieval England.*

91 Madox, *Exchequer* 1, pp. 613–4 and nn.; *Rishanger,* p. 229; *Flores* 3, p. 132,
duplicated in TCC MS R 5. 41, fo. 99^v (100); *Ann. Lond.*, p. 146.

92 Bodl. Lib., MS Laud Misc. 529, fo. 100^v; TCC MS R 5. 41, fo. 88^{r-v} (89), duplicating *Flores* 3, pp. 131–2; *Nicholai Trevet Annales*, p. 409; *Froissart* 1, ed. Luce,
p. 114 (see Maunde Thompson, *Chronicon*, Notes p. 179); *EC,* p. 106–9; Denholm
Young, *Papers*, p. 92 ("Feudal Society in the Thirteenth Century"); on the Arthurian cult, ibid. chapter 5 ("The Tournament in the Thirteenth Century"); and *inter
alia* for the numbers knighted: ibid., pp. 127–8 ("Song of Carlaverock"); Loomis,
"Edward I Arthurian enthusiast." For a more cautionary note: Powicke, *Thirteenth
Century,* pp. 515–16. Bodl. Lib., MS Lat. hist. c 4 (R) records the knighting of the
prince and of Gaveston. The household expenses for the relevant week were about
two and a half times those of the previous week (£167 12s 3d as against £65 8s.
2½d).

93 *EC*, p. 112; Barbour, *Bruce* 2, ll. 346–467 (pp. 28–31); *Nicholai Trevet Annales*,
pp. 409–10; *Flores* 3, p. 133; TCC MS R 5.41, fos. 99^v(100)–100^r; *CDS* 2, nos.
1786, 1789.

94 *EC*, p. 113; Barbour, *Bruce* 2, ll. 346–467 (pp. 28–31); *Nicholai Trevet Annales,*
   p. 409; *Rishanger*, p. 229; *Guisborough,* pp. 367–8. The prince's itinerary can be
   followed from 1–2 December 1305, when he was at Edgware and Langley, until
   his return to the latter place on 6 November 1306: Bodl. Lib. MS. Lat. hist. c 4.
   Denholm Young, *Papers,* p. 130 ("Song of Carlaverock") suggests that "commili-
   tones," the word used by Guisborough, could refer to some sort of *corps d'lites.* I
   have found the word in other contexts but suspect it to be a non-technical reference to what at one time were called "young bloods." For the naval forces see
   Stanford Reid, "Sea Power in the Anglo-Scottish War," especially pp. 7–14.

95 Barbour, *Bruce* 2, ll. 452–7 (p. 31).

96 *Rishanger,* p. 230.

97 Barbour, *Bruce* 2, ll. 71–6 (p. 58).

98 Barrow, *Bruce,* p. 161; *Scalacronica,* ed. Stevenson, pp. 131–2, ed. Maxwell, pp.
   32–3; Bower, *Scotichronicon* 2, pp. 233, 236, ed. Watt 6, pp. 322–3, 328–9; *CDS*
   2, nos. 1829, 1833.

99 Barbour, *Bruce* 3, ll. 721–63; 4, l. 1 (pp. 55–6); *EC*, p. 115; Barrow, *Bruce,* chapters 9–10 and maps 8–9, pp. 147, 167.

100 *Lanercost,* p. 205: "In omnibus istis factis non fuit rex Angliae et Scotiae in Sco-
   tia, sed filius suus cum exercitu supradicto. Rex autem, proper senectutem et
   debilitatem, lento gradu, ... appropinquavit cum regina versus marchiam Scotiae."
   EC, p. 117.

101 *EC*, p. 118; *Foedera* I ii, p. 1009; Richardson and Sayles, *Parliament,* pp. 430–1
   (Carlisle Parliament). Prince Edward had sent him (1302-03) by the hand of Walter Langton a magnificent choir cope embroidered with pearls. PRO E101/363/18,
   fo. 21ᵛ; *CDS* 2, no. 1413 (the earliest printed account) with this item at p. 369.

102 *EC*, p. 116; *CFR 1272–1307,* pp. 543–4.

103 *EC*, p. 117 (citing BL Add. MS 22923, fo. 14ᵛ). Barker, *Tournament,* pp. 135,
   167, citing the same MS, fos. 1ᵛ–2ᵛ, 7ᵛ, 8ʳ, 10ᵛ, 15ʳ.

104 *EC*, p. 126; *Lanercost,* p. 207; Barrow, *Bruce,* p. 173; Phillips, *Pembroke,* p. 24.
   Itinerary, ed. Safford, 3 p. 286.

105 *Scalacronica* ed, ed. Stevenson, p. 110, ed. Maxwell, pp. 5–6; *EC*, p. 31; Stones,
   "English Chroniclers and Scotland," pp. 324–8, remarking on the secrecy of the
   arrangements and the comparative silence of the chroniclers. The text of Birgham
   is in *Documents,* ed. Stevenson, 1 no. 108, and the matter is fully discussed by
   Reid, "Margaret Maid of Norway."

106 I owe the suggestion to Chaplais, "Some Private Letters of Edward I," p. 83 (citing *Les Registres de Nicolas IV*).

107 *EC*, pp. 32, 43; Powicke, *Thirteenth Century,* pp. 659–60, 664–5.

108 *Foedera* I ii, pp. 794–6, 894–5 et seq.; *Treaty Rolls* I, pp. 135–487 (nos. 358–70);
   Guisborough, pp. 317–22, 331–2; *Rishanger*, pp. 395–7, especially p. 396; Fawtier, *Capetian Kings,* p.154 (with an incorrect year for the marriage); Prestwich,
   Edward I, pp. 395–6, 521. Dubois in his *Summaria* advocated marriage alliances
   in preference to war, also the maintenance of royal jurisdiction. I am indebted to

Doherty, "Isabella," for pointing me towards the philosophical, though irritatingly
unspecific, Dubois. Keeler, *Geoffrey of Monmouth,* pp. 56–7, established the
source of Rishanger's account of the feast and prints parallel texts. Doherty discusses the situation in chapter 1 and prints at App. p. 332, document 1 (from
Arch. Nat. Paris J. 654 no. 8), in support of the idea that Isabella's marriage was
tied to the return of Gascony.

109 *Treaty Rolls* 1, pp. 154–66, nos. 384–95; *Foedera* 1 ii, pp. 952–4; *EC,* pp. 43, 88
and n. 2, 104, 119–20; *Letters,* pp. 143–5 (nos. 645–50); Powicke, *Thirteenth
Century,* p. 654.

110 *Letters,* pp. xlviii, 144–5 (no. 648): "ac matrimonium cum eadem per verba de
presenti pro nobis et nostro nomine contrahendi." For the similar appointment of
Henry de Lacy and Aymer de Valence in 1307, see *Foedera* 2 i, p. 12. Doherty,
"Isabella," chapter 1, traces the course of the marriage negotiations between 1298
and 1307. His overall thesis is that Edward I was dragging his feet in the matter.
Isabella appointed her proxies, including her uncle the count of Evreux, 3 December 1308. Ibid., p. 15, citing BN Coll. Brienne 7007, fo. 1.

111 *EC,* pp. 120–1; *Guisborough,* pp. 370–1; Richardson and Sayles, *Parliament,* pp.
436–7, especially p. 436 para. 2 (Carlisle Parliament). According to the newsletter
the cardinal was given extensive powers of correction in all dioceses, of hearing
confession and of granting absolution, even in the most horrible cases – excepting
vows of crusade and "great sins of religion" (heresy) – with authority to relax
penance imposed by the bishops. His excessive demand for procurations was
regarded as "outrageous."

112 Polistoire, fo. 232^r (BL Harl. MS 636). See fos. 232^r–3^v for the mini-biography.

113 *EC,* p. 42 (citing BL MS 7965, fo. 76^r). He was paid twelve pence a day apart
from four days during which he had been supplied with food.

114 BL Cotton MS Cleopatra D. IX, fos. 83–5 (printed Haskins, "Chronicle," pp. 73–81):
"accessit ad eum quidam Petrus de Gaualstona nomine, de eadem provincia oriundus
[i.e., Flandria *sic*], tantamque graciam coram rege invenit quod officium armigeri in
curia sua gessit familie regis ascriptus absque mora. Quem filius regis intuens in eum
tantum protinus amorem iniecit quod eum eo firmitatis [*recte* fraternitatis] fedus iniit
et pre ceteris mortalibus indissollubile dileccionis vinculum secum elegit et firmiter
disposuit innodare" (ibid., fo. 83^r, p. 75). Compare Bodl. Lib. MS Laud. Misc. 529,
Evesham version of Higden's *Polychronicon,* fo. 100^v. Pierre Chaplais has argued in
Piers Gaveston that the relationship between Edward and Gaveston is wholly explicable in terms of such a bond of fraternity. Had this been so it seems strange that the
concept was not commented upon favourably in mitigation of the king's conduct.

115 PRO E101/360/17 (the roll endorsed inaccurately[?] "anno 29"). See Johnstone,
"Wardrobe and Household Accounts," p. 42 and n.

116 *EC,* p. 116; *CFR 1272–1307,* pp. 543–4. The mandate in *CFR* points to Gaveston's interests in no fewer than ten counties.

117 *Letters,* p. 70 (no. 286). Letter to his sister Elizabeth, countess of Hereford, asking
for her intervention with the queen so that the latter might persuade her husband.

118 *Scalacronica*, ed. Stevenson, p. 131, ed. Maxwell, p. 33; *Guisborough*, pp. 382–3.

119 Moorman, "Edward I at Lanercost Priory," pp, 165, 171–2. On 4 March preparations were on foot for a move to Carlisle after over 22 weeks at the priory.

120 *Foedera* I ii, p. 1010.

121 *EC*, pp. 122–5, especially pp. 122–3.

122 *EC*, pp. 122–5; *Guisborough*, pp. 382–3: "Et apprehensis capillis utraque manu, dilaceravit eos in quantum potuit, et in fine lassus ejecit eum." Another chronicler perhaps confusing the later event, suggests that the proposed gift was the earldom of Cornwall. Haskins, "Chronicle" (BL Cotton MS Cleopatra D. IX), p. 75.

123 *EC*, p. 125, citing Edward's lavish gifts embellished with coats of arms for a forthcoming tournament. BL Add. MS 22923, fo. 10^v. For Piers's stay at Crécy May-July see ibid., fol 4^r, and for the itinerary of the prince at the time ibid., fo. 14^v. The conditions laid down for Gaveston's exile are in *Foedera* I ii, p. 1010; *CCR 1302–1307*, pp. 526–7.

124 *CCR 1302–1307*, pp. 506, 516, 530–1.

125 *EC*, pp. 97–8; *Ann. Lond.*, p. 138.

126 *Letters*, pp. xl–xliv, 30 (no. 113); *Abbreviatio Placitorum*, pp. 256–7.

127 *Letters*, pp. xl, 30 (no. 113); *EC*, p. 98: "If the itineraries of father and son are marked on a map containing colours, the faithfulness with which the prince carried out his expressed intention becomes visible."

128 *Letters*, pp. xliii–xliv, 31 (no. 114), 32 (nos. 119, 120), 60 (no. 239), 61 (no. 240), 74 (no. 299); *EC*, p. 99.

129 Galbraith, "St. Edmundsbury Chronicle," p. 75 (fo. 201^v): "Filius regis diucius perhendinans loca peciit in eodem monasterio ad immorandum secreciora. Frater enim noster factus est in capitulo. Multum enim sibi placuit loci regalitas et crebra fratrum solacia. Singulis enim diebus peciit liberacionem monachilem videlicet sicut in refectorio reficiuntur fratres sibi exhiberi. Ferunt utique eum dixisse nunquam sibi loci magnalia dulciaque fratrum complacuisse consorcia. Duodecimo tamen die valefaciens fratribus ad patrem suum properavit."

130 *Letters*, p. 122 (no. 531).

131 *Vita*, p. 40: "O qualis speratur adhuc princeps Wallie! Tota spes evanit dum factus est rex Anglie." Powicke, *Thirteenth Century*, pp. 514, 516, argues that the king was only too well aware of his son's inadequacies. It would have been hard to measure up to Edward I's standards, but Johnstone justly points out that in his own youth he had been thought irresponsible and given to outbursts of temper – as indeed he continued to be. *EC*, chapter 1.

132 Catto, "Andrew Horn," p. 375; *Ann. Lond.*, p. 151.

CHAPTER TWO

1 E.g., *Ann. Dunst.*, p. 313; *Ann. Wigorn.*, p. 491; *Ann. London.*, p. 104 (for the Falkirk round table); Keeler, *Geoffrey of Monmouth*, App. 5, especially pp. 134–5; Denholm-Young, *Papers*, pp. 117–19 and nn. ("Tournament in the Thirteenth Century").

2 Wace, *Le Roman de Brut,* ll. 9994–10007; Laȝamon *Brut* (EETS) 2, ll. 11427ff.
(pp. 597–9). I owe these references to Denholm-Young, *Papers* (1969), p. 108 n.1
("Tournament"), who cites, for the literary aspects, *CHEL* 1, pp. 234–5, 265.

3 *Flores* 3, p. 59: "Portio Dominicae Crucis magna, quae lingua Wallensium dicebatur *Croizneth,* domino Edwardo regi Angliae cum multis famosis reliquiis trade-
batur ... Corona quondam famosi regis Britonum Arthuri regi Angliae cum multis
aliis jocalibus reddebatur. Sic ad Anglicos gloria Wallensium, invite Anglorum leg-
ibus subditorum per Dei providentiam est translata." Cf. *Ann. Waverley,* p. 401;
Ann. Wigorn., p. 409. Taylor, *Studies,* pp. 283–4 and n. 49, suggests that its likeness may be preserved in a sixteenth century boss in the nave vault of St. George's
chapel, Windsor. Frequent offerings of five shillings were made by Edward I to the
cross during the campaign of 1300 in conjunction with three shillings to the
thorn(s) of the crown of Christ (*spinam/spinas de corona Christi*): SA MS 119, pp.
32 (bis), 36 (bis), 39; *Liber Quotidianus,* pp. xxx–xxxi, 32, 42, 64, 365–6.

4 Barrow, *Bruce,* p. 61 n. 34; Powicke, *Thirteenth Century,* p. 610.

5 Barrow, *Bruce,* p. 73; Legge, "La Piere d'Escoce"; Watson, "The Coronation Stone
of Scotland"; "The Black Rood of Scotland." Hunter, "King Edward's Spoliations
in Scotland," has useful documentation (PRO E101/354/9 m. 1). See also *CDS* 2,
no. 840; Stones, *Anglo-Scottish Relations,* no. 25.

6 Southern, "History as Prophecy," p. 160. Cf. Reeves, *Prophecy,* p. 505 and her
Conclusion in general.

7 See, in particular, Keeler, *Geoffrey of Monmouth.* She is concerned only with the
Latin chroniclers, analyzed as follows: those who draw from Geoffrey de Monmouth without questioning his historical value; those who make use of him but
question individual passages; those (by far the largest group) who do not explicitly
call Geoffrey's historical reliability into question but who make use of him for
some specific purpose, usually political; and lastly (here she adduces as examples
only John of Fordun and John of Whetehamstede), those chroniclers who were
aware of the fictitious character of his work and who expose it. For the *Brut* chronicle: Brie, *Geschichte und Quellen,* and in brief, Eckhardt, *Prophetia Merlini,* pp.
36–9. Some revision of Brie's analysis is to be found in Smallwood, "Prophecy of
the Six Kings."

8 Taylor, *Political Prophecy,* chaps. 1–2, discusses the possible date (before 1135)
and the sources of the *Libellus Merlini,* as well as the manner in which it differs
from the *Historia.*

9 Taylor, ibid., pp. 16–21.

10 Ibid., pp. 48–51; *Brut,* pp. 72–6.

11 Ibid.; Smallwood, "Prophecy of the Six Kings," pp. 575, 580.

12 Eckhardt, *Prophetia Merlini,* pp. 11–13, gives a sampling of such commentaries
dating from the twelfth century to the early fifteenth and edits a Middle English
example from the latter century, though that particular prophecy does not go
beyond Henry III.

13 Smallwood, "Prophecy of the Six Kings," argues that there are eight main versions

of the work, comprising the "original" and revised prose versions, the English prose translation, the English couplet version with two revisions, the Welsh prose translation, and the Latin version. He dates the "original" prose (Anglo-Norman) version to about 1312 and its revision to about 1327 (incorporated into the Anglo-Norman *Brut*). The two earliest of the surviving MSS of the longer *Brut* he assigns to the 1330s. He enumerates seven MSS (A–G) of the "original" prose version, stating that the only printing (said to be of breathtaking inaccuracy) is by Taylor, *Political Prophecy*, pp. 160–4, from BL MS Harley 746 (C), fos. 1^v–3^r. The dates he assigns are at variance with the view of Taylor, Robbins, and Scattergood that the prophecy is a propaganda piece directed against Henry IV ("Prophecy of the Six Kings," pp. 671–2).

14 The bear and ragged staff were to feature as the badge of the Beauchamps of Elmley and Warwick. Neville, "Law of Treason," p. 18 n. 89, cites various examples of out-putters from PRO Just. 3.

15 *Brut*, pp. 243–7 (chapter 211). Cf. Smallwood, "Prophecy of the Six Kings," pp. 576–8. He considers the comments about the military successes of the 'boar' to be a "fortuitous" anticipation of Edward III's activities.

16 The prophecy is discussed by Taylor, *Political Prophecy*, pp. 51–8, Curley, "The Cloak of Anonymity," p. 361, describes it as "for the most part simply a historical retrospect of English affairs beginning during the reign of Edward II." Rigg, "Bridlington's Prophesy: a New Look," provides yet another assessment and suggests, were Ergome not to be accepted as author, some alternative dating of particular incidents.

17 Curley. "Cloak of Anonymity," p. 361; "Fifteenth-Century Glosses," p. 322.

18 Thought to have died *ca.* 1160. The line "Si veram scribam, verum crede me fore scribam", declaring authorship, occurs in the proem to the prophecy (l. 9, *John of Bridlington*, p. 129). See Meyvaert, "John Erghome," pp. 659–60. For the saintly prior (1320–79): Purvis, "St. John of Bridlington," *Journal of the Bridlington Augustinian Soc*iety (1924), a reference I owe to Genet, *Four English Political Tracts*, pp. 45–6.

19 *John of Bridlington*, p. 123 n. 1; James, "Catalogue," p. 11; Curley, "Cloak of Anonymity," pp. 366–7.

20 Curley, "Cloak of Anonymity," pp. 366–7, 369 n. 42, where, referring to his thesis (PhD Chicago 1973, pp. 279–317) he claims that thirty-one lines are missing from Wright's edition. See also ibid., pp. 368–9, where he summarizes the arguments for and against Ergome's authorship of the prophecy; *Bridlington*, pp. xxiv–xxvi, 91–2; "Item versus vaticinales de eodem." James, "Catalogue," pp. 11–12, wrote: "Both the metrical prophecy and the exposition of it are deplorable productions from a literary point of view." Gwynne, "John Erghome and the Black Prince," *English Austin Friars*, p. 135, expressed a similar view of their quality. This may be so, but there is an admirable clarity in Ergome's expository argument.

21 *John of Bridlington* (first preamble, p. 125): "a canonico regulari secundum communem opinionem vulgi."

22 *HBC*, p. 465; *Westminster Abbey MSS*, pp. 85–6. For Ergome see Gwynne, "John
    Erghome and the Black Prince," pp. 129–38 and especially 134–8; Emden, *Biog.
    Oxon.*, s.v. "Erghome." A later writer on these matters, Curley, "Cloak of
    Anonymity," provides a bibliography on the question of authorship (p. 361 n. 2)
    and discusses fully the various attributions. Curley, "Fifteenth-Century Glosses,"
    dates Ergome's composite work 1362 X April 1364.

23 The quotation is from Curley, "Fifteenth Century Glosses," p. 322. Cf. Taylor,
    Political Prophecy, pp. 52–3.

24 *John of Bridlington*, pp. 132–3. This notion of a substituted child is common
    among the chroniclers. For references see *EC*, p. 130 nn. 6–7.

25 *Polychronicon* 8, p. 298.

26 *John of Bridlington* (expositio), pp. 132–7.

27 Edited from Bodl. Lib. MS Laud 622 by E.J. Furnivall.

28 Emerson, "Date of Adam Davy's Dreams."

29 This is obscure, since Clement V's coronation was in 1305, that of his successor,
    John XXII, in 1316.

30 Candlemas (2 February), also called "Wives feast day."

31 "Date of Adam Davy's Dreams," pp. 11–16.

32 When at Langdon Abbey on 28 August 1325, Edward expressed his "special devo-
    tion" to St Thomas in his grant of the advowson of Tonge church to the Canterbury
    monks. Canterbury Register Reynolds, fo. 142ᵛ.

33 For Edward II's reception of embassies from the ruler of Iran and the king of
    Armenia urging a crusade, see Phillips, "Edward II and the Prophets," p. 193 n. 23.

34 For which see Taylor, *Political Prophecy*, pp. 35–6; Scattergood, "Adam Davy's
    Dreams and Edward II," pp. 255–7. Martyrdom is also alluded to by Phillips,
    "Edward II and the Prophets," p. 193 n. 24.

35 For Horn's prophecy (s.a. 1307) see *Ann. Lond.*, p. 151. "The Prophecy of the
    Eagle and the Hermit" is from BL MS Arundel 57, fo. 5ʳ; Scattergood, "Adam
    Davy's Dreams and Edward II," p. 257; Taylor, *Political Prophecy*, pp. 95–6 n. 43.
    There were also unfavourable poems on the times; for instance "The Simonie,"
    edited by Wright, *Political Songs*, pp. 323–45, but since 1991 available in a mod-
    ern edition. Cf. Hardwick, *Poem on the Times of Edward II;* Ross, "On the Evil
    Times of Edward II." "The Simonie" blames all classes of society for the state of
    affairs: Edward is portrayed as victim.

36 Scattergood, "Adam Davy's Dreams and Edward II," p. 254.

37 *Chronicles Edward I and II* 2, pp. i–xviii, 3–21. This "commendatio" is inserted in
    other MSS e.g. TCC R. 5 41, fos. 102ᵛ (103)–110ʳ (111). Compare *Flores* 3, p.
    137, which contains much material in common with the TCC MS but not this item.
    See also D'Avray, *Death and the Prince*, especially pp. 70–9 and index s.v.
    "Edward I."

38 *PL* 207, Ep.66.

39 Hardy, *Materials* 3, pp. 282, 309, suggests that he could be John Bever, a West-
    minster monk, but since he does not prefix "frater" to his name, it is more likely

that John was a secular clerk. No monk of that name is mentioned in Pearce, *Monks of Westminster.*

40 Norfolk escheated to the Crown with Roger Bigod's death *sine prole* in 1306, Cornwall with that of Edmund of "Almaine" in 1300.

41 Tout, *Place,* p. 33.

42 Ibid. and *idem, PHE* 3, p. 237.

43 Legg prints the papal letter in Latin and English in *Coronation Records,* pp. 69–76, from Vatican Archives Reg. Vat. 110, fos. 136^r–7^v. The precise reference I owe to Phillips, "Edward II and the Prophets," p. 196 nn. 29, 30, who also explains how Legg mistook the date, though in view of Orleton's embassy I was already aware of this error. For Edward's offerings at Canterbury see chapter 1, p. 12.

44 Phillips, "Edward II and the Prophets," pp. 197–8 n. 33.

45 Margaret, born 11 September 1275, was married 1290 and died in 1318.

46 For Bishop Grosseteste's letter to Henry II about the gifts conferred by unction see Legg, *Coronation Records*, pp. 66–8.

47 Phillips, "Edward II and the Prophets," pp. 197–8; Haines, *John Stratford,* p. 125.

48 Phillips, "Edward II and the Prophets," p. 198 n. 35, where the references are given.

49 Haines, *Church and Politics,* pp. 20–2. When writing that book I was unaware that Orleton was carrying the bishop's letters about the oil. His other (principal?) concerns were apparently the matter of homage for Aquitaine, the canonization of Thomas Cantilupe, and the Scottish question. The six bulls he brought back early in 1320 are enumerated, ibid., p. 22. None has reference to the holy oil.

50 Phillips, 'Edward II and the Prophets', p. 198, citing *Foedera* 2 i, pp. 387, 399, 424. Edward asked for the appointment of John de Wrotham in place of Wisbech. *Liber Epistolaris,* 245.

51 Sandquist, "Holy Oil of St. Thomas," p. 336; Bloch, *Les Rois Thaumaturges,* p. 243, who considered the oil of St Thomas to be no more "qu'une médiocre imitation"; Oppenheimer, "The Legend of the Sainte Ampoule." Marc Bloch also demonstrates (pp. 97–9) that Edward II continued his father's practice of "touching" the sick and that in the time of Edward III the distinguished theologian Bradwardine testified to the miracles thereby performed.

52 See, for instance, Sandquist, "Holy Oil of St. Thomas."

53 Hereford Cathedral MS P.5. xii, fos. 99^v–107^v, "Cecidit corona capitis." The rubric and endnote to another copy of this sermon in Lambeth MS 61, fos. 143^r–47^v ascribe it to M. Henry de Harclay. The sermon very possibly dates from 29 December 1314, shortly before Gaveston's burial at Langley 2 January 1315 (BL Cotton MS Cleopatra D. III, fo. 56^v). See Haines, *John Stratford,* p. 288 n. 64; "Some Sermons at Hereford"; Kemp, "History and Action." For the Harclay family see Pelster, "Heinrich von Harclay," p. 209, who considers Henry to be probably a younger brother of Andrew; also Summerson, *Carlisle* 1, pp. 230–56.

54 MS P.5. xii, fo. 104^r, from *De oneribus prophetarum:* "Barachie filius in Thoma rursus occiditur." See Matthew 23:35; Luke 11:51; 2 Chronicles 24:20–1.

55 MS P.5. xii, fo. 103^r.

56 *Const. Hist.* 2, pp. 313–14.

57 *Vita,* pp. 39–40

58 *Polychronicon* 7, pp. 299, 301, and compare the parallel English version printed there from BL Harleian MS 2261. Higden's original Latin is at pp. 298, 301. Ranulf Higden is recorded to have entered St Werburgh's in 1299, so that he could have been born, as was Edward II, in the 1280s. He apparently died in 1364. Taylor, *Ranulf Higden,* pp. 1–2. This author (p. 45 n. 4) considers Higden's work to be of little value (apart from its celebrated character sketch of Edward) between 1300 and 1352. The first version was written "almost certainly" in the 1320s, the "short text" ending in 1327 (ibid., pp. 45 n. 4, 96, 110). Other character sketches of this kind are to be found in *Bridlington,* p. 91, *Melsa* 2, p. 286, and *Knighton* 1, p. 40 (derived from Higden). For the highly derivative nature of the earlier part of *Knighton* see now H.G. Martin's introduction to the edition covering the period 1337–96.

59 *Chronicon,* p. 29; *Vita et Mors,* p. 315. Baker writes that Isabella did not wish to see him and prevented his children from doing so.

60 Historia Roffensis, fos. 46^v–7^r. Although Despenser was ribbed by the king on account of Hethe's forthright comments, that no animosity existed between Despenser and Hethe is suggested by the latter part of the conversation reported by Dene.

61 Tout, *Collected Papers* 2 (Westminster Chronicle), pp. 289–90 (citing Chetham MS no. 6712, fo. 295^v), 299–300. The note as to authorship is also in the fifteenth century BL Cotton MS Cleopatra A. XVI, fo. 139^r. See *Flores* 3, p. 232: rubric marking the point where the canon of St Paul's, Adam Murimuth, took over (*inchoatio Adae Merimouth sancti Pauli*).

62 Gransden, *Historical Writing* 2, pp. 17–18. See also the same writer's "Continuation of the Flores" and "Propaganda." In Gransden's view this portion of the chronicle may even have been written at the express command of Isabella and Mortimer. It is certainly strongly pro-Mortimer at the time of his escape from the Tower (*Flores* 3, p. 217). See also Tait's introduction to *Chronica Johannis de Reading,* pp. 1–8, though now outdated in part.

63 The statement in the Chetham MS is at fo. 295^v; Gransden, *Historical Writing* 2, p. 18 and n., also cited by Tout, n. 61 above.

64 Gransden, *Historical Writing* 2, pp. 17 n. 83, 18: "It could merely signify the point at which Robert's death halted his work, not the date when he died" (I find this hard to interpret); Tout, *Collected Papers* 2, pp. 292–3; Pearce, *Monks of Westminster,* p. 70. It seems unlikely that there were two monks named Robert of Reading given the information in this last source.

65 Tait, *Chronica Reading,* pp. 5–7, 18. Against this, Gransden, *Historical Writing* 2, p. 18 n. 87, suggests "very tentatively" that Murimuth himself may have used a Westminster exemplar, notably for the account of the deposition that, she thinks, "so exactly corresponds with the theme of Reading's chronicle." For a summary of

the argument ending with the suggestion that the chronicle from 1298 to 1326 may have been the work of a single author, see now Taylor, *English Historical Literature*, pp. 77–80.

66 *Flores* 3, pp. 157: where he condemns papal policy for inflicting injuries on Canterbury and the monastic Order (*Injurias quas ecclesiae Christi Cantuariae et ordini monastico* [Clement V] *continue studuit irrogare*); 177–8, 191–2.

67 Ibid., pp. 155–6, 191–2.

68 Haines, *Church and Politics*, pp. 109–10, 183–4.

69 *Flores* 3, pp. 182–3, and compare *Murimuth*, p. 25, or in greater detail, *Graystanes* (*Scriptores Tres*), pp. 98–9, 118–19; *HBC*, p. 76; Maddicott, *Lancaster*, pp. 241–2, 264, 293–5; Haines, *Archbishop Stratford*, p. 187. For the stewardship of England see Vernon Harcourt, *His Grace the Steward*, especially chapter 5 and p. 163 (letters patent of Lancaster's appointment).

70 *Flores* 3, p. 199; Tout, *Chapters* 2, p. 273. For Badlesmere see below especially chapters 5–6.

71 Ibid., pp. 172–3, 205, 212–14. Gray, *Scalachronica*, ed. Stevenson, p. 140, ed. Maxwell, p. 51, thought that Banaster acted at Edward's instigation, though such does not appear to have been the case. See Maddicott, *Lancaster*, pp. 175–6.

72 *Flores* 3, pp. 205, 223.

73 Ibid., 191, 196, 205–6, 223.

74 Ibid., pp. 149–50, 161–7, 171–2, 227. *CPR. 1313–1317*, p. 186, has a mandate to the sheriff of Oxford against vagabond Dominicans with instructions to prohibit publication of scandalous writings against the Order.

75 Ibid., pp. 169, 193, 232; Gransden, *Historical Writing* 2, p. 18 and n. 88. Other irritations are noted by Tout, *Collected Papers* 2, pp. 297 and n. 2, who discusses the exchequer reforms at pp. 301–4. See also *idem, Chapters* 2, pp. 211–12. Barbara Harvey, *Westminster Estates*, p. 44, points out that the offerings at the abbey were at a low ebb during Edward II's reign, only a shade over thirty six pounds in 1317–18, and that in 1319 the king fined the abbey forty pounds for appropriating Morden church without licence. Ibid., p. 411 n. 6 (from *CPR 1317–21*, p. 344). For Eye see ibid., index s.v.; "Burgoyne" is mentioned in SA MS 122, pp. 75–6.

76 For the robbery see the bibliography in Tout, *Chapters* 2, p. 57 nn. 3–4, and for Reading's criticisms, *Flores* 3, pp. 192–3, 201, 210, 214, 218, 221–2, 228. Compare *Scotichronicon*, ed. Watt 7, pp. 12–13, 175 Notes (44–56, in particular 47), where Bower (here following Fordun) makes no aspersions.

77 *Lanercost*, pp. 227–8; *Brut y Tywysogion* (Peniarth MS), p. 123, and see Mackie, "Bannockburn," pp. 189–90.

78 Barbour, *Bruce* 13, ll. 295–8 (p. 234); *Trokelowe*, p. 86; "hausto spiritu acriore, in hostes more leonis, sublatis catulis, irruit truculenter et, more animosi militis, multorum sanguinem gladio vibrante effudit." For a summary of Argentan's career: *Scotichronicon*, ed. Watt 7, p. 192 Notes (31).

79 Cook, *Portrait of St Albans*, p. 44 (and personal observation); Liber Benefactorum

BL MS Cotton Nero D. VII, fo. 6ᵛ; *Chronica St Albani* 3, p. 433; McCullough, "Saints Alban and Amphibalus." See below, chapter 8, n. 115.

80 *Scalachronica,* ed. Stevenson, p.142, ed. Maxwell, p. 56.

81 See, in particular, Fryde, *Tyranny and Fall,* chapters. 6–7; Buck, *Stapeldon,* chapter 8; also below chapter 6.

82 See below, chapter 11.

83 Davies, *Baronial Opposition,* p.77; Johnstone, "Eccentricities of Edward II," pp. 264–7; Childs, "Welcome my Brother," p. 160; Hill, *The King's Messengers,* pp. 74–7, has a lengthy piece on Robert of Newington, who was a king's messenger.

84 Some of these contra indications are advanced by Prestwich, *Three Edwards,* p. 79. For Edward's address in French to the mayor and sheriffs of London see *Ann. Lond.,* pp. 208–9; for the demand in 1320 see Stuart, "Interview between Philip V and Edward II" (printed from PRO C47/29/9/25); Haines, *John Stratford,* p. 127 n. 23. The English chroniclers do not record the dramatic incident at Poissy in June 1313 (Pontoise?). *Itinerary EII.,* p. 99, shows Edward there throughout June but at Poissy in July) to be found in *RHGF* 23 (*Chronicon Ste Catherinae*), p. 409.

85 Davies, *Baronial Opposition,* p. 80.

86 Ibid., pp. 80–1.

87 Bodl. Lib. MS Douce 128, fos. 156ʳ, 158ʳ⁻ᵛ: "Et issint fust le Roy venge de lui pur la mort Ser Peres de Gavestone;" *Historia Anglicana* 1, pp. 167–8. At the time of Gaveston's death the author of the *Vita* remarks, p. 30, that Edward determined to destroy those who had killed him. Indeed, this determination constitutes a consistent theme in that chronicler's version of events, see for example ibid., pp. 76, 104, 126. The same idea occurs in *Scalachronica,* ed. Stevenson, pp. 148–9, ed. Maxwell, p. 67, as also in *Lanercost,* p. 244: "in vindictam mortis Petri de Gaverstoun quem comes fecerat decollari," and *Anonimalle Chronicle,* pp. 108–9. Those who knew the king best said that but for this reason the earl would not have been precipitately executed. BL Royal MS. 13 E. IX (Walsingham).

88 Tout, *PHE* 3, p. 241, regarded Gaveston as not "specially vicious." Stubbs, *Const. Hist.* 2, p. 319, had written virtually the same thing, adding that it was a matter of a strong will dominating a weak one. Prestwich, *Three Edwards,* p. 80, writes: "it is hard to doubt a sexual element in his friendships with Gaveston and Despenser." Of this, I think, there can be no question. On the other hand, more recently (1994) Dr Chaplais has attempted to explain his conduct as determined throughout by his pact of brotherhood with Gaveston, a factor that has been noticed previously but not so systematically worked out. Undoubtedly this did constitute an element in Edward's relationship with Gaveston, stemming from his adolescence in Edward I's reign; but it is hardly conclusive, particularly when his subsequent relationship with Despenser is taken into account. Moreover, if such a pact of fraternity be regarded as more specifically concerned with knighthood and comradeship in arms, Edward would sit uneasily within such a framework. There were other kinds of fraternity that survived for centuries: see for example, Wiseman, *Ritual Brotherhood in Renaissance Florence.* The problem has lately (1997) been discussed by

E.A.R. Brown, "Ritual Brotherhood": with respect to Gaveston especially pp. 359, 378–81. For her, sexual activity is neither a necessary part of the king's close association nor is it proven. But if not, how to explain the king's extraordinary conduct? See nn. 89, 95 below.

89 *Melsa* 2, p. 355: "Ipse quidem Edwardus in vitio sodomico nimium delectebat"; Winchester Cartulary, fo. 4^v (no. 233); *Responsiones,* cols. 2763–5; *Exeter Register Grandisson* 3 (App.), pp. 1540–47.

90 Froissart, *Chroniques* (ed. Luce) 1, p. 247 (Rome MS), and compare Le Bel, *Chronique,* p. 27, from which Froissart largely derived his account; Maunde Thompson, *Chronicon,* p. 212 (notes). See below chapter 7 n. 50. For the Templars see Barber, "Charges against the Templars" (below chapter 3, n. 23).

91 *HBC,* p. 39; Blackley, "Adam," p. 77 (from BL MS Stowe 553, fos. 27^r, 113^r); Given Wilson and Curteis, *Royal Bastards*: Valente, "Lament of Edward II," p. 433 n. 56.

92 *CPR 1327–30,* pp. 437–8; *Foedera* 2 ii, p. 771. Doherty, "Isabella," p. 287, citing Froissart, *Chroniques* (ed. Luce) 1, p. 88. This matter is discussed by Harding, "Isabella and Mortimer," pp. 124–5. There could have been other reasons for her taking precautions at a time of manifest unrest.

93 *Knighton* 1, p. 434; *Willelmi Capellani de Brederode,* p. 177. I owe the last reference to Doherty, "Isabella," pp. 138–9. In SA MS 122, the entries reveal mutual gifts, letters, privy dining, the care taken over forty seven caged goldfinches awaiting her arrival, and numerous royal visits: pp. 1, 8, 25, 28–9, 40, 43, 45–6, 51, 65, 75, 92. The cost of one of these visits by water to Eleanor at Sheen (p. 40) was £67 17s. Eleanor had been at court for some considerable time and is mentioned in the 1311–12 wardrobe book, Bodl. Lib. MS Tanner 197, fo. 12^r, as being paid expenses while outside the Curia on a journey to Alnwick. At the time of her marriage in 1317 in the chapel of Windsor Park, royal oblations of three pounds were distributed over the heads of Hugh Despenser and his countess. Stapleton, "A Brief Summary of Wardrobe Accounts," p. 337.

94 The queen had sent letters of support for Eleanor's chaplain, John de Sadington. *Stonar Letters and Papers* 1, p. 3, no. 3, 7 Feb. (1326?).

95 Chaplais, *Gaveston,* especially his conclusions at pp. 109–14. He allows that there is no conclusive evidence for a pact of the kind suggested but argues that circumstances point to one. *Ann. Paul.,* p. 263, uses the term "adoptivus frater" (in a technical sense?) to explain the king's attitude. Brown, "Ritual Brotherhood," p. 360, observes that a distinction between adoptive (*adoptivus frater*) and ritual brotherhood (*fedus fraternitatis*) "was not observed so punctiliously in the West as it seems to have been in the East." See above, n. 88, and Keen, "Brotherhood in Arms"; also Jordan's provocatively entitled *The Invention of Sodomy in Christian Theology,* which is perhaps not sufficiently detached.

96 *Lanercost,* pp. 236–7. Compare *Vita,* pp. 86–7; *Anonimalle Chronicle,* pp. 94–5.

97 "Poidras" is the name in Bodl. Lib. MS Douce 128, fo. 157^r, and the *Anonimalle Chronicle.* Powderham is in Devon. These sources state that the imposter's parents came from Exeter only a short distance away. See Childs, "Welcome my Brother."

98 *Chronicon*, pp. 9, 189 (Notes); Knowles and Hadcock, *English Religious Houses*, p. 236; *VCH Oxon.* 2, p. 139; *CPR 1317–1321*, p. 75.

99 *Lanercost*, pp. 236–7; *Ann. Paul.*, pp. 282–3; Bodl. Lib. MS Douce 128, fo. 157^r. This last has "community," which I have adopted as the translation of "universitas" in *Lanercost*.

100 Ibid. *Ann. Paul.* says that he confessed to having acted at the instigation of the devil and to have believed in the magical arts for seven years and gives the date of his death as 20 July. The Douce MS and the *Anonimalle Chronicle* have the eve of St James (24 July).

101 *Vita*, pp. 136–7; *John of Bridlington*, pp. 132–3; *EC*, p. 30 and especially n. 7; *Melsa* 2, pp. 335–6.

102 Worcester Register Cobham, fos. 62^{r-v}; edition p. 97.

103 Ibid., fo. 62^v, p. 98.

104 *Lanercost*, pp. 420–2 (Notes). See also the hard-hitting mandate (1317) of Pope John to his nuncios complaining about the encroachments of royal officials: Wright, *Reynolds*, App. 7, pp. 333–41.

105 *Guisborough*, p. 381: "Benedictus deus omnipotens qui post regem sapientissimum dedit nobis principium boni regis." *Lanercost*, p. 215. For the events following Edward III's return in December 1340: Haines, *John Stratford*, chapter 3, "The Crisis of 1341."

106 Robinson, "Edward II a Degenerate?," p. 446 n. 4.

107 *Scalacronica*, ed. Stevenson, pp. 136, 150, 152–3; ed. Maxwell, pp. 45, 70, 74–6; *Brut*, p. 220.

108 *John of Bridlington*, p. 137: "Sic credo quod iste rex impediatur per amorem mulierum a regno Franciae et pascuis suis."

109 For this threat see Winchester Cartulary, fo. 4^v no. 233: "Quod si domina Isabella regina Anglie tunc uxor legitime regis predicti ad ipsum regem personaliter accederet idem rex ipsam reginam interficeret et quod in una caligarum portavit cultellum ad hoc specialiter destinatum, quodque si aliud paratum non haberet unde predictam reginam interficere posset ipsam ad mortem dentibus strangularet." See for printed transcripts: *Responsiones*, col. 2766, *Exeter Register Grandisson* 3 (App.), p. 1542.

110 BL MS Cotton E. IV 9.

111 *Vita*, p. 136. For Lisle see Aberth, *Criminal Churchmen*, and my article forthcoming in the New DNB. For the 1341 crisis see n. 105 above.

112 See chapter 1, n. 38.

113 Göttingen MS 740, fo. 221^r, ed. Eckhardt 2, p. 1063 ll. 39412–27.

CHAPTER THREE

1 *Lanercost*, p. 209

2 PRO E101/373/5,7; *Itinerary EII*, p. 21. The royal wardrobe was at Lambeth 8–9 July 1307, at Pontefract on the sixteenth, at Carlisle on Wednesday the nineteenth.

3 *Lanercost*, p. 207; *Guisborough*, p. 379: "Celaveruntque sui mortem regis quousque veniret filius eius et magnates terre, et incarcerabantur multi qui mortem regis predicaverant."

4 *CFR 1272–1307*, pp. 558–9; *CDS* 3, no. 2; *Lanercost*, pp. 209, 412 (Notes) – a transcript of the Greenfield document; Richardson, "English Coronation Oath [2]," pp. 62–3 n. 91; Beardwood, *Trial of Langton*, p. 11. One of Langton's letters is dated 23 July. For Edward's assumption of the Crown by hereditary right see Stubbs, *Const. Hist.* 2, p. 315 n. 3; *Foedera* 2 i, p. 1 (proclamation of the king's peace). The *Historia Anglicana* 1, p. 119, claims that Edward succeeded: "non tam jure haereditario quam unanimi assensu procerum et magnatum."

5 *Itinerary EII*, p. 21. *CFR 1272–1307*, p. 559, gives 20 July as the date of the king's return to Carlisle. *Lanercost*, p. 209, also gives this date and at this juncture is precise about chronology.

6 *Flores* 3, p. 138.

7 The chancellor sealed writs of course until the feast of St James the Apostle (25 July), having no certain knowledge of the king's death prior to that day. On the following Saturday (29 July) he received orders from Edward. Beardwood, *Trial of Langton*, p. 11; *CFR 1272–1307*, p. 559.

8 *Ann. Paul.*, p. 257 (cf. Bodl. Lib. MS Lat. hist. d.4, fo. 203^r), gives the date of Langton's arrest as some three days after (*post triduum*) the cortège's arrival at Waltham, i.e., 7 August. No other printed chronicle is so precise. *Murimuth*, p. 11, stands alone in his statement that Langton was escorted to prison by two friars, J. and R. (or "K") Feltone, who subsequently came to a bad end. This incident, he adds, provided the occasion for Pope Boniface's constitution against those who assaulted bishops.

9 *Historia Anglicana* 1, p. 119. On 4 October a proclamation was issued in the name of Treasurer Reynolds and of Gaveston, urging all who had complaints against Langton to put them in writing for delivery to the clerk of Bereford, chief justice of the Common Pleas. *Letter Book C*, p. 156.

10 *Bridlington*, p. 273: "Cumque venisset apud Waltham juxta Londonias, et esset cum corpore, rex novus et dominus Petrus conjuraverunt contra eum, pro eo quod in vita patris noluit eis omnia ad libitum ministrare de thesauro patris regis mortui." This is also in *Guisborough*, p. 383. The Pauline annalist (*Ann. Paul.*, p. 257) states that he was given (*datus*) to Gaveston: "qui sibi erat inimicissimus," having been exiled, "quasi per eum." He adds that all his lands, money, horses and farm stock were made over to the favourite. Beardwood contends that corroboration is lacking for Langton's self-aggrandizement. See *Trial of Langton*, p. 25; *Records of the Trial*, p. 2 n. 5. *Lanercost*, p, 210, describes Langton as "virum utique discretum inter omnes de regno." For the king's creation of Gaveston as "chief secretary" see *Ann. Paul.*, p. 238; Bodl. Lib. MS Lat. hist. d.4, fo. 203^v. The favourite's movements at the time of the old king's death are given by Hamilton, *Gaveston*, p. 139 n. 1. He is said to have reached Carlisle shortly after 1 August.

11 Beardwood, *Trial of Langton*, p. 13, citing PRO Just. 1/1344 m. 25: pleas concern-

ing Langton before Brabazon and others at Windsor, Westminster, and the Tower.

12 Tout, *Chapters* 2, pp. 192–3; 6, pp. 7, 18, 20. Baldock continued to act 8 July–2 August 1307. Langton was acting by 18 August.

13 *Lanercost*, p. 209. *Guisborough*, p. 379, states that homage and fealty were received by the king at Roxburgh, which place does not appear in his printed itinerary at this point.

14 *Foedera* 2 i, pp. 4, 6.

15 Phillips, *Pembroke*, p. 25.

16 In 1297, although guardian of Scotland, Earl Warenne "corrupcionem aeris causans, dixit se ibi non posse cum sanitate manere." *Guisborough*, p. 294.

17 *Foedera* 2 i, pp. 11–12: the accompanying *magistri* were John de Berwick and Robert de Pickering, canons of York; Barbour, *Bruce* 8, ll. 359–62 (p. 143): "Sa schamfull that he vencust was, / That till Inglande in hy he gais / Richt till the King, and schamfully/ He gaf up that his wardanry."

18 *Itinerary EII*, p. 23 and n.; *Foedera* 2 i, p. 2 (*English Royal Documents*, p. 61 no. 8b: section of the charter only); *Vita*, p. 1; *CDS* 5, nos. 515, 521, pp. 221, 223.

19 *Lanercost*, p. 210; *Parl. Writs* 2 ii, pp. 1–14; *HBC*, p. 456.

20 *Guisborough*, p. 379 (the statute is printed in Stubbs, *Select Charters*, pp. 470–2); Parry, *Parliaments*, p. 70; *Foedera* 2 i, p. 4; *Parl. Writs* 2 i, pp. 14–15; Stubbs, *Const. Hist.* 2, p. 316 n. On 28 November 1307 collectors were appointed for the counties: *CPR 1307–1313*, pp. 22–4. Richardson, "Early Coronation Records [2]," p. 3, states: "We cannot doubt that Edward II's letter to Clement V of 16 December [*Foedera* 2 i, p. 23; *Concilia* 2, pp. 200–1] pressing for Winchelsey's reinstatement follows a decision reached in the Parliament." Doubtless this was so, but why was the interval a couple of months? In his letter to the pope the king remarked: "Idem archiepiscopus non sit obnoxius."

21 *Lanercost*, p. 210, *Hemingburgh* 2, pp. 267–8; *Guisborough*, pp. 379–80 and n. 1; *Langtoft*, pp. 380–3. At this stage BL MS Lansdowne 239 ends the third book "compiled by Walter Hemingburgh, canon of Gisbourn." Compare CCC MS 5. 41, fo. 110ᵛ (111); *Flores* (Tintern MS), p. 330.

22 *Itinerary EII*, p. 25. He was there from 10 November until the first day of December. Pembroke was at Langley 22 November. Phillips, *Pembroke*, p. 323 (from PRO C53/94 m. 8).

23 *Foedera* 2 i, pp. 18–20, 23–4 (Templars in Wales, Scotland and Ireland). For an account of proceedings taken against the Templars in the provincial councils of Canterbury and York, as well as for a bibliography, see *Councils & Synods II*, pp. 1240–43. and index s.v. "Temple, Order of." Barbour, "Charges against the Templars," regards the accusations as propaganda and suggests similarity to those brought against the Waldensians.

24 *Itinerary EII*, p. 26 & n.(a); *Vita*, p. 2; *Ann. Paul.*, pp. 258–9 (Bodl. Lib. MS Lat. hist. d.4, fo. 203ᵛ – a variation of the *Flores*); *Foedera* 2 i, p. 24. *Trokelowe*, p. 65: "Vilissime conculcavit, et victoriam campi sibi inperpetuum dedecus adquisivit;

quas quidem victoria maculam posuit in sua gloria, majorisque odii seminarium adaugebat." Lancaster's presence at Wallingford is disputed by his biographer, Maddicott, *Lancaster*, p. 75. Similarly Phillips, *Pembroke*, p. 25, states that Valence was in France at the time. For the marriage see Dodge, *Gaveston*, pp. 57–61.

25 He sailed from Dover on Monday, 22 January 1308 and from Wissant to Boulogne the following day. *Ann. Paul.*, p. 258; *Flores* 3, p. 141; *Foedera* 2 i, p. 29.

26 PRO E101/373/7; *RHGF* 21, p. 650. Both are cited in *Itinerary EII*, p. 27. For details of the marriage settlement and of the political implications of the liaison: E.A.R. Brown, "Political Repercussions," and "Marriage of Edward II."

27 PRO E101/373/7. In *Ann. Paul.*, p. 258 (Bodl. Lib. MS Lat. hist. d.4, fo. 103^v) some of the king of France's gifts are enumerated: a ring of his realm (*annulum regni sui*), a couch (*cubile*) more beautiful than any other, and choice warhorses.

28 Now printed from transcripts in Bodl. Lib. Dugdale MS 18, fos. 1^v, 80^r, by Phillips, *Pembroke*, App. 4, pp. 316–7.

29 *Itinerary EII*, p. 28. Edward left Boulogne 3 February 1308 and sailed from Wissant on the seventh. *Ann. Paul.*, p. 258; *Ann. Lond.*, p. 152; *Foedera* 2 i, p. 31. See also Maunde Thompson, *Chronicon* (Notes), pp. 179–80.

30 *Lanercost*, p. 210, states that Edward had an improper familiarity with Gaveston, calling him "brother." Cf. *Ann. Paul.*, p. 259 (Bodl. Lib. MS Lat. hist. d.4 fos. 203v–4r): "Rex vocavit Petrum, pre timore nimio fratrem suum; vulgus vero eum regis ydolum vocitabit, cui displiceret ut patri timuit, et ut superiori studuit complacere." There were two kings, one nominal, the other real (*duos reges in uno regno, istum verbaliter istum realiter conregnare*). The *Vita*, p. 28, says that the king had adopted Gaveston as his brother "adoptaverat in fratrem."

31 *Vitae Arch. Cant.*, p. 17: "B. Thomae martyri totum statum suum specialiter recommendans." However, this writer, whoever he was, liked to cast archbishops in the role of emulators of Becket. This is cited in Richardson, "Early Coronation Records [2]," p. 5 n. 1. The liberties of the church of Durham, confiscated by Edward I were restored to Bek on 4 September 1307; *Foedera* 2 i, p. 5.

32 On the other hand, if the chronicle evidence is accurate, Henry Lacy, the earl of Lincoln, did not appreciate Edward's defects at the time, or at least was prepared to give him the benefit of the doubt. See text below.

33 *Foedera* 2 i, p. 23; *Concilia* 2, pp. 290–1. See n. 20 above.

34 For this endemic problem see Haines, *Ecclesia anglicana,* chapter 5.

35 *CPL* 2, p. 33; *Lit. Cant.* 3, p. 386 (no. 47); *Concilia* 2, pp. 291–2; *HMCR* 8 Rep. App. 1, p. 351. Richardson (needlessly?) doubts the statement in *Ann. Paul.*, pp. 259–60, that the pope proposed a cardinal to crown the king and that the latter countered by requesting that the ceremony be performed by the archbishop of York with the bishops of Durham and London. There could, of course, be some confusion with Winchelsey's suggestion about choosing one of three bishops, although that does come later in the same account. It might equally refer to a previous papal arrangement. The one we actually know about involved only the archbishop of York. Richardson's suggestion that the Pauline annalist confused this with the

story of Becket's oil over a decade later appears improbable. See Richardson, "Early Coronation Records [2]," pp. 3 nn. 3, 5; 6 n. 3; 4 n. 2; *Winchester Register Woodlock* 1, pp. 253–4; Stubbs, *Const. Hist.* 2, p. 316 n. 4.

36 *Lit. Cant.* 3, p. 386 no. 47 (CCL Reg. 1, fo. 282ʳ): "Revocacio commissionis facte archiepiscopo Eboracensi per sedem apostolicam pro coronacione regis Edwardi filii regis Edwardi."

37 *Foedera* 2 i, p. 26. See n. 35 above for arrangements about crowning the king. Reynolds had been appointed treasurer 22 August 1307. *CPR 1307–1313*, p. 1.

38 *Lit. Cant.* 3, p. 386 (no. 48) and see nn. 35–6 above.

39 BL MS Cotton Vitellius C. XII fo. 231ʳ⁻ᵛ (printed by Richardson, "Early Coronation Records [2]," pp. 8–9; "Tribus episcopis commissionem suam ut unus eorum, quem rex eligere vellet, ipsum regem vice sua coronaret quod ad vestram notitiam satis credimus pervenisse."

40 *Winchester Register Woodlock* 1, pp. 245–6, 253–4; 2, p. 937; *Parl. Writs* 2 ii, p. 20; *Foedera* 2 i, p. 32.

41 For Richardson's critique of Wilkinson's arguments with respect to these matters see "English Coronation Oath," p. 59 n. 75. The former's emphatic statement that "the king did not know that Winchelsey was detained by sickness, presumably at Poitiers," is at least questionable.

42 Richardson, "Early Coronation Records [2]," p. 4 and n. 6. Stubbs, *Const. Hist.* 2, p. 316 n. 4, cites Lambeth MS 1106 (continuation of Matthew of Westminster) after noting the delay of a week (*Ann. Paul.*, pp. 259–60).

43 Bertie Wilkinson, as we shall see, viewed the postponement as a consequence of baronial discontent. He disliked at least two of the suggestions put forward by Richardson: the fact that the archbishop's messenger failed to deliver his letters and that the king writing on 9 February (*Foedera* 2 i, p. 32) could have expected the archbishop to respond in time for the coronation on the eighteenth. Wilkinson, "Coronation Oath of Edward II," especially pp. 454–6. Compare, Richardson, "English Coronation Oath," p. 59 n. 75.

44 For the coronation see the bibliography in Wilkinson, *Const. Hist.* 2, p. 8; also Wickham Legg, *English Coronation Records* and *Three Coronation Orders*. The Cotton Vitellius MS makes no mention of the ecclesiastical element in the procession.

45 This process is detailed in Richardson, "Early Coronation Records [2]" (BL MS Cotton Vitellius C. XII), p. 9, and from the close roll entry in *Foedera* 2 i, p. 36; *Parl. Writs* 2 ii, App. pp. 10–11.

46 *Ann. Lond.*, p. 152; *Parl. Writs* 2 i, p. 178, cited Stubbs, *Const. Hist.* 2, p. 3.

47 *Ann. Paul.*, p. 260. For variations in the list of those attending see Maunde Thompson, *Chronicon* (Notes), p. 181. For Marigny: Favier, *Enguerran de Marigny*, p. 121.

48 The offering subsequently made by the queen (see text below) was a mark weight of gold in the form of a pilgrim receiving the ring. See Richardson, "Early Coronation Records [2]," p. 7 n. 2, for the origins of this. Edward the Confessor and the

pilgrim are depicted on the south face of the second pier of the nave in St Albans abbey.

49 Compare Galbraith, "Literacy," p. 17, ascribing Edward's taking the oath in French to "stupidity or laziness" as does Stubbs, *Const. Hist.* 2, p. 318 (whom Wilkinson cites "Coronation Oath of Edward II," p. 405 n.1); Wilkinson, "Notes on the Coronation Records," p. 586; Richardson and Sayles, "Early Coronation Records [1]," pp. 130–45. The Canterbury scribe gives both the Latin and French forms of the oath (D. and C. Cant. MS K.11, printed *SR* 1, 168) and does seek to explain the linguistic variation on grounds of literacy.

50 BL Harleian MS 2901 (Liber Regalis). See Richardson, "Early Coronation Records [2]," pp. 7, 10–11.

51 *Foedera* 2 ii, p. 36. For problems about the identification of the redeemed sword with *Curtana* see Legg, *English Coronation Records,* pp. xli–xlii; Richardson, "Early Coronation Records [2]," p. 8.

52 Legg, *English Coronation Records*, pp. 99, 122; Richardson, "Early Coronation Records [2]," p. 10.

53 Richardon, "Early Coronation Records [2]," p. 10 (BL Cotton MS C. XII).

54 *Ann. Paul.*, pp. 260–2; *Croniques de London*, p. 34 and n. Favier, *Enguerran de Marigny*, p. 121, suggests that one of the secret matters entrusted by the French king to his representatives at the coronation "qui grandement touchent nostre honeur et le votre" was Gaveston's position.

55 This hypothesis was first ventilated by Wilkinson in "The Coronation Oath of Edward II" (1933). He expanded it in his "Coronation Oath and the Statute of York." See also *idem*, "Notes on the Coronation Records" and *Const. Hist.* 2, introducion and chapter 1; ibid. 3, p. 60.

56 Printed by Phillips, *Pembroke*, App. 4. See n. 28 above.

57 Wilkinson, *Studies*, pp. 67–8: Maddicott, *Lancaster,* pp. 72–3. Harriss, *King, Parliament and Public Finance*, pp. 161–4. Maddicott, unlike Phillips, thinks that Pembroke, irritated by his supersession as lieutenant of Scotland (see text above) was one of the leaders of the "opposition group," hence his association with this document.

58 Phillips, *Pembroke*, pp. 25–8. Compare Denholm-Young, *History and Heraldry*, pp. 130–1.

59 See, in particular, Wilkinson, "The Coronation Oath of Edward II"; "Notes on the Coronation Records"; Richardson, "The English Coronation Oath [1 and 2]"; Hoyt, "The Coronation Oath of 1308, the Background of *Les leys et les custumes*" and "The Coronation Oath of 1308." This last prints the two versions side by side, French (*oratio recta*) and Latin (*oratio obliqua*) at pp. 355–6, and at p. 354 n. 1 provides a bibliography up to that time (1956). See also Graves, *Bibliography*, pp. 173–4. The Latin oath is in *Foedera* 2 i, p. 33, from the coronation roll; for the French: ibid., p. 36, and *Parl. Writs* 2 ii, App. p. 10. The MSS are cited *inter alios* by Wilkinson, "Notes on the Coronation Records," p. 582 nn. 2–3.

60 Some manuscripts have "queles le poeple eslira," but not I think, *pace* Wilkinson,

BL Cotton MS Vitellius C. XII (*auera esleuz*). It is erroneous to suggest that the illustration from CCC MS 20 (frontispiece to Legg, *English Coronation Records*) could refer to 1327 because both archbishops were supposedly present only in that year. Melton is not recorded to have been at Edward III's coronation (see below, chapter 7, n. 101). In fact the archbishop of York appears not to have attended the coronations of the first three Edwards. Further, I see no good reason to argue that the oath in MS Vitellius C. XII should be assigned other than to the coronation of 1308. Wilkinson, "Notes on the Coronation Records," pp. 586–9.

61 Hoyt, "Coronation Oath of 1308" citing Prynne, *Vindication* 1, p. 56; 2, pp. 74–80; Brady, *Introduction to Old English History*, p. 36. Their views are summed up by Taylor, *The Glory of Regality*.

62 Hoyt (*op. cit.*, p. 368) regards the Brady/Prynne argument as "unreal."

63 Ecclesiastical authorities were clearly responsible and the fourth recension, says Richardson, "English Coronation Oath," pp. 45–6, is associated with Westminster Abbey, the interests of which are preserved by the rubrics.

64 "Early Coronation Records [1]," p. 136; "Early Coronation Records [2]," pp. 2 and n. 5, 10. Wilkinson, *Const. Hist.* 2, pp. 90–1, regards Richardson's suggestion that the oath was no hasty improvisation but a preliminary to the preparation of books for the coronation as contradicting that author's statement that the second form of the fourth recension was "botched." It is really only the rubrication that is at issue here.

65 Hoyt, "Coronation Oath of 1308," pp. 355–6ff., 362.

66 Ibid., pp. 363–4, 369, 377.

67 Ibid., p. 381, and in general, pp. 377–83. Hoyt claims (p. 366): "The weight of the evidence of the chronicles is, therefore, for what it is worth, against any influence of dissension between Edward II and his magnates upon the drafting of the coronation oath."

68 Hughes, "Antiphons and Acclamations: The Politics of Music," and "The Origins and Descent of the Fourth Recension," especially pp. 197–207, 210.

69 Richardson, "English Coronation Oath," pp. 58–9, 65; Historia Roffensis, fo. 50^r.

70 *Ann. Paul.*, p. 260. It should be noted, however, that the *Historia Anglicana* 1, p. 121, here dependent on BL Royal MS 13 E. IX, a St Albans manuscript, says much the same more briefly. Compare Bodl. Lib. MS Rawlinson B. 152, fo. 2^r (a version of the *Historia*). Hoyt, "Coronation Oath of 1308," pp. 373–4, n. 3, demonstrates how Walsingham's (printed) version modified that of the Pauline annalist. But surely, in view of the marriage with Isabella, there is no problem about the French nobles joining with their English counterparts "to discuss the state of the realm"?

71 *Flores* 3, p. 142; *Bridlington*, p. 32.

72 *Ann. Paul.*, p. 260: "Primo die Quadragesimae": 3 March 1308 at Westminster.

73 Ibid., pp. 262–3.

74 *Guisborough*, p. 381: "Benedictus deus omnipotens qui post regem sapientissimum dedit nobis principium boni regis."

75 Ibid., pp. 381–2. Maddicott, *Lancaster*, p. 74 and n. 3, deduces (from PRO E101/373/5,7) that the earl was dining regularly with the king at this time and was as yet no enemy of Gaveston.

76 *HBC*, p. 552; Parry, *Parliaments*, pp. 70–1.

77 Ibid. *Ann. Lond.*, p. 153, states that the parliament met on "Hockday," 30 April.

78 *Ann. Paul.*, p. 263; *Vita*, p. 5. *Guisborough*, p. 384, says there was a great altercation between king and earls, the latter gaining the upper hand. For discussion of the April Parliament, see Maddicott, *Lancaster*, pp. 81–4.

79 *Ann. Lond.*, pp. 153–4; *Bridlington*, pp. 33–4 (Latin version: "Homagium et sacramentum"). Richardson and Sayles, *Governance of Mediaeval England*, pp. 467–8 (translation 468–9) print the document from BL Burney MS 277, fo. 5^v, which has the rubric: "Le primer enprise e l'ordenaunce mustre par le cunte de Nicole au Roy." Quotations in the text are from his version.

80 Gaveston is not named in the Burney MS, which employs the circumlocution "la persone dount home parle." *Bridlington*, p. 34, has "quantum ad personam domini Petri de Gavestone," although this is not regarded by the editor as part of the document itself.

81 Dene, in the Historia Roffensis, fo. 36^r, suggests that the original document (assigned to 1311) contained Gaveston's name and that a copy from which it was removed was attributed by Badlesmere to Despenser, since it was considered treasonable (see chapter 5 below). *Ann. Lond.*, p. 153, clearly associates it with the parliament of 1308 and follows it with a writ for Gaveston's banishment and with Winchelsey's excommunication (pp. 154–6). For Winchelsey's return: *Bridlington*, p. 33; *Melsa* 2, p. 280.

82 Wilkinson, *Const. Hist.* 2, p. 100, regards it as possibly a prelude to formal indictment of Gaveston at the Easter Parliament of 1308. Richardson considered that it might have been concocted after Gaveston's death, hypothesizing further that it could have been a partisan document from baronial extremists. "English Coronation Oath," pp. 66–7. Compare Maddicott, *Lancaster*, pp. 81–3, who accepts the declaration as having been presented by Lincoln in parliament.

83 Richardson, "English Coronation Oath," p. 67, citing *SR* 1, p. 182 (re Despenser) and Roberts, "Edward II and Gaveston's Jewels," p. 15, where the barons deny any suggestion of compelling the king; it was neither true nor did they wish to proceed in that way (*quod non est verum, nec placet eis iste modus*). Compare Historia Roffensis, fo. 35^r.

84 See the argument in Doherty, "Isabella," chapter 2 especially pp. 20–32. At p. 25 he claims that Edward's enforced acceptance of the awards of 1299 and 1303, coupled with Gaveston's anti-French advice, were probably the source of Edward's annoyance with Philip prior to the marriage and of his treatment of Isabella after it. *Bridlington*, p. 32, remarks that Edward married; "sub spe pacis et recuperationis terrarum in partibus transmarinis ... sed completo matrimonio, terras in Gasconia et alibi, ut praedicitur, injuste primitus occupatus, detinuit sicut prius." For Adam see Blackley, "Adam," p. 76, and, for uncertainty as to his date of birth, Valente, "Lament of Edward II," p. 433 n. 56.

85 Doherty, "Isabella," p. 24, citing (the text, dated 8 July 1307 X 24 January 1308, is ibid., p. 332 no. 1) BN Arch. Nat. J 654 no. 8; Coll. Brienne, fos. 67^r–70^v. Philip threatened to repossess all the lands of the English king across the Channel.

86 *Ann. Paul.*, pp. 258, 262–3. For the king of France's presents see n. 27 above.

87 LRO Dii/56/1 no. 42, cited by Maddicott, *Lancaster*, p. 83. See also the comments of E.A.R. Brown, "Political Repercussions," pp. 583–5, and ibid., "Documents", pp. 589–95.

88 LRO Dii/56/1 no. 39, printed in Maddicott, *Lancaster*, App. 1, pp. 335–6.

89 Ibid. The word "libras" here is much more likely to have been "livres turnois", as Maddicott, *Lancaster*, pp. 83–4 and 84 n. 1, points out. Even so, it would have been an immense amount and is doubtless exaggerated.

90 Phillips, *Pembroke*, pp. 28-0, who argues that "Pembroke's sympathies still lay with the King as they had done at Boulogne in January 1308."

91 *CPR 1307–1313*, pp. 9, 51; *CFR 1307–1319*, p. 18.

92 Doherty, "Isabella," p. 30, citing BN Arch. Nat. J 356, nos. 1, 7, 29.

93 An account of the election is in Pearce, *Wenlok*, pp. 218–24. See also Maddicott, *Lancaster*, pp. 85–6;*Wenlok Documents*, ed. Harvey, pp. 9, 120, 201, 212; Pearce, *Monks of Westminster*, s.v. "Aldenham," "Bolton," "Hadham," "Kedyngton," "Persore," "Wenlok," respectively pp. 70, 77, 63–4, 73–4, 62, 60–1; WAM nos. 5453, 5460, 9456, 9499D, E, 12777. Chaplais, *Gaveston*, App. 1, provides relevant transcripts from WAM 5460 (and see his text pp. 61–8). Monastic elections are discussed in Haines, *Ecclesia anglicana*, chapter 2.

94 *Foedera* 2 i, pp. 134, 41–2. For the bishop of St Andrews' treason: *Flores* 3 (Merton MS). p. 324; TCC R.541, fo. 100^r (101); Stones, *Anglo Scottish Relations*, no. 35. For that of his colleague of Glasgow: Barrow, *Bruce*, index s.v. "Wishart." These matters will be dealt with in chapter 9. The quotation is from Menache, *Clement V*, p. 278.

95 The most active among the earls appears to have been the veteran Henry de Lacy (Lincoln), but Phillips, *Pembroke*, p. 29, insists that Valence continued to sympathize with the king. *Vita*, p. 4, makes no exception for Valence but says that the earl of Gloucester remained neutral and that Hugh Despenser (presumably the elder) made himself odious to the barons who were working for the common benefit of the realm.

96 *Ann. Lond.*, p. 154; *Foedera* 2 i, p. 44.

97 *Bridlington*, p. 34.

98 Maddicott, *Lancaster*, p. 82, argues: "The fourth clause of the coronation oath had clearly been intended, not primarily to safeguard Edward I's concessions to the baronage, but to ensure that in any future struggle the King would be held to observe the magnates' decision."

CHAPTER FOUR

1 "The III Considerations," in *Four English Political Tracts*, p. 192

2 Treharne, *The Personal Role of Simon de Montfort*, p. 413

3 *Melsa* 2, p. 326: "ultra omnes in regno post regem immo quasi rex, potens, in opere et sermone."

4 Maddicott, *Lancaster*, p. 70; *Ann. Paul.* p. 259; CCC MS 174, fo. 122^v; *Brut* 1, p. 205. The *Vita*, p. 1 (cf. pp. 15–16) records Lincoln's argument that the earldom "quod cum corona habebat posset separare" and claims that the greater part of the barons did not consent. As Maddicott points out, op. cit., p. 71, there was disparagement of the royal line. Harriss, *King, Parliament and Public Finance*, chapter 6, discusses the concept of the royal fisc. The status of the *Brut* as a source for the period 1307–33 is analyzed by Taylor, *English Historical Literature*, App. 1.

5 CCC MS 174, fos. 121^r, 123^r; *Brut* 1, p. 202.

6 Phillips, *Pembroke*, pp. 24, 27–8. Clifford was appointed marshal on 3 September 1307 and became warden of Scotland on 20 August 1308. *Foedera* 2 i, pp. 5, 58.

7 *Vita*, p. 4; BL MS Cotton Vitellius C. XII, fo. 231^v (Richardson, "Early Coronation Records [2]," p. 10); Maddicott, *Lancaster*, pp. 6 (for the young Lancaster's relationship with Edward), 74–6. For the Lancastrian stewards and the background to the office: Vernon Harcourt, *His Grace the Steward*, chapters 5–6.

8 *Vita*, p. 15. Compare *Melsa* 2, p. 326.

9 *Bridlington*, p. 33; *Ann. Paul.*, p. 259. According to the former (p. 32), it was due to Gaveston that aliens occupied the most influential and rewarding positions, "domus regis officia secreta et pinguia." Maddicott, *Lancaster*, pp. 78–9, considers patronage *vis à vis* Gaveston and concludes: "It is this undercurrent of conflict over patronage which undoubtedly lies beneath the magnates' more personal and obvious grievances against the favourite."

10 *Murimuth*, p. 11; Bodl. Lib. MS Lat. hist. d. 4, fo. 203^r (*Ann. Paul.*, p. 257); MS Laud Misc. 529, fo. 93^r (101): "spretis consiliis aliorum nobilium in eorum precipue quorum consilio pater suus pre ceteris utebatur." He had spurned the councils of the other nobles, particularly of those on whom his father had relied. *The III Considerations*, p. 102, an English translation of a French tract of 1347, makes much use of "Roboam," distinguishing between the old and wise councillors and the youthful attendants appropriate to recreational activities. For the barons as councillors: Baldwin, *King's Council*, pp. 91–102. Baldwin's suggestion (following *Blaneford*, p. 148) that after his disgrace Stratford was rapidly restored to greater favour than before is not borne out by the facts.

11 Hamilton, *Gaveston*, pp. 44–5, 144 n. 67. See also Maddicott, *Lancaster*, pp. 78–9; *CPR 1307–1313*, pp. 25–6, 31, 56, 60, 79, 80 (bis), 83, 106, 137, 180–1, 202, 205–6, 356.

12 See above, chapter 3 n. 93.

13 Hamilton, *Gaveston*, pp. 45–6.

14 Gaveston's regency is examined by Hamilton, *Gaveston*, pp. 45–6.

15 BL Harleian MS 636 (*Polistoire*), fo. 232^r. The relevant quotation is Englished in Hamilton, *Gaveston*, p. 46, and given in the original French at pp. 144–5 n. 76.

16 CCC MS 174, fo. 123^r; *Brut* 1, p. 206. Compare the version in Leland, *Collectanea* 2, p. 473.

17 *Guisborough*, p. 383. See also Haskins, "Chronicle of the Civil Wars," pp. 75–6. Stubbs, *Const. Hist.* 2, p. 321 and n. 2.

18 *Foedera* 2 i, pp. 203–5, in French and Latin. For a version in English see Hamilton, *Gaveston*, App. 2, pp. 119–27. A ruby set in gold and said to be worth £1,000 was found in Gaveston's possession at his capture. Chaplais, *Piers Gaveston*, pp. 90–1, 99–108, and App. II (a list of 193 precious items from PRO C66/138 m. 3 (cf. *Foedera* loc. cit.), does not accept the chroniclers' view and a common modern assumption that these had come into Gaveston's ownership.

19 Davies, *Baronial Opposition*, pp. 56ff.; Maddicott, *Lancaster*, p. 67. Prestwich, *The Three Edwards*, pp. 82–3, regarded Edward as having "many advantages" at his accession.

20 For Lancaster: Maddicott, *Lancaster*, pp. 75–7; for Richmond: Lyubimenko, *Bretagne*, p. 104. Gloucester's predicament as brother-in-law, which allegedly forced him to be neutral, is explained in *Vita*, p. 4, although the Trevet continuator (ed. Hall, p. 4) categorizes Gloucester as "opposition" (together with Pembroke), as does *Lanercost*, p. 211. Phillips, *Pembroke*, pp. 208–9, does not accept his subject's opposition, perhaps somewhat against the weight of the chronicle evidence. At most it was a temporary alienation. In general see Hamilton, *Gaveston*, p. 50; Maddicott, *Lancaster*, p. 84.

21 *CFR 1317–1319*, pp. 17–19, 21; *CPR 1307–1313*, pp. 5, 51–2. Maddicott, *Lancaster*, pp. 77–8; Hamilton, *Gaveston*, pp. 48–9. For Clifford, Tibetot, and Botetourt, see Dugdale, *Baronage* 1, pp. 338–9; 2, pp. 39, 46. Botetourt has been considered a bastard of Edward I on the basis of Hailes Abbey chronicle BL MS Cleopatra D. III, fo. 51^r (*HBC*, p. 38), but as this was written over an erasure it has been discounted by Given-Wilson/Curteis, *Royal Bastards*, pp. 135–6.

22 Maddicott, *Lancaster*, p. 78; Hamilton, *Gaveston*, p. 49. Despenser's unpopularity on account of his adhesion to Gaveston "studio placendi et cupiditate lucrandi" is explained in *Vita*, p. 4.

23 *Itinerary EII*, p. 29; PRO E101/373/7; *Foedera* 2 i, p. 43; Maddicott, *Lancaster*, p. 78 and n. 6 citing PRO E403/143 m. 2.

24 *Vita*, p. 5; *Foedera* 2 i, p. 44; *CPR 1307–1313*, p. 71. The writ is incorporated in *Ann. Lond.*, p. 154. Only a few days before, 9 May, the earl of Leicester was granted the stewardship of England for himself and his heirs in perpetuity.

25 *Ann. Paul.*, p. 263.

26 Hamilton, *Gaveston*, pp. 146–7 n. 1.

27 Ibid., p. 53; *Ann. Lond.*, pp. 154–5; *Salisbury Register Gandavo* 1, pp. 237–30; Denton, *Winchelsey*, p. 257.

28 *Vita*, p. 6; *Foedera* 2 i, pp. 48–9; *CPR 1307–1313*, pp. 74–9. For details of these grants: Hamilton, *Gaveston*, p. 147 nn. 3–4.

29 *Foedera* 2 i, p. 48. This grant involved *inter alia* the manors of Burstwick and Skipton-in-Craven (Yorkshire), the honour of the High Peak (Derbyshire) and Carisbrooke Castle (Isle of Wight). Hamilton, *Gaveston*, pp. 53–5, gives a full

account and provides sketch-maps to show the location of Gaveston's Gascon and English lands.

30 PRO C62/84 m. 2; E404/1/3; E403/143; *CChW* 1, p. 275, all cited by Hamilton, *Gaveston*, p. 147 n. 8.

31 *Vita*, p. 6; *Foedera* 2 i, p. 51, 16 June 1308.

32 *Bridlington*, p. 15. Hamilton, *Gaveston*, p. 148 n. 19, rightly dismisses the claim in *Lanercost*, p. 211, that the barons assembled in arms at Northampton about 2 June when the king and Gaveston were there. Edward was in fact at Langley and was nowhere near Northampton in either May or June. *Itinerary EII*, pp. 31–2, from PRO E101/373/7; Maddicott, *Lancaster*, p. 88.

33 *Itinerary EII*, pp. 31–2; *Ann. Lond.*, p. 156; *Lanercost*, pp. 211–12; *CCR 1308–1313*, p. 68; *Foedera* 2 i, pp. 103–4: 13 February 1310. For the use of such blanks and for Edward's demands for the great seal so that he could use it in person for Gaveston's concerns in 1308 and 1312 see Dickinson, "Blank Charters," especially pp. 385–6; Maxwell-Lyte, *Historical Notes*, p. 320. The use of blank charters forms part of the recitation of Gaveston's misdeeds in article 20 of the Ordinances. Hamilton, *Gaveston*, p. 161 n. 72, dismisses the blank charter charge with respect to Gaveston's lieutenancy in Ireland on the grounds that the Irish seal would have been at his disposal.

34 It is as well covered by Hamilton as surviving records permit. See *Gaveston*, chapter 4, and chapter 10 below.

35 *Vita*, p. 6.

36 *Itinerary EII*, p. 37; Bodl. Lib. Bodley MS Lat. hist. c. 5 (R); *Ann. Paul.*, p. 264; *Ann. Lond.*, p. 156. Jean de Bretagne the father was also duke of Brittany (1286–1305), but that title passed to Arthur (duke 1305–12) and only in 1312 to Jean de Bretagne (ob. 1341), who became earl of Richmond on his uncle's death in 1334. The percentage figures for Gloucester's testing are 1307-08: 20; 1308-09: 51.9; 1309–10: 83.8; 1310–11: 86.4. Corresponding figures for Richmond are less impressive, viz.: 25.0; 22.2; 21.6; 9.1. Gaveston was not a regular witness, his highest figure being 13.6 percent for 1310–11. See Hamilton, "Charter Witness Lists," App. 1 (p. 8).

37 Hamilton, *Gaveston*, pp. 67, 152 n. 3; Maddicott, *Lancaster*, pp. 90–1; *Foedera* 2 i, p. 45.

38 Maddicott, *Lancaster*, p. 91, writes that Hereford witnessed charters from 2 June (1308} onwards. The percentage figures are for 1307-08: 27.5; 1308-09: 59.3; 1309–10: 16.2; 1310–11 (none recorded): Hamilton, "Charter Witness Lists," App. 1 (p. 7). Idem, *Gaveston*, p. 152 n. 6, citing PRO C53/95/m. 14, states that he first appears on the charter rolls as a witness on 2 August.

39 Bodl. Lib. Bodley MS Lat. hist. c. 5 (R); Maddicott, *Lancaster*, p. 92, citing *CPR 1307–1313*, pp. 123, 286, for Lacy's loans to the king of 600 and 3,000 marks, repayable by bonds issued in 1309 and 1310. But the significance of Lacy's loans should not be exaggerated. They do indicate "friendliness," but many others oblig-

ed the king. For instance, Reynolds lent a thousand pounds, Sandale, the treasurer, three thousand marks and Hugh le Despenser the same amount. The last came to be owed over £2,544 and the Genoese merchant Antonio de Pessagno some £7,380. *CPR 1307–1313,* pp. 376, 481, 506, 509–12.

40 Bodl. Lib. Bodley MS Lat. hist. c. 5 (R).

41 *Vita,* pp. 6–7; Hamilton, "Charter Witness Lists," App. 1 (p. 7).

42 LRO Dii/56/1, printed Maddicott, *Lancaster,* pp. 335–6; Bodl. Lib. MS Lat. hist. c. 5 (R); Hamilton, "Charter Witness Lists," App. 1 (p. 8). For Pembroke's position compare Maddicott, ibid., pp. 91, 94–5 (who thought he had "executed a complete volte–face") and Phillips, *Pembroke,* pp. 28–9 (who rejects the notion of a volte-face and argues that "Pembroke's sympathies still lay with the king as they had done at Boulogne in January 1308").

43 *Foedera* 2 i, p. 68.

44 Ibid., p. 44; Doherty, "Isabella," p. 34, citing PRO E401/141 m. 7; /144 mm. 1, 4–5, 8; /146 mm. 1, 4–5; *CPR 1307–1313,* p. 74; ibid. *1317–21,* pp. 115–6, 201–3.

45 *Foedera* 2 i, pp. 49–50.

46 Ibid., p. 51

47 Ibid., pp. 53–4, 59, 64–5, 70–1. For the many benefices enjoyed by Raymond in England see Wright, *Reynolds,* pp. 292–3.

48 *Itinerary EII,* p. 39. Bodl. Lib. Bodley MS Lat. hist. c. 5 (R) shows Louis dining on Sunday the third and Thursday the twelfth of November.

49 *Foedera* 2 i, p. 63.

50 Ibid.

51 Ibid., p. 65.

52 *Salisbury Register Gandavo,* pp. 314–16; *Hereford Register Swinfield,* pp. 451–2. For the improved relationship with the pope: Hamilton, *Gaveston,* pp. 69–70.

53 Bodl. Lib. Bodley MS Lat. hist. c. 5 (R): "Iste die venit comes Cornubie usque Cestr'." The *Vita,* p. 7, suggests that Gaveston avoided ambushes by returning through Wales.

54 Parry, *Parliaments,* p. 71; Maddicott, *Lancaster,* pp. 95–7; Hamilton, *Gaveston,* p. 72; *Itinerary EII,* pp. 44–5. Lancaster tested forty percent of charters for the regnal year 1307-08, only 7.4 percent (of fifty charters) during the following year. Hamilton, "Charter Witness Lists," App. 1 (p. 8).

55 Stubbs, *Const. Hist.* 2, p. 323.

56 Maddicott, *Lancaster,* p. 97.

57 Stubbs, *Const. Hist.* 2, pp. 323–4; Maddicott, *Lancaster,* pp. 97–9. *Rot. Parl.* 1, pp. 443–5, contains the articles and the responses to them.

58 As Maddicott, *Lancaster,* p. 99, points out, various chroniclers ascribe the petitions to the earls and barons, e.g., *Ann. Paul.,* p. 267; *Ann. Lond.,* p. 157; *Guisborough,* p. 384. In fact it is arguable, with Maddicott, that they were drawn up "by a combination of knights, burgesses, and magnates" – the last being dominant.

59 *Guisborough,* p. 384; *Parl. Writs* 2 ii, pp. 24–36.

60 *Ann. Paul.*, p. 267; *Ann. Lond.*, p. 157; Stubbs, *Const. Hist* 2, pp. 324–5; Hamilton, *Gaveston*, p. 72.

61 *CChW 1244–1326*, p. 291; Parry, *Parliaments,* p. 72 n. v; Stubbs, *Const. Hist.* 2, p. 325 and n. 1; Denton, *Winchelsey*, p. 258. Winchelsey was irritated by Gaveston's recall and the bull revoking his excommunication.

62 *Ann. Lond.*, pp. 157–65; *SR* 1, pp. 154–6; Stubbs, *Const. Hist.* 2, p. 325 n. 1. Maddicott, *Lancaster*, pp. 106–9 (also index s.v. "prises and purveyance"), has a digression on the significance of prises for Edward's situation. See also his "English Peasantry and the Demands of the Crown." William of Pagula, Leonard Boyle demonstrated, was the author *c.* 1330 of a condemnation of this "diabolicum prerogativum" (*De Speculo Regis Edward III*, ed. Moisant). Much of the examination into the use and abuse of purveyance in the half century after the regulatory statute of 1362 is also applicable to the reign of Edward II, when the weight of both purveyance for war and for the household of the king and queen must have been extremely burdensome. See Boyle, "William of Pagula and the *Speculum* "; Given-Wilson, "Purveyance of the Royal Household 1362–1413."

63 Denton, *Winchelsey*, p. 257; Haines, "Political Involvement of Bishops"; Hamilton, *Gaveston*, p. 73. With respect to Hamilton's comment, it should be remarked that the phrase in Clement V's bull "Non monitum ... nec super aliqua fraude convictum" is merely a recension of Edward's petition on his behalf.

64 *Guisborough*, p. 384.

65 *Bridlington*, p. 35.

66 *Vita*, pp. 7–8; Maddicott, *Lancaster*, p. 92. Among the earls Gilbert de Clare was the most frequent witness of charters during 1309–10, 1310–11. Hamilton, "Charter Witness Lists," p. 7.

67 Bodl. Lib. MS Fairfax 10, fo. 105^r (a French version of Trevet cited by Maddicott, *Lancaster*, p. 104, but not as such). BL MS Cotton Nero D. X, has a similar statement but in Latin.

68 Maddicott, Lancaster, p. 105, citing PRO C53/96/mm. 10–11. Oddly Warwick was a *testis*. For Lancaster's limited witnessing 1308–09, 1309–10, 1311–12 see Hamilton, "Charter Witness Lists," p. 8. Gaveston occurs even more infrequently.

69 CCC MS 174, fo. 123^v; *Brut* 1, pp. 206–7. Compare the English *Brut* versions cited by Maunde Thompson, *Chronicon*, pp. 183–4 (Notes) in which "Robert" de Clare also occurs. See next note.

70 *Pace* Hamilton, *Gaveston*, pp. 75, 155 n. 59. (influenced by Denholm-Young's argument, *Vita*, p. 8 n. 1, relying on *Ann. Lond.*, p. 133), also Tout, *Place*, pp. 12–13. The epithet "whoreson" would seem to have been applied to a Clare earl of Gloucester, as the *Brut* suggests, not to Monthermer. Were the latter intended, this remark (contrary to the suggestion of most chroniclers) would antedate 1307, when Gilbert de Clare had livery of the earldom. Nor, perhaps, was it all that "vicious," but probably a common oath. Edward I had applied it, as has been shown, to his own son when Prince of Wales. Further, Monthermer did not die until 1325. *HBC*, pp. 463, 501; Dugdale, *Baronage* I, pp. 217–18. Lincoln had died

by 5 February 1311 a *terminus ad quem* for this list. Also, Monthermer was the king's brother-in-law, hence his sons Thomas and Edward were royal nephews. He remained loyal to the king and was well rewarded for doing so, as the patent rolls bear witness. In consequence he was less likely to have been the butt of Gaveston's wit.

71 Maddicott, *Lancaster*, pp. 105–6.

72 Hamilton, *Gaveston*, pp. 74–5.

73 *Guisborough*, pp. 384–5; Parry, *Parliaments*, p. 72.

74 Hamilton, *Gaveston*, pp. 75–6.

75 *Guisborough*, pp. 384–5; Parry, *Parliaments*, p. 72.

76 *Vita*, pp. 8–9.

77 Ibid.; *Itinerary EII*, p. 54.

78 *Foedera* 2 i, p. 103; Hamilton, *Gaveston*, p. 77.

79 *Ann. Lond.*, pp. 168–9; *Liber Custumarum*, pp. 198–9.

80 Maddicott, *Lancaster*, p. 111.

81 *Ann. Lond.*, pp. 169–72; *Foedera* 2 i, p. 105; *Rot. Parl.* 1, p. 445. The text of the royal grant from *Ann. Lond.*, p.169, is: "plein poair de ordiner lestat de nostre roiaume et de nostre houstial suzdit; en tiele manere qe les ordinaunces soient faitz al honour de Dieu, et al honour et profist de seinte eglise, et al honour et profist de nous et al profist de notre poeple, selon droit et reson, et le serment qe nous faimes a nostre coronement."

82 *Vita*, p. 10. Compare *Guisborough*, p. 385; *Ann. Paul.*, p. 26.

83 *Ann. Lond.*, pp. 170–2, and see *Parl. Writs* 2 ii, App. pp. 26–7; *CCR 1307–1313*, p. 253.

84 *Ann. Lond.*, p. 172; Wilkinson, *Studies*, chapter 9; Davies, *Baronial Opposition*, chapter 11; Tout, *Chapters* 2, chapter 8, sect. 3 and in general, ibid. 6, index s.v. "Ordinances: The Ordinances (1310–11)."

85 *Ann. Lond.*, pp. 172–3; *Foedera* 2 i, p. 113; *Rot. Parl.*1, p. 446; Wilkinson, *Studies*, pp. 233–6.

86 *Ann. Lond.*, pp. 172–3.

87 *SR* 1, p. 157; *Rot. Parl.* 1, pp. 281–6 (London 5 October 5 Edw. II, 1311); *English Historical Documents 1189–1327*, pp. 527–39; Wilkinson, *Const. Hist.* 2, pp. 127–32 (partial).

88 Specifically the chancellor, chief justices of both benches, the treasurer, chancellor and chief baron of the exchequer, steward of the household, keeper of the wardrobe and the comptroller, a clerk suitable for keeping the privy seal, the chief keeper of forests this side of and beyond Trent, the king's chief clerk of the common bench. Maddicott, *Lancaster*, p. 119, when discussing the non-clerical emphasis of the Ordinances, overlooks no. 12, but see Denton, *Winchelsey*, p. 264; McFarlane, *Nobility*, pp. 234–5 (dependent on *Vita*, pp. 62–3, for Warwick's supposed capabilities). The barons were capable of making their own tendentious claim to lack of appropriate "literacy." See n. 156 below.

89 *Vita*, pp. 19–20.

90 *Bridlington*, pp. 40–1, for example, concentrates on these personal elements, which may well have seemed most important to contemporaries, or at any rate most easily comprehensible. Davies, *Baronial Opposition*, pp. 369–71, cautions that these clauses "were not actuated solely by personal motives." For the Frescobaldi and their financial operations: Kaeuper, "The Frescobaldi of Florence."

91 Davies, *Baronial Opposition*, pp. 376–7; Tout, *Chapters* 2, pp. 229–30, who argues that there was no novelty in these limitations on the judicial powers of the household.

92 Wilkinson, *Const. Hist.* 2, p. 119

93 Clause 1, with which is coupled the clergy's franchises (heading the Ordinances). See Wilkinson, "Coronation Oath of Edward II," p. 405; *Foedera* 2 i, p. 36. Davies, *Baronial Opposition*, p. 374, points out that the Mirror of Justices (ed. E.J. Whittaker, Selden Soc. 7 1893, p. 155) advocated twice-yearly parliaments "for the salvation of the souls of trespassers" rather than having them summoned rarely and at the king's will.

94 See Hurnard, *The King's Pardon for Homicide*.

95 The restriction on protection and pardon were considerable limitations on the king's rights. Davies, *Baronial Opposition*, pp. 373–4.

96 Rubricated in *Ann. Lond.*, p. 198, as the "Ordinationes comitum secundae" and printed ibid., pp. 198–202. Neither this nor the first set of Ordinances, concludes the chronicler, was properly observed (*nec istae nec primae incolumes servatae sunt*).

97 Davies, *Baronial Opposition*, p. 495, considered this committee to be ineffective: "the appointment of a committee of five to hear complaints against the royal officers, was almost useless as an executive body, and little trace, if any, is left of its action."

98 Maddicott, *Lancaster*, pp. 97–9, 118–19; Tout, *Chapters* 2, p. 227.

99 Stubbs, *Const. Hist.* 2, p. 329.

100 Prestwich, "Ordinances of 1311," and see his "A New Version of the Ordinances."

101 Stubbs, *Const. Hist.* 2, p. 331.

102 Wilkinson, *Studies*, chapter 11, p. 227, citing Davies, *Baronial Opposition*, p. 350, who continues, in line with his underlying thesis: "before any successful attack could be made it was essential for the barons to obtain some control over the executive or provide an alternative remedy."

103 Wilkinson, *Studies*, pp. 227–8.

104 Ibid., pp. 228–33; *Ann. Lond.*, p. 198.

105 Ibid., pp. 236–7; Tout, *Chapters* 2, pp. 235–60.

106 *Vita*, p. 17.

107 Maddicott, *Lancaster*, p. 117, citing BL Cotton MS Nero C. VIII, fo. 55ᵛ.

108 *Sempringham*, pp. 344–5: "les ordinaunces le dit counte de Lancastre"; Bodl. Lib. MS Lyell 17 (French *Brut*), fo. 115ᵛ; CUL MS Gg I. 15, fo. 187ᵛ (see chapter 8 n. 61 below); *Croniques de London*, pp. 46 (citing BL Harleian MS 565, fo. 2ʳ), 54.

109 *Ann. Lond.*, p. 202; *Vita*, pp. 20–1.

110 BL Cotton MS Nero C. VIII, fo. 65ʳ (wardrobe book); *Trokelowe*, pp. 68–9; *Historia Anglicana* I, p. 126. I owe these references and some discussion to Hamilton, *Gaveston*, pp. 91–2.

111 Hamilton, *Gaveston*, p. 91, citing *Foedera* 2 i, p. 144; *CCR 1307–1313*, p. 441. See also *Anonimalle Chronicle*, pp. 84–5.

112 *Ann. Paul.*, p. 271. BL Cotton Nero C.VIII, fo. 84ᵛ, gives the birth of Margaret's daughter as February with the christening at the end of the month when the court was entertained by minstrels (see text below and n. 127). Chaplais, *Gaveston*, pp. 76–7, argues for a birth about 12 January and suggests that Gaveston came to celebrate the churching of his wife forty days thereafter.

113 *Foedera* 2 i, p. 151; *CPR 1307–1313*, p. 405; *Vita*, p. 21: he was thought "to be lurking now in the king's apartments, now at Wallingford, now at Tintagel Castle." But this chronicler wrongly states that the pair celebrated Christmas together at York. See *Itinerary EII*, p. 80, for Edward's movements.

114 *Ann. Lond.*, p. 202, where Windsor is possibly an error for Westminster. Maddicott, *Lancaster*, pp. 121–2, thought that Gaveston was probably with the king at the latter place for Christmas, but Hamilton, *Gaveston*, p. 93, points out that on 23 December Edward paid a messenger one pound for delivering a letter from Gaveston and returning with the reply (BL Cotton MS Nero C. VIII, fo. 84ʳ).

115 *Vita*, p. 21.

116 *Ann. Lond.*, pp. 198–202; *Liber Custumarum*, pp. 682–90 (with differing rubric); CCL MS K.11 (dorse), according to Wilkinson, *Studies*, p. 235 n. 3, provide the only copies extant. Maddicott, *Lancaster*, p. 118 n. 6, mentions BL Cotton Ch. 43 D.18, the Canterbury MS and the Acland Hood MS in *HCMR* 6, App. p. 235, as the "only three contemporary copies." See also Davies, *Baronial Opposition*, p. 382.

117 *Ann. Lond.*, p. 202: "Istis ordinationibus jam promulgatis, nec istas nec primas incolumes servatas sunt."

118 *Foedera* 2 i, pp. 153–4; *Ann. Lond.*, p. 203. Edward forced the chancery clerks "sub gravi forisfactura" to append the seal to the documents effecting Gaveston's rehabilitation. See Maxwell Lyte, *Historical Notes*, p. 320, and n. 33 above.

119 *Foedera* 2 i, p. 154: writs issued to sheriffs throughout England.

120 Maddicott, *Lancaster*, pp. 122–3, citing PRO SC1/37/218. Writs for the restoration of Langton's lands were dated 24 January 1312 (*Foedera* 2 i, p. 154). He was sworn as treasurer on the twenty-third – but in accordance with the Ordinances only until the next Parliament (Tout, *Chapters* 6, p. 20; *CPR 1307–1313*, p. 413). These facts mentioned by the York correspondent would serve to date his letter to the last week of January, but it is odd that the writer says that the king arrived at York "this Thursday" (27 January), since by then he had been there for some considerable time. *Itinerary EII*, p. 81.

121 *CPR 1307–1313*, p. 413; *Parl. Writs* 2 ii, p. 46; *Ann. Lond.*, p. 203. Maddicott, *Lancaster*, p. 123, gives further information.

122 *Vita*, p. 22, colourfully describes Winchelsey's action as striking Gaveston with the sword of anathema: "gladium suum arripuit et Petrum anathemate percussit, ut sic lata sententia evacuaretur gratia."

123 Davies, *Baronial Opposition*, no. 16 pp. 551–2. The grounds of interference were that Langton had not taken the oath to maintain the Ordinances and, subsequently, that the treasurer should be appointed with the assent of the baronage.

124 *Ann. Lond.*, p. 204. Denton, *Winchelsey*, pp. 247–68, discusses the archbishop's role as Ordainer. For the occasions on which Edward is reported, or rumoured, to have been seeking Scottish help see chapter 9 below.

125 *Vita*, pp. 22–3.

126 *Ann. Lond.*, p. 204: "seductorem Petrum caperent et regem informarent"; *Lanercost*, p. 218.

127 *Itinerary EII*, pp. 81–2; BL Cotton MS Nero C. VIII, fo. 84^v. See n. 112 above.

128 Hamilton, *Gaveston*, p. 94, citing at p. 163 nn. 31–3, PRO E101/373/26 fo. 51 (details payments for preparations by carpenters, a smith, royal porters, and others at Scarborough Castle); SC8/286/14296 (one of a gathering of Gascon petitions); BL Cotton MS Nero C.VIII, fo. 88^r; *Foedera* 2 i, p. 156 (restoration of Wallingford); *CPR 1307–1313*, p. 514; ibid., *1313–1317*, p. 45. Caillou was to continue to work for the king after Gaveston's death: see *War of Saint-Sardos*, index s.v., and for this family see Pole-Stuart (PhD thesis), "Gascony."

129 *Itinerary EII*, p. 82 (from BL Cotton MS Nero C. VIII).

130 Maddicott, *Lancaster*, p. 125, citing gifts of venison by the queen to Lancaster and Hereford early in 1312 (BL Cotton MS Nero C. VIII, fos. 138^v, 148^v); Blackley and Hermansen, *Household Book*, pp. 137, 139, 215). Doherty, "Isabella," p. 40, regards such gifts as no indication of political allegiance. Presumably, though, they did have some connotation of friendship, regard, conciliation, or reconciliation. The part played in medieval life by "douceurs" would make an interesting topic.

131 Doherty, "Isabella," pp. 38–41, citing PRO E403/159/m. 5 for the queen's expenses.

132 Ibid., p. 41, where Doherty claims that Isabella's true feelings towards Gaveston at the time are unclear. Perhaps, he suggests, that as potential mother to the heir to the throne and as mistress of a substantial household she was willing to tolerate him. *Ann. Paul.*, p. 272, gives the date of Louis' arrival as the eve of the Exaltation of the Holy Cross, i.e. 13 September. See n.173 below.

133 Bodl. Lib. MS Tanner 197, fo. 54^v. Forty marks were paid for dragging the king from his bed on the morning after Easter: "Johanne de Vilar. et Alicie de Leygrave [the king's *nutrix*] et aliis domicellis camere regine trahentibus regem de lecto suo die lune in crastino Pasche [i.e., 27 March 1312]." See also fo. 54^r for payment of a further ten marks to Alice, and chapter 1 above n. 12

134 *CPR 1307–1313*, p. 454; *CFR 1307–1319*, p. 129; BL Cotton MS Nero C. VIII, fo. 98^r.

135 *CPR 1307–1313*, p. 454; Hamilton, *Gaveston*, pp. 94–5.

136 *Itinerary EII*, p. 84; *Bridlington*, p. 42. *Melsa* 2, p. 327, gives 10 April as the date
     of the king's departure for Newcastle with Gaveston, Henry de Beaumont, and
     Edmund de Mauley (de Malo Lacu).

137 BL Cotton MS Nero C. VIII, fo. 86^r; Hamilton, *Gaveston*, pp. 95, 164 n. 50.

138 *Vita*, pp. 22–3 (where the author does not specifically ascribe leadership to Lan-
     caster); *Trokelowe*, pp. 69–70; *Historia Anglicana* 1, p. 131 (Bodl. Lib. MS
     Rawlinson B.152, fo. 6^r); Maddicott, *Lancaster*, p. 123 n. 7; *Melsa* 2, p. 326.
     suggests that at the instance of the archbishop Lancaster attempted to counteract
     the king's ineptitude: "Thomas Lancastriae comes, qui ipsius archiepiscopi ani-
     matus hortatu, cum suis adhaerentibus conatus est regiis obsistere ineptiis"; Göt-
     tingen MS 740, fo. 218^v, ed. Eckhardt 2, ll. 38975–7: "Aftre Pers fulharde
     enchaste/ lo þe erel of Lancastre Thomas/þoru comun assent ladesman he was"
     (adding capitalization but not punctuation).

139 The chroniclers report his "nocturnal theft" and clandestine journeying through
     woodland. *Vita*, p. 23: "Sic Thomas de nocte volat, sub luce moratur,/ Ut lateat,
     modicum cursum ne fama loquatur"; *Lanercost*, p. 218: "dimissa via alta, per
     nemerosa loca Angliae veniens latenter"; *Bridlington*, p. 42; *Itinerary EII*, p. 85.

140 *Lanercost*, p. 218; *Bridlington*, p. 42; *Vita*, pp. 23–4; *Trokelowe*, p. 75; *Itinerary
     EII*, p. 85; *Foedera* 2 i, p. 169.

141 *Trokelowe*, pp. 75–6; *Historia Anglicana* 1, p. 131 (Bodl. Lib. MS Rawlinson
     B.152, fo. 6^v). Hamilton, *Gaveston*, p. 164 n. 52, assumes that there was a per-
     sonal meeting between the queen and Lancaster.

142 Blackley and Hermansen, *Household Book*, pp. xxiv–xxvi, 130–5, 218–21, 237.
     Compare Maddicott, *Lancaster*, p. 125; Hamilton, *Gaveston*, pp. 95–6, 164 n.52;
     Doherty, "Isabella," pp. 42, 92. I am indebted to Doherty for the notion of a pos-
     sible confusion between the incidents of 1312 and 1322. For the latter he cites
     RHGF 20 (*Continuator of Guillelmus de Nangiaco*), p. 633. But this last source
     does not name Tynemouth, merely a strong maritime castle: "quoddam castrum
     fortissimum, cui mare adjacet."

143 Maddicott, *Lancaster*, pp. 125–30; Phillips, *Pembroke*, pp. 32–7; Hamilton,
     Gaveston, pp. 93–9; Harcourt, *His Grace the Steward*, s.v. "Gaveston." The
     fullest chronicle account is *Vita*, pp. 23–4, but the *Flores* 3, pp. 150–3, 336, has
     additional details, while *Ann. Paul.*, p. 271, states uniquely that Gaveston escaped
     from Pembroke's custody.

144 Maddicott, *Lancaster*, p. 125, following *Vita*, pp. 23–4. His argument (also
     adopted by Hamilton, *Gaveston*, p. 96: "a strategic error of the first order"), that
     had king and favourite stayed together "the forcible seizure of Gaveston would
     have been much more difficult," is open to question. It would have hazarded the
     royal person a second time (the first being at Newcastle) and precipitated a crisis
     similar to that which followed the battle of Lewes (1264). In the event, Gaveston
     was not forcibly seized at Scarborough nor was the castle "newly fortified,"
     merely put into a state of defence "victualibus et armis munito" (*Bridlington*, p.
     42; *Ann. Lond.*, p. 204) and inadequately at that.

145 *Vita*, pp. 23–4 (suggesting that Lancaster took advantage of the king's separation
     at Knaresborough from Gaveston at Scarborough); *Ann. Lond.*, p. 204; *Bridling-*
     ton, pp. 42–3; *Flores* 3, pp. 150–3, 336 (describes Pembroke and Warenne as act-
     ing "ex parte ordinatorum regni et pacis Anglie"); *Lanercost*, p. 218; *Trokelowe*,
     p. 77; *Historia Anglicana* I, pp. 131–3 (Bodl. Lib. MS Rawlinson B.152, fos.
     6ʳ–7ʳ); *Foedera* 2 i, p. 169. The Tintern MS of the *Flores*, p. 336, makes Gave-
     ston rather than the king the briber of Pembroke. The *Flores* is clearly to be pre-
     ferred to the *Vita* (p. 24) in implying that Pembroke acted on behalf of Lancaster
     and the other dissidents. See n. 148 below.
146 *Historia Anglicana* I, p.132 (Bodl. Lib. MS Rawlinson B.152, fo. 6ᵛ).
147 *Vita*, p. 24.
148 *Ann. Lond.*, pp. 204–6; CCL Reg. I, fos. 365ʳ–6ʳ (*Lit. Cant.* 3, App. no. 52, pp.
     388–92). Phillips, *Pembroke*, p. 33 n. 3, names another Canterbury text: BL
     Harley MS 636, fo. 233ʳ (*Polistoire*). That Pembroke acted on his own initiative
     (*Vita*, p. 24) is belied by the text of the document itself and by the fact that Lan-
     caster was on hand when the arrangement was made. See *Pembroke*, p. 34; Mad-
     dicott, *Lancaster*, p. 126; n. 145 above.
149 *Trokelowe*, p. 76; *Historia Anglicana* I, p. 132 (Bodl. Lib. MS Rawlinson B.152,
     fos. 6ᵛ–7ʳ).
150 *HBC*, p. 553; Parry, *Parliaments*, p. 75. Venue changed to Westminster by writs
     of 8 July.
151 *Vita*, pp. 24–5 (according to which there was no resistance to Warwick); *Flores* 3,
     pp. 151–2. 336; *Melsa* 2, pp. 327–8; *Anonimalle Chronicle*, pp. 86–7; *Ann.*
     Lond., pp. 206–7 (a lengthy account of the "surrender" of Gaveston caught
     unawares "nudis pedibus"); *Bridlington*, p. 43, hints at Pembroke's connivance at
     the abduction. *Ann. Paul.*, p. 271, alone says that Gaveston escaped and was
     recaptured by Warwick. The exchange in the *Flores* (p. 152) between Gaveston
     and Warwick is scarcely credible in the circumstances. Gaveston, catching sight
     of his pursuer through a window at Deddington, is said to have taunted him with
     the nickname "Black Dog of Arden," receiving the response – addressed to the
     "traitor" – that he was no dog but the earl of Warwick.
152 "Qui ipsum Petrum decollari fecerunt inter Wotton et Warewyk sub monte vocato
     le Blakelowe ibi [ubi?] est crux que vocatur Gaverstonescros." Bodl. Lib. MS
     Dugdale 12, p. 53 (from fo. 50ᵛ of a lost register of Stoneleigh Abbey). The date
     given in this source is the eve of St Bartholomew, i.e. 10 June. MS Dugdale 18,
     fo. 17ᵛ, gives 13 Kal. July (19 June). The spot is still commemorated.
153 *Vita*, pp. 29–30; *Flores* 3, pp. 152–3. Surviving copies of such letters are in
     Davies, *Baronial Opposition*, no. 138, p. 598 (Lancaster safeguarding Hereford,
     but marked "vacatur"); *CDS* 3, no. 275 (Warwick safeguarding Hereford); Bodl.
     Lib. MS Tanner 90, fo. 1ʳ (Botetourt safeguarding Warwick, in a more expansive
     form, dated 18 June at Warwick, specifying the action at Deddington): "la queu
     prise est bonne et droiturele." See Maddicott, *Lancaster*, pp. 128–9, who points
     out (p. 128 n. 7) the obscurity of Hereford's part in all this.

154 *Ann. Lond.*, p. 207; *Bridlington*, pp. 43–4. The latter remarks that the revocation of the Ordinances was not known in the county: "de quarum revocacione illi comitatui non constabat." If this is not just the chronicler's way of legitimizing the earls' action it must indicate negligence or deliberate non-compliance on the sheriff's part, under Warwick's aegis as Maddicott, *Lancaster*, p. 128, suggests. But *Bridlington*, p. 43, also remarks: "quae quidem revocatio non omnibus innotuit, quibus publicatio fuerat nuntiata."

155 *Vita*, pp. 26–7; *Flores* 3, p. 153. According to Bodl. Lib. MS Dugdale 12, p. 53 (fo. 50^v of a Stoneleigh Abbey register not known to be extant), after describing the capture of Gaveston by Lancaster and Warwick, comments on the illegality of the earls' actions: "Et quia predicti comites de Lancaster. et Warr. in se regiam potestatem assumebant prefatum Petrum sine legis iudicio aut parum regni sic ut premittitur perimendo, prefatus rex per brevia sua ipsos comites ad parliamentum suum citari fecit apud Westmonasterium."

156 *Vita*, p. 28; *Ann. Lond.*, pp. 207, 236: where Warwick is described at the time of his death in 1315 as "homo discretus et bene literatus, per quem totum regni Angliae sapientia praefulgebat." According to the St Albans' tradition (*Historia Anglicana* 1, pp. 132–3; *Trokelowe*, p. 77) it was one of profound counsel (Warwick?) who cut the knot and decided that it were better for one man to die than that wars should bring turmoil to the people (compare John 11:50). It was presumably just a negotiating device for the barons to suggest – as will be noticed below – in response to Cardinal Arnaud Nouvel's letters, that "se litterarum notitiam non habere, sed in militia et in usu armorum eruditos esse; quare dictas litteras non curabant videre" (*Trokelowe*, p. 78). See n. 88 above and text below.

157 E.g. *Trokelowe*, p. 76; *Vita*, p. 26.

158 *Vita*, pp. 25–6.

159 Ibid., p. 26.

160 Ibid., pp. 27–8; *Flores* 3, pp. 151–3, 336–7 (Tintern); *Ann. Lond.*, pp. 207–8; *Bridlington*, p. 44; *Trokelowe*, p. 77. The *Flores* emphasizes Pembroke's part in opposing the earls, who had caused him to betray his trust, while *Lanercost*, p. 219, suggests that he was incensed that someone placed in his custody should be killed unbeknown to him.

161 *Vita*, pp. 30–2.

162 Maddicott, *Lancaster*, pp. 129–30.

163 *Ann. Lond.*, pp. 208–9. See chapter 2 n. 84 above.

164 *Ann. Lond.*, pp. 209–10; *CPL 1305–1342*, pp. 104, 107; PRO E101/375/8 mm. 7–9; *Itinerary EII*, p. 89, which shows the court to have been at Dover between about 5 and 9 August.

165 *CPR 1307–1313*, p. 489; *Foedera* 2 i, pp. 173, 175–6; *Parl. Writs* 2 i, p. 88; PRO E101/375/8 m.7.

166 *Vita*, pp. 29–30 (this legalistic authority remarks that to meet force with force for one's own protection is lawful); *Flores* 3, p. 337 (Tintern MS), p. 210; *Ann. Lond.*, p. 210.

167 *HBC*, p. 553.

168 *Ann. Paul.*, pp. 271–2; *Trokelowe*, p. 78. See n. 156 above, also Maddicott, *Lancaster*, p. 134.

169 On 24 December 1312 Testa became cardinal priest of St Cyriacus in Thermis; d'Aux, cardinal bishop of Albano. Cristofori, *Storia dei Cardinali*, p. 302. These cardinals rank respectively fourth and sixth in the table compiled from the Roman Rolls (PRO C70/2–6) by Dr Wright on the basis of the yearly average of letters directed to them from England. Of all the cardinals, Testa received by far the highest number of letters – 107 in 13 years and 9 months. Wright, *Reynolds*, App. 4, especially p. 310, and see n. 186 below.

170 *Foedera* 2 i, pp. 175, 196–7, 205. Walter Maidstone, future bishop of Worcester, was a member of this embassy.

171 *Foedera* 2 i, p. 178; *Vita*, pp. 32–3.

172 *Vita*, p. 32; *Lanercost*, p. 219.

173 According to *Ann. Paul.*, pp. 271–2, the cardinal arrived 29 August and Louis of Evreux on 13 September. See also Maddicott, *Lancaster*, p. 134 n. 3, citing PRO E101/375/2 for their dining with the king (at Westminster) on 6 and 15 September respectively – also with Isabella. See nn. 132 above, 183 below.

174 *Vita*, pp. 32–3.

175 *Vita*, pp. 33–4.

176 *Vita*, pp. 34–8.

177 *Itinerary EII*, p. 90; *Ann. Lond.*, pp. 215–17.

178 Phillips, *Pembroke*, chapter 11, and Maddicott, *Lancaster*, pp. 130–54, go over the ground more minutely than would be appropriate here.

179 Roberts, *Edward II, the Lords Ordainers*, pp. vi–vii; *Foedera* 2 i, p. 180; *CPR 1307–1313*, p. 498; *Trokelowe*, pp. 77–8; Maddicott, *Lancaster*, p. 134; Phillips, *Pembroke*, p. 47 n. 1, suggests that the French clerks were William de Novo Castro and Raymond de Suspiriano rather than Richardson's suggestion, "English Coronation Oath," p. 69, that they were the M. Gerard de Curton and M. Richard Tybetot, clerks of the king of France, present for the "peace" indenture of 20 December 1312 (Roberts, *Edward II, the Lords Ordainers*, p. 21 and n. 188 below). Pembroke had been paid for a ship to carry Suspiriano and de Novo Castro (also named in the indenture), who are described as being clerks of the French king in PRO E101/375/8 fo. 9, cited by Maddicott, *Lancaster*, p. 136 n. 2. "De Novo Castro" is said to be a knight in *Ann. Lond.*, p. 225. However, Suspiriano or Subirani was in 1314 Edward's envoy to the Curia, not Philip's: see *Foedera* 2 i, p. 240.

180 *Ann. Lond.*, pp. 211–15. Richardson, "English Coronation Oath," pp. 69–70, comments on the lawyer's arguments. He contends that the contrast between the position of Edward I and Edward II "lies in the difference between the forms of oath to which the two kings had sworn at their coronations." For ecclesiastical elections see Haines, *Ecclesia anglicana*, chapter 2.

181 See Phillips, *Pembroke*, pp. 47–8, for this association of the earls.

182   *Ann. Lond.*, p. 211.

183   A safe conduct had been issued on 8 October 1312 at the instance of the media-
        tors (the cardinal, the count of Evreux, and the bishop of Poitiers) for the earl of
        Hereford, Robert de Clifford, John Botetourt, John de Heselarton, Adam de Her-
        wynton, and Michael de Meldon (the last three clerks) to come to them for dis-
        cussions. Another was issued on 6 November to last until the twenty-third (omit-
        ting the two last names), another on 11 November (Henry Percy is added) and
        another on 16 December for Clifford, Lancaster, Warwick, Hereford, Percy, and
        Botetourt to travel throughout the realm, but without arms and caparisoned hors-
        es. *CPR 1307–13*, pp. 502, 507–8, 509, 516–17.

184   Roberts, *Edward II, the Lords Ordainers*, pp. 15–17. The names (at p. 17) follow
        the "Rationes Baronum," which object to the insufficiency of the security
        promised to them, and the "Memoriale de litteris specialibus faciendis" in pur-
        suance of an agreement between the parties.

185   For the de la Pole/Charlton quarrel see Morgan, "Barony of Powys," also *Rot.
        Parl.* 1, pp. 355–6, for this "gravis dissensio." The various matters for which Lan-
        caster sought solution are detailed in a letter on his behalf to the cardinal:
        Roberts, *Edward II, the Lords Ordainers*, pp. 7–9. The response is at ibid., pp.
        9–10. The cardinal, a skilful diplomat, avoided comment on the derogatory epi-
        thets applied to Gaveston. These further points at issue are aired by Maddicott,
        Lancaster, pp. 137–44; Phillips, *Pembroke*, pp. 53–8.

186   To give them their proper titles, since there has been some confusion on the
        point: Arnaud Nouvel, cardinal bishop of St Prisca (1310–17), and the Gascon
        Arnaud d'Aux, bishop of Poitiers, who between 24 December 1312 and 24
        August 1320 was cardinal bishop of Albano, and who acted as papal chamber-
        lain. In January 1314 Aux was granted a royal pension of fifty marks a year for
        his "fructuosa servitia et matura consilia." *Foedera* 2 i, p. 241; Wright, *Reynolds*,
        pp. 286, 299.

187   Roberts, *Edward II, the Lords Ordainers*, p. 17; *Ann. Lond.*, p. 221.

188   The terms of the settlement are given in French in *Ann. Lond.*, pp. 221–5 (in
        Latin in Roberts, *Edward II, the Lords Ordainers*, pp. 17–21), and in English
        summary in *CPR 1307–13*, pp. 191–2. They are dated 20 December 1312 at Lon-
        don in the cardinal bishop of St Prisca's chamber. Others present were the bishop
        of Poitiers (himself in a few days to become a cardinal), Cobham, bishop of
        Worcester, the earl of Pembroke, John de Crombwell or Cromwell, two clerks of
        the French king (see n. 179 above), Raymond Subirani (de Suspiriano), William
        de Novo Castro, knight, M. Roger de Northburgh, John Walwayn and Michael de
        Meldon. The response of the earls, incorporating a number of reservations, is in
        Ann. Lond., pp. 225–9.

189   Phillips, *Pembroke*, pp. 49–50.

190   Roberts, *Edward II, the Lords Ordainers*, pp. 4–6; *Foedera* 2 i, pp. 203–5;
        Hamilton, *Gaveston*, App. 2 pp. 119–27.

191   On the basis of cap. 1, which demands a receipt, Maddicott, *Lancaster*, p. 148

(see also p. 336), wished to date the earls' response to 23 X 27 February. On the twenty-third the jewels etc. were taken from Clifford's house to the Tower. The schedule of the horses and jewels for which an acquittance is recorded is dated the twenty-seventh. *Foedera* 2 i, pp. 203–5, *CPR 1307–13*, p. 525; Hamilton, *Gaveston*, App. 2. But as Phillips, *Pembroke*, p. 59 n. 1, points out, the parliament is referred to in the past tense, which would require the response to be dated 18 March X 29 May (the next parliament). In that case it would be more likely to approximate to the earlier than the later date.

192 *Ann. Lond.*, pp. 225–9, esp. pp. 226–7, 229.

193 Ibid., pp. 225–9.

194 Haines, *Church and Politics*, p. 13 nn. 29–30; Phillips, *Pembroke*, pp. 40–1.

195 Phillips, *Pembroke*, p. 41. Clement V had empowered the cardinal of St Prisca and Bishop Arnaud not only to make peace but also to annul the Ordinances: BL Cotton MS Nero C.VIII, fo. 57^r; *CPL 1305–1342*, pp. 103–4, 106, 117.

196 *Vita*, pp. 38–9; *HBC*, p. 39; Phillips, *Pembroke*, pp. 62–4. In late May Louis de Clermont, count of Clermont, and other magnates dined with the king; on the following day with the queen. PRO E101/375/2 m. 9.

197 *RHGF* 23 (*Chronicon Ste Catherinae*), p. 409. *Vita*, pp. 38–9, is uncertain as to whether the king of Navarre was to be crowned or knighted and states that the earl of Gloucester was appointed keeper in Edward's absence.

198 *RHGF* 23 (*Chronicon Ste Catherinae*), p. 409, gives a graphic description of Edward's action in saving himself and his wife from a nocturnal conflagration: "Et quadam nocte lectus in quo praedictus rex Anglorum et ejus uxor erant totus inflammatus est igne. Quae ut rex Angliae percepit cito toto corpore nudo surrexit, et uxorem suam inter brachia sua composuit, et sic gratia Dei liberati a combustione fuerunt." See also Doherty, "Isabella," pp. 50–3; Trease, "Spice and Apothecaries," p. 46. For the royal itinerary at this time: *Itinerary EII*, pp. 98–9; PRO E101/375/2 mm. 9–10.

199 Ibid.: "Regina, uxor domini Ludovici, regis Navarrae, filii praedicti regis Franciae, et cum ipsa eodem modo uxores fratrum domini Ludovici (quod regina Anglorum prima percepit) in adulterio deprehensae sunt cum duobus milititus fratribus, Philippo scilicet et Galtero de l'Auney [i.e., Margaret with Philip and Blanche wife of Charles with Walter]." This incident and Isabella's visit have been exhaustively examined by Brown, "Diplomacy, Adultery and Domestic Politics," pp. 53–6, where she states that it will also feature in her forthcoming *Adultery, Charivari, and Political Criticism in Early Fourteenth Century France.*

200 *Vita*, pp. 42–3 (which is explicit on the topic of Edward's delaying tactics); *Foedera* 2 i, pp. 230–3; *Statutes* 1, p. 169.

201 *Vita*, pp. 43–4. Archbishop Stratford and Kilsby were to follow a similar festive routine after their reconciliation: Haines, *John Stratford*, p. 326. For Marigny's role see Favier, *Un Conseiller de Phillipe le Bel*, pp. 122–4.

202 *Vita*, p. 44.

203 Maddicott, *Lancaster*, pp. 151–3, summarizes the events leading to "Edward's victory."

204 *Ann. Lond.*, pp. 200–1.

205 *Trokelowe*, pp. 77, 79–80: "Ab illo ergo die crevit amor filii, et evanuit memoria Petri": From that day the love of her son grew, while the memory of Peter faded.

206 *Ann. Paul.*, p. 273; *Vita*, pp. 36–7. *Trokelowe*, p. 79, suggests that the French nobles wanted the baby to be called Louis. Had it been so it might have assisted future pretensions.

207 Reynolds's election is graphically described in the *Vita*, pp. 45–6.

208 Phillips, *Pembroke*, p. 65. Enguerran fell from grace and was hanged during Philip V's reign (*RHGF* 22, *Ex anonymo regum Franciae*, p. 19). For him see Favier, *Un Conseiller de Phillipe le Bel*, especially pp. 121–6 for his relations with Edward II; for Pessagno, Fryde, "Antonio Pessagno of Genoa." Isabella was also in contact with Testa (by letter): Blackley and Hermansen, *Household Book*, p. 145.

209 *Vita*, pp. 49–50 (where the barons are said to have wished to decide about the Scottish campaign in Parliament so as not to infringe the Ordinances); Phillips, *Pembroke*, pp. 72–3; and see below.

210 Inge and Henry Spigurnel were the justices delivering the Warwick gaol before whom Gaveston was brought to give a semblance of judicial trial to Gaveston's death "by authority of the Ordinances." *Bridlington*, pp. 43–4.

211 Bodl. Lib. MS Dugdale 18, fos. 17^v–18^r. See also BL MS Cotton Cleopatra D. III, fo. 56^v; *Trokelowe*, p. 88; *Itinerary EII*, p. 122, which shows that the king remained at Langley for some two and a half weeks.

CHAPTER FIVE

1 Treharne, *Baronial Plan of Reform*, pp. 412–13.

2 *Ann. Paul*, p. 57; *Melsa* 2, pp. 331–2. The suggestion in *Knighton* (1, p. 410) that the king had not wanted the earl to attend the Bannockburn campaign (he had planned to capture him at Pontefract on his victorious return) should be treated with caution in view of that chronicler's bias. The same caution should be extended to the remarks of the author of the Tintern *Flores* (3, p. 338) that Lancaster and "complices sui," the other absentees (Warwick, Arundel and Warenne) feared for their own safety. The *Flores* is fiercely "anti-Edward." Bannockburn is dealt with in the context of Scottish affairs in chapter 9.

3 Phillips, *Pembroke*, pp. 74–6, discusses the earl's participation. The chronicle evidence is contradictory, but it is suggested that Pembroke may have emerged with some credit from the retreat.

4 Maddicott, *Lancaster*, chapter 5. Hamilton, "Charter Witness Lists," App. 1 (p. 11), shows Lancaster (following a total absence) witnessing 43.9 percent of charters in the regnal year 1314–15, 33.3 percent in 1315–16, but only 4.8 percent in 1316–17.

5 For what follows immediately I am indebted to the analysis of Harriss, *King, Parliament and Public Finance*, chapter 7.

6 Harriss (loc. cit., p. 169) argues that the Ordainers avoided an explicit connection between restraining grants and purveyances. They did not want to abolish grants, merely those of which they did not approve. Not only were they jockeying for retention among themselves but in his turn the king argued that such resumption should not be prejudicial to the Crown. In a sense any such attempt to restrict the king's freedom of action in such matters was prejudicial. For the tract on purveyance attributed respectively to Archbishops Islip and Mepham, but most recently to William of Pagula, see Tait, "On the Date and Authorship," Boyle, "William of Pagula and the *Speculum Regis Edwardi III*, " pp. 329–36; Denholm Young, "Authorship of the *Vita*," pp. 269–70.

7 These matters are discussed by Maddicott, "The English Peasantry."

8 Historia Roffensis, fos. 35ᵛ–6ʳ; *Lit. Cant.* 3, pp. 402–3; See Haines, "Bishops and Politics ... Hethe," p. 603 n. 78.

9 Haines, *John Stratford*, p. 247.

10 Davies, *Baronial Opposition*, pp. 400–7. The various petitions that ensued, as well as the resumptions and commissions for perambulation, are detailed there.

11 *CCR 1313–18*, p. 166; *CPR 1313–17*, p. 290; *Reg. Palat. Dunelm.* 4, pp. 75, 89–94; Harriss, *King, Parliament and Public Finance*, p. 172.

12 Harvey, *Cuxham*; Kershaw, *Agrarian Crisis*, p. 117. For an overall view: Jordan, *The Great Famine*, particularly pt. 1: "A Calamity 'Unheard of Among Living Men'."

13 *CChW 1244–1326*, p. 436.

14 *Flores* 3, pp. 160–1; *Trokelowe*, pp. 89–98; Baker, *Chronicon*, p. 9, laments the famine: "eodem tempore in Anglia nimis invaluerunt pestilencia et fames, quaterio frumenti xl solidos sterlingorum appreciato." The author of the *Vita* (pp. 69–70) vacillated between blaming scarcity on the wickedness of the people (following Jeremiah) and the effect of Saturn being in the ascendant. The highest price that Thorold Rogers, *Six Centuries of Work and Wages*, pp. 215–18, found during the period was on 30 May 1316 at Leatherhead, when wheat was sold at 13s. 4d. a quarter. A Canterbury-based chronicler doubles that figure (n. 16 below). In fact it varied widely below the forty shillings of Baker and the *Anonimalle Chronicle*, while Knighton notes forty-four shillings in Leicester market (1, p. 411). For some caveats about Thorold Rogers's work see Fischer, *Great Wave*, pp. 392–3. In general: Jordan, *The Great Famine*; Lucas, "The Great European Famine"; Kershaw, "The Great Famine," especially pp. 89–92, for the various prices vouchsafed by chroniclers. In 1322 there was further scarcity. The prices per quarter in Kent were then: wheat twenty-three shillings, barley sixteen shillings, and oats eighteen shillings. Historia Roffensis, fo. 39ᵛ (compare nn. 16–17 below).

15 "Tanta fuit sterilitas bladique tota terra fame pene consumebatur. Nichil tamen sensit ex eo ecclesia Roffensis nec defectum in esculentis et poculentis paciebatur, sed

satis habuit domino providente." Historia Roffensis, fo. 2^v. The reference may be
more particularly to the monastery.

16 For a comprehensive critical analysis of "The Crisis of the Fourteenth Century,"
concerned with prices, population and other economic aspects, see Fischer, *Great
Wave*, pp. 448–54, also pp. 23–40 for an overall assessment. To what extent these
economic movements in themselves affected Edward's fall would be hard indeed
to determine.

17 TCC R.5 41 fo. 113^r (114). "Tanta caristia erat in Anglia ut illi qui solebant de
bonis suis propriis seipsos et familiares honeste sustinere per vicos et plateas per-
rexerunt mendicantes. Illo enim tempore summa [a quarter] frumenti [wheat]
vendebatur pro ii marcis et summa ordei [barley] pro xvis. premaxima mortalitas
hominum erat; (fo. 113^v (114) anno domini millesimo CCCmoXVIIIo maxima
mortalitas animalium, de genere boum in toto regno Anglie." *Anonimalle Chronicle*, pp. 90–1, records (for London?) forty shillings a quarter of wheat "badly
cleaned and poorly weighed," while two small onions fetched a penny in Cheapside. See also the detailed analysis of Farmer in "Crop Yields, Prices and Wages"
and "Grain Yields on Westminster Abbey Manors."

18 Bodl. Lib. MS Top. Devon d.5, fo. 5^v. After noting the promotion of an abbot at
the mother house of Beaulieu on 30 September 1314: "In cuius tempore bussellus
frumenti pro iiis. iiid. et aliquando pro iiiis. vendebatur et buselli grossi salis pro
iiiis. viiid. Fames enim erat valida et inaudita et mortalitas hominum sed precipue
pauperum, et magna mortalitas armentorum maxima et inaudita, videlicet bovum,
vaccarum et vitulorum per multos annos durans, ubicumque enim ambulabant vel
stabant pre vehementi dolore eos interius anxiante quasi lacrimantes rugiendo
intuentibus conquerebantur, et ita subito corruentes exspirabant de domo ista."

19 Bodley MS. Lyell 17, fo. 113^r; *Anonimalle Chronicle*, pp. 88–91; Maddicott, *Lancaster*, pp. 163–4.

20 *Rot. Parl.* 1, p. 295; *Foedera* 2 i, pp. 263, 266. Kershaw, "Agrarian Crisis," pp.
106–17, gives many details of the decline in livestock and of oxen for ploughing, a
development only accentuated by the problems of this particular time. In many
instances plough-horses had to be substituted for oxen.

21 Graphs illustrating these changes have been collected in Fischer, *Great Wave*, pp.
18–22, 26–7.

22 Maddicott, *Lancaster*, pp. 172–4.

23 *Flores* 3, p. 172.

24 Maddicott, *Lancaster*, p. 175; *Vita*, pp. 64–6.

25 *Ann. Paul.*, p. 279:

26 Tupling, *South Lancashire*, pp. xlii-li, for this and what immediately follows.

27 Compare Historia Roffensis, fo. 36^v: "cum vexillo regis deplicato." On the displaying of banners, a sign of "public war," see Keen, *Laws of War*, pp. 92–107, especially 106–7. In this case the display was unauthorized, a usurpation of authority,
hence traitorous.

28 Some differing chronicle accounts are discussed by Tupling, op. cit., pp. xlvi n. 5,

xlvii, n.1. He concludes that the earl had no knowledge of Banaster's death, but see *Guisborough*, pp. 397–8, who claims that Banaster's hiding place was discovered by scouts (*exploratores*) of the earl and this coincides with the Coram Rege roll edited by Tupling, pp. 38, 46.

29 The following recapitulation of events makes use of other documents, but it is not always easy to square these, particularly chronologically, with the narrative of the *Vita*.

30 The monks were granted licence to elect on 8 July 1316, Sandale being duly elect- ed on the twenty-sixth. *Le Neve* 4, p. 45. For the earl's movements at this time see Phillips, *Pembroke*, pp. 102–3.

31 At that time there were new troubles in Bristol of a different kind: "fugientes miraculos," which prompted the government's repressive action. *Foedera* 2 i, pp. 536–7.

32 *Vita*, p. 74, comments on the risk to life and possessions incurred by anyone resist- ing the king: "Quid est regi resistere nisi propriam vitam contemnere et omnia bona pariter amittere?"

33 A more complex account emerges from Fuller's article, "The Tallage of 6 Edward II." He diligently searched the public records in manuscript and provides tables of the names and assessments of those townsmen who were "Partisans of the King and Constable" and of those who constituted "The Party of the Townsfolk." Some of the more important of these references are now: *CPR 1313–16*, pp. 68–9, 289, 574, 604–5; *CFR 1307–19*, pp. 147, 169, 172, 286, 308–9; *Foedera* 2 i, pp. 200, 225; *Rot. Parl.* 1, pp. 359–62. For the charters of 1312, 1317 (two) 1321 (two) and 1322 (ratification of Edward I's charter, 7 February 1322 Gloucester) see *Bristol Charters* 1, pp. 48–69.

34 *Polychronicon* 7, pp. 299, 301.

35 Beverley Smith, "Edward II and the Allegiance of Wales," p. 149, citing PRO E101/376/7 fo. 12^r. The king was at Clipstone from 22 December and for the greater part of January 1316. *Itinerary EII,* pp. 135–6.

36 Beverley Smith, "Edward II and the Allegiance of Wales," pp. 139, 149. See chap- ter 10 below.

37 *Trokelowe*, pp. 91–2: "audaciam resistendi a victoria Scotorum sibi assumentes, foedusque et fiduciam eis ineuntes."

38 The *Vita*, p. 68, insists that Llywelyn's surrender was unconditional. For expenses May-July 1316 paid for the captive Llywelyn and his sons: SA MS 120, p. 53, and for the rounding up of his forfeited flocks in September, ibid., p. 29.

39 Davies, *Baronial Opposition*, pp. 31–2. The Tintern *Flores* has a fairly full account of the affair and of the traitor's death meted out to Llywelyn: *Flores* 3, pp. 339–40, 343. For the charge against Despenser of encroachment on the royal power: *SR*. 1, p. 183.

40 Charlton was chamberlain at least by 1313. His closeness to the king and the favours he enjoyed incurred the enmity of the barons who sought to have him removed. His rise to power is detailed by Davies, *Baronial Opposition*, pp. 215–16. See also Morgan, "Barony of Powys."

41 Morgan, "Barony of Powys"; Davies, *Baronial Opposition*, pp. 215–7, 285, 418, 571 no. 36 (transcript of PRO C81/82/2430); *CPR 1313–17*, p. 548 (10 October 1316).

42 For the later stages of the dispute in Powys: Morgan, "Barony of Powys," pp. 26–42; Fryde, *Tyranny and Fall*, p. 80. See chapter 7.

43 There is much information about this parliament. *Rot. Parl.* 1, pp. 350–4, has a lengthy entry; see also Parry, *Parliaments*, pp. 79–81 – "more formally and regularly recorded than the proceedings in any former parliament" (ibid., p. 81 n. *l*). It may be, as Maddicott suggests (*Lancaster*, p.180), that this has exaggerated its importance in the minds of historians. William Ayrminne, clerk of the chancery, was specially deputed to draw up a memorandum of proceedings.

44 *Vita*, p. 69.

45 See Davies, "Statute of Lincoln and Sheriffs"; *Baronial Opposition*, pp. 523–4.

46 Davies, *Baronial Opposition*, pp. 408–14; *Rot. Parl.* 1, pp. 350–1. But see *Flores* 3, p. 341 (Tintern MS): "Sed mala voluntas regis versus comitem Lancastriae semper duravit."

47 Ibid., pp. 413, 419 – where the relevant passage from the parliament roll is given in the text..

48 *Bridlington*, p. 49. Davies examines Lancaster's three conditions and their implications, *Baronial Opposition*, pp. 419–21.

49 *Rot. Parl.* 1, p. 351. For taxation references see chapter 1 n. 90

50 *Foedera* 2 i, pp. 283–4: Lincoln, 7 Feb. 1316; *CCR 1313–18*, p. 327.

51 *Vita*, p. 69; *Le Livere de Reis*, p. 332. Compare *Bridlington*, p. 49. What conclusion should be drawn from the fact that Walwayn, putative author of the *Vita*, was at the parliament as a trier of petitions, yet reported Lancaster's new status "in an off-hand fashion"? Maddicott advances this fact as an argument for the earl's new position not being considered "extraordinary" (*Lancaster*, p. 181). It could, of course, be an argument against Walwayn's authorship, otherwise quite convincing. Many issues were in fact dealt with but by fewer nobles than would ordinarily have responded to the summons.

52 Historia Roffensis, fo. 79[v]: "per unum diem cum aliis octo episcopis muros respiciendo ibi moram traxit et videns quod ibi nichil profecit rediit apud Bromlegh." Presumably he sought leave before withdrawing.

53 Pembroke left for France in mid-May 1315 and with Bishop Stapeldon, Antonio Pessagno and M. Henry of Canterbury appeared before Louis X at Vincennes on 8 June, among other matters to hear the responses to various petitions concerning Aquitaine. Doubtless the question of homage was also raised. Phillips, *Pembroke*, p. 86; Buck, *Stapeldon*, pp. 124–5.

54 Davies, *Baronial Opposition*, p. 415.

55 The contention of Maddicott, "The English Peasantry," especially pp. 15–34, and see above.

56 *CFR 1307–19*, p. 275 (12 April 1316: mandate to collectors of customs); *Cal. Letter Bk. E*, p. 60. See Davies, *Baronial Opposition*, pp. 405–6, 416–7, 426; Maddi-

cott, *Lancaster*, p. 182. The difficulty of any permanent resumption against the royal will is indicated by Davies, op. cit., pp. 406–7 n. 2, citing PRO Escheator's account (north of Trent) E153/3/18.

57 *CCR 1313–18*, p. 166; *Reg. Palat. Dunelm.* 4, pp. 74–6. Ireland was suffering from the Bruce invasion. See chapter 10 below.

58 The council met 18 July. Parry, *Parliaments*, p. 82, and the cardinals d'Eauze and Fieschi were in London by the end of June. See Haines, *John Stratford*, p. 126 and below.

59 *Foedera* 2 i, p. 335; *Parl. Writs* 2, ii, p. 171; *RDP* (App.) 3, p. 267.

60 Phillips, *Pembroke*, pp. 96–7. For Lancaster's letter: *Murimuth*, pp. 271–6 (French version with translation in an appendix to the printed chronicle from BL Claudius E.VIII, fo. 256^{r-v}); *Bridlington*, pp. 50–2 (Latin version).

61 The claim that he was not sufficiently well: "eo quod non vigemus nec valemus aliqualiter laborare" (*Bridlington*, p. 51) contradicts his other excuses about Scottish incursions and that matters of importance should not be discussed other than in parliament, by interpretation an assembly with all the peers of the realm, not just a few.

62 These matters are discussed by Phillips, *Pembroke*, 97–9, and Maddicott, *Lancaster*, pp. 186–9, 331–2.

63 Maddicott, *Lancaster*, p. 187, suggests that it may have been as a consequence of the king's demand that fifty pound landholders served at their own expense.

64 SA MS 120, p. 39. These were carried by Roger de Bray, a "scutifer" of the household, who returned to Beverley on 17 September.

65 Maddicott, *Lancaster*, pp. 186–8; *Itinerary EII*, pp. 146–7.

66 *CFR 1307–19*, p. 331.

67 Parry, *Parliaments*, pp. 81–2; Maddicott, *Lancaster*, p. 345.

68 The situation over a century later provides parallels. Watts, "The Counsels of King Henry VI" writes (p. 293): "In the minds of the fifteenth-century nobility, then, counsel had a firm place, but it was as a perpetual stream flowing freely to the monarch. It could not be borne by a fixed group except under short-lived revolutionary circumstances or in the absence of an adult king."

69 According to the Trevet continuator, p. 20 (cited Maddicott, *Lancaster*, p. 191), the younger Despenser, Amory, and Audley are an addition to the list of those taking part in these council meetings. For the clerical element see Haines, *John Stratford*, p. 125.

70 *Flores* 3, p. 178: "surrexerunt alii tres sub umbra regis alarum sperantes, fautores mendacii ipso Petro nequiores" and, lower down, "factus est novissimus error peior priore."

71 *Ann. Lond.*, p. 146.

72 Bodl. Lib. MS Douce 128, fo. 157^r; *Documents*, ed. Cole, p. 4; Tout, *Chapters* 6, p. 45; Davies, *Baronial Opposition*, pp. 431–3 (he considers the "curialists" to have been formed by Pembroke into the "middle party"), 544–5; Phillips, *Pembroke*, pp. 132–3, who rejects the concept of a "middle party" in the sense advocat-

ed by Davies and Tout. Maddicott, *Lancaster*, 193–5, considers the five courtiers (the Despensers, Amory, Audley, Montagu) as "perhaps being conscious of form- ing a distinct and compact political group, almost a 'party' in the modern sense," and cites their mutual recognizances in June 1317 in support of this view. He pro- vides a detailed summary of the various grants they enjoyed by royal favour.

73 Phillips, *Pembroke*, p. 132 n. 5, cites PRO C81/100/4231 for the order on 12 May 1317 for partition; livery of the portions did not occur until 15 November 1317: *CFR 1307–19*, p. 350; Davies, *Baronial Opposition*, p. 431. The Despenser portion is detailed in Clark, *Cartae de Glamorgan* 3, pp. 1048–56.

74 *Vita*, p. 68; SA MS 120, p. 35; *Flores* 3, p.178; Tout, *Chapters* 6, p. 42. For the family see G.E.C. *Complete Peerage*, 9 (s.v. "Montagu"), 11 (s.v. "Salisbury"); Dugdale, *Baronage* 1, pp. 643–53; Douch, "Career of William Montague" (thesis).

75 Maddicott, *Lancaster*, pp. 56, 102.

76 *Ann. Lond.*, p. 152; *Vita*, p. 2. Oddly the latter source does not record Warenne's part in the Scarborough siege.

77 See Fairbank, "Last Earl of Warenne."

78 Ibid.

79 *Select Cases before King's Council 1243–1482*, pp. lxvi–lxix, 27–32 (MS Holkham Misc. 29, fos. 229^r–31^r). Matilda de Neyrford, widow of Sir William de Neyrford, was Warenne's mistress, and a case of divorce with her as "actrix" had been brought into the court of the archdeacon of Norfolk "in dedecus ipsius domini regis manifestum et contemptum." Warenne's wife Joan was the king's niece and in the company of the queen when cited in the lower chapel of the palace of West- minster in contravention of the exemption of the palace. The case was in the Court of Arches in 1316, when the king paid M. Simon de Inven3ano two shillings a day for 142 days to prosecute the case on behalf of the countess. SA MS 120, p. 26.

80 The evidence is examined by Phillips, *Pembroke*, pp. 111–15, especially p. 115 n. 1. Jean de Lamouilly, who had provided Edward with the capacity to use gunpow- der when besieging Stirling in 1304 is said to have kidnapped Pembroke as a con- sequence of Edward I's meanness in rewarding him for his services. Prestwich, *Edward I*, p. 155.

81 Fairbank, "Last Earl of Warenne," pp. 199–200; *CChW 1244–1326*, pp. 576–8. Warenne was to die in 1347 without legitimate heirs. His title passed to his nephew, Richard FitzAlan.

82 *Melsa* 2, p. 335. Alice had married Sir Ebles (Ebulo) Lestraunge by 10 November 1324 and on his death (1335) made a vow of chastity. Once again she was "abduct- ed," this time by Sir Hugh de Frene (Lord Frene), whom she later married. On his death (between December 1336 and January 1337) the pope instructed Bishop Burghersh to enforce the vow negated by Frene's "ravishment." She died without issue on 2 October 1348. *GEC Complete Peerage* 5, pp. 572–4; 7, pp. 687–8; *HBC*, p.470 ; *CPL 1305–42*, p. 544.

83 Maddicott, *Lancaster*, p. 197 n. 6 (citing *Historia Anglicana* 1, p. 148), makes the point that the St Albans chronicle suggests that the abduction had the king's assent

and that of many others, but that one version (BL MS Royal 13 E. IX) changes the unlikely "plurimis Anglorum" to "plurimis aulicorum" – courtiers.

84 *Vita*, p. 80: "quod possit sine offensione vestra de iniuria sibi illata vindictam sumere et satisfactionem qualem poterit impetrare."

85 *Vita*, p. 81.

86 *CPL 1305–42*, pp. 414, 430, 439. Wright, *Reynolds*, App. 7, pp. 333–41, prints the bull sent to the nuncios in 1317 detailing the various *gravamina*.

87 TCC MS R.5 41, fos. 113^{r-v} (114). Clearly this Canterbury chronicler was either present himself or had the details from someone who was. The king gave generous gifts to a number of cardinals and to Otto de Grandisson who accompanied the nuncios. Gaucelme de Jean, the papal vice-chancellor, the pope's "nepos," received forty pounds, as well as other gifts including provisions. SA MSS 120, pp. 102, 105–6; 121, p. 66; Wright, *Reynolds*, nos. 11, 17, pp. 290–1, 293–6, for summary biographies.

88 *Hereford Reg. Orleton*, p. 16; Haines, *John Stratford*, p. 126.

89 *Reg. Palat. Dunelm.* 4, pp. xliv–xlv, 391–6; *Liber Epistolaris*, 163; *Le Neve* 6, p. 107; 12, s.v. "Beaumont," "Kynardesley"; *Graystanes* (SS), pp. 98–100; Smith, *Episcopal Appointments*, pp. 23–6; Middleton, *Gilbert de Middleton*.

90 Interestingly the author of the *Vita* does not even mention the Durham election and certainly casts no suspicion on Lancaster with respect to the Middleton affair.

91 Involvement with the Scots is well attested by the chroniclers: *Graystanes* (SS), p. 100; *Melsa* 2, p. 333; Castleford chronicle, fo. 220^r, ed. Eckhardt 2, p. 1060 ll 39228–29; *Lanercost*, pp. 233–4, does not implicate the Scots in the affair.

92 BL Cotton MS Domitian A. XX, fo. 42^r; *Melsa* 2, p. 334. The *Scalacronica*, ed. Stevenson, p. 144; ed. Maxwell, p. 60 (compare Stapleton, "Brief Summary of Wardrobe Accounts," pp. 328, 330), suggests that the cause of the rebellion was the earlier arrest of Middleton's cousin, Sir Adam de Swinburne, but despite the general reliability of Sir Thomas Gray with respect to northern affairs this seems to be an oversimplification. For Edward's report to the pope, 10 September 1317, *Liber Epistolaris*, 168; *Foedera* 2 i, p. 341: *Dolenter audivimus*.

93 The matter is closely examined by Maddicott, *Lancaster*, pp. 204–7; more recently (1992) and with different conclusions by Prestwich, "Gilbert de Middleton." In chapter 9 below this incident is further discussed in the context of Scottish affairs.

94 See Maddicott, *Lancaster*, pp. 207–8, for details. He cites *inter alia* the chronicle of St. Werburgh, Chester, from White Kennett, *Parochial Antiquities*, p. 376; PRO SC8/157/7833, /177/8829–31; Watson, *Memoirs of the Earls of Warren* 2, pp. 26–7.

95 On 29 August 1317 in a letter from Aldington to the Canterbury chapter Reynolds rejoiced in the fact that at last the king was setting out for Scotland for the salvation of the Church and people of those parts. He ordered that prayers be offered for his success. HMCR *Var. Coll.* 1, p. 267. On 4 September at Edward's request Reynolds urged that prayers and masses be said in his diocese for victory. Priests so doing were to have forty days' indulgence, while thirty days were promised to

all who took part in prayers, pious works, etc., with that intention. See Wright, *Reynolds*, pp. 353–4.

96 *Vita*, pp. 80–1. As Maddicott, *Lancaster*, p. 208, states, this had the effect of transferring the claim made by the Ordainers to the earl himself.

97 Maddicott, *Lancaster*, pp. 208–9. He prints the agreement in App. 1, pp. 336–7, as does Phillips, *Pembroke*, App. 4, pp. 319–20, who discusses it ibid., chapter 5.

98 Maddicott, *Lancaster*, p. 209, regards them as "not entirely in the King's favour."

99 *Cont. Trivet*, p. 23.

100 *Vita*, p. 82; *Cont. Trivet*, p. 24; *Flores* 3, pp. 180–1; *Foedera* 2, 1, p. 479. However, the claim put into the mouth of Pembroke by the author of the *Vita* can hardly be an accurate depiction of Lancaster's attitude: "Regnum et feodum, et universa que possidet, comes ipse relinqueret priusquam huiusmodi proditionem inchoaret." Events were shortly to prove otherwise.

101 Maddicott, *Lancaster*, p. 213, suggests that about 30 November a meeting of clergy "accepted the Ordinances as a basis for peace-making." He cites *Flores*. 3, pp. 182[–3] and *Ann. Paul.*, p. 281. The bias of the former is anti-Edward and distinctly pro-Lancaster, but the latter makes no mention of this aspect. What it does indicate is that at this time ecclesiastics were more particularly concerned with Archbishop Melton's provocative act in carrying his cross elevated throughout Kent and London, a move to which Reynolds responded by placing the city under an interdict for the duration of his stay. See Haines, *Ecclesia anglicana*, chapter 5. On the twenty-seventh – the day of Melton's departure – Cardinal Fieschi celebrated mass and published the bull for a truce with the Scots (see chapter 9 below). The following day Reynolds excommunicated all who impeded the peace of the realm (this would have included Lancaster) and those who seized ecclesiastical property (certainly the Scots).

102 For details of these arrangements, the generous nature of which could only anger Lancaster, see Maddicott, *Lancaster*, pp. 210–11. Badlesmere's indenture is recorded as an expense in SA MS 121, p. 40. He was to receive 600 marks a year, 5,000 in time of war. *CPR 1317–21*, p. 14, 3 August 1317, records an annual fee of 1,000 marks a year to be taken for four years from the first fruits of vacant benefices, granted to the king by the pope.

103 Davies, *Baronial Opposition*, pp. 433–4, 563–4 (App. no. 42); Maddicott, *Lancaster*, pp. 211–13; Phillips, *Pembroke*, pp. 142–7.

104 Stapleton, "Brief Summary of Wardrobe Accounts," p. 344; Maddicott, *Lancaster*, index s.v. For Tyeys see Banks, *Baronia Anglica* 1, p. 436 s.v. "Tyes." Richard d'Amory was apparently associated with the elder Despenser: Davies, *Baronial Opposition*, pp. 209–10 and index s.v. "Damory."

105 *Foedera* 2 i, pp. 356–7, 365; Parry, *Parliaments*, p. 82; Maddicott, *Lancaster*, p. 213. The king took the opportunity to make a pilgrimage to Canterbury where he was to be found on 14 June. HMCR *Var. Coll.* 1, p. 267; Wright, *Reynolds*, p. 387. These sources confirm that R.L. Poole's conjectured date "1318" in *Var. Coll.*, is in fact correct.

106 See chapter 9 below.

107 *Bridlington*, p. 54. At that time the king was moving from Sheen to Windsor. *Itinerary EII*, p. 166. Compare *Knighton*, pp. 412, 421, who writes that the king and queen, the archbishop of Canterbury with all his comprovincial bishops, as well as the earls and barons, were met at Leicester by Lancaster. King and earl kissed and were reconciled.

108 See Haines, *Church and Politics*, pp. 121–2; Phillips, *Pembroke*, pp. 155–7, whose footnotes provide references for the meeting; Maddicott, *Lancaster*, pp. 213–14. The concerned king had already issued a mandate on 18 February 1318 from Sheen (Archbishop Reynolds was there at the time) directing the clergy not to do anything in derogation of his authority at their London convocation (23 February) but to leave matters touching him until the Lincoln Parliament, which in the event did not take place. *CPR 1317–21*, p.104; *Foedera* 2, i, p. 356. *Bridlington* omits Bishop Cobham of Worcester from those present at Leicester, but see *Worcester Register Cobham*, pp. 7, 229, 252, which show that he was there between 4 and 10 April and presumably for a short while thereafter.

109 The *Vita*, p. 85, declared that the archbishop and the earls, since Lancaster's mind was immovable, specifically granted on the king's behalf that the Ordinances were to be observed. A charter was drawn up and sealed to that effect. Lancaster for his part promised fealty to the king but excepted the dispute with Warenne: "domino regi et suis debitam fidelitatem et securitatem sub fide promisit, excepta querela quam contra comitem Warenne de raptu uxoris dudum instituit." This is really only a condensed version of the information in *Bridlington*.

110 *Bridlington*, pp. 54–5. See also *Flores* 3, pp. 183–4; *Knighton* 1, pp. 413–21, who states that the articles given there were confirmed by the cardinals in London..

111 Maddicott, *Lancaster*, p. 216, writes that the town fell a few days after the Leicester meeting, but see Barrow, *Bruce*, p. 389, which gives the date as 1–2 April. The second of April is the date given by *Ann. Paul.*, p. 282. Stubbs, *Const. Hist.* 2, p. 342, regarded its capture as "the signal for reconciliation."

112 Salisbury, "Political Agreement," pp. 78–83, from PRO C49/4/26; Phillips, *Pembroke*, App. 4, pp. 320–1, from PRO C49/4/27.

113 *Ann. Paul.*, p. 282; *Flores* 3, p. 184. It may be no coincidence that at this time the Pauline annalist, like some other chroniclers, inserts a piece about an imposter who claimed to be the real king. The Lanercost chronicler, who was particularly concerned about the lack of royal activity on the border with Scotland, can only have echoed the truth when he quoted the imposter's claim to have been told by the spirit of the Lord (*quidam spiritus Domini*): "Edwardus rex in nullo penitus a populo est dilectus." *Lanercost*, p. 237.

114 This unsealed document (in draft form with some aberrations) is printed from PRO SC1/63/183, by Phillips, *Pembroke*, pp. 321–2.

115 These were far-ranging: "donationes terrarum, tenementorum, balliviarum, wardarum, maritagiorum et escaetarum, ac remissiones firmarum, debitorum et

aliorum." The document is printed by Maddicott, *Lancaster*, App. 1 p. 337, from PRO E159/91 m. 64d; E368/88 m. 92.

116 Simon of Ghent, the Salisbury diocesan, acting for Archbishop Winchelsey, published them in St Paul's churchyard.

117 *Parl. Writs* 2 i, pp. 501–3.

118 Thompson, "An Alert in 1318," p. 168.

119 *Knighton* 1, pp. 413–21.

120 Maddicott, *Lancaster*, p. 220, gives the PRO references for these incursions: SC8/177/8829–30 – Warenne's petitions against his fellow earl. The council merely advised Warenne to do what he could on his own. It is difficult to accept Lancaster as a single-minded reformer in view of the fact that he was, as in this case, prepared to give preference to his personal territorial advantage over his political aims. See Maddicott's admission of this, ibid., p. 223.

121 This could refer to the initial but temporary restraint on the king's power to make grants in 1310. Davies, *Baronial Opposition*, pp. 359–60, 372.

122 *Knighton* 1, p. 415: "tenuz pur nules, e le pernoure puny en le parlement par agarde de Baronage."

123 Ibid., pp. 415–21.

124 Maddicott, *Lancaster*, p. 223, who cites the letter (overlooked by Wilkinson and Edwards, in their work on the Treaty of Leake), giving the reference PRO E101/377/7. It is printed HMCR *Var. Coll.* 1 (Canterbury), pp. 220–1. The earl was to come to Northampton within ten days of the letter's date. Elements of the administration had arrived at Northampton by 30 June in preparation for an assembly there: *Itinerary EII*, p. 168.

125 HMCR *Var. Coll.* 1, p. 220.

126 This statement by Reynolds is useful since it helps distinguish two men of the same name who were almost contemporaneous (see Emden, *Biog. Oxon.*, s.v.), but Wright, *Reynolds*, only records a relationship with the other Bosco, who was rector of Harrow, Middlesex.

127 *Parl. Writs* 2, i, p. 504.

128 HMCR *Var. Coll.* 1, pp. 267–8.

129 Ibid., pp. 268–9.

130 *Vita*, p. 88, excepts Hugh Despenser (the younger?) and Warenne from those who humbled themselves before the earl to receive his grace. According to this chronicler the queen, the earl of Hereford, and other nobles "quos comes Lancastriae reputabat fideles," played a part in the peacemaking. Reynolds, who was on the spot, makes no mention of the queen.

131 This is an interesting statement. Parliament in response to writs of 25 August met at York on 20 October. There seems to have been an intention of issuing another summons to Lincoln following the revocation of 8 June. See Parry, *Parliaments*, p. 82; Stubbs, *Const. Hist.* 2, p. 343 n. 3, citing *Documents*, ed. Cole, p. 4.

132 HMCR *Var. Coll.* 1, pp. 269–70. For Reynolds's whereabouts at this time see Wright, *Reynolds*, p. 387.

133 I have viewed the preliminaries to Leake mainly through the eyes of one of the major participants, Reynolds, who expressed himself clearly on the topic. For detailed analyses see Davies, *Baronial Opposition*, chapter 5 and pp. 447–50; Edwards, "Negotiating of the Treaty," pp. 360–78; Wilkinson, "Negotiations preceding the Treaty," pp. 333–53. Some of the details and conclusions have been revised by Maddicott, *Lancaster*, pp. 218–29, and Phillips, *Pembroke*, pp. 165–77.

134 Both quotations are from Davies, *Baronial Opposition*, pp. 448–9.

135 See Haines, *Church and Politics*, pp. 123–5, for a consideration of the bishops' involvement.

136 The indenture is printed in *Documents*, ed. Cole, pp. 1–2, and see *CCR 1318–23*, pp. 112–13; *Foedera* 2 i, p. 370.

137 See Maddicott, *Lancaster*, p. 227.

138 Phillips, *Pembroke*, pp. 172–3.

139 Davies, *Baronial Opposition*, p. 496: "When the influence of the younger Despenser grew the king followed him and his father rather than the committee."

140 Phillips, *Pembroke*, p. 173. See below. The claim was advanced at the York parliament of 1318 and subsequently. According to Davies, *Baronial Opposition*, p. 21, the high-water mark came in 1319.

141 *Vita*, p. 89.

142 The roll of the York Parliament is printed in *Documents*, ed. Cole, pp. 1–54. See also *Rot. Parl. Inediti*, pp. 64–80. The editors of the latter print a document [C] unique among surviving parliamentary miscellanea, containing a statement of the various petitions: for the great council (*coram magno concilio*), for the king's personal attention (*coram rege*), those concerning the king's debts, those not yet been carried out fully, and those that had been expedited. Unfortunately the substance of the petitions is not recorded.

143 Maddicott, *Lancaster*, p. 232; Powicke, *Military Obligation*, pp. 145–6.

144 Maddicott, *Lancaster*, p. 229. According to Davies, *Baronial Opposition*, pp. 450–1 n. 9, Michael de Meldon, Lancaster's steward, was apparently "the effective representative of Lancaster." For notices of Belers, a baron of the exchequer, see Tout, *Chapters* 6, s.v.; Davies, *Baronial Opposition*, index s.v. "Beler."

145 Ely (Hothum, the chancellor), Norwich (Salmon), Coventry and Lichfield (Walter Langton), Winchester (Sandale), Worcester (Cobham), Salisbury (Martival), Exeter (Stapeldon), Bath and Wells (Droxford), Durham (Beaumont), Carlisle (Halton), and one unreadable name. The missing name was not Orleton of Hereford, who did not expect to be back from a Continental mission and had appointed a proctor. It could well have been John Langton of Chichester, a regular.

146 For what follows, apart from *Documents*, ed. Cole, I have relied principally on Davies, *Baronial Opposition*, pt. 2, chapter 6, and Tout, *Chapters* 2, chapter 8, sect. 3, together with the modifications made by Maddicott, *Lancaster*, pp. 229–39; Phillips, *Pembroke*, pp. 176–7, but I have naturally gone back to the sources cited. Atholl (Strathbogie) had had his earldom forfeited by Bruce in 1314.

147 This is the complement of the committee in *Documents*, ed. Cole, p. 3. But ibid.,
    p. 12, the bishops are said to have been nominated by the king and associated
    with Hereford, together with the other lords with the addition of Badlesmere. An
    entry in SA MS 121, p. 17, states that (in April 1318) Northburgh, keeper of the
    wardrobe, had been sent from Wallingford to Westminster to treat with the coun-
    cil "de statu hospicii."

148 Davies, *Baronial Opposition*, p. 460, notes (citing *CPR 1317–21*, pp. 247–8;
    CChR 1300–26, pp. 297–8, 399, 403) that between 1 and 16 November 1318,
    188 of his adherents were granted charters.

149 *Bridlington*, p. 56.

150 *Rot. Parl. Inediti*, pp. 68–70. The bishop was allowed custody of the chattels of
    fugitives and felons, despite the fact that this was of loss to the king.

151 *CPR 1317–21*, p. 227. For this and the following changes and confirmations in
    office see Davies, *Baronial Opposition*, pp. 453–4.

152 The chronicler seems to be referring to some of its deliberations: *Vita*, p. 91. In
    December 1318 Walwayn was appointed an envoy to the Low Countries. Den-
    holm-Young, "Authorship of the Vita," p. 281. This is almost a parallel with
    Orleton's position in 1328. He too left the treasurership (though apparently of his
    own volition) and became engaged on diplomatic business overseas.

153 *CFR 1319–27*, p. 78.

154 Ibid., pp. 389–93; *Vita*, p. 91, regards the whole administrative and judicial sys-
    tem as corrupt from the lord chief justice downwards. *Bridlington*, p. 56, while
    noting the sweeping nature of the changes, merely remarks that they took place
    on a single day.

155 They are considered in detail by Tout, who continues his discussion of the house-
    hold until 1326. *Chapters* 2, pp. 245–81, especially p. 245 and ibid. 6, index s.v.
    "Ordinances and Statutes: of York (1318)."

156 *SR*. 1, p. 177.

157 For details see Maddicott, *Lancaster*, pp. 230–1.

158 Ibid., pp. 233–7, from which the following abbreviated account is derived.

159 *Vita*, p. 88; "et omnes hii, contra quos diceret se comes habere querelam, ad arbi-
    trium comitis satisfacerent, et super hoc fideiussores, cautionem aut pignora
    prestarent"; *CCR 1318–23*, p. 177. As Maddicott points out, Davies, *Baronial
    Opposition*, p. 435 n. 5, was confused by these payments acknowledged as due to
    Lancaster on 23 November 1318.

160 Somerville, *Duchy of Lancaster* 1, pp. 26, 337; Fairbank, "The Last Earl
    Warenne," pp. 212–13. The *Vita*, p. 93, remarks of this unequal exchange that it
    was made to avoid a greater peril: "Iacturam fecit ut evitaret maius periculum,
    quia de duobus malis minus malum est eligendum."

161 *Vita*, p. 93.

162 The *Vita*, pp. 87–8, while noting these dangers, does not mention the fact that
    Lancaster in his own interest would have been quite happy to ignore them.

163 *Bridlington*, p. 55, having wondered at the nature of the arrangements that

allowed lawbreakers to go free (see text above), noted the mutual exchange of a kiss of peace between king and earl and their apparent reconciliation: "sicut astantibus apparuit, concordati sunt."

164 Wright, *Reynolds*, did not give much attention to the business of convocation and provincial council but the action of the clergy at this time clearly harks back to earlier reticence – in view of the decree *Clericis laicos* – to accept royal taxation save in cases of *urgens necessitas*. See Denton, *Winchelsey*, chapter 4 and ibid., index s.v. "necessity; taxation."

165 *HBC*, p. 594; *Murimuth*, p. 30; *Ann. Paul.*, 286.

166 The *Brut*, p. 211, kaleidoscoping events, considered that the younger Despenser was made king's chamberlain at York at this time, but his appointment had been renewed in the York assembly of 20 October 1318, as mentioned above.

167 The hereditary stewards from Geoffrey, earl of Essex (1140–44), by way of Simon de Montfort (the sixth steward) and Thomas of Lancaster (the eighth), are conveniently listed in Harcourt, *His Grace the Steward*, index s.v. "Stewards, hereditary." The patent roll grant of 9 May 1308 to Thomas (*ad predictum comitatum Leycestrie ut dicitur pertinentem*) is printed ibid., p. 163 (also in *Foedera*, 2 i, p. 38). The "Tract" is ibid., pp. 164–7.

168 Davies, *Baronial Opposition*, pp. 312–13.

169 Maddicott, *Lancaster*, p. 242.

170 This copy is of a later date than 1321: it speaks of the time "regis Edwardi filii regis Henrici", i.e., Edward I. The earliest MS copy cited by Harcourt is from Richard II's reign, when it was again pertinent. That does not, of course, mean that the original could not have been composed in Thomas's time. The cooperation of steward and constable occurs in other parts of the tract. A French version has been printed by Hardy, "On the treatise *Modus*," pp. 259–74.

171 Harcourt, *His Grace the Steward*, p. 122. The earl of Warwick was a minor in 1321.

172 Maddicott, *Lancaster*, pp. 243–7, discusses the size of the army and of Lancaster's contingent, and its payment, at length.

173 *Vita*, p. 104. The author likened the earl to Achilles, sulking in his tent.

174 Clark, *Cartae de Glamorgan* 3, p. 1064: "par le procurement et par le compassement le counte de Lancastre fist taunt le dit counte qe le roi se remua." See chapter 9 below.

175 Maddicott, *Lancaster*, pp. 247–50.

176 Haskins, "Chronicle of Civil Wars," p. 77.

177 *Vita*, pp. 95, 97–8.

178 Ibid., p. 102.

179 *Flores* 3, pp. 192–3.

180 Maddicott, *Lancaster*, pp. 251–2.

181 See the unfriendly *Flores* 3, pp. 192–3. Castleford chronicle, fo. 220^v, ed. Eckhardt 2, p. 1061 ll. 39272–85, gives a vivid impression of the strength of the royal army.

182 *Vita*, pp. 102–3.

183 See chapters 9, 11 below.

184 *Parl. Writs* 2 i, pp. 215–16; Parry, *Parliaments*, p. 84. On 5 (6?) November an *inspeximus* and confirmation of grants to Durham Cathedral Priory was tested by Archbishop Melton, Chancellor Hothum, John of Brittany (Jean de Bretagne), earl of Richmond, Pembroke, Despenser junior, and Ralph de Monthermer.

185 *Vita*, p. 104; *Le Livere de reis*, p. 337; BL MS. Cotton Nero D. X, fo. 110ᵛ. This last, Trevet, puts the earl's conduct down to the fact of the Scottish truce.

186 There was nothing clandestine about the meeting, scarcely the "occultus locus" of the *Modus*. Writs were sent to the two archbishops, 16 bishops, 30 heads of regular houses, 9 earls, 98 barons, as well as judges and members of the council, but not to knights of the shire or burgesses.

187 Maddicott, *Lancaster*, p. 254, citing PRO C53/106 m. 5 (roll of 13 Edward II 1319–20); *Itinerary EII*, p. 192 (which does not cite this reference).

188 Haines, *Church and Politics*, pp. 158–9, for a summary of his subsequent position.

189 *Bridlington*, pp. 66–7. The convincing claim that the younger Despenser influenced the appointment of Baldock as chancellor in 1323 is in the *Brut*, p. 231.

190 *CPR 1317–21*, p. 417; BL Add. MS. 17362, fo. 40ᵛ. For this and further details see Buck, *Stapeldon*, pp. 131–3.

191 *Flores* 3, p. 191: Badlesmere was made steward of the household and Despenser king's chamberlain (*custodem vero sui capitis in officio camerarie constituit*). For the dates of their appointment: Tout, *Chapters* 6, pp. 42, 45.

192 For what follows in this paragraph and for the relevant references see Haines, *Church and Politics*, pp. 19–26.

193 Elements of the government were there on 6 February 1320 in the process of moving south to Westminster. *Itinerary EII*, p. 193.

194 For the Winchester and Lincoln vacancies see *Le Neve* 4, p.45, ibid. 1, p. 1; Smith, *Episcopal Appointments*, pp. 35–6.

195 *Bridlington*, p. 60; BL Cotton MS Nero D. X, fo. 110ᵛ. "Ad presenciam pape deductus est a quo impetravit absolucionem domini regis Angl[ie] et optinuit a iuramento prestito super ordinacionibus observandis alias London. factis per comites et barones." Maddicott, *Lancaster*, pp. 255–6, suggests that Trevet's circumstantial account may indicate his presence at the papal audience. The cardinals were duly canvassed by letters of 28 February 1320, but without any detail of the nature of the business, said to be "negocia nos specialiter tangencia": PRO SC1/32/79–82.

196 "Euntem vero illum versare cum domina regina et cum multa alia ac decenti commitiva nobilium et magnorum. Dominus Bartholomeus de Badlesmere regis senescallus in castrum suum de Chileham gloriose recepit ac splendide comminavit, necnon in eius et suorum recessu magnifice remuneravit quemlibet nobilium iuxta status sui decenciam donis honorando. Veniens igitur dominus rex cum suis apud Dovoriam deliberavit cum suis de homagio faciendo se excusare et

nuncios ad regem Francie ac ulterius ad curiam Romanam pro negociis regni des-
tinare. Mittens tunc [*sic*] dominum Edmundum ipsius fratrem, dominum
Hugonem le Despenser patrem, dominum B. de Badlesmere, magistrum Adam de
Hereford. ipsius loci episcopum, ac curiam Romanam per regem Francie transe-
untes ... magnifice sunt recepti." Historia Roffensis, fos. 33^v–4^r. The chronology
is confused: as stated above in the text the embassy had already set out in March.

197 *Itinerary EII*, p. 197.

198 Haines, *Church and Politics*, p. 25; Buck, *Stapeldon*, p. 132–3.

199 "Apud Westm[onasterium] parliamento convocato omnes episcopi provincie
Cant. plene personaliter ac omnes magnates regni excepto comite Lancastrie
interfuerunt." Historia Roffensis, fo. 34^r. Bishop Cobham affirms that the archbishop of Canterbury and seventeen provincial bishops attended. *Worcester
Reg.Cobham*, p. 98 (fo. 62^v).

200 The nature of this bull must remain uncertain. It is possible that it was brought by
Bishop Orleton, who had recently returned from Avignon and who was at the
parliament, where in conjunction with Bishops Droxford and Cobham he acted as
a receiver of petitions for Ireland, Gascony, and the Isles. Haines, *Church and
Politics*, pp. 126–7; *CPL 1305–42*, p. 442.

201 *Historia Roffensis*, fo. 34^v; *Ann. Paul.*, p. 290. The latter names Nicholas de Segrave as Lancaster's representative.

202 "Ubi tria digne dolenda per querelam omnium congregatorum proposita fuerunt,
videlicet quod propter periurium iuratorum in assisis et in inquisicionibus coram
iusticiariis et ordinariis et quod communiter in regno homines rapti fuerunt et
ducti quo nesciebatur, ita quod nunquam postea comparuerunt. Necnon propter
falsitatem magnorum et cupiditatem fovencium et manutenencium huiusmodi
iuratores, raptores et communes latrones ita quod nulla iusticia in regno fiebat,
regnum in puncto periclitandi fuit, de quo remedium petebatur. Et ordinatum fuit
quod prelati periurios excommunicarent et absolucionem sibi reservarent et quod
iusticiarii dicti Trailebastoun in singulis comunitatibus raptores et fautores
punirent. Et quia maiores de regno se et suos per hoc timebant multum fuisse
gravatos atque lesos quilibet in patria sua sicut dominus B[adlesmere] in Kancia
procuravit et impedivit iusticiarios ne venirent." Historia Roffensis, fo. 34^{r-v}, and
see *CPR 1317–21*, p. 548: commission for dealing with these matters.

203 *Worcester Register Cobham*, pp. 97–8 (fo. 62^{r-v}). In the letter to the cardinal the
phrasing is somewhat different, ending: "et in multis articulis subtiliter ex sua
discrecione supplevit, ubi deficere quicquam vidit; propter que mirabiliter gens
nostra letatur, ad spem magnam morum eius melioracionis adducitur, magis ad
unitatem et concordiam excitatur." Compare Cobham's account with that of
Trevet: BL Add. MS 17362, fos. 39^v–40^v. An English rendering of these letters is
in chapter 2 above.

204 *Worcester Register Cobham, loc. cit.* ; *Foedera* 2 i, p. 441: 19 January 1321.

205 Maddicott, *Lancaster*, p. 257.

206 Ibid., p. 257 n. 7, citing PRO E159/94 m. 22.

207 In *Worcester Register Cobham*, p. 98, immediately following the letters about the king's behaviour in parliament, is a letter addressed to Archbishop Reynolds extolling Winchelsey's virtues and mentioning Lancaster's "eager requests" for his canonization.

208 Griffiths, *Principality of Wales*, pp. 14–15, 245–6, 258–61, 279–80.

209 The Glamorgan charter is dated 21 November 1318: *CChR 1300–26*, p. 399. See also Davies, *Baronial Opposition*, pp. 93–4, 102–4.

210 *CPR 1317–21*, pp. 257, 415, 456. See Davies, *Baronial Opposition*, p. 473; Maddicott, *Lancaster*, p. 260.

211 Dugdale, *Baronage* 1, p. 420; *Ann. Paul.*, pp. 292–3.

212 *CPR 1317–21*, p. 464. Another man who had served Braose as a steward was Robert de Prestbury who, leaving his service, took advantage of the 1321–22 revolt forcibly to occupy Braose's lands in Plympton, Devon. Waugh, "Profits of Violence," pp. 853–4.

213 *Ann. Paul.*, p. 293; *CFR 1319–27*, p. 40; *Vita*, p. 108.

214 *Vita*, pp. 108–9: "et barones talia allegantes lese maiestatis videbatur arguere."

215 *CFR 1319–27*, pp. 41–2.

216 According to the *Vita*, p. 109, Roger Clifford blamed Despenser for the disinheritance of his mother. Another chronicler (TCC MS R.5 41, fo. 114^r (115) indicts John de Crumwell or Cromwell. Baker names the principal opponents of Despenser as Hereford, Maurice de Berkeley, Badlesmere, Amory, and Tyeis (a Lancaster retainer). He also implicates Pembroke "occulte" and Lancaster "ardenter et manyfeste." *Chronicon*, p. 11.

217 Griffiths, *Principality of Wales*, gives a biographical sketch of both M. Rhys ap Hywel and John Yweyn, pp. 97–8, 258. Rhys survived into the next reign, but Yweyn was captured by the magnates in Neath Castle in 1321 and was put to death at Swansea. See also Maddicott, *Lancaster*, pp. 262–3.

218 Griffiths, *Principality of Wales*, pp. 99–101, provides a lengthy sketch of his life.

219 Maddicott, *Lancaster*, pp. 262–3. One of those forbidden in late January to attend the meeting allegedly planned by Hereford was the northerner John de Clavering, an informant for the writer of the letter from Newcastle mentioned in the text below. Significantly he was not at the later Pontefract or Sherburn assemblies.

220 See chapter 9 below.

221 *Ancient Correspondence concerning Wales*, pp. 180–1, 259.

222 PRO C49/5 m. 6 (writ of 1 March 1321 forewarning the constables and justices in North and South Wales, and ordering the treasurer to see to the victualling of castles); *CPR 1317–21*, p. 569; *CCR 1318–23*, p. 292. *Knighton* 1, 196: "regem velut murelegum per festucam quocumque voluerit circumduxit."

223 *Itinerary EII*, p. 208; *Parl. Writs* 2 i, p. 231; Haines, *Church and Politics*, pp. 25–6. Giffard likewise does not appear to have come. See Butler, "Last of the Brimpsfield Giffards," p. 81, citing *SR.* 1, p. 182.

224 TCC R.5 41, fo. 114^r (115).

225 *Parl. Writs* 2 i, pp. 231–2; *CChW 1244–1326*, p. 519; *CFR 1319–27*, p. 50. This, according to Yweyn, brought Hereford to a more cooperative frame of mind: Clark, *Cartae Glamorgan* 3, p. 1075. These sources are cited by Maddicott, *Lancaster*, pp. 265–6. See also Davies, *Baronial Opposition*, pp. 475–6, who notes (from *CCR 1318–23*, pp. 314, 367–8) that Hereford in the heat of the moment had replied that unless Despenser were removed he would not come to the king, who was nearby at Gloucester, but that he subsequently sent the abbot of Dean (*recte* Dore) to the king with a more conciliatory response. See TCC R.5 41, fo. 114^r (115), for a fuller account.

226 Maddicott, *Lancaster*, p. 263; Smith, "Revolt of Somertone," pp. 76–83. Walkfare's behaviour was neither disinterested nor confined to his Lancastrian sympathies; he effectively ruined the finances of Binham by extorting pensions for himself and his son.

227 The pardon subsequently issued (see below) was for all lawless activity since the first week of Lent (8 March 1321).

228 TCC MS R.5 41, fo. 114^r (115). Maddicott, *Lancaster,* p.268 n. 1, uses the version in Leland, *Collectanea* 1, p. 272.

229 Bodl. Lib. MS Laud Misc. 529, fo. 106^r; *Wigmore Chronicle*, p. 352.

230 *Lanercost*, p. 241; Historia Roffensis, fo. 35^r: "favente eis T. comite Lancastrie." In general see Maddicott, *Lancaster*, pp. 267–8.

231 Historia Roffensis, fo. 35^r: "asserentes quod pro utilitate regis et regni hoc fecerunt et in assercionem huius rei vexillum regis erectum ubilibet in castris locis et terris ponentes, omnia in manibus regis verbaliter capientes, ad eius utilitatem ut dicebant occupata detinebant." See n. 27 above.

232 *Worcester Register Cobham*, pp. 101–2. About this time thieves had broken into the cathedral at Worcester, damaged the shrine of St Oswald, and carried off precious jewels donated by those who had thankfully witnessed the saint's miracles. Nothing was sacred any more. Ibid., p. 100.

233 *Ann. Paul.*, p. 292: "et pro libito suo officiarios in domo domini regis amovit, et alios in loco eorum constituit irrequisito consensu et assensu magnatum regni."

234 Baker, *Chronicon*, p. 11: "qui dixerant Hugonem, alterum regem, immo regis rectorem, animam regalem, ad instar Petri de Gaveston, incantasse, et de regis familiaritate ita presumpsisse quod nonnullos nobiles frequenter a regis colloquio artaret; quibusdam quoque nonnunquam pro diversis negociis se ipsos tangentibus regem alloquentibus, regia benignitate preoccupata, ipse responderet, responsiones non optatas set adversas votis, regis tantummodo pretendens commoditatem, ipsis refunderet."

235 "Adepto ergo huiusmodi officio post modicum tempus crudelem omnino se exhibuit in tantum ut nulli patuit gracias cum domino rege colloquendi aut pro negociis suis quamquam arduis et celeriter expediendis cum eo tractandi, nisi prius predicto domino Hugoni in magna quantitate pecunie foret satisfactum. Acquisivit sibi per rigorem et austeritatem maneria plura, et possessiones, et thesaurum infinitum." This chronicle goes on to impute to the Despensers an agree-

ment with the Scots at Stirling about the death of the earl of Gloucester, whose
lands the younger Hugh coveted, as well as the detention of the king and counselling him to take flight. In addition, at Berwick the younger Despenser is
alleged to have sold the queen to the Scots and then to have imputed such misdeed to Lancaster. One need not take tittle-tattle of this sort too seriously. Haskins, "Chronicle of the Civil Wars," p. 77.

236 *Lanercost*, p. 241. Compare *Flores* 3, p. 194: "Nam Hugo Dispensarius junior,
qui custos capitis regis exstiterat, in arcum pravum conversus igneque cupiditatis
intus accensus, ad integrum honorem comitatus Gloucestriae per fas vel nefas
obtinendum totis desideriis anelabat." See also the *Anonimalle Chronicle*, pp.
92–3: "nul homme purra aprocher au roi sanz la volunte le dist sire Hugh, et ceo
pur grandement doner de soen. Et si nul desiroit parler ove le roi il noseroit pas
en nul manere fors soulement en la presence de meismes celi sire Hugh."

237 *Bridlington*, pp. 61–5, has by far the longest account of the whole affair and is
used here to provide an outline of what is alleged to have happened..

238 Maddicott, *Lancaster*, p. 269, examines these connections. What is clear is that
no Marchers are enumerated.

239 As will be seen from what follows the clergy must have been uneasy about the
summons in view of the fact that the situation was clearly a threatening one,
despite the declaration that all was in the interests of peace.

240 *Bridlington*, p. 65.

241 Maddicott, *Lancaster*, pp. 173–4, citing DL 41/1/37 m. 7 for record of the indenture in Lancaster's possession. The number "25" is also the number given for the
baronial supporters outside London. See below, n. 253.

242 This is clearly the understanding of the Rochester chronicler who records (Historia Roffensis, fo. 35ʳ) that all the prelates beyond Trent and the earl of Hereford
were at Sherburn "cum maioribus supranominatis," i.e., the Marchers. His view is
that their purpose was to pursue the Despensers as traitors, considering this to be
useful to the king.

243 Maddicott, *Lancaster*, pp. 269–79, discusses the whole matter. He points out that
Wilkinson, although he had copies of the Sherburn indenture, did not know that it
was in fact sealed at Sherburn on 28 June 1321 (Sunday after St John 14 Edward II).

244 BL Cotton MS Nero D. X, fo. 111ʳ.

245 Wright, *Reynolds*, p. 394.

246 *Trokelowe*, pp. 177–8.

247 Parry, *Parliaments*, p. 84.

248 The bishops could well have been Walter Langton, who died before the end of
the year, and possibly Cobham. The latter was in London on 13 May. *Worcester
Register Cobham*, pp. 236, 257.

249 *HBC*, p. 555; Parry, *Parliaments,* p. 84. A council was summoned to Oxford for
10 May, but this was altered to Westminster for 17 May.

250 PRO SC8/106/5268 (petition of the elder Despenser); Maddicott, *Lancaster*,
p.279; *Parl. Writs* 2 ii, p. 226

251 Wright, *Reynolds*, p. 355. This indulgence is printed from Canterbury Reg. Reynolds, fo. 70ᵛ, by Wilkins, *Concilia* 2, p. 507.

252 *Blaneforde*, p. 109; *Concilia* 2, p. 507.

253 Hereford, the Mortimers, Mowbray, Giffard of Brimpsfield, Clifford, Tyeis, Amory and Audley "cum aliis barnettis circiter viginti quinque." Dene adds later: "favente eis comite Lancastrie qui semper de parliamento se absentavit." Historia Roffensis, fo. 35ʳ⁻ᵛ.

254 "Venientes igitur ad parliamentum totam patriam in itinere devastantes, abbates priores rectores cives mercatores et diciores patrie de Marchia artantes ad con-tribuendum eis, ecclesias ubique et patriam depauperarunt." Ibid.

255 "Fuerant omnes induti tunicis viridis quarum quarta pars brachii dexteri crocei coloris fuit, quasi fuissent per predictos patrem et filium quateronati." Another mention of such distinctive livery occurs at the time of Sir Roger de Elmbridge's condemnation in 1322, who was hanged in the livery given by the barons to knights as a distinguishing mark (*Vita*, p. 120). According to one version of the indictment against the Despensers the younger Hugh himself had endeavoured to win over John de Grey, seemingly an exact reversal of what actually may have happened. Historia Roffensis, fo. 35ʳ; Maddicott, *Lancaster*, pp. 282–3 n. 2.

256 For these events and those immediately following see Haines, *Church and Politics*, pp. 127–31. The most important chronicle sources are the Historia Roffensis and for events from 29 July, the Pauline annalist. Either Dene was present or else he had a very detailed account from Bishop Hethe soon after the events described with some precision.

257 *Ann. Paul.*, pp. 294–7. After 14 August there is an insertion about a royal visit to St. Paul's for the feast of the Commemoration of that church's patron saint (30 June 1321).

258 The bishops mentioned are Canterbury (Reynolds), London (Gravesend), Ely (Hothum), Salisbury (Martival), Lincoln (Burghersh), Hereford (Orleton), Exeter (Stapeldon), Bath and Wells (Droxford), Chichester (John Langton), Rochester (Hethe).

259 Historia Roffensis, fo. 35ᵛ: "Et pur ceo vous prient qe vous lez meneez en par-lement en respounz a resceyure par agard dez piers ceo qil ount deservy ... et qe eoux soyent exile hors de terre pur touz iours et eoux et lour heyrs desherytes com faus et tretres atteyns et esproues."

260 Ibid., fos. 35ᵛ–6ʳ: "et tresoun de soun lige seignur et de la corone en contre sa foy. Adinventa fuit ista racio anno domini Mᵒ CCCᵐᵒ undecimo et facta in ordi-nacionibus pro domino Petro de Gaverston, hic tamen subducto nomine Petri ad colorandum factum suum, predicto H[ugoni] filio imputebant. Tunc episcopus Roffen. de hiis valde admirans, quesivit a domino R. de Grey an recepit huiusmo-di de domino Hugone. Qui dixit quod eam invenit in bursa sua inter alias cedulas. Ab illo enim tempore episcopus facta eorum detestabatur et suspecta habebat."

261 Maddicott, *Lancaster*, pp. 278–83, discusses the whole business at length. Is it really possible to argue that Badlesmere may have persuaded the opposition

leaders that the *Homage et serment* declaration "was more useful as ammunition against the younger Despenser than as a statement of their own principles"?

262 TCC MS R.5 41, fo. 115^r (116), seems to have placed Edmund of Woodstock's creation out of chronological order, but he remarks interestingly: "Et ne dictus B[adlesmere] maximus foret pre ceteris in Cancia sicut solebat dominum E[dmundum] de Wodestoke fratrem suum de London. comitem Kanc. fecit."

263 "Instantissime tunc barones per mediatorem comitem de Penbrok et omnia verba pro eis facientem contra regem egerunt ut pater et filius H[ugo] et H[ugo] in exilium deportarentur et eorum heredes exheredarentur. Ad quod cum rex respondisset hoc esse iniustum et contra iuramentum suum quemquam exheredari sine responso et melius fuisse eos ad tempus in Hibernia moraturos, quousque corda magnorum essent sedata. Dolendum esse viros generosos et nobiles sic iudicari. Adiecit comes Penbroch. quod de duobus eligeret rex aut guerram suorum vel exilium duorum, et quod necessario unum perficere, oporteret rex inquam plebis multitudini parcere preferens quam duobus, precibus prelatorum, comitum, baronum, justiciariorum, ac omnium ibi congregatorum non tantum victus sed vi metu ac necessitate compulsus." Historia Roffensis, fo. 36^v. Compare John 11: 50.

264 Technically speaking this was an award delivered in parliament by the lay magnates. It was not a statute in that it did not receive royal assent, but as will be seen from the text of the chroniclers, contemporaries were inclined to call it such and the language used is confusing. The *Vita*, p. 114, states that a statute was enacted, while *Bridlington*, p. 69, recites the process, in which the barons are said to have asked for a statute.

265 TCC R.5 41, fo. 114^v (115); *Anonimalle Chronicle*, pp. 100–1.

266 Historia Roffensis, fo. 36^v.

267 The abbot of Langdon was a good friend of the king.

268 *Ann. Paul.*, pp. 296–7, suggests that in August 1321 Despenser was cruising about in the Thames off Gravesend and that at night he came to the king and advised him to delay agreement with the barons.

269 Historia Roffensis, fo. 37^r. The story in *Ann. Paul.*, p. 298, is that on 30 September 1321 the sailors of Winchelsea captured the port of Southampton, claiming assistance against foreigners. They were given two ships but, still dissatisfied, they proceeded to burn seventeen others. There is no mention of Despenser's involvement.

270 TCC R.5 41, fo. 114^v (115); *Anonimalle Chronicle*, pp. 100–1. The *Vita*, pp. 115–16, says that he was a sea monster (*belua marina*) and waylaid all merchant ships. His capture of a Genoese dromond was to have repercusssions for Edward III, who had to pay compensation at a time when he was anxious to secure the help of the Genoese shipbuilders. See Haines, *John Stratford*, pp. 243–4.

271 Historia Roffensis, fo. 37^r: "ut plures possent depredare." See n. 27 above

272 *Vita*, pp. 112–13: "Considera, inquit, domine rex, potentiam baronum, imminens adverte periculum, nec frater nec soror te tibi debet esse carior."

273 Ibid.: "utile est ut malis hominibus evacuetur patria, et ad hoc, domine rex, prestitisti iuramentum in coronatione sua ... sin autem, et a petitionibus eorum aures avertis, regnum forsan et nos omnes consequenter amittes." Here the barons use the same argument as the king himself.

274 The *Vita*, p. 114, does not state that the prelates did not consent, a point made clear by the Rochester chronicler.

275 *Vita*, pp. 114–15; *Bridlington*, pp. 70–1, 73: "Ecce! nunc [etc.]" See n. 303 below.

276 Maddicott, *Lancaster*, pp. 289–92; Pronay and Taylor, *Parliamentary Texts*, p. 27 n. 54, where it is argued that "version A" of the *Modus* in the common law books never appears alone with the "Tract on the Steward" in the earliest copies of the *Vetera Statuta*. The texts of the two version are printed at pp. 67–91 (B), 103–14 (A) respectively.

277 For the most recent text (including that of the related Irish *Modus*), and for some discussion of the varied views of scholars, see Pronay and Taylor, *Parliamentary Texts*, pp. 13–152. For interpretation see *inter alios*, Morris, "Date of the *Modus*"; Galbraith, "*Modus Tenendi Parliamentum*"; Roskell, "A Consideration of Aspects and Problems of the *Modus*"; Taylor, "The Manuscripts of the *Modus*" (who lists the principal works seeking to date the document at p. 676 n. 2); Richardson and Sayles, *Irish Parliament*, pp. 137–8, who argued (in 1941) for the priority of the Irish *Modus* and for a date during the reign of Richard II. This last argument was followed up in 1981 (the year following the Pronay and Taylor publication) by Sayles in his "*Modus Tenendi Parliamentum*, English or Irish?," more recently (1998) by Kerby-Fulton and Justice, "Reformist Intellectual Culture in the English and Irish Civil Service," who likewise prefer the later date and an Irish context and have robustly questioned some of the reasoning and conclusions of Pronay and Taylor.

278 Pronay and Taylor, *Parliamentary Texts*, p. 25. However, ibid., n. 46, this statement is repeated but with the terminal date "about 1332." Both are misleading. Also at n. 47, commenting on the fact that the "B version" writes of the "rotuli" of parliament (in the 1320s there were regularly more than one), rather than the "rotulus" of "version A" (ibid., pp. 78, 114), the word "roluti" should read "rotuli." The *Modus* itemizes six graded elements (*gradus*) in parliament of which the third consists of the clergy's proctors (ibid., pp. 78, 109).

279 See Denton and Pooley, *Representatives of the Lower Clergy*, App. 5, listing summonses between 1295 and 1340; also McHardy, "Representation of Lower Clergy," who argues for the "invisibility" of clerical proctors in the later fourteenth century rather than their absence. Maddicott, *Lancaster*, p. 291, states that the normal procedure was to summon two clerical proctors from each diocese, not from each archdeaconry (as in the *Modus*), but App. 5 in Denton and Pooley shows that not infrequently one or more proctors were appointed for archdeaconries, although at other times one was deputed from each archdeaconry. Kerby-Fulton and Justice in the most recent discussion of the *Modus*,

"Reformist Intellectual Culture," appear not to have been aware of the Denton and Pooley book.

280 Maddicott, *Lancaster*, p. 291.

281 Pronay and Taylor, *Parliamentary Texts*, p. 28: "No copy of the *Modus* has been found in association with materials other than the technical texts of the law of the land and the procedure at court."

282 Maddicott, *Lancaster*, esp. pp. 290–91.

283 Ibid., p. 290; *HBC*, p. 473.

284 BL Add. MS. 49359.

285 Kerby-Fulton and Justice, "Reformist Intellectual Culture," p. 163.

286 "in armis [*domini* cancelled by subpunctuation] domini B. de Badlesmere ex alia parte."

287 "cum xix militibus linia armatura sub supertunicis armigeri vero illius ferro palam discooperti."

288 These details are (uniquely?) to be found in the Canterbury-based chronicle TCC MS R.5 41, fo. 115^r (116). For them Maddicott, *Lancaster*, p. 293, cites a printed version from Leland, *Collectanea* I, pp. 272–3. Maddicott thought Cromwell "an ardent loyalist." He had certainly suffered at the hands of the Despensers' enemies.

289 *CPR 1317–21*, pp. 128, 131–2. *Documents*, ed. Cole, pp. 341–2, 346–7, reveals an intention of adding Leeds to Isabella's dower. Reversion to her was granted in 7 Edward II (1313–14): Wykeham Martin, *Leeds Castle*, pp. 116–17 and App. 7–12A. For the grant (1 November 1317) to Badlesmere: *CPR 1317–21*, pp. 46, 128. When, in the 1327 parliament, Badlesmere's widow, Margaret, petitioned for the return of Leeds or the manor of Adderley, Isabella chose to retain the castle. *Rot. Parl. Inediti*, p. 165 no. 50.

290 The Historia Roffensis (fo. 37^r) provides this detail: "ipse cum armata potencia et machinis sequi se paravit." *Ann. Paul.*, p. 299, claimed that Edward's army numbered 30,000. *Sempringham*, p. 339, suggests an even more unlikely 60,000.

291 "Unde dominus B. de Badlesmere quasi cum eis confusus reversus est. Cum autem nunciatum fuisset obsessis desperati fuerunt et in vigilia Omnium Sanctorum dictum castrum in manibus domini regis reddiderunt graciam et misericordiam ab eo postulantes. Sed dominus rex accepit obsessos, videlicet [dominam] de Badlesmere cum unico filio suo Egidio nomine et cum filiabus suis, et dominum Bartholomeum de Burgesshe militem et uxorem eius et Thomam de Aldon constabularium illius castri et ad turrim London statim fecit adduci." TCC R.5 41, fo. 115^v (116). See also Historia Roffensis, fo. 37^{r-v}.

292 Phillips, *Pembroke*, p. 255.

293 The above details are almost entirely from TCC R.5 41, fos. 115^v–16^r (116–7), but see also *Ann. Paul.*, pp. 298–9; *Lit. Cant.* 3, pp. 402–4: enquiry about Badlesmere's retention of Tonbridge and Leeds castles against the king's will and writ to the sheriff of Kent for the punishment of Badlesmere and his adherents.

294 *Flores* 3, pp. 191, 199. Maddicott, *Lancaster*, pp. 264, 293–4, 300, discusses this hostility to Badlesmere, which seriously weakened the baronial cause.

295 *Vita*, p. 116: "plures transgressiones sibi imposuit."

296 See also Baker, *Chronicon*, p. 12, who provides a more compressed account.

297 "B. de Badlesmere faciente verbum quod archiepiscopus et episcopi regem adirent comitante eis comite predicto [Pembroke], castrumque de Ledes, salvis sibi uxore filiis parentibus amicis omnibusque aliis in castro existentibus, cum catallis et custodia castri usque ad proximum parliamentum regi liberarent. Dicebat insuper quod prerogativa que regi debetur si ingressus castri ei negetur. Regina non est nisi uxor et sponsa regis, non potest neque debet vendicare, adiciendo quod forisfactum castri per denegacionem ingressus regi factam, in parliamento et non aliter secundum Magnam Cartam per pares regni adiudicari debet." Historia Roffensis, fo. 37^v.

298 Ibid., fos. 37^v–8^r: "Tandem animo mitigati [barones] miserunt duos milites, scilicet dominos Hugonem de Knowle et Willelmum Wyne cum episcopis ad interessendum securitati faciende de expositis per prelatos, quibus libenter annuerunt, comiti Lancastrie dum placeret, illis nichilominus de capcione castri de Ledes et suspensione hominum plurimum conquerentes, totum quod accidit comiti de Penbrok. imputabant minas ei inferendo."

299 Compare *Vita*, p. 116 and TCC R.5 41, fo. 116^v (117). It is arguable that Maddicott, *Lancaster*, p. 294, uses the latter chronicler's statement to the effect that Lancaster would not help the barons unless they abandoned Badlesmere, citing the printed version in Leland, *Collectanea* 1, p. 274, slightly out of context. The context was the revolt in the Marches, not the siege of Leeds. In a somewhat confused account the *Anonimalle Chronicle*, pp. 104–5, states (after the fall of Leeds) that Hereford and others went to Pontefract to seek Lancaster's help.

300 Haines, *Church and Politics*, pp. 132–3.

301 *CCR 1318–21*, p. 410; *CPR 1321–24*, p. 37.

302 *Bridlington*, pp. 70–1. This is undated but was presumably used to influence the prelates in the December 1321 convocation mentioned below.

303 Ibid., p. 73. "Ecce! nunc qualiter legum conditores facti sunt legum corruptores. Comes namque Lancastriae in parliamento Eboraci induxit dominum regem ad pardonandum sectam pacis suae versus ipsum et alios malefactores suos ad numerum circiter mille personarum, et tamen idem comes prius juraverat super quibusdam ordinationibus tenendis ne dominus rex in casibus emergentibus de morte ulli remitteret sectam pacis."

304 *Vita*, p. 117; Phillips, *Pembroke*, pp. 217, 220.

305 *Itinerary EII*, p. 219; *Ann. Paul.*, p. 301; Baker, *Chronicon*, p. 12; *Trokelowe*, p. 111. TCC R.5 41, fo. 116$^{r–v}$ (117). This last states that Giffard intercepted six wagons full of arms and kept them. Edward allegedly then destroyed Brimpsfield Castle on his way to Cirencester, although it is situated to the north-west of that town: "versus castrum dicti Johannis [Giffard] videlicet Bremmesfeld properavit et funditus demollivit." On 26 December, while Edward was enjoying the

Christmas festival, a writ of aid was issued in favour of the sheriff of Gloucester and Robert de Aston, appointed to destroy the castle. *Parl. Writs* 2 i, p. 270 (cited in Butler, "Last of the Brimpsfield Giffards").

306 *Vita*, p. 117, states that the king had an "exercitum copiosum." This chronicler in recording the help given by the king's half-brothers suggests that they were dexterous knights considering their age (*pro etate strenui*) – both had recently reached their majority.

307 TCC R.5 41, fo. 116ᵛ (117): "Et barones apud Gloucestr. innumerabili exercitu quasi in quadruplo plus quam rex habuit in comitiva sua ibi fuerunt. Postea dominus rex processit versus Gloucestr. Quo audito barones a villa recesserunt et sic in partibus illis ante regem semper fugerunt totam patriam devastantes, nec regi voluerunt resistere licet manum tunc forciorem et populum valenciorem habuerunt." According to this account the king spent the whole of Christmas at Shrewsbury, which was certainly not the case. He seems to have been at Worcester by the end of January and at Shrewsbury only on the fourteenth. *Itinerary EII*, pp. 219–20.

308 PRO Just. 1/1388/mm. 2v, 5r; KB27/255/Rex m. 87d. *Rot. Parl.* 2, pp. 427–8, is an *inspeximus* of the King's Bench record. For further details of this intriguing episode and Orleton's defence see Haines, *Church and Politics*, pp. 134–7; "A Defence Brief for Bishop Orleton." Maddicott, *Lancaster*, p. 204, is content to accept the indictment at face value. For Mortimer's and the other barons' behaviour see Waugh, "Profits of Violence," pp. 848–51, who did not realize that the unnamed sheriff (*Vita*, pp. 119–20) was Roger de Elmbridge – see n. 255 above. "Hambury in Saltmarsh" (Waugh, p. 850) should be "Henbury," "Minchampton" (p. 857) "Minchinhampton."

309 *Vita*, p. 118, states that FitzWarin (FitzWarren) commanded the cavalry of the royal army.

310 TCC R.5 41, fos. 116ᵛ–17ʳ (117–8); Maddicott, *Lancaster*, pp. 304–5.

311 BL MS Nero D. X, fo. 111ᵛ – supplemented, despite chronological inaccuracy, by TCC R.5 41, fo. 116ᵛ (117) – provides a surprisingly detailed account. See also *Melsa* 2, p. 340; *Vita*, p. 119. For that interesting but violent character, Robert Ewer, who according to the *Vita* (pp. 117–18), commanded the king's infantry, see the editor's thumbnail sketch, *Vita* p. 117 n. 4 and, for this chronicler's detailed account of his last days, pp. 127–9. Captured in Southampton, he had died from the rigours of imprisonment before January 1323. His erratic later career can be followed in the many entries in *CPR 1317–21*, ibid., *1321–24*, index s.v.

312 The Gervase continuator rather deliberately mentions Lancaster's position as steward: "dominum Thomam comitem Lancastrie et Leycestrie senescallumque Anglie."

313 TCC R.5 41, fo., 116v (117): "in societate eorum nullo modo venire."

314 *Murimuth*, p. 35, gives "Salopiam," allegedly "per mediationem fraudulentem." Fryde, "Tyranny and Fall," p. 54, gives 22 January at Shrewsbury, but without

reference. Historia Roffensis, fo. 38^v, supplies Ross [-on-Wye] as the place of their surrender. TCC R.5 41, fo. 117^r (118), states that the Mortimers "credentes certive graciam et favorem similiter et terras suas optinuisse, salutato rege missi sunt statim a rege custodiri."

315 See *inter alia*, *Wigmore Chronicle*, p. 352; BL Cotton MS Nero D. X, fo. 111^v; *Anonimalle Chronicle*, pp. 106–7 (somewhat garbled); *Melsa* 2, p. 340; *Flores* 3, p. 202: allegedly the Mortimers were "carcerali custodiae artius mancipari." For modern accounts with fuller references, Haines, *Church and Politics*, pp. 134–5 nn. 3–4; Phillips, *Pembroke*, pp. 221–2; Maddicott, *Lancaster*, pp. 305–6; Edwards, "Sir Gruffydd Llwyd," pp. 589–601; Parry, "Note on Sir Gruffydd Llwyd," pp. 316–18.

316 TCC R.5 41, fo., 117r (118), *Vita*, p. 119.

317 *Vita*, p. 119.

318 Haines, *Church and Politics*, p. 137.

319 *Itinerary EII*, pp. 220–1.

320 *Vita*, pp. 119–20, which does not give his name. TCC R.5 41, fo. 118^r (119), after details of Boroughbridge, names him Roger de Elmesbregge, mentioning his hanging at Gloucester (by royal grace he was not drawn as a traitor). He then describes the terrifying death of Badlesmere. See also n. 255 above.

321 Maddicott, *Lancaster*, p. 306, considered this to have been a tactical move in view of the actions of its constable, William de Aune, who had kept his master informed of what was happening in the North. Surely, however, the news must have reached the king well before he reached Gloucester (ibid., p. 307), very nearly a month later.

322 Maddicott, *Lancaster*, p. 307.

323 *Lanercost*, p. 242: "rex, per industriam aliquorum sibi adhaerentium, cives Londoniae et alios australes tam comites quam barones et milites cum magnis donis et promissis parti suae attraxit, et dictis duobus exulibus reditum et suam pacem concessit, et eam fecit apud Londonias publice proclamari. Quo rumore audito pars comitis Lancastriae castrum regis de Tykehil cum magno exercitu obsedit, et sic mota et incepta est guerra in Anglia."

324 TCC R.5 41, fo. 117^r (118): "habito consilio cum emulis comitum et baronum videlicet cum dicto H[ugone] Spencere patre et H[ugone] filio et non cum spiritu sancto."

325 *Lanercost*, p. 242.

326 *Parl. Writs* 2 i, p. 566 (cited by Maddicott, *Lancaster*, p. 308). For Melton's activities see Haines, *John Stratford*, index s.v.

327 *Vita*, pp. 120–1. The king's response was to the effect that he preferred first to deal with the internal rebels. For details of the Scottish raids see chapter 9 below.

328 PRO KB27/254, printed in Tupling, *South Lancashire*.

329 Historia Roffensis, fo. 38^v.

330 Ibid., fo. 39^r: the royal army advanced "magna penuria et angaria ac magno discrimine viarum cum paucis apud Burton super Trente pervenit."

331 *Vita*, p. 122.

332 Bodl. Lib. MS Laud Misc. 529, fo. 107^r. Lichfield does not feature in *Itinerary EII*, p. 222.

333 TCC R.5 41, fo. 117^{r-v} (118).

334 Ibid., fo. 117^v; Baker, *Chronicon*, p. 13.

335 *Brut*, p. 216, gives the precise date with a flourish, and names the leaders of the royal forces as the Despensers, Pembroke and Arundel.

336 *Vita*, p. 122.

337 The *Vita* is hardly realistic with respect to numbers. The copyist gave the size of the royal army as 300,000, clearly a mistake (for 30,000?), but he did not (*pace* his editor) estimate the baronial force as 30,000 strong. What he suggests is that this number offered to renounce their fealty to Despenser and to obey the orders of those occupying his lands (*obedire mandatis vestris*). At Boroughbridge he suggests that Lancaster's force was more than seven times that of Harclay. *Vita*, pp. 110–11, 122 and n. 4, 125. Compare Maddicott, "Thomas of Lancaster and Sir Robert Holland," p. 467.

338 *Brut,* pp. 216–17. Maddicott, "Thomas of Lancaster and Sir Robert Holland," p. 472, shows that Holland had received many manors (some twenty-five), thanks to the earl; he was not only the "manager of Lancaster's affairs" but also "his closest friend and confidant."

339 TCC R.5 41, fo.117r (118), gives the name of his escort as Nicholas de Cryel.

340 For a lengthy notice of Holland's life see Tupling, *South Lancashire*, pp. xxix–xxxiii. See also Maddicott, *Lancaster*, p. 310, and index s.v.; "Thomas of Lancaster and Sir Robert Holland."

341 Baker, *Chronicon*, p. 13. For a discussion of this chronicler see Haines, *Church and Politics*, pp. 105–7, and Maunde Thompson's introduction to his edition of the *Chronicon*. The Bodleian Library's transcript was at one time in possession of the Bohun family and Baker was an ardent admirer of Hereford, sympathetic to Lancaster and antagonistic to the Despensers but not to Edward II. His baronial sympathies appear to have landed him in prison by 1326.

342 Maddicott, *Lancaster*, p. 310, citing PRO DL 34/1/25.

343 *Brut*, p. 216.

344 TCC R.5 41, fo.117v (118); *Vita*, p. 123. The former source suggests that because the earls' banners were still flying from a tower of Pomfret Castle, the besiegers initially thought that they were still there.

345 *Brut*, p. 217.

346 *Lanercost*, p. 243.

347 *Brut*, pp. 217–19.

348 *CCR 1318–23*, p. 522.

349 *Lanercost*, p. 243; *Brut*, pp. 219, 245; *Vita*, p. 123–4. The account in the *Vita* suggests that Lancaster's men were already settling into their lodgings, which they then left to confront Harclay.

350 *Lanercost*, pp. 243–4.

351 Haskins, "Chronicle of Civil Wars," p. 78.

352 *Lanercost*, p. 244; *Vita*, pp. 123–6; *Anonimalle Chronicle*, pp. 106–7. The *Brut*, pp. 219–20, makes Lancaster retire into a chapel to place himself upon God's mercy, whereupon he was leaped upon and taken prisoner. This source is particularly anxious to expound the earl's piety.

353 *Brut*, pp. 221–2.

354 Ibid., pp. 221–3; *Ann. Paul.*, p. 302; *Foedera* 2 i, pp. 478–9. However, Haskins, "Chronicle of the Civil Wars," p. 78, lists Richmond, Pembroke, Arundel, Kent, both Despensers, with whom Malberthorpe – "in cuius ore verba fuerunt posita" – was associated. Malberthorpe, justice between 1320 and 1331, was among the justices who served on the commission of January 1324 to enquire as to the Contrariants in Herefordshire, Worcestershire and Gloucestershire. PRO Just. 1/1388. He was present at the council that met at Bishopthorpe (York) on 30 May 1323. The full list of those attending is given in Davies, *Baronial Opposition*, App. 94, pp. 584–5, and see ibid., p. 292. See also Fryde, *Tyranny and Fall*, p. 60, citing *Le Livere de Reis*, p. 343; *CPR 1327–30*, p. 32.

355 *Brut*, p. 222 (and BL Harl. MS. 2279 cited in Baker, *Chronicon*, notes p. 191); *Vita*, p. 126: "Fortis est hec curia, et maior imperio, ubi non auditur responsio nec aliqua admittitur excusatio."

356 The Bridlington chronicler says that after the Trent had been crossed Despenser prostrated himself and asked the king's pardon for his people, arguing that were Edward to unfurl his standard general war would pervade the country. It was, however, alleged that the earl had unfurled his banners (*vexillis explicatis*). *Bridlington*, pp. 75, 77. Bishop Orleton also made the point, when accused of aiding Mortimer, that it was not a time of war. Haines, "Defence Brief," p. 235. For the procedure see Keen, "Treason Trials"; *Laws of War*, pp. 104–7.

357 *Lanercost*, p. 244

358 *Vita*, p. 98.

359 *Lanercost*, p. 244: "in perpetuo carcere detentus vel in exilium missus, nisi causa alia praecessisset."

360 *Vita*, pp. 125–7.

361 *Lanercost*, p. 244: "decollatus, sicut fecerat idem Thomas comes Petrum de Gaverstoun decollari"; *Vita*, pp. 126–7, citing 2 Samuel. 2:23, 3:27; Judges 1: 6–7.

362 TCC R.5 41, fo. 118^r (119); *Foedera* 2 i, pp. 478–9. The *Brut*, p. 224, adds John Page, an esquire, as does *Anonimalle Chronicle*, pp. 108–9 (*vadlet al dite counte*). And see Maddicott, *Lancaster*, p. 312.

363 Where the crowd, mocking his pseudonym "King Arthur," shouted traitor and snowballed him. *Brut*, p. 221.

364 *Lanercost*, p. 244: "homo generosior, ut dicebatur, et unus nobilior inter Christianos et ditior comes mundi."

365 Stubbs, *Const. Hist.* 2, p. 349.

366 On 7 March Archbishop Reynolds published at St Paul's letters – said to have

been forged – containing details of an agreement between the earls and the Scots. They were recited by a clerk of his, T. de Stowe, although no clerk of this name is recorded by Wright, *Reynolds. Ann. Paul.*, p. 302. *Bridlington,* p. 78, reports evidence of a confederation with Bruce vouched for by one John de Denum, a royal agent, but concludes: "non affirmo, sed an sit verum nec ne nescio. Deus novit." It is also claimed that an incriminating indenture was found on Hereford's body at Boroughbridge: *Foedera* 2 i, p. 479. Certainly Harclay's strategy was to prevent the rebels' juncture with the Scots. Maddicott, *Lancaster*, pp. 301–3, examines the evidence for Lancaster's collusion and considers it "very strong."

CHAPTER SIX

1 *Brut*, pp. 224–5 (somewhat modernized); CCC MS 174, fo. 134^r.
2 "... distringent et gravabunt nos modis omnibus quibus poterunt, scilicet per capcionem castrorum, terrarum, possessionum et aliis modis quibus poterunt." Cap. 61 (completed by cap. 63). I have used the text in Holt, *Magna Carta*, App. IV.
3 Ibid., cap. 39 (compare 1225 reissue, cap. 29).
4 Stubbs, *Const. Hist.* 2, p. 351.
5 *Vita*, pp. 124–6; chapter 1, n. 98 above, where the *Scotichronicon* records that the young prince witnessed hangings at Durham.
6 Fryde, *Tyranny and Fall*, p. 60.
7 *Vita*, pp. 116–17.
8 Fryde, *Tyranny and Fall*, p. 60.
9 *Bridlington*, p. 78. Fryde, *Tyranny and Fall*, p. 61, adds William Suly, who elsewhere is said to have been killed at Boroughbridge.
10 For his trial see Haskins, "Chronicle of Civil Wars," p. 80 n. 1; "Judicial Proceedings against a Traitor." Butler, "Last of the Brimpsfield Giffards," pp. 94–5, suggests on the information provided by Fane, "Boyton Church," pp. 237–8, that he may in fact have been decapitated rather than hung, as suggested by a skeleton discovered in 1853 below an indent for a fourteenth century brass in Boyton church. However, this is no more than conjecture.
11 A local source, Historia Roffensis, fo. 39^r, is highly critical of him: "ignobilis Thomas Colpeper de novo factus miles non immeritus."
12 Not "Cambridge," as in Fryde, *Tyranny and Fall*, p. 61.
13 Badlesmere was captured at Stowe Park, a manor of the bishop of Lincoln, his nephew Henry Burghersh. *Brut*, pp. 220–1. His particularly brutal treatment is detailed in TCC R.5 41, fo. 118^r (117): "xviiio kalen. Maii [14 April 1322] iudicatus fuit ad mortem per recordum domini regis et ipsa die extra castrum Cant. ad caudas equorum miserabiliter per mediam civitatem usque ad furcas [gallows] de Bleen trahitur, et ibi suspensus est, et postea decollatus corpore sine capite ibidem iterum suspenso, et caput eius in hasta positum super portam fuit civitatis Cant. que Burgate appellatur, iudicium pronunciantibus iusticiariis ad hoc assignatis."
14 The *Brut*, p. 224, TCC R.5.41, fo. 118^r (117), Historia Roffensis, fos. 39^{r-v}, and

Baker, *Chroniculum*, pp. 171–2, collectively supply these names. According to the *Vita*, pp. 119–20, the punishment of Elmbridge (not specifically named) for treason was mitigated by the king while at Gloucester (apparently in mid-February 1322), and he was hanged instead. See above chapter 5, n. 255. There are variants in the list given by Stubbs, *Const. Hist.* 2, p. 350 n. 3. Palgrave's list from the Borough-bridge Roll in *Parl. Writs* 2 ii, pp. 194–201, is criticized for accuracy and arrange-ment by Gibbs, "Battle of Boroughbridge," pp. 222–6. He asterisks those who either cannot be shown to have been at the battle or who can be proved not to have been there and names the six who were supposedly hanged but in fact survived.

15 Baker, *Chroniculum*, p. 172; Haskins, "Chronicle of the Civil Wars," p. 80, has the same names except that William Trussell merely "evasit"; *Croniques de London*, p. 44 gives John de Twyford rather than "de Kingston", but in Haskins, "Chronicle of the Civil Wars," p. 81, Twyford is among those incarcerated.

16 *Murimuth*, p. 43; *Ann. Paul.*, p. 306.

17 *Vita*, p. 125; *Lanercost*, p. 245: "quatuor autem capti et cito liberati, decem incar-cerati sed postea liberati. Milites etiam quindecim tracti fuerunt et suspensi, et unus mortuus in lecto, quinque fuerunt cito liberati, et sexaginta et duo capti et incarcerati, sed postea liberati."

18 Baker, *Chroniculum*, p. 172. The barons are: Hugh d'Audley the younger, John de Wilington, Gilbert Talbot, John Mauduit, Edmund Hakelut, John de Sapy, Robert de Wateville (of Essex), Philip de la Beche, John de Beck, and Henry de Ley-bourne.

19 Haskins, "Chronicle of Civil Wars," pp. 80–1. This provides the fullest list as fol-lows: three slain, twenty-two hanged, one died anyway (from wounds: "propria morte"), four surrendered, five escaped, eighty-three imprisoned – a total of 118 names. This can be compared with the less-than-reliable list in *Parl. Writs* 2 ii, App., pp. 200–1. See also the "Boroughbridge Roll," in GEC *Complete Peerage*, App. 2, pp. 597–602, and the critique by Gibbs, "Battle of Boroughbridge." See above n. 14.

20 The sentence, pronounced on 2 August 1322, is in PRO E163/24/12, the judges being Walter de Norwich, William de Herle, Walter de Friskeney, John de Stonor and Hamo de Chigwell, the mayor of London. This document is printed by Davies, *Baronial Opposition*, App. no. 44, p. 565. See also *Croniques de London*, p. 45; *Anonimalle Chronicle*, pp. 110–11; Haines, *Church and Politics*, p. 143, n. 39.

21 *Ann. Paul.*, p. 312, gives the date of his death correctly as 3 August 1326 and says that his body was transported to his castle of Chirk for burial with his ancestors. According to the *Wigmore Chronicle*, p. 351, it was laid to rest by Bishop Orleton at the Mortimers' foundation, Wigmore Abbey. See also Haines, *Church and Poli-tics*, p.161.

22 Haines, *Church and Politics*, pp. 108–9, 143 nn. 39, 42; Fryde, *Tyranny and Fall*, pp. 160–1; *Croniques de London*, p. 45; *Ann. Paul.*, pp. 305–6; *Wigmore Chronicle*, p. 352. The account in the *Brut*, p. 231, is that the morning after St Laurence (i.e., 11 August) was fixed for Mortimer's execution and that he escaped

the day before. See the references collected in Baker, *Chronicon*, Notes p. 193, also the citations below at n. 177 for a fuller account. A chapel, dedicated to St Peter ad Vincula, was subsequently built in the outer ward of Ludlow Castle (*Wigmore Chronicle* loc. cit.), a Mortimer stronghold, where Roger (owner of the castle from 1314) was to make extensive alterations. Shoesmith and Johnson, *Ludlow Castle*, pp. 44, 47, 170.

23 PRO KB27/254 Rex m. 37. The names of the imprisoned, eighteen of them, are detailed by Fryde, *Tyranny and Fall*, pp. 62–3, but with the omission of John Knoynt, and again at p. 160, this time including him. Among the prisoners were Thomas Gurney, Bartholomew Burghersh, and Giles Badlesmere, son of Bartholomew.

24 *Vita*, pp. 129–31, and see below.

25 Fryde, *Tyranny and Fall*, pp. 63–4.

26 Historia Roffensis, fo. 39ᵛ: "Summa expensarum suarum xxxiii libras per v septimanias, eundo redeundo et morando, cum xi equis." It would have been more had he not performed part of the journey by boat, for there was a great lack of provisions. See above, chapter 5, nn. 14–16.

27 Parry, *Parliaments*, p. 85.

28 Baldwin, *King's Council*, p. 472 (dated 15 October from *Parliamentary Proceedings* vol. 10): Davies, *Baronial Opposition*, pp. 582–3; Ormrod, "Agenda for Legislation," pp. 3–4 and App. C. The last two from PRO C49/5/10.

29 *SR* 1, p. 190.

30 See, in particular, Davies, *Baronial Opposition*, chapter 10, especially pp. 511–17; Lapsley, "The Commons and the Statute of York"; "The Interpretation of the Statute of York" (two parts); Clarke, *Medieval Representation*, who also regards the *Modus Tenendi Parliamentum* as "contemporary and semi-official evidence as to the nature and organization of parliament" (Lapsley, p. 24); Haskins, *Statute of York*; Wilkinson, *Studies*, cap. 2; Richardson and Sayles, "Early Records of English Parliaments"; Trueman, "The Statute of York and the Ordinances of 1311"; Clementi, "That the Statute of York is no longer Ambiguous."

31 See Lapsley, "Interpretation," App. pp. 50–1.

32 This is the date of the letters patent permitting the appointment of the Ordainers. Davies, *Baronial Opposition*, pp. 359–61, gives the text in part (from *Foedera* 2 i, p. 105). This text is closely followed in the first paragraph paraphrased above.

33 Stubbs, *Const. Hist.*, 2, p. 352; Ormrod, "Agenda for Legislation," pp. 1–3.

34 Dene regretfully writes (Historia Roffensis, fo. 39ᵛ): "Ordinaciones vero facte per archiepiscopum R[obertum] de Wynchelsee, prelatos, comites, barones, iusticiarios, cives, burgenses, ad quarum observacionem tota fere communitas regni fuit iurata ibi sunt dampnate, exceptis sex de quibus facta sunt sex statuta imitate nomine ordinacionis in statutum."

35 Davies, *Baronial Opposition*, p. 492. For what follows concerning the statute incorporating certain elements of the Ordinances see ibid., pp. 492–5.

36 This refers to the legislation of 28 Edward I and appears to concern §2 of the *Articuli super Cartas*, *SR* 1, pp. 137–8.

37 *Lanercost*, pp. 246–8. The Scottish situation at this time is discussed in detail at chapter 9 below.

38 "Nam armiger militem, miles baronem, baro comitem, comes regem, in omni fere cultu antecedere nititur et laborat. Porro dum sumptus deficit, quia patrimonium non sufficit, ad predam se convertunt, vicinos spoliant, subditos expilant, et in ipsos Dei ministros infamem questum exercent. Hinc est quod magnates terre vel cadunt in bello, vel moriuntur sine filio, aut sexus femineus hereditatem dividit, et nomen patris imperpetuum evanescit." *Vita*, p. 57 (my translation in the text).

39 Waugh, "The Profits of Violence," p. 856, citing Hilton, *A Medieval Society*, pp. 248–53.

40 See the graphs in Fischer, *The Great Wave,* pp. 36, 38. Bishop Hethe found his travel expenses to the York Parliament of 1322 were heavy and his biographer commented: "Quia hoc anno erat magna caristia bladi. Valuit summa frumenti in Kancia xxiiii s., ordei xvi s., avene xviiis." Historia Roffensis, fo. 39^v. The corresponding figures for 1315 in *Sempringham*, p. 333, are similar, viz. twenty-four shillings, sixteen shillings, twenty shillings. Compare the valuation of a Canterbury-based chronicler for the earlier period in chapter 5, n. 17.

41 Waugh, "Profits of Violence," pp. 843–7.

42 PRO Just.1/1388/ m. 6d. See Haines, *Church and Politics*, p. 136 n. 13.

43 Powicke, *Military Obligation*, especially pp. 118–33, 137, 150–1.

44 *Parl. Writs* 2 ii, p. 542. Forty shillings was the fine later levied on many minor Contrariants.

45 Waugh, "Profits of Violence," p. 851. The allegation that Orleton sent men willingly to Ledbury is at least questionable. Some of those named were clearly Mortimer's retainers and doubtless coerced by him. See Haines, "Defence Brief."

46 Historia Roffensis, fo. 39^r: "Scriptum fuit prelatis et religiosis ac amicis suis pro subsidio habendo ad defensionem contra rebelles. Cui episcopus Roffensis per J. de Delham senescallum suum xx libras mittens, et quia parum fuit, vel quia pauperi episcopo pepercit, eas tamen remisit."

47 Waugh, 'Profits of Violence', pp. 851–2, citing PRO E368/92, m. 113; E13/45, m. 6.

48 Fryde, *Tyranny and Fall*, p. 69. The background here is quite heavily dependent on chapter 6 of this book but with modifications, additions and some corrections. See my review in *Speculum* 56 (1981), pp. 135–7.

49 Waugh, "Confiscated lands of Contrariants" (London PhD); Fryde, *Tyranny and Fall*, incorporates material from this thesis.

50 *CPR 1321–24.*, p. 151

51 Ibid., pp. 158–60.

52 For his career and possible authorship of the *Vita* see Denholm-Young, "Authorship of *Vita Edwardi Secundi* ."

53 For some notice of these retainers: Maddicott, *Lancaster*, index s.v.

54 PRO Just.1/1388, mm. 2d, 7d; Haines, *Church and Politics*, pp. 182–3, n. 12; Tout, *Chapters* 3, pp. 11 n. 1, 15 n. 3.

55 Maddicott, *Lancaster*, p. 319.

56 *CPR 1321–24*, p. 46; ibid. *1324–27*, p. 121; *CCR 1318–23*, p. 519. Fryde, *Tyranny and Fall*, p. 73, suggests that Amory's inexplicable detention may have been "the work of a bungling sheriff." Interestingly, Richard d'Amory became justice of North Wales for the early months of the Isabella-Mortimer regime. Tout, *Chapters* 6, pp. 59–60.

57 *CFR 1319–27*, p. 100; PRO Just. 1/1388, m. 2d, and for Gilbert Talbot, ibid., m. 7d, where he claims (in 1324) to have received a pardon with restoration of all his lands; Haines, "Defence Brief," pp. 240–1 (HCM no. 1373E).

58 Maddicott, *Lancaster*, pp. 64–5; PRO SC8/65/3249 (Eleanor Percy's petition on Dalton's behalf); *CPR 1321–24*, p. 135.

59 He is named in PRO Just.1/1388, m. 11d, as a Wiltshire Contrariant.

60 Fryde, *Tyranny and Fall*, p. 76. Knoville is listed among those captured in Haskins, "Chronicle of the Civil Wars," p. 81 s.v. "Kneuvile."

61 Fryde, *Tyranny and Fall*, pp. 76–7; Waugh, "Profits of Violence," p. 843 n. 1, lists among his sources: accounts of forfeited lands: PRO SC6/1145–48, enrolled in E358/14–16. In addition, he notes, some individual surveys have survived in E142 (Ancient Extents); SC11 and SC12 (Rentals and Surveys). The proceedings of the justices are enrolled in Just.1/295, /317, /1037 and /1388 – most of which material pertains to Worcestershire, Herefordshire, and Gloucestershire.

62 The Painswick attack is discussed by Phillips, *Pembroke*, pp. 261–7.

63 Waugh, "Profits of Violence," pp. 857–9.

64 One of these is recorded in Beardwood, *Langton Records*, p. 231. See also *Historia et Cartularium Gloucestrie* 3, pp. 271–2. These sources, together with PRO references are cited in Waugh, "Profits of Violence," p. 858 n. 73.

65 Bellamy, "The Coterel Gang"; Stones, "The Folvilles."

66 PRO Just.1/295 m. 1d. I owe this reference to Waugh, "Profits of Violence," p. 860 n. 86.

67 *CPR 1321–24*, p. 52; *CCR 1318–23*, p. 620.

68 PRO Just.1/1388, m. 10d; KB27/257/ Rex m. 11; E372/170 m. 31d. I owe the last two references to Waugh, "Profits of Violence," p. 862 nn. 103–4.

69 *CCR 1323–27*, p. 262.

70 *Hereford Register Swinfield*, pp. 423–4, 431–2

71 PRO CP40/244 m. 85; /249, m. 219. These references I owe to Waugh, "Profits of Violence," p. 862 n. 98.

72 PRO E368/92 m. 49; *Cal. of Letter Books E*, p. 150

73 Waugh, "Profits of Violence," pp. 860–1, citing PRO CP40/244 m. 62d; /256, m. 71d. See also CP40/246/ m. 35, where those named in the attack *vi et armis* included Richard and Thomas Irby and Thomas Broun, parson of Hope Mansel. Henley, by 1313 a canon of Hereford (*Hereford Register Swinfield*, p. 486, not mentioned in *Le Neve* 2, p. 26, 4, p. 47), was accused in 1324 of having sent his valet, Thomas de la Walle, in aid of Roger Mortimer during the 1321–22 rebellion. The jurors acquitted him. PRO Just.1/1388, m. 2; HCM 1373F (printed in Haines, "Defence Brief," p. 241).

74 The bishop's mandate of excommunication (see next note) declares that they burned them on the spot and took away the charcoal.

75 *Hereford Register Orleton*, pp. 227–8, 231–3.

76 PRO SC8/232/11584.

77 Orleton, in response to the king's mandate sent towards the end of June 1322, asked to be excused from making the arduous journey to a theatre of war. He wisely failed to appear before the king on 16 August, because Edward was in the war zone at Alnwick, but on 21–23 August he did appear initially before Chancellor Salmon and later before him and the treasurer, Stapeldon. On the second occasion he handed to them a written explanation of events. This is endorsed with an acknowledgment of the document's receipt but not of acceptance of the excuse. PRO SC1/34/151^{r-v}: "et dictus cancellarius ea recepit ut valeant quatenus valere poterint set pro finali excusacione ipsius episcopi Herefordensis ea admittere non audebat."

78 PRO KB27/250/Rex m. 16d; SC1/32/118 (Mandate dated 23 September 1322 from Newcastle summoning Orleton to appear to answer for his contempt in issuing a sentence of excommunication. Transcript in Smith (see below). A fuller account of the above is to be found in Haines, *Church and Politics*, pp. 140–2, also Smith, *Episcopal Appointments*, pp. 131–3. Other PRO sources, apart from the two above, are: SC8/232/11584 (compare *Calendar of Ancient Petitions*, pp. 384–5); SC1/34/151. The case about the alleged excommunication of the king's men was adjourned from one term to another until virtually the end of the reign: KB27/251/Rex m. 6; 252/Rex m. 12; /253 Rex m. 13; /254 Rex m. 25d etc.

79 *Rule of St Benedict*, pp. 14, 16: the fourth type of monk were the Gyrovagi or wanderers "qui tota vita sua per diversas provincias ternis aut quaternis diebus per diversorum cellas hospitantur, semper vagi et numquam stabiles, et propriis voluntatibus et gulae illecebris servientes." An apt description of Prior Irby.

80 *Worcester Reg. Cobham*, p. 150.

81 Bannister, introduction to *Hereford Register Orleton*, p. xxvi; Stones, "Date of Roger Mortimer's Escape." The apparent confusion between "Rogeri evasionem" and "regis eversionem" is explained in Haines, "Defence Brief," pp. 233–4, n. 8.

82 Haines, *Church and Politics*, p. 143. The judicial enquiry into the escape (see PRO KB27/254/ Rex m. 37) makes no mention of Orleton. See n. 177 below.

83 In practice many who had received pardons were none the less required by the justices to answer a second time.

84 KB 27/255/Rex m. 87d; *Rot. Parl.* 2, p. 427; Tupling, *South Lancashire*.

85 HCM nos. 1373 D–G (printed Haines, "Defence Brief," pp. 240–2). D: "qe ieo suy tant comme il plest a dieu evesqe et prestre et dey oyer confessiones et conseils de salutz des almes, dont nul seculer justice ne nulle homme terrein ne deit ne ne poet avoir conissance." Also PRO Just.1/1388 mm. 2d, 5.

86 Further details and references are given in Haines, *Church and Politics*, pp. 143–6. The principal ones are PRO KB27/255/ Rex m. 87d; Just. 1/1388/ mm. 2d, 5; *Rot. Parl.* 2, pp. 427–9. See also Usher, "Career of a Political Bishop," and "Adam de Orleton" (unpublished thesis).

87 *Blaneforde*, pp. 141–2; Harcourt, *His Grace the Steward*, pp. 305–6. The Close Roll entry (*CCR 1327–30*, pp. 44–5) is printed in *Rot. Parl.* 2, p. 429, and *Foedera* 2 ii, pp. 689–90, the important phrase being: "Licet idem episcopus inquisitionem aliquam, inde faciendam, se non posuisset nichilominus praefati justiciarii ad inquisitionem praedictam capiendam processerunt."

88 PRO SC8/161/8043. This *mutatis mutandis* coincides with that prefacing the 1327 annulment process. *Rot. Parl.* 2, p. 428 (*inspeximus* 3 Edward III of the annulment process of 1327).

89 The process as delivered to chancery (C49/6/5) described Mortimer as a man "qui levavit de guerra." In fact, as has been shown, both sides avoided such designation by the convention of not elevating their banners. In any case, Hervy de Staunton's commission did not extend to those who made war, only to trespasses.

90 Usher, "Political Bishop," p. 40; Haines, *Church and Politics*, p. 147 n. 59; *Hereford Register Orleton*, p. 306.

91 *CPR 1327–30*, p. 365; *Hereford Register Orleton*, p. 306.

92 *CPR 1321–24*, p. 398.

93 Ibid., p. 452.

94 Irby was a monk of St Peter's, Gloucester, of which the Hereford priory was a dependency.

95 *Hereford Register Orleton*, pp. 275–6, 305–9. Tuitory appeal was a process whereby a plaintiff could have his suit removed from the local ordinary's jurisdiction to that of the provincial court of Canterbury, but only for a limited time pending permission to appeal to the papal curia. The large number of *testes* summoned to the court included men, Canon James de Henley and Adam Irby among them, who were ranged on either side of the case.

96 PRO E352/119/29; E372/170/48

97 *CFR 1319–27*, p. 269. John de Toucester or Towcester was with the king to the last. In October 1326 he was one of those in the Forest of Dean who were paid to spy out the queen's coming. SA MS 122, p. 90.

98 *Blaneforde*, p. 142; *Salisbury Register Martival*, pp. 155–6, nos. 537–8; BL Cotton MS Vitellius E. IV 9 (Orleton's complaint to Pope John XXII). Inge, formerly sheriff of Glamorgan and a justice, was a supporter of the Despensers and mentioned as an unsuitable judge in the charges against them: Fryde, "Edward III's Removal of his Ministers," p. 158; *Tyranny and Fall*, index s.v. Nonetheless, he survived into the next reign.

99 *CPL 1305–42*, p. 280; *Lettres Communes Jean XXII*, no. 30267; Haines, *Church and Politics*, pp. 49–54.

100 BL Cotton MS Vitellius E.IV 9. This largely illegible document is partly paraphrased in Haines, *Church and Politics*, pp. 150–1 n. 77. Recently, with the aid of modern technology, I have been able to read much more of it. The letter deplores the "Herodiana sevicia" of the king, the sustained persecution by "ille vir" (presumably Baldock). It describes Irby as a demoniac monk and the younger Despenser [?] as, "the knight notable for his malice rather than his

ancestry." For Stratford: Haines, *John Stratford*, pp. 148–9. Fryde, "John Stratford and the Crown," points out (p. 156) that the ten thousand pounds was
regarded as a permanent debt to the king, but that two thousand pounds was to be
paid, the remainder being a bond for Stratford's future good behaviour. Stratford
was also forced to enter into recognizances to both the younger Despenser and
Baldock. See the table appended to Fryde's article. Archbishop Melton's register
contains a copy of an acquittance to Stratford, not mentioned by Fryde. It is
dated 4 February 1327, and is for a hundred pounds, being part payment of a recognizance of a thousand marks. Borthwick Institute, University of York Reg. 9B,
William Melton, fo. 716^v (dlxxvi).

101 See Haines, *Church and Politics*, pp. 137–8. Much of what is known about Abbot
William is noted in *VCH Kent* 2, pp. 169–71. He was for a time excommunicated
at the behest of the abbot of Prémontré, but in 1325 the king granted his house
the advowson of church of Tonge (formerly belonging to Badlesmere "the king's
enemy") which was then appropriated. Canterbury Register Reynolds, fos. 142^v,
144$^{r–v}$, 155^v.

102 Haines, *John Stratford*, pp. 142–9.

103 Haines, *Church and Politics*, pp. 158–9; Taylor, "Judgment on Hugh Despenser,"
pp. 70, 75.

104 Haines, *John Stratford*, p. 152 n. 169. See also chapter 11 below for this papal
mission in the context of Gascon affairs..

105 *Worcester Register Cobham*, pp. 168–70. Letter to Cardinal Vitale Dufour, probably written about the end of March 1324. For Burghersh: *CCR 1323–27*, p. 86. In
general, Haines, *Church and Politics*, pp. 150–3.

106 Historia Roffensis, fos. 46^v–7^r. "Rex dixit episcopo: 'Quando vis petere aliquid a
me? Multa fecisti pro me et domino Hugone et nunquam retribui tibi. Multa feci
pro hiis qui ingrati sunt michi, quos promovi ad statum magnum et facti sunt
michi hostes in capite et ideo domine Hugo precipio tibi quod si episcopus Roffensis quicquam habeat facere fiat.' Ad quod dictus Hugo 'Domine libentissime,
quia bene meruit et erga vos semper bene se habuit'."

107 Aberth, *Criminal Churchmen*, and see my review in *Albion* 29 (1987), pp. 465–7.

108 Phillips, *Pembroke*, pp. 238–9 The Countess of Pembroke's letters, the first about
the burial of her husband, the second a petition as executor regarding the loss by
reason of the bad counsel of Hugh Despenser and others of goods and chattels in
the earl's chapel and wardrobe to the tune of £20,000 and more. PRO
C81/1329/6925 and SC8/66/3265–6, references provided by Phillips. A further
petition is on behalf of Nicholas FitzMartin, apparently a descendant of the
Nicholas Martin of Cemaes, who in 1277 was a tenant within the liberty of the
earldom of Pembroke, and mentioned as such ibid., p. 249. The later Martin is
not there recorded as being in the earl's retinue.

109 Davies, *Baronial Opposition*, p. 340.

110 Tout, *Chapters* 6, pp. 10–11, 21, 50. Melton had served Edward I and his
second wife Margaret of France and is described by Tout on his undertaking the

controllership of the wardrobe in 1307 as the "wisest of the *garderobarii* of Edward of Carnarvon" (ibid. 2, p. 225). For his lengthy career see ibid. 6, index s.v.

111   Ibid., p. 21; *CCR 1318–23*, pp. 219–20.

112   These details are in Tout, *Chapters* 6, pp. 9–11, 21, 50. After Baldock the privy seal passed through several hands: Robert Wodehouse (from 8 July 1323), Robert Aylestone (from 3 October 1323 until 16 May 1324), William Ayrminne (?May /August 1324 until January /February 1325), Henry Cliff – a clerk, loyal to the Despensers, who frequently had custody of the great seal – April-July 1325; William Harleston, from October 1325 until the following October, the end of Edward's personal reign. See also Saul, "Despensers and Downfall of Edward II," p. 11.

113   Tout, *Chapters* 2, pp. 348, 357–8.

114   Fryde, *Tyranny and Fall*, p. 106.

115   *Chronicon*, pp. 16–17. Baker cites the Latin tag "Illum quem metuit quisque perire cupit." See Ennius cited Cicero, *De Officiis*, 2, 7, 23; Ovid, *Amores*, 2 ii, 10.

116   *Vita*, p. 136. Of this plot we seemingly learn nothing from other sources.

117   Interestingly, Stapeldon is not noted as being in this rogues' gallery. Cliff was both Despenser's clerk and the king's. The family may have come from Despenser's manor of Cliff in the parish of Hemingburgh, near Selby in York-shire. He was granted pardon in March 1327, but had died by the following year. See Tout, *Chapters* 3, p. 5 nn. 2–3. For some of Cliff's nefarious activities see Fryde, *Tyranny and Fall*, pp. 110, 115. Why "William Clif" should be thought to have spread rumours of Lancaster's miracles (ibid., p. 153) and sought sanctuary is not clear. Either the rumour was malicious or he was an *agent provocateur*.

118   *Bridlington*, pp. 66–7; *CCR 1318–23*, pp. 492–5..

119   Waugh, "For King, Country, and Patron," p. 24.

120   Phillips, *Pembroke*, App. 2, pp. 295–311.

121   But see Maddicott, *Lancaster*, chapter 2, where the earl's retinue is discussed in detail, but without tabular material. The index is also invaluable in this connection.

122   Tout, *Chapters* 3, p. 4: "the wholesale desertion of Edward II by every section of the official class, the household, the local administration, the chancery and the exchequer."

123   However, Waugh, "Despensers and Downfall of Edward II," pp. 4–8, argues that the Sussex knights Sir John de Ratindon, Sir Ralph de Camoys, and Sir Robert de Etchingham, as well as Sir Ingelram Berenger and Sir John de Handlo contin-ued in the service of one or other of the Despensers until their fall.

124   Phillips, *Pembroke*, pp. 300, 302. Holland seems to have continued his lawless-ness. The elder Despenser petitioned for redress on account of damage inflicted on property at Loughborough on 4 July 1322 by him and William de Bredon. PRO SC8/106/5268.

125 Saul, *Knights and Esquires*, pp. 44, 65, 80; "Despensers and Downfall of Edward II," p. 11.

126 For what immediately follows I have relied on Waugh, "For King, Country, and Patron."

127 Ibid., p. 24 n. 4.

128 Ibid., tables 1–2.

129 Davies, *Baronial Opposition*, p. 315.

130 Saul, "Despensers and Downfall of Edward II," p. 3.

131 Tout, *Place of Edward II*, p. 144; also idem, *Chapters* 3, pp. 11–12 for the reversal of those attributed to the Despensers. Melton was keeper of the privy seal 1307–11 [–1312?], keeper of the great seal 1310, controller of the wardrobe 1307–14, keeper 1314–16, treasurer 1325–6. Op. cit. 4, pp. 7, 21, 26, 28, 50, 84–5.

132 Roger Northburgh was keeper of the wardrobe 1316–22, Roger Waltham between 1322 and 1323. Tout, *Chapters* 6, p. 26, also index s.v..

133 See Buck, "Reform of the Exchequer"; *Stapeldon*, chapter 8.

134 Saul, "Despensers and Downfall of Edward II," p. 3.

135 Davies, *Baronial Opposition*, pp. 36–7; *CFR 1319–27*, pp. 152–73, 233–5, 240, 280–1, 293–5; *Rot. Parl.* 2, p. 10.

136 Fryde, *Tyranny and Fall*, pp. 108–9, and App. 1 (pp. 228–32), where the properties and acquisitions of both Despensers are more fully listed together with the relevant sources.

137 Saul, "Despensers and Downfall of Edward II," pp. 7–8; Fryde, *Tyranny and Fall*, pp. 107–8 and App. 1, provides much statistical information; Maddicott, *Pembroke*, pp. 22–3, and in general chapter 1; Rees, *Caerphilly Castle* (1937), pp. 28–31, summarizes the treasure stored in the castle at the time of its surrender in 1327 and (1974 ed.), gives an English rendering of Langton's account. See below chapter 7, n. 55.

138 Fryde, *Tyranny and Fall*, p. 108: "One object of expenditure is still wonderfully visible today in the magnificent work which he carried out on the Clare fortress of Caerphilly. Built on a remarkable scale and with the highest quality of stonework, surrounded by a moat which is like a great lake, it remains one of the most dramatic fortresses in the British Isles."

139 Harvey, *English Mediaeval Architects*, pp. 15, 154, 267; Rees, *Caerphilly Castle* (1937), pp. 51–5 and plan; (1974 ed.), p. 139, where it is suggested that Despenser may have prepared the apartments for Edward's reception.

140 See chapter 5 above.

141 Saul, "Despensers and Downfall of Edward II," pp. 16–22.

142 Ibid., pp. 28–29.

143 Putnam, *Shareshull*, pp. 19–20, citing Foss, *Judges* s.v., and Holdsworth, *History of English Law* 2, pp. 556 ff.

144 Saul, "Despensers and Downfall of Edward II," p. 25; Davies, *Baronial Opposition*, pp. 121–2 and index s.v.; Tout, *Place of Edward II*, p. 130.

145 For him see Haines, *Church and Politics*, p. 88.

146 Saul, "Despensers and Downfall of Edward II," p. 23

147 Kaeuper, "Law and Order in Fourteenth-Century England," especially pp. 744–7.

148 Saul, "Despensers and Downfall of Edward II," p. 30; Haines, *John Stratford*, p. 170; *Croniques de London*, p. 51.

149 Waugh, "King, Country, and Patron," pp. 26–8 and n. 10.

150 Fryde, *Tyranny and Fall*, pp. 20, 105, 209, and in general ibid., chapter 7.

151 Historia Roffensis, fo. 46^v: "asserens quod rex Anglie non habuisset parem in diviciis si regina et episcopus Norwycen. et eorum complices discordiam inter reges non suscitassent."

152 *Brut*, p. 225 (CCC MS 174, fo. 134^{r-v}). Compare e.g., *Flores* 3, pp. 217–18, *Vita*, p. 136 (see text for n. 116 above). BL Add. MS 35,114 lists many precious articles formerly belonging to Badlesmere, Harclay and Elmbridge, e.g., fos. 7^r, 13^r–14^v.

153 Harriss, *King Parliament and Public Finance*, p. 524; Fryde, *Tyranny and Fall*, p. 75; Willard, *Parliamentary Taxes*, p. 344; Lunt, *Financial Revenues to 1327*, pp. 410–11. Childs, "Finance and Trade," pp. 19–22, incorporates these figures and others into her preliminary discussion of Edward II's finances, pointing out that the basis for much of his income had been established by Edward I, even though he also bequeathed a heavy burden of debt to his son.

154 Wright, *Reynolds*, pp. 186–7, 191, 264.

155 Buck, *Stapeldon*, chapter 8, especially relevant here pp. 177ff.

156 Childs, "Finance and Trade," describes in some detail the importance of this aspect of income. She analyses the major sources of Edward II's revenue in round figures as follows: seven lay subsidies £266,044; clerical and papal grants between £203,297 and £271,364, while the customs revenue she estimates at some £240,328, about a third of other traditional sources. Ibid., p. 28.

157 Waugh, "For King, Country and Patron," pp. 40–41 and nn. 84–6.

158 Buck, *Stapeldon*, chapter 8, especially pp. 166–7, discusses Stapeldon's responsibility for policy and decides that the king, or whoever determined policy, was in overall control.

159 Fryde, *Tyranny and Fall*, p. 89. Davies, *Baronial Opposition*, p. 177, argued somewhat differently but to much the same effect. "The king's position in the administrative machinery was fundamental and concentric. Every department was subject to his influence, and, following closely his influence, was the influence of the household officials and the king's personal advisers, whether drawn from the great earls like Pembroke, the baronage, as the Despensers, the lesser baronage, as Badlesmere, or the official class, as Melton and Baldock."

160 Buck, *Stapeldon*, p. 166.

161 *Vita*, p. 136.

162 Davies, *Baronial Opposition*, p. 340: "they acted together in close sympathy for they had a common administrative ability to bind them together," yet it was "seldom that the Despensers obtruded themselves." This is not to exclude the king's

personal animus in specific situations. Thus, when in 1322 Orleton presented his "excuses" in the chancery at York (in the presence of Stapeldon and Baldock), the document was endorsed "dictus cancellarius ea recepit ut valeant quatenus valere poterint set pro finali excusacione ipsius episcopi Hereford. ea admittere non audebat." For fear of the king, Despenser, or both? Orleton subsequently appeared before Edward himself. PRO SC1/34 fo. 151d (under ultraviolet light). In this case there was personal vindictiveness.

163 See, for instance, the many letters addressed to Despenser in *War of Saint-Sardos*, also chapter 11 below.

164 For this and for much of what immediately follows see Buck, *Stapeldon*, chapter 8. Details of the effects of exchequer reforms on the wardrobe are discussed by Tout, *Chapters* 2, pp. 258–81.

165 Dorothy M. Broome's Manchester thesis on Belers is cited by Tout, *Chapters* 2, p. 186 n. 4.

166 *CPR 1321–24*, pp. 108, 144–5, 161, 178. See Fryde, *Tyranny and Fall*, pp. 80–1 (not p. 50 as indexed), and ibid., chapter 7.

167 Tout, *Chapters* 2, p. 219 n. 1; 3, p. 19.

168 The writ is printed from PRO E159/97 Trinity m. 4, by Davies, *Baronial Opposition*, no. 38 pp. 562–3. Belers's instigation is stated in *Flores* 3, pp. 231–2.

169 At the time of Belers's death (*interfectus mirabiliter*) the Pauline annalist describes him as "miles, et justitiarius domini regis et ejus consiliarius capitalis," *Ann. Paul.*, p. 310. See also *Croniques de London*, p. 49 and n. He was murdered by the Folville gang, for which see Stones, "The Folvilles."

170 Tout, *Chapters* 2, pp. 186, 219n., 220–1, 267–8; Davies, *Baronial Opposition*, pp. 532–4.

171 Buck, *Stapeldon*, pp. 167–70.

172 Ibid., p. 171. The clergy declined to make a grant in 1323 and 1324, the laity in 1324 and 1325.

173 Ibid., pp. 177–80.

174 *Vita*, pp. 127–9; Fryde, *Tyranny and Fall*, pp. 153–5. Ewer's punishment *peine forte et dure* followed from his refusal to plead (mute of malice). Pollock and Maitland, *History of English Law* 2, pp. 650–2.

175 *Foedera* 2 i, p. 514, The justices appointed were Henry le Scrope, John de Stonore and John Bourchier. A mandate of 14 November 1323, following Mortimer's escape, implicates him in the "three castles conspiracy," naming Roger de Wauton as his agent at Wallingford. *CPR 1321–24*, p. 349.

176 *Vita*, pp. 129–31. *Sempringham*, pp. 346–7, has a quite different account in which Berkeley's wife took the castle on 11 January and held it for a fortnight. After which Edmund de la Beche, Hodgkin de Wandon, and John Maltravers were captured and taken to the king.

177 PRO KB27/254/Rex m. 37. Segrave, admitting that he had been duped, declared "ipse seductus fuit per quendam vallettum suum in quo fiduciam habuit et se confidit ut de se ipso et qui fuit de covina ipsius Rogeri ad predictam evasionem

faciend[um], ipso Stephano penitus hec ignorante." *Knighton* I, p. 429, names
him as Girard de Alspaye.

178 *Ann. Paul.*, pp. 305–6; *Croniques de London*, pp. 45, 47; CUL Gg I 15 (French
   Brut), fos. 186ᵛ, 187ᵛ; Haines, *Church and Politics*, pp. 143–4; and n. 22 above.
   For the judicial enquiry see PRO KB27/254/Rex m.37, also *Parl. Writs* 2 ii, pp.
   249, 288, implicating Richard de Betoyne and Gisors. There is information about
   the Gisors family in Thrupp, *Merchant Class of Medieval London*, App. pp.
   345–6. She does not mention Bokton or a family of that name.

179 *Ann. Paul.*, p. 311. See chapter 8, n. 56.

180 Haines, *John Stratford*, p. 288 and nn.; "Some Sermons at Hereford," pp. 426.
   430.

181 *Vita*, pp.120–1.

182 See chapter 9 below for Harclay in the context of the Scottish wars.

183 *Chronicon*, pp. 17–18, 21; *Vita et Mors*, pp. 306, 308.

184 The position of those bishops who suffered various degrees of government persecution is discussed by Haines, *Church and Politics*, pp. 154–8, 173. In a letter to
   the pope of 3 June 1326 Edward explained that measures had been taken against
   Bishops Orleton, Burghersh, Ayrminne, and Archbishop Bicknor through their
   baronies in accordance with the laws and customs of the realm.

185 At the Lent Parliament of 1324 there was some relaxation of punitive measures:
   the bodies of the hanged were allowed burial and Lancaster was permitted to
   have the earldom of Leicester. *Ann. Paul.*, p. 306; *Foedera* 2 i, p. 546 (11 March
   1324).

186 The king is said to have been at Winchester at the time. He was there early in
   May 1325. *Itinerary EII*, p. 271.

187 *Vita*, pp. 138–40.

188 Many examples of such disturbances are mentioned in Fryde, *Tyranny and Fall*,
   chapter 11, who discusses the Coventry case in some detail using *Select Cases in
   the Court of King's Bench* 4, p. 155. The extraordinary coincidence is that the
   younger Despenser complained to the pope against the practice of witchcraft
   employed against him. *CPL 1305–42*, p. 461.

189 *Ann. Paul.*, p. 306.

190 Historia Roffensis, fos. 46ʳ, 47ʳ. "Nunquam postea regem vidit. Corda omnium
   ab eo eversa fuerunt"; "omnes maiores regni et totus populus sediciosus, qui
   semper sunt et fuerunt proni ad sedicionem." The latter quotation is a comment
   following the queen's landing in September 1326.

191 *Foedera* 2 i, p. 624. It is tempting to think that this was somehow connected with
   the then current struggle about the wearing of the pallium and/or the elevation of
   the metropolitical cross in the jurisdiction of Canterbury, but there is no evidence
   to that effect. Another pallium was requested from the pope.

192 *Chronicon*, pp. 18–19: "timentes ne, sui contubernio privati inciderent in manus
   hostiles vicinorum, quibus sciebant se ipsos odiosos." See also *Murimuth*, p. 45:
   the Despensers "propter odium communitatis regni et nobilium qui perfecto

odio oderant illos, dederunt consilium, et praevaluerunt, ut filius regis transiret."

193 *Vita*, p. 138.

194 Historia Roffensis, fo. 45^v.

195 *Brut*, p. 234.

196 *Vita*, p. 135. For further details about Isabella's mission see below chapter 11.

197 *Vita*, pp. 144–6: "cum ante recessum tuum et in ipso recessu hillarem sibi faciem ostenderis, et litteras amicabiles postea ei transmisseris quas in pleno parliamento in argumentum fidei protulit coram multis"; compare *Foedera* 2 i, p. 615, where a similar letter is dated 1 December 1325.

198 PRO SC1/37/45. In any case Joan Mortimer seems to have been kept in reasonable comfort. In 1326 she was conducted with her two damsels, a laundress, a chamberlain, a cook and a groom from Skipton Castle to that of Pontefract, *CMRE*, pp. 306–7. Davies, *Baronial Opposition*, p. 107; Perroy, *Hundred Years War*, p. 58, writes of Isabella as "a daughter of Philip the Fair, whose wickedness was matched by her misconduct," whom Edward "banished from his court"; Doherty, "Isabella," pp. 98–9, discusses the relationship of the queen and Mortimer.

199 *War of Saint-Sardos*, p. 5 (no. 6). See also, pp. 72 (no. 54), 103 (no. 87), 179–81, 194, 196 (no. 167).

200 Blackley, "Isabella and the Bishop of Exeter," gives details of the bishop's mission; also Buck, *Stapeldon*, chapter 7, especially p. 157 n. 207. On 1 December 1325 the king, after lamenting the non-return of his wife and son, apologized to Charles for the hasty departure of Stapeldon on account of threats by the king's enemies and those banished to France. *Foedera* 2 i, p. 615.

201 *Vita et Mors*, p. 307: "eam, illicitis complexibus Rogeri de Mortuomari delinitam." With slight verbal variation this is also in Baker's *Chronicon*, p. 20.

202 *CCR 1323–27*, p. 543.

203 TCC MS R.5 41, fo. 120^r (119), and Isabella's letter to the archbishop of 5 February 1326 specifically naming the younger Despenser: *Responsiones*, cols 2767–8; *Exeter Register Grandisson* 3 (App.), p. 1547; *Froissart* ed. Lettenhove 18, pp. 9–10. For much of what immediately follows, with references, see Haines, *John Stratford*, pp. 167–70.

204 Brut (CCC MS 174), fo. 139^v; Historia Roffensis, fo. 46^v; *Wigmore Chronicle*, p. 352: the exile of Isabella, the young Edward, and Edmund earl of Kent, "per regni comitatus publicari et mandari fecit"; TCC MS R.5 41, fo. 121^r (120): "regina ac filium in foro London. tanquam proditores fecit publice proclamari." A similar statement is in the Lichfield Chronicle (see n. 232 below). The king denied such reports in letters to the pope: *Foedera* 2 i, p. 625 (15 April 1326), to whom he had sent William de Weston, canon of Lincoln, to explain the situation, ibid., p. 616 (5 December).

205 Historia Roffensis, fo. 46^v. The parallel is certainly tempting, but surely an instance with so devastating a sequel for the king would not have been chosen. It

can only be a coincidence that the story ends not so far from the apocryphal tale of Edward himself given in chapter 8 below. A later example would be the fate of Eleanor of Aquitaine at the hands of Henry II.

206   *Willelmi Capellani de Brederode*, p. 177. See above chapter 2, n. 93.

207   See n. 209 below and chapters 8, n. 27 and 11, n. 148.

208   *Croniques de London*, p. 49: "En cele temps la reyne usa simple apparaille come dame de dolour qe avoit son seignour perdue. Et pur langwis q'ele avoit pur maintener la pées, le commune poeple mult la pleinoit."

209   *Responsiones*, col. 2767–8. The document is from Lambeth MS 1213, pp. 300–6. The version in *Exeter Register Grandisson* 3 (App.), p. 1547, is from the Winchester Cartulary. The letter is enigmatic but behind it may lurk the rumour, whether based on fact or not it is impossible to tell, that Despenser was trying to engineer the queen's divorce. It is possible – as Doherty suggests, "Isabella," p. 137 – that the king's message to the queen and her son contained in *CCR 1323–27*, p. 577, constituted a veiled threat of divorce.

210   *CPR 1321–24*, p. 349: 14 November 1323.

211   *CCR 1323–27*, pp. 578–9.

212   *Foedera* (H) 2 ii, pp. 158: "qui portavit sectam dicti filii nostri et in ipsius comitiva, publice, coram tota gente Parisius in solempnitate coronationis [regine], ad Festum Pentecostes ultimo preteritum [11 May 1326] in magnum contemptum et vituperium nostri et omnium nostrorum." *Foedera* 2 i, pp. 630–1 (French version) with corresponding letter to Isabella. The Pauline annalist records that the kings of Bohemia [?], Navarre, and Castile were present at the coronation as well as many magnates. The coronation of Charles himself had taken place on 21 February 1322. In that year, having secured an annulment of his marriage to the adulterous Blanche on the grounds of spiritual consanguinity, he married Mary of Luxemburg, daughter of the Emperor Henry VII, and thirdly on 5 July 1324 Jeanne of Evreux. *War of Saint-Sardos*, p. 190 and nn. 2–3.

213   TCC MS R.5 41, fo. 121^(r–v) (120): "Interea regina Anglie constituit magistrum filii sui dominum R[ogerum] de Mortuo Mari qui prius evasit de turri London."

214   According to a Flemish chronicle Charles wished the queen to leave. *RHGF* 22 (*Chronique anonyme* intitulée "Anciennes Chroniques de Flandre"), p. 421, and in general for Isabella's sojourn in France, ibid., pp. 420–9. See also Perroy, *Hundred Years War*, p. 58.

215   *Foedera* 2 ii, p. 686; PRO SC1/49/55; *Journaux du Trésor de Charles IV*, col. 1508 no. 9419. See Doherty, "Isabella," p. 127. The loans repaid to the Bardi in 1327 were substantial, viz. two thousand pounds and £360 6s. 8d. See also Perroy, *Hundred Years War*, p. 58 (without MS references); *RHGF* 20 (*Guillelmus de Nangiaco*), p. 638: "interim vero rex Franciae pro se et retenta familia expensas et necessaria faciebat ministrari."

216   Fryde, *Tyranny and Fall*, p. 181; Viollet, "Comment les femmes ont été excluses, en France, de la succession à la coronne"; Perroy, *Hundred Years War*, chapter 4.

217 Haines, *Church and Politics*, pp. 31, 39, 183, 229; *John Stratford*, pp. 195, 298–9; Déprez, *Les Préliminaires*, p. 36.

218 PRO SC1/49/47. Letter from Reynolds to Edward dated 20 January [1326] from his palace of Otford reporting the rumout that with the alliance of France and Hainault invasion could be expected shortly. Early in 1325 Charles had been complaining about Edward's attempts to conclude alliances with Spain, Aragon and the count of Hainault, to the prejudice of the French king. *War of Saint-Sardos*, p. 130 (no. 124).

219 *War of Saint-Sardos*, pp. 72–3 (no. 54). On 15 August 1326 Sturmy was again instructed to patrol north of the Thames and to report anything suspicious: *Foedera* 2 i, p. 638.

220 *Lit. Cant.* 1, p.181; Chaplais, *Diplomatic Practice* pt. 1, 1 no. 169 and p. 315 n. 35; *Foedera* 2 i, pp. 616–7, 626, *Ann. Paul.*, p. 312.

221 TCC MS R.5 41, fo. 121ᵛ (120). On 25 April 1326 Reynolds had been constrained to issue a statement from Otford denying the rumour that the nuncios would be in danger of losing life, limb, and property. *Hereford Register Orleton*, pp. 359–61; Wright, *Reynolds*, p. 358 n. 73.

222 He was at Saltwood for most if not all the first week of June. *Itinerary EII*, p. 285. Reynolds was there on the seventh and then at Canterbury 9–13 June. Wright, *Reynolds*, p. 409.

223 TCC MS R.5 41, fo. 121ᵛ (120); Haines, *John Stratford*, pp. 167–8.

224 Ibid.: "In capitulo ecclesie Christi Cant. cum archiepiscopo Cant. et cum aliquibus suffraganeis qui erant de consilio regis tractatum habuerunt." The Rochester chronicler says in general terms that they were discussing Isabella's possible return but with only moderate success (*qui modicum ibi proficientes*). Historia Roffensis, fo. 46ᵛ. According to the Pauline annalist they sailed on the eleventh *Ann. Paul.*, p. 312.

225 *Foedera* 2 i, p. 629; *CCR 1323–27*, p. 570; Historia Roffensis, fo. 46ᵛ: "Rex pro eis multitociens misit, sed Rogerus de Mortuomary redire desuasit mortem comminans si redierit." See the earlier letter written by Edward to his wife, dated 1 December 1325, in which he details her excuses, denies their relevance, and encourages her to return. *Foedera* 2 i, p. 615.

226 But see Fryde, *Tyranny and Fall*, p. 177.

227 For some notice of him see Bree, *Cursory Sketch*, pp. 14–16; SA MS 122, p. 91, where he is recorded as admiral towards the west in August 1326.

228 *Foedera* 2 i, p. 637; TCC MS R.5 41, 121v (120). The manuscript's rubrics in the chronicle at this point are instructive: "Nota preceptum regis" and "Malum maximum." The impression is that the situation had so degenerated that the king was acting in person. There is a lacuna at the point where the name of the town where the expedition landed should have been inserted. It was apparently Barfleur, and there was a raid on nearby Cherbourg Abbey (Doherty, "Isabella," p. 152, citing Roncière, *Histoire de la Marine Française* 1, p. 384). *Ann. Paul.*, p. 313, relates that a hundred men were sent from London to Porchester and another hundred

from Kent. This expedition is more fully discussed by Fryde, *Tyranny and Fall*, pp. 184–5, who suggests that a possible reason for the raid (probably in the first fortnight of September 1326) was the capture of Prince Edward who subsequently was loosely described as having been "in those parts." She goes on to claim that "there is no mention in any known source of Edward's presence with Isabella when she landed." In fact there are several. *Ann. Paul.*, p. 314, is unequivocal in naming him among those "venientes cum domina regina," as are *Bridlington*, p. 86, and *Lanercost*, p. 255. For the pardons subsequently issued for this raid: *CPR 1327–30*, p. 10: 10 February 1327. It may have been intended to pre-empt an attack. Reynolds, for instance, thought that a hostile fleet was assembling in Normandy: PRO SC1/49/92 (January 1326).

229 *Foedera* 2 i, pp. 586–9, 590–1, 623, 625 etc. See chapter 11 below.

230 *Exeter Register Stapeldon*, p. 169; Buck, *Stapeldon*, p. 126

231 PRO SC1/49/46–7 (Prior Eastry's correspondence); *Foedera* 2 i, pp. 617–8.

232 *Brut*, pp. 234–5; CCC MS 174, fo. 140^{r-v}; *CCR 1323–27*, p. 569. The Lichfield Chronicle states, p. 204, that the queen and her son were publicly branded as "hostes publicos regis Anglie et regni" and mentions the bribery of the "Twelve Peers." Incidentally, the English king could himself claim to be one. See also *Historia Roffensis*, fo. 47^{r}: "quosdam potenciores de Francia muneribus allexit ut reginam caperent ad Angliam remittendam," and *Lanercost*, p. 255: "maxima summa pecuniae missa est in Franciam, ad diversos proceres et magnates ut facerent reginam Anglie caute capi cum filio suo."

233 Doherty, "Isabella," p. 141. The story of Isabella's sojourn in France and subsequent departure found its way into Walsingham's *Historia Anglicana*, p. 179, and into a number of French sources listed by Doherty, including *Recueil des Historiens* 23 (*Chroniques de Flandres*), pp. 419–20. Jean le Bel, *Chronique* 1, pp. 14–15 ff. describes Jean de Hainault's behaviour in the chivalric terms popular at the time.

234 *Historia Roffensis*, fo. 47^{r}; *War of Saint-Sardos*, p. 269, and index s.v. "Brittania, John de"; *Foedera* 2 ii, pp. 158, 162–3; Lyubimenko, *Jean de Bretagne;* Haines, *John Stratford*, pp. 169 and n. 29, 189.

235 E.g., *Foedera* 2 i, pp. 634–5, mandates of 18 and 20 July.

236 *RHGF* 20 (*Guillelmus de Nangiaco*), p. 640: Despenser "per omnes portus incudaverat ut si ipsam ad ipsorum aliquem applicari contigeret, utpote regali et regalibus praeceptis inobediens tanquam rea criminis caperetur. Quod perpendens regina assumpto secum domino Johanne de Hanonia ..." This chronicler suggests that the queen retired to Ponthieu and that some time after the Assumption (15 August) she went to Hainault.

237 *Foedera* 2 i, pp. 637, 640; Haines, *John Stratford*, p. 169 n. 28.

238 *Foedera* 2 i, p. 640. Charles IV had been as unsuccessful as his predecessors in subduing the Flemings.

239 *Table Chronologique des Chartes et Diplomes*, p. 220; *Groot Charterboek der Graaven Van Holland* 2, pp. 393–4, both cited in Doherty, "Isabella," pp. 144–5.

According to Fryde, *Tyranny and Fall*, p. 185 (from *Bronnen tot de Gescheidenis*, p. 201) in the event the invasion force was tucked into ten fishing vessels. This seems at best improbable bearing in mind the amount of baggage and the transport of horses: it certainly conflicts with known details of preparation for the invasion force.

240   For the Boroughbridge Roll see n. 19 above; Gibbs, "Battle of Boroughbridge;" *CFR 1319–27*, p. 108; *Knighton* 1, pp. 431–2. As has been shown, five of the invading force – Percy, Maltravers, Botetourt, Kingston, and Trussell fled following Boroughbridge. Beaumont and Cromwell (Crombwell) had been present at the young Edward's performance of homage, Maltravers was closely associated with the Berkeleys as son-in-law of the imprisoned Maurice de Berkeley, hence brother-in-law of Thomas de Berkeley (who succeeded as Lord Berkeley in 1326). Thomas was to marry (firstly) Margaret a daughter of Roger Mortimer. Walkfare, who had escaped from Corfe, and Trussell, were staunch "Lancastrians," while Cromwell, a long-term "royalist," had mysteriously sought Badlesmere's protection prior to the siege of Leeds Castle. John de Ros had at one time been in Thomas of Lancaster's retinue, John Botetourt a baronial supporter and after Leake a councillor. John de Kingston was a Contrariant. The earl of Kent feared to return because of his concessions to the king of France: "ubi comes Cancie regem Anglie sic obligavit quod ad Angliam redire non audebat": Historia Roffensis, fo. 46^r.

241   TCC R.5 41, fo. 122^r (121); *Brut*, p. 235; *Ann. Paul.*, p. 314.

242   Bodl. Lib. MS Holkham Misc. 29, fo. 43^r; *Le Livre de Reis*, p. 354. *CCR 1318–23*, p. 717; Davies, *Baronial Opposition*, pp. 291–2.

243   For what follows see in more detail Fryde, *Tyranny and Fall*, pp. 183–4. I have used the same sources e.g. PRO C49/5/17 (details of the assignments for defence) and *Parl. Writs* 2 ii, pp. 754–5. Other details are to be found in *Foedera*.

244   The bishop's biographer, as the Rochester chronicler may be termed, does not mention Hethe's involvement at this or any other stage, nor *pace* Fryde, *Tyranny and Fall,* is there mention of it in PRO C49/5/17.

245   SA MS 122, p. 51; *Foedera* 2 i, pp. 633 (10 July), 637, 639.

246   Ibid.

247   *Foedera* 2 i, p. 637; *Concilia* 2, pp. 532–3; Wright, *Reynolds*, p. 358; Haines, *John Stratford*, pp. 169–70.

248   *CPR 1324–27*, pp. 302, 315–16, 327; *Foedera* 2 i, pp. 639, 643–4. In August 1325 John Sturmy had been appointed admiral from the mouth of Thames to the North. In February 1326 he was engaged in securing ships and supplies from Lynn, and on 18 July was ordered to patrol the area north of the Thames and to report anything suspicious. SA MS 122, p. 51; Bree, *Cursory Sketch*, pp. 18–19; *Foedera* 2 i, p. 638.

249   Some of the principal mentions of the Watevilles are: *Foedera* 2 i, pp. 230, (1313 pardon as Lancaster adherent), 471 (1321 at Bridgnorth with the rebels); 565–6 (August 1324 commissioner of array); 643–4 (September 1326 "nostre cher et

foial"); 646 (October 1326 at Bristol with queen); 648–9 (December 1326 ordered "per ipsum regem nunciante regina" to restore the manor of Swaffham to the earl of Richmond); BL Egerton Roll 8724 lists Badlesmere's retainers; Gibbs, "Battle of Boroughbridge," p. 223. See also Fryde, *Tyranny and Fall*, index s.v.; Saul, "Despensers and Downfall of Edward II," pp. 13–14; Banks, *Baronia Anglica*, pp. 155–6.

250 *Foedera* 2 i, pp. 565–6, 643–4, 646; *Memorials of St. Edmunds* 2, pp. 327–8; *Ann. Paul.*, p. 314: "quasi peregrinando." Fryde, *Tyranny and Fall*, pp. 185–6, 266 nn. 43–4, among other details, cites PRO E372/171/m.43, for the (Orton) Wateville's expenses for 13 days during October paid by the king while ill at Cippenham (in Burnham, Bucks.), but SA MS 122, p. 89, records his being there "malades a les custages le roi" for the thirteen days between 27 July and 8 August 1326 and, confusingly, at his house without Aldgate on 31 July, ibid., p. 77.

251 *Ann. Paul.*, p. 314.

252 *CMemR*, no. 2100; *CPR 1324–27*, p. 344; *Foedera* 2 i, pp. 648–9, 760.

253 Ibid: "tota communitas comitatuum Northfolck et Suthfoch sibi [regine] obediebat."

254 This may be the explanation of the (confused?) suggestion in the *Croniques de London*, p. 51, that the sailors, who disliked Despenser, refused to fight and made a piratical raid on Normandy.

255 Göttingen MS 740, fo. 221ʳ, ed. Eckhardt 2, p. 1063 ll.39354–5 (*Itinerary EII*, p. 289); *Murimuth*, pp. 46–7; *Flores* 3, p. 233. This view about the bishops is accepted by Fryde, *Tyranny and Fall*, p. 186, but see Haines, *Church and Politics*, pp. 160–1, 227 (Orleton's itinerary). Burghersh's itinerary, derived from his register, shows him to have been at Buckden 8–16 August 1326, Liddington (near Uppingham) 20–24 August, Stowe Park 8–9 September, Ramsey 15–16 September, Banbury 17–22 September, Biddlesden, 26 September, Liddington 28–29 September. There is an interval before he appears at Gloucester on 21 October, after that he is found at Westbury, convenient to Bristol, on 25–26 October, together with other supporters of Isabella.

CHAPTER SEVEN

1 Le Bel, *Chronique* 1, pp. 17–19.

2 The first letter was apparently dated 29 September. *Croniques de London*, pp. 51–2; *Great Chronicle*, pp. 29–30; *Chronicle of London*, pp. 50, 152–3 n. K. The French chronicler, William de Nangiaco, implying that the queen sought to come peacefully, says that the king "obstinatus in malo animo" had no wish to receive her peaceably "sed indignanter remandavit sibi displicere quod cum manu armata visa esset terram Angliae subintrare, praesertim cum eam regni et regis assereret inimicam. Quibus auditis regina sibi de cetero magis timuit." *RHGF* 20 (*Guillelmus de Nangiaco*), p. 641.

3 Isabella uses the title "By the grace of God queen of England, lady of Ireland, and countess of Ponthieu."

4 CUL MSS Ff. II.26 (English *Brut*), fos. 89ᵛ–90ʳ; Gg. I.15, fo. 190ʳ⁻ᵛ (French *Brut*); Hh VI.9 c. 213, fos. 101ʳ–2ʳ ; *Brut*, pp. 236–7; *Croniques de London*, p. 51; *CPMR*, pp. 41–2; Galbraith, "Extracts," pp. 211–12. The letter of 6 October is now printed (in Old French with English translation) in *Anonimalle*, pp. 124–7. The king apparently left London on 2 October: Tout, *Chapters* 3, p.2 n.2. On the third he was at Ruislip, while on the fourth at the Tower livery of various *jocalia* was made to the treasurer and chamberlains of the exchequer. SA MS 122, pp. 88, 93.

5 *Lanercost*, pp. 225, 425 (Notes); *Memorials of St Edmund* 2, p. 328; *Ann. Paul.*, p. 314; Lichfield Chronicle, p. 205: "Pro victualibus et aliis sibi necessariis plene et fideliter persolvebant. propter quod omnes populus tocius regionis ubicumque regina transibat sibi adhesit."

6 Perhaps, however, one should not have too much sympathy for Catel in view of the behaviour of his villainous family, which included M. Richard Baldock (brother of Robert) and Richard Catel, a kinsman, who allegedly dressed up as monks for nefarious purposes. Kaeuper, "Law and Order," pp. 734–5 (from PRO SC8/31/1539).

7 *Memorials of St Edmund* 2, p. 328; *Ann. Paul.*, pp. 314–15; CUL MS Gg. I.15, fo. 192r; SA MS 122, pp. 88–90; Tout, *Chapters* 3, p. 7. Tout emphasizes the continuity of the exchequer amidst the disturbances in London.

8 The bull was the fifth of those secured by Orleton: "Item quinta bulla directa archiepiscopis et episcopis de excommunicando omnes invadentes regnum Anglie et eorum valitores et fautores": PRO E159/93/77. The bull is that printed in *Foedera* 2 i, p. 413. TCC MS R.5 41, fo. 122ᵛ (121): "Aliqui tamen audientes dictam pronunciacionem bulle pecierunt datam bulle"; *Ann. Paul.*, p. 315; Baker, *Chronicon*, p. 21; Historia Roffensis, fo. 47ᵛ: "Receperat episcopus Roffensis sicut ceteri prelati et maiores regni litteras regine ut ad eam pro utilitate regni accelerarent"; Haines, *John Stratford*, pp. 170–1.

9 Baker, *Chronicon*, pp. 21–2. He is suspect on account of his concern to incriminate the bishops. Despite his claim neither Orleton nor Burghersh was with the queen in the earliest stages. For Baker the king was "amicicie cultor fidelissimus," so he stood by his friends, the Despensers and the rest.

10 TCC MS R.5 41, fo. 122ʳ (121).

11 *Croniques de London*, pp. 41–2; *Ann. Paul.*, p. 291; *Eyre of London 1321*; Davis and Weinbaum, "Sources for the London Eyre of 1321," pp. 35–8; Cam, "Cases of Novel Disseisin in the Eyre," pp. 95–105.

12 See Haines, *John Stratford*, pp. 164–92; "The Political Involvement of English Bishops."

13 While Hethe and Stapeldon were discussing the fluid state of affairs a great black dog appeared: "dum simul considerent de varietate seculi confabulantes venit quidam canis magnus ad Roffen. multum bonum sibi faciens, et statim ivit ad Exonien. multum meliorem ei faciens, ita q[uod] ad pedes episcopi proiecit Exon.,

quod armigeri dicti episcopi episcopo perpendentes malum futurum." And so it proved three days later.

14 These events are discussed more fully in Haines, *John Stratford*, pp. 170–6; *Church and Politics*, pp. 161–4; Buck, *Stapeldon*, chapter 10.

15 Genesis 3.15: "Inimicias ponam inter te et mulierem, et semen tuum et semen illius, ipsa conteret caput tuum."

16 Orleton was defending himself in 1334 against the allegedly false claim that he had "put enmity between the queen and her husband" and that the sermon was directed against their relationship. Baker, *Chronicon*, p. 23, inimical to Orleton, wrote that the bishop's text was "Capud meum doleo" (4 Kings 4:19) and implied that he was arguing that the "head" needing to be removed was the king's. For Orleton's appeal: Haines, "Looking Back in Anger."

17 Orleton may well have been MA of Oxford, for he demonstrated an interest in the university: his legal studies were probably abroad. Haines, *Church and Politics*, p. 3.

18 *Ann. Paul.*, p. 316, says that his head was sent to the queen at Bristol.

19 "Sub vexillo filii, non animo malicioso set male ducti." Baker, *Chronicon*, p. 23. Baker, though disliking the queen intensely, whom he describes as being at this juncture "potentissima," did not wish to attribute any wrongdoing to the under age Edward.

20 Ibid.; *Murimuth*, p. 47. Wake, son in law of Henry of Lancaster, was to be appointed constable of the Tower and justice of the forest south of Trent, another northerner, John Ros, became steward of the king's household (February 1327). Tout, *Chapters* 3, pp. 10–11.

21 *Murimuth*, p. 48; TCC MS R.5 41, fo. 123ᵛ (122); Baker, *Chronicon*, pp. 22–3.

22 TCC MS R.5 41, fo. 123ᵛ (122): "Eodem die [24 October?] misit rex litteras credencie per duos fratres domine regine pro vita secum existencium in navi salvanda. Cui eadem regina cito rescripsit." SA MS 122, p.90, details the king's movements..

23 *CPR 1324–27*, p. 332

24 Baker, *Chronicon*, remarks: "virago [Isabella] iussit comitem predictum sine questione seu responsione finali supplicio detorqueri."

25 TCC MS R.5 41, fo. 124ʳ (123), giving the date of his death as the vigil of Saints Simon and Jude, i.e., 26 October; *CPR 1324–27*, p. 332; Baker, *Chronicon*, pp. 24–5.

26 *Ann. Paul.*, pp. 317–18; *Bridlington*, p. 87: "Proht dolor! quod tantus vir, praeminens temporibus suis sensu et probitate pollens, deberet desipere in extremis."

27 Parry, *Parliaments*, p. 91; *Foedera* 2 i, p. 646; Tout, *Chapters* 3, p. 1 n. 2 gives the formula used: "Teste Edwardo, filio nostro primogenito, custode regni," with the warrant "per ipsum custodem et reginam."

28 Fryde, *Tyranny and Fall*, pp. 183, from PRO C49/5/17; *Parl. Writs* 2 ii, pp. 754–5.

29 *Croniques de London*, p. 52, includes the king as well as the queen and her son: "Fut la cry fait en Chepe qe les enemis le roy et la reigne et lour fitz deveroient

tout voider la vile sur peril qe puet avenir." Doubtless the Despensers and their supporters were indicated by this wording. See n. 33 below.

30 CUL Gg.I.15, fo. 192^r.

31 "le meir mercy criant à jointes meyns ala à la Guldhalle, et graunta à le commune lur demaunde." *Croniques de London*, pp. 51–2.

32 Tout, *Chapters* 3, p. 2. For the plaque see below, chapter 8 n. 61.

33 *Anonimalle Chronicle*, pp. 126–9; *Brut*, pp. 237–8. There is support for the latter version in *Bridlington*, p. 66: the king sent Stapeldon to London to draw the citizens to the king. Other accounts suggest that on seeing the disturbed state of the city Stapeldon was so terrified that he merely sought sanctuary from the mob. See the account derived from Lambeth MS 1106 in *Exeter Register Grandisson* 3 (App.), pp. 1537–39.

34 In one version the bishop's brother, Richard Stapeldon, is among the victims. In fact he died in 1332. *Croniques de London*, pp. 53–4 n., citing BL MS Cotton Faustina A. VIII, fo. 163^r; Buck, *Stapeldon*, genealogical table, p. 11.

35 In *Croniques de London*, p. 54, he is called "Segrave," the name of an earlier bishop. This is followed by Buck, *Stapeldon*, p. 215.

36 *Croniques de London*, p. 49, has details of the preparations made for its defence.

37 The Gervase continuator records the release, among others, of the younger Despenser's wife, TCC MS R.5 41, fo. 123^{r-v} (122). See also *Croniques de London*, p. 54, which has a somewhat different list of released prisoners..

38 It is interesting to note this inclusion by the Gervase continuator of the king, diplomatically not viewed as an "enemy."

39 CUL MS Gg.I.15, fo. 192^v; TCC MS R.5 41, fos. 122^v–3^r (121); *Ann. Paul.*, pp. 315–17, 321–2; *Croniques de London*, pp. 51–4. For William de Cliff's earlier unpopularity see Tout, *Chapters* 2, pp. 301–2 n.6, and for Henry de Cliff's allegiance, Ibid. 3, p. 5 n. 2.

40 *CPMR*, p. 16 n. 1. Earlier, for example in 1323, he is termed "mayor of the merchants of the staple of wool": *CPR 1321–24*, p. 314, and see Lloyd, *English Wool Trade*, chapter 4, especially pp. 116–20.

41 Ibid., pp. 15–17.

42 Haines, *John Stratford*, pp. 174–5; *CMRE*, no. 832; Davies, *Baronial Opposition*, p. 568 no. 49 (transcript of Stratford's appointment).

43 *Croniques de London*, pp. 55–6; *Ann. Paul.*, p. 318; Haines, *John Stratford*, pp. 174–7; Thrupp, *Merchant Class*, p. 71. For Betoyne's and Gisors's involvement see *Ann. Paul.*, pp. 305–6; *Parl. Writs* 2 ii, pp. 249, 288.

44 These names are given in *Ann. Paul.*, p. 319. See also Rees, *Caerphilly Castle* (1937), pp. 27–8. For the connection of Wyther and Beck with Lancaster see Maddicott, *Lancaster*, index s.v. For Holden, an important chamber clerk and controller of the wardrobe: Tout, *Chapters* 6, index s.v. He lost his office but was pardoned 22 April 1327 at the request of Henry of Lancaster: *CPR 1327–30*, p. 97; *CCR 1327–30*, p. 125.

45 *Responsiones*, col. 2766; *Exeter Register Grandisson* 3 (App.), p. 1546: "sponte venit ad dictum comitem Lancastrie."

46 Haines, *Church and Politics*, p. 166. The seal, delivered to the queen at "Marcle," was used between 30 November and 28 January 1327 in the name of the keeper of the realm, the duke of Aquitaine. Tout, *Chapters* 6, pp. 10–11; *Itinerary EII*, p. 291.

47 *Bridlington*, p. 87; Baker, *Chronicon*, p. 25; TCC R.5 41, fo. 124ʳ (123). For the Charlton-de la Pole conflict see chapter 5 above. *Lanercost*, p. 256, says the trial was secret: "et quasi in occulto adjudicatus est morti, et postea decollatus."

48 *Itinerary EII*, pp. 291–2.

49 *Knighton* 1, pp. 436–7, 441; *Ann. Paul.*, pp. 319–20; TCC R.5 41, fo. 124ʳ⁻ᵛ (123).

50 The second quotation "Quid gloriaris etc. usque penultimum ver. [*verbum* or *versum*?] psalmi", refers to Vulgate Psalm 51 v.1 ff. "Quid gloriatur in malicia qui potens est in iniquitate." The circumstantial account is from TCC R.5 41, fo. 124ᵛ (123). "In crastino vero [24 November] dominus H[ugo] filius ad mortem condempnabatur et per mediam civitatem Herefordie ad caudas equorum trahebatur super cratum habentem quatuor rotas, deinde suspensus in patibulo, et semivivus dimissus decollatur, abscisisque genitalibus et evisceratis in igne cremati sunt, ac postea trunco quatuor partes secto, caput palo positum super pontem London[ie] affigitur. Quadrifica vero membra ad quatuor partes Anglie sunt transmissa." That in Despenser's case his genitals were cut off and burned is without doubt an indication of what was thought to be his homosexual relationship with the king, as Jean le Bel openly declares (Froissart follows him almost verbatim): Le Bel, *Chronique* 1, pp. 27–8; *Froissart* ed. Luce 1, pp. 34–5 (illustrated from Bibliothèque Nationale MS Fr. 2643, fo. 97ᵛ, in *Chronicles of the Age of Chivalry*, ed. E. Hallam, p. 215). The twelfth century saw corresponding punishment meted out to the ravisher of a nun of Watton according to the story told by Ailred of Rievaulx, *Patrologia Latina* 195, cols. 789–96. See also the "Life of St William," pp. 289–90.

51 See chapter 6 above.

52 Haines, *Church and Politics*, pp. 111–12, 167, 179; for Irby's subsequent fate: Worcester Register Montacute 1, fo. 4ʳ⁻ᵛ; 2, fos. 5ʳ, 7ᵛ.

53 Taylor, "Judgment of Hugh Despenser," pp. 70–7.

54 Ibid., pp. 71, 76.

55 Rees, *Caerphilly Castle* (1974), pp.109–21, provides from John Langton's account a full inventory (in English) of the goods of Edward II. A large barrel containing a thousand pounds belonged to the younger Despenser, while a further twenty-six barrels each contained five hundred pounds. Thomas de Berkeley was allotted five hundred pounds for the former king's upkeep (ibid., p. 113). By early 1329 Eleanor de Clare, Hugh le Despenser's widow, had married William la Zouche de Mortimer, who had abducted her, whether willingly or not is unclear, from Hanley Castle in Worcestershire. Rees, *Caerphilly* (1937), p. 32.

56 According to Historia Roffensis, fo. 47ᵛ, the queen returned to Oxford and then

proceeded to Wallingford. At an undetermined date both Isabella and Mortimer undertook vows, possibly in gratitude for their success, to visit the shrine of St. James at Compostella. Both subsequently secured papal bulls of relaxation: Isabella in November 1328 for other *pietatis opera*, Mortimer in October 1330, just prior to his fall. Vatican Archives Reg. Aven. 31, fo. 219^{r-v}; 38, fo. 690^r.

57 Interestingly Ayrminne is described by Orleton (writing in 1334) as bishop-elect at the time. In fact he had been consecrated 15 September 1325, although he did not receive his temporalities until 6 February 1327.

58 The quotation is from CUL Gg I 15, fo. 193^v. Lancaster's title was formally restored on 3 February 1327.

59 Orleton's statement is confirmed by Historia Roffensis, fo. 47^v: "In nataliciis domini pro victoria potita fecit eum predicare puplice per episcopum Herfordensem Adam de Orleton quod metu mortis quam rex ei intemptaverat marito adherere non audebat."

60 *Responsiones*, cols. 2766–7; *Exeter Register Grandisson* 3 (App.), p. 1547; Haines, *Church and Politics*, p. 168 and n. 45. It was alleged against Orleton in 1334, at the time of his promotion to Winchester, that he had originated the idea.

61 *Knighton* 1, p. 457; *Rot. Parl.* 2, pp. 52–3 (App. B below); Haines, *Church and Politics*, p. 176.

62 See for instance Historia Roffensis, fo. 49^r: "Tunc per totum regnum in civitatibus, villis, burgis atque oppidis malefactores et pred[at]ores surrexerunt, ad depredandum, comburendum, devastandum et prophanandum, ecclesias, cathedrales, monasteria et ecclesias conventuales ac paganis ferociores sancta sanctorum conculcantes, res et ornamenta eorum distrahentes hostiliter ecclesias invadentes religiosas personas male tractantes, sub colore adhesionis regine nimia crudelia exercuerunt."

63 TCC R.5 41, fo. 124^v (123), has the twelfth; Haines, *John Stratford*, p. 177.

64 *Ann. Paul.*, p. 324; TCC R.5 41, fos. 124^v–5^r (123–3); Haines, *John Stratford*, pp. 177–8 n. 73. The details of the nuncios' mission and the early stages of the bishop's promotion are in *Exeter Register Grandisson* 1, pp. 315–23. The date of their arrival (10 December) is at p. 320, where at n. 1 there is a transcript of their safe conduct of 30 November. For the summons: Lincoln Register Burghersh 2 (Reg. 5), fo. 390^r (*Concilia* 2, p. 534, inchoate version of the Register Burghersh entry).

65 Historia Roffensis, fo. 49^r: "In quo [parliamento] per Herford. episcopum adherentibus sibi multis aliis episcopis propositum fuit quod si regina regi adhereret occideretur."

66 Baker, *Chronicon*, p. 29: "Quot amorosa teleumata [κήληματα, charms?] voce submissa tamquam alter Orfeus concinuit, set incassum." There is no basis for the insinuation about Orleton, who was not in a position to give any such advice.

67 The dating of the Kenilworth missions is difficult, since the differing accounts remain irreconcilable. See Haines, *Church and Politics*, pp. 169–72. The Gervase continuator claims that Orleton had come (or returned) to parliament to deliver his address *after* visiting Kenilworth and witnessing the renunciation of homage: "et

qualiter regem alloquebatur evidenter exposuit," and lower down the folio: "et homagia magnatum sibi ... adnullabantur." The "fiats" for the new king took place after the three addresses, for which see below. The logic of this is that any subsequent visit made to the king merely acquainted him with what had happened in parliament. It raises the question whether there was time for a mission from parliament between the seventh and the thirteenth, the date of the formal deposition. If not, as from this account seems inescapable, the king's renunciation took place before the parliament, which merely justified and/or sanctioned it. But confusingly this version of the proceedings gives the text of William Trussell's renunciation of homage (French version) after the "fiats" (see n. 85 below). TCC R.5 41, fos. 125^r–6^r (124–5). However, *Bridlington*, pp. 90–1, dates the renunciation of allegiance 27 January 1327, and provides a Latin version. This makes more sense, but would scarcely have allowed sufficient time for those involved to return for the coronation. Claire Valente, who does not mention Bridlington, suggests that the withdrawal of homage took place at Kenilworth on January 20 or 21. The Pipewell chronicler says the twentieth (n. 88 below). "Deposition and Abdication," p. 860.

68 *Lit. Cant.* I, pp. 203–5. Eastry suggests that the second mission should consist of two earls, two barons, four burgesses, and four knights "per communitatem totius regni ad hoc specialiter electos." See n. 88 below.

69 Baker, *Chronicon*, pp. 26–8; Historia Roffensis, fos. 49^r–50^r; *Lanercost*, pp. 257–8; TCC R.5 41, fos. 123^{r-v} (122). Precise references to these particular sources will not usually be given in what follows.

70 Haines, *Church and Politics*, pp. 168–76; *John Stratford*, pp.178–87; where the relevant literature is cited.

71 Baker's exemplar, Murimuth, likewise writes of three bishops, but does not name them. *Murimuth*, p. 51.

72 The Pipewell chronicle names Gravesend as one of the three. This is inherently unlikely. See above and n. 67.

73 Proverbs 13 [*recte* 11:13]: "Ubi non est gubernator populus corruet."

74 Citing Paralipomenon 2:6 [*recte* 2 Par. 6:21]: "Audi preces populi tui."

75 Compare 4 Kings 4:19 "caput meum caput meum."

76 A writ of 11 January ordered Richard d'Amory to summon twenty-four men from North Wales. The knights of the shire attended for sixty-nine days. Parry, *Parliaments*, p. 91.

77 *Ann. Paul.*, p. 322, merely mentions his arrival on 13 January at the Guildhall, while *Murimuth*, p. 50, says that he travelled with the queen to London. There is no record of his role in parliament.

78 TCC MS R.5 41, fo. 126^r(125); Historia Roffensis, fo. 49^{r-v}. The claim that the Lichfield chronicler believed that Reynolds actually deposed the king (Fryde, *Tyranny and Fall*, p. 200, citing Bodley MS 956, fo. 205^r) is misleading. He was merely an agent announcing the decision arrived at by prelates and barons with a nod to "the people." Stratford's theme, a traditional one, is cited in Walther, *Carmina Medii Aevi Posterioris* I, no. 3839.

79 Stubbs edited a version of the *Chronicon* for Edward's reign as the *Vita et Mors Edwardi Secundi regis Angliae conscripta a generosissimo milite Thoma de La Moore.* In the preface to his edition of the *Chronicon* Maunde Thompson explains this misconception and dispels any prospect of finding a "lost French original."

80 See Haines, *John Stratford*, index s.v. "Laurence." A much revised biography of More is to appear in the *New DNB*.

81 This portrayal of a pious, self-sacrificing Edward justifiably arouses suspicion in view of the tone Baker generally adopts with respect to the king, whom he clearly regards as a martyr.

82 It is possible that we have here a kaleidoscoping of two separate visits to Kenilworth. The first to gain the king's consent, the second, a delegation from parliament for the renunciation of homage. *Lanercost*, pp. 257–8, clearly distinguishes two missions.

83 Dene has a slightly different version of the king's behaviour in response to the renunciation of homage: "ubi [Kenilworth] rex qui fuit genibus provolutis manibus levatis peciit veniam de commissis et ut eum vivere sinerent et non occiderent humiliter peciit." Historia Roffensis, fo. 49^v.

84 Baker (dependent here on de la More), *Chronicon*, p. 28. Virtually the same statement is in *Murimuth*, p. 51: "ipse cum fletu et ejaculatu respondit quod ipse multum doluit de eo quod sic demerit erga populum sui regni; sed ex quo aliter esse non potuit, dixit quod placuit sibi quod filius suus fuit toti populo sic acceptus quod ipse sibi succederet, regnaturus pro eo."

85 The text of Trussell's renunciation is in various places, e.g. *Ann. Paul.*, p. 324; *Knighton* 1, pp. 441–2; *Lit. Cant.* 3, p. 414. The "reliable version" printed in *Rot. Parl. Inediti*, is the same, other than orthographically, as that provided by the Gervase continuator (compare *Anonimalle*, pp. 49 (introduction), 132–3). See n. 67 above. The English *Brut* has a very different account of proceedings, claiming that the king was in the custody of Bishop Hothum and Sir John Percy, that he gave his "power to ordain a parliament," resolutely refused to attend himself, and that Hothum "yielded up fealty and homage [*sic*] for all the archbishops and bishops of England and for all the clergy" (bishops did not perform homage): *Brut*, pp. 241–2; (CCC MS 174, fos. 144^r–5^r).

86 *Chronicon*, p. 28; Lloyd, *English Wool Trade*, p. 117.

87 See, in particular, Clarke, "Committees of Estates."

88 Historia Roffensis, fo. 49^v; *Lanercost*, p. 258. The Pipewell Chronicle (BL MS Cotton Julius A.1, fo. 56^{r-v}), dates the formal visit for renunciation at Kenilworth to 20 January. According to this the delegation comprised twenty-one persons: three bishops (of London, Winchester and Hereford – Gravesend, Stratford and Orleton), two abbots, and the same number of earls, barons, justices, barons of the Cinque Ports, justices (Scrope and Boussier – Bourchier), four London burgesses and the same number of knights of the realm.

89 I had thought the subject of "amabat" might be the king, but it must be the queen, who was indeed fond of the Franciscans, in whose London house she was buried.

Edward's favourite Order was the Dominican. On this reading she was not trying
to avoid upsetting the king unduly.

90 *Murimuth*, p. 51. That citizens went to Kenilworth from London is confirmed by
    CPMR, p. 30, which records fifty pounds as expenses for those going, including
    John de Gisors, Reginald de Conduit, John Hauteyn and others not named.

91 *Croniques de London*, p. 57. Both the date and the archbishop's role are confirmed
    by CUL Gg I 15, fo. 194^r, "a Weymoustre devaunt le poeple plusours articles
    countre le roi par qe le poeple graunta et cria qil de deveroit regner mes qe son fiz
    duk Guyenne serroit." The latter continues by claiming that the king *faute de
    mieux* gave his blessing: "et se assenta car il ne poeit autrement faire et resigna a
    lui la coronne et lui dona sa benisoun."

92 *Responsiones*, cols. 2765–6. A more satisfactory version from the Winchester Car-
    tulary was transcribed by F.J. Baigent and published as a supplement to *Exeter
    Register Grandisson* 3 (App.), pp. 1545–6, and again recently by C. Valente in her
    article "The Deposition and Abdication of Edward II," pp. 880–1, she being
    unaware of the documents in the Grandisson appendix. See Haines, "Looking
    Back in Anger."

93 Stubbs, *Const. Hist.* 2, pp. 364–6. Another more recent precedent could have
    been that of Henry II of Cyprus: Peters, "Henry II", especially pp. 772–4 and
    n. 33.

94 Watt, "Medieval Deposition Theory," pp. 197–214, is concerned with papal
    authority and the deposition of Emperor Frederick. In the 1399 situation, a pre-
    cise correlation has been made between the canon law and the justification for
    Richard II's deposition. Caspary, "The Deposition of Richard II and Canon
    Law," pp. 190–201. At p. 199 n.40, the "Articles of Deposition" concerning
    Edward II are quoted by Caspary from Orleton's *Responsiones* in Twysden, *His-
    toriae Anglicanae*, cols. 2763–8. He argues that the phrase "il deguerpist son
    royaume" ("il guerpy soun Roialme" in the Grandisson register version, *Exeter
    Register Grandisson* 3 (App.), pp. 1545–6) would not mean, as is regularly sup-
    posed, "deserted his realm" but as "guilty of [its] neglect and dilapidation." But
    the contemporary allegation that the king had deserted the realm is independent-
    ly vouched for by Prior Eastry: "sum tristis effectus quod princeps imperium et
    regimen regni sui deserens ad foranea se transtulit, si sit ita, quod Deus avertat."
    Lit. Cant. 1, p. 202.

95 It could be that Louis de Beaumont was at the parliament since two of his petitions
    were presented. *Rot. Parl. Inediti*, pp. 100, 110–16.

96 It is noted that the abbot of Waltham "non venit nec iuravit."

97 *CPMR*, pp. 11–14.

98 Historia Roffensis, fo. 49^r; *Memorials of St Edmund* 2, pp. 329–54, 357–61; 3, pp.
    38–47; Lobel, "Rising at Bury St. Edmunds," pp. 215–31. *Ann. Paul.*, p. 332, dates
    the attack on Abingdon Abbey 27 April, and also mentions the riot that took place
    at Merton College, Oxford, between the masters and the "community of
    scholars."

99 Historia Roffensis, fo. 50ʳ; *CPMR*, p. 11; *Croniques de London*, p. 58; *Ann. Paul.*, p. 323, where he is said to have made public protestation that if he had offended against them in anything he would submit to their regulation. He was also shamed into giving them fifty "dolia" of wine for their goodwill.

100 This time there is no question about the tense of "eligo," not in Dene's mind anyway. See above chapter 3, nn. 59–61.

101 Historia Roffensis, fo. 50ʳ. *Ann. Paul.*, pp. 324–5, mentions the participation of Gravesend and Stratford. In *Foedera* 2 ii, p. 684, the participants from English sees are given as: Hothum (Ely), Orleton (Hereford), Stratford (Winchester), John Langton (Chichester), Beaumont (Durham), Cobham (Worcester), Burghersh (Lincoln), Ayrminne (Norwich). In view of Dene's detailed account of officiants, as well as for other reasons, it is odd that Gravesend and Hethe are omitted. It seems that Archbishop Melton was not there, despite the statement by Froissart (Rome MS) that he was together with twelve bishops and forty-eight (*quarante wit*) abbots. *Froissart* ed. Luce 1, p. 254. See *Ann Paul.*, 324–5, for a further brief account of the coronation. The quotation is from BL MS Claudius A.V, fo. 41ʳ.

102 *Bridlington*, p. 95

103 Bodl. Lib. MS Holkham Misc. 29, fo. 44ᵛ.

104 This was not wide of the mark in at least one instance, a petition that the eyres in the Tower be held in accordance with the laws in being in the time of King John and King Henry [III]. *Rot. Parl. Inediti*, p. 132.

105 Historia Roffensis, fo. 50ʳ⁻ᵛ.

106 *Rot. Parl.* 2, pp. 7–11; *Rot. Parl. Inediti*, pp. 106–79; Haines, *Church and Politics*, pp. 178–9.

107 See Lancaster's critique of the government in *Brut*, pp. 254, 258 (CCL MS 174, fos. 152ᵛ–3ʳ, 155ᵛ); *Croniques de London*, p. 62.

108 See Fryde, *Tyranny and Fall*, p. 253 n. 92; Tout, *Chapters* 6, p. 42. The subsequent line of stewards expectedly consists of strong Mortimer supporters: Maltravers, Wysham, Maltravers again, Turplington. Ibid., pp. 42–3.

109 Tout, *Chapters* 6, p. 11, dates Burghersh's chancellorship from 12 May, *HBC*, p. 86, from 2 July 1328.

110 *Brut*, pp. 254–5; (CCC MS 174, fo. 153ʳ); *Rot. Parl.* 2, p. 52.

111 *Ann. Paul.*, pp. 325–32.

112 *CPMR*, p. 31.

113 Haines, *John Stratford*, pp. 189–90, and chapter 11 below..

114 See chapter 11 below.

115 *CPL 1305–42*, p. 484, 13 July 1327; Haines, *Church and Politics*, pp. 27–8.

116 Ibid., pp. 28–31, where Orleton's promotion is more fully discussed. Bransford is a village on the River Teme just outside Worcester.

117 Harding, "Isabella and Mortimer," App. I. Hothum is said to have witnessed 80 for the period 4 Feb. 1327 to 7 Jan 1328, 57 between 27 Jan. 1328 and 14 Jan. 1329 and 24 between 25 Jan. 1329 and 18 Feb. 1330. He suggests that Lancaster,

whose witnessing fades out after the second of these periods, may also have been dissatisfied by the tardiness with which his lands were restored. Ibid., pp. 60–1.

118 *Responsiones*, col. 2767; *Exeter Register Grandisson* 3 (App.), p. 1546.

119 See chapter 8 below for more detailed treatment.

120 *Murimuth*, p. 56.

121 BL Cotton MS Galba E. IV, fo. 183ᵛ; *Croniques de London*, p. 61 and n.; *HBC*, p. 36; *Ann. Paul.* pp. 338–9 (where the date is given as 30 January).

122 *Ann. Paul.*, p. 340, also claims that Thomas de Wake became king's chamberlain.

123 *Murimuth*, pp. 56–7; *Croniques de London*, p. 61 (giving York as the location of the marriage and an incorrect date); Barrow, *Bruce*, p. 260.

124 Baker, *Chronicon*, p. 40. For details of the treaty see below, chapter 9.

125 Ibid., p. 41: "auxilio Scotorum regnum et matrem regis usurparet."

126 *Brut*, p. 256 (CCC MS 174, fo. 153ʳ), where it is claimed that when Edward was "put out of his realm" he was not "put out of the fealties and services of the realm of Scotland."

127 *Avesbury*, p. 284: "Sic se quasi regem supra alios, in quantum potuit, extollebat, nesciens quod paucitas dierum suorum finiretur in brevi."

128 *Croniques de London*, p. 61. Dene is equally condemnatory. After mentioning the concession of a tenth "pro victoria concessa" he adds: "Nam thesaurus totus regni quem rex colligerat pater exhaustus fuit." Historia Roffensis, fo. 50ᵛ. See also *Brut*, p. 259 (CCC MS 174, fos. 155ᵛ–6ʳ), Lancaster's complaint.

129 Tout, *Chapters* 4, pp. 230–33, especially p. 232 n. 1, citing *CPR 1327–30*, pp. 66–9, which lists the grants made to the queen.

130 See Fryde, *Tyranny and Fall*, p. 208.

131 Orleton was subsequently granted custody of the lands of Laurence, while a minor – he was born 20 March 1320 – in recompense for money owed him by Edward III. Laurence was recognized as earl on 13 October 1339. Haines, *Church and Politics*, p. 63 n. 8; *HBC*, p. 477.

132 *Murimuth*, p. 57; *Avesbury*, p. 284; *Wigmore Chronicle*, p. 352; *Knighton* 1, p. 449; Barber and Barker, *Tournaments*, p. 31.

133 *Brut*, p. 262 (CCC MS 174, fo. 157ᵛ).

134 Griffiths, *Principality of Wales*, p. 102.

135 *Ann. Paul.*, pp. 342–3; *Avesbury*, p. 284; *Brut*, p. 260 (CCC MS 174, fo. 156ʳ): "against all the barons' will in England, in prejudice of the king and of his crown"; Haines, *John Stratford*, p. 197 n. 25.

136 *Brut*, pp. 261–2 (CCC MS 174, fo. 157ʳ⁻ᵛ). The statement in the translation of the *Anonimalle Chronicle*, p. 145, that "Sir Geoffrey through madness even called himself [*sic*] king" is nonsensical.

137 Buck, *Stapeldon*, p. 170, from PRO E101/332/18, 20. A week later, he notes, an inventory revealed the extent of the valuables stored beneath St John's chapel in the Tower. See also Galbraith, "The Tower as an Exchequer Record Office."

138 Ibid., p. 171.

139 Fryde, *Tyranny and Fall*, pp. 208–9, 270, citing PRO E101/332/21, 26; /383/8

fos. 5^{r-v} (wardrobe book); E403/220, /225 (issue rolls) under dates 9 and 23 February 1327. Harding, "Isabella and Mortimer," p. 296, delineates the decline in cash resources of the treasury from the £54,839 or so at the time of Melton's handing over to Stratford (November 1326), to the minuscule £4 12s. 11d. when he resumed the treasurership on 1 December 1330. The author of the *Brut* deprecated the encroachments on the king's revenue and treasure: *Brut*, pp. 257, 259 (CCC MS 174, fos. 154^v, 155^v–6^r).

140 Fryde, *Tyranny and Fall*, p. 210.

141 The various sums are enumerated by Maunde Thompson in his notes to Baker's *Chronicon*, p. 214.

142 *Knighton* 1, p. 447: Lancaster "qui deputatus et ordinatus est capitalis custos et supremus consiliarius in tempore coronationis ... non potuit ei appropinquare nec quicquam consilii dare"; and see *Melsa* 2, p. 358. The new edition of Knighton (ed. H.G. Martin), dealing with the "contemporary" portion 1337 to 1396 (by which time the author had died), has an extensive introduction. Prior to 1337 the chronicle is mainly a conflation of Higden (itself a compilation) and Guisborough (the published edition of which ends in 1312).

143 For discussion of Mepham's political involvement see Haines, "An Innocent Abroad," and for details of his election ibid., pp. 358–60.

144 Haines, *John Stratford*, p. 196; *CPMR*, p. 79; Parry, *Parliaments*, p. 93; *HBC*, p. 556. The *CPMR* entry is a government-inspired account of proceedings.

145 *CPMR*, pp. 70–1.

146 *CPMR*, pp. 36, 38, 66, 68, 79–80; Winchester Register Stratford, fo. 110^r.

147 *CPMR*, p. 68. The entries recording the sending of these letters are marked "cancelled"; *HBC*, p. 556.

148 *CPMR*, pp. 30–1, 68–9.

149 Haines, "An Innocent Abroad," p. 560; *John Stratford*, p. 480; *Le Neve* 4, p. 342; *CPMR*, p. 80; *CCR 1327–30*, p. 321.

150 *Brut*, p. 257 (CCC MS 174, fo.154v); *Ann. Paul.*, p. 343–4; Maddicott, "Thomas of Lancaster and Sir Robert Holland," p. 469; Haines, *John Stratford*, p. 202.

151 It seems incredible that the staunch Lancastrian Wither or Wyther could be identifiable as this "Thomas Wether, knight," of SA MS 122, p. 90, who was later captured with the king's party. He took an oath (under duress?) as "prive chivaler mons[ieur] Hughe qe servientast sur le corps nostre seignur privement en la chambre le roi devant le roi et le dit mons[ieur] Hughe qil ne lerreit iames la compaignie mons[ieur] Hugh' tant come la vie lui durast et nul autre ne servireit sil ne fuisse le corps nostre seignur le roi: de donn xx mareks." Fryde, *Tyranny and Fall*, p. 191, makes no comment about this phenomenon but duly indexes him, ibid. pp. 218, 222, as being the same person. Ostensibly Wyther had made a double *volte-face*.

152 Historia Roffensis, fo. 51^v, has the dismissive comment: "Parliamentum apud Sar. ubi archiepiscopus novus modum et mores hominum totaliter ignorans, comitibus Kancie et Lancastrie et eorum sequele qui contra reginam et Rogerum

de Mortuo Mari regnantes sub colore utilitatis regni se partem facientes cepit adherere. Multa locutus est sed parum profecit."

153 *CPMR*, pp. 71–2; *Brut*, p. 260 (CCC MS 174, fo 156v).

154 Baker, *Chronicon*, p. 42.

155 Chancellor Burghersh was associated with Hervy in the commission for opening parliament. Parry, *Parliaments,* p. 93. For what follows concerning the parliament and Lancaster's armed demonstration at Winchester, see *CPMR*, pp. 80–3. It is, of course, the government's view as expressed in a letter sent to London where it was published on 20 December. Bishop Grandisson excused himself from attendance at Salisbury, claiming in a letter of 12 October to the king: "Vous avez si bon Counsail de noz honourables freres Evesques et autres Grants qe y serront, qe nostre presence tendrait petite ou nul value illoeques." *Exeter Register Grandisson* 1, pp. 179–80. See also Harding, "Isabella and Mortimer," pp. 165–6 and ibid., n. 1.

156 Baker, *Chronicon*, p. 42. For other particulars concerned with the situation at Salisbury: Harding, "Isabella and Mortimer," pp. 175–6; Fryde, *Tyranny and Fall*, pp. 219–21.

157 *CPMR*, pp. 81–2. These details are contained in a letter from the court, then at Gloucester. This is dated 16 December. Other elements of the letter are discussed below.

158 Stratford's flight is recounted in *Vitae Arch. Cant.*, p. 19 (Lambeth MS 99, fo. 136^r); Haines, *John Stratford*, pp. 198–200.

159 *Ann. Paul.*, p. 343, says the royal party reached London "about St Nicholas" (6 December) and stayed a week. Holmes, "Rebellion of Lancaster," p. 84, suggests 21 November–1 December as roughly marking the period of their stay.

160 *CPMR*, pp. 77–8.

161 *Lit. Cant.* 1, p. 272; *Ann. Paul.*, p. 343; Historia Roffensis, fos. 51^v–2^r.

162 An account of one William de la Marche, king's sergeant, is for expenses of coming from Rickmansworth on 5 January to Worcester with men-at-arms, hobelers, and footsoldiers, to aid the king against his enemies. From Worcester he travelled by way of Leicester to Bedford, clearly with the royal forces. Transcription from PRO E101/18/12 is in Holmes, "Rebellion of Lancaster," p. 87 n. 2.

163 See chapter 11. This document does not mention the highly contentious treaty with Scotland. That this was included in Lancaster's complaints against the Mortimer-Isabella regime – he did not hold the king responsible for the government's action – is maintained by the *Brut*, where Joan of the Tower is said to have been disparaged. *Brut*, pp. 257–9 (CCC MS 174, fo. 155^r–6^r).

164 *CPMR*, pp. 77–83. Misled by the rubric in *CPMR*, I have previously assumed that it was published on the feast, 21 December.

165 The queen owed a debt of gratitude to Sir Thomas Roscelyn of Edgefield and Walcott in Norfolk, for he had been one of her supporters in 1326. *Knighton* 1, pp. 431–2.

166 *Ann. Paul.*, p. 343; Holmes, "Rebellion of Lancaster," p. 88 (transcript of PRO C49/6/13, a manifesto justifying the seizure of Lancaster's lands).

167 *CPMR*, p. 84. A text is in *Lit. Cant.* 3, pp. 414–6 (from CCL Reg. I, fo. 427^{r-v}). The phrase omitted at the turn of the page is supplied by Holmes, "Rebellion of Lancaster," p. 87 n. 9.

168 *CPMR*, p. 85.

169 Gravesend is omitted at this point, apparently in error.

170 *Ann. Paul.*, p. 343–4.

171 His itinerary shows him to have been at Guildford on 8 January, at Farnham on the twelfth. Haines, *John Stratford*, p. 481.

172 *CPMR*, pp. 85–6; Holmes, "Rebellion of Lancaster," pp. 84, 86, 88.

173 *Knighton* 1, p. 450. He adds Stratford to the Lancastrian force, but is not sufficiently precise at this point.

174 *Foedera* 2 ii, p.754; *Brut,* p. 260 (CCL MS 174, fo. 156^{v}); Haines, *John Stratford*, p. 205 n. 66.

175 Historia Roffensis, fo. 52^{r}: "Alioquin dicti comites et eorum adherentes in vi armata regi occurrere, resistere et eum vi comprimere se velle asserebant." Dene was not one to invent little background touches, so this account has a ring of authenticity.

176 Compare Malachi 4:5–6.

177 Aldon is mentioned later (1337) in the same chronicle, in conjunction with Thomas de Cobham and others in a royal commission. Historia Roffensis, fos. 74^{v}–5^{r}.

178 As we know from other sources these were the knights Trussell, Wyther (Wither), Roscelyn, and Beaumont, who had been excluded in the ultimatum of 29 December. PRO KB27/276/Rex m. 24

179 *Knighton* 1, pp. 450–1; Historia Roffensis, fo. 52^{r-v}; Haines, *John Stratford*, pp. 203–5; "An Innocent Abroad," pp. 561–5. That Mepham engineered the submission is alleged by Baker, *Chronicon*, pp. 42–3: "procurante archiepiscopo Cantuariensi, apud Bedeford gracie regis se submiserunt."

180 Historia Roffensis, fo. 52^{v}; *Knighton* 1, pp. 450–1; TCC R.5 41, fo. 127^{v} (128); *Brut,* p. 260 (CCC MS 174, fo. 156^{v}); Maunde Thompson in *Chronicon*, Notes p. 220. Fryde, *Tyranny and Fall*, "Epilogue," especially p. 219, contrasts Knighton and the government *pièce justificative*, but takes no account of the Historia Roffensis, possibly the most valuable source for the last stages of the "quasi-rebellion." Her inclusion of Orleton as a confederate is suspect. For the confiscations and the recognizance's demanded: *CFR 1327–37*, pp. 116–17; *CCR 1327–30*, pp. 528–31.

181 Baker, *Chronicon*, pp. 42–3.

182 As apparently implied in Fryde, *Tyranny and Fall*, p. 224.

183 See Haines, *John Stratford*, pp. 205–6 and ibid., nn. 65–6; *CCR 137–30*, p. 425.

184 *CPR 1327–30*, pp. 472, 484, 547; PRO KB27/276/Rex m. 24.

185 *Ann. Lond.*, pp. 245–51. In the November 1330 parliament the Londoners suc-

cessfully petitioned for the redress of those grievances they had suffered because of the Winchester and Bedford affairs and at the hands of the justices of oyer and terminer. *Rot. Parl.* 2, pp. 54–5; *Foedera* 2 ii, p. 804.

186 Baker, *Chronicon*, pp. 36–9.

187 *Knighton* 1, pp. 451–2. See chapter 11 below.

188 Historia Roffensis, fo. 53^r: "In vigilia novi festi corporis Christi dedit obviam regi de partibus transmarinis redeunti, et in festis corporis Christi et sancti Johannis Baptiste missas regis celebravit in ecclesia cathedrali Roffen[si] et utroque die cum rege comedit. Cui Rogerus de Mortuo Mari magnum vultum fecit, rogans episcopum ut ad consilium regis apud Wyndesore veniret. Sed illic venire se excusavit quia difficile grave et sumptuosum foret pauperi episcopo Roffen[si] parliamenta regis et consilia ubique in regno sequi, nec sufficiunt facultates episcopatus eius id facere, sufficit tamen sibi Lond. ad parliamentum venire." For the feast of Corpus Christi see Pfaff, *New Liturgical Feasts*, index s.v.

189 *Croniques de London*, p. 62 and n.

190 Historia Roffensis, fo. 56^r. Chronological order is difficult here since this entry (without mention of the year) is sandwiched between details of Edward II's being still alive and the closing of parliament "on the morrow." There was no Westminster Parliament at this time. The correct date is in BL MS Cotton Galba E.IV, fo. 183^v.

191 One of the less reliable statements in a government manifesto at the time of the "Lancastrian rebellion" is that the rebels were guilty of sending people disguised as "freres de Pye," or as other religious, who went about mocking the king. Holmes, "Rebellion of Lancaster," p. 88 (from PRO C49/6/13). Presumably the "Pied friars" are intended here, but if so it is an odd choice as there were very few indeed of them at this or any other time. That Lancaster's supporters would have mocked the king is inherently unlikely. They were anxious to assert their loyalty and to disengage him from Mortimer's tentacles. It does suggest, however, that Mortimer could have been sufficiently unscrupulous to adopt a ruse of this kind to trap Kent.

192 A lengthy account of the affair is in the *Brut*, pp. 263–7 (CCC MS 174, fos. 158^r–61^r). In view of the deliberately public funeral, how could the earl not have known of the king's death? The pope was to point out this obvious fact. Those who had given aid to Kent "a la deliverance faire de nostre seign[eur] le roi qi mort est" were duly pardoned at the Westminster Parliament of November 1330: *Rot. Parl.* 2, p. 54.

193 Haines, "An Innocent Abroad," p. 583; *Knighton* 1, p. 452. Kent was buried in the church of the Friars Minor, but subsequently his widow, Margaret, and her son received papal permission (13 April 1331) to have the body exhumed and buried at Westminster in which abbey church "regalium defunctorum Anglie consueverunt corpora sepeliri." Vatican Archives, Reg. Aven. 38, fo. 711^v.

194 See chapter 8 below for an examination of the whole elaborate hoax.

195 *Murimuth*, App. (from BL MS Cotton Claudius E.VIII), pp. 253–7 (Kent's con-

fession); *Foedera* 2 ii, pp. 783 (justificatory letter to the pope), 787, 796 (implication of Rhys ap Gruffydd); *Rot. Parl.* 2, p. 54 (petition of 1330 for rehabilitation, which mentions only one secular by name, William la Zouche).

196 Lincoln Register Burghersh 5, fos. 403^{r-v}, 429^{r-v}; Historia Roffensis, fo. 56^r; *Concilia* 2, pp. 558–9: Haines, "An Innocent Abroad," pp. 576, 596. Other aspects of the Lambeth assembly are mentioned below.

197 *Brut*, p. 267 (CCC MS 174, fo. 161^r), and see Fryde, *Tyranny and Death*, p. 225. But it could be argued against Fryde that the adjournment of cases against lesser offenders in this matter was due to fear of provoking too wide a hostile reaction, rather than to Edward's intervention. We do not know how much the king was able to effect on his own, but he was beginning to kick against the pricks.

198 *Murimuth*, p. 60.

199 Historia Roffensis, fo. 56^v; *Bridlington*, p. 101. *Ann. Paul.*, p. 349, adds that the infant was baptised by Bishop Burghersh of Lincoln.

200 *Brut*, p. 268 (CCC MS 174, fo. 161^v). Harding, "Isabella and Mortimer," records (p. 54 and n., citing PRO E101/382/8) that orders for the dubbing of knights at Edward III's coronation included the requirement that Thomas de Useflete, supervisor of the wardrobe – the man who had made provision for Edward II's funeral – should provide robes "tanquam pro comitibus" for Mortimer's three sons Edmund, Roger and Geoffrey. For Mortimer's aggrandizement and that of his family: ibid., pp. 96–116. The author cites B. Penry Evans, "The Family of Mortimer," University of Wales Ph.D. 1934, in his bibliography. See also Holmes, *Estates of Higher Nobility*, index s.v.

201 Tout, *Chapters* 3, p. 29.

202 *Foedera* 2 ii, p. 785; *CPR 1327–30*, p. 470; *CCR 1330–33*, p. 41. It is notable that Bury, as former keeper of the wardrobe, on 23 Oct. 1330 was allowed the "money, gold and silver vessels, jewels and other things" which had been delivered to Isabella, Philippa and Mortimer by *viva voce* order. *CCR 1330–33*, p. 67. Harding, "Isabella and Mortimer," App. III, provides a transcription from the account of William de Shaldeford (Shalford) and John de Piercebridge (PRO E372/179/ m.22) of Mortimer's plate, jewels etc. found at Ludlow and Wigmore. Compare Larking,Way ed., "An Inventory of the Effects of Roger de Mortimer," pp. 69–80 (from a roll of the Queen's Remembrancer).

203 Woodhouse, archdeacon of Richmond, acted as treasurer 16 September 1329–30 November 1330; Melton, then archdeacon of York, from 26 November 1330 (entered office 1 December) until 1 April 1331. Tout, *Chapters* 6, p. 21. The figures I owe to Fryde, *Tyranny and Fall*, pp. 223–4, 273, citing PRO E101/384/1, fo. 9 (account book of Bury), E101/333/3). Tout, *Chapters* 6, p. 86, gives tentative sums (here adjusted to the nearest £) for the income of the kings wardrobe as follows: 1326–28 (Woodhouse) £89,908; 1328–29 (Bury), £21,280; 1329–31 (Garton), £36,327. The great wardrobe figures are (receipts with expenses in brackets): 25 January 1327–24 January 1328, £4,505 (£4,574); 1328–29, £4,961 (£3,642); 1329–30, £2,872 (£3,894); 1330–31, £4,058 ((£6,697). Ibid., p. 105.

204 Fryde, *Tyranny and Fall*, pp. 223–4, 273 (from PRO E404/2/10). Zouche was
     keeper 26 January 1329–15 July 1334. Tout, *Chapters* 3, p. 53 n.2; 6, p. 35.
     Harding, "Isabella and Mortimer" in App. II, pp. 387–8, lists (a) the loans made
     by the Bardi (in excess of £44,400) and (b) by the de la Poles, Richard and
     William (just short of £14,500).

205 *Ann. Paul.*, p. 348; *Historia Roffensis*, fo. 56ʳ; *Lit. Cant.* I, pp. 323–30; Haines,
     "An Innocent Abroad," p. 583; and see above.

206 Charlton had his property pillaged at the time of the 1326 disturbances in the
     City. *Croniques de London*, pp. 53, 55 n. For his concern with the wool staple
     see Lloyd, *English Wool Trade*, p. 117 and index s.v. "merchants."

207 *Ann. Lond.*, pp. 247–51.

208 *CFR 1327–37*, p. 116. This particular grant is marked as vacated because surren-
     dered. But see ibid., p. 129, *CPR 1327–30*, pp. 386, 392.

209 Tout, *Chapters* 3, p. 29–30, n. 6; *CCR 1327–30*, p. 425: Harding, "Isabella and
     Mortimer," App. I lists Montacute as a witness twelve times between 25 Jan.
     1329 and 18 Feb. 1330 and 33 between 27 Jan. and 16 Oct. 1330. For Montacute
     and his family: Douch, "The Career of William Montague"; *GEC* 9 (s.v. "Mon-
     tague"), 11 (s.v. "Salisbury"); Haines, "Simon de Montacute." He married
     Catherine (Katharine), a sister of Bishop Grandisson of Exeter: sculptured heads
     of all three are to be seen in the Lady Chapel in the former collegiate church of
     Ottery St Mary.

210 Tout, *Chapters* 3, pp. 28–9; Johnson and Jenkinson, *English Court Hand*, plate
     XXIIB, and (transcript) pp. 174–5; *English Diplomatic Practice* pt. 1, no. 18;
     Crump, "Arrest of Roger Mortimer," pp. 331–2. Bury was to be rewarded when
     Edward III in December 1330 wrote to the pope, again in his own hand, asking
     preferment for one who "nobis, a pueritia nostra impendit multipliciter laboribus
     indefessis." William de Montacute was sent to Avignon to recommend him. *Foed-
     era* 2 ii, p. 804.

211 *Murimuth*, pp. 60–1: "viro utique competenter illiterato et minime personato,
     quem si papa vidisset, nunquam eum, ut creditur, tantum apicem promovisset."

212 Parry, *Parliaments*, pp. 94–5; *Ann. Paul.*, p. 350; *Rot. Parl.* 2, pp. 52–3 (Mor-
     timer's indictment); *Scalacronica*, ed. Stevenson, p. 157; Tout, *Chapters* 3, p. 29.
     One of the longest accounts of the events at Nottingham is in the *Brut* BL Harl.
     MS 2279 (in Notes to *Chronicon*, pp. 226–9). See nn. 216–17 below.

213 *Chronicon*, pp. 45–6; *Scalacronica*, ed. Maxwell, p. 85.

214 The same word was used to describe Gaveston.

215 Baker, *Chronicon*, p. 46, describes him as "speculator" or spy, who knew every
     passage of the castle.

216 The account in Dene, Historia Roffensis, fo. 56ᵛ, runs: "Regina mater episcopus
     Lyncoln[iensis] et Rogerus de Mortuo Mari in camera ipsius super lectum ipsius
     regine sedebant consulentes et titubantes de insidiis." Turplington had succeeded
     John Maltravers in the office of steward as recently as 1 August 1330. The
     Scalacronica, ed. Maxwell, pp. 86–7, states that they entered by the open postern

"and mounted the stairs of the second court without meeting anybody." They then passed first to a hall and then a private chamber.

217 This is a conflation of the accounts given by Baker, *Chronicon*, pp. 29, 45–6, which states that the door of the queen's chamber was open, and that she was preparing for bed, and those in versions of the *Brut*, pp. 268–71 (CCC MS 174, fos. 161ᵛ–3ᵛ), BL MS Harley 2279 (in Notes to *Chronicon*, pp. 226–9). According to Baker the plea was addressed to her son whom she could not see, although she guessed he was there. The conspirators apart from Montacute and Neville included according to *Brut*, p. 269 (also version in CUL Ee. IV. 32, fo. 141ʳ), the brothers Bohun (Sir Humphrey and William *sic*), Ralph Stafford, Robert Ufford, and William de Clinton. Walkfare's participation is vouched for by *Calendar of Ancient Petitions Wales*, p. 253 and *CPR 1330–34*, p. 172. See also *Foedera* 2 ii, pp. 799–800; *Scalacronica*, ed. Stevenson, p. 157, ed. Maxwell, pp. 86–7; Tout, *Chapters* 3, pp. 29–30; 6, p. 43.

218 Baker, *Chronicon*, pp. 46–8, also p. 25 where Despenser is twice designated (ironically?) earl of Gloucester; *Murimuth*, pp. 63–4. The lengthy official version is in *Rot. Parl.* 2, pp. 52–3. See the summary of this last in App. B below.

219 Tout, *Chapters* 3, p. 11 and n. 3. For the establishment of staples or fixed markets for the trade in wool, whether in England or abroad, see Lloyd, *The English Wool Trade*, index s.v. "staple" and especially chapter 4.

220 Tout, *Chapters* 3, p. 11 n. 4, gives the details; see also 4, pp. 230–1. There were only two escheators by 26 February 1327, when William Trussell became escheator south of Trent.

221 Cam, "The General Eyres of 1329–1330," p. 152; Putnam, "Transformation of the Keepers"; *Shareshull*, p. 60; Kaeuper, "Law and Order," pp. 745 and n. 45. Stones, "Geoffrey le Scrope," p. 11, comments on the views of Cam and Putnam.

222 Rogers, "MS of Eyre of Northampton." Stones, "Geoffrey le Scrope," pp. 11–12, argues the difficulty of assigning policy to a particular person and concludes that "Scrope's part" in the law and order campaign "as in politics, may prove to have been dictated substantially by considerations of immediate advantage to the Government of the day."

223 Kaeuper, "Law and Order," especially pp. 744–6 and graph p. 741; Stones, "Geoffrey le Scrope," pp. 10–15.

224 When Edward III became king *de facto* as well as *de iure*, he was prompt to announce his intention of governing "by right and reason" (*solonc droiture et reson*) and to act with the common consent of the magnates. *Foedera* 2 ii, pp. 799–800, Nottingham 20 October 1330.

225 Harding, "Isabella and Mortimer," App. I, lists John de Eltham as witnessing charters 66 times between 27 January and 16 October 1330; Maltravers as witnessing 56 times, Ingham 54, Mortimer 57 and Burghersh 72. See also ibid., pp. 70–76, 85–87 for the domination of these men and their rewards. Eltham, however, was a juvenile, doubtless under the thumb of his mother and Mortimer. Born in 1316 he had been created earl in 1328 at the same time as Mortimer. The only

bishops (other than Burghersh) who witnessed an appreciable number of times were Hothum (12), Orleton (12) – engaged in diplomatic activity at this juncture – and Northburgh (15).

CHAPTER EIGHT

1 English *Brut* (anonymous) chronicle, p.263. Slightly adapted and with partially modernized spelling.
2 BL Cotton MS Galba E. IV, fo. 183ᵗ. Much of what follows in this chapter is derived from my article "Edwardus *Redivivus*: the 'Afterlife' of Edward of Caernarvon" (1996), which retains independent value. Some aspects are omitted here but there is additional material. My *Death of a King* is intended as a more popular examination of aspects of this mystery. The Cuttino and Lyman article appeared in *Speculum* in 1978. For the despatch of news of Edward's demise see n. 99 below.
3 "Where is Edward II?," p. 529; Bent, "Where did Edward II die?," p. 381. Cuttino and Lyman appear to have been unaware of Bent's comments (see next note).
4 "Where is Edward II?" provides an English translation at pp. 526–7, a Latin text at pp. 537–8. My English rendering differs only slightly and my reading of the Latin text is in agreement apart from a few orthographical details. There have been earlier Latin texts and translations. Alexandre Germain first brought the document to a wider audience. See his "Lettre de Manuel de Fiesque concernant les dernires annes du roi d'Angleterre Édouard II," pp. 109–27, also that society's publication no. 37, December 1877, pp. 118–20. News of the document percolated to England where Theodore Bent published it in 1880 both in *Macmillan's Magazine* (March) and in *Notes and Queries*, "Where did Edward II die?," pp. 381–3, 401–3 (translation at pp. 402–3). Sir Henry Ogle referred to it in a paper delivered for him in 1890 at the Society of Antiquaries of Newcastle-on-Tyne and subsequently (having translated an article in *Nuova Antologia* by Costantino Nigra), provided a text in that society's *Proceedings*. Stubbs, *Chronicles of Edward I & II*, 2, introduction pp. ciii–cviii, had already printed Germain's Latin text and discussed its validity.
5 The Latin reads: "monitu matris vestre," where one might expect something like "innotum matri vestre" – unknown to his mother. Isabella would not have issued a warning, since she was in hot pursuit of her husband. Moreover, in the light of the story that follows the composer of the letter could scarcely have cast Edward III's mother in a favourable light at this point.
6 The coronation, as we have seen, took place on Sunday 1 February.
7 "Where is Edward II?," p. 540, suggests that Edward reached Corfe in September 1328 and left for Ireland in March or April 1330, But there is no indication in the document of any such interval following the death of the porter and the king's putative escape in September. It runs: "Et postquam exivit carceres castri antedicti fuit receptatus in castro de Corf."

8 "Where is Edward II?," pp. 541–2, conjectures Edward's arrival at Melazzo d'Acqui (*castrum Melasci* of the MS) about June or July 1331 and at the abbey of Sant' Alberto di Butrio near Cecima supra Voghera (*castrum Cecime*) about December 1334. This identification of place names is adopted by Cuttino and Lyman from Anna Benedetti, *Edoardo II d'Inghilterra* .

9 Ughelli, *Italia Sacra* 4, col. 804, has 6 Kal. July (26 June); Gams, *Series Episcoporum*, p. 826, although *inter alia* citing *Italia Sacra,* gives 25 June (p. 826).

10 "Where is Edward II?," p. 542, derived from *CPR 1334–1338,* p. 116.

11 *Hemingby's Register*, no. 75, pp. 85–6, and for biographical notes, pp. 198–9.

12 *Grande Dizianario Enciclopedico,* s.v.

13 *Le Neve Fasti* 12, index s.v. "Fieschi (Flisco)."

14 These and other details are to be found with references in *Le Neve* and *Hemingby's Register*, see nn. 9, 13 above. "Where is Edward II?," p. 544, gives a summary genealogical table of the "Fieschi connection."

15 *Foedera* 2 ii, pp. 946–7; *CPR 1334–1338,* pp. 247, 321, 328–9; cf. *Ann. Paul.,* p. 300; Haines, *John Stratford,* pp. 243–4

16 "Where is Edward II?," p. 544, citing (ibid. n.71) *Foedera* 2 i, p. 274. For Luca di Fieschi see Wright, *Reynolds,* no. 11, pp. 290–1.

17 SA MS 122, p. 90; *Itinerary EII*, pp. 290–1. Bliton was to be implicated in the so-called conspiracy of the earl of Kent in 1330. *Chronicon*, p. 44. See above chapter 7 also n. 85 below.

18 *Anonimalle Chronicle*, pp. 130–1, stigmatizing those with Edward as "his enemies"; Baker, *Chronicon*, p. 22, names the earl of Gloucester, instead of Arundel, as one of the royal companions – ironically a title coveted by the younger Despenser. See ibid., p. 197 (Notes) for Le Bel's idea that a miracle was responsible for the adverse wind.

19 See Haines, *Church and Politics,* pp. 11–12, 165–6. For Arundel see Given Wilson, "Wealth and Credit: Earls of Arundel, 1306–1397," pp. 1–26 especially 2–5. The Gervase continuator (TCC MS R.5 41), fo. 124^{r-v} (123), gives details of the barbarities inflicted, notably on the younger Despenser (see above chapter 7 n. 50), a story retold by Froissart (ed. Luce, 1, pp. 34–5) following Le Bel, *Chronique* 1, pp. 27–8.

20 *Murimuth*, p. 52; Baker, *Chronicon*, p. 30; *Brut* ; p. 253 (CCC MS 174, fo. 152^r). This version of the *Brut* suggests (in error?) that Edward died at Corfe, but Berkeley is named later with cross reference to the earlier passage, ibid., p. 268 (fo. 159^r); French Brut (CCC Oxford MS 78, fo. 169^r) printed by Galbraith, "Extracts," p. 216. A version of an anonymous Flemish chronicle (*Chroniques de Flandre, RHGF* 22, p. 425 n. 4) states that the king was taken to "Tourf," which can be interpreted as Corfe.

21 PRO SC1/35/207; Tanquerey, "Conspiracy of Dunheved," pp. 119–24; Denholm-Young, *Collected Papers* ("Authorship of *Vita* "), especially pp. 286–7; Smith, "Rise of the Berkeleys," pp. 76–8; *CPL 1305–1342,* pp. 253, 479. Tanquerey, followed by Tout, Cuttino, Natalie Fryde and others, including myself, misled by the

PRO index, thought incorrectly that the letter was sent by Walwayn. There has been confusion about the responsibility of Berkeley for the king's safe-keeping. Berkeley does not seem to have been deprived of such custody, nor is Murimuth's suggestion that Berkeley and Maltravers shared custody by alternate months (*Murimuth*, p. 52) corroborated by any other source. Berkeley's fine alabaster effigy (he died in 1361) lies on his tomb in the south aisle of Berkeley church beside that of his second wife Katharine, daughter of John Cliveden and widow of Sir Peter de Veel, a Gloucestershire knight.

22 *Brut*, p. 249 (CCC MS 174, fo. 149ᵛ), slightly modernized orthography here and in other quotations from this MS: "The frere Prechouris to hym were goode friends evermore and caste and ordeyne bothe nyght and day hou they myght bringe him out of prisoun." Gaveston was, as we have seen, buried at the Dominican house at Langley. *Vita*, pp. 58–9; Hamilton, *Gaveston*, pp. 99–100, 166 n. 79, for royal gifts to the Dominicans.

23 PRO SC1/35/207; Tanquerey, "Conspiracy of Dunheved," pp. 119–20; *CPR 1327–1330*, pp. 80, 156–7.

24 Said to be parsons (rectors) respectively of *Dadynton* (Deddington, Oxfordshire, the place from which Gaveston had been abducted?) and Beadewell (Bedwell, Hertfordshire, or Bidwell, Bedfordshire?).

25 "Ad rapiendum dominum E. de Carnarvan, nuper regem Angliae, patrem nostrum, et ad levandum populum nostrum de guerra contra nos." *Foedera* 2 ii, p. 714, 20 August 1327. Aylmere was imprisoned at Oxford, hence the sheriff's involvement.

26 *CPL 1305–1342*, p. 474; SA MS 122, p. 34.

27 *Lanercost*, pp. 254, 260, where Dunheved's mission is reported to have been at the behest of the younger Despenser and included (at first mention) among the events of 1325, where it is assumed to have been one of the reasons prompting the queen's journey to France. This is unlikely in view of the anxiety of the king and councillors that she should act as an emissary to the king of France. Dene in the Historia Roffensis, fo. 46ᵛ, records that Bishop Hethe rejected the precedent propounded by the king that a disobedient queen could be deposed from her dignity (*a dignitate regali deposita fuit*).

28 *Ann. Paul.*, p. 337; PRO E101/29/64 (for the attempt on Kenilworth Castle). The *Brut* adds that Dunheved died in Pontefract Castle, but gives no date. *Brut*, p. 249 (CCC MS 174, fo. 149ᵛ).

29 Dunheved's depredations by way of Cirencester, Oxfordshire and Chester are noted by Tout, "Captivity and Death," pp. 157–8.

30 This account is mainly from personal observation. See also Faulkner, "Berkeley Castle," pp. 197–200; Clark, *Medieval Military Architecture in England* 1, pp. 228–39; Hamilton Thompson, *Military Architecture*, index s.v. "Berkeley;" Oman, *Castles*, pp. 84–8. The castle is illustrated in Brown, *Castles from the Air*, pp. 50–2, and in Sackville West, *Berkeley Castle*.

31 Baker, *Chronicon*, p. 33; Higden, *Polychronicon* 8 (Trevisa), pp. 324–7.

32 The earliest mention of *Le Canonbury* street in *EPNS Gloucs.* 2, p. 212, is 1492.

The name is derived from the lands of the Augustinian canons of Bristol in the town. Alkington is Southeast of Berkeley.

33 Berkeley Mun., select rolls 39 and 40 [copy]. See n. 36 below.

34 *Foedera* 2 ii, p. 801. Deverel is said to have been drawn and hung at London (1332) for the earl's death (*prodicione collacionis*): Lichfield Chronicle, p. 209.

35 *Brut*, p. 253 (CCC MS 174, fo. 152ʳ), which states that Mortimer granted the wardship of the king to Gurney (*Toiourneye*, but Gorney later in the MS) and Maltravers. This source also confuses Sir Thomas Berkeley with Sir Maurice Berkeley, his father, or possibly his younger brother of the same name. Subsequently the Friars Preacher are said to have suggested to Edmund, earl of Kent, that his "brother" was alive at Corfe under the guardianship of Gurney. Ibid., p. 263.

36 Berkeley Mun., select rolls 39–40 [the latter a copy of 39 by W. F. Shrapnel, sometime steward of Berkeley]. Roll 39 is that of the steward of Berkeley, apparently William Aside, for the period 1 January 1326 to 30 September 1327. See also Jeayes, *Descriptive Catalogue*, pp. 274–5 (extracts).

37 *Murimuth*, pp. 53–4.

38 *Lanercost*, p. 260: "Mortuus est, vel morte propria naturali vel ab aliis violenter inflicta." See also n. 58 below.

39 For discussion of Baker and other chroniclers of the time see Haines, *Church and Politics*, chapter 4, and in general, Gransden, *Historical Writing II*, chapter 1.

40 *Chronicles of Edward I & II*, 2, pp. lviii–lxxv, 297–319. Referred to hereafter as *Vita et Mors* (from Camden's edition collated with BL MSS Cotton Vitellius E. V and Harleian 310, Bodl. Lib. 761). This last is the principal MS used by Maunde Thompson in his edition of Baker's *Chronicon*.

41 Baker, *Chronicon*, introduction pp. vi–ix.

42 Haines, *John Stratford*, index s.v. "Laurence."

43 *CPR 1324–1327*, p. 331: Haines, *Church and Politics*, p. 105.

44 See Haines, *Church and Politics*, chapter 4 "Orleton and the Chroniclers," especially p. 104..

45 Ibid., p. 109 and n. 36.

46 Ibid., p. 106.

47 At the commencement of the "Passion sequence" Baker addresses his patron de la More as *miles reverende*, explaining that because of Edward's enemies still alive he cannot reveal the full facts. But he then continues with the details learned, so he says, from Bishop after 1349. Clearly this points to a subsequent revision of the text. The story of the king's being forcibly shaved in ditch-water is also to be found in a version of the *Brut*, but there the man responsible is said to be Sir Thomas Gurney. Galbraith, "Extracts," p. 216.

48 Baker, *Chronicon*, p. 31.

49 "Where is Edward II?," p. 523; Tout, "Captivity and Death," p. 163, considered him "indistinguishable" from his namesakes

50 *CPR 1321–1324*, pp. 17, 377; *1338–1340 et seq.* indices s.v.

51 This sergeant may be identifiable as the William Bishop who in 1335 paid forty

shillings for a horse for the king's use: BL Cotton MS Nero C. VIII (Wardrobe
Book 9 Edward III), fo. 211^r. He is possibly the sergeant who gave a receipt, 12
July 1355, for expenses of £46 13s. 4d. The document is sealed with a fine round
heraldic seal in red wax, the arms being surmounted by a mitre. PRO E47/170.

52 CCC MS 174, fos. 152^{r-v}; Baker, *Chronicon*, p. 33.

53 Westminster chronicle (BL Cotton Cleopatra A. XVI), fo. 144^r, cited in *Chronica
Johannis de Reading*, p. 78: "quomodo vel quali morte fama confessioque carnifi-
cum manifestavit quod in lecto tabulis oppressus, cornu accepit violenter in ano
per medium quoque veru ferreum in visceribus, sicque cruciatus expiravit."

54 For Mortimer's indictment see *Rot. Parl.* 2, pp. 52–3; *Knighton* 1, pp. 454–8.

55 *Froissart* (Rome MS), ed. Luce, 1, p. 247.

56 *CPR .1327–1330*, pp. 42, 125; *Ann. Paul.*, p. 311. See for Walkfare: PRO
C81/177/4121; Maddicott, *Lancaster*, pp. 263–4.

57 Moore, "Documents," pp. 216–7, 223 (text of Chancellor's roll 1 Edward III, the
particulars for which are said to be no longer extant). Dr. Arnold Taylor kindly
provided me with a transcript of the particulars of the account of John Darcy, the
cousin, concerning other arrangements for burial of the king's father.

58 BL MS Cotton Claudius A. V, fo. 41^v. Compare the Lanercost chronicler's enigmatic remark in n. 38 above.

59 *Historia Gloucestriae* 1, pp. 44–5; Moore, "Documents," p. 233; Smyth, *Lives of
the Berkeleys* 1, pp. 292–3.

60 WAM no. 20344, Beby's expense account.

61 *Chroniques de London*, p. 46; *Anonimalle Chronicle*, pp. 114–15; Bodl. Lib. MS
Lyell 17, fo. 115^v: "la table qe le dit comte de Lancastre avait fait peindre et pen-
dre sur une piler en remembrance qe le roi avait graunte et afferme les orde-
nances'; *Flores* 3, pp. 213–4: "statuam in similitudinem ipsius [Lancaster]
armatam in brevi tabula lignea protractam, consimilia copiose miracula refulsere."

62 PRO E101/624/14.

63 Moore, "Documents," p. 226.

64 Brown, "Death and the Human Body," pp. 267–8 and n. 193, writes that "a sense
of the unbridgeable gulf between the living and the dead manifested itself in the
occasional veiling of the corpse's face during the funeral procession," and suggests
that a wax effigy may have been used at Henry III's funeral in 1272.

65 Kantorowicz, *The King's Two Bodies*, pp. 373, 420–1; "Where is Edward II?," p.
525, citing Giesey, *Royal Funeral Ceremony*, p. 82; Moore, "Documents," p. 222.

66 J. H. Cooke in *Notes and Queries*, pp. 489–90.

67 Gardner, *English Medieval Sculpture*, p. 357; "Alabaster Tombs of the Gothic Period," pp. 6, 23, 64; *Age of Chivalry*, pp. 416–7 no. 497. An earlier detailed description is that of Roper, *Monumental Effigies of Gloucestershire*, pp. 142–6. See now
Welander, *Gloucester Cathedral*, chapter 8.

68 Smyth, *Lives of the Berkeleys* 1, p. 293, citing the receiver's roll for 2 Edward II.

69 Moore, "Documents," pp. 218–19, 226 and n. Clearly suspicion arises that
Glanville's "oversight" was deliberate.

70 Kingsford, *Grey Friars*, p. 74.

71 Stow, *Survey* I, pp. 630–1. *Murimuth*, p. 62, agrees that Mortimer was buried there initially but adds that the body was subsequently taken to Wigmore. Archaeologists have recently sought in vain for his burial place among the ruins of the abbey church. The *Wigmore Chronicle*, p. 352, after declaring that Edward III "debite non remuneravit" makes no mention of the manner of Mortimer's death but says that he was buried at the Greyfriars in Shrewsbury on 29 (vigil of St Andrew) November 1331. But it was the Franciscans of Coventry who were licensed (7 November 1331) to deliver the body for burial at Wigmore, a move for which his widow, Joan, had petitioned. *Foedera* 2 ii, p. 829; *Calendar of Ancient Petitions Wales*, p. 89.

72 Kingsford, *Grey Friars*, pp. 75, 198.

73 Blackley, "The Tomb of Isabella," pp. 161–4. The funeral service was conducted in the Minorites' church by Archbishop Islip. The tombs were all sold in the autumn of 1547. It seems to me unsatisfactory to dismiss the friar's story of the heart as "legend." For death and burial practices see Brown, "Death and the Human Body," pp. 221–70 esp. p. 253; Bradford, *Heart Burial*, especially pp. 105–8; Hallam, "Royal Burial," pp. 359–80.

74 *Foedera* 2 ii, p. 697, 10 March 1327. He had been granted protection to accompany the king abroad in 1325. *CPR. 1324–1327*, p. 167.

75 *CCR. 1327–1330*, pp. 446, 448, 485; *CChR, 1327–1341*, p. 190, where he is described as the king's (Edward III's) "leech."

76 BL Add. MS 38006: wardrobe account of Robert de Tong, treasurer of the household of Eleanor on her journey to Nijmegen; Safford ed., "Expenses of Eleanor," pp. 111–40, especially 129, 135. Information from copy of a letter of 5 October 1978 sent by Dr. A.J. Taylor to Professor Cuttino, and passed on to me by the former.

77 PRO E36/203, fos. 88ᵛ–9ʳ, pp. 178–9. This reference I owe to Cuttino and Lyman, "Where is Edward II?," p. 530 n. 43, themselves indebted to Pierre Chaplais. Should the "December" of the MS be "September"?

78 *Ann. Paul.*, pp. 282–3; *Bridlington*, pp. 86–7; *Lanercost*, pp. 236–7; *Historical Collections of London*, p. 74. For an earlier instance (1315–16) see PRO E368/86 m.93.

79 Details are in Cuttino and Lyman, "Where is Edward II?," p. 531ff. The article includes a plan of the abbey and photographs of parts of it, including three of the empty tomb claimed as a resting place for the bones of Edward of Caernarvon.

80 Ibid. "Qui fu sepolto finch furono trasportate in Inghilterra e collocate nel mausoleo di Glocester le sue Ossa da Eduardo III."

81 Ibid. and see (for an earlier period) Geary, *Furta Sacra*.

82 *A Catalogue of the Records of St. Peter's Abbey*, p. 163: D936A17 Account Book of Marshall Allen. H. Haines, *Guide to the Cathedral of Gloucester*, prints the memorandum which is also to be found in various guidebooks, e.g. (from Haines) Thurlow, *Gloucester and Berkeley*.

83 See, for example, the enigmatic mandate in *Foedera* 2 ii, p. 775.

84 *Chronicon*, pp. 43–4.

85 Those named by Baker as being involved were the provincials of the Dominicans and of the Carmelites (John Baconthorpe), the Carmelite friar Richard de Bliton, Stephen Gravesend, bishop of London, and Robert de Taunton, archbishop Melton's clerk. For others implicated, Archbishop Melton among them, see Haines, *John Stratford*, p. 212 n.109; for their rehabilitation: *Rot. Parl.* 2, pp. 31–3, 54.

86 *Ann. Paul.*, p. 349, records a rumour that Edward "in transmarinis partibus vivere et in brevi supervenisse"; *Murimuth*, p. 60; *Bridlington*, p. 100; *Historia Roffensis*, fos., 55v, 56r. Hethe's devastation at the news of the earl's death is recorded by Dene: "apud Hallyng. ibi sedit cogitativus et tremebundus dolens de morte comitis Kancie, qui decapitatus fuit apud Wynton. in quadragesima precedenti iussu regine regnantis quia comes dixit se velle fratrem suum regem iuvasse et ei succurrisse si fuisset vivus." The bishop who had the same sympathies as those now being pursued by the government was clearly not deluded.

87 *Rot. Parl.* 2, p. 52.

88 *Brut*, p. 263 (CCC MS 174, fo. 158ᵛ).

89 See Edwards, "The Cult of St. Thomas of Lancaster," for a recent discussion of this phenomenon of popular sainthood. In 1319 Lancaster had himself launched a campaign for Winchelsey's canonization. Reynolds supplied a schedule of his predecessor's miracles, but this was omitted from Register I of the cathedral priory. *Lit. Cant.* 3, pp. 398–401 nos 58–61.

90 *CPL 1305–1342*, p. 499. See also *Foedera* ii, p. 783, a "royal letter" of 24 March 1330 complaining about the friar [Dunheved] who had conjured up a demon who told him that the former king was alive. The story is also in *Lanercost*, p. 265.

91 *Rot. Parl.* 2, p. 57; *Murimuth*, p. 63.

92 Confirmation of Mortimer's sojourn at Abergavenny is lacking. The court and the core of the bureaucracy appear to have been in Lincoln, where parliament was summoned to assemble on 15 September 1327. See n. 99 below.

93 Tout, "Captivity and Death," App. 11, pp. 182–9: "A Welsh Conspiracy to Release Edward II." For William de Shalford see Jones, *Medieval Mason*, pp. 21n., 25, 147, 149, 190, also n. 94 below. Ockley's origin are obscure, but he had held lands in Ireland, which were restored in 1327. On occasion he is called "Ogle," the same name as a Northumberland family. See n. 4 above.

94 In May 1331 Shalford was appointed a commissioner to examine the complaints of Englishmen in North Wales who claimed to be oppressed by Sir Rhys ap Gruffydd, a local supporter of Edward II, so it may be that Shalford was deliberately targeted in view of his alleged misdeeds as Mortimer's lieutenant. A later commission suggests that he retained Edward III's confidence. *CPR 1330–1334*, pp. 61, 143, 322–3. For the context see Beverley Smith, "Edward II and the Allegiance of Wales," pp. 170–1.

95 Tout, "Captivity and Death," p. 189; *CPR 1330–1334*, p. 208. It may be noted that one of Hywel's sureties was John de Eccleshale from Staffordshire, a particular

friend of John Stratford's and mentioned in his will. Haines, *John Stratford*, index s.v. For comments on the Welsh "mainprises": Beverley Smith, "Edward II and the Allegiance of Wales," p. 170 n.

96   For this family see Gurney, *Record of the House of Gournay*, which has a slightly inaccurate genealogical table. Another such table faces p. 270 in Batten, "Stoke sub-Hamden." See also Saul, *Knights and Esquires: the Gloucestershire Gentry*, pp. 69–71.

97   PRO KB27/254/Rex m. 27; *CPR 1324–27*, p. 6: 23 July 1324. The Gurney castle of Culverhay, still a substantial earthwork, is on a spur of land just north of Englishcombe village. *County of Avon Historic Landscape Survey of Englishcombe*, pp. 8–9, provides a plan..

98   *Rot. Parl.* 2, p. 57. Gurney, like Maltravers, was a retainer of Thomas de Berkeley. See n. 96 above. My article "Sir Thomas Gurney of Englishcombe in the County of Somerset, Regicide?" is forthcoming. It could be that his responsibility for Edward's death is not susceptible of proof. Berkeley, who must have known the truth, lied his way out of the matter. See also Manco, *Englishcombe*, pp. 1–5.

99   Smyth, *Lives of the Berkeleys* 1, p. 292. Select roll no. 39 [40 copy], 1 Jan. 1326–30 Sept. 1327. This was the roll of the steward (William Aside?), and contains record of a payment to Gurney for travelling to Nottingham to notify the king and Queen Isabella of Edward's death. The sum is not now legible but Smyth (p. 293) gives it as 31s. 1d. He also makes the deduction that Gurney set out on 22 September. There is no date in the account. Dene (Historia Roffensis, fo. 51ʳ) states that Gurney delivered the message to the queen on 22 September at the Lincoln Parliament, which terminated the following day. Harding, "Isabella and Mortimer," p.145 and n., cites PRO DL 10/253 – a letter (in Edward's name) mentioning that the news reached him at Lincoln during the night of 23 September. According to Smyth (p. 297) Berkeley "by a second direction [from Mortimer] brought back by Gurney kept secret the king's death till All Saints [1 November] following." I find no confirmation of this. See also Jeayes, *Descriptive Catalogue*, pp. 274–5; Tout, "Captivity and Death," pp. 168–9.

100   Dugdale, *Baronage* 1, p. 357; Smyth, *Lives of the Berkeleys*, p. 297. Gurney was a wanted man only after Mortimer's arrest in October 1330. Releases from Thomas ap-Adam, lord of Beverstone, dated respectively 13 and 28 August 1329 were made to a Hugh de Gurney, the later one being cancelled (Berkeley MSS General Charters nos. 2683, 2729). For ap-Adam's connection with the family and for Hugh: Gurney, *Record of the House of Gournay*, pp. 686, 689, 691. Thomas de Gurney's grants of lands in Beachley, "Gorste" (Aust) and Tidenham to Thomas lord Berkeley is undated (Berkeley MSS no. 2597) but is assigned to "early Edward III." A slip catalogue of names is in the County Record Office at Gloucester.

101   *Foedera* 2 ii, p. 801; *CPR 1330–1334*, p. 144.

102   Hunter, "Measures for Apprehension," pp. 274–97, provides the basis for most of what follows. Compare Gurney, *Record of the House of Gournay*, especially App.

CXII-CXIII. The latter is dependent on Hunter but does not adopt his justifiable scepticism about the chroniclers.

103 *CPR 1330–1334*, p. 70; Galbraith, "Extracts," pp. 203–17 especially 216–7. Sir John de Belhouse, knight, and his father, Thomas, are mentioned earlier in *Rot. Parl.* 1, p. 323.

104 *Foedera* 2 ii, pp. 819–20; Hunter, "Measures for Apprehension," p. 279. The accounts of Giles of Spain are printed ibid., pp. 288–91.

105 Hunter, "Measures for Apprehension," pp. 283–6. Thweng's accounts are at pp. 291–4. For apprehending Gurney Cornwall was granted the bailiwick of the porter of Norwich Castle. *CPR 1330–1334*, p. 464 (13 August 1333).

106 *CFR 1327–37*, pp. 193–5 (order for confiscation of the lands of Mortimer, Ingham and Bereford); *Foedera* 2 ii, pp. 799–800. Fryde, *Tyranny and Fall*, p. 206, claimed that Gurney was "murdered in or off the coast of Gascony" (see Baker, *Chronicon*, pp. 34, 211–12). But there is clear evidence that every effort was made by the king's emissaries to keep him alive: *Acta Aragonensia* 3, pp. 747–8; Hunter, "Measures for Apprehension," p. 285. On the other hand, Galbraith was prepared to accept the statement in a version of the French *Brut*, "Extracts," p. 217, that Oliver ordered Gurney's execution. For Ingham's long and distinguished career: *GEC* 7, s.v.

107 Tout, "Captivity and Death," p. 178, argued the young king's complaisance, followed by McKisack, *Fourteenth Century*, p. 95. More recently Fryde, *Tyranny and Fall*, p. 206, states inexplicably that "Nobody was ever convicted of the king's murder."

108 Hunter, "Measures for Apprehension," p. 275; *Chroniques de London*, pp. 63–4 and n. Tout, "Captivity and Death," p. 98.

109 *Rot. Parl. Inediti*, pp. 285–6; "Where is Edward II?," p. 530.

110 For her life settlement: *Foedera* 2 ii, p. 835, 29 March 1331.

111 *Chronicles of Edward I & II* 2, introduction p. cviii.

112 See above n. 66.

113 Murray, "Confesion as a Historical Source," p. 283: "In the thirteenth century the highest authorities thought nothing of quizzing the confessor of a supposedly holy person, especially just after the latter's death, to make sure he or she really *was* holy, and could be prayed to or for accordingly."

114 Modernized. For the three parallel versions see *Polychronicon* 8, pp. 325–7.

115 "Edwardus Karnerivan [sic?] cui dominus nostris temporibus specialiter benedixit ut inter sanctos merito numeretur. Istud monasterium semper protexit regali potentia et donis multiplicibus decoravit." St Albans Abbey, *Liber de Benefactoribus*, BL Cotton MS Nero D. VII, fo. 6ᵛ, illustrated with a bearded figure holding a floriated sceptre in the right hand, as do Edward III and Edward, Prince of Wales (below in the MS); in his left hand the cup "magnam argenteam et auratam" which he donated to the refectory of the house. The text of the *Liber* is printed in an appendix to *Trokelowe, Chronica Sancti Albani* 3: this extract at p. 433. The Carmelites of Oxford, a learned Order, also benefited from Edward's

generosity: the gift of Beaumont manor and support for twenty-four brothers (moved from his manor of Sheen), each to receive five marks from the Exchequer. *Rot. Parl.* 2, p. 35; Knowles and Hadcock, *Med. Religious Houses*, p. 198 and n.

116 *Lanercost*, p. 426 (Notes). Baston, a collector of pontage at Hethbeth Bridge, near Nottingham, was pardoned about this time for his part in the death of two notorious felons.*CPR 1338–40*, pp. 21, 69.

117 See, for instance, *Fälschungen im Mittelalter*.

CHAPTER NINE

1 For much of what follows I have been guided by the excellently balanced work of G.W.S. Barrow, *Robert Bruce* (1988 ed.), as well as that by A.A.M. Duncan, editor *inter alia* of the *Acta* of Robert Bruce (hereafter *Acts of Robert I*). McNamee, *Wars of the Bruces*, covers the period 1306–30: the rise and fall of "Scottish Hegemony." An overall view of Scottish history is provided by Croft Dickinson (revised Duncan), *Scotland to 1603*. E.L.G. Stones, in *Anglo-Scottish Relations*, provides texts of documents to supplement the earlier work of Prynne, Rymer, Palgrave, Stevenson and Bain. The work of the last has been expanded, corrected and provided with modern PRO references in a supplementary volume (*CDS* 5). Stones and Simpson have exhaustively covered the events and texts for the period 1290–1296 in their two–volume study *Edward I and the Throne of Scotland* (hereafter *Throne of Scotland*). I have also made use of *Anglo-Scottish Relations, 1174–1328*, ed. Stones. Various instruments are to be found in *Rotuli Scotiae* (*Rot. Scot.*), the *Registrum Magni Sigilli Regum Scotorum* (*RMS*), the *Acts of the Parliaments of Scotland* 1 (1124–1423) (*APS*) and for the fealties of 1291–1296 *Instrumenta Publica* (see also the lengthy narrative account of the "Great Cause" in *Rishanger*). The most helpful Scottish chronicles are Barbour's *Bruce*, supplemented by the sketchy Fordun, *Chronica*, popularly known as the *Scotichronicon*, and by Walter Bower's amplification of this strongly biased account: "Non Scotus est, Christe, cui liber non placet iste" (2, p. 513). The apposite volumes (6–7, 1991, 1996) of the new edition under the general editorship of D.E.R. Watt with invaluable notes are cited in addition to Goodall's Bower, a parallel text of which is in Watt's edition. Apart from Rishanger the most informative English chroniclers are Walter of Guisborough (*Guisborough*) – a house founded by the Bruce family – which is sporadically detailed; Sir Thomas Gray's *Scalacronica* (ed. Stevenson in Norman French, Maxwell in English), which for the period is seemingly based on his father's predilections; and the so-called *Lanercost Chronicle*, basically a work of the Franciscans (Little, "Chronicles of the Mendicant Friars"). This last is particularly informative about Scottish and border events. The *Vita* has useful Scottish material for Edward II's reign. Scottish documents (Exchequer) PRO E39 are noted in *L&I* 49. Many of them were transferred (as were other documents earlier) in 1949 to the General Register House in Edinburgh (now Scottish Record Office, Register Series: SRO RH5).

2 Baker, *Chronicon,* p. 40.

3 Barrow, *Bruce*, pp. 1–2, provides a reconstruction of Alexander's doomed visit in foul weather to see his young second wife.

4 Stones, "Records of the Great Cause"; *Anglo-Scottish Relations*, no. 19. For a revised chronology of the Great Cause 5 May? 1291–26 December 1292: *Throne of Scotland* 1, pp. 109–10 and App. ix–x. See also for the period 1286–92, Young, *Bruce's Rivals the Comyns*, chapter 5.

5 It was a judgment in his court rather than the "arbitration" of the chroniclers: Stones, "English Chroniclers of Scotland," p. 324. See the discussion in Dickinson and Duncan, *Scotland to 1603*, pp. 145–6, and Barrow, *Bruce*, pp. 30–1; also Stones, *Anglo-Scottish Relations* no. 14; *Throne of Scotland* 1, pp. 7–8, and for texts, ibid. 2, pp. 3–6. In 1321 the Scots claimed that Edward had taken the initiative in 1291: Lineham, "Fourteenth Century History of Anglo-Scottish Relations." Genealogical tables of the thirteen claimants are in *Scotland to 1603*, p. 153 table 5; Barrow, *Bruce*, p. 382; *Throne of Scotland* 1, fig. 4.

6 This last is the form adopted by Barrow, *Bruce*, p. 32. The phrase is translated literally (the good people of Scotland) by Stones, *Anglo-Scottish Relations*, nos. 15, 16, who comments p. [53] n. 2. Some of those who encountered it, e.g. the rubricator of nos. 15 and 16, understood it to refer to the magnates; *Rishanger*, p. 242, claims that it was the *communitas* that responded to Edward I.

7 "Evasive" is used by Stones, "Records of the Great Cause," p. 107. For Barrow, *Bruce*, p. 32, this misses the point. It constituted, he thought, a "polite reminder" that in a feudal realm only the king could make decisions affecting its status. This, however, could be interpreted as a complementary rather than an opposing view.

8 Barrow, *Bruce*, pp. 32–3, discusses the question. The text of the Scottish reply is in Stones, *Anglo-Scottish Relations*, no. 16. See also *Throne of Scotland* 2, pp. 30–1

9 *Rot. Scot.* 1, pp. v–vi, has a facsimile and translation of a mandate for livery of Berwick to the steward of the household, Walter de Beauchamp. Edward's claim to overlordship, his intention to hear the case as suzerain and the lack of Scottish arguments in contradiction of Edward's claim, as delivered by Chancellor Burnell in a statement at Holywell Haugh (Norham), are in *Throne of Scotland* 2, pp. 30–7. Bruce the Competitor's acceptance of Edward's jurisdiction is ibid., pp. 40–3, 52–3 (Balliol). Edward reserved his right as a claimant, should he wish to proceed as such: ibid., p. 58. Balliol and eight other claimants accepted Edward's jurisdiction, ibid., pp. 66–8. On 6 June 1291 the Competitors agreed to the seisin of Scotland and its castles to the English king and 104 auditors were chosen: ibid., pp. 74–5, 77. Edward by letters patent of 6 June 1291 (Glasgow MS) agreed to maintain the status quo while the kingdom was in his hands and to make restoration to the king appointed: ibid., p. 88. Further letters patent, 12 June 1291, whereby Edward guaranteed his future actions: ibid., pp. 98–9. See also *CDS* 2, nos. 503–4; ibid. 5, nos. 91–5 pp. 145–6.

10 *Throne of Scotland* 2, pp. 92, 94, 102–5. Edward's declaration with respect to Scottish suits is at ibid., p. 119 from the Close Roll.

11 Dickinson and Duncan, *Scotland to 1603*, p. 146.

12 For the historical argument assembled by Edward I with the help of the monasteries and incorporated in the rolls produced by John de Caen and Andrew de Tong (or Tange) see *Throne of Scotland* 1, App. x and 2, App. A; *Documents*, ed Palgrve, nos. 23–40. The Tong or Tange rolls and processes together with instruments from the time of Edward II "super superioritate et directo dominio dicte terre Scotie" were to be transported by Tong for twelve days' negotiations between July and November 1316 (he was retained for 140 days in all) and was paid for a further 225 (less 16 concerned with his own affairs) between 25 November and the following 7 July. Tong could have been unwell or had possibly died when his son Robert appeared for the compotus at York 7 December 1319: SA MS 120, pp. 36, 53.

13 Stones, "Records of the Great Cause"; *Anglo-Scottish Relations*, no. 19; *Throne of Scotland* 2, pp. 240–9. Writs (19 November 1292) were issued for the seisin of Scotland and the castles to Balliol: ibid., p. 250; also *Rot. Scot.* 1, pp. 11a–12a. The written pleadings of the Competitors are given from *Rishanger* at ibid. App. B. The seal of Scotland as used since Alexander III's death was broken, but significantly its pieces were to be kept in the English treasury as evidence of English suzerainty.

14 Barrow, *Bruce*, p. 49.

15 *Throne of Scotland* 2, pp. 248–9, 254–9; *Guisborough*, p. 239; *Foedera* I ii, pp. 781–2.

16 *Throne of Scotland* 2, pp. 260–3; *Anglo-Scottish Relation*, no. 20; *CDS* 2, nos. 653–5.

17 E.g. Dickinson and Duncan, *Scotland to 1603*, p. 150; Barrow, *Bruce*, pp. 30, 184–5.

18 The text of this treaty (18 July 1290) is in *Documents*, ed. Stevenson, no. 108. Essentially it was a marriage treaty (Prince Edward of England and Margaret of Norway), but it specifically reserved the individual rights, laws and customs of Scotland, and declared that the northern kingdom was to remain free, without subjection, and separate from that of England.

19 *Throne of Scotland* 2, pp. 264–7; *Foedera* I ii, p. 783.

20 Ibid., pp. 268–9; *Foedera* loc. cit..

21 2 January 1293, Newcastle. *Throne of Scotland* 2, p. 272 n. 3.

22 Ibid., pp. 270–2; Dickinson and Duncan, *Scotland to 1603*, pp. 150–1.

23 But the statement in the Tong (Tange) roll that the parliament was held in what was later known as York House is questionable; the editors suggest a confusion with the assembly of June 1294, *Throne of Scotland* 2, p. 282 n.2. For a "Narrative of Edward I's disputes with John Balliol, 1293–1296": ibid. pp. 279–85; also *Rot. Scot.* 1, p. 176 et seq. The Macduff case (see next note) was only one of a number appealed to English courts.

24 *Throne of Scotland* 2, pp. 283–4; Stones, *Anglo-Scottish Relations*, no. 21; Bower, *Scotichronicon* 2, pp. 152–3, ed. Watt 6, pp. 40–3; *HBC*, p. 549 (bibliographical

note). There is uncertainty about the precise details. The adjournment in King's
Bench was until May 1294 (*HBC*, p. 549, *CPR 1292–1301*, p. 102), allegedly (see
text) he sent others to the parliament of November 1295. See *Throne of Scotland* 2,
p. 284 n. 3; Stones, no. 21, p. [67], nn. 1, 3.

25 *Foedera* I ii, p. 807; *Throne of Scotland* 2, p. 284 n. 2. Homage, Edward declared,
   had been rendered "solonc fourme de la pees."

26 *Foedera* I ii, p. 804 (summons to English host 29 June 1294); Barrow, *Bruce*, pp.
   62–3. For the Welsh revolt: Powicke, *Thirteenth Century*, pp. 440–2; Edwards,
   "Battle of Maes Madog"; Guisborough, pp. 250–2; chapter 1 above.

27 Barrow, *Bruce*, pp. 63–5; Nicholson, "Franco-Scottish and Franco-Norwegian
   Treaties of 1295." The text of the latter (22 October 1295) is in *Documents*, ed.
   Stevenson, 2 no. 343. At ibid., no. 344 is Balliol's agreement not to go to war with
   Norway while France was engaged with England or Germany. *Guisborough*, pp.
   264–9, gives the text of the Franco-Scottish treaty and the appointment of the
   Scottish proctors. See also *Foedera* I ii, pp. 822, 830–2; Bower, *Scotichronicon* 2,
   pp. 153–6, ed. Watt 6, pp. 44–50; *APS* I, pp. 451–3. Balliol's son Edward was to
   marry the daughter of Charles, brother of Philip IV.

28 *Guisborough*, p. 264 and Fordun, *Chronica* I, pp. 327–8; 2, pp. 321–2, give Scone.
   Barrow, *Bruce*, p. 338 n. 47, gives reasons for opting for Stirling.

29 *Lanercost*, pp. 161–2; *Guisborough*, p. 264; Fordun, *Chronica* I, pp. 327–8; Barrow, *Bruce*, pp. 63–4. But as will be seen from English affairs (e.g. in 1318 and
   1327) there is nothing peculiarly Scottish about the "symmetry" in the composition
   of this council.

30 See *APS* I, pp. 451–3 and n. 28 above; *Lanercost*, p. 166, and Barrow, *Bruce*, p.
   338 n. 51. The chronicler in conventional terms castigates the Scottish envoys, the
   bishops of St. Andrews and Dunkeld as "mercenarii ... non pastores."

31 *Scalacronica*, ed. Stevenson, p. 121, ed Maxwell, p. 14; *Lanercost*, p. 167, which
   has "Gedewrth" (Jedburgh) instead of Stirling; Dickinson and Duncan, *Scotland to
   1603*, pp. 151–2; *Anglo-Scottish Relations*, ed. Stones, no. 24.

32 *Anglo-Scottish Relations*, ed. Stones, no. 23; *Guisborough*, pp. 275–6. Bower,
   Scotichronicon 2, pp. 156–7 (ed. Watt 6, pp. 50–53): "Iste rex Johannes intrusus
   per dolum et potenciam regis Angliae, non stetit per quatuor annos rex sub maxima
   servitute et bondagio regis Anglie."

33 *Guisborough*, pp. 269–70; Barrow, *Bruce*, p. 69.

34 *Anglo Scottish Relations*, ed. Stones, no. 27.

35 *Guisborough*, pp. 270–4; Barrow, *Bruce*, pp. 69–71; *Scalacronica*, ed. Stevenson,
   pp. 121–2, ed. Maxwell, p. 14;.

36 *Scalacronica* (see previous note); *Guisborough*, pp. 274–5; Barrow, *Bruce*,
   p. 72.

37 *Guisborough*, pp. 276–81; *Lanercost*, pp. 175–9; *Scalacronica*, ed. Stevenson, pp.
   122–3, ed. Maxwell, p. 16. Barrow, *Bruce*, p. 70 map. 3, using *Documents*, ed.
   Stevenson, 2 no. 352, is able to provide the royal itinerary for the 1296 campaign
   with dates. A general account of "The Scottish Wars, 1296–1307" is chapter 12 in

Prestwich, *Edward I.* For the 1296 campaign ibid., pp. 469–73, and for the numbers involved, p. 470 n. 4.

38 For this see Prestwich, "English Campaign in Scotland in 1296," citing the Hagnaby chronicle (BL Cotton MS Vespasian B. XI, fo. 41ʳ); Stones and Blount, "The Surrender of King John of Scotland," printing two "forms of peace" from the Hailes Abbey chronicle (BL Cotton MS Cleopatra D. III, fo. 51ᵛ).

39 *CDS* 2, no. 754; *Foedera* I ii, p. 841. *Documents*, ed. Stevenson, 2 no. 372; *Anglo-Scottish Relations*, ed. Stones, no. 24; *Guisborough*, pp. 280–1; Bower, *Scotichronicon* 2, pp. 167–8, ed. Watt 6, pp. 76–9; Simpson, "Toom Tabard."

40 *Scalacronica*, ed. Stevenson, p. 123, ed. Maxwell, p. 17; Barrow, *Bruce*, p. 74.

41 *CDS* 2, no. 823; *Instrumenta Publica*, nos. 60–174; *Documents*, ed. Stevenson, 2 nos. 43–106; *Guisborough*, pp. 281–4; *Foedera* I ii, p. 844; Barrow, *Bruce*, pp. 76–8; A. McAndrew, "The Sigillography of the Ragman Rolls," *PSA Scot.* 129 (1999), pp. 663–752.

42 *Documents*, ed. Stevenson, 2 nos. 447–9, 452–5; *Scalacronica*, ed. Stevenson, pp. 123–4, ed. Maxwell, p. 18, which tells how the chronicler's father was left stripped as a corpse overnight at Lanark; *Guisborough*, pp. 294–5; Barrow, *Bruce*, pp. 83, 342 n. 81, gives other references, but *CDS* 2, no. 418, must be an error.

43 Barrow, *Bruce*, p. 82 map. 4; *Lanercost*, pp. 303–6.

44 Barrow, *Bruce*, pp. 87–9; Fisher, *Wallace*, pp. 49–56; Watson, *Under the Hammer*, p. 49. The fullest account of the battle is in *Guisborough*, pp. 298–303; *Lanercost*, p. 190; also, briefly, *Scalacronica*, ed. Stevenson p. 124, ed. Maxwell, p. 19.

45 *Guisborough*, pp. 325–8; *Lanercost*, pp. 191–2; *Scalacronica*, ed. Stevenson, p. 125, ed. Maxwell, p. 21; Fisher, *Wallace*, chapter 6; Barrow, *Bruce*, pp. 96–103 (with campaign map); Watson, *Under the Hammer*, pp. 62–7.

46 For the suggested connection between Wallace's defeat and his resignation as Guardian see Fisher, *Wallace*, chapter 7, also Bower, *Scotichronicon* 2, p. 174, ed. Watt 6, pp. 92–5: *De conspiracione contra custodem concepta per magnates.*

47 E.g. facsimile charter of 29 March 1298 in *APS* I, between pp. 452 and 453.

48 The bull is printed from the original, PRO SC7/6/10, *Anglo-Scottish Relations*, ed. Stones, no. 28, who notes other variations.

49 Ibid., nos. 12 p.[40]; 6, pp. [17]-[18].

50 Ibid., no. 28 p.[87].

51 For a summary biography of Sarden: *Biog. Oxon.* s.v. He was summoned to parliament 1299–1301.

52 *Anglo-Scottish Relations*, ed. Stones, no. 29 from PRO C47/31/15–16.

53 The king's response to the pope's bull is printed ibid., no. 30 (where other versions are noted). See also, Powicke, *Thirteenth Century*, pp. 693, 702.

54 *Anglo Scottish Relations*, ed. Stones, no. 31 from BL Cotton MS Vespasian F. VII. Also printed *Lanercost*, App. pp. 517–21. For a critical appraisal of the Scottish appeal to the papacy see Goldstein, "The Scottish Mission to Boniface VIII in 1301."

55 His son, Edward, was to be for some years in England at Edward II's expense. In 1316 Thomas de Brotherton, the king's half-brother, entertained Edward in his

household, accounting for 140 days at ten shillings a day between 8 July and 24 November 1316. SA MS 120, p. 30, also ibid., p. 45.

56 *Anglo-Scottish Relations*, ed. Stones, no. 33 (from Close Roll PRO C54/122/m. 13d), where the editor (confusingly?) translates "terre d'Escoce" as "realm of Scotland"; *CDS* 2, nos. 1691–2, ibid. 5, no. 259 p. 168 (1 October 1309: advising of the French king's transfer of the former King John to Bailleul).

57 *Anglo-Scottish Relations*, ed. Stones, p.[120] n.1. Barrow, *Bruce*, p. 134, is also favourably impressed by Edward's attempt to construct a constitution by agreement. Elsewhere he describes the period 1304-06 as one in which Edward returned to his conciliatory policy of 1296: "The Aftermath of War," pp. 119–20.

58 Bower, *Scotichronicon* 2, pp. 229–30, ed. Watt 6, pp. 312–17; *CDS* 2, nos. 1685, 1730; *Documents*, ed. Palgrave, p. 295. *Ann. Lond.*, pp. 139–42, details the "trial" of Wallace at Westminster and subsequent barbarous death. His head was placed on London Bridge and his quarters distributed to Newcastle, Berwick, Stirling and Perth, though a different distribution (Aberdeen instead of Stirling) is suggested by *Lanercost,* p. 203. For a modern account: Fisher, *Wallace*, chapter 10.

59 See above, chapter 1 n. 90, for references to Comyn's murder. Bruce's biographer generously considers this to be "out of character" and possibly unpremeditated. Barrow, *Bruce*, pp. 147–8. For the Comyns and their position in Scottish history see Young, *Bruce's Rivals the Comyns*, especially chapter 8.

60 *Lanercost*, pp. 206–7; *CDS* 2, nos. 1895–6 (royal letters of February 1307), 1923 (expeditions mounted against Bruce), 1926, 1979. Moorman, "Edward I at Lanercost Priory," describes the ruinous nature of the court's long stay and lists some of the medication prescribed for the ailing king.

61 Barbour, *Bruce* 7, ll. 400–87, pp. 126–9. There is another anecdote of this kind, but concerning ferrymen, in *Scalacronica*, ed. Stevenson, pp. 132–3, ed. Maxwell, p. 35.

62 Barbour, *Bruce* 8, ll. 1–408, pp. 133–44, 413–4 nn.; *Guisborough*, p. 378.

63 *Guisborough*, p. 378; *CDS* 2, no. 1935.

64 The tentative suggestion of Barrow, *Bruce*, p. 172.

65 *CDS* 2, no. 1926, ibid. 5, p. 77 from PRO C47/22/5(71). Barrow, *Bruce*, pp. 172–3, quotes this in a modified form.

66 *Ann. Paul.*, p. 265

67 Barrow, *Bruce*, p. 165.

68 On the matter of Bruce's whereabouts in the winter of 1306–7 see Barrow, *Bruce*, pp. 166–71; Barnes and Barrow, "The Movements of Robert Bruce." There is an excellent description of the physical aspect of medieval Scotland in Barrow, *Kingship and Unity*, chapter 1. For contemporary comment: *Chronicles of the Picts and Scots*, pp. 214–5, from BL Cotton MS Nero D.II.

69 *Itinerary EII*, p. 22; *CPR 1307–1313*, p. 44.

70 Barrow, *Bruce*, pp. 173–8.

71 *Lanercost*, p. 212. Compare Barbour, *Bruce* 9, ll. 472–631 pp. 161–5; Fordun, *Chronica* 1, p. 345; 2, p. 337.

72 *Guisborough*, p. 384.

73 *CPR 1307–1313*, p. 81; *Foedera* 2 i, pp. 51–2; Maddicott, *Lancaster*, pp. 106–7. See chapter 10 for Wogan's activities.

74 *CPR 1307–1313*, p. 83; *Foedera* 2 i, p. 51; Hamilton, *Gaveston*, pp. 55–7, 147 (where other references are given); Richardson and Sayles, *Administration of Ireland*, pp. 11–12 and list of "chief governors," pp. 82–5 (PRO E101/235/11 being cited for Gaveston's appointment). See below, chapter 10, for his performance in office.

75 *Lanercost*, p. 213.

76 Ibid., pp. 213–4; *Foedera* 2 i, pp. 63–4.

77 *Lanercost*, p. 212; Barbour, *Bruce* 9, ll. 632–71, pp. 165–6 (compare Fordun, *Chronica* 1, p. 345; 2, p. 337); *APS* 1, p. 459; *Foedera* 2 i, p. 79; *Ann. Lond.*, p. 266 (where Philip does not give Bruce his regal title but addresses him as "dear friend"); Barrow, *Bruce*, pp. 182–3, 187.

78 *Lanercost*, p. 213. Parliament had last met at Northampton in October 1307.

79 *Foedera* 2 i, p. 79.

80 Ibid., pp. 82–7.

81 *CPR 1307–1313*, p. 203. Compare *Simonie*, A 295–300.

82 *Vita*, p. 8. But *Itinerary EII*, p. 54, places the court and household at nearby St. Albans.

83 *Vita*, p. 10: "de consilio suo ... expugnare disposuit." The Ordainers were to require that consultation precede war.

84 *Foedera* 2 i, p. 106. Robert de Clifford had been appointed warden 15 December 1309: ibid., p. 100.

85 Ibid., pp. 106, 108.

86 Ibid., p. 109. The earl of Ulster was appointed 18 June 1310.

87 *CDS* 5, nos. 532–3, 536–9, 541, 557–61, 563–5, pp. 226–31; *Foedera* 2 i, pp. 109, 115, 120. There were no fewer than sixteen "refusals."

88 *CDS* 5, nos. 534–5, p. 226.

89 *CDS* 5, no. 543, pp. 227–8.

90 *Vita*, p. 11. Edward's letter in *Foedera* 2 i, p. 110, is dated 5 July 1310; *CDS* 5, no. 526, p. 224, dates it 7 July [1309]. See also *Foedera* 2 i, pp. 111–12; *Treaty Rolls* 1, no. 496; Barrow, *Bruce*, p. 183. Philip IV's letter in response to Edward's gave Bruce the title "King of Scots." A note deprecating this is on the dorse.

91 *Foedera* 2 i, pp. 114–17; *Vita*, pp. 10–12; *Lanercost*, p. 214. The barons and the fleet were to be at Berwick by the Nativity of the BVM (8 September). Simon de Montacute was appointed to command the fleet, Lincoln's appointment as lieutenant of the realm is dated 1 September 1310. Five days later, from Newcastle, Humphrey de Bohun, the constable, was summoned to perform his service as such in Scotland. For Pembroke's attitude: Phillips, *Pembroke*, p. 31.

92 *Itinerary EII*, pp. 62–4; *CDS* 3, no. 122.

93 *CDS* 3, no. 166, from PRO C47/22/6(5); ibid. 5, no. 166 p. 81: 6 October 1310; *Vita*, pp. 12–14; *Itinerary EII*, pp. 65–75; *Foedera* 2 i, p. 120.

94 *HBC*, p. 470; *Ann. Paul.*, p. 269; *CDS* 3, no. 204; ibid. 5, p. 82 (chancellor to Jean de Bretagne, earl of Richmond); *Lanercost*, p. 215: "Gavestoun, qui ibi praesens cum rege advenerat, sed comes nec eum osculari voluit nec etiam salutare, de quo ipse non modicum est gravatus." Maddicott, *Lancaster*, p. 115, discusses the fealty incident, dismissing the criticism of the chronicle evidence by Somerville, *Duchy of Lancaster*, p.23. At ibid., p. 116, Maddicott gives a possible explanation of the friction between Lancaster and Gloucester.

95 *CDS* 3, p. 197, from PRO C47/22/6(7); ibid. 5, p. 82: Chancellor Reynolds to Jean de Bretagne.

96 *CDS* 3, nos. 201–2, 204–5; ibid. 5, p. 82. For Abernethy's appointment, 15 June 1310, see *Foedera* 2 i, p. 108.

97 *Lanercost*, p. 214.

98 *CDS* 3, no. 201, from PRO C47/22/10(8); ibid. 5, p. 82: William Melton to Chancellor Reynolds.

99 *CDS* 3, no. 202, from PRO C47/22/6(9); ibid. 5, p. 82: John de Sandale to Chancellor Reynolds [?].

100 *Foedera* 2 i, pp. 132, 139; *Itinerary EII*, pp. 75–6.

101 *Lanercost*, pp. 216–17. *CDS* 3 nos. 203–4, from PRO C47/22/6(9); *CDS* 5, p. 82: Chancellor Reynolds to Jean de Bretagne; ibid. 3, no. 203; ibid. 5, p. 82; *CChW* I, p. 352.

102 *Lanercost*, pp. 216–17.

103 See the argument in Rogers, "Edward III and the Dialectics of Strategy," pp. 85–90.

104 Ibid., p. 217 and, for a list of the various truces negotiated throughout the north of England between 1311 and 1328, see Scammell, "Robert I and the North of England," p. 386 n. 1, 393 n. 2 (Durham).

105 *Lanercost*, p. 217.

106 Neville, "Political Allegiance of the Earls of Strathearn," especially pp. 138–9, 145–9.

107 Supposedly, as will be seen later, in 1326 he planned to seek refuge in Scotland.

108 *Vita*, p. 22.

109 *Lanercost*, pp. 219–20; *Anglo-Scottish Relations*, ed. Stones, no. 37; Graystanes (SS), p. 94, who writes of the "Schavaldos insurgentes" whom Bishop Kellaw either hanged or forced to flee, and the Scottish invasion while Kellaw was at parliament in London. This author states that the truce was made with the Scots for a thousand marks. Scammell, "Robert I and the North of England," p. 393 n. 2, details all discoverable Durham truces between 1311 and 1327 and calculates (ibid., pp. 395–401) the probable tribute paid by the area. Reference to the Western Marches' plight in McNamee, "Buying off Robert Bruce," p. 78, would appear more appropriate to 1313 than 1312. Edward was abroad only in the former year.

110 *Vita*, pp. 30–1, 36; *Foedera* 2 i, p. 187. The cardinal baptised the baby, the others were among those named as godfathers.

111 *Lanercost*, pp. 220–1.

112 Ibid., p. 221.

113 Barrow, *Bruce*, p. 190 and, for maps, nos. 9, 12, pp. 167, 234–5.

114 *Lanercost*, p. 221.

115 Barrow, *Bruce*, pp. 191, 194–5.

116 *Lanercost*, p. 222.

117 *Foedera* 2 i, pp. 215–6, 217–22; *Itinerary EII*, pp. 98–102; *Vita*, pp. 38–9.

118 *Lanercost*, p. 223; Barbour, *Bruce* 10, ll. 352–505, pp. 178–82; *Scalacronica*, ed. Stevenson, p. 140, ed. Maxwell, pp. 51–2. *CDS* 3, pp. 406–8, gives the muster roll of the garrison 1311–12. The constable, William de Fillinge (*CDS*) or Guillemin de Fenes, a Gascon, was a courageous defender of the "grete toure," the last to fall. Badly wounded, he surrendered on terms and died shortly afterwards. There may be some confusion in *Vita*, p. 48, at this point, which castigates the perfidy either at Roxburgh or Edinburgh of a "certain Gascon," said to be Gaveston's cousin, Peres Lebaud, who was sheriff of Edinburgh when the castle was taken.

119 *Lanercost*, p. 223; Barbour, *Bruce* 10, ll. 506–787, pp. 182–90.

120 *Lanercost*, p. 223; Barbour, *Bruce* 10–11, ll. 804–25, 1–20. pp. 190–1; *Vita*, pp. 48–9.

121 Barbour, *Bruce* 11, ll. 38–41, p. 192.

122 *Vita*, p. 49. Unlike Barbour's this account mentions only the royal grief, not the advantageous nature of the truce.

123 Ibid., pp. 49–50; *Melsa* 2, pp. 330–1.

124 *Foedera* 2 i, pp. 245–6.

125 Ibid., pp. 244–9; *CDS* 5, nos. 1705–1737, pp. 361–5. Barrow, *Bruce*, pp. 203–9, outlines the preparations in some detail and analyses the likely strength of the opposing armies. In chapter 12 he provides the best recent overall account of the battle with plans of the field.

126 *Trokelowe*, p. 83 (see chapter 1 above); *Historia Anglicana* 1, pp. 138–9.

127 *Lanercost*, p. 224; Summerson, *Carlisle* 1, pp. 214–5. McNamee, "Buying Off Robert Bruce," pp. 76–89, has further details and prints a PRO document detailing the sums raised. For the raiding of northern England 1311–22 and its defence during that period: McNamee, *Wars of the Bruces*, chapters 3–4 (with sketch-maps).

128 *Itinerary EII*, pp. 111–13. The *Vita*, p. 50, suggests that the king awaited the army's arrival at Berwick but that the earls of Lancaster, Warenne and Warwick failed to come.

129 *Flores* 3, p. 338; *Vita*, p. 50; *Melsa* 2, p. 330.

130 *Lanercost*, pp. 224–5.

131 *Vita*, pp. 50–1; *Ann. Lond.*, p. 231; *Scalacronica*, ed. Stevenson, p. 141, ed. Maxwell, p. 53; Barrow, *Bruce*, p. 218, who gives an account of the combat from Barbour, *Bruce* 12, ll. 27–54, pp. 211–12. Barbour calls Sir Henry "cosyn" to the earl. Gray's account of the initial encounter is somewhat different.

132 *Lanercost*, p. 225.

133 Barrow, *Bruce,* map. 10 p. 205, distinguishes King's Park and New Park. This is the latter (see next note), which is further away (south) from Stirling. For Seton see *Scotichronicon* ed. Watt 7, p. 171 Notes (17).

134 *Scalacronica*, ed. Stevenson, pp. 141–2, ed. Maxwell, pp. 53–6. Compare Barbour, *Bruce* 11, ll. 498–626, pp. 205–9. Barbour suggests that a much inferior force under Moray assaulted Clifford's troops as they skirted New Park, whereupon Douglas joined in the fray, Ibid., ll. 627–55, pp. 209–10.

135 *Lanercost*, pp. 225–6.

136 *Vita*, pp. 52–3; Baker, *Chronicon*, p. 8: "Scoti redimendum libenter reservassent, si per togam proprie armature, quam tunc non induebat, ipsum cognovissent."

137 *Lanercost*, pp. 227–8. This chronicler suggests that many were killed while pursuing the Scots, whilst the *Vita*, p. 55, states that the greater part of the Scottish army was preoccupied with plunder, thus allowing the English to seek safety in flight.

138 See chapter 2 above. *Vita*, p. 54: "Porro dum vexillum regis abire conspicitur, totus exercitus cito dispergitur."

139 *Vita*, pp. 52–4; Baker, *Chronicon*, pp. 7–9; *Flores* 3, p. 151; *Lanercost*, pp. 226–8. A list of the English knights killed has been inserted in *Ann. Lond.*, p. 231. It is difficult to square these and other conflicting accounts, which are imprecise or silent about Pembroke's escape. His biographer argues that the most likely outcome was that he accompanied the king who, according to the *Vita*, fled to Dunbar and hence by ship to Berwick.

140 *Flores* 3, p. 158; *Vita*, p. 53. Barrow, *Bruce*, p. 368 n. 85, mentions that the statement in the *Flores* has been described by Denholm-Young as "surely rubbish," citing *Vita*, p. 27 [*recte* p. xxvii n. 1]. The latter points out that Hereford had been reinstated as constable subsequent to his refusal to serve in 1310. The quarrel was real enough and TCC MS R.5 41, so far as I know not quoted in the matter, does assume at fo. 113ᵛ (114), as does the *Vita*, that the basis of Hereford's claim was his office of constable: "Porro in crastino comes Herefordie cuius interest primam habere aciem racione constabularie Anglie Scotos invasit et eorum exercitum viriliter penetravit. Quo sic reverso comes Glovernie aliquid arduum et quasi probitate dignum facere satagens precipitanter in Scotos minus caute insiliens, lanceis eorum oppositis et hinc inde cancellatis in fronte sui exercitus qui vulgariter dicitur *scheltroun* infigitur aculeis et sic confossus de cella sua violenter eripitur."

141 *Vita*, p. 51, with respect to the first day's battle. Gloucester was unhorsed later in the day. The *Scalacronica*, ed. Stevenson, p. 141, ed. Maxwell, p. 53, says that Gloucester commanded the van on the first day.

142 *Vita*, p. 52.

143 Barrow, *Bruce*, p. 226.

144 *Scalacronica*, ed. Stevenson, p. 142, ed. Maxwell, p. 55. The *Vita*, p. 56, also recalls Courtrai.

145 For Barbour's account of Bannockburn see *Bruce* 11–13, ll. 434ff., pp. 204–47. The sunken pits are described ibid., ll. 348–73, pp. 201–2, and compare *Melsa* 2, p. 331.

146 Edward as prince would have learned something of the terrain in 1303. See chapter 1 above. The constable of Stirling is known to have discussed the nature of the area with the English commanders prior to battle.

147 Baker, *Chronicon*, pp. 8–9.

148 The defeat was the appropriate punishment for evil, luxury and pride remarked the London annalist. *Ann. Lond.*, p. 231: "Et istud totum factum est propter peccata enormia Anglorum, videlicet propter superbiam permaximam, luxuriam, gulam, avaritiam et cetera vitia." For the Meaux chronicler (*Melsa* 2, pp. 331–2) disaster was attributable not only to pride but also to the fact that the barons had come contrary to the Ordinances and were therefore excommunicate. The sole Ordainer who escaped, he suggests, was Pembroke and he "nudus sine armis."

149 *Trokelowe*, p. 87.

150 *Lanercost*, p. 228; *Acts of Robert I*, no. 41: Ordinance for perpetual disinheritance, Cambuskenneth 6 November 1314.

151 *Itinerary EII*, pp. 114–18; *Vita*, pp. 57–8. Maddicott, *Lancaster*, p. 166, citing Lambeth MS. 1213, fos. 32^v–33^r, for an exchange of letters between Edward and Bruce; *Rot. Scot.* 1, pp. 132–4. In any case, the continued successful raiding by the Scots at this time argues a lack of sincerity on Bruce's part, and perhaps of desperation on Edward's.

152 *Lanercost*, p. 228, which has "John," who was his father, a Competitor in 1291. See *Scotichronicon* ed. Watt 7, p. 161 Notes (2).

153 Lanercost, pp. 228–9.

154 Ibid., pp. 229–30.

155 Ibid., pp. 230–2. For a modern account with sketch map: Summerson, *Carlisle* 1, pp. 216–19.

156 *Scalacronica*, ed. Stevenson, p. 149, ed. Maxwell, p. 68. Harclay's capture is made fun of by Barbour, *Bruce* 16, ll. 509–22, p. 292: he makes nothing of his hero's defeat at Carlisle. Summerson, *Carlisle* 1, p. 219.

157 Maddicott, *Lancaster*, pp. 169–74. For the gathering of Pembroke's force he cites *Vita*, p. 60; PRO E101/15/6, /376/7 fo. 60; *Parl. Writs* 2, i, pp. 453–4. See also Powicke, *Military Obligations*, p. 142.

158 *Lanercost,* p. 232.

159 Ibid., pp. 232–3; *Melsa* 2, p. 333. A quarter of wheat (frumentum) was sold for forty shillings (*Lanercost*). The account roll of Coombe (Hants.) for 1306-07 gives four shillings as the price per quarter, for 1307-08 it is six shillings and eight pence. *English Lands of Bec*, pp. 146, 159. In 1322 the price in Kent rose to twenty-four shillings: Historia Roffensis, fo. 39^v. Local variations were doubtless considerable. For further details of prices see chapter 5 above.

160 SA MS 120, p. 25. John de Sapy was sent to the Mortimers on 10 August and to Pembroke in September. In November he joined Edmund Bacon, another

household knight, on a mission to the earls of Hereford and Pembroke, then at Newcastle. Phillips, *Pembroke*, p. 328, shows that Pembroke was at Durham on 6 November.

161 SA MS 120, p. 29. The envoys' account was for the period 17 November–6 December 1316.

162 Barbour, *Bruce* 15, ll. 315–400, pp. 270–3, 457 (n.); *Scalacronica*, ed. Stevenson, p. 143, ed. Maxwell, p. 58. Compare *Gascon Rolls*, no. 1749.

163 Barbour, *Bruce* 16, ll. 331–488, pp. 287–91, 461 (n.). Sir Thomas, from Burton Constable, is made an earl by Barbour, who confuses him with his principal, the earl of Arundel.

164 Barbour, *Bruce* 15, ll. 400–500, pp. 273–7, 458 (n.); *Scalacronica*, ed. Stevenson, p. 143, ed. Maxwell, p. 58 and n.; *CDS* 3, p. xxv and no. 527. Compare *Bridlington*, p. 56.

165 Barbour, *Bruce* 16, ll. 535–658, pp. 292–6; Barrow, *Bruce*, p. 238.

166 *Lanercost*, p. 234; *Ann. Paul.*, pp. 281, 283; *Vita*, pp. 78–9; Haines, *Church and Politics*, p. 160. For Eure's association with Lancaster: Maddicott, *Lancaster*, index s.v.

167 Maddicott, *Lancaster*, p. 203 n. 2 (indenture of 29 December 1317, i.e. after Middleton's attack, hence surely indicating approval, from Bodl. Lib. MS Dugdale 18, fo. 39ᵛ). Eure's indenture (n. 171 below) makes him a prime opponent of Louis de Beaumont's provision.

168 Ibid., pp. 202–4.

169 He does seem to have been a "magister," but not much is known about him. See *Le Neve* 12, index s.v. "Kynardesley," for his canonries.

170 *Graystanes* (SS), pp. 97–9, giving the fullest chronicle account: *Le Neve* 6, p. 107; Smith, *Episcopal Appointments*, pp. 23–5; Maddicott, *Lancaster*, p. 204.

171 Middleton, *Sir Gilbert*, pp. 24–7 (the indenture survives as Durham misc. ch. no. 4238). Eure received pardon as a follower of Lancaster 1 November 1318, but his lands were to be forfeited as an adherent of Sir Gilbert Middleton. *CPR 1317–21*, pp. 227, 231; ibid., *1358–61*, p. 261. For many details about him see *Sir Gilbert*, index s.v., also Prestwich, "Gilbert de Middleton."

172 *Trokelowe*, p. 100. See also the narrative in *Historia Anglicana* 1, pp. 150–3; *Graystanes* (SS), pp. 100–1.

173 Middleton, *Sir Gilbert*, identifies the place as Rushyford [Rushyworth], p. 28 and map opposite. *Melsa* 2, p. 333, describes Sir Gilbert Middleton as "confoederatus cum Scottis." See also chapter 5 above, especially nn. 90–2.

174 Middleton, *Sir Gilbert*, pp. 13, 57–8; Prestwich, "Gilbert de Middleton," p. 187.

175 See Phillips, *Pembroke*, p. 127, who argues that although some of his servants and former servants were involved that does not of itself implicate him.

176 Maddicott, *Lancaster*, pp. 204–5. He cites *Melsa* 2, p. 333; Castleford chronicle, fo. 220ʳ [ed. Eckhardt 2, pp. 1059–60 ll. 39195–227], as evidence for Middleton's involvement with Bruce – the cardinals thought so. Prestwich, "Gilbert de Middleton," p. 184, argues that the evidence to support Scottish collusion 'lacks

solidity'. He dubs the reported presence of Moray and Douglas at Rushyworth a "late story." See above chapter 5 nn. 91–3.

177 *Bridlington*, p. 52.

178 Middleton, *Sir Gilbert*, chaps. 5–6, 11. For his death ibid., pp. 57–61; *Melsa* 2, pp. 333–4. Phillips, *Pembroke*, pp. 125–8 discusses the affair. On 7 September Middleton had a secret meeting with Lancaster in Durham cathedral priory, the monks averting their gaze, but the earl could do nothing for him and Lancaster subsequently adopted a law-abiding aspect by conducting the cardinals to safety. See *Graystanes* (SS), pp. 100–1; Maddicott, *Lancaster*, p. 206.

179 Duncan, *Declaration of Arbroath*, pp. 23–5; Middleton, *Sir Gilbert,* p. 30. The Br Adam incident is from York Reg. Melton, fo. 500ᵛ (see printed edition 3, nos. 21, 141: fo. 522ᵛ; also 3, nos. 3–5, fo. 459ᵛ, for the record of the publication of the bull, 27 November 1317); Hill, "An English Archbishop and the Scottish War," pp. 65–6; "John XXII's Excommunication of Robert Bruce," pp. 136–7.

180 *Ann. Paul.*, pp. 281, 283–4; *Vita*, pp. 89–90, where the author relates an apt miracle: when Bruce's chaplain was forced to celebrate mass the host was plucked from his hand. PRO SC7/56(1 no.1): faculty for the cardinals to make a two-years truce 1 May 1317, which follows *Rex excelsus*, 17 March 1317, empowering the same cardinals to negotiate peace between Edward II and Bruce: *York Register Melton* 3, no. 21; SC7/56(1 no. 4): transcript of faculty *Crescit facile* for the above to excommunicate Bruce 29 May [1318], published at Nottingham in August; *CPL 1305–42*, p. 432; *Concilia* 2, pp. 471–4, 480–2; *Foedera* 2 i, pp. 308, 317–8, 362–3; *Exeter Register Stapledon*, pp. 351–4, 361–2. See Hill, "John XXII's Excommunication of Bruce," p. 137 (from York Register Melton, fos. 502ʳ–3ᵛ); *York Reg. Melton* 3, index s.v. "Bruce."

181 *Acts of Robert I*, intro. p. 148; *Foedera* 2 i, pp. 362–3, 370, 384, 388, 390; *Whethamstede* 2, p. 352.

182 Lawlor, "Absolution of Robert Bruce," pp. 325–6, who on the basis of the document he cites (TCC MS. E.2 28, p. 396) considered the matter "canonically resolved" in 1310; *Acts of Robert I*, no. 567 pp. 148, 698n., where 1311 is suggested as the date; *Foedera* 2 i, pp. 407–8, 412–13. The fourth bull brought from Avignon by Orleton in February 1320 was for the citation of Scottish prelates, the fifth for the excommunication of invaders of the English realm, while the sixth was for Bruce's excommunication. See Haines, *Church and Politics*, pp. 22–3; Hill, "John XXII's Excommunication of Bruce," p. 137. The entry (from PRO E159/93/m. 77) is wrongly dated 1321 in *CDS* 3, no. 725 and ibid. 5, p. 90. For a number of documents concerned with the denunciation before the pope of the bishops of Glasgow (Wishart) and St Andrews (Lamberton) see *Documents*, ed. Palgrave, nos. 145–6, 148–50, 152.

183 *CDS* 3, nos. 307, 391, 420–1, 481, 521, 562, 618, 636–7, 1396; ibid. 5, nos. 606[?], 682, 815, 818. For details see Barrow, *Bruce*, pp. 28–9, 49, 191–3, 255–9, 317, 321. *Lanercost*, p. 210, records the grant of the Isle of Man to

Gaveston s.a. 1307. This appears to be an error. It was granted to Henry de Beaumont in 1310 and 1311: *CPR 1307–13*, pp. 300, 461; *HBC*, pp. 64–5.

184   SA MS 121, p. 16. M. Robert Baldock, archdeacon of Middlesex (an earlier
mention than any in *Le Neve*), with the earl of Angus, William de Ros, Roger
Northburgh and John de Benstead, were engaged in such a mission between 21
March and 24 April 1318.

185   *Lanercost*, pp. 234–6, 238; *Melsa* 2, p. 335; *APS* 1, pp. 465–6; Barrow, *Bruce*, p.
294.

186   *CDS* 3, no. 663; *CChW* 1, p. 501; *Itinerary EII*, p. 187. See chapter 5 above.

187   Barbour, *Bruce* 17, ll. 379–81, p. 307.

188   Ibid., ll. 589–854, esp. 589–609, pp. 313–19.

189   *CDS* 3, nos. 663–5. The *Anonimalle Chronicle*, pp. 94–7, has additional details.

190   *CDS* 3, no. 668; ibid. 5, p. 89, giving the reference PRO C47/22/10(34). (compare E101/15/27) and correcting the date from October to August-September.
Some 8,080 men assembled: 120 crossbowmen, 1,520 archers, 3,000 English and
2,040 Welsh foot, and 1,040 hobelars or light horsemen. Some soldiers were paid
from 1 August and disbanded 24 September. This did not include Lancaster's
contingent.

191   *Vita*, pp. 95–6; *Trokelowe*, p. 103; *Flores* 3, pp. 188–9; Haskins, "Chronicle," p.
77.

192   *Lanercost*, p. 239.

193   Barbour, *Bruce* 17, ll. 539–44, p. 311.

194   *Trokelowe*, pp. 103–4; *Lanercost*, p. 239; *Anonimalle Chronicle*, pp. 94–9; *Vita*,
pp. 96–7, which claims the Scots blinded the English with the smoke from burning hay; *Bridlington*, pp. 58–9; *Melsa* 2, pp. 336–7, has a lengthy account of the
loss and subsequent recovery of the archiepiscopal cross. See also, *Brut*, pp.
211–12. For Melton see Hill, "An English Archbishop and the Scottish War."

195   *Lanercost*, pp. 239–40 (the statement has an element of contradiction);
Trokelowe, p. 104. Maddicott, *Lancaster*, p. 248, gives the date the news reached
Berwick from *Cartae de Glamorgan* 3, p. 1064.

196   Barbour, *Bruce* 17, ll. 843–85, p. 315; *Vita*, pp. 97–9; Phillips, *Pembroke*, p. 185,
citing E101/378/3 m. 3 for the date of departure; Maddicott, *Lancaster*, pp.
246–51 esp. p. 249 (see *Cartae de Glamorgan* 3, pp. 1063–5, for Lancaster's
forcing Edward to withdraw). Most of the soldiers were paid off on 24 September. See n. 190 above.

197   *Historia Anglicana* 1, pp. 155–6; *CDS* 5, no. 654, p. 248; *Lanercost*, p. 422
(Notes), a transcript of Despenser's letter to his sheriff in Glamorgan. It is, of
course, possible that Edward was foolish enough to promise to bestow honours
on his "favourites." We have no means of checking the report, although in general terms it is repeated by the far from impartial *Flores* (3, p. 188).

198   *Lanercost*, p. 240.

199   Ibid. Some rough statistical estimate of the damage done to the counties of
Northumberland, Cumberland, Westmorland, Lancashire and Yorkshire between

1307 and 1327 is given by Willard, "The Scotch Raids and the Fourteenth-Century Taxation." He concludes that although the sums paid for subsidies are not capable of precise comparison, it is clear that on occasion nothing could be paid. There were considerable differences between 1307 and the end of the reign. For the travails of the Northwest between 1316 and 1322 (with sketch-map) see Summerson, *Carlisle* 1, pp. 220–30. For some time the bishop of Carlisle could not reside in his diocese. In general see the list of charts and maps (p. x) in McNamee, *Wars of the Bruces*.

200 Fo. 220r, ed. Eckhardt 2, p. 1061 ll. 39258–61.

201 *Lanercost*, p. 240; *CDS* 3, nos. 677, 681; ibid. 5, nos. 656–7 pp. 248–9. The truce, dated 22 December 1319 is Englished in no. 657 from PRO C47/22/13(6). A and B texts are printed in *Acts of Robert I*, no. 162. Neither mentions Harbottle by name. See also *Foedera* 2 i, pp. 409–10, 416, and for Harbottle's destruction ibid., p.455; *CDS* 3, nos. 738–9; *CPR 1321–24*, pp. 21–2.

202 *Acts of Robert I*, nos. 440, 569. The editor comments that the phraseology seems appropriate to a papal bull calling for peace, hence it was intended for the eye of John XXII as well as Edward II. Denholm-Young had previously suggested Edward I as the addressee.

203 Duncan, "The Making of the Declaration of Arbroath," p. 174. There is a photo-graph of the "file copy" from the Scottish Record Office in the same author's *The Nation of Scots and the Declaration of Arbroath*, centre fold. See also Simpson, "The Declaration of Arbroath Revitalised."

204 *APS* 1, pp. 474–5; Donaldson, "The Pope's reply to the Scottish Barons," pp. 119–20 (text in Theiner, A., *Vetera Monumenta*, no. 433, Rome 1864, summary in *CPL 1305–42*, p. 428); *Scotichronicon* ed. Watt 7, pp. 165–7 Notes to pp. 5–7 of text (3–18); Duncan, *The Nation of Scots*; "The Making of the Declaration of Arbroath," which is illuminating for historical context; Macquarrie, "The Ideal of the Holy War in Scotland"; Haines, *Church and Politics*, pp. 22–3.

205 The political leanings of Cobham are unclear. He did remain loyal to the last, although only too well aware of the king's faults. He was summoned to Westminster for Hilary (13 January) as a preliminary to making the journey to the north, but received insufficient notice. His reply (significantly?) is dated from the younger Despenser's manor of Wootton Bassett. He was given permission to proceed directly to the north from his cathedral city. *Worcester Register Cobham*, pp. 99–100. By contrast, Halton was much involved with Lancaster, perhaps inevitably in view of the situation of his bishopric. See *Biog. Oxon.* s.v. Safe conducts were issued by Bruce on 26 January: *CDS* 3, no. 722; ibid. 5, p. 90 from PRO C47/22/10(38). Halton was denied his expenses on the grounds that he was too close to his own bishopric and the negotiations were also for its own good. Ibid., no. 743; 5, p. 90 from PRO SC8/103/5117.

206 *Anglo-Scottish Relations*, ed. Stones, no. 38 a-j; *CDS* 5, nos. 666–76, pp. 250–1; Lineham, "Fourteenth Century History of Anglo-Scottish Relations" – important for giving the Scottish view of what happened in 1291 (see n. 9 above).

207 *Vita*, pp. 97–9, which suggests that at the time of the siege of Berwick Scots and Lancastrian forces passed through each other's lines unhindered. Maddicott, *Lancaster*, p. 302, accepts at face value the earl's offer (in 1319) to purge himself. A fair one, thought *Vita*, p. 102, because there was rumour but no specific charges. But this has to be taken in conjunction with the earlier comments in that chronicle.

208 *CDS* 3, no. 746; *CPR 1318–23*, p. 525; *Foedera* 2 i, pp. 463, 472, 474, 478–9 (indictment of Lancaster); *Trokelowe*, pp. 112–24; *Ann. Paul.*, p. 302; *Bridlington*, p. 78. Maddicott, *Lancaster*, pp. 301–3, discusses the matter at length.

209 *Lanercost*, p. 242: "Noluit enim pugnare pro regno illius qui eum voluit impugnare."

210 *Lanercost*, pp. 241–2; *CDS* 3, no. 749; Vita, pp. 120–1. For Harclay's commission: *CDS* 3, no. 745; *CPR 1321–24*, p. 71; *Foedera* 2 i, p. 473. The January raid may well have been planned with Lancaster's stance in mind. After Boroughbridge *Lanercost* suggests that Harclay thought that the earl would seek help from the Scots.

211 *CPR 1321–24*, pp. 97, 205; *CCR 13–18–23*, pp. 529–30, 556–7, 690, 719–20.

212 Barrow, *Bruce*, pp. 317–19, dwells on the "piety" of the Scots king. He had much, even by the standards of the day, which he needed to expiate on his final pilgrimage to Whithorn. In Scotland, England and Ireland he performed notorious acts of sacrilege, that need to be set against this notion of a "devout" king. His care for the saints and their shrines was selective. Nor can this be entirely ascribed to an attitude of mind common in those times.

213 *Lanercost*, p. 246.

214 The wardrobe account for 1322–3, lists a number of disbursement "pro armatura et alia necessaria" purchased for Adam. These were on 6 June, 4 July, and 10 July at York, 3 August at Newcastle, 19 August at Mussleborough and 18 September at Newcastle once again, dates indicative of the king's short-lived expedition. Blackley, "Adam, Bastard Son," pp. 76–7.

215 *CDS* 3, nos. 751–2, 754–5; *CPR 1321–24*, pp. 119–21.

216 Baker, *Chronicon*, p. 14, says that Edward entered Scotland on the feast of St. James (25 July). Historia Roffensis, fo. 39^v, gives this as the date for the army's assembly at Newcastle. See *Itinerary EII*, pp. 228–9, which has the king at Thirsk on that date and at Newcastle by 3 August.

217 *CDS* 3, nos 756–7; *Foedera* 2 i, p. 489; *Lanercost*, p. 247.

218 *Flores* 3, pp. 209–10; Baker, *Chronicon*, p. 14; *Lanercost*, p. 247; Barbour, *Bruce* 18, ll. 291–332, pp. 330–1; Fordun, *Chronica* 1, pp. 349–50; 2, pp. 341–2; *Scotichronicon* ed. Watt 7, pp. 10–13, 175 Notes (32–9).

219 For the situation in the Northwest see Tupling, *South Lancashire*, pp. xxxv–xxxix.

220 The king was at Byland and Rievaulx on 13–14 October 1322, at Bridlington on the fifteenth. *Itinerary EII*, p.232 and nn. a-d.

221 *Bridlington*, pp. 79–81; *Lanercost,* pp. 247–8; *Scalacronica*, ed. Stevenson, p. 149, ed. Maxwell, p. 69. "The Scots were so fierce and their chiefs so daring, and the English so badly cowed, that it was no otherwise between them than as a hare before greyhounds." For a detailed account: Barrow, *Bruce*, pp. 243–4.

222 *Brut*, pp. 226–8.

223 *CPR 1321–24*, pp. 93, 140; *Foedera* 2 i, p. 481; *CDS* 3, no. 756; *Lanercost*, p. 248.

224 Summerson, *Carlisle* 1, pp. 235–7; *Lanercost*, pp. 248–9. The royal almoner, the Carmelite friar Richard de Bliton, was one of those used by the king in this business as a messenger.

225 *Foedera* 2 i, p. 473: Gloucester 9 February 1322. This did require him (naturally enough) "ad certiorandum nos de hiis quae inde tractata fuerint." *CDS* 5, no. 691, p. 254: 26 February 1323. Walter de Strikeland was commissioned to receive all who wished to abandon the alliance with Harclay and to return to the king's fealty prior to Palm Sunday (20 March).

226 Duncan, *Acts of Robert I*, no. 315, prints three texts, A, B and C. A is the Bergen text; B is also printed in Stones, *Anglo-Scottish Relations*, no. 39 from PRO E.159/96/m. 70 (French); C is from *Bridlington*, pp. 82–3. See also the summarized text in *Lanercost*, pp. 248–9.

227 Duncan's B text; *Anglo-Scottish Relations*, ed Stones, no. 39, p.[154].

228 *Anglo-Scottish Relations*, ed. Stones, p.[155]; *Acts of Robert I*, p. 481 (text A).

229 E.g. *Bridlington*, p. 82; *Anglo-Scottish Relations*, ed. Stones, pp. [155–6] (French).

230 At the time Bruce did not have a direct male heir. His heir male was Robert, son of his daughter Marjorie.

231 Failing Edward's acceptance, the twelve persons "shall act according to their judgement for the common profit of one realm and the other." *Anglo-Scottish Relations*, ed. Stones, pp.[156–7]. For a discussion of the treaty: Summerson, *Carlisle* 1, pp. 243–8.

232 *Foedera* 2 i, p. 502, Cowick 8 January 1323: "Unde vehementer cogimur admirari, praecipue quod, nobis inconsultis, tractatus hujusmodi fieri permisistis;" ibid., p. 505, Newark 1 February 1323 (mandate for arrest); *CDS* 3, nos. 800–3; *CPR 1321–24*, p. 234; *CCR 1318–23*, p. 692.

233 *CDS* 5, no. 683 p. 252.

234 *Lanercost*, pp. 248–51, 424 (Notes); *Brut,* pp. 226–8.

235 *Acts of Robert I*, no. 222 from PRO C47/22/4(166); *CDS* 3, no. 807; *Foedera* 2 i, pp. 510–11.

236 *CDS* 5, no. 683 pp. 252.

237 *Acts of Robert I*, no. 448; *CDS* 5, no. 683 pp. 252–3; *CDS* 3, no. 809; ibid. 5, p. 91 from PRO C47/22/10(41–2); *Foedera* 2 i, p. 518.

238 *Lanercost*, p. 252; *Acts of Robert I*, no. 232; CDS 3, no. 810 (from PRO C81/1329(6524); *Foedera* 2 i, p. 519. Phillips, *Pembroke*, pp. 230–1, gives an account of the negotiations, particularly of the part played by Valence himself.

239 *Foedera* 2 i, p. 521.

240 *Acts of Robert I*, no. 232.

241 Bodl. Lib. MS Holkham Misc. 29, fo. 43^r; *Foedera* 2 i, p. 520. Among the chron-
     iclers the *Flores* (3, pp. 215–6) is particularly critical of the truce.

242 *Acts of Robert I*, no. 232; Barrow, *Bruce*, pp. 249–50. The editor of the *Acta* sug-
     gests that Bruce was reluctant to accept Edward's ostensible claim to be able to
     determine the peace and to impose sentences. But this clause is not dissimilar in
     intent to that which is to be found in the 1328 treaty. After 25 November 1324
     letters were being prepared by the chancery asking for absolution of the Scots
     during the peace negotiations (*CDS* 3, no. 855, *CChW* 1, p. 560). For the imposi-
     tion of such sentences see Hill, "John XXII's Excommunication of Bruce," pp.
     135–8, using material from Archbishop Melton's register. I would doubt, howev-
     er, if Bruce "quite clearly believed that he had never been excommunicated
     because he was not the person described in the papal letters" (p. 137). The caveat
     "lawfully" (ibid., p. 138) is more to the point. He knew perfectly well that he was
     the person intended but it would have been impolitic to receive such letters and
     clearly better to adopt a subterfuge (on a technical point) than to express open
     defiance. He was anxious enough for absolution for political if no other reasons.
     See nn. 180–2 above.

243 *Acts of Robert I*, no. 232 (comment). The editor has E and R texts. See *Foedera* 2
     i, pp. 521, 524; Johnson, "Preliminary Draft of the Text."

244 *War of Saint-Sardos*, pp. ix, 176.

245 Ibid., p. 177–9.

246 Ibid., pp. ix–xiii.

247 Haines, *John Stratford*, pp. 133–46. Barrow, *Bruce*, p. 250, was so irked by these
     representations as to expostulate: "With staggering effrontery, the English king
     demanded among other things, that no one in Scotland [i.e. no Scotsman] should
     be made bishop in the Scottish church." But from Edward's (doubtless unaccept-
     able) viewpoint the demand was logical enough. He did not acknowledge Bruce
     as king. Scottish bishops, as is well known, were political activists in Bruce's
     cause. Eaglescliff possibly never visited his diocese but performed the services of
     a suffragan in that of York: Hill, "An English archbishop and the Scottish War,"
     p. 60

248 Ibid., pp. 142–3. While there may have been a degree of attempted double-deal-
     ing on Edward II's part in keeping the sentences alive, Barrow, *Bruce*, p. 250, is
     incorrect in his assertion "Yet in the very next year (1324) Edward II sent a pow-
     erful mission to the papal curia, headed by the newly appointed bishop of Win-
     chester, John Stratford." His curial embassy had ended in the late summer of
     1323. Thereafter Stratford was *persona non grata* with the government and only
     at the end of 1324, 10 December, did he leave for Paris (not Avignon) on quite
     different business. See Haines, *John Stratford*, pp. 151–3, 471–3.

249 *Foedera* 2 i, p. 541; *Instrumenta Misc.*, no. 994.

250 *Foedera* 2 i, p. 561; *CDS* 3, no. 845; *CPR 1324–27*, p. 6.

251　*CDS* 3, nos. 845–6, 848; *CPR 1324–27*, pp. 6, 23; *Vita*, pp. 131–2.

252　*CDS* 3, nos. 851–2; *Foedera* 2 i, pp. 577–8.

253　*Vita*, pp. 132–4.

254　*CDS* 3, nos. 882–3; *CCR 1323–27*, pp. 466, 476; *Foedera* 2 i, p. 626; Summerson, *Carlisle* 1, pp. 259–60.

255　*APS* 12, pp. 5–6.

256　*Lanercost*, pp. 256–7. It is alleged that some similar offer was made in 1312. See Frame, *Lordship in Ireland*, p. 140.

257　*Lanercost*, pp. 258–9; *CDS* 3, nos. 907, 913–4, 922 from PRO E30/1536(1); ibid., (5); nos. 1782–4, 1786–8, 1798–9, p. 369; *Foedera* 2 i, pp. 689, 695–6, 702–3, 708–9; *CPR 1327–30*, pp. 15, 33; Le Bel, *Chronique* 1, pp. 36–7.

258　Barbour, *Bruce* 19, ll. 190–202, 230–8, pp. 343–4; *CDS* 3, nos. 887–9, 923 (*Foedera* 2 i, p. 719) giving the date of Balliol's safe conduct as 12 July; *CPR 1324–27*, pp. 324, 352, 354, 617; *CPR 1327–30*, p. 137; Barrow, *Bruce*, pp. 252, 372 n. 76. Barrow (pp. 251–2) seems too partial to Bruce at this point. On 4 March 1327 the English government had appointed the abbot of Rievaulx and Ivo de Aldeburgh to treat for peace, i.e., prior to their "unilateral" confirmation of the truce (Fordun, *Chronica* 1, pp. 351–2; 2, p. 344, records the sending of envoys "under a show of treating for secure peace"). It was seldom possible to regulate piracy and the English often complained of it themselves – sometimes at the hands of their own nation. That it was officially inspired is not proven. The problems already facing Edward's government in 1326 do not require stressing. It is clear that in 1327 Bruce was the aggressor, and that for internal political reasons, if no others, the government of Isabella and Mortimer desired peace in the North.

259　*Lanercost*, p. 259; Barbour, *Bruce* 19, ll. 240, 350, pp. 344, 347. For the date(s) of the Scottish incursion(s) see references to Barrow, *Bruce*, in nn. 265–6 below.

260　*Lanercost*, p. 529; *CDS* 3, 919; *CCR 1327–30*, p. 212.

261　*Lit. Cant.* 1, pp. 223–4; Le Bel, *Chronique* 1, p. 43.

262　Le Bel, *Chronique* 1, p. 70; *Lanercost*, pp. 259–60;: "ita doluit ut fleret" (the lachrymose tale is also in *Scalacronica*, ed. Stevenson, p. 155, ed. Maxwell, p. 81). Baker, *Chronicon*, p. 35, gives an account of the riot in York. See also *Bridlington*, p. 96; CCC MS 174, fo. 150[r]; *Brut*, p. 250. Four score is said to have been the number that died and were buried at St Clement's church. An inquest found that the English had started the fight.

263　Rogers, "Edward III and the Dialectics of Strategy," p. 87, remarks: "this expedition was deeply engraved on the consciousness of the young king, and did much to shape his understanding of the craft of war. The more so, since the end result of the military failure was the *turpis pax*."

264　Baker, *Chronicon*, p. 35; *French Chronicle*, p. 60 and n. ; CCC MS 174, fos. 150[v]–1[r], 155[v], 163[v]; Haines, *John Stratford*, pp. 193–4.

265　Barrow, *Bruce*, pp. 252, 372 n.78, gives this date. *CDS* 3, nos. 920, undated [ca.

4 July 1327], printed *Lanercost*, (App. LI) p. 539; 921 from C81/146(1079); *CDS* 5, p. 93. *CDS* 3, no. 918, points to the fact that an English army was in process of formation on 15 June to fend off a threatened Scottish incursion.

266 Barrow, *Bruce*, pp. 252–3, 372–3 nn. 78–84; Barbour, *Bruce*, editor's notes to book 19, pp. 478–87; *Scalacronica*, ed. Stevenson, pp. 153–5, ed. Maxwell, pp. 79–82; Le Bel, *Chronique* I, pp. 48–75. For Rokeby's reward of a hundred pounds a year: *CDS* 3, no. 936; *Foedera* 2 ii, p. 717.

267 *Scalacronica*, ed. Stevenson, p. 156, ed. Maxwell, p. 83. Gray puts down the arrangement by Isabella and Mortimer as one of the causes of their undoing.

268 *Lanercost*, p. 262; Haines, *John Stratford*, p. 195 n. 16.

269 David (the future David II), that new sword (*novus ensis*): Bower,*Scotichronicon* 2, pp. 279–80, ed. Watt 7, pp. 12–15) was born 5 March 1324, Joan of the Tower 5 July 1321 – not specifically named by Bruce in this document. *HBC* pp. 39, 59.

270 *Anglo-Scottish Relations*, ed. Stones, no. 40; "Anglo-Scottish negotiations of 1327." See also Nicholson, "The Last Campaign of Robert Bruce," who concludes of the letters patent of 1 March: "Embodied in these was the substance of everything for which Bruce had fought, and a renunciation of the Scottish policy followed by Edward I and his successors."

271 *Anglo-Scottish Relations*, ed. Stones, no. 41 (a), (b).

272 Ibid., no. 41 (c); n.275 below; Stones, "The English Mission to Edinburgh"; "An Addition to the *Rotuli Scotiae* "; "Historical Revision: The Treaty of Northampton." According to the last there have been four principal misconceptions with respect to the treaty documents handed down by Lord Hailes in his *Annals of Scotland*: 1. That there was provision for the return of the Stone of Scone; 2. That the payment of twenty thousand pounds was compensation for Scottish plundering; 3. That agreement was reached about confiscated estates; 4. That each party agreed to pay two thousand pounds to the papacy should it fail to keep the agreement.

273 See *Anglo-Scottish Relations*, ed. Stones, p.[168] n. 1, for the misunderstanding of this clause which led to the notion that the transfer of documents to Scotland from the PRO in 1937 and later was a belated fulfillment of the Northampton treaty. See also end of n. 1 above.

274 *APS* I, pp. 484–7; *Foedera* 2 ii, pp. 734–5, 741–2; *Anglo-Scottish Relations*, ed. Stones, no. 41 (c); *Acts of Robert I*, nos. 342–5 (from PRO C71/12/mm. 3–4). In a separate document, *Acta* no. 343, Bruce put himself under obligation to pay the vast (impossibly large?) sum of one hundred thousand pounds should he fail to complete the David-Joan marriage by Michaelmas 1338 (when David would be of age to give his own consent); non-payment would result in cancellation of the recognition of Scottish independence. Obviously this was somewhat of a smokescreen. The marriage was celebrated at Berwick on 17 July 1328 (not the twelfth, as in Barrow, *Bruce*, p. 260); *Lanercost*, p. 261; Bower, *Scotichronicon* 2, ed. Watt 7, pp. 42–3; *HBC*, p. 59.

275 *Lanercost*, p. 261; *Scalacronica*, ed. Stevenson, pp. 155–6, ed. Maxwell, pp. 82–3; Baker, *Chronicon*, p. 216 (Notes); Legg, *Early Coronation Records*, no. 11 pp. 77–8 (transcript from Bodl. Lib., MS Rawlinson D.809, fo. 394ʳ).

276 According to the *Scalacronica*, ed. Stevenson, p. 156, ed. Maxwell, p. 83, it was agreed by Edward that all his adherents in Scotland should be disinherited except Wake, Percy and Beaumont. Percy was granted his lands by Bruce, 28 July [1328], doubtless as a *quid pro quo* in helping to negotiate the peace: *Anglo-Scottish Relations*, ed. Stones, no. 42. Wake and Beaumont were implicated in Lancaster's rising of 1328, but negotiations, citing the treaty (*tractatus pacis*), were under way in 1330–32: *CDS* 3, nos. 1013, 1023, 1029, 1050–1 (*Foedera* 2 ii, pp. 804, 809); ibid. 5, p. 94; *CCR 1330–33*, pp. 174, 294; Stones, "Historical Revision: the Treaty of Northampton," pp. 57–9.

277 Stones, "Sir Geoffrey le Scrope," p. 9.

278 See the extract from the version in BL Cotton MS Tiberius A.VI, fo. 184ʳ, in Taylor, "French Brut and Edward II," pp. 436–7.

279 For a critique of the supposed involvement of Orleton see Haines, *Church and Politics*, pp. 109–10.

280 Baker, *Chronicon*, p. 41; *CPMR*, p. 80.

281 For monies paid to Isabella: *CDS* 3, nos. 997 (ten thousand marks), 1002 (five thousand marks); *Foedera* 2 ii, p. 785; *CPR 1327–30*, p. 470; Balliol's protection, 16 October 1330: ibid., 1010 (*Foedera* 2 ii, p. 799); final payment of ten thousand marks (16 July 1330): ibid., 1007 (*Foedera* 2 ii, p. 795).

282 *CDS* 3, nos. 1022, 1024, 1034–6.

283 *CDS* 3, nos. 1059, 1064.

284 These derogatory nicknames and the unpopularity of the peace are commented upon by Maunde Thompson, Baker, *Chronicon*, pp. 215–6.

CHAPTER TEN

1 Warner ed., *The Libelle of Englyshe Polycye*, ll. 698–701

2 For the broad outline of this chapter I have been dependent principally on such writers as Cosgrove, Frame, Otway-Ruthven, Phillips, J. A. Watt, and Richardson and Sayles, whose works are listed in the Bibliography, as well, of course, as printed documents and the chroniclers. I hope to have done my bit to counter the stricture that for the period 1216–1360 "with one or two exceptions, English historians tend to ignore the lordship, or to allot it at best a few uneasy pages": Frame, "England and Ireland, 1171–1399," p. 139.

3 Prestwich, *Edward I*, pp. 13–14 and index s.v. "Ireland"; O'Sullivan, "Italian Merchant Bankers and the Collection of Customs," pp. 168–85. Otway-Ruthven remarks, *History of Medieval Ireland*, p. 224: "Throughout Edward I's Scottish wars Ireland had been a source of both men and supplies to the English Crown, and continued to be so under Edward II."

4 For the text of the Falaise treaty see Stones, *Anglo-Scottish Relations*, pp. 1–5. Barrow, *Feudal Britain*, chapters 15, 21, provides an overview of Scottish history between 1153 and 1314.

5 See Prestwich, *Edward I*, chapter 7, Barrow, *Feudal Britain*, chapters 14, 19; and for South Wales, Griffiths, *Principality of Wales*, introduction and pp. 1–17.

6 The text is printed from *Ralph de Diceto* 1, ed. Stubbs, RS 68, p. 300 in *Pontifica Hibernica*, pp. 15–16, and the sources cited ibid., n. 4. See also *English Historical Documents* 2, pp. 776–80, nos. 159–62, and n. 9 below.

7 Richter, "The First Century of Anglo-Irish Relations," especially pp. 195–8, 203–10, discusses the intentions and implications of the bull. He suggests that papal views as to the "primitive" nature of the Irish church were duplicated in the case of Wales.

8 Cheney and Semple ed., *Selected Letters of Innocent III*, no. 67, pp. 177–83. The falling-off of direct contact between the Irish reguli and the English king during the thirteenth century is discussed by Frame, "England and Ireland, 1171–1399," pp. 144–47

9 Watt, "Negotiations between Edward II and John XXII," pp. 3–5; Lydon, "A Land of War," pp. 242–3; Walsh, *FitzRalph*, pp. 8–10; Frame, *Lordship in Ireland*, p. 12. The Remonstrance, an indictment of English rule in Ireland, was a political document which has been said to have some relationship to Robert Bruce's letter to the kings of Ireland and the Declaration of Arbroath. Doubtless the pope would not have got very far with a threat of this kind, even with such a weak king as Edward II, but the latter preferred to have papal support so far as possible. Equally, the pope was not looking for conflict.

10 These matters are discussed at length in Otway-Ruthven, *History of Medieval Ireland*, chapter 3.

11 Lydon, "A Land of War," NHI chapter 9, p. 240 n. 2.

12 However misleading the term may be, I have used it for convenience in view of its widespread adoption.

13 Cosgrove, *"Hiberniores ipsis Hibernis,"* pp. 7, 14, citing *Statutes of Ireland*, p. 210.

14 Ibid., pp. 1–14.

15 Colledge, *Latin Poems of Richard Ledrede*, has edited the poems and written an introduction detailing the bishop's career. Ledred's indictment of heretics became confused with political divisions reflected in Ireland during Edward II's reign and that of Isabella and Mortimer. Stemmler ed., *The Latin Hymns of Richard Ledrede*, provides another aspect of his devotional work.

16 These and other matters are discussed compactly by Frame, "Les Engleys nes en Irlande" (see in particular the works on the common law cited in the footnotes to p. 87) and at considerable length on a British canvas by R. R. Davies, "The Peoples of Britain and Ireland 1100–1400" I-IV, and earlier in "Domination and Conquest," the Wiles lectures (Belfast). See also Phillips, "The Anglo-Norman Nobility." Questions similar to those raised with respect to Irish identity could equally be posed of present-day "multi-racial" societies.

17 Otway-Ruthven, *History of Medieval Ireland*, p. 130.

18 Watt, "Negotiations between Edward II and John XXII," pp. 1–3, citing *Foedera* 2
    i, pp. 615–6. With respect to his advocacy of Alexander Bicknor as archbishop of
    Dublin, the king subsequently changed his mind in view of the archbishop's
    actions in Gascony, as he did with respect to some occupants of English sees when
    he found them or their close relatives unsatisfactory in the secular sphere. For a
    general review of the question of royal rights and the Irish church (or better, the
    "Church in Ireland"), see Otway-Ruthven, *History of Medieval Ireland*, chapter 4
    "The Medieval Irish Church"; Watt, "English Law and the Irish Church."

19 An anti-Irish complaint on this score has been attributed to Henry de London,
    archbishop of Dublin. See Otway-Ruthven, *History of Medieval Ireland*, pp.
    131–2. London is the man believed to have brought a copy of the Salisbury con-
    suetudinary to Ireland: Haines, *Ecclesia anglicana*, p. 264 n. 1. In the case of Eng-
    land the personnel is well known thanks to the revised *Le Neve*, but detailed analy-
    sis is scattered.

20 Otway-Ruthven, *History of Medieval Ireland*, pp. 136–7.

21 This document is printed by Watt, "Negotiations between Edward II and John
    XXII," pp. 16–18, from a microfilm of Barberini Latini MS no. 2126 in the Vati-
    can Library.

22 Cosgrove, "Hiberniores ipsis Hibernis," pp. 8–10.

23 Clyn, *Annals*, p. 20; Lydon, "The Braganstown Massacre"; Otway-Ruthven, *Histo-
    ry of Medieval Ireland*, p. 245.

24 Sayles, "The Rebellious First Earl," pp. 203–29. Sayles is at pains to dispel the
    impression given by Curtis in his *History of Ireland* of a patriot leader of Anglo-
    Ireland.

25 Richardson and Sayles, "Irish Revenues," p. 98.

26 For the de Burgh family see Orpen, "The Earldom of Ulster," especially *JRSAI* 43,
    pp. 30–46.

27 Richardson and Sayles, *Administration of Ireland*, pp. 82–5, lists the governors for
    the period until 1330 under their various titles such as Justiciar, Deputy Justiciar,
    King's Lieutenant etc., as well as the treasurers, chancellors etc.; see also *HBC*.

28 O'Sullivan, "Italian Merchant Bankers in Ireland," pp. 184–5, citing *Rot. Parl.* 1,
    p. 281; *CCR 1307–13*, p. 415; Lydon, "Impact of the Bruce Invasion," pp. 275–7,
    and more minutely, idem., "Enrolled Account of Bicknor" and "Edward II and the
    Revenues of Ireland"; Richardson and Sayles, "Irish Revenue."

29 Lydon, "A Land of War," pp. 262–3.

30 *Chronicon*, p. 4: "in re militari satis excercitatus."

31 Hamilton, *Gaveston*, pp. 56–7; Richardson and Sayles, *Administration of Ireland*,
    pp. 11–12, 82.

32 *Ann. Lond.*, p. 156: "pompose se gerens, mores novellos saeculo inauditos adinve-
    niens, mirabili varietate vitam adduxit"; *Murimuth*, p. 12: "regaliter vixit, et fuit
    bene dilectus, erat enim dapsilis et largus in muneribus dandis, et honoribus et sibi
    adhaerentibus procurandis"; *Lanercost*, pp. 211–12, makes much of the king's gifts

to the favourite, claiming that "dedit etiam sibi multas cartas sigillatas magno sig-
illo suo, sed vacuas, in quibus facere posset scribi quicquid vellet." See above
chapter 4 n. 33. Baker, *Chronicon*, p. 4, states that he went "cum valida manu" and
a stipend to be paid by the exchequer.

33 *Statutes of Ireland*, pp. 244–57.

34 On his arrival his chaplain Walter de London delivered two thousand pounds to
Treasurer Bicknor. Hamilton, *Gaveston*, pp. 62, 150 nn. 46–8, citing PRO
E101/235/11(m.1), 12; Lydon, "Enrolled Account of Bicknor."

35 This matter is discussed by Hamilton, *Gaveston*, pp. 63–5; "The Murage of
Dublin."

36 Hamilton, *Gaveston*, pp. 59–61, 149–50 nn. 33–43; Lydon, "A Land of War," pp.
262–3; Orpen, "Castrum Keyvini," p. 17; "Novum Castrum McKynegan," pp.
135–6; *Chart. of St. Mary's*, 2, p. 338. Other manuscript and printed sources are
detailed by Hamilton.

37 For what follows I have used more particularly Otway Ruthven, *History of Ireland*,
chapter 7 "The Bruce Invasion and its Aftermath;" Lydon, "The Bruce Invasion of
Ireland"; "Impact of the Bruce Invasion"; Phillips, "The Mission of John Hothum
to Ireland"; "Documents of the Bruce Invasion"; Frame, "Bruces in Ireland";
Nicholson, "A Sequel to Edward Bruce's Invasion of Ireland." The details of
Bruce's connections with Irish families and with Ulster are to be found in Orpen,
"The Earldom of Ulster," *JRSAI* 43, pp. 30–46.

38 These and other views have recently been discussed by McNamee, *Wars of the
Bruces*, chapter 5, especially pp. 190–4: "Celtic Alliance – or Anglo-Norman
Adventurism?" (also n. 64 below); and see Barrow, *Bruce*, pp. 314–17.

39 Barrow, *Bruce*, p. 57. He suggests (pp. 18, 25–6) that the mysterious "Turnberry
Band" (1286) may indicate some early plan of the Bruces with respect to Ireland.

40 Nicholson, "Sequel to Edward Bruce's Invasion," pp. 31, 38–9; Barrow, *Bruce*, pp.
147 (map of Bruce's possible movements in 1306), 314, 379 n. 9; Lydon, "Impact
of the Bruce Invasion," p. 283 and n. 2 (referring to an earlier edition of Barrow's
Bruce).

41 *Chart. of St. Mary's* 2, p. 342, says that Bruce sent galleys to Ulster on 31 May
"cum suis piratis ad depredandum." They were vigorously put to flight.

42 Lydon, "Impact of the Bruce Invasion," pp. 283–5; Wood, "Letter from O'Neil to
MacCarthy"; Phillips, "Documents," pp. 269–70 (from BL MS Harleian 655). This
last (s.a. 1314) states that Edward Bruce was invited by a magnate of Ireland with
whom he had been brought up, presumed (Barrow, *Bruce*, p. 332 n. 31) to be
O'Neill of Tyrone.

43 Compare the interpretation of Edward III's strategy in France: Rogers, "Edward III
and the Dialectics of Strategy."

44 There is a graphic account of their depredations coupled with those of the native
Irish in *Annals of Loch Cé* 1, pp. 564–9. Lydon, "Impact of the Bruce Invasion,"
pp. 282–3, suggests a second front as Robert Bruce's likely strategy. For the argument against Scottish devastation as not being exceptional and no worse than that

of the Anglo-Irish magnates – one might add of the Irish themselves: Frame, "Bruces in Ireland," p. 9.

45 Lydon, "Bruce Invasion of Ireland," p. 111, lists the "causes" of Ireland's weakness under Edward II and beyond, the last of which is the Bruce invasion.

46 Compare the analysis of Frame, "Bruces in Ireland," especially pp. 3–17.

47 Frame, "Bruces in Ireland," p. 14, summarizes the arguments for the viability of the Irish adventure.

48 See chapter 5 above.

49 The description is that of Barrow, *Bruce*, p. 293.

50 There are three useful maps of the Bruce expeditions in Lydon, "Impact of the Bruce Invasion," p. 281, based on *Historical Atlas of Scotland*, pp. 168–9.

51 Otway-Ruthven, *History of Medieval Ireland*, p. 226; *Chart. of St. Mary's* 2, p. 344; Phillips, "Documents," pp. 257–65: transcripts of this and other letters from the Anglo-Irish magnates in response to anxious enquiries from the king. See also Lydon, "Impact of Bruce Invasion," p. 282 n. 3.

52 Mandeville wrote plaintively to Edward II about the loss of castles and lands to the Scots, pointing out the good service he had rendered to the king and his father. He had intended to come to England, but on receiving the king's letter requesting his aid against the royal enemies decided to remain. Phillips, "Documents," pp. 260–1.

53 Dillon, "The Inauguration of O'Conor," p. 186,

54 *Annals of Loch Cé* 1, pp. 568–71.

55 Ibid., pp. 565–6, 578–9; Sayles, "Siege of Carrickfergus," pp. 94–5.

56 *Chart. of St. Mary's* (*Annals*), pp. cxxxi, 345, 347. Clyn, *Annals*, p. 12, gives an account of the sack of Dundalk and of the looting of the Franciscan friary.

57 *Chart. St. Mary's* 2, p. 345.

58 See the reports of de la Roche and John de Barry in Phillips, "Documents," nos. 9, 18, pp. 258, 264–5. The justiciar disbanded the royal host at Carlingford, probably on 18 July. The earl's insistence may have stemmed from a number of reasons, but it was also common sense in view of the difficulty of provisioning so large a force.

59 *Annals of Loch Cé* 1, pp. 566–71; *Chart. of St. Mary's* (*Annals*) 2, pp. 345–6; Otway-Ruthven, *History of Medieval Ireland*, pp. 226–7.

60 *Chart. of St. Mary's* 2, p. 347, says the engagement took place about the feast of St. Andrew (30 November).

61 Ibid., p. 347; *Rot. Parl.* 1, p. 385; Otway-Ruthven, *History of Medieval Ireland*, p. 228.

62 At the Hilary session of pleas of the Crown held before Edmund Butler, Walter and Hugh de Lacy denied that they had encouraged Bruce to come to Ireland. They were acquitted, but further indicted for advising Edward Bruce about the best route to take through Leinster and for staying with his forces. Subsequent proceedings were held before Mortimer as king's lieutenant in July 1317. Many others were also indicted for having raised the standard of Hugh de Lacy against that of the king. *Chart. of St. Mary's* (App. II 1) 2, pp. 407–9; (App. II 2), pp. 410–12; (Annals), p. 298.

63 As suggested by Phillips, "John de Hothum," p. 68, who gives details.

64 The king ordered the provisioning of Welsh castles and defensive measures on the coast in view of the Irish invasion as early as 21 June 1315. *CCR 1313–18*, p. 186. See Smith, "Gruffydd Llwyd and the Celtic Alliance." McNamee, *Wars of the Bruces*, pp. 190–4, examines "Celtic propaganda" and Edward Bruce's letters to the princes of Wales.

65 Phillips, "Documents"; "John de Hothum," pp. 67, 80 n. 46.

66 Parry, *Parliaments*, p. 79; Phillips, "John de Hothum," p. 63. For what follows I have relied almost exclusively on Phillips' detailed account of Hothum's mission. His informative footnotes with numerous manuscript references provide the necessary corroboration. For Hothum's administrative activity in England see Tout, *Chapters* 6, index s.v. "Hotham."

67 For whom see my forthcoming article in the *New DNB*.

68 Lydon, "Bruce Invasion of Ireland," pp. 114–15.

69 Hothum's expense accounts are printed in Phillips, "Documents," pp. 266–8.

70 Otway-Ruthven, *History of Medieval Ireland*, p. 229. Apparently he was acting upon an earlier order of the council.

71 John FitzThomas was created earl of Kildare 14 May 1316, but died 12 September, being succeeded by his son and heir Thomas FitzJohn. *HBC*, p. 494.

72 Ibid., p. 349.

73 Phillips, "Documents," no. 4, pp. 251–3. This is largely mirrored by another letter in the name of a clerk as well as Hothum, ibid. no. 7, pp. 255–7. The Annals record the death of a "nobilis armiger," Haymond le Grace, and of William Prendergast, knight. *Chart. of St. Mary's* 2, p. 347.

74 Phillips, "Documents," no. 5, pp. 253–5; *Chart. of St. Mary's* (Annals) 2, p. 348. The latter claims that they swore "simul pro morte et vita" to hold with the king, to bring peace in so far as they could, and to kill Scotsmen.

75 Phillips, "John de Hothum," p. 74.

76 Phillips, "Documents," no. 7, pp. 255–7.

77 *Chart. of St. Mary's* 2, p. 349; Orpen, "Novum Castrum McKynegan," pp. 135–6.

78 Ibid., pp. 296–7; Clyn, *Annals*, p.13; Reid, "Sea-Power," especially pp. 19–20; Sayles, "Siege of Carrickfergus"; Lydon, "Impact of Bruce Invasion," pp. 289–90.

79 *Chart. of St. Mary's* 2, p. 298. This annal gives "Monday before All Saints" (i.e. 25 October) as the date of the skirmish. All Saints fell on a Monday in 1316.

80 Frame, "Bruces in Ireland," p. 23, regards this as a reasonable inference.

81 Barrow, *Bruce*, pp. 312–17, discusses some of these problems.

82 *Chart. of St. Mary's* 2, p. 298.

83 The earl of Ulster is supposed to have ambushed the Scots at his manor of Ratoath (Otway-Ruthven, *History of Medieval Ireland*, p. 230), but this has been taken to be "a dubious tradition" (Lydon, "Impact of Bruce Invasion," p. 291).

84 For this account, from PRO SC 6/1239/13, see Frame, "The Campaign against the Scots in Munster."

85 *Chart. of St. Mary's* 2, pp. 298–302.

86 *Annals of Loch Cé* 1, pp. 594–5.

87 Otway-Ruthven, *History of Medieval Ireland*, p. 236.

88 *Chart. of St. Mary's* 2, p. 359.

89 *Annals of Loch Cé* 1, p. 595. They are not mentioned in the fuller account in *Chart. of St. Mary's* 2, pp. 359–60.

90 Walter, Hugh, Robert and Aumary de Lacy are mentioned, John had already been imprisoned by Mortimer for earlier treachery. For the proceedings against the de Lacys see *Chart. of St. Mary's* 2, App. II, pp. 407–16.

91 Ibid.; Mac Iomhair, "Two Old English Chronicles," pp. 89–90; *Knighton* 1, pp. 411–12. Bermingham was created earl of Louth 12 May 1319. The title died with him. *HBC*, p. 495.

92 *Annals of Loch Cé* 1, p. 595.

93 Lydon, "Impact of Bruce Invasion," pp. 297–8.

94 *Chart. of St. Mary's* 2, p. 361.

95 The ecclesiastical estates in the vicinity of Dublin are mapped in the endpaper of *Gwynn Studies*, to illustrate Otway-Ruthven, "Medieval Church Lands of County of Dublin." Those of the archbishop are particularly prominent. They certainly suffered at the hands of the Bruces and also of the native Irish. Ireland lacked a lay magnate anxious to salve his soul in this pious direction. See also Ó Conbhuí, "The Lands of St. Mary's Abbey," pl. 1.

96 Clyn, *Annals*, p. 14; Rashdall, *Universities* 2, pp. 325–7, citing FitzMaurice and Little ed., *Materials for the History of the Franciscan Province of Ireland*, pp. xxviii, 107–9; Gwynn, "The Medieval University of St. Patrick's, Dublin," pp. 199–212, 437–54.

97 Lydon, "Impact of Bruce Invasion," p. 297.

98 *Foedera* 2 i, p. 417; *Statutes of Ireland*, pp. 281–91, 307.

99 For what follows I am indebted particularly to Sayles, "The First Earl of Desmond."

100 See chapter 9 above.

101 Otway-Ruthven, *History of Medieval Ireland*, p. 241; Wood, "Muniments of Edmund de Mortimer," pp. 337–47. For Mortimer's surrender see chapter 5 above.

102 *Annals of Loch Cé* 1, pp. 594–5 and n. 7; Otway-Ruthven, *History of Medieval Ireland*, p. 141.

103 Otway-Ruthven, *History of Medieval Ireland*, pp. 141–2, who declared that "The face of Irish politics had been dramatically changed"; Orpen, "Earldom of Ulster," p. 34. Pembroke's lands in Kilkenny and Wexford are mapped by Phillips, *Pembroke*, (map. 2), and the Wexford officials detailed at pp. 292–3, also index s.v. "Ireland." For the Carrick earldom: *HBC*, p. 491.

104 The explosion in 1922 which virtually demolished the Irish medieval public records destroyed the indictments against FitzThomas, but copies were preserved in those of the court of King's Bench for 25 Edward III, Trinity term 1351, PRO KB27/364/mm. 18d–23. These indictments are listed by Sayles, "Earl of Desmond," App. II; that for the Clonmel enquiry of February 1332, is no. 5 at m. 18.

105 Colledge, *Latin Poems of Richard Ledrede*, p. xxiii, who treats fully of this matter so far as it concerned Ledred, assigns this meeting to 1327 and hence the conspiracy is said to be against the young Edward III. His reference is to PRO KB27/364/m.18, so this is somewhat puzzling. By May 1327 one of those named as conspirators, the earl of Kildare, was justiciar, an appointment he owed to the government of Mortimer and Isabella acting in Edward III's name.

106 FitzJohn was first deputy-justiciar 30 September 1320–30 June 1321, then justiciar until 1 October 1321. He was succeeded by Bermingham, who held office 28 August 1321–25 August 1323 (appointed 21 May 1321, *CPR 1317–21*, p. 588) according to the list for this period in Richardson and Sayles, *Administration of Ireland*, pp. 82–5. Compare *HBC*, p. 162.

107 *HBC*, pp. 493, 495.

108 PRO KB27/364/m.18; Sayles, "Earl of Desmond," pp. 207, 213, 228 App. II, no. 2

109 Outlaw was acting justiciar in 1328 (John Darcy became justiciar about May 1329), deputy justiciar 17 July 1330–2 June 1331, while Anthony Lucy was justiciar 3 June 1331–3 December 1332), during part of which time the earl of Ulster, William de Burgh, acted as king's lieutenant. Sayles, "Earl of Desmond," App. I.

110 *Chart. of St. Mary's* 2, pp. 374–5.

111 There was a similar allegation in 1344. This time a letter was supposed to have been sent by Desmond to the kings of France and Scotland asking them to send help to ensure joint action against the king of England, or so the indictment ran. Sayles, "First Earl of Desmond," p. 219, 228 App. II no. 25, citing KB27/364/m. 20 (1346)

112 T.F. Tout in *DNB* s.v. "FitzGerald, Thomas", cited by Colledge, *Latin Poems of Richard Ledrede*, p. xxiv.

113 Lydon, "Braganstown Massacre," pp. 5–16, especially 5–6;

114 Sayles, "Earl of Desmond," p. 207. Otway-Ruthven, *History of Medieval Ireland*, p. 246, considered him "a difficult and unsatisfactory man." Ironically he was himself to be accused of heresy.

115 Colledge, *Latin Poems of Ledrede*, pp. xxv–xxix.

116 Ibid., p. xix; *Proceedings against Kyteler* : Otway-Ruthven, *History of Medieval Ireland*, pp. 242–3, 245; *Chart. of St. Mary's* 2, pp. 364–5. Ledred, who is recorded to have become a centenarian, was bishop between 1317 and about 1361.

117 *CCR 1327–30*, pp. 206–7; PRO SC1/38/76. These references cited by Otway-Ruthven, *History of Medieval Ireland*, pp. 244–5 n. 77.

118 PRO SC1/42/69, cited Colledge.

119 Colledge, *Latin Poems of Ledrede*, pp. xxvi–xxxiv, recites the lengthy story of Ledred's troubles.

120 Haines, *Church and Politics*, pp. 80–1 n. 146.

121 Greeves, "Robert I and the de Mandevilles," pp. 61–2; Otway-Ruthven, *History*

of Medieval Ireland, pp. 244; Nicholson, "A Sequel to Edward Bruce's Invasion." PRO SC1/38/76 provides a copy of the Mandeville agreement (indenture 12 July 1327).

122 These details and many more are to be found in Otway-Ruthven, *History of Medieval Ireland,* p. 247, while the equally blood-curdling events in Ulster and the far north between 1328 and 1330 are related in the *Annals of Loch Cé* 1, pp. 6–15.

123 Otway-Ruthven, *History of Medieval Ireland,* pp. 247–9; *Early Statutes,* pp. 322–8.

124 Otway-Ruthven, "Partition of the de Verdon lands in Ireland."

125 Otway-Ruthven, *History of Medieval Ireland,* chapter 8 (followed in chapter 9 by the "attempt at recovery," 1349–76); *NHI* chapter 13. All these, of course, are chapter headings attempting to set the scene for what follows.

126 Richardson and Sayles, "Irish Revenue," pp. 87–100. In the "Table of Receipts by Treasurers, 1278–1384," the relevant figures (taken from PRO E372, Pipe Rolls) are as follows: 18 Apr. 1305–23 Jan. 1308, £12,984; 24 Jan. 1308–15 Apr. 1314, £22,155; 15 Apr. 1314–1 Aug. 1321, £18,566; 1 Aug. 1321–9 Sept. 1321, £184; 9 Sept. 1321–29 1322, £1,021; 29 Apr. 1322–29 Sept. 1325, £8,553; 29 Sept. 1325–20 Jan. 1326, £595; 4 Oct. 1326–19 Dec. 1327, £3,282; 19 Dec. 1327–31 March 1331, £5,380.

CHAPTER ELEVEN

1 Cuttino, *Diplomatic Administration,* p. 28.

2 Trabut-Cussac, "Les archives de la Gascogne anglaise," p. 97.

3 For much of what follows in this chapter I acknowledge, apart from older works, the recent researches of Pierre Chaplais, notably in his collected *Essays in Medieval Diplomacy,* his *English Diplomatic Practice,* and his edition of documents for *The War of Saint Sardos.* Chaplais's twenty-two collected essays (I–XXII), are here referred to by their number, short title (e.g. *Essays* IV "Le Duché-Pairie"), and original pages, as in chapter 1. The *Gascon Rolls* are, of course, invaluable. On perusing them Trabut-Cussac, "Les archives de la Gascogne anglaise," p. 97, was prompted to remark that they enabled him: "de constater comme souvent les decisions adoptées [by Edward II] répondent mal aux nécessitées du moment." See also Prestwich, *Edward I,* chapter 11 "The Duke of Aquitaine, 1273–94." Here too, Dr Doherty has provided invaluable insights into Isabella's whereabouts and activities.

4 Chaplais, *Essays* I, "Treaty of Paris and the Royal Style," pp. 235–53.

5 The use of the terms Gascony, Guienne or Guyenne, Aquitaine, is somewhat confusing. Strictly speaking the duchy of Guienne was a fief of the French king before the break with King John in 1202. By the treaty of 1259 only part of the duchy – the three bishoprics of Limoges, Cahors and Périgueux – was to be restored to Edward I (though this was not done prior to 1294). This part alone, according to

the 1259 treaty, merited the designation "duchy of Guienne." In 1286–7 the English envoys claimed that only if these lands were returned could the English king be called duke of Aquitaine. Gascony, however, claimed the status of a free allod (*franc-alleu*) that formed no part of France but of the Empire. See Chaplais, *Essays* III, "Le Duché-Pairie," pp. 30–32.

6 Chaplais, *Essays* II, "Le Traité de Paris de 1259," pp. 121–37, especially 125–6, 130–3, 135; *Essays* III, "Le Duché-Pairie," pp. 7–13.

7 Chaplais, *Essays* III, "Le Duché-Pairie," pp. 11–13, 15 and ibid., nn. 27–8.

8 Chaplais, *Diplomatic Practice* pt 1, 2 no. 235 (a) (b). In 1298, prior to June, a "factum" drawn up by M. Raymond de la Ferrière was prepared for Edward's justification (*ad innocenciam regis Anglie ostendendam*), and presented to the pope in that year and again in 1302. Ibid., no. 237 (from PRO C47/29/4/9).

9 Chaplais, *Essays* III, "Le Duché-Pairie," pp. 26–8; Cuttino, "Another Memorandum Book," p. 96. The treaty, sealed at Paris, is termed "of Montreuil" by Trabut-Cassac, *L'Administration Anglaise*, p.110.

10 Chaplais, *Essays* III, "Le Duché-Pairie," pp. 34–8. For the negotiations leading up to the peace and alliance, as well as its proclamation in England, see idem, *Diplomatic Practice* pt. 1, 2 no. 252 (a) (b) (c), 291, 294. No. 252 (b) is the English exemplar of the articles of the treaty, Paris 20 May 1303. Also *Treaty Rolls* 1, no. 394.

11 Trabut-Cassac, *L'Administration Anglaise*, pp. 112, 116–7. He gives a lengthy account of the unhealthy state of the Gascon inheritance "continuellement menacé dès avant 1294 par les officiers français." On the other hand Renouard, *Histoire de Bordeaux*, in book 3 covering the period 1303–1372, claims that the town for a century and a half enjoyed "une prospérité sans cesse croissante."

12 See chapter 1 above and Johnson, "The Homage for Guienne in 1304." Prince Edward was at that time being introduced to campaigning in Scotland.

13 Chaplais, *Essays* IV, "Le Duché-Pairie," p. 139 n. 18, citing PRO C47/29/5/10. For a recent assessment of this pope and his policies: Menache, *Clement V*.

14 See Cuttino, *Diplomatic Adminisitration*, chapter 2. Emden, *Biog. Oxon.* 3, p. 2196, provides a brief account of him.

15 Cuttino, *Diplomatic Administration*, pp. 64–5; Chaplais, *Essays* IV, "Le Duché-Pairie," p. 139 n. 19, citing PRO C47/32/19 m. 1.

16 Cuttino, *Diplomatic Administration*, chapter 3, treats of this process (pp. 62–87) and of its many problems, as well as those of Périgueux (pp. 87–100) and Agen (pp. 100–111).

17 Ibid., pp. 84–5 and 85 n. 1, citing C47/28/2/41; /3/5, 46, 49; 30/3/23, 27–8; 30/1/17; /4/3.

18 Cuttino, *Diplomatic Administration*, p. 13.

19 *Ann. Paul.*, pp. 258, 262; and see above, chapter 4. Chaplais, *Gaveston*, pp. 9–10, argues that Philip "the Fair" would not have given away his twelve-year-old daughter to a sodomite, a view that would militate against the suggestion in *Ann. Paul.* that he preferred the bed of Gaveston to that of his princess. But would

Philip have been sufficiently aware of the degree of the king's infatuation? See above, chapter 2 nn. 87–8, 95.

20 Chaplais, *Diplomatic Practice* pt. 1, 1 p. 56 n. 37, no. 42.

21 *Foedera* 2 i, pp. 101–2, 113, 120–1, 125; Chaplais, *Diplomatic Practice* pt. 1, 2 no. 348 (a) (b) (c); *Gascon Rolls*, nos. 408–13, 419–21, 429–37, 441, 449, 462, 477–8, 494.

22 Chaplais, "Court of Sovereignty," especially pp. 134–40; Kicklighter, "English Gascony and the Parlement of Paris." Only in the next reign did the English king seek to solve the problem by establishing a Court of Sovereignty, prospectively at Saintes (which was recaptured by the French) and then at Bordeaux.

23 The bishoprics of Cahors, Limoges and Périgueux, the Agenais, Quercy and part of Saintonge were to be restored by the terms of the Treaty of Paris 1259. See Chaplais, *Essays* II, "Le Traité de Paris de 1259," pp. 123–4. For the appointment of proctors to resume the process of Montreuil (Thomas de Cobham and Gilbert de Middleton) and of Périgueux (Cobham, Middleton, Walter de Stapeldon and John de Cromwell): idem, *Diplomatic Practice* pt. 1, 2 no. 323, and cf. 252, 367; *Gascon Rolls*, nos. 438–9.

24 Cuttino, *Diplomatic Administration*, p.97; *Gascon Rolls*, no. 494. The treatment of the Jews in the English continental possessions has been regarded as a precedent for their expulsion by Edward I from England in 1290. See the recent study by Mundill, *England's Jewish Solution*.

25 Chaplais, *Essays* IX, "Conflict Franco-Anglais," pp. 280–5.

26 Haines, *Church and Politics*, pp. 11–13; *Treaty Rolls I*, p. 197 n. 1; *Gascon Rolls*, no. 494.

27 *Gascon Rolls*, nos. 438–9.

28 For Weston's distinguished career as a diplomat and his particular involvement with Gascony, which was just beginning at this time, see Emden, *Biog. Oxon.* s.v. For Canterbury see Haines, *Church and Politics*, pp. 4 n. 85, 26 n. 97, 38 n. 64, and for his responsibility for the calendar, *Gascon Calendar*, intro. pp. viii–ix; Cuttino, *Diplomatic Administration*, pp. 121–26; "Henry of Canterbury." He appears to have been a clerk who served Edward before he became king: Tout, *Chapters* 2, pp. 168, 171. Weston, Canterbury and Burton are frequently mentioned in Cuttino, op. cit. index s.v.

29 For the Ferrers-d'Albret dispute: *Gascon Rolls*, nos. 734–5, 834 (Edward's mandate to his envoys, dated London, 4 February 1313, by which time the seneschal had been dead for some months), 1162, 1299. Much later (24 June 1326) instruction was given for the granting of "grace" to d'Albret and his family: *Foedera* 2 i, p. 632.

30 See above, chapter 4 nn. 177, 186.

31 *Gascon Rolls*, nos. 836–41; *Gascon Calendar*, nos. 187–9; Buck, *Stapeldon*, pp. 123–4; Phillips, *Pembroke*, pp. 61–2 citing at nn. 2, 6, Arch. Nat. J. 633 no. 35, J. 918 no. 18. A copy of the latter (for arrangement of a face-to-face meeting) is in the Gascon register BL Cotton MS Julius E. 1, fo. 45^r.

32 *Vita*, pp. 38–9. The chronicler's earnest wish that the king might return safely suggests that his account was written at the time and not subsequently revised.

33 According to Doherty, "Isabella," pp. 41–4, the king and Isabella seem to have been on reasonable terms at this time.

34 *Itinerary EII*, pp. 98–9.

35 See above chapter 4.

36 Phillips, *Pembroke*, p. 63, citing *inter alia Grandes Chroniques* 8, pp. 288–9.

37 *Foedera* 2 i, p. 220; *Gascon Rolls*, nos.1080–81. These letters were intended to be conciliatory Edward I's ordinance of 1285 had threatened to cause a crisis, but with Philip III's death Edward paid a personal visit to his successor, Philip IV, performed homage, and concluded an amicable agreement. Chaplais, *Essays* III "Le Duché-Pairie," pp. 23–5.

38 Doherty, "Isabella," p. 51, citing *Foedera* 2 i, p. 215, BL Cotton MS Julius E.1, fo. 325[r].

39 *CPR 1313–17*, p. 4. Pessagno was assigned the customs throughout the realm and the issues of the vacant archbishopric of Canterbury in order to repay Enguerran de Marigny. He was to continue in the service of Edward III. See Larson, "Payment of Envoys," p. 407, and in general, Fryde, "Antonio Pessagno of Genoa."

40 Doherty, "Isabella," p. 52, citing Bib. Nat. Lat. MS 8504 fos. 1[v]–2[r].

41 *Itinerary EII*, p. 102; *Foedera* 2 i, p. 222. On 1 July 1313 at Pontoise Edward had appointed commissaries to open parliament and to conduct its business: viz. Archbishop Reynolds, the bishop of Bath and Wells (Droxford), and the earls of Gloucester (Gilbert de Clare) and Richmond (Jean de Bretagne). *CPR 1307–13*, pp. 594–5.

42 *Foedera* 2 i, p. 238.

43 *Itinerary EII*, p. 107.

44 *Foedera* 2 i, p. 237; *Parl. Writs* 2 i, pp. 421–3.

45 *Foedera* 2 i, pp. 240, 242–4. For Elias Jonestone see Cuttino, *Diplomatic Administration*, index s.v., and for his accounts ibid., pp. 194–209.

46 TCC R.5 41, fo. 112[v]. This chronicler (or his copyist) has III Kal' March, an error for XIII Kal'; *Ann. Paul.*, p. 275. For other references: Wright, *Reynolds*, p. 368.

47 *Foedera* 2 i, p. 244; *CPR 1313–17*, p. 85; PRO E101/375/9 provides the queen's itinerary; E36/187, p. 53; Doherty, "Isabella," pp. 54–5; Phillips, *Pembroke*, p. 86. The memorandum explaining why the "supplicaciones et querele proponende sunt nomine domine nostre Regine" and the petitions themselves are printed from PRO C47/27/8/31, E30/1530, in an appendix to Brown, "Diplomacy and Domestic Politics," pp. 78–83.

48 Doherty, 'Isabella', pp. 50–1, citing *Chronique de Pays Bas* 2, pp. 138–9; Cordier, "Annales de l'Hôtel de Nesle," p. 46. See also *RHGF* 20 (*Guillelmus de Nangiaco*), p. 607; ibid., 23 (*Chronicon Ste Catherinae*), pp. 408–9, with details of the adulteries; *Scalacronica*, ed Stevenson, p. 137, ed. Maxwell, pp. 45–7. Brown, "Diplomacy, Adultery and Domestic Politics," pp. 53–5, does not accept Isabella's role in revealing the scandal. See above chapter 4, n. 199.

49 TCC R.5 41, fo. 113ᵛ; *Murimuth*, p. 22.

50 See above chapter 6, n. 209.

51 *Ann. Paul.*, p. 277.

52 It is also possible that they tendered Edward's excuses for not coming to the coronation.

53 *York Register Greenfield* i, p. 76: "In civili sapiencia solempniter regendo tam in cismarinis quam ultramarinis partibus famosus ubilibet divulgatus." Cited by Emden, *Biog. Oxon.* s.v. "Pykering." A king's clerk since 1302 when he began his diplomatic work in France. In 1307 he had been one of those negotiating the marriage of Isabella.

54 Buck, *Stapeldon*, pp. 125–6; *Gascon Rolls*, p. 544; *Gascon Calendar*, nos. 1925–6. M. Thomas de Cambridge (Cantebrigg', Cauntebrugge) and John de Benstead were sent to Gascony to raise a subsidy for the Scottish war.

55 SA MS 120, p. 28. He was paid for the period 8 July–30 November 1316 (146 days), principally in London. For much of the term the king was absent, mainly in the North. Jonestone had a further assignment of 27 days between 11 June and 7 July 1317. ibid. p. 50.

56 Chaplais, *Essays* X, "Un message de Jean de Fiennes à Edouard II," pp. 145–8. This includes transcripts of two documents: PRO C81/97/3974, SC8/34/155. Among the clerks specially summoned were Robert Baldock and John Stratford. For Burton's mission 26 November to 6 December 1316 and his summons to Clarendon for 13 February: SA MS 120, p. 44. The question of succession to the French Crown is discussed by Petit, *Charles de Valois*, pp. 166–75. See also Brown, "The Ceremonial of Royal Succession in Capetian France: the Double Funeral of Louis X."

57 *Foedera* 2 i, p. 304: Edward's reply Clipstone, 20 December 1316; *Itinerary EII*, p.148. Meanwhile, John de Benstead and Thomas de Cantebrigg' had left England on 9 November 1315 and were subsequently in the Agenais and Gascony. An account of their proceedings was sent to the king from Bordeaux, 26 January 1316. *Gascon Rolls*, pp. 568–70.

58 SA MS 121, pp. 14–15.

59 *Foedera* 2 i, p. 360; *CCR 1313–18*, p. 622.

60 *Foedera* 2 i, p. 365; *CPR 1317–21*, p. 162, *Treaty Rolls* I, no. 575; SA MS 121, p. 15.

61 The SA MS reads "Norht." (seemingly Northampton), but the court was clearly at Nottingham at that time and much occupied with more immediate matters. *Itinerary EII*, p.171.

62 SA MS 121, pp. 18–20

63 Haines, *Church and Politics*, p. 20.

64 The summonses were dated 24/25 August: *HBC*, p. 554.

65 *Foedera* 2 i, pp. 371, 372–3; *Treaty Rolls* I, nos. 577–8. Nothing of Orleton's movements transpires, indeed they appear to be lost for the time between his sealing of the Treaty of Leake on 9 August and 18 October, when he appears in

London. Meanwhile simultaneous negotiations were in train with the papacy and in Flanders. Antonio de Pessagno was in France, and together with Henry de Canterbury in Gascony. SA MS 121, pp. 16–20.

66 *Liber Epistolaris*, 159 (dated *c.* March 1319) and ibid., 236; *Foedera* 2 i, p. 390.

67 *HBC*, p. 555. Writs of summons were issued on 20 March.

68 *Foedera* 2 i, pp. 390, 395. The alternatives are outlined by Chaplais, *Essays* IV, "Le Duché-Pairie," pp. 151–2.

69 BL Add. MS 17362, fo. 13^r. Orleton's itinerary as so far known shows him to have been at Avignon on 19 June and also on 8 September. Haines, *Church and Politics*, p. 219.

70 Buck, *Stapeldon*, p. 127, citing PRO E159/92 Recorda Trinity m. 7d, for the documents he carried with him.

71 *Treaty Rolls I*, nos. 597ff.; *Foedera* 2 i, pp. 390, 395.

72 For what follows immediately: Chaplais, *Essays* IV, "Le Duché-Pairie," pp. 152–3.

73 On 28 February 1320 the elder Hugh Despenser, Bartholomew Badlesmere and Adam Orleton had been sent with oral messages. Chaplais, *Diplomatic Practice* pt. 1, 1 no. 45; Haines, *Church and Politics*, pp. 23–4 n. 85, citing PRO SC1/32/78–82 (letters of accreditation dated 28 February to various cardinals).

74 BL Add. MS 17362, fo. 12^r.

75 *Ann. Paul.*, p. 289; *Itinerary EII*, p. 197; PRO SC1/45/193. Chaplais, e.g. *Diplomatic Practice* pt. 1, 1 no. 46, gives Brugg's name (Bridges?) as "de Bures," a rendering found in some manuscripts. But see Emden, *Biog. Oxon.* 3 (App.), p. 2156.

76 *Winchester Chartulary*, pp. 62–4 no. 127; 64–5, nos. 128–9.

77 PRO C47/29/9/25.

78 *Ann. Paul.*, pp. 289–90; *Itinerary EII*, p. 200.

79 Haines, *Church and Politics*, pp. 25–6. Natalie Fryde is not quite fair to Edward in suggesting (*Tyranny and Fall*, p. 140) that he was "too preoccupied with the fate of his favourite's lands." Edward was dealing with unbridled lawlessness. Nor is she fair to Orleton who was certainly *not* the king's "enemy" at this time. It could also be said that envoys were at other times kept waiting around on account of more immediate matters.

80 Baker, *Chronicon*, p. 15, alleges that Despenser and Baldock kept details of the French envoys' message from the king, but that after the envoys had gone they suggested that Edward perform homage. Whereupon Andrew de Florencia, acting as notary of the French king, thinking that King Edward did not consider the citation to be lawful, drew up a process for the seizure of Guienne and Ponthieu. This is accepted by Fryde, *Tyranny and Fall*, pp. 140–1, but it is more likely to be a piece of Baker's fanciful invention designed to blacken Despenser and Baldock.

81 They left Dover 28 November 1323 and were back in London on 25 January 1324. *The War of Saint-Sardos*, p. 177 n. 1 citing PRO E403/206 m. 2. For Schor(e)dich (Shoreditch), a king's councillor from 1321 and engaged in diplomatic affairs concerning France and Avignon, both in Edward II's reign and that of his son, see Emden, *Biog. Oxon.*, s.v. "Shordich."

82 *War of Saint-Sardos*, pp. xi–xii. Charles IV knew of the burning of Saint-Sardos on 1 November, but the news took about another three weeks to reach Edward.

83 *War of Saint-Sardos*, introduction pp. xi–xii, 176–9 (no. 167).

84 Ibid., introduction pp. xii, 3–6, 7–11, 15–17, 39–41 (nos. 4–6, 9, 10, 14, 28).

85 Ibid., introduction p. xi, citing at n. 3 PRO SC8/267/13303.

86 Chaplais regarded the postponement as dangerous in that Charles might well have seized Edward's fiefs *pro defectu hominis*, as he eventually did. *War of Saint-Sardos*, introduction p. ix.

87 Ibid. p. 180 n.1; *Foedera* 2 i, p. 547.

88 Ibid., pp. 180–1.

89 Ibid., p. 179.

90 *CPR 1321–24*, p. 349: 14 November 1323.

91 *War of Saint-Sardos*, pp. 27–38 (no. 26).

92 Ibid., pp. 38–9 (no. 27).

93 Ibid., p. 188 n. 1, providing much of the text of PRO C47/30/6/17. A full account of this mission is in Chaplais, *Diplomatic Practice* pt. 1, 1 pp. 103–16 no. 68.

94 Ibid., pp. 42–3 (no. 29): "prietz especialment nostre dit frere qil voille aver regard a nostre personne e de nos enfantz ... e especialment del alliance qe se fit par nostre persone qe tout le munde seet qe ele fu faite pur pees e amur nurir e maintenir entre les deux roiaumes."

95 Eryom was prebendary of Ulleskelf (1322–38): *Le Neve* 6, p. 84, where he is not entitled *magister*.

96 *War of Saint-Sardos*, p. 189 n.1; *CPR 1321–24*, pp. 425–7.

97 *War of Saint-Sardos*, p. 42: "les plus privetz le roi." This description is used in the draft instructions for the queen mentioned above.

98 See Phillips, *Pembroke*, pp. 133–4.

99 Quite apart from his irritation at Edward's infatuation with Gaveston there was his enmity for Enguerran de Marigny, who favoured the English connection, and whose fall and execution in 1315 (*RHGF* 20, *Chroniques de St. Denis*, p. 696) Charles was instrumental in bringing about. For Marigny, who was treated ungratefully much as was Jacques Coeur about a century later (though he escaped with his life), see Favier, *Un Conseiller de Philippe le Bel: Enguerran de Marigny*.

100 Baker, *Chronicon*, p. 15.

101 *War of Saint-Sardos*, p. 190 n. 1.

102 *Foedera* 2 i, p. 561. Segrave died at Bayonne 3 September 1325. See *War of Saint-Sardos*, p. 88 n. 1 citing BL Add. MS 7967, fo. 30; PRO E101/381/14.

103 *War of Saint-Sardos*, pp. 190–1 n. 2, provides details of the sequence of events.

104 Ibid., p. 191 n. 1, citing Gascon Roll 36, m. 30; Haines, *John Stratford*, pp. 150 nn. 161–2.

105 See Haines, *John Stratford*, p. 151 n. 162; Buck, *Stapeldon*, p. 152 n. 167; Taylor, "Judgment of Hugh Despenser," p. 76; *Vita*, pp. 135, 142; CCC MS 174 fo.

147ᵛ, stating that the queen was cut off with twenty shillings a day, which "sore annoyed" her brother. Compare *Brut*, p. 232, where this detail is omitted.

106 Doherty, "Isabella," pp. 101–2 for this (citing PRO E403/201 mm. 14–15) and further details about Isabella's financial state, also Buck, *Stapeldon*, p. 152 nn. 166–8. Charles's council could not conceive how such a move could either benefit the English king or harm his French counterpart: *War of Saint-Sardos*, pp. 130–1.

107 Historia Roffensis, fo. 46ʳ: "prope Grenewych. habuit obviam totam familiam regine de Francia revertentem." The "split household" is discussed by Doherty, "Isabella," p. 127.

108 See Doherty, p. 127, who cites SA MS 122, pp. 46, 49, 52. These instances concerned respectively a clerk of the [king's] chapel, a royal squire, and the marshal of the hall in the royal household.

109 The text of the truce is in *War of Saint-Sardos*, pp. 61–3 (no. 47). It is said to have been concluded by the counsel of Bicknor, and William Weston, described as king's councillors, and by that of John de Wisham, Robert de Wateville, Oliver Ingham and Robert de Echingham, knights.

110 Haines, *Church and Politics*, p. 157; *War of Saint-Sardos*, pp. 74–5 (no. 56).

111 *War of Saint-Sardos*, pp. 75–7 (no. 57).

112 Ibid., pp. 58–61 (nos. 43–6). This letter is addressed: "Chier piere en Dieu" – possibly Baldock, the chancellor, although this form is regularly used to bishops.

113 Ibid., pp. 101–2, 108–9 (nos. 85, 95).

114 Ibid., pp. 69–72 (no. 52). The king was at Porchester for the last three weeks of September and the first of October. *Itinerary EII*, pp. 262–3.

115 Ibid., pp. 118–9 (no. 109).

116 Ibid., pp. 68–9 (no. 51). The archbishop was himself at Mortlake on 31 October, but thereafter at Lambeth. Wright, *Reynolds*, p. 403.

117 *HBC*, p. 555; Parry, *Parliaments*, p. 89.

118 *Itinerary EII*, pp. 263–55.

119 This document (from PRO E30/1582) was printed in *Rot. Parl. Inediti*, pp. 94–8, as pertaining to the June Parliament of 1325, also held at Westminster, and mentioned below. Chaplais has produced cogent reasons for regarding this as an error: *War of Saint-Sardos*, pp. 95–8.

120 *War of Saint-Sardos*, p. 89 (no. 71).

121 *Ann. Paul.*, p. 308; Worcester Register Cobham, fo. 96ʳ. See also *Foedera* (H) 2 ii, pp. 109, 118, 120; *Treaty Rolls I* (from PRO C76/10), pp. 246–48 (no. 638).

122 BL Egerton MS 2814; PRO E101/381/4, cited in *War of Saint-Sardos*, p. 192 n. 1. For what follows see Haines, *John Stratford*, pp. 150–55.

123 *Foedera* 2 i, p. 579; *Lettres secrètes Jean XII*, nos. 2293, 2297–8, 2300ff.; *CPL 1305–42*, pp. 465–6; Worcester Register Cobham, fo. 96ʳ (edition, p. 173). See chapter 6, p. 157, for other details of this papal mission.

124 Details of the threats against him as he attempted to join nobles and prelates and

to stay for that purpose in the London house of the Franciscans are in Orleton's fire-damaged letter: BL Cotton MS Vitellius E. IV 9.

125 *War of Saint-Sardos*, pp. 192–4 (no. 167). No. 167 details the lengthy negotiations conducted between 17 August 1323 and 3 May 1325.

126 That the king was at Langley on the twelfth is not supported by *Itinerary EII*, p. 267. He would appear to have been at Melbourne in Derbyshire and probably not at Langley until 22 January. However, the calculation of expenses for 286 days (see text and next note) is accurate. Stratford's summary oral report on behalf of his colleagues is illustrated in Chaplais, *English Diplomatic Practice* pt. 2, pl. 14 (from PRO E30/1535). See also ibid. pt. 1, no. 106 (b) and p. 432 n. 61.

127 These details, as well as others concerning the journeys of the other envoys, are in *War of Saint-Sardos*, pp. 181–2 n. 1 from PRO E101/309/28. See also *CPR 1321–24*, pp. 339, 403–4.

128 PRO E403/ 206, m. 10; /207/m. 4 ; *Foedera* 2 i, pp. 545–6.

129 He had been arrested and imprisoned in the Châtelet in Paris on 21 December 1323. *War of Saint-Sardos*, p. 6 (no. 7) from PRO SC1/34/95. For his name and those of other proctors see lists in Kicklighter, "English Gascony and the Parlement," App. pp. 131–36.

130 *War of Saint-Sardos*, pp. 182–4.

131 ibid., no. 124; Chaplais, *Diplomatic Practice* pt. 1, no. 153 (a) (b). The bishop complained that prior to his leaving England he had not been informed of the summons to Edward to perform homage to Charles IV.

132 *Vita*, pp. 135–6; TCC MS R.5 41, fo. 120ʳ. Compare *Murimuth*, p. 42, who mentions only Edmund of Woodstock, the earl of Kent, who was already there, and says that the duke's forces put up as much resistance as possible. *Foedera* (H) 2 ii, pp. 134–5 etc. More precise details can be gathered from PRO E101/16/37, /40/1,3; /17/3, /381/4; BL Add. MS 7967, fo. 17ᵛ, cited in *War of Saint-Sardos*, pp. 101 n. 1, 210 nn. 1–2.

133 *War of Saint-Sardos*, pp. 207–14 (nos. 169–7).

134 See Chaplais, *Diplomatic Practice* pt. 1, 2 note at pp. 473–81.

135 Ibid., p. 130 (no. 124): report of the bishops of Norwich and Winchester (Stratford), and of the earl of Richmond. The three other points raised by Charles were: the failure of Edmund of Woodstock to keep his agreement (La Réole) though it was allegedly favourable to the English side, the English king's sheltering of those banished from France, even appointing them to office in Guienne, and the removal, even imprisonment, of Queen Isabella's entourage.

136 *War of Saint-Sardos*, pp. 109–10 (no. 96); Chaplais, *Diplomatic Practice* pt. 1, 2 no. 253.

137 *War of Saint-Sardos*, pp. 140–2, 214–17 – recital of negotiations 22 May 1325 (nos. 132, 178); *Foedera* 2 ii, pp. 124–6; Chaplais, *Diplomatic Practice* pt. 1, 2 nos. 253–4 and p. 502 n. 79. For some background to policy with respect to Aragon and Castile see Goodman, "England and Iberia in the Middle Ages."

138 In 1320 marriages with the young Edward and Thomas of Brotherton, Edward

II's half brother, had been mooted. See Chaplais, *Diplomatic Practice* pt. I, I
nos. 47, 55, 58.

139 Joan was born 5 July 1321, she was to marry David Bruce in 1328.

140 *Foedera* 2 i, pp. 548–9, 573, 585–7, 589–9; *CPR 1324–27*, p. 104; *Acta Aragonensia* I, pp. 499–500 (dated 1324 instead of 1322); *War of Saint-Sardos*, pp.
230 –1, 275–7 (nos. 196, App. V, 1–3).

141 *War of Saint-Sardos*, pp. 127–8 (no. 122), 134 n.1, 135 n.3. For Pessagno, an
accomplished financier, see Fryde, "Antonio Pessagno of Genoa."

142 *Foedera* 2 i, pp. 591–2; *Murimuth*, p. 43; Baker, *Chronicon*, pp. 17–18.

143 They are called the earls of Winchester and Gloucester [*sic*]. The elder Despenser
was made earl in 1322. The younger Despenser had aspirations, but he was never
earl of Gloucester, despite his possessions in the region. The title was dormant
between 1314 and Hugh d'Audley's creation in 1337.

144 Baker, *Chronicon*, p. 19. A Canterbury chronicler points out that the younger
Despenser had had reason to flee from France on an earlier occasion when he
had secretly crossed the Channel in the habit of the abbot of Langdon. He was
forced to return to England: "Parisium pervenit, sed timens pelli sue et Almer-
icum comitem de Penebrok qui tunc ibi erat quod aliqua de eo sinistra loquebatur
in curia regis Francie furtive recessit ad mare." TCC R.5 41, fo. 115^v. The French
Brut is precise on the matter, suggesting that a ship was all ready for the king to
board, but the younger Despenser feared "les grauntz de la terre et auxi de cote la
commune fist graunt dolour et auxi se pleint pitousement ou Roi et dist qe sil
passat outre il serreit mis a mal mort en sa absence." CUL Gg. I. 15, fo. 189^v.

145 *Chronicon*, pp. 16–18.

146 *Vita*, pp. 134–5.

147 TCC R.5 41, fo. 120^v: "pacem non posse nisi per eam tam cito reformari."

148 Dunheved was made a papal chaplain 16 September 1325 when conventional
attributes are ascribed to him: "Religionis zelus, morum decor, vite puritas, litterarum sciencia, et alia virtutum merita." Vatican Archives Reg. Aven. 24, fo. 40^r
(no. vii). He remained a firm supporter of Edward II until his own death.

149 *Lanercost*, p. 254, has: "Ipsi etiam instigaverant regem." However, it is uncertain
who were intended to be the subjects (the Despensers?); ostensibly "ipsi" would
refer to Baldock, Dunheved and his accompanying religious.

150 Ibid. At p. 260 the chronicler mentions this a second time in the context of Dunheved's attempts to liberate Edward II and to reinstate him as king.

151 *War of Saint-Sardos*, pp. 195–6 (no. 167).

152 Ibid., pp. 195, 198 (no. 167).

153 For the queen's itinerary see Hunter, "Journal of Queen Isabella," pp. 245ff.; *War
of Saint-Sardos*, App. 3, pp. 267–79. The suggestion, Fryde, *Tyranny and Fall*, p.
147, that the queen was unduly dilatory with the business in hand overlooks the
details of negotiations which merely culminated on the last day of May, the day
after, she says, that Isabella first met her brother.

154 "Les messages nostre seint' piere le pape qi touz jours estoient presentz es

dites busoignes et bien et dilegeaument se ount portez." *War of Saint-Sardos*, p. 199.

155 *Foedera* 2 1, p. 597; *War of Saint-Sardos*, pp. 199–200: report from Bishop Stratford and William Ayrminne from Poissy 31 March 1325.

156 Historia Roffensis, fo. 44^v: "multas machinas contra regem procurans reginam non facere pacem." He does, however, date the Westminster Parliament to 7 July [1325] rather than 25 June.

157 The king was at Beaulieu Abbey between 4 and 27 April 1325. *Itinerary EII*, p. 270.

158 The various documents are collected in *War of Saint-Sardos*, pp. 198–207. The executor of William of Oterhampton, responsible for royal provisioning at Portsmouth, claimed allowance for men-at-arms and sailors sent to Gascony between 8 March 1325 and 16 July following. *CMRE*, p. 307.

159 *Foedera* 2 i, p. 599.

160 *Foedera* 2 i, pp. 601–2; Chaplais, *Diplomatic Practice* pt. 2, pl. 15–16: respectively the English version of the articles of agreement and the English ratification.

161 Ibid., 2 i, pp. 602–3; *Treaty Rolls* 1, pp. 259–64 (nos. 660–2); *Lettres secrètes Jean XII*, no. 2536; Chaplais, *Diplomatic Practice* pt. 1, 2 no. 300 (a) (b) (c)

162 Ayrminne is recorded to have reached the queen on 18 May (*War of Saint-Sardos*, App. 3, p. 267). The Rochester chronicler states that at a Westminster Parliament convoked for 7 July (Translation of Blessed Thomas) – clearly an error – the king, the younger Despenser, and Chancellor Baldock explained how Ayrminne had been given by the king "potestatem omnimodam ad tractandum terminandum consenciendum et concedendum de terra Vasconie et ad faciendum omnia sicuti et rex presens fuisset," together with the bishops of Winchester (Stratford), Norwich (Salmon) and Exeter (Stapeldon), but that the terrified Stapeldon had fled to England. The chronicler is erratic in his chronology; Stapeldon's flight came towards the end of September, but Dene goes on to detail happenings in the parliament of 25 June, followed by Stapeldon's removal from office. Historia Roffensis, fos. 44^v–5^r.

163 Historia Roffensis, fo. 45^r: "Rex Anglie congregatis in parliamento consiluit an procuratorium revocare debuit, quod facere non potuit, vel procuratoris factum confirmare, vel pro homagio faciendo transfretare, cui finaliter consultum fuit quod transfretaret, et sic dissolutum est parliamentum." The *Vita*, pp. 138–9, added that unless the king performed homage Gascony would be seized and those concerned (*nos omnes*) accused of treason.

164 Ibid.; *Vita*, p. 139.

165 Historia Roffensis, fo. 45^v. This account, taken from the chronicle, the author of which was in regular personal contact with the bishop, is particularly illuminating. That in TCC R.5 41, fo. 120^v–21^r, is somewhat different. According to this the king had every intention of going but the king of France suggested that he might like to send his son instead. This is not very convincing. The response

awaited was one to the English envoys' suggestion. "Responsum a suis qui erant in curia Francie expectabat. Habitoque responso ad Dovor. pervenit et ex communi consensu episcoporum et comitum diffinitum est quod rex mare transiret et homagium faceret regi Francie pro terris suis. Rex autem precepit milites suos et familiam suam cum victualibus suis mare transire, habuitque in proposito suo mare transisse. Interim rex Francie scripsit regi Anglie per litteras suas patentes quod si ipse venire non potest filium suum primogenitum Edwardum nomine mitteret et ab eo homagium pro terris Vasconie ac eciam pro aliis in regno suo libenter acciperet. Similiter illud consulerunt nuncii regis Anglie qui erant in partibus illis ut filium suum mitteret ad vitandum pericula que possent evenire."

166 *Foedera* 2 i, p. 606. Chaplais, *Essays* IV, "Le Duché-Pairie," p. 136, generously suggests that the evidence is insufficient to assume that Edward was feigning but that the malady, if such it was, came "fort à point."

167 The various problems inherent in such an arrangement were examined at length by the lawyers. *War of Saint-Sardos*, pp. 245–7 (no. 215).

168 *Treaty Rolls* 1, pp. 256–7 (nos. 654–5).

169 Ibid., pp. 258–9 (no. 659). In 1322 a marriage had been mooted between Prince Edward and a daughter of Charles of Valois. Chaplais, *Diplomatic Practice* pt. 2, pl. 12(b).

170 *Treaty Rolls* 1, p. 258 (no. 658). See Haines, *John Stratford*, pp. 158–61 (and ibid., chapter 3), for further details of the bishop's participation in continental affairs.

171 PRO SC1/32/101 (notification to the duchy of the grant); *CPR 1324–27*, pp. 173–4; *Foedera* 2 i, pp. 607–8: Dover 10 September; Chaplais, *Diplomatic Practice* pt. 1, 1 no. 49 and ibid., pp. 68–9 nn.

172 *War of Saint-Sardos*, p. 241 (no. 211); Chaplais, *Essays* IV, "Le Duché-Pairie," p. 157.

173 *Foedera* 2 i, p. 609; *Itinerary EII*, p.276.

174 *War of Saint.-Sardos*, pp. 241–2 (no. 212), "emancipatus seu liberatus a patria potestate et factus major annis et habilis ad regendum, gubernandum et administrandum terram."

175 The Rochester chronicler is scathing about the appointment, considering it to have been a reward for acting for the French king against the English one. Historia Roffensis, fo. 45ʳ.

176 *War of Saint-Sardos*, pp. 243–5 (no. 213) and p. 269 (Isabella's itinerary).

177 Ibid., p. 249 (no. 216).

178 *Rochester Register Hethe*, pp. 356–9; Lincoln Register Burghersh 5, fo. 384ᵛ; Wright, *Reynolds*, pp. 57–8 (no. 70).

179 *War of Saint-Sardos*, p. 277 n. 1, from PRO KB27/265 Trinity 19 Edw. II, Rex m. 23d; *Foedera* 2 i, p. 622; *Diplomatic Practice* pt. 1, 1 no. 185 and p. 335 n.

180 Both Historia Roffensis, fo. 46ᵛ, and *Vita*, pp. 140–41, give details. Grassi, "William Airmyn and the Bishopric of Norwich" provides a reasonable defence

of his conduct. See also Smith, *Episcopal Appointments*, pp. 41–5; *Foedera* 2 i, pp. 641–2; *Lettres secrètes de Jean XXII*, nos. 2535, 2544.

181 Historia Roffensis, fo. 46ᵛ: "Valde conquestus est dictus H[ugo] de Spenser episcopo [Hethe] de domino W[illelmo] Norwycensi episcopo quod regem tradiderat Anglie et ideo factus est episcopus, asserens quod rex Anglie non habuisset parem [interlineated] in diviciis si regina et episcopus Norwycensis et eorum complices discordiam inter reges non suscitassent."

182 *Foedera* 2 i, p. 632; Haines, *John Stratford*, p. 166.

183 *Foedera* 2 ii, pp. 700–1, 703.

184 PRO C47/29/10 no. 21. He claimed expenses for 365 days.

185 The chronological arrangement is not easy to follow at this point in the chronicle. The parliament is said to have been about the time of the Purification (2 February) in London. In fact it met at Westminster on 9 February in 1329. *HBC*, p. 556. However, Orleton and Ayrminne's embassy set out in February 1330, in other words just after the Purification – but in the year following. Parliament in 1330 met at Winchester on 11 March. Haines, *Church and Politics*, pp. 31–2.

186 Philip, son of Charles of Valois, succeeded as king of France and Navarre, following a brief regency, on 1 April 1328. He was crowned on 29 May. Baker, *Chronicon*, pp. 36–9, has a lengthy section on the iniquity of Charles, his unpleasant death, news of which was brought to Edward II on 30 December 1325 (SA 122, p. 45), and on the succession to the French Crown to the detriment of the English king "quem [Philippus] scivit fuisse de iure." One version of the *Chronicon* (pp. 39–40 n. 13) retails the story of Charles [*sic*], count of Evreux (Averoys), who on Philip's accession, claimed Navarre through his wife Jeanne, daughter of his suffocated mother-in-law, Margaret. To prove her legitimacy by ordeal Jeanne was thrown nude to hungry lions who "ut filiam regiam venerantes non tetigerunt."

187 Haines, *Church and Politics*, p. 31; Perroy, *Hundred Years War*, pp. 80–1. According to *CPMR.*, p. 78, the decision to send the two prelates was taken at the parliament which met on 24 April at Northampton.

188 Pirenne, "La première tentative."

189 Chaplais, *Essays* IV, "Le Duché-Pairie," pp. 158–9.

190 Historia Roffensis, fo. 55ᵛ. "Et quia Norwycensis episcopus tempore regis patris in curia Francie potestate quam habuit de rege Anglie male usus est ac male regem inbrigavit, licet in eodem parliamento de illa briga se excusare nitebatur per reginam regis matrem, et ipsa regina sic responderit: *Ego sum femina, quid scivi vel facere potui cum sim iuris ignara, et tu clericus et nuncius regis discrecius egisse debuisti, tibi et non michi est imputandum, igitur sicut malum in Francia seminasti sic et metes.* Et sic missus est cum episcopo Wygorniensi ad curiam Francie ad sanandum quod wlneravit."

191 Chaplais, *Essays* IV, "Le Duché-Pairie," p. 158.

192 *Foedera* 2 ii, pp. 760, 765; Déprez, *Les préliminaires*, pp. 45–6; Haines, *John Stratford*, pp. 207–8; Stones, "Geoffrey le Scrope," p. 16: this veteran envoy was

at the preliminary negotiations at Abbeville and was present at the homage ceremony.

193 For Walwayn and Shordich (Shoreditch) see *Biog. Oxon.* 3, App. s.v. The latter was DCL and subsequently knighted.

194 *Foedera* 2 ii, p. 778: 5 February 1330.

195 Ibid. pp. 791–2, 794; Déprez, *Les préliminaires*, pp. 57–8 ff.; Haines, *Church and Politics*, pp. 32–3.

196 *Foedera* 2 ii, pp. 813, 815–6; Cuttino, *Diplomatic Administration*, pp. 15–16, *Winchester Chartulary*, pp. 62–5, nos. 127–9. Haines, *Church and Politics*, pp. 33–4; *John Stratford*, pp. 218–20.

197 *Les préliminaires*, p. 73. See Haines, *John Stratford*, pp. 218–19.

198 Historia Roffensis, fo. 57^v, emphasizes the foolhardiness and irregularity of this journey: "Rex cum paucis videlicet undecim equitibus [scarcely 15 according to Murimuth] cum malis retro sellas [*sic*] absque consilio vel consensu parium et communitatis regni occulte mare transiens ad regem Francie, honorifice est receptus, sed ab omnibus regnicolis Francie et Anglie pro modo et periculo eundi plurimum vituperatus." Compare *Murimuth*, p. 63, which has "cum mantellis et sine harnesiis."

199 Déprez, *Les préliminaires*, pp. 75–7; Haines, *John Stratford*, pp. 219–20.

200 *Murimuth*, p. 148.

201 *Chronicon*, p. 75.

CHAPTER TWELVE

 1 See, in particular, Prestwich, *Edward I*, chapters 19–20.

 2 Doherty, "Isabella," p. 104, discusses this situation.

 3 *Bridlington*, p. 32.

 4 *Vita*, p. 143. The translation from the Latin is mine.

 5 These are discussed cursorily by Prestwich, *Edward I*, and in detail by Trabut-Cussac, "L'Administration anglaise en Gascogne," especially pp. 110–37.

 6 Henry II, son of Geoffrey of Anjou, married Eleanor of Aquitaine. Their son John married secondly Isabella of Angoulême. Their issue, Henry III, married Eleanor of Provence, whose son was Edward I. Edward married firstly Eleanor of Castile, whose last child was Edward II, secondly Margaret of France.

 7 Prestwich, *Edward I*, p. 336; Chaplais, *Essays* IV, "Le Duché–Pairie," pp. 137, 141–2.

 8 Smith, "Edward II and the Allegiance of Wales," especially pp. 140–45; Griffiths, *Principality of Wales* I, pp. 97, 102.

 9 Ibid., p. 165; *Murimuth*, p. 49. The chronicler says that he was captured with the aid of Welshmen in whom he had trusted, who did not go unpaid (*non sine pecuniae interventu*). There is a biographical note on Rhys in Griffiths, *Principality of Wales* I, pp. 97–8. He had been implicated in the 1321–22 revolt as a follower of Roger d'Amory. As a result a large part of his lands fell to the younger Despenser.

10 There is no need to take at face value the panegyric sent to the pope: "dum rebus agebat humanis, honestus extitit, affectabilis et benignus, justus, providus et fidelis, pie compationis, et misericorditer intelligens super pauperes et afflictos, ac Divini nominis more succensus, et in solidate fidei confirmatus, quadam floruit praerogativa constantiae singularis." *Foedera* 2 ii, p. 695: 29 February 1327.

11 Maddicott, "Thomas of Lancaster and Sir Robert Holland," especially p. 455.

12 Gibbs, "Battle of Boroughbridge," pp. 223–4: "It will be observed that of the forty-seven persons above enumerated who engaged in open rebellion, only ten suffered the death penalty, and having regard to the times and the very serious nature of the rebellion it is clear that no unusual or unnecessary severity was exercised."

13 SA MS 122, pp. 92–3.

14 Saul, "The Kingship of Richard II," pp. 37–57, especially 49–50.

15 Details of Richard's efforts to secure his great-grandfather's canonization are summarized in *Diplomatic Correspondence*, p. 210, and a letter to Pope Urban dated by the editor 1385X1389 is printed at pp. 62–3 (no. 95). See also Given-Wilson, "Richard II, Edward II," pp. 568–9 and n. 1, containing bibliography. Richard held a parliament at the abbey in 1378. Representations (subsequently restored) of his badge, the white hart, were painted on the Norman pillars that flank Edward's tomb and which were modified to accommodate it. For an overall context see Vauchez, *Sainthood in the Later Middle Ages*, especially index s.v. "Edward II."

Bibliography

MANUSCRIPT SOURCES

Berkeley Castle

These MSS were examined at the Record Office in Gloucester thanks to the kindness of D.J.H. Smith, County Archivist for Gloucestershire and honorary archivist of Berkeley Castle.

Cambridge

Corpus Christi College MS 174. Version of English *Brut* chronicle called the "Peterhouse Chronicle." Used by Barnes in his *Edward III* and by Caxton, *Chronicles of England*, London 1480

Trinity College Cambridge MS R.5 41. Canterbury-based chronicle, continuator of Gervase, containing elements from the Merton *Flores*,with which it is at many points identical

University Library:

Dd.VII 14   Misc. including "Sententia lata super Petrum de Gavestone" (fo. 207)

Ee. IV. 32   English *Brut* (see also Ee. IV, 31)

Ee.V. 31   Register of Prior Henry de Eastry

Ff.II.26   English *Brut*. (Contains material not in the *Brut* printed by Brie q.v., including the text of a letter sent to the mayor and citizens of London from Baldock on 6 October.)

Gg.I.15   French *Brut* (ending 1326). See London, British Library, Cotton MS. Tiberius A. VI.

Hh.VI.9   English *Brut*. (Includes the letter sent by Queen Isabella at cap. 213, fos. 101–2, and a detailed account of Edmund of Woodstock's "treason" at cap. 225, fos. 110^V–12^V.)

Canterbury

CATHEDRAL LIBRARY
Register I

Durham

UNIVERSITY LIBRARY
M.Phil. thesis; D. A Harding, "The Regime of Isabella and Mortimer 1326–30,"
   1985

Hereford

CATHEDRAL LIBRARY
MS P.5 XII, fos. 99^V–107^V Contains prophecies
1373 A-H,   Orleton's "defence brief"

London

BRITISH LIBRARY
Add. MSS.
 (inter alios)
7967   Contains details of Gascon affairs
9951   Wardrobe Book 14 Edward II (1320–21)
17362   Wardrobe Book 13 Edward II (1318–20)
35114   Wardrobe receipt book 17 Edward II (1323–24)
38006   Wardrobe account of Robert de Tong, treasurer of Eleanor, daughter of
        Edward II

Cotton MSS:
   Claudius A. V, Peterborough chronicle
   Cleopatra A. XVI, Westminster based chronicle
   Cleopatra C. III, extracts from Dunmow Priory chronicle
   Cleopatra D. III, Hales [Hailes] Abbey chronicle. Also Harleian MS 3725 Cleopatra
      D. IX, "Fragmenta de bellis et causis bellorum civilium tempore Edward II," fos.
      81^V–6^r. (Mini-chronicle 1295–1321 at fos. 83^r–5^r: printed Haskins, "Chronicle of
      the Civil Wars," q.v.)
   Domitian A. XII, anonymous chronicle
   Faustina A. VIII
   Faustina B. V, Historia Roffensis. Probably he work of William Dene, archdeacon of
      Rochester
   Galba E. IV, Henry of Eastry's register
   Julius A. I (item 6), French chronicle (Pipewell) with other material from Edward's

reign at fos. 51–63. (See Clarke, "Committees of Estates," pp. 44–5, and Richardson, "Affair of the Lepers," q.v.)

Julius E. I, register of Gascon material

Nero C. VIII, Wardrobe Book 9 Edward III 1310–11; Queen Isabella's 1311–12

Nero D. VII, St Albans Book of Benefactors

Nero D. X, Trevet's chronicle. (Attributed apparently by Sir Robert Cotton, but the name "fratris Nicholai Trivett" occurs on fo. 113 when Murimuth's chronicle takes over and there is a warning about the latter's eccentric dating from Michaelmas (*Murimuth*, introuction p. xx.)

Tiberius A. VI, fos. 168–84 (Similar to the long version of French *Brut* and printed, partly in translation, by Hearne, *Collectanea* 2, pp. 455–70, as the "Pakington chronicle.")

Vespasian B. XI. Hagnaby chronicle at fols. 1–61. (Extract in Stones, "English chronicles and Scotland," pp. 345–8.)

Vespasian C. XIII (fo. 60$^{\text{r-v}}$ has Spanish negotiations)

Vespasian F. VII

Vitellius E. IV 9. Mutilated fragment of letter sent by Bishop Orleton to the pope.

Egerton MS 2814 Wardrobe Roll 18–19 Edward II (1324–25)

Egerton Roll 8724 (lists Badlesmere's retainers)

Harleian MSS:

155, so-called Chronicle of Thomas Rudborne, monk of Winchester

530, miscellaneous extracts, including some from Dunmow Priory

636, Polistoire of Christ Church, Canterbury

655, containing a chronicle which is a variant of the *Polychronicon*

1240, at fo. 35ff. (xxxvii) charges against Mortimer and their reversal, s.v. Wiggemore

2901 (Liber Regalis)

Royal 12 D. XI, fo. 21^{r}. (Copy of letter of William Montacute thanking the pope for promotion of his brother Bishop Simon de Montacute.)

Stowe MS 553, Wardrobe book 16 Edward II (1322–23)

INSTITUTE OF HISTORICAL RESEARCH

MA theses:

K. Edwards, "The Personnel and Political Activities of the English Episcopate during the Reign of Edward II," University of London 1937. (Summarised in *BIHR* 16 (1938–39), pp. 117–19.)

G. A. Usher, "Adam de Orleton." University of Wales 1953

R. Douch, "The Career, Lands and Family of William Montague, Earl of Salisbury, 1301- 44," University of London 1951. (Summarised in *BIHR* 24 (1951), pp. 85–8.)

Ph.D. theses:

J. F. Lydon, "Ireland's Participation in the Military Activities of English Kings in the Thirteenth and early Fourteenth Centuries," London 1955

E. Pole-Stuart, "Some Aspects of the Political and Administrative History of Gascony, 1303–27," London 1927

S.L. Waugh, "The Confiscated Lands of Contrariants in Gloucestershire and Herefordshire in 1322: an Economic and Social Study," London 1975

LAMBETH LIBRARY

MS 99 Vitae Archiepiscoporum q.v.

MS 242

MS 1213, contains Orleton's *Apologia* or *Responsiones* printed by Twysden in *Historiae Anglicanae* q.v. (Extracts from this manuscript are also in the edition of Exeter Register Grandisson, vol. 3, Appendix, from the Winchester Cartulary.)

PUBLIC RECORD OFFICE

Chancery

C47	Chancery Miscellanea. Bundles 27–32 Diplomatic Documents
C49	Parliamentary and Council Proceedings
C53	Charter Rolls
C54	Close Rolls
C62	Liberate Rolls
C66	Patent Rolls
C70	Roman Rolls
C71	Scotch Rolls
C76	Treaty Rolls
C81	Chancery Warrants for the Great Seal

Common Pleas

CP25	Feet of Fines
CP40	De Banco Rolls

Duchy of Lancaster

DL41	Miscellanea

Exchequer

E13	Plea Rolls
E30	Diplomatic Documents
E36	Wardrobe Books
E39	Scottish Documents
E101	Accounts Various
E142	Ancient Extents
E159	Memoranda Rolls (King's Remembrancer)
E163	Exchequer Miscellanea
E175	Parliamentary and Council Proceedings
E313	Letters Patent (Original)
E352	Chancellor's Rolls (Pipe Office)
E358	Miscellaneous Accounts
E368	Memoranda Rolls (Lord Treasurer's Remembrancer)

E372   Pipe Rolls
E401   Receipt Rolls
E403   Issue Rolls (Pells of Issue), /1-/1692
E404   Privy Seals and Warrants for Issue
Just. Itinerant
J[ust].1   Assize Rolls
King's Bench
KB27   Coram Rege Rolls
Special Collections
SC1   Ancient Correspondence
SC6   Ministers' and Receivers' Accounts
SC7   Papal Bulls
SC8   Ancient Petitions
SC10   Parliamentary Proxies
SC11   Rentals and Surveys
SC12   Rentals and Surveys

SOCIETY OF ANTIQUARIES

SA MS 119, wardrobe book 28 Edward I, 1299–1300 (see *Liber Quotidianus Garder-obae,* ed. J. Topham)

SA MS 120, wardrobe book 10 Edward II, 1316–17 (see *Archaeologia* 26 (1836), pp. 318–45): Roger de Northburgh, keeper, Thomas Charlton contrarotulator

SA MS 121, wardrobe book 11 Edward II, 1317–18 (*Liber cotidianus* of Thomas Charlton contrarotulator)

SA MS 122, chamber account 18–20 Edward II (1324–26)

(The above MSS are cited by the modern pagination)

WESTMINSTER ABBEY

WAM, no. 20344, Br Beby's expense account

Oxford

BODLEIAN LIBRARY

MS Lat. hist. c.4, 5 Roll of household accounts of Prince Edward of Carnarvon 1305–6 and of Edward II 1308–9

MS Lat. hist. d. 4 MS volume belonging to St Edmundsbury (14th cent.with extracts from *Murimuth, Flores,* and material included in *Ann. Paul.*)

MS Top. Devon d. 5, Cartulary of Newenham Abbey (contains epitaph for Bp. Stapeldon)

Ashmole MS 860 (contains a summary of the Sherburn indenture)

Bodley MS 956, Lichfield chronicle

Douce MS 128, French *Brut*

Holkham MS Misc. 29, material concerning court of King's Bench

Laud MS Misc. 529, Evesham version of Higden's *Polychronicon*

Lyell MS 17, French *Brut*

Rawlinson B 152 Chronicle (version of *Historia Anglicana*)

Tanner MS 90 (contains Botetourt's letters patent in support of the earl of Warwick's capture of Gaveston)

Tanner MS 197, wardrobe book 1311–12

D.Phil. theses:

R. Highfield, "The Relations between the English Crown 1349–1378 – from the death of Archbishop Stratford to the Outbreak of the Great Schism," 1951

J.R. Maddicott, "Thomas of Lancaster 1307–22," 1967

P.[C.] Doherty, "Isabella, Queen of England 1296–1330," 1977

Winchester

WINCHESTER CATHEDRAL LIBRARY

Winchester Cartulary, vol. 2, and see *Chartulary of Winchester Cathedral*, ed. Goodman

France

Montpellier

ARCHIVES DÉPARTMENTALES D'HÉRAULT

Liber A, Cartulaire de Maguelone

Germany

Göttingen

UNIVERSITY LIBRARY

MS Göttingen Hist. 740 (microfilm), Castleford Chronicle. (See below "*Castleford's Chronicle*" ed. C.D. Eckhardt.)

Italy

VATICAN ARCHIVES

In general see L.E. Boyle, *A Survey of the Vatican Archives and of its Medieval Holdings*, Toronto 1972; C. Burns, *Sources of British History In the Instrumenta Miscellanea of the Vatican Archives*, Archivum Historiae Pontificae 9, Rome 1971

RV   Registra Avenionensia

RV   Registra Vaticana

IM   Instrumenta Miscellanea (for no. 5947 see Roberts, *Edward II, the Lords Ordainers and Piers Gaveston's Jewels and Horses, 1312–13*, CS 3rd. ser. 41, Miscellany 15 (1929)

PRINTED SOURCES

Reference

Cappelli, A. ed., *Cronologia, Cronografia e Calendario Perpetuo*, Milan 1983

Carte, T., *Catalogue des Rolles gascons, normans et françois*, 2 vols. London 1743

Corson, Livingston, *A Finding List of Political Poems referring to English Affairs of the XIIIth and XIVth Centuries*, New York 1910 rep. 1970

Gams, P.B.B., *Series Episcoporum*, Ratisbon 1873

Gough, H., *The Itinerary of Edward I, 1272–1307*, 2 vols. Paisley 1900 and see Safford

Graves, E.B., *Bibliography of English History to 1485*, Oxford 1975

Hallam, E.M., *The Itinerary of Edward II and his Household, 1307–1328, L&I Soc.* vol. 211 (1984)

Hardy, T.D., *Descriptive Catalogue of Materials Relating to the History of Great Britain and Ireland* (to 1327), RS 3 vols. London 1862–71

Harvey, J., *English Mediaeval Architects, a Biographical Dictionary Down to 1550*, n.p. 1987

Knowles, D., Hadcock, R.N., *Medieval Religious Houses*, London 1953

Livingstone, M., *A Guide to the Public Records of Scotland*, Edinburgh 1905 (Supplementary accession 1905–1946, in *SHR* 26 (1947), pp. 26–46.)

Lydon, J. F., P. McNeill, R. Nicholson ed., *An Historical Atlas of Scotland c. 400–1600*, St. Andrews 1975

Midmer, R., *English Mediaeval Monasteries (1066–1540)*, Athens Georgia 1979

Mirot, L., Déprez, E., *Les ambassades anglaises pendant la guerre de cent ans; catalogue chronologique, 1327–1450, BEC*59 (1898), pp. 550–77; 60 (1899), pp.177–214; 61 (1900), 20–5

Molinier, A., *Les Sources de l'Histoire de France*, vol. 3 *Les Capétiens (1180–1328)*, Paris 1903

Parry, C.H., *The Parliaments and Councils of England*, London 1839

Pirenne, H., *Bibliographie de l'histoire de Belgique*, 3rd edn Bruxelles 1931

Pollock, S.F, Maitland, F.W., *The History of English Law*, 2 vols. Cambridge 1952

Renouard, Y., *Gascon Rolls preserved in the Public Record Office 1307–1317*, London 1962

Safford, E. ed., *The Itinerary of Edward I*, parts 1–3, *L&I Soc.* vols. 103, 132, 135, 1974, 1976–7, and see Gough

Ughelli, F., *Italia Sacra sive de Episcopis Italiae*, 2nd edn 10 vols. in 9 Venice 1717–22

Venn, J. and J.A., *Alumni Cantabrigiensis*, 5 vols. Cambridge 1922–53

Vulgate Bible, see Colleections of Documents s.v. "*Biblia Sacra*"

Walther, H., *Carmina Medii Aevi Posterioris Latina, Lateinische Sprichwörter und Sentenzen des Mittelalters*, 5 vols + 2 of indices Göttingen 1963–9

Collections of Documents, Calendars and Catalogues

NOTE: Printed episcopal registers printed prior to about 1981 are readily identifiable in D. M. Smith, *Guide to Bishops' Registers of England and Wales*, London 1981, and in the footnotes here are identified merely by the name of the diocese and bishop: e.g. *Hereford Reg. Swinfield* (in Italics for printed registers, otherwise Romans). Similarly, editions of papal registers can be identified in L.E. Boyle, *A Survey of the Vatican Archives*, Toronto 1972. Volumes of the *Victoria History of the Counties of England* are referred to as merely as *VCH* with the name of the county and the volume number. For *Foedera* see Abbreviations.

Abbreviatio Placitorum, see *Placitorum Abbreviatio*

Acta Aragonensia, ed. H. Finke, 3 vols. Berlin/Leipzig 1908–22

Actes concernant les rapports entre les Pays-Bas et la Grande Bretagne de 1293 a 1468, ed. P. Bonenfant, *Bulletin Comm. Royale d'Histoire*, 109 (1944), pp. 51–125

(The) Acts of the Parliaments of Scotland I (1124–1423), London 1844

(The) Acts of Robert I, King of Scots 1306–1329, ed. A.A.M. Duncan, Edinburgh 1988 (vol. 5 of *Regesta Regum Scottorum*)

Age of Chivalry, ed. J. Alexander, P. Binski, London 1987

Ancient Kalendars and Inventories of the Exchequer, ed. Sir F. Palgrave, 3 vols.London 1836 (Contains Bishop Stapeldon's Calendar of Documents, I, pp. 1–155.)

Anglo-Scottish Relations, 1174–1328: Some Selected Documents, ed. E. L. G. Stones, London 1965

(The) Berkeley Manuscripts, John Smyth, ed. Sir John Maclean, 3 vols Gloucester 1883–5 (Vol. I: *The Lives of the Berkeleys* .)

Biblia Sacra iuxta vulgatam versionem, ed. R. Weber, 2 vols. Stuttgart 1983

Book of Prests, 1294–5, ed. E. B. Fryde, Oxford 1962

Bristol Charters vol. I, ed. N. D. Harding, *Bristol Record Society* (1930)

Caerlaverock: The Siege of Caerlaverock, 1300, ed. N.H. Nicolas, London 1828; also ed. T. Wright, London 1864

Calendar of Ancient Correspondence Concerning Wales, ed. J. G. Edwards, Cardiff 1935

Calendar of Ancient Petitions Relating to Wales, ed. J. G. Edwards, Cardiff 1975

Calendar of Documents Relating to Ireland, 1171–1307, ed. H.S. Sweetman, London 1875–6

Calendar of Documents Relating to Scotland preserved in HM Public Record Office, ed. J. Bain, 5 vols. Edinburgh 1881–88, 198- [vol. 3 1307–1357]

Calendar of Documents and Records Illustrating the History of Scotland, ed. Sir F. Palgrave, London 1837

Calendar of the Justiciary Rolls, Ireland, ed. J. Mills et al., vol. 3 1307–1314, Dublin 1905

Calendar of Letter Books of the City of London, E (1314–1337), ed. R.R. Sharpe, London 1902

Calendar of Plea and Memoranda Rolls ... of the City of London, 1323–1364, ed. A.H. Thomas, Cambridge 1926

Cartae et alia munimenta quae ad Dominium de Glamorgancia , ed. G. T. Clark rev. G.L. Clark, 6 vols. Cardiff 1910

Catalogue of the Records of the Dean and Chapter including the former St. Peter's Abbey, ed. I.M. Kirby, Gloucester 1967

Chartulary of Winchester Cathedral, ed. A. W. Goodman, Winchester 1927 (See also the extracts in *Winchester Register Grandisson* 3, App.)

Collectanea, J. Lelandi, ed. T. Hearne, vols. 1–2, London 1774

County of Avon Historic Landscape Survey of the Manor of Englishcombe, Bristol 1983

Descriptive Catalogue of the Charters and Muniments ...at Berkeley Castle, ed. I. H., Jeayes, Bristol 1892

Diplomatice Correspondence of Richard II, ed. E. Perroy, CS 3rd ser. 48 (1933)

Documents Illustrating the Crisis of 1297–8 in England, ed. M.C. Prestwich , CS 4th ser. 24 (1980)

Documents Illustrating the Rule of Walter de Wenlok, ed. B. F. Harvey, CS 4th ser. 2 (1965)

Documents Illustrative of English History in the Thirteenth and Fourteenth Centuries, ed. H. Cole, London 1844

Documents Illustrative of the History of Scotland 1286–1306, 1307–1357, ed. J. Stevenson, 3 vols. Edinburgh 1870–87

Documents and Records Illustrating the History of Scotland, ed. Sir F. Palgrave, London 1837

Edward I and the Throne of Scotland 1290–1296, E.L.G. Stones, G.G. Simpson, 2 vols. Oxford 1978 (An invaluable modern collection of source material.)

English Historical Documents 1189–1327, ed. H. Rothwell, 1975

English Medieval Diplomatic Practice, ed. P. Chaplais pt. 1, 2 vols.; pt. 2 Plates, London 1975, 1982

English Royal Documents: King John-Henry VI 1199–1461, ed. P. Chaplais, Oxford 1971

(The) Eyre of London 14 Edward II, A.D. 1321, ed. H.M. Cam, 2 vols. Selden Society 26, part 1(1968), pt. 2 (1969)

Fälschungen im Mittelalter (Schriften der Monumenta Germaniae Historica 33), Hanover 1988

Four English Political Tracts of the Later Middle Ages, ed. J-P.Genet, CS 4th ser., 18 (1977)

(The) Gascon Calendar of 1322, ed. G. Cuttino, CS 3rd. ser. 70 (1949)

Gascon Rolls (Rôles Gascons) 1307–1317, ed. Y. Renouard, R. Fawtier, London/Paris 1962

Groot Charterboek der Graaven van Holland en Zeeland ..., ed. F. Van Mieris, 4 vols. Leiden 1753–6.

Hemingby's Register, ed. H.M. Chew, Devizes 1963

(The) Household Book of Queen Isabella of England for the fifth regnal year of Edward II, 8 July 1311 to 7 July 1312, ed. F.D. Blackley, G. Hermansen, Edmonton Alta 1971

Instrumenta Publica (See PRO E39 documents noted in *L&I Soc.* vol. 49, many of them transferred to the General Register House, Edinburgh in November 1949)

Irish Historical Documents 1172–1922, ed. E. Curtis, R.B. McDowell, London 1943

John of Bridlington, in Wright, *Political Poems* 1, pp. 123–215

(Les) Journaux du Trésor de Charles le Bel, ed. J. Viard, Paris 1917

(Les) Journaux du Trésor de Philippe IV, ed. J. Viard, Paris 1940

(The) Latin Hymns of Richard Ledrede, ed. T. Stemmler, Mannheim 1975

(The) Latin Poems of Richard Ledrede O.F.M., Bishop of Ossory 1327–1360, ed. E. Colledge, Toronto 1974

(Calendar of) Letter Books of the City of London, C-E *c.* 1291–1337, ed. R.R. Sharpe, London 1901-04

Letters of Edward, Prince of Wales, 1304–1305, ed. H. Johnstone, Roxburghe Club 1931

Lettres de Rois, Reines et autres personnages des cours de France et d'Angleterre, vol. 2 (1301–1515), ed. J.J. Champollion-Figeac, Paris 1839–47

Lettres secrètes et curiales du Pape Jean XXII (1316–1334) relatives à la France, ed. A. Coulon, S. Clémencet, vol. 3 fasc. 6–9 Paris 1961–67

Liber Custumarum, Liber Horn, see *Munimenta Gildhallae*

(The) Liber Epistolaris of Richard de Bury, ed. N. Denholm-Young, Roxburghe Club 1950 (Cited as *Liber Epistolaris* with number of entry.)

Liber Quotidianus Contrarotuloris Garderobae, 28 Edward I, ed. J. Topham, London 1787. See Manuscript Sources, *Society of Antiquaries*

List of Welsh Entries in the Memoranda Rolls, 1282–1343, Cardiff 1974

Littere Wallie, ed. J.G. Edwards, Cardiff 1940

(The) Lives of the Berkeleys see *(The) Berkeley Manuscripts*

(The) Mabinogion, trans. T.P. Ellis and J. Lloyd, 2 vols. Oxford 1929 (Contains "The Dream of Macsen Wledig," 1, pp. 135–50)

(The) Manuscripts of Westminster Abbey, ed. J.A. Robinson, M.R. James, Cambridge 1909

Materials for the History of the Franciscan Province of Ireland, 1230–1450, ed.E.B. FitzMaurice and A.G. Little, Manchester 1920

"(The) Middle English Prose *Brut*: A Location List of the Manuscripts and Early Printed Editions," L.M. Matheson, in *Analytical and Enumerative Bibliography* 3 (1979), pp. 254–66

Modus Tenendi Parliamentum, ed. T.D. Hardy, London 1846

Monasticon Anglicanum, Dugdale, W., rev. J. Caley et al., 6 vols. in 8, London 1817–30

Munimenta Gildhallae Londoniensis: Liber Albus, Liber Custumarum et Liber Horn, ed. H.T. Riley, 3 vols. RS 12, 1859–62

(The) Muniments of the Dean and Chapter of Canterbury in *HMCR* Various Collections 1, pp. 205 ff.

Northern Petitions, ed. C.M. Fraser, SS 194 (1981)

Original Letters illustrative of English History, ed. H. Ellis, 3 vols. London 1824, 2nd. edn 1825

Parliamentary Texts of the Later Middle Ages, ed. N. Pronay, J. Taylor, Oxford 1980

Parliamentary Writs, ed. Sir F. Palgrave, 2 vols., London 1827–34

Parry, *Parliaments*, see Printed Sources, Reference

Placitorum Abbreviatio, Richard I-Edward II, ed. G. Rose, W. Illingworth, RC 1811

(A) Poem on the Times of Edward II, ed. C. Hardwick, Percy Society 1849

Political Poems and Songs Relating to English History, ed. T. Wright, RS 2 vols.London 1859–61

Political Songs of England, ed. T. Wright, London 1839, CS o.s. 6

Proceedings against Alice Kyteler, A Contemporary Narrative of the, ed. T. Wright, CS (1843)

Records of the Trial of Walter de Langeton, Bishop of Coventry and Lichfield 1307-1312, ed. A. Beardwood, CS 4th ser. 6 (1969)

Records of the Wardrobe and Household, ed. B.F. and C.R. Byerly, 2 vols.1977, 1986

Registrum Magni Sigilli Regum Scotorum: The Register of the Great Seal of Scotland 1306–1424, ed. J.M. Thompson, Edinburgh 1912

Registrum Palatinum Dunelmense 4, ed. T.D. Hardy, RS London 1878

Rôles Gascons, see *Gascon Rolls*

Roll of the Household Expenses of Richard de Swinfield, Bishop of Hereford, 1289- 90, ed. J. Webb, 2 vols. CS (1854–5)

Rotuli Parliamentorum, 6 vols. London 1783, index (ed. J. Strachey) 1832

Rotuli Parliamentorum Anglie Hactenus Inediti, ed. H. G. Richardson, G. O. Sayles, CS 51 (1935)

Rotuli Scaccarii Regum Scotorum 1, 1264–1359, 1878

Rotuli Scotiae 1, 1814

Rouse Roll, The, ed. W Courthope, London 1859

Rule of St Benedict, ed. J. McCann, London 1963

Select Cases before the King's Council 1243–1482, ed. I.S.Leadam, J.F. Baldwin, Selden Society 35 (1918)

Select Cases in the Court of King's Bench (1272–1422), ed. G. O. Sayles, 7 vols., Selden Society vols. 4–6, 74 (1955), 76 (1957), 82 (1965)

Select Charters, ed. William Stubbs rev. H.W.C. Davis, 9th edition Oxford 1942

Selected Documents see *Anglo Scottish Relations* above

Selected Letters of Pope Innocent III, ed. C.R. Cheney, W.H. Semple, Edinburgh 1953

(The) Simonie: a Parallel Text Edition, ed. D. Embree, E. Urquhart, Heidelberg 1991

Sir Christopher Hatton's Book of Seals, ed. L.C. Lloyd, D.M. Stenton, Oxford 1950

Sources of British History in the Instrumenta Miscellanea of the Vatican Archives, ed. C. Burns, Archivum Historiae Pontificae 9, Rome (1971)

South Lancashire in the Reign of Edward II, ed. G.H. Tupling, Chetham Society (1949)

Statutes of Ireland : Early Statutes of Ireland 1, King John to Henry V, ed. H. F. Berry, London 1907

Stonar Letters and Papers 1290–1483, ed. C.L. Kingsford, 2 vols. CS 19–20 (1919)

Table chronologique des Chartes et Diplomes, ed. A. Wautier, Brussels 1896

Testamenta Vetusta , ed. N. H. Nicholas, 2 vols. London 1826

Treaty Rolls I, 1234–1325, ed. P. Chaplais, London 1955

(The) War of Sardos, ed. P. Chaplais, CS 3rd. ser. 87 (1954)

Wenlock Documents, see *Documents*

Westminster Abbey MSS see *(The) Manuscripts of Westminster Abbey*

William Worcestre, Itineraries, ed. J. H. Harvey, Oxford 1965

Winchester Chartulary, see *Chartulary*

Chronicles

Anglia Sacra, ed. H. Wharton, 2 vols. London 1691 (Includes a version of
    Graystanes.)

Ann. Dunst.: Annales de Dunstaplia , see *Annales Monastici* 3

Ann. Lond., Annales Londonienses, in *Chronicles of Edward I and II*

Ann. Osney, see *Annales Monastici* 4

Ann. Paul., Annales Paulini, in *Chronicles of Edward I and II*

Ann. Waverley, see *Annales Monastici* 2

Ann. Wykes, Wygorn., see *Annales Monastici* 4

Annales Breves Hiberniae, Thaddeo Dowling, ed. R. Butler, Dublin 1849

Annales Hiberniae, Jacobi Grace, see *Jacobi Grace*

"Annales de Hotel de Nesle," H. Cordier, in *Mémoire de l'Institut National de France*
    41 (1920)

Annales Monastici, ed. H. R. Luard, 5 vols. RS 36, London 1864–9

(The) Annals of Connacht, ed. A.M. Freeman, Dublin 1944

(The) Annals of Inisfallen, ed. S. MacAirt, Dublin 1951

(The) Annals of Ireland by Friar John Clyn and Thady Dowling, ed. R. Butler, *IAS*
    1849

Annals of Loch Cé 1014–1590, ed. W. A. Hennessey, 2 vols. RS 54, London 1871

Annals of Ulster, ed. W. M. Hennessey, B. MacCarthy, 4 vols. Dublin 1887–1901

(The) Anonimalle Chronicle 1307–41, ed. W.R. Childs, J. Taylor, *YAS* Record ser.
    147, Leeds 1991 (A French *Brut* chronicle). This edition is the one cited in
    footnotes

(The) Anonimalle Chronicle 1333 to 1381, ed. V.H. Galbraith, Manchester 1927

Baker, see *Chronicon Galfridi de Baker*

Barbour, *Bruce: The Bruce by John Barbour,* ed. W. M. Mackenzie, London 1909

Blaneford: *Johannis de Trokelowe et Henrici de Blaneforde Chronica Annales,* see
    Chronica Monasteri Sancti Albani 3

Bridlington, in *Chronicles of Edward I and II* 2 and see *John of Bridlington*

Brut, The, or The Chronicles of England edited from MS Rawlinson B 171 Bodleian
    Library, 2 vols. EETS Orig. ser. 131, 136, London 1906–8

Brut y Tywysogion, (Peniarth MS 20 Version), ed. T. Jones, Cardiff 1941

Brut y Tywysogion, or The Chronicle of Princes (Red Book of Hergest version), ed. T. Jones, Cardiff 1955

Castleford Chronicle, *"Castleford's Chronicle" or "The Boke of Brut,"* ed. C.D. Eckhardt 2 vols. Oxford for *EETS* 305–6, 1996. (A third volume of notes etc. is to follow.) See under Manuscript Sources Germany, Göttingen

Caithréim Thoirdhealbhaigh, ed. S. H. O'Grady, London 1929

Chartularies of St. Mary's, Dublin and Annals of Ireland, 1162–1370, ed. J. T. Gilbert, 2 vols. RS 80, London 1884, 1886

Chronica Johannis de Reading et anonymi Cantuariensis 1346–1367, ed. J. Tait, Manchester 1914

Chronica Monasterii Sancti Albani, ed. H. T. Riley, 7 vols. RS 28, London 1863–76

Chronicle of Glastonbury: Cronica sive antiquitates Glastoniensis ecclesie, ed. J.P. Carley trans. D. Townsend, Woodbridge 1985 (also *British Archaeological Reports* 47(i) 1978.)

Chronicle of London, [ed. E. Tyrell, N.H. Nicolas], London 1827

Chronicles of the Age of Chivalry, ed. E. Hallam, Twickenham 1995

Chronicles of Edward I and Edward II, ed. W. Stubbs, 2 vols. RS 76, London 1882–3

Chronicon Galfridi de Baker de Swynebroke, ed. E. Maunde Thompson, Oxford 1889

Chronicon Henrici Knighton, ed. J.R. Lumby, vol. 1, RS 92, 1889. (New edition of the "contemporary" portion of the chronicle 1337–96 with valuable introduction, ed. G. H. Martin, Oxford 1995.)

Chronicon sanctae Catherinae de Monte Rotomagi, in *RHGF* 23, pp. 397–415

Chronique anonyme intitulée "Anciennes Chroniques de Flandre," Extraits d'une, in *RHGF* 22, pp. 329–429

Chronique anonyme: Ex anonymo regum Franciae chronico, in *RHGF* 22, pp. 16–21

Chronique anonyme finissant en 1328, Extraits d'une, in *RHGF* 21, pp. 146–58

Chronique de Guillaume de Nangis (Continuatio), in *RHGF* 20, pp. 583–646. (Also *Chronique latine de Guillaume de Nangis de 1113 à 1300 avec les continuations de cette chronique de 1300 à 1368)*, ed. H. Géraud, 2 vols *SHF* 33, 35, Paris 1830.)

Chronique de Jean le Bel, ed. J. Viard, E. Déprez, 2 vols. Paris 1904–5

Chronique normande du XIVᵉ siècle, ed. A. and E. Molinier, *SHF* Paris 1832

Chroniques de Flandre, Extraits de, see *Chronique anonyme*

Chronique de Pays Bas, de France, d'Angleterre et de Tournai, ed. J-J. Smet, *Recueil des Chroniques de Flandre* 3, Brussels 1856

Chroniques de St. Denis, in *RHGF* 20, pp. 654–724

Coggeshall: Radulphi de Coggeshall Chronicon Anglicanum, ed. J. Stevenson, RS 66, London 1875

Cont. Trivet, see *Trevet Continuator*

Cotton: Bartholomaei de Cotton Historia Anglicana, ed. H.R. Luard, RS 16, London 1859

Croniques de London, ed. G.J. Aungier, CS o.s. 28, London 1844

Flores Historiarum, ed. H. R. Luard, 3 vols. RS 95, London 1890

Fordun: Chronica Johannis de Fordun, Chronica Gentis Scotorum, ed. W.F. Skene,

Edinburgh 1871–82. (See also *Scotichronicon* ed. Watt where Bower's dependence on Fordun and other chroniclers is detailed.)

French Chronicle of London see *Croniques de London*

Froissart, Jean, Chroniques, ed. Kervyn de Lettenhove, 25 vols. in 26 (vols. 2 to 1339, 18 Pièces justificatives), Brussels 1867–77

Froissart, Jean, Chroniques, ed. S. Luce, G. Reynaud, 11 vols. Paris 1869–99

Gervase continuator, see under Manuscript Sources, Cambridge

Gesta Abbatum Monasterii Sancti Albani a Thoma Walsingham, ed. H.T. Riley, vol. 2 1290–1349, RS 28, London 1867, and see *Historia Anglicana, Trokelowe*

Giraldus Cambrensis: Giraldi Cambrensis Opera, vols. 4 ed. J.S. Brewer, 8 ed. G.F. Warner, RS 21, London 1873, 1891

Glastoniensis Chronica: Johannis Glastoniensis Chronica, ed. T. Hearne, 2 vols. Oxford 1726. (See also *Chronicle of Glastonbury*.)

(Les) Grandes Chroniques de France, ed. J. Viard, vol. 8 (Philippe le Hardi–Philippe V le Long), *SHF* Paris 1934

Graystanes, see *Historia Dunelmensis Scriptores Tres*

(The) Great Chronicle of London, ed. A.H. Thomas, I.D. Thornley, London/Aylesbury 1938

Guillelmus de Nangiaco, see *Nangiaco*

Guisborough: The Chronicle of Walter de Guisborough, ed. H. Rothwell, CS 99, London 1957

Hemingburgh: Chronicon domini Walteri de Hemingburgh, vulgo Hemingford nuncupati, ed. H.C. Hamilton, London 1849

Historia et Cartularium Monasterii Gloucestriae, ed. W.H. Hart, RS 33 vol.1, London 1863

Historia Anglicana: Thomae Walsingham Historia Anglicana, vol. 1 1272–1381, see *Chronica Monasterii Sancti Albani* 1

Historia Aurea, see Secondary Sources s.v. Galbraith

Historia Dunelmensis Scriptores Tres, Galfridus de Coldingham, Robertus de Graystanes, et William de Chambre, SS 1839

(The) Historia Regum Britanniae of Geoffrey of Monmouth, ed. A. Griscom, London/New York/Toronto 1929

Historia Roffensis, in *Anglia Sacra* , and see Manuscript Sources, *British Library,* Cotton MS Faustina B.5

Historiae Anglicanae Scriptores Decem, ed. R. Twysden, London 1652 [Contains Orleton's *Apologia* or *Responsiones* and Thorne's chronicle.]

Historic and Municipal Documents, Ireland, 1172–1320, ed. J. T. Gilbert, RS 53, London 1870

Holinshed: [Raphael] Holinshed's Chronicle of England, Scotland and Wales, intro. by V.F. Snow, 6 vols. London 1807–8, rep. 1965–76 (Edward II in vol. 2, pp. 546–88.)

Istore et croniques de Flandres, ed. Kervyn de Lettenhove, 2 vols. Brussels 1879–80

Jacobi Grace, Kilkenniensis, Annales Hiberniae, ed. R. Butler, *PIAS* 1842

Jean le Bel, see *Chronique de*

John of Bridlington see *Political Poems*, ed. Wright

Knighton, see *Chronicon Henrici Knighton*

Lanercost: Chronicon de Lanercost, ed. J. Stevenson, Edinburgh 1839

Langtoft: The Chronicle of Pierre de Langtoft, ed. T. Wright, 2 vols. RS 47, London 1866–68

Le Livere de Reis de Brittanie e le Livere de Engleterre, ed. J. Glover, RS 42, London 1865

Le Roman de Brut de Wace, ed. I. Arnold, *Société des Anciens Textes Français* 80, Paris 1938

Lichfield Chronicle, see *Manuscript Sources* Oxford, Bodl. Lib. Bodley MS 956

"Life of St William," *Historians of the Church of York*, ed. J. Raine, vol. 2, RS 71, London 1886

Memorials of St. Edmund's Abbey, ed. T. Arnold, 3 vols. RS 96, London 1890–96

Murimuth: Adae Murimuthi Continuatio Chronicarum Robertus de Avesbury De Gestis Mirabilibus regis Edwardi Tertii, ed. E. Maunde Thompson, RS 93, London 1889

Nangiaco (Nangis), Guillelmus de, *Continuatio Cronici Guillelmi de*, see *Chronique de*

Nicholai Trevet Annales, ed. T. Hog, London 1845

"Pakington chronicle," version of the French *Brut* printed by J. Leland in translation, and which he attributed to William Pakington, *Collectanea* 2, ed. Hearne, London 1774, pp. 455–70

Polistoire see Manuscript Sources, *British Library*

Polychronicon Ranulphi Higden, Monachi Cestrensis, 9 vols. RS 41, London 1865–86

Recueil des chroniques de Flandre, vol. 3, see *Chronique de Pays-Bas*

Recueil des Historiens des Gaules et de la France, ed. A.C. Bouquet, L. Delisle et al., esp.vols. 22–23, Paris 1840-, Facsimile Farnborough 1967–8

Responsiones: see *Historiae Anglcanae*, ed. Twysden

Rishanger: Willelmi Rishanger Chronica et Annales, see *Chronica Monasterii S. Albani* II

Saint Edmundsbury, Chronicle of, see Secondary Sources s.v. Galbraith, and see *Memorials of St. Edmund's Abbey*

Scalacronica: A Chronicle of England and Scotland (1066–1362), ed. J. Stevenson, Maitland Club, Edinburgh 1836

Scalacronica, ed. and trans. H. Maxwell, Glasgow 1907

Scotichronicon: Johannis de Fordun Scotichronicon cum Supplementis et Continuatione Walteri Boweri, ed. W. Goodall, Edinburgh 1759. (A new edition 9 vols. under the general editorship of D.E.R. Watt has recently (1998) been completed. The relevant volumes, 6 Books XI-XII, ed. and trans. N.F. Shead, W.B. Stevenson et al., Aberdeen 1991; 7 Books XIII-XIV, ed. and translated Watt with U. Morét, N. F. Shead, Edinburgh 1996, are cited in the footnotes.)

Sempringham Chronicle, see *Le Livere de reis*

Stow, J., *Annales*, 1601

Thorne: *Chronica Guillelmi Thorne Monachi Sancti Augustini Cantuariae*, in *Historiae Anglicanae*, ed. Twysden

Trevet Continuator: Nicolai Triveti Annalium Continuatio, ed. A. Hall, Oxford 1722, and see *Nicholai Trevet*

Trokelowe: *Johannis de Trokelowe et Henrici de Blaneforde Chronica Annales*, see *Chronica Monasteri Sancti Albani* 3

Vita Edwardi Secundi/The Life of Edward II, ed. N. Denholm-Young, Edinburgh/London 1957

Vitae Arch. Cant.: *Stephani Birchingtoni Monachi Cantuariensis Historia de Archiepiscopis*: ed. H. Wharton, *Anglia Sacra* 1 q.v. (Lambeth MS 99)

Walsingham, see *Gesta Abbatum, Historia Anglicana*

Wigmore Chronicle, in Dugdale, *Monasticon* vol. 6i (cited). See also *The Anglo-Norman Chronicle of Wigmore Abbey*, ed. and translated J.T. Dickinson and P.T. Ricketts, *Transactions of the Woolhope Naturalists' Field Club* (1969)

Willelmi Capellani in Brederode Chronicon, ed. C. Pynacher Herdyk, Historisch Genootschap 20, Amsterdam 1904

SECONDARY SOURCES

Aberth, J., *Criminal Churchmen in the Age of Edward III: the Case of Bishop Thomas de Lisle*, Pennsylvania 1996

– "Crime and Justice under Edward III: the Case of Thomas de Lisle," *EHR* 107 (1992), pp. 283–301

Alexander, J.J.G., Gibson, M.T. ed., *Medieval Learning and Literature. Essays Presented to Richard William Hunt* , Oxford 1976

Alexander, J.W., "A History Survey: Norman and Plantagenet Kings since World War II,"*JBS* 24 (1985), pp. 94–109

Altschul, M., *A Baronial Family in Medieval England: the Clares, 1217–1314,* Baltimore 1965

Anderson, A.R., *Alexander's Gate, Gog and Magog, and the Inclosed Nations*, Cambridge Mass. 1932

Archer, R.A., "The Estates and Finances of Margaret of Brotherton, c.1320–1399," *HR* 60 (1987), pp. 264–80

Armand D'Herbomez, see Herbomez

Bailey, D.S., *Homosexuality and the Western Christian Tradition,* London 1955

Baker, J.H., *The Legal Profession and the Common Law: Historical Essays,* London 1986

– *The Order of Serjeants at Law: a Chronicle of Creations,* Selden Society supp. ser. vol. 5 , London 1984

Baker, R.L., *The English Customs Service, 1307–1343: A Study of Medieval Administration,* TAPhS n.s. 51 pt. 6, Philadelphia 1961

– "The Establishment of the English Wool Staple in 1313," *Speculum* 31 (1956), pp. 444–53

Baldwin, J.F., "The Household Administration of Henry Lacy and Thomas of Lancaster," *EHR* 42 (1927), pp. 180–200

– "The King's Council," in *English Government at Work*, Willard, Morris ed.

– *The King's Council in England during the Middle Ages*, Oxford 1913

Balfour Melville, E.W.M., see Melville

Ball, F.E., *The Judges in Ireland*, 2vols., London 1926

Banks, R.W., "King Edward II in South Wales (with documents)," *Arch. Camb.* 4 5th ser. (1887), pp. 161–82

– "The Marriage-Contract of King Edward II," ibid. pp. 53–7

Barber, M., "Propaganda in the Middle Ages: The Charges against the Templars," *NMS* 17 (1973), pp. 42–57

– *Tournaments,* Harmondsworth 1978

– *The Trial of the Templars,* Cambridge 1978

– "The World Picture of Philip the Fair," *JMH* 8 (1982), pp. 13–27

Barber R., Barker J, *Tournaments*, Woodbridge 1989

Barker, J.R.V., *The Tournament in England 1100–1400*, Woodbridge 1986

Barnes, J., *The History of ... Edward III*, Cambridge 1688

Barnes, P.M., Barrow, G.W.S., "The Movements of Robert Bruce between September 1307 and May 1308," *SHR* 49 (1970), pp. 46–59

Barron, C., "The Tyranny of Richard II," *BIHR* 41 (1968), pp. 46–69

Barrow, G.W.S., "The Aftermath of War: Scotland and England in the late Thirteenth and Early Fourteenth Centuries,"*TRHS* 28 (1978), pp. 103–25

– *Feudal Britain: The Completion of the Medieval Kingdoms 1066–1314*, London 1965

– "The Idea of Freedom in Late Medieval Scotland," *Innes Review* 30 (1979), pp. 26–32

– "A Kingdom in Crisis: Scotland and the Maid of Norway," *SHR* 69 (1990), pp. 128–41

– *The Kingdom of the Scots: Government and Society from the Eleventh to the Fourteenth Century*, London 1973

– "Lothian, 1296–1320," *SHR* 55 (1976), pp. 151–71

– Review of Stones, *Anglo Scottish Relations, SHR* 46 (1967), pp. 58–61

– *Robert Bruce*, London 1988

– "The Scottish Clergy in the War of Independence," *SHR* 41 (1962), pp. 1–22

– "Wales and Scotland in the Middle Ages," *WHR* 10 (1981), pp. 302–19

Barrow, G.W.S., Stewart, G.W., *Kingship and Unity: Scotland 1000–1306*, London 1981

Bassett, M., "Newgate Prison in the Middle Ages," *Speculum* 18 (1943), pp. 233–46

Batten, J., "Stoke-sub-Hamden," *PSANHS* new ser. 40 (1894), pp. 236–71 [Gurney genealogical table facing p. 270]

Bean, J.M.W., " 'Bacheler' and Retainer," *Medievalia et Humanistica* new ser. 3, ed. P.M. Clogan (1972), pp. 117–31

– *The Decline of English Feudalism, 1215–1540*, Manchester 1968

- *From Lord to Patron: Lordship in Late Medieval England*, Manchester 1989
- "The Percies and their Estates in Scotland," *Arch. Ael.* 4th ser. 35 (1957), pp. 91–9

Bearwood, A., "The Trial of Walter Langton, Bishop of Lichfield 1307–1312," *TAPhS* n.s. 54 pt. 3, Philadelphia 1964
- *Records of the Trial of Walter de Langeton* , see Collections of Documents

Beckett, J.C., *The Anglo-Irish Tradition*, 1976

Behrens, B., "Origins of the English Resident Ambassador in Rome," *EHR* 49 (1934), pp. 640–56

Bellamy, J.G., *Bastard Feudalism and the Law*, London 1988
- "The Coterel Gang: an Anatomy of a Band of Fourteenth-Century Criminals," *EHR* 79 (1964), pp. 698–717
- *Criminal Law and Society in Late Medieval and Tudor England*, Gloucester 1984
- *The Law of Treason in England in the Later Middle Ages*, Cambridge 1970

Benedetti, A., *Edoardo II d'Inghilterra all' Abbazia di S. Alberto di Butrio*, Palermo 1924

Bent, J.T., "Where did Edward II die?," *Notes & Queries*, 6th ser. 2 (1880), pp. 381–3, 410–13

Bertrand de Broussillon, A., *La maison de Craon (1050–1480)*, 2 vols. Paris 1893

Bingham, C., *The Life and Times of Edward II*, London 1973

Birch, W. de Gray, *A History of Neath Abbey*, Neath 1902

Birdsall, P., "Non Obstante, a Study of the Dispensing Power of English Kings," in *Essays in History and Political Theory in Honor of Charles H. McIlwain*, Cambridge Mass. 1936, pp. 37–76

Birley, A.R., "Magnus Maximus and the Persecution of Heresy," in *Wilkinson Essays*, Powicke, Sandquist ed., pp. 13–43

Blackley, F.D., "Adam, Bastard Son of Edward II," *BIHR* 37 (1964), pp. 76–7
- "Isabella and the Bishop of Exeter," in *Wilkinson Essays*, Powicke, Sandquist ed., pp. 220–35
- "Isabella of France, Queen of England (1308–1358) and the Late Medieval Cult of the Dead," *CJH* 14 (1980), pp. 25–47
- "The Tomb of Isabella of France, wife of Edward II of England," *Bulletin of the International Society for the Study of Church Monuments* 8 (1983), pp. 161–4 (typescript)

Blackley, F.D., Hermansen, G. ed., *The Household Book of Queen Isabelle of England for the Fifth Regnal Year of Edward II, 8 July 1311 to 7 July 1312*, Edmonton Alta. 1971

Blake, J.R., "Medieval Smuggling in the North-East: some Fourteenth-Century Evidence," *Arch. Ael.* 4th ser. 43 (1965), pp. 243–60

Bloch, M., *Les Rois Thaumaturges*, Strasbourg/Paris 1924

Boardman, S., "Chronicle Propaganda in Late medieval Scotland: Robert the Steward, John of Fordun and the 'Anonymous Chronicle'," *SHR* 76 (1997), pp. 23–43

Boas, G., *Vox Populi: Essays in the History of an Idea*, Baltimore 1969 (See also Menache, *Vox Dei*.)

Bolton, J.L., *The Medieval English Economy 1150–1500*, London 1980

Bond, E.A., "Extracts from the Liberate Rolls, relative to Loans supplied by the Italian Merchants to the Kings of England in the 13th and 14th Centuries," *Archaeologia* 28 (1840), pp. 207–326

– "Notices of the Last Days of Isabella, Queen of Edward the Second, Drawn from the Account of the Expenses of her Household," Collectanea *Archaeologia* 35 (1854), pp. 453–69

Booth, P.H.W., *The Financial Administration of the Lordship and County of Chester 1272–1377*, Manchester 1981

Boswell, J., *Christianity, Social Tolerance and Homosexuality in Western Europe : Gay People from the beginning of the Christian Era to the Fourteenth Century*, Chicago/London 1988.

Boulton, D., *The Knights of the Crown: the Monarchical Orders of Knighthood in Later Medieval Europe 1325–1520*, Woodbridge 1987

Boyette, P.E., "Wanton Humour and Wanton Poets: Homosexuality in Marlowe's Edward II," *Tulane Studies in English* 22 (1977), pp. 33–50

Boyle, L. E., "William of Pagula and the *Speculum Regis Edwardi*," *MS* 32 (1970), pp. 329–36

Bradford, C.A., *Heart Burial*, London 1933

Bree, J., *The Cursory Sketch of the State of the Naval, Military and Civil Establishment etc.*, London 1791

Breeze, D.J., Introduction to "Studies Commemorative of the Anniversary of the Maid of Norway," *SHR* 69 (1990), pp. 117–19

Brie, F.W.D., *Geschichte und Quellen der mittelenglischen Prosachronik, the Brute of England*, Marburg 1905

Brodwin, L.L., "Edward: Marlowe's treatment of Love," *ELH* 31 (1964), pp. 139–55

Brooke, C.N.L., "Geoffrey of Monmouth as a historian," in Brooke et al. ed., *Church and Government*, pp. 77–91

Brooke, C.N.L. et al. ed., *Church and Government in the Middle Ages*, Cambridge 1976

Broome, D.M., "Auditors of the Foreign Accounts of the Exchequer, 1310–1327," *EHR* 38 (1923), pp. 63–71, 39 (1324), p. 482 (addendum).

– "Exchequer Migrations to York in the 13th and 14th Centuries," in *Essays*, Little, Powicke ed., pp. 291–300

Broussillon, see Bertrand de Broussillon

Brown, A.L., "The authorisation of Letters under the Great Seal," *BIHR* 37 (1964), pp. 125–56

Brown, E.A.R., "The Ceremonial of Royal Succession in Capetian France: the Double Funeral of Louis X," *Traditio* 34 (1978), pp. 227–71

– "Death and the Human Body in the Later Middle Ages: the Legislation of Boniface VIII on the Division of the Corpse,"*Viator* 12 (1981), pp. 221–70.

– "Diplomacy, Adultery, and Domestic Politics at the Court of Philip the Fair: Queen Isabelle's Mission to France in 1314," in *Documenting the Past*, Hamilton, Bradley ed., pp. 53–83

- "The marriage of Edward II of England and Isabelle of France: a Postscript," *Speculum* 64 (1989), pp. 373–9
- "The Political Repercussions of Family Ties in the Early Fourteenth Century: The Marriage of Edward II and and Isabelle of France," *Speculum* 63 (1988), pp. 573–95
- "Ritual Brotherhood in Western Medieval Europe," *Traditio* 52 (1997), pp. 357–81
- "Royal Necessity and Noble Service and Subsidy in Early Fourteenth-Century France: the Assembly of Bourges of 1318," in ΠΑΡΑΔΟΣΙΣ: *Studies,* Fletcher, Schulte ed., pp. 135–68

Brown, R.A., *Castles from the Air*, Cambridge 1989

Brown, R.A., Colvin, H.M., Taylor, A.J., *The History of the King's Works, I The Middle Ages*, London 1963

Brückmann, J., "The *Ordines* of the Third Recension of the Medieval Coronation Order," in Powicke, Sandquist ed., *Wilkinson Essays*, pp. 99–115

Brundage, J.[A], *Law, Sex, and Christian Society in Medieval Europe*, Chicago 1987 *and see* Bullough, Brundage

Bryant, W.N., "Some Earlier Examples of Intercommuning in Parliament," *EHR* 85 (1970), pp. 54–8

Buck, M., *Politics, Finance and the Church in the Reign of Edward II: Walter de Stapeldon Treasurer of England*, Cambridge 1983
- "Reform of the Exchequer 1316–1326," *EHR* 98 (1983), pp. 241–60

Bullock-Davies, C., *A Register of Royal and Baronial Domestic Minstrels 1272–1327*, Woodbridge 1986

Bullough, D. A., Storey, R. L., *The Study of Medieval Records: Essays in Honout of Kathleeen Major*, Oxford 1971

Bullough, V.L., *Sexual Variance in Society and History*, New York 1976, Chicago 1980

Bullough, V.L., Brundage, J.A., *Sexual Practices and the Medieval Church*, Buffalo 1982

Burrt, J., "Account of the Expenses of John of Brabant and Thomas and Henry of Lancaster, A.D. 1292–3," CS o.s. 55, Miscellany 2 (1853), pp. iii-xvi, 1–18

Butler, R., "The Last of the Brimpsfield Giffards and the Rising of 1321–22," *TB&GAS* 76 (1957), pp. 75–97

Cam, H.M., "Cases of Novel Disseisin in the Eyre of London in 1321," reprinted in *Law-Finders*, pp. 95–105
- *Law-Finders and Law-Makers in Medieval England*, New Jersey/London 1962 repr. 1979
- *Liberties and Communities in Medieval England*, London 1963, contains "The general eyres of 1329–30" (from *EHR* 39 (1924), pp.241–52), pp. 150–62
- "Recent Work and Present Views on the Origins and Development of Representative Assemblies," in *Relazioni del X Congresso Internazionale di Scienze Storiche*, Florence 1955, pp. 8–25, 44–5
- *Studies in the Hundred Rolls: Some Aspects of Thirteenth Century Administration*, *Studies in Social and Legal History* 6, 1921

Camden, W., *Britannia* , 2 vols. London 1722

Capra, P., "Les Bases Sociales du pouvoir anglo-gascon au milieu du xive siècle," *Le Moyen Age* 81 (1975), pp. 273–99, 447–73

Carpenter, C., "The Beauchamp Affinity: A Study of Bastard Feudalism at Work," *EHR* 95 (1988), pp. 514–32

Carr, A.D., "Anglo-Welsh Relations, 1066–1282," in *England and her Neighbours 1066–1453:: Essays in Honour of Pierre Chaplais*, Jones, Vale ed., pp. 122–38

– *Medieval Anglesey*, Anglesey Antiquarian Society, Llangefni 1982

Carus-Wilson, *England's Export Trade, 1275–1547*, Oxford 1963

Cary, H[enry] Viscount Falkland [attrib.], *The History of ... Edward II King of England ...with the rise and fall of ...Gaveston and the Spencers*, London 1680

Caspary, G.E., "The deposition of Richard II and the Canon Law," *Proceedings of the Second International Congress of Medieval Canon Law*, Kuttner S., Ryan, J.J. ed., Monumenta Iuris Canonici, Series C: Subsidia I, Vatican City 1965, pp.189–201

Cassan, S.H., *Lives of the Bishops of Winchester*, 2 vols., London 1962

Catto, J.I., "Andrew Horn: Law and History in Fourteenth-Century England," in Davis, Wallace Hadrill ed., *The Writing of History in the Middle Ages*, pp. 367–91

Catto, J.I., ass. ed. Ralph Evans, *The History of the University of Oxford* 1, Oxford 1984

Cavanaugh, S.H., "Royal Books: King John to Richard II," *The Library* 10 (1988), pp. 304–16

Chaplais, P., "The Court of Sovereignty of Guyenne (Edward III-Henry VI) and its Antecedents," in Hamilton, Bradley ed., *Documenting the Past*, pp. 137–53

– "English Arguments concerning the Feudal States of Aquitaine in the 14th Century," *BIHR* 21 (1948), pp. 203–13

– *Essays in Medieval Diplomacy and Administration*, London 1981. The articles cited are as follows: I "The Making of the Treaty of Paris (1259) and the Royal Style"; II "Le Traité de Paris de 1259 et l'Inféodation de la Gascogne Allodiale"; III "Le Duché-Pairie de Guyenne: l'Hommage et les Services Féodaux de 1259 à 1303"; IV "Le Duché-Pairie de Guyenne: l'Hommage et les Services Féodaux de 1303 à 1337"; V "La Souveraineté du Roi de France et le Pouvoir Législatif en Guyenne au Début de XIVe Siècle"; VI "Les Appels Gascons au Roi d'Angleterre sous le Règne d'Edouard Ier (1272–1307)"; IX "Règlement des Conflits Internationaux Franco-Anglais au XIVe Siècle (1293–1377)"; X "Un Message de Jean de Fiennes à Edouard II et le Projet de Démembrement du Royaume de France (Janvier 1317)"; XIII "Documents Concernant l'Angleterre et l'Ecosse Anciennement Conservés à la Chambre des Comptes de Lille (XIIe-XVe Siècles)."

– *Piers Gaveston, Edward II's Adoptive Brother*, Oxford 1994

– "Some Private Letters of Edward I," *EHR* 77 (1962), pp. 79–86.

Chareyron, N., *Jean le Bel: Le maître de Froissart, grand imagier de la Guerre de Cent Ans*, Brussels 1996

Cheney, C.R., *Medieval Texts and Studies*, Oxford 1973

– *Notaries Public in England in the Thirteenth and Fourteenth Centuries*, London 1972

– *The Papacy and England 12th–14th Centuries*, London 1982

Chew, H.M., *The English Ecclesiastical Tenants in Chief and Knight Service, especially in the Thirteenth and Fourteenth Centuries*, Oxford 1932

Cheyette, F.L., "The Sovereign and the Pirates, 1332," *Speculum* 45 (1970), pp. 40–68

– "The Professional Papers of an English Ambassador on the Eve of the Hundred Years' War," in *Economies et Sociétés au Moyen Age. Mélanges offerts à Edouard Perroy*, Sorbonne 1973

Chibnall, A.C., *Master Richard de Badew and the University of Cambridge 1315–40*, Cambridge 1963

Chibnall, M.M., *The English Lands of the Abbey of Bec*, Oxford 1946

Childs, W.R., *Anglo-Castilian Trade in the Later Middle Ages*, Manchester 1978

– "Finance and Trade under Edward II," in *Politics and Crisis*, Taylor, Child ed., pp. 19–37

– " 'Welcome, My Brother': Edward II, John of Powderham and the Chroniclers, 1318," in *Church and Chronicle in the Middle Ages*, Wood, Loud ed., pp. 149–63

Clanchy, M.T., *England and its Rulers 1066–1272*, Oxford 1983

Clark, G.T., *Medieval Military Architecture in England*, London 1884

Clarke, M.V., "Committees of Estates and the Deposition of Edward II," in *James Tait Essays*, Edwards et al. ed., pp. 27–45

– *Fourteenth Century Studies*, Oxford 1937

– "Irish Parliaments in the Reign of Edward II," *TRHS* ser. 4, 9 (1926), pp. 29–62, rep. in *Studies*, pp. 1–35

– *Medieval Representation and Consent*, London 1936

Clementi, D., "That the Statute of York is no longer Ambiguous," *Album Helen Cam* 2, Louvain/Paris 1961, pp. 93–100

Clough, C.H. ed., *Profession, Vocation, and Culture in Later Medieval England: Essays dedicated to the Memory of A.R. Myers*, Liverpool 1982

Cobban, A.B., "Edward II, Pope John XXII and the University of Cambridge," *BJRL* 47 (1964–5), pp. 49–78

– *The King's Hall within the University of Cambridge in the Later Middle Ages*, Cambridge 1969

Colvin, H.M. (general editor), *The King's Works*, see Brown R.A.

Connolly, P., "An Account of Military Expenditure in Leinster, 1308," *Analecta Hibernica* 30 (1982), pp. 3–5

Cook, G.H., *Portrait of St. Albans*, London 1951

Cooke, J.H., *Notes & Queries* 6th ser. 2 (1880), 489–90

Cosgrove, A., "Hiberniores Ipsis Hibernis," in *Studies in Irish History*, Cosgrove, McCartney ed., pp. 1–14

– ed., *A New History of Ireland: II Medieval Ireland 1169–1534*, Oxford 1987

Cosgrove, A., MacCartney, D. ed., *Studies in Irish History presented to R. Dudley Edwards*, Dublin 1979

Cosgrove, A., McGuire, J.I., *Parliament and Community*, Belfast 1983

Costain, T.B., *The Three Edwards*, New York 1958

Coulson, C., "Structural Symbolism in Conventual Crenallation: An Essay in the Sociology and Metaphysics of Medieval Fortification," *Medieval Archaeology* 26 (1982), pp. 69–100

Coulton, G.G., *Five Centuries of Religion*, 4 vols., Cambridge 1923/1929/30

– *Medieval Panorama*, Cambridge 1947

Cox, E.L., *The Eagles of Savoy*, Princeton 1974

Cristofori, E., *Storia dei Cardinali di Santa Romana Chiesa*, Rome 1888

Crump, C.G., "The Arrest of Roger Mortimer and Queen Isabel," *EHR* 26 (1911), pp. 331–2

Curley, M.J., "The Cloak of Anonymity and the *Prophecy of John of Bridlington*," *Modern Philology* 77 (1980), pp. 361–9

– "Fifteenth Century Glosses on *The Prophesy of John of Bridlington*: a Text, its Meaning and Purpose," *MS* 46 (1984), pp. 321–39

– "A New Edition of John of Cornwall's *Prophetia Merlini*," *Speculum* 57 (1982), pp. 217–49

Curtis, E., "The Clan System among English Settlers in Ireland," *EHR* 25 (1918), pp. 116–20

– *History of Mediaeval Ireland from 1086 to 1513*, 2nd. edn London 1938

Cuttino, G.P., *English Diplomatic Administration*, Oxford 1940, 2nd edn 1971 [cited]

– "Henry of Canterbury," *EHR* 57 (1942), pp. 298–311

– "King's Clerks and the Community of the Realm," *Speculum* 29 (1954), pp. 395–409

– "Mediaeval Parliament Reinterpreted," *Speculum* 41 (1966), pp. 681–7

– "A Memorandum Book of Elias Joneston," *Speculum* 17 (1942), pp. 74–85

– "Another Memorandum Book of Elias Joneston," *EHR* 63 (1948), pp. 90–103

– "A Reconsideration of the *Modus tenendi parliamentum*," in *The Forward Movement*, Utley ed., pp. 31–60

Cuttino, G.P., Lyman T.W., "Where is Edward II?," *Speculum* 53 (1978), pp. 522–44

Dales, R.C., "Henry of Harclay on the Infinite," *JHI* 45 (1984), pp. 295–301

Dalrymple, D. [Lord Hailes], *Annals of Scotland*, 3 vols., Edinburgh 1819

Daniell, C., *Death and Burial in Medieval England, 1066–1550*, London/New York 1997

Davies, J.C., "The Statute of Lincoln 1316, and the Appointment of Sheriffs," *Law Quarterly Review* 33 (1917), pp. 78–86

– *The Baronial Opposition to Edward II*, Cambridge 1918

– "The Despenser War in Glamorgan," *TRHS* 3rd. ser. 9 (1915), pp. 21–64

– "The First Journal of Edward II's Chamber," *EHR* 30 (1915), pp. 662–80

– ed., *Studies presented to Sir Hilary Jenkinson*, London 1957

Davies, R.G., Denton, J.H. ed., *The English Parliament in the Middle Ages: a tribute to J.S. Roskill*, Manchester 1981

Davies, R. R., *Domination and Conquest: The Experience of Ireland, Scotland and Wales 1100–1300*, Cambridge 1990

– "The Law of the March," *WHR* 5 (1970–71), pp. 1–30

- *Lordship and Society in the March of Wales, 1282–1400*, Oxford 1978
- "The Peoples of Britain and Ireland 1100–1400," parts 1–4, (presidential addresses) *TRHS* 6th ser. 4–7 (1994–7), pp. 1–20, 1–20, 1–23, 1–24.

Davies, W., *Patterns of Power in Early Wales,* Oxford 1990

Davis, J., Weinbaum, M., *see* Weinbaum

Davis, R.H.C., Wallace Hadrill, J.M. ed., *The Writing of History in the Middle Ages: Essays Presented to Richard William Southern*, Oxford 1981

D'Avray, D.L., *Death and the Prince: Memorial Preaching Before 1350*, Oxford 1994

Dean, R.J., "MS. Bodl. 292 and the Canon of Nicholas Trevet's Works," *Speculum* 17 (1942), pp. 243–9
- "Nicholas Trevet, Historian," in *Medieval Learning* , Alexander, Gibson ed., pp. 328–52
- Review of F. Ehrle, *Nikolaus Trivet, sein Leben*, in *Medium Aevum* 10 (1941), pp. 161–8

Denholm-Young, N., "The Authorship of the *Vita Edwardi Secundi*," *EHR* 71 (1956), pp. 189–211 (*Collected Papers* 1969, pp. 267–89)
- *Collected Papers on Mediaeval Subjects*, Oxford 1946, 2nd edn Cardiff 1969
- *The Country Gentry in the Fourteenth Century*, Oxford 1969
- "Feudal Society in the Thirteenth Century," *History* 29 (1944), pp. 107–19
- *History and Heraldry, 1254–1310*, Oxford 1965
- "Richard de Bury 1287–1345," *TRHS* 4th ser. 20 (1937), pp. 135–68 (*Collected Papers* 1946, pp. 1–25)
- *Seignorial administration in England*, Oxford 1937

Denton, J.H., "Canterbury episcopal appointments: the case of Walter Reynolds," *JMH* 1 (1975), pp. 317–27
- "The Clergy and Parliament in the Thirteenth and Fourteenth Centuries," in Davies et al. ed., *The English Parliament*, pp. 88–108
- "The Making of the 'Articuli Cleri' of 1316," *EHR* 101 (1987), pp. 564–95
- *Robert Winchelsey and the Crown, 1294–1313: a Study in the Defence of Ecclesiastical Liberty*, Cambridge 1980
- "Walter Reynolds and Ecclesiastical Politics 1313–1316: a postscript to *Councils and Synods II*," in Brooke et al. ed., *Church and Government* , pp. 247–74

Denton, J.H., Dooley, J.P., *Representation of the Clergy in Parliament 1295–1340*, Woodbridge 1987

Déprez, E., *Etudes de diplomatique anglaise de l'avènement d'Edouard 1er à celui de Henri VII, 1272–1485*, Paris 1908
- *Les préliminaires de la Guerre de Cent Ans*, Bibliothèque des Ecoles Françaises d'Athènes et de Rome 96, Paris 1902

Dibben, L.H., "Secretaries in the Thirteenth and Fourteenth Centuries," *EHR* 25 (1918), pp. 430–44

Dickinson, J.G., "Blanks and Blank Charters in the Fourteenth and Fifteenth Centuries," *EHR* 66 (1951), pp. 375–87

Dickinson, W.C., Duncan, A.A.M., *Scotland from the Earliest Times to 1603*, 3rd edn

Oxford 1977

Dillon, M., "The Inauguration of O'Conor," in *Gwynn Studies*, Watt et al. ed., pp. 186–202

Dimitresco, M., *Pierre de Gavaston, comte de Cornouailles*, Paris 1898

Dodge, W.P., *Piers Gaveston: a Chapter in Early Constitutional History*, London 1899

Doherty, P. [C.], "The Date of the Birth of Isabella, Queen of England 1308–1358," *BIHR* 48 (1975), pp. 246–8, and see Manuscript Sources, Oxford D.Phil. theses

Dolley, R.H.M., *Anglo-Norman Ireland ca. 1100–1318*, Dublin 1972

Donaldson, G., "The Pope's reply to the Scottish Barons in 1320,"*SHR* 29 (1950), pp. 119–20

Donaldson, G., Nicholson, R., *The Edinburgh History of Scotland, 2 The Later Middle Ages*, Edinburgh 1978

Douie, D.L., "The Canonisation of St. Thomas of Hereford," *Dublin Review* 229 (1955), pp. 275–87

Dubois, P., *Summaria Brevis et Compendiosa*, ed. H. Kampf , Leipzig/Berlin 1936

Du Boulay, F.R.H., *The Lordship of Canterbury*, London 1966

– ed., "The Pipe Roll account of the See of Canterbury (1292–5)," in *Kent Records* 18 (1964), pp. 41–57

Duchesne du Cange, C., ed. A. le Suer, *Histoire des comtes de Ponthieu et de Montreuil*, Abbeville 1917

Dugdale, W., *Baronage of England*, London 1675–6

– *The History of St. Paul's Cathedral*, 2nd edn London 1716

Dumville, D.N., "Sub-Roman Britain: History and Legend," *History* 62 (1977), pp. 173–92

Duncan, A.A.M., "The Early Parliaments of Scotland," *SHR* 45 (1966), pp. 36–58

– "The Making of the Declaration of Arbroath," in *The Study of Medieval Records*, Bullough, Storey ed., pp. 174–88

– *The Nation of Scots and the Declaration of Arbroath (1320)*, Historical Association London 1970

– Review of Stones, *Anglo-Scottish Relations*, in *EHR* 81 (1966), pp. 184–201

– "The War of the Scots, 1306–1323," *TRHS* 6th ser. 2 (1992), pp. 125–51

Eckhardt, C.D., *The "Prophetia Merlini" of Geoffrey of Monmouth: a Fifteenth-Century Commentary*, Speculum Anniversary Monographs 8, Cambridge Mass. 1982

Edwards, J. "The Cult of 'St.' Thomas of Lancaster and its Iconography,"*YAJ* 64 (1992), pp. 103–22

– "The Cult [etc.]: a Supplementary Note," *YAJ* 67 (1995), pp. 187–91

Edwards, J.G., "The Battle of Maes Madog and the Welsh Campaign of 1294–5," *EHR* 39 (1924), pp. 1–12

– "Confirmatio Cartarum and baronial grievances in 1297," *EHR* 58 (1943), pp. 147–71, 273–300

– "Edward 1's Castle-Building in Wales," *PBA* 32 (1946), pp. 15–81

– "The Negotiating of the Treaty of Leake, 1318," in *Poole Essays* , Davis ed.

– "The Personnel of the Commons under Edward I and Edward II," in *Tout Essays*,

Little, Powicke ed., pp. 197–214; reprinted *Historical Studies*, Fryde, Miller ed., pp. 150–67

– *The Principality of Wales 1267–1967, A Study in Constitutional History*, Denbigh 1969

– "Sir Gruffydd Llwyd," *EHR* 30 (1915), pp. 589–601

Edwards, J.G., Galbraith, V.H., Jacob, E.F. ed., *Historical Essays in Honour of James Tait*, Manchester 1933

Edwards, K., "Bishops and Learning in the reign of Edward II," *CQR* 138 (1944), pp. 57–86

– "The Personnel and Political Activities of the English Episcopate ...," see *Institute of Historical Research* MA thesis

– "The Political Importance of the English Bishops during the Reign of Edward II," *EHR* 59 (1944), pp. 311–47

– "The Social Origins and Provenance of the English Bishops during the Reign of Edward II," *TRHS* 5th ser. 9 (1959), pp. 51–79.

Ehrlich, L., *Proceedings against the Crown (1216–1377)*, in *Oxford Legal Studies* 6, Vinogradoff ed.

Elliott-Binns, L., *Medieval Cornwall*, London 1955

Elvey, G.R., "The first fall of Sir John Molyns," *Records of Buckinghamshire* 19 (1972), pp. 194–8

Emerson, O.F., "The Date of Adam Davy's 'Dreams'," *MLR* 21 (1926), pp. 187–9

Fairbank, F.R., "The Last Earl of Warenne and Surrey," *YAJ* 19 (1907), pp. 193–264

Falkland [attrib.] *see* Cary

Fane, A., "Boyton Church and the Vale of Wylye,"*WA&NHSM* 1 (1854), pp. 233–8

Farmer. D., "Crop Yields, Prices and Wages in Medieval England," *Studies in Medieval and Renaissance History* 6 (1983). pp. 115–55

– "Grain Yields on Westminster Abbey Manors, 1271–1410," *CJH* 18 (1983), pp. 331–4

Faulkner, P.A., "Berkeley Castle," *Arch. Jnl.* 122 (1965), pp. 197–201

Favier, J., *Un Conseiller de Philippe le Bel: Enguerran de Marigny*, Paris 1963

Fawtier, R., trans L. Butler, R.J. Adam, *The Capetian Kings of France*, London 1964

– "Un parlement franco-anglais en 1308," in *Recueil des travaux offert a M. Clovis Brunel*, Paris 1955, 1, pp. 422–4

Fischer, D. H., *The Great Wave*, Oxford 1997

Fisher, A., *William Wallace*, Edinburgh 1986

Fletcher, H.G., Schulte M.B. ed., ΠΑΡΑΔΟΣΙΣ: *Studies in Memory of E. A. Quain*, New York 1976

Flint, V. I. J., "The *Historia regum Britanniae* of Geoffrey of Monmouth, Parody and Purpose. A Suggestion," *Speculum* 54 (1979), pp. 447–68

Foreville, R., *Le Jubilé de Saint Thomas Becket, du xiiie au xve siècle (1220–1470)*, Paris 1958

– *Thomas Becket dans la tradition historique et hagiographique*, London 1981

Foss, E., *The Judges of England*, 9 vols. 1848–64

Fowler, D.C., "New Light on John Trevisa," *Traditio* 17 (1962), pp. 289–317

– *The Life and Times of John Trevisa, Medieval Scholar*, Seattle/London 1995.

Frame, R., "The Bruces in Ireland," *IHS* 19 (1974–5), pp. 3–37

– "The Campaign against the Scots in Munster," *IHS* 24 (1985), pp. 361–72

– *Colonial Ireland 1169–1369*, Dublin 1981

– "England and Ireland 1171–1399," *Chaplais Essays*, Jones, Vale ed., pp. 139–55

– *English Lordship in Ireland 1318–1361*, Oxford 1982

– "English Officials and Irish Chiefs in the Fourteenth Century," *EHR* 90 (1975), pp. 748–77

– "*Les Engleys nées en Irlande* : The English Political Identity in Medieval Ireland," *TRHS* 6th ser. 3, 1993, pp. 83–103

– "The Judicial Powers of the Irish Keepers of the Peace," *IS* new ser. 2 (1967), pp. 308–26

– *The Political Development of the British Isles, 1100–1400*, Oxford 1990

– "Power and Society in the Lordship of Ireland, 1272–1377," *P&P* 76 (1977), pp. 3–33

Fryde, E.B., "The Deposits of Hugh Despenser the Younger with Italian Bankers," *EcHR* 2nd ser. 3 (1951), pp. 344–62

– "Loans to the English Crown, 1328–31," *EHR* 70 (1955), pp. 198–211

Fryde, E. B., Miller, E. ed., *Historical Studies of the English Parliament*, 2 vols. Cambridge 1970

Fryde, N.M., "A medieval robber-baron, Sir John Moleyns of Stoke Poges, Buckinghamshire," in *Medieval Legal Records*, Hunnisett, Post ed., pp. 198–99

– "Antonio Pessagno of Genoa, King's Merchant of Edward II in England," in *Studi in Memoria di Federigo Melis*, 5 vols. Naples 1978, 2, pp. 159–78

– "John Stratford, Bishop of Winchester and the Crown, 1323–30," *BIHR* 44 (1971), pp. 153–9

– *The Tyranny and Fall of Edward II, 1321–1326*, Cambridge/New York 1979

– "Welsh Troops in the Scottish Campaign of 1322," *BBCS* 26 (1974), pp. 82–5

Fuller, E.A., "The Tallage of 6 Edward II, December 16, 1312, and the Bristol Rebellion," *TB&GAS* 19 (1895), pp. 171–278

Funck-Brentano, F., "Mémoire sur la bataille de Courtrai (1302, 11 Juillet)," *Mémoires de l'Institut AIBL* 10 (1893–7), pp. 235–326

Furnivall, E.J. ed., "Adam Davy's Five Dreams about Edward II" [Laud MS 622], *EETS* 69, London 1878

Galbraith, V.H., "Extracts from the *Historia Aurea* and a French *Brut* 1317–47 ," *EHR* 43 (1928), pp. 203–17

– "Good Kings and Bad Kings in Medieval English History," *History* n.s. 30 (1945), pp. 119–32

– "The Literacy of Medieval English Kings', *PBA* 21 (1935), pp. 201–38

– "The *Modus tenendi parliamentum*," *JW&CI* 16 (1953), pp. 81–99, rep. in *Kings and Chroniclers: Essays in English Medieval History*, London 1982

– "The St. Edmundsbury Chronicle, 1296–1301," *EHR* 58 (1943), pp. 61–78

– "The Tower as an Exchequer Record Office in the Reign of Edward II," in *Tout Essays*, Little, Powicke ed., pp. 231–47

Galloway, J., *Eleanor of Castile and the Monuments erected in her Memory*, London 1914

Gardner, A., "Alabaster Tombs of the Gothic Period," *Arch. Jnl.* 80 (1923), pp. 1–80

– *Handbook of English Medieval Sculpture*, Cambridge 1937

Germain, A., *Lettre de Manuel de Fiesque, concernant les dernières années du roi d'Angleterre Edouard II*, Montpellier 1878

Gibbs, V., "The Battle of Boroughbridge and the Boroughbridge Roll," *Genealogist* n.s. 21 (1905), pp. 222–6

Giesey, G.E., *Royal Funeral Ceremony in Renaissance France*, Geneva 1960

Gillingham, J., Holt, J.C. ed., *War and Government in the Middle Ages: Essays in Honour of J.O. Prestwich*, Woodbridge 1984

Given-Wilson, C., *The English Nobility in the Late Middle Ages: the Fourteenth Century Political Community*, London/New York 1987

– "Richard II, Edward II and the Lancastian Inheritance," *EHR* 109 (1994), pp. 53–71

– "Wealth and Credit, Public and Private: the Earls of Arundel, 1306–1397," *EHR* 106 (1991), pp. 1–26

Given-Wilson C, Cuteis, A., *The Royal Bastards of Medieval England*, London 1984

Goldstein, R.J., "The Scottish Mission to Boniface VIII in 1301: A Reconsideration of the Context of the Instructiones and Processus," *SHR* 70 (1991), pp. 1–15

Goodman, A., *A History of England from Edward II to James I*, London 1977

– "England and Iberia in the Middle Ages," in *Chaplais Essays* , Jones , Vale ed., pp. 73—966

Goodman, A, Gillespie J. ed., *Richard II: The Art of Kingship*, Oxford 1999

Grabowski, K., *Chronicles and Annals of Mediaeval Ireland and Wales: the Clonmacnoise-group texts*, Woodbridge 1984

Gransden, A, "Childhood and Youth in Medieval England," *NMS* 16 (1972), pp. 3–19

– "A Fourteenth Century Chronicle from the Grey Friars at Lynn,"*EHR* 72 (1957), pp. 270–78

– *Historical Writing in England c. 550-c.1307, London 1974*

– *Historical Writing in England II: c.1307 to the Early Sixteenth Century*, London 1982

Grant, A., *Independence and Nationhood: Scotland 1306–1469,* New History of Scotland 3, London 1984

Grassi, J.L., "William Airmyn and the Bishopric of Norwich," *EHR* 70 (1955), pp. 550–61

Green, M.A.E., *Lives of the Princesses of England*, 6 vols. London 1849–55

Greeves, J.R.H., "Robert I and the De Mandevilles of Ulster," *Dumfrieshire Transactions* 3rd ser. 34 (1957), pp. 59–73

Griffiths, J., *Edward II in Glamorgan*, London 1904

Griffiths, R.A., *The Principality of Wales in the Later Middle Ages I , South Wales 1277–1536,* Cardiff 1972

Gurney, D., *The Record of the House of Gournay,* London 1848, (Supplement) 1858

Gwynn, A., *The English Austin Friars in the Time of Wyclif*, London 1940

– "The Medieval University of St. Patrick's, Dublin,"*Studies* 27 (1938), pp. 199–212, 437–54

Haines, H., *A Guide to the Cathedral Church of Gloucester*, 1867, 2nd. edn rev. F.S. Waller [1880]

Haines, R.M., "An Innocent Abroad: the Career of Simon Mepham, Archbishop of Canterbury, 1328–33," *EHR* 112 (1997), pp. 555–96.

– *Archbishop John Stratford: Political Revolutionary and Champion of the Liberties of the English Church ca. 1275/80–1348*, Toronto 1986

– "Bishops and Politics in the Reign of Edward II: Hamo de Hethe, Henry Wharton and the *Historia Roffensis*," *JEH* 44 (1993), pp. 586–609

– *The Church and Politics in the Fourteenth Century: the Career of Adam Orleton c. 1275–1345*, Cambridge 1978

– "Conflict in Government: Archbishops versus Kings 1279–1348," in *Aspects of Late Medieval Government*, J.G. Rowe ed., Toronto 1986, pp. 213–45

– *Death of a King: An Account of the Supposed Escape and Afterlife of Edward II, King of England, Lord of Ireland, Duke of Aquitaine*, Scotforth, Lancaster 2002

– "A Defence Brief for Bishop Adam de Orleton," *BIHR* 50 (1977), pp. 232–42

– "*Edwardus Redivivus*: The 'Afterlife' of Edward of Caernarvon," *TB&GAS* CXIV (1996), pp. 65–86

– "The Episcopate of a Benedictine Monk: Hamo de Hethe, Bishop of Rochester (1317–1352)," *RB* 102 (1992), pp. 192–207

– "Looking Back in Anger: A Politically Inspired Appeal Against John XXII's Translation of Bishop Adam de Orleton to Winchester (1334)," *EHR* 116 (2001), pp. 389–404

– Review of Hamilton, *Piers Gaveston*, q.v., *CJH* 24 (1989), pp. 388–90

– Review of Raban, *England under Edward I and Edward II*, q.v., *CJH* 37 (2002), pp. 109–10

– "Some Criticisms of Bishops in the Fourteenth and Fifteenth Centuries," in *Miscellanea Historiae Ecclesiasticae* 8, ed. B. Vogler, *BRHE* fasc. 72 (1987), pp. 169–80

– "Simon de Montacute, brother of William, Earl of Salisbury, Bishop of Worcester (1333–37), of Ely (1337–45)," in *Fourteenth Century England I*, Saul ed., pp. 37–71

– "Some Sermons at Hereford Attributed to Archbishop John Stratford," *JEH* 34 (1983), pp. 425–37

Hall, G.D.G., "The Frequency of General Eyres," *EHR* 74 (1959), pp. 90–2

Hallam, E.M., *The Itinerary of Edward II*, see Printed Sources, Reference

– "Royal Burial and the Cult of Kingship in France and England, 1066–1330," *JMH* 8 (1982), pp. 359–80

Hallam, H.E., *The Agrarian History of England and Wales*, vol. 2 1042–1350, rep. New York 1988

Hamilton, J.S., "Charter Witness Lists for the Reign of Edward II," in Saul ed., *Fourteenth Century England I*, pp. 1–20

- "Edward II and the Murage of Dublin: English Administrative Practice versus Irish Custom," in Hamilton, Bradley ed., *Documenting the Past*, pp. 85–97
- *Piers Gaveston, Earl of Cornwall 1307–1312*, Detroit 1988

Hamilton, J. S., Bradley P.J. ed., *Documenting the Past: Essays in Medieval History presented to George Peddy Cuttino*, Bury St. Edmunds 1989

Hammer, C.I., "Patterns of Violence in Fourteenth-Century Oxford," *P&P* 78(1978), pp. 3–23

Hanawalt, B.A., *Crime and Conflict in English Communities, 1300–1348*, Cambridge Mass. 1979
- "Economic Influences on the Pattern of Crime in England, 1300–1348," *AJLH* 18 (1974), pp. 281–97

Hand, G.J., *English Law in Ireland, 1290–1324*, Cambridge 1967
- "English Law in Ireland, 1172–1351," *Northern Ireland Legal Quarterly* 13 (1972), pp. 393–422

Harding, A., *The Law Courts of Medieval England*, London 1973

Hardy, T. D., "On the treatise entitled 'Modus Tenendi Parliamentum' with special reference to the unique French Version ...," *Arch. Jnl.* 19 (1862), pp. 259–74

Harcourt, L.W.V., *His grace the Steward and the Trial of Peers*, London 1907

Harriss, G.L., *King, Parliament, and Public Finance in Medieval England to 1369*, Oxford 1975
- "The Formation of Parliament, 1272–1377," in Davies et al. ed., *The English Parliament*, pp. 29–60
- "Parliamentary Taxation and the Origins of Appropriation of Supply in England 1207–1340," in *Gouvernés et Gouvernants* (Société Jean Bodin, Brussels 1965), pp. 165–79
- "War and the Emergence of the English Parliament, 1297–1360," *JMH* 2 (1976), pp. 35–56

Hartshorne, C.H., "Caernarvon Castle," *Arch. Jnl.* 7 (1850), pp. 237–65
- *The Itinerary of King Edward II*, privately printed 1861

Harvey, B.F., *Westminster Abbey and its Estates in the Middle Ages*, Oxford 1977 and see *Documents Illustrating the Rule of Walter de Wenlok*

Harvey, P.D.A., *A Medievel Oxfordshire Village: Cuxham 1240–1400*, Oxford 1965

Haskins, G.L., "A Chronicle of the Civil Wars of Edward II," *Speculum* 14 (1939), pp. 73–81
- "The Doncaster Petition of 1321," *EHR* 53 (1938), pp. 478–85
- "Judicial Proceedings against a Traitor after Boroughbridge," *Speculum* 12 (1937), pp. 509–11
- *The Statute of York and the Interest of the Commons*, Oxford 1935

Hauck, K., Mordek, H. ed., *Geschichtsschreibung und geistiges Leben im Mittelalter Festschrift für Heinz Löwe zum 65 Geburtstag*, Koln/Wien 1978

Hay, D., "The Divisions of the Spoils of War in Fourteenth Century England,"*TRHS* 5th ser. 4 (1954), pp. 91–109

Helmholz, R.H., *Canon Law and English Common Law*, Selden Society, London 1983

– *Canon Law and the Law of England*, London 1987 (Contains *inter alia* the article "Crime" below.)

– "Canonical Defamation in Medieval England," *AJLH* 15 (1971), pp. 255–68

– "Crime, Compurgation and the Courts of the Medieval Church," *Law and History Review* 1 (1983), pp. 1–26

Henneman, J.B., *Royal Taxation in 14th-century France: the Development of War Financing 1322–1356*, Princeton 1971

Henniger, M.G., *Relations: Medieval Theories, 1250–1325*, Oxford 1989

Herbomez, Armand d', "Notes et Documents pour servir à l'histoire des rois fils de Philippe le Bel," *BEC* 59 (1898), pp. 497–532, 689–711

Higournet, C., "Paysages, mise en valeur, peuplement de la banlieue sud de Bordeaux à la fin du xiiie siècle," *Rev. d'histoire de Bordeaux* 26 (1977), pp. 5–25

Hill, M.C., *The King's Messengers 1199–1377*, Stroud 1994

Hill, R.M.T., "An English Archbishop and the Scottish War of Independence," *Innes Review* 22 (1971), pp. 59–71

– "Belief and Practice as Illustrated by John XXII's Excommunication of Robert Bruce," *SCH* 8 (1972), pp. 135–8

– "The Theory and Practice of Excommunication in Medieval England," *History* 42 (1957), pp. 1–11

Hilton, R.H., *A Medieval Society: the West Midlands at the End of the Thirteenth Century*, London 1966

– "Small Town Society in England before the Black Death," *P&P* 105, pp. 53–78

Holdsworth, W.S., *A History of English Law*, 12 vols. London 1922–38

Holmes, G.A., *The Estates of the Higher Nobility in Fourteenth-Century England*, Cambridge 1957

– "A Protest against the Despensers 1326," *Speculum* 30 (1955), pp. 207–12

– "The Rebellion of the Earl of Lancaster, 1328–9," *BIHR* 28 (1955), pp. 84–9

Holt, J.C., *Magna Carta*, Cambridge 1965.

Howard, Sir R., *Historical Observations upon the Reigns of Edward I, II, III and Richard II ...*, London 1689

Howarth, S., *The Knights Templar*, London 1982

Howell, M., "Regalian Right in Wales and the March: The Relation of Theory to Practice," *WHR* 7 (1974–75), pp. 269–88

Hoyt, R.S., "The Coronation Oath of 1308," *EHR* 280 (1956), pp. 353–83

– "Coronation Oath of 1308; The Background of *Les leys et les custumes*," *Traditio* 11 (1955), pp. 235–58

Hubert, Sir F., *The Deplorable Life and Death of Edward the Second, King of England ...*, London 1628

Hughes, A., "Antiphons and Acclamations: The Politics of Music in the Coronation Service of Edward II, 1308," *The Journal of Musicology* 6 (1988), nos.149–68

– "The Origins and Descent of the Fourth Recension of the English Coronation Oath," in *Coronations: Medieval and Early Modern Monarchic Ritual*, J. M. Bak ed., Berkeley/Oxford 1990, pp. 197–216

Hughes, R., "The Parliament of Lincoln, 1316," *TRHS* 10 (1896), pp. 41–58

Hunnisett, R.F., Post, J.B. ed., *Medieval Records edited in memory of C.A.F. Meekings*, London 1978

Hunt, R.W., Pantin, W.A., Southern, R.W. ed., *Studies in Medieval History presented to F.M. Powicke*, Oxford 1948 rep. 1969

Hunter, J., "Journal of the Mission of Queen Isabella to the Court of France and of her long residence in that Country," *Archaeologia* 36 (1855), pp. 242–57

– "King Edward's Spoliations in Scotland in 1296: The Coronation Stone," *Arch. Jnl.* 13 (1856), pp. 245–55

– "On the Measures taken for the Apprehension of Sir Thomas Gournay, one of the Murderers of King Edward the Second, and on their final Issue," *Archaeologia* 27 (1838), pp. 274–97

Hurnard, N., *The King's Pardon for Homicide*, Oxford 1969

Hutchison, H.F., "Edward II and his Minions," *History Today* 21 (1971), pp. 542–9

– *Edward II: the Pliant King*, London 1971

Illsley, J.S., "Parliamentary Elections in the Reign of Edward I," *BIHR* 49 (1976), pp. 24–40

Ivens, R.J., "Deddington Castle, Oxfordshire, and the English honour of Bayeux," *Oxoniensia* 49 (1984), pp. 101–19

James, M.R., "The Catalogue of the Library of the Augustinian Friars at York,"in *Fasciculus Ioannis Willis Clark dicatus*, Cambridge 1909, pp. 1–96 (re John Erghom, pp. 9–15)

Janelle, P., *L'Angleterre catholique à la veille du Schisme*, Paris 1935

Jewell, H.M., *English Local Administration in the Middle Ages*, Newton Abbot 1972

Johns, C.N., *Caerphilly Castle (Castell Caerffili)*, Cardiff 1978

Johnson, C., "The Homage for Guienne in 1304," *EHR* 23 (1908), pp. 728–9

– "A Preliminary Draft of the Truce of Bishopthorpe, 1323," *EHR* 35 (1920), pp. 231–3

– "Robert Bruce's Rebellion in 1306," *EHR* 33 (1918), pp. 366–7

Johnson, J.H., 'The King's Wardrobe and Household' in *The English Government at Work, 1327–1336*, Willard, Morris ed., pp. 206–49

– "The System of Account in the Wardrobe of Edward II," *TRHS* 4th ser. 12 (1929), pp. 75–104

Johnstone, H., "The County of Ponthieu, 1279–1307," *EHR* 29 (1914), pp. 435–52

– "The Eccentricities of Edward II," *EHR* 48 (1933), pp. 264–7

– *Edward of Carnarvon, 1284–1307*, Manchester 1946

– "England: Edward I and Edward II," in *CMH* 7, pp. 393–433

– "Isabella, the She-Wolf of France," *History* 21 (1936–7), pp. 208–18

– "The Parliament of Lincoln, 1316," *EHR* 36 (1921), pp. 53–7, 480

– "The Queen's Household," in *The English Government at Work* , Willard, Morris ed., pp. 250–97

– "The Wardrobe and Household Accounts of the Sons of Edward I," *BIHR* 2 (1925), pp. 37–45, see Collections of Documents *Records of the Wardrobe and Household*

Jones, F., *The Princes and Principality of Wales*, Cardiff 1969

Jones, M., Vale, M. ed., *England and her Neighbours 1066–1453: Essays in Honour of Pierre Chaplais*, London 1989

Jones, J.P., *The Medieval Mason*, Manchester 1933

Jordan, M.D., *The Invention of Sodomy in Christian Theology*, Chicago 1997

Jordan, W.C., *The Great Famine, Northern Europe in the Early Fourteenth Century*, Princeton N.J. 1996

Jordan, W.C., McNab, B., Ruiz, T.F. ed., *Order and Innovation in the Middle Ages: Essays in Honor of Joseph R. Strayer*, Princeton N.J. 1976

Kaeuper, R.W., "Law and Order in XIVth Century England: the Evidence of Special Commissions of Oyer and Terminer," *Speculum* 54 (1979), pp. 734–84

– *War, Justice and Public Order, England and France in the Later Middle Ages*, Oxford 1988

Kantorowicz, E., "Inalienability: A Note on Canonical Practice and the English Coronation Oaths in the Thirteenth Century," *Speculum* 29 (1954), pp. 488–502

– *The King's Two Bodies*, London/Princeton 1957

Keeler, L., *Geoffrey of Monmouth and the Late Latin Chroniclers 1300–1500*, Los Angeles 1946

Keen, D., *Cheapside before the Great Fire*, n.p. 1985.

Keen, M.H., "Brotherhood in Arms," *History* 47 (1962), pp. 1–17

– *Chivalry*, Newhaven 1984

– "Chivalry, Heralds and History," in *Writing of History*, Davis, Wallace-Hadrill ed., pp. 393–414

– *England in the Later Middle Ages*, Oxford 1973

– *The Laws of War in the Late Middle Ages*, London 1965

– *The Outlaws of Medieval Legend*, Toronto 1977 (rep. 1979), London 1987

– "Treason Trials under the Laws of Arms," *TRHS* 5th ser. 12 (1962), pp. 85–103

Keeney, B.C., *Judgement by Peers*, Cambridge Mass. 1952

– "The Medieval Idea of the State; the Great Cause, 1291–2," *Toronto Law Journal* 7 (1949), pp. 48–71

– "Military Service and the Development of Nationalism in England, 1272–1327," *Speculum* 22 (1947), pp. 534–49

Kemp, E.W., *Counsel and Consent*, London 1961

– "History and Action in the Sermons of a Medieval Archbishop," in *The Writing of History*, Davis, Wallace-Hadrill ed., pp. 349–65

Kennett, White, *Parochial Antiquities*, Oxford 1695, 2 vols. 1818

Kerby-Fulton, K., Justice, S., "Reformist Intellectual Culture in the English and Irish Civil Service: the *Modus Tenendi Parliamentum* and its Literary Relations," *Traditio* 53 (1998), pp. 149–202

Kershaw, I., "The Great Famine and Agrarian Crisis in England 1315–1322," in *Peasants, Knights and Heretics*, Hilton ed., pp. 85–132 [also *P&P* 59 (1973)]

Kervyn de Lettenhove, *Histoire de Flandres,* vol. 2 1278–1383, Bruges 1853

– *Histoire de Flandre,* vol 3 1304–84, Brussels 1847

Kicklighter, J.A., "English Bordeaux in Conflict: the Execution of Pierre Vigier de la Rouselle and its Aftermath, 1312–14," *JMH* 9 (1983), pp. 1–14

– "English Gascony and the Parlement of Paris: a Study of Anglo-Gascon Legal Representatives, 1259–1337," in Hamilton, Bradley ed., *Documenting the Past*, pp. 119–136

– "French Jurisdictional Supremacy in Gascony: one aspect of the Government's Response," *JMH* 5 (1979), pp. 127–34

Kingsford, C.L., *The Grey Friars of London: Their History with the Register of their Convent and an Appendix of Documents*, BSFS 6, Aberdeen 1915

Kirby, J.L., "The Rise of the Under-Treasurer of the Exchequer," *EHR* 72 (1957), pp. 666–77

Knox, H.T., "The Bermingham Family of Athenry," *JnGaA&HS* 10 (1917–18), pp. 139–54

Knut, H., "Norwegian Foreign Policy and the Maid of Norway," *SHR* 69 (1990), pp. 142–56

Kuttner, S. ed., *Proceedings of the Third International Congress of Canon Law*, Vatican 1971

Labarge, M.W., *Gascony, England's First Colony, 1284–1453*, London 1980

Lampe, David, "The Poetic Strategy of the *Parlement of the Thre Ages*," *The Chaucer Review* 7 (1972–3), pp. 173–83

Lapsley, G.[T.], *The County Palatine of Durham*, Harvard Historical Studies, Cambridge Mass. 1924 (also N.Y. 1900)

– "Knights of the Shire in the Parliaments of Edward II," *EHR* 34 (1919), pp. 25–42, 152–71

– [ed. H. Cam and G. Barraclough], *Crown Community and Parliament in the Later Middle Ages*, Oxford 1951 [reprints *inter alia* his articles "The Statute of York," "Knights of the Shire"]

Larking, L.B., ed. Way A., "An Inventory of the Effects of Roger de Mortimer at Wigmore Castle and Abbey, Herefordshire. Dated 15 Edward II, A.D. 1322," *Arch. Jnl.* 15 (1858), pp. 69–80

Larson, A., "Payment of 14th-Century English Envoys," *EHR* 54 (1939), pp. 403–14

Lawlor, H.J., "The Absolution of Robert Bruce," *SHR* 19 (1921–2), pp. 325–6

Lawrence, C.H., *The English Church and the Papacy in the Middle Ages*, London 1965

Leadman, A.D.H., "The Battle of Byland Abbey," *YAJ* 8 (1884), pp. 475–80

Legg, L.G.W., *English Coronation Records*, Westminster 1901

Legge, M.D., "La Piere d'Escoce," *SHR* 38 (1959), pp. 109–13

Lehugeur, P., *Philippe le Long, roi de France (1316–1322)*, Paris 1897

Leland, J., *Itinerary*, ed. L.T. Smith, London 1907–10 and see Collections of Documents, *Collectanea*

Lepage, Y.G., "François Villon et l'homosexualité," *Le Moyen Age* 92 (1986), pp. 69–89

Le Patourel, J., "Edward III and the Kingdom of France," *History* 43 (1958), pp. 173–89

Lettenhove, Kervyn de, see Kervyn

L'Heureux, L., "A Royal Progress during Times of Political Unrest, the itinerary of King Edward II of England for the years 1317–1318, 1321–1323," Typescript

Lineham, P., "A Fourteenth-Century History of Anglo-Scottish Relations in a Spanish Manuscript," *BIHR* 48 (1975), pp. 106–22

Little, A.G., "The Authorship of the Lanercost Chronicle," *Franciscan Papers, Lists and Documents*, Manchester 1943, pp. 42–54

– "Provincial Priors of the Dominican Order in England," *EHR* 8 (1893), pp. 519–25

Little, A.G., Powicke, F.M., *Essays in Medieval History Presented to Thomas Frederick Tout*, Manchester 1925

Lizerand, G., *Clément V et Philippe IV le Bel*, Paris 1910

Lloyd, S.D., review of Hamilton, *Piers Gaveston*, q.v., in *History* 75 (1990), pp. 297–8

Lloyd, T.H., *The English Wool Trade in the Middle Ages*, Cambridge 1977

Lobel, M.D., "A Detailed Account of the 1327 Rising at Bury St. Edmund's and the Subsequent Trial," *Proc. Suffolk Institute of Archaeology and Nat. Hist.* 21 (1933), pp. 215–31

Longley, K.M., "The Scottish Incursions of 1327: a Glimpse of the Aftermath. (Wigton Church Accounts, 1328–9)," *TC&WAAS* 83 (1983), pp. 63–72

Loomis, R.S., "Edward I, Arthurian Enthusiast," *Speculum* 28 (1953), pp. 114–27

Lucas, H.S., "A Document Relating to the Marriage of Philippa of Hainault in 1327," in *Etudes d'histoire dédiées à la mémoire de Henri Pirenne par ses anciens élèves*, Brussels 1937, pp. 199–207

– "The Great European Famine of 1315, 1316, and 1317," *Speculum* 5 (1930), pp. 343–77, rep. in *Essays in Economic History* 1, E.M. Carus-Wilson ed., London 1954 pp. 49–72

– "John Crabbe: Flemish Pirate, Merchant and Adventurer," *Speculum* 29 (1945), pp. 334–50 [See also Melville]

– *The Low Countries and the Hundred Years War*, Michigan 1929

Lunt, W.E., "Clerical Tenths levied in England by Papal Authority during the Reign of Edward II," in *Haskins Essays*, Taylor, LaMonte ed., pp. 157–82

Lydon, J.F., "The Braganstown Massacre, 1329," *JCLA&HS* 19 (1977), pp. 5–16

– "The Bruce Invasion of Ireland," in *Historical Studies* 4, G.A. Hayes-McCoy ed., 1963, pp.111–25

– "The Impact of the Bruce Invasion, 1315–27," *NHI* Cosgrove ed., chap. 10, pp. 275–302

– "Edward II and the Revenues of Ireland in 1311–1312," *IHS* 14 (1964–5), pp. 39–57

– ed., *England and Ireland in the Later Middle Ages: Essays in Honour of Jocelyn Otway-Ruthven*, Blackrock, Co. Dublin, 1981

– ed., *The English in Medieval Ireland: Proceedings of the First Joint Meeting of the Royal Irish Academy and the British Academy, Dublin 1982*, Dublin 1984

– "The Enrolled Account of Alexander Bicknor, Treasurer of Ireland 1308–1314," *An. Hib.* 30 (1982), pp. 9–46

– "The Hobelar: an Irish Contribution to Medieval Warfare," *IS* 2 (1954), pp. 12–16

– *Ireland in the Later Middle Ages*, Dublin 1973

– "Ireland's Participation in the Military Activities of English Kings in the Thirteenth and early Fourteenth Centuries," see *Institute of Historical Research* Ph.D. theses

– "Irish Levies in the Scottish Wars, 1296–1302," *IS* 5 (1961–2), pp. 207–17

– *The Lordship of Ireland in the Middle Ages*, Dublin 1972

– "A Land of War," *NHI* Cosgrove ed., chap. 9, pp. 240–74

Lyon, B., "What Made a Medieval King Constitutional?," *Wilkinson Essays*, Sandquist, Powicke ed., pp. 157–75

Lyubimenko, I.I., *Jean de Bretagne, comte de Richmond*, Lille 1908

Macgregor, P., ed. Stapleton B., *Odiham Castle 1200–1500*, Gloucester 1982

Mac Iomhair, An tAthair D., "Two English Drogheda Chronicles," *JCLA&HS* 15 (1961), pp. 88–95

Mackenzie, W.M., *The Medieval Castle in Scotland*, London 1927

Macquarrie, A., "The Ideal of the Holy War in Scotland, 1296–1330," *Innes Review* 32 (1981), pp. 83–92

Maddicott, J.R., "The County Community and the Making of Public Opinion in Fourteenth-Century England," *TRHS* 28 (1978), pp. 27–43

– *The English Peasantry and the Demands of the Crown, 1294–1341*, P&P Supp, 1, Oxford 1975

– *Law and Lordship: Royal Justices as Retainers in Thirteenth and Fourteenth Century England*, P&P Supp. 4, Oxford 1978

– "Parliament and the Constituencies, 1272–1377," in Davis et al. ed., *The English Parliament*, pp. 61–87

– "Forms of Social Protest in Early Fourteenth-Century England," in *England in the Fourteenth Century*, Ormrod ed., pp. 130–44

– *Thomas of Lancaster 1307–1322: A Study in the Reign of Edward II*, London 1970

– "Thomas of Lancaster and Sir Robert Holland: a Study in Noble Patronage," *EHR* 86 (1971), pp. 449–72

Madox, T., *The History and Antiquities of the Exchequer*, 2nd. edn 2 vols., London 1767 rep. New York 1969

Manco, J., *The Parish of Englishcombe: A History*, Englishcombe P.C., Bath 1995

Marlowe, Christopher, *Edward the Second*, 1594 (Marlowe Society Reprints 1925)

Martin, C. Wykeham, *The History and Description of Leeds Castle, Kent*, Westminster 1869

Mate, M., "The Effects of War on the Economy of Canterbury Cathedral Priory 1294–1340,"*Speculum* 57 (1982), pp. 761–78

Maskell, W., *Monumenta Ritualia Ecclesiae Anglicanae,* London 1847.

Massingberd, W.O., "An Account of the Family of Bek, of Lusby," *AASRP* 24 (1897) pt. 1, pp. 33–53

Matthew, G., "Ideals of Knighthood in late Fourteenth-Century England," *Powicke Studies*, Hunt et al. ed., pp. 354–62

Maxwell-Lyte, H.C., "Burci, Falaise and Martin," *PSANS* 4th ser. 5, p. 20

– *Historical Notes on the Use of the Great Seal*, London 1926

Mayr-Harting, H., "The Foundation of Peterhouse, Cambridge (1284), and the Rule of St. Benedict," *EHR* 103 (1988), pp. 318–38

McKerral, A., "West Highland Mercenaries in Ireland," *SHR* 30 (1951), pp. 1–14

McFarlane, K.B., "Bastard Feudalism," *BIHR* 20 (1945), pp. 161–80

– "Had Edward I a 'Policy' towards the Earls?," *History* 50 (1965), pp. 145–59

– *The Nobility of Later Medieval England*, Oxford 1973

– "Parliament and Bastard Feudalism," *TRHS* 4th ser. 26 (1944), pp. 53–79

McKisack, M., *The Fourteenth Century*, Oxford 1959

– "London and the Succession to the Crown during the Middle Ages," in *Powicke Studies*, R.W. Hunt et al. ed., pp. 76–89

McCulloch, F., "Saints Alban and Amphibalus in the Works of Matthew Paris: Dublin Trinity College MS 177," *Speculum* 56 (1981), pp. 761–85

McNamee, C. [J.], "Buying Off Robert Bruce: An Account of Monies Paid to the Scots by Cumberland Communities in 1313–14," *TC&WAAS* n.s. 92 (1992), pp. 77–89

– *The Wars of the Bruces: Scotland, England and Ireland 1306–1328*, East Linton 1997

– "William Wallace's Invasion of Northern England, 1297," *NH* 26 (1990), pp. 40–58

Melville, E.W.M. Balfour, "Two John Crabbs," *SHR* 38 (1959), pp. 31–4.

Menache, S., *Clement V*, Cambridge 1998.

– "Mythe et symbolisme au début de la Guerre de Cent Ans: vers une conscience nationale," *Le Moyen Age* 38 (1893)), pp. 85–97

– "Isabella of France, Queen of England – a Reconsideration," *JMH* 10 (1984), pp. 107–24

– *The Vox Dei*, Oxford/New York 1990

Mertes, K., *The English Noble Household, 1250–1600: Good Governance and Politic Rule*, Oxford 1988

Meyvaert, P., "John Erghome and the *Vaticinium Roberti Bridlington*," *Speculum* 41 (1966), pp. 656–64

Middleton, A.E., *Sir Gilbert de Middleton*, Newcastle 1918

Midgley, M., *Ministers' Accounts for the Earldom of Cornwall 1296–7*, 2 vols. CS 3rd. ser. 66, 68 (1942, 1945)

Miller, E., Hatcher J., *Medieval England: Rural Society and Economic Change, 1086–1348*, London 1978

Mills, M. H., review of Ramsay, *A History of the Revenues*, *EHR* 41(1926), pp. 429–31

Mitchell, S.K., *Taxation in Medieval England*, New Haven 1951

Mohl, R., *The Three Estates in Medieval and Renaissance Literature*, New York 1933

Mollat, G., *La Collation des bénéfices ecclésiastiques à l'époque des Popes d'Avignon*, Paris 1921

– *The Popes at Avignon 1305–1378*, (Paris 1950) Edinburgh/London 1963

Monahan, A.P., *Consent, Coercion and Limit: the Medieval Origins of Parliamentary Democracy*, Kingston/Montreal 1987

Monroe, W.H., "Two Medieval Genealogical Roll-Chronicles in the Bodleian Library," *Bodleian Library Record* 10 (1978–82), pp. 215–21

Moor, C., Knights of Edward I, *Harleian Society* 81–4 (1929–32)

Moore, M.F., *The Lands of the Scottish Kings in England: the Honour of Huntingdon, the Liberty of Tyndale, and the Honour of Penrith*, London 1915.

Moore, S.A., "Documents relating to the Death and Burial of Edward II," *Archaeologia* 50 (1887), pp. 215–26

Moorman, J.R.H., "Edward I at Lanercost Priory, 1306–7," *EHR* 67 (1952), pp. 161–74

Morgan, P., *War and Society in Medieval Cheshire 1277–1403*, Manchester 1987

Morgan, R., "The Barony of Powys 1275–1360," *WHR* 10 (1980), pp. 1–32.

Morris, J.E., "Cumberland and Westmorland Levies in the Time of Edward I and Edward II," *TCWAAS* n.s. 3 (1903), pp. 317–25

– *The Welsh Wars of Edward I*, Oxford 1901

Morris, R. H., "The Investiture of the Prince of Wales," *Arch. Cambrensis*, 6th ser. 11 (1911), pp. 220, 232–3 (1301 charter).

Morris, W.A., "The Date of the 'Modus tenendi parliamentum'," *EHR* 49 (1934), pp. 407–22

– "Magnates and Community of the Realm in Parliament, 1264–1327," *Mediaevalia et Humanistica* 1 (1943), pp. 58–94

– "The Sheriff," in *The English Government at Work, 1327–1336* 2, Morris, Strayer ed., pp. 41–108

Morris, W.A., Strayer, J.R. ed., *English Government at Work, 1327–1336*, Cambridge Mass. 1947

Munch, P. A., "Concordia Facta inter Anglicos et Scotos, 3 January 1322/3," *PSAS* 3 (1857–60), pp. 454–62

Mundill, R.R., *England's Jewish Solution: Experiment and Expulsion, 1262–1290*, Cambridge 1998.

Murray, A., "Confession as a historical source in the Thirteenth Century," in Davis, Wallace-Hadrill ed., *The Writing of History in the Middle Ages*, pp. 275–322

– *Reason and Society in the Middle Ages*, Oxford 1978

Myers, H.A., *Medieval Kingship*, Chicago 1982

Nelson, J.L., *Politics and Ritual in Early Medieval Europe*, London 1986

Nelson, L.H., *The Normans in South Wales 1070–1171*, Austin Texas, 1966

Neville, C.J., "The Political Allegiance of the Earls of Strathearn during the War of Independence," *SHR* 65 (1986), pp. 133–53

– "The Law of Treason in the English Border Counties in the Later Middle Ages," *Law and History Review* 9 (1991), pp. 1–30

Nicholson, R.G., *Edward III and the Scots: the Formative Years of a Military Career 1327–35*, London 1965

– "The Franco-Scottish and Franco-Norwegian Treaties of 1295," *SHR* 38 (!959), pp. 114–32

– "The Last Campaign of Robert Bruce," *EHR* 77 (1962), pp. 233–46

– *Scotland: The later Middle Ages*, Edinburgh 1974

– "A Sequel to Edward Bruce's Invasion of Ireland," *SHR* 42 (1962), pp. 30–40

Nicolas, N.H., *History of the Battle of Agincourt*, London 1827

Nigra, C., "Uno Degli Edoardi in Italia," *Nuova Antologia* 92 ser. 4 (1901)

O'Mahony, C.K., *The Viceroys of Ireland, the Story of the Long Line of Noblemen*, London 1912

Oman, C., *Castles*, London 1926

Oppenheimer, F., *The Legend of the Sainte Ampoule*, London n.d.[1953]

Ormrod, W.M., "Agenda for Legislation, 1322-c. 1340," *EHR* 105 (1990), pp. 1–33

– ed., *England in the Fourteenth Century*, Woodbridge/Dover New Hampshire 1986

– *The Reign of Edward III: Crown and Political Society in England 1327–1377*, New Haven/London 1990

Orpen, G.H., "Castrum Keyvini," *JRSAI* 38 (1908), pp. 17–27

– "The Earldom of Ulster," *JRSAI* 43–5 (1913–15), pp. 30–46, 133–43; 50 (1920–21), pp. 167–77; 51–2 (1921–2), pp. 68–76

– *Ireland under the Normans (1169–1333)*, 4 vols. Oxford 1911–20

– "Novum Castrum McKynegan, Newcastle, County Wicklow," *JRSAI* 33 (1908), pp. 126–40

O'Sullivan, M. D., "Italian Merchant Bankers in Ireland," *Gwynn Studies*, Watt et al.ed., pp. 168–85.

Otway Ruthven, A.J., "The Partition of the de Verdon lands in Ireland in 1332," *PRIA* 66C (1967), pp. 401–45

Otway-Ruthven, A.J., Jocelyn, A., *A History of Medieval Ireland*, London 1980

Owen, E., *A Roll of those who did Homage and Fealty to the First English Prince of Wales in 1301*, Cardiff 1901 [See now *in extenso CPR 1343–45*, pp. 227–34.]

Owst, G.R., "Sortilegium in English Homiletic Literature of the Fourteenth Century," in *Jenkinson Studies*, Davies J.C. ed., pp. 155–77

Palmer, C.F.R., "The King's Confessors 1256–1450," *The Antiquary* 22 (1890), pp. 114–20, 159–61, 262–6; 23 (1891), pp. 24–6.

Palmer, R.C., *The County Courts of Medieval England*, Princeton N.J. 1982

– *The Wilton Dispute, 1264–1380: a Social-Legal Study of Dispute Settlement in Medieval England*, Princeton N.J. 1984

Parry, B.P., "A Note on Sir Gruffydd Llwyd," *BBCS* 19 (62), pp.316–18

Parsons, J.C., *The Court and Household of Eleanor of Castile in 1290*, Toronto 1977

– "The Year of Eleanor of Castile's Birth and her Children by Edward I," *MS* 46 (1984), pp. 245–65

Partington, J.R., *A History of Greek Fire and Gunpowder*, Cambridge 1960

Payling, S.J., "Inheritance and Local Politics in the Later Middle Ages: the Case of Ralph, Lord Cromwell, and the Heriz Inheritance," *NMS* 30 (1986), pp. 67–95

Pearce, E.H., *Thomas de Cobham*, London 1923

– *The Monks of Westminster*, Cambridge 1916

– *Walter de Wenlock*, London 1920

Pegues, F.J., "A Monastic Society at Law in the Kent Eyre of 1313–1314," *EHR* 87 (1972), pp. 548–64

Pelster, F., "Heinrich von Harclay, Kanzler von Oxford und seine Quästionen," in *Mis-*

cellanea Francesco Ehrle: Scritti di Storia e Paleografia I, Studi e Testi 37, Vatican 1924, pp. 307–35

Perkins, C., "The Wealth of the Knights Templars in England and the Disposition of it after their Dissolution, "*AHR* 15 (1909–10), pp. 252–63

Peters, E.M., "Henry II and Cyprus, *Rex inutilis*: A footnote to the *Decameron* 1.9," *Speculum* 72 (1997), pp. 763–75

– *The Shadow King: Rex Inutilis in Medieval Law and Literature 751–1327*, New Haven 1970

Petit, J., *Charles de Valois, 1270–1325*, Paris 1900

Petit, K., "Le marriage de Philippa de Hainaut, reine d'Angleterre (1328)," *Le Moyen Age* 36 (1981), pp. 373–85

Pfaff, R.W., *New Liturgical Feasts in Later Medieval England*, Oxford 1970

Philip, J.R., "Sallust and the Declaration of Arbroath," *SHR* 26 (1947), pp. 75–8

Phillips, J.R.S., "The Anglo-Norman Nobility," in *The English in Medieval Ireland*, Lydon ed., pp. 87–104

– *Aymer de Valence, Earl of Pembroke 1307–1324*, Oxford 1972

– "Documents on the Early Stages of the Bruce Invasion of Ireland, 1315–1316," *PRIA* 79 (Dublin 1979), pp. 247–70

– "Edward II and the Prophets," in *England in the Fourteenth Century*, Ormrod ed., pp. 189–201

– "The 'Middle Party' and the Negotiating of the Treaty of Leake: a Reinterpretation," *BIHR* 46 (1973), pp. 11–27

– "The Mission of John de Hothum to Ireland, 1315–1316," in *England and Ireland in the Later Middle Ages*, Lydon ed., pp. 62–85

Pirenne, H., "La première tentative pour reconnaître Edouard III comme roi de France," *Annales de la Société d'histoire de Gand*, 1902, pp. 5–11

Plucknett, T.F.T., "The Origin of Impeachment," *TRHS* 4th ser. 24 (1942), pp. 64–8

– *Statutes and their Interpretation in the first half of the Fourteenth Century*, Cambridge 1922

– *Studies in English Legal History*, London 1983

Pollard, A.F., "Receivers of Petitions and Clerks of Parliament," *EHR* 57 (1942) pt. 1, pp. 202–226

Powel, D., *The History of Cambria now called Wales*, appended at pp. 376–401 to: *Princes of Wales of the Blood Royall of England*, London 1584

Powicke, M., *The Thirteenth Century*, Oxford 1962

Powicke, M.R., "Edward II and Military Obligation," *Speculum* 21 (1956), pp. 83–119

Powicke, M.R., Sandquist T.A. ed., *Essays in Medieval History Presented to Bertie Wilkinson*, Toronto 1967

Prestwich, M.[C.], "Cavalry Service in Early Fourteenth Century England," *Prestwich Essays*, Gillingham, Holt ed., pp. 147–58

– "The Crown and the Currency: the Circulation of Money in Late Thirteenth and early Fourteenth Century England," *Numismatic Chronicle* 142 (1982), pp. 51–65

– *Edward I*, London 1988

- "Edward I and the Maid of Norway," *SHR* 69 (1990), pp. 157–74
- "English Armies in the Early Stages of the Hundred Years War: a Scheme in 1341," *BIHR* 56 (1983), pp. 102–13
- "English Castles in the Reign of Edward II," *JMH* 8 (1982), pp. 159–79
- "Gilbert de Middleton and the Attack on the Cardinals, 1317," in *Warriors and Churchmen in the High Middle Ages: Essays presented to Karl Leyser*, T. Reuter ed., London 1992
- "A New Version of the Ordinances of 1311," *BIHR* 57 (1984), pp. 189–203
- "The Ordinances of 1311 and the Politics of the Early Fourteenth Century," in *Politics and Crisis*, Taylor, Childs ed., pp. 1–18
- *The Three Edwards: War and State in England 1272–1377*, London 1981 (orig. pub. 1980)
- *War, Politics and Finance under Edward I*, London 1972

Prestwich, M., Coulson, C., *Castles: a History and Guide*, Blandford 1980

Prynne, W., *An Exact Abridgement of the Records in the Tower of London ... collected by Sir Robert Cotton*, London 1657
- *Exact Chronological Vindication of Our King's Supreme Jurisdiction ...* 3 vols. London 1670

Putnam, B.H. ed., *Kent Keepers of the Peace 1316–1317*, Kent Archaeological Society, Records Branch, Ashford 1933
- *The Place in Legal History of Sir William Shareshull, Chief Justice of the King's Bench 1350–1361*, Cambridge 1950

Queller, D., *The Office of Ambassador in the Middle Ages*, Princeton 1967

Raban, S., *England Under Edward I and Edward II, 1259–1327*, A History of Medieval Britain ser. Malden, Mass. 2000
- *Mortmain Legislation and the English Church 1279–1500*, Cambridge 1982

Ramsay, J. H., *A History of the Revenues of the Kings of England, 1066–1399*, 2 vols. Oxford 1925 [and see Mills]

Ramsay, J., *The Genesis of Lancaster 1307–99* 1, Oxford 1913

Rashdall, H., rev. F.M. Powicke, A.B. Emden, *The Universities of Europe in the Middle Ages*, Oxford 1936

Rayner, D., "The Forms and Machinery of the Commune Petititon in the Fourteenth Century," *EHR* 56 (1941), pp. 198–233, 549–70

Redstone, V.B., "Some Mercenaries of Henry of Lancaster," *TRHS* 3rd ser. 7 (1913), pp. 151–66

Rees, W., *Caerphilly Castle*, Cardiff 1937 (new edition *Caerphilly Castle; and its place in the Annals of Glamorgan* [with additions], Caerphilly 1974)

Reeves, M., *The Influence of Prophecy in the Later Middle Ages. A Study in Joachimism*, Oxford 1969

Reid, W.S., "Margaret Maid of Norway and Scottish Queenship," *RMS* 8 (1982), pp. 75–96
- "The Scots and the Staple Ordinance of 1313," *Speculum* 34 (1959), pp. 598–610

– "Sea-power in the Anglo-Scottish War 1296–1327," *Mariner's Mirror* 46 (1960), pp. 7–23

Renouard, Y., "Edouard et Clément V d'après les rôles Gascons," *Annales du Midi* 67 (1955), pp. 119–41

– *Histoire de Bordeaux*, 3 *Bordeaux sous les rois d'Angleterre*, Bordeaux 1965

Rezneck, S.,"The Early History of the Parliamentary Declaration of Treason," *EHR* 42 (1927), pp. 497–513

Richardson, H., "The Affair of the Lepers," *Medium Aevum* 10 (1941), pp. 15–25

Richardson, H.G., "The *Annales Paulini*," *Speculum* 23 (1948), pp. 630–40

– "Early Coronation Records" [2], *BIHR* 16 (1938–9), pp. 1–11. For [1] see Richardson and Sayles

– "The English Coronation Oath," *Speculum* 24(1949), pp. 44–75

– "English Institutions in Medieval Ireland," *IHS* 1 (1938–9), pp. 382–92

– "Irish Revenue, 1278–1384," *PRIA* 62 (1962), pp. 87–100

Richardson, H.G., Sayles G.O., *The Administration of Ireland 1172–1377*, Dublin 1963

– "Early Coronation Records" [1], *BIHR* 13 (1935–6), pp. 129–45 and for [2] see Richardson above

– "Early Records of the English Parliaments," *BIHR* 6 (1929), pp. 71–88, 129–55

– *The English Parliament in the Middle Ages*, London 1981

– *The Governance of Mediaeval England from the Conquest to Magna Carta*, Edinburgh 1963 rep. 1964

– *The Irish Parliament in the Middle Ages,* Philadelphia 1941

– "Irish Revenue, 1278–1384," *PRIA* 62C (1961–2), pp. 87–100

– "The King's Ministers in parliament 1272–1307," *EHR* 46 (1931), pp. 529–50.

– "The Parliament of Lincoln, 1316," *BIHR* 12 (1934), pp. 105–7

– "Parliaments and Great Councils," *LQR* 77 (1961), pp. 213–36, 401–26

Richter, M., "The First Century of Anglo-Irish Relations," *History* 59 (1974), pp. 195–210

Riesenberg, P.M., *Inalienability of Sovereignty in Medieval Political Thought*, New York 1956

Rigg, A.G., "John of Bridlington's Prophesy: A New Look," *Speculum* 63 (1988), pp. 596–613

Robbins, R.H. ed., *Historical Poems of the Fourteenth and Fifteenth Centuries*, New York 1959

Roberts, E.A., *Edward II, the Lords Ordainers and Piers Gaveston's Jewels and Horses, 1312–13*, CS Miscellany 15 (1929)

Roberts, B.F., "Geoffrey of Monmouth and Welsh Historical Tradition," *NM* 20 (1976), pp. 29–40

Robinson, J.A., *Two Glastonbury Legends: King Arthur and Joseph of Arimathea*, Cambridge 1926

Rogers, C. J., "Edward III and the Dialectics of Strategy, 1327–1360," *TRHS* 6th ser. 4, pp. 83–102

Rogers, J. E. Thorold, *Six Centuries of Work and Wages: the History of English Labour*, London 1908

Rogers, R.V., "The John Rylands Library Manuscript of the Eyre of Northampton, 3 Edward III (1329)," *BJRL* 34 (1951–2), pp. 388–431

Roncière, C. de la, *Histoire de la Marine français*, Paris 6 vols in 8, vol. 2 *La Guerre de Cent Ans* (1900)

Roper, I.M., *The Monumental Effigies of Gloucestershire and Bristol*, Gloucester 1931

Roskell, J.S., "A Consideration of Certain Aspects and Problems of the English *Modus Tenendi Parliamentum* ," *BJRL* 50 (1968), pp. 411–42

Ross, C., *Patronage, Pedigree and Power in Later Medieval England*, Gloucester 1979

Ross, T.W., "On the Evil Times of Edward II, A New Version from Bodley MS 48," *Anglia* 85 (1957), pp. 173–93

Rosser, G., *Medieval Westminster 1200–1540*, Oxford 1989

Rothwell, H., "The Confirmation of the Charters, 1297," *EHR* 60 (1945), pp. 16–35, 177–91, 300–15

– "Edward I and the Struggle for the Charters, 1297–1305," in *Powicke Studies*, Hunt et al. ed., pp. 319–32

Rubin, M., *Charity and Community in Medieval Cambridge 1200–1500*, Cambridge 1986

Russell, F.H., *The Just War in the Middle Ages*, Cambridge 1975

Russell, J.C., "The Canonisation of Opposition to the King in Angevin England," in *Haskins Anniversary Essays*, Taylor, LaMonte ed., pp. 279–90

Sackville West, V., *Berkeley Castle,* Derby 1985

Safford, E.W. ed., "(An) Account of the Expenses of Eleanor, sister of Edward III, on the Occasion of her marriage to Reynold, Count of Guelders," *Archaeologia* 77 (1927), pp. 111–40

Salisbury, E., "A Political Agreement of June, 1318," *EHR* 33 (1918), pp.78–83

Salt, M.C.L., "List of English Embassies to France, 1272–1307," *EHR* 44 (1929), pp. 263–70

Sanders, I.J., *English Baronies: a study of their origin and descent, 1086–1327*, Oxford 1960

Sandquist, T.A., "The Holy Oil of St. Thomas of Canterbury', in *Wilkinson Essays*, Powicke, Sandquist ed., pp.330–44

Saul, N., 'Conflict and Consensus in English Local Society," in *Politics and Crisis*, Taylor, Child ed., pp. 38–58

– "The Despensers and the Downfall of Edward II," *EHR* 99 (1984), pp. 1–33

– "The Kingship of Richard II," in *The Art of Kingship*, Goodman, Gillespie ed., pp. 37–57

– *Knights and Esquires: the Gloucestershire Gentry in the Fourteenth Century*, Oxford 1981

– *Scenes from Provincial Life: Knightly Families in Sussex 1280–1400*, Oxford 1986

– "The Religious Sympathies of the Gentry in Gloucestershire, 1200–1500," *TB&GAS* 98 (1980), pp. 99–112

Saul N. ed., *Fourteeth Century England I*, Woodbridge 2000

Sayers, J. E., "Proctors representing British Interests at the Papal Court, 1198–1415," in Kuttner ed., *Proceedings*, pp. 143–63

Sayle, C.E., "Kings Hall Library," *PCAS* 24 NS 18 (1921–2), pp. 54–76

Sayles, G.O., "The Formal Judgements on the Traitors of 1322," *Speculum* 16 (1941), pp. 57–63

– *The King's Parliament of England*, London 1975 (Contains at cap. 6, pp. 94–108 "The Ordinances of 1311: the reaction against Bureaucracy.")

– "The Legal Proceedings against the First Earl of Desmond," *AH* 23 (1966), pp. 3–47

– "*Modus Tenendi Parliamentum*, English or Irish," in Lydon ed., *England and Ireland*, pp. 122–52

– "The Parliament of Lincoln, 1316," *BIHR* 12 (1935), pp. 105–7

– "The Rebellious First Earl of Desmond," in *Gwynn Studies*, Watt et al. ed., pp. 203–29

– *Scripta Diversa*, London 1982

– "The Siege of Carrickfergus Castle," *IHS* 10 (1956), pp. 94–100

Scammell, J., "The Origin and Limitations of the Liberty of Durham," *EHR* 81 (1966), pp.449–73

– "Robert I and the North of England," *EHR* 73 (1958), pp. 385–403

Scattergood, V.J., "Adam Davy's Dreams and Edward II," *Archiv für das Studium der neueren Sprachen Literaturen* 206 pt. 4, Braunschweg 1969, pp. 253–60

Scattergood, V.J., Sherborne, J.W., *English Court Culture in the Middle Ages*, London 1983

Schramm, P.E., trans. Legg, L.G.W., *A History of the English Coronation*, Oxford 1937

Seyer, S., *Memoirs of Bristol* , 2 vols. Bristol 1823

Seymour, W., "Battle of Bannockburn, 1314," *HT* 23 (1973), pp. 564–71

Sharpe, M., "Some Glimpses of Gloucestershire in the Early Fourteenth Century," *TB&GAS* 93 (1974), pp. 5–14

Simpson, G.G., "The Declaration of Arbroath Revitalised," *SHR* 56 (1977), pp. 11–33

– "Why was John Balliol called 'Toom Tabard'?," *SHR* 47 (1968), pp. 196–9

Smallwood, T.M., "The Lament of Edward II," *MLA* 68 (1973), pp. 521–9

– "The Prophecy of the Six Kings," *Speculum* 60 (1985), pp. 571–92

– "An Unpublished Early Account of Bruce's murder of Comyn," *SHR* 54 (1975), pp. 1–10

Smit, H. J. ed., *Bronnen Tot de Geschiedenis von den Handel met Engeland, Schotland en Ierland, 1150–1485*, Rijks Geschiedkundige Publicatien 65, The Hague 1928

Smith, J. Beverley, "Edward II and the Allegiance of Wales," *WHR* 8 (1976), pp. 139–71

– "Gruffydd Llwyd and the Celtic Alliance 1315–18," *BBCS* 26 (1976), pp. 463–78

– "The Lordship of Glamorgan," *Morgannwg:TGLHS* 1 (1957), pp. 9–37

– "The Rebellion of Llywelyn Bren," *Glamorgan County History* 3, pp. 72–86

Smith, W.E.L., *Episcopal Appointments*, Chicago 1938.

Smith, W.J., "The 'Revolt' of William de Somercote," *EHR* 69 (1954), pp. 76–83

– "The Rise of the Berkeleys: an Account of the Berkeleys of Berkeley Castle 1243–1361," *TB&GAS* 70 (1951), pp. 76–8

Smyth, J., *Lives of the Berkeleys*, see Collections of Documents *The Berkeley Manuscripts*.

Southern, R.W., "Aspects of the European Tradition of Historical Writing 3: History as Prophecy," *TRHS* 22 (1972), pp. 159–80

Staford, P., *Queens, Concubines and Dowagers*, Athens 1983

Stanford Reid, see Reid

Stapleton, T., "A Brief Summary of the Wardrobe Accounts of the tenth, eleventh, and fourteenth years of Edward II," *Archaeologia* 26 (1836), pp. 318–45

Stitt, F.B., "A Dunstable Tournament 1308–9," *Ant. Jnl.* 33 (1952), pp. 202–3

Stones, E.L.G., "The Anglo-Scottish Negotiations of 1327," *SHR* 30 (1951), pp. 49–54

– "The Appeal to History in Anglo-Scottish Relations between 1291 and 1401," *Archives* 9 (1969), pp. 11–21, 80–3

– "The Date of Roger Mortimer's Escape from the Tower," *EHR* 61 (1951), pp. 97–8

– "English Chroniclers and the Affairs of Scotland, 1286–1296," in *Writing of History*, Davis, Wallace-Hadrill ed., pp. 323–48

– "The English Mission to Edinburgh in 1328," *SHR* 28 (1949), pp. 121–32

– "Historical Revision: The Treaty of Northampton, 1328," *History* 38 (1953), pp. 54–61

– "The Folvilles of Ashby-Folville, Leicestershire, "*TRHS* 5th ser. 7 (1957), pp. 117–36

– "The Records of the 'Great Cause' of 1291–92," *SHR* 35 (1956), pp. 89–109

– "Sir Geoffrey le Scrope, c. 1285–1340, Chief Justice of the King's Bench," *EHR* 69 (1954), pp. 1–17

Stones, E. L. G. ed., *Anglo-Scottish Relations, 1174–1328: Some Selected Documents*, London 1965

Stones, E.L.G., Blount, M.N., "The Surrender of King John of Scotland to Edward I in 1296: Some New Evidence," *BIHR* 48 (1975), pp. 94–106

Stones, E.L.G., Keil, I.J.E., "Edward II and the Abbot of Glastonbury: a New Case of Historical Evidence solicited from the Monasteries," *Archives* 12 (1976), pp. 176–82

Stones, E.L.G., Simpson, G.G., see Collections of Documents *Edward I and the Throne of Scotland*

Stow, J., ed. J. Strype, *A Survey of the Cities of London and Westminster*, 2 vols. London 1754

Strayer, J.R., Rudisill, G, "Taxation and Community in Wales and Ireland, 1272–1327," *Speculum* 29 (1954), pp. 410–16

Strayer, J.R., Queller, D. ed., *Post Scripta: Essays in Honour of Gaines Post , Studia Gratiana* 15, Rome 1972

Stuart, E. P., "The Interview between Philip V and Edward II at Amiens in 1320," *EHR* 41 (1926), pp. 412–15

Stubbs, W., *The Constitutional History of England*, 3 vols. Oxford 1874–78

Studer, P., "An Anglo-Norman Poem by Edward II, King of England," *MLR* 16 (1921), pp. 34–46

Summerson, H., *Medieval Carlisle: The City and the Borders from the late Eleventh to the mid-Sixteenth Century*, 2 vols. C&WAAS extra ser. 25, Kendal 1993

– "Crime and Society in Medieval Cumberland," *TC&WAAS* 82 (1982), pp. 111–24

Sutherland, C.H.V., *English Coinage, 600–1900*, London 1973

Tait, J., "The Date and Authorship of the *Speculum Regis Edwardi III*," *EHR* 16 (1901), pp. 110–15.

Tanqueray, F.J., "The Conspiracy of Thomas Dunheved, 1327," *EHR* 31 (1916), pp. 119–24

Taylor, A., *The Glory of Regality*, London 1820

Taylor, A.J., "The Birth of Edward of Caernarvon and the Beginnings of Caernarvon Castle," *History* n.s. 35 (1950), pp. 256–61

– *Caernarvon Castle and Town Walls*, 1975 rep. 1981 [For evidence supporting his conclusions: *Antiquity* 26 (1952), pp. 25–34.]

– "The Castle of St. Georges-d'Esperanche," *Ant. Jnl.* 33 (1953), pp. 33–47 (*Studies*, pp. 29–43)

– *Studies in Castles and Castle Building,* London 1985

[Taylor, C.], *Bannockburn*, National Trust for Scotland, Edinburgh 1987

Taylor, C.H., LaMonte, J.L. ed., *Anniversary Essays ... by students of C.H. Haskins*, Boston 1929

Taylor, J., *English Historical Literature in the 14th Century*, Oxford 1987

– "The French *Brut* and the Reign of Edward II," *EHR* 72 (1957), pp. 423–37

– "The French Prose *Brut*: Popular History in Fourteenth-Century England," in *England in the Fourteenth Century*, Ormrod ed, pp. 247–54

– "Higden and Erghome: Two Fourteenth-Century Scholars," in *Economies et sociétés au moyen âge: mélanges offerts à Edouard Perroy*, Sorbonne sér. Etudes 5, Paris 1973, pp. 644–9

– "The Judgment of Hugh Despenser, the Younger," *Medievalia et Humanistica* 12 (1958), pp. 70–7 [from BL MS Cotton Julius A. 1].

– "Letters and Letter-Collections in England, 1300–1420," *NMS* 24–25 (1980–1), pp. 57–70

– "The Manuscripts of the 'Modus Tenendi Parliamentum'," 83 (1968), pp. 673–88

– *The Universal Chronicle of Ranulf Higden*, Oxford 1966

Taylor, J., Childs, W. ed., *Politics and Crisis in Fourteenth-Century England*, Gloucester 1990

Taylor, R., *The Political Prophecy in England*, New York 1911

Templeman, C., "Edward I and the Historians," *CHJ* 10 (1950), pp. 16–35

Thompson, A. Hamilton, *Military Architecture in England during the Middle Ages*, London 1912

Thompson, M. W., "An Alert in 1318 to the Constable of Bolingbroke Castle, Lincolnshire," *Mediaeval Archaeology* 9 (1965), pp. 167–8

Thorald Rogers, see Rogers

Thrupp, S. L., *The Merchant Class of Medieval London*, Michigan 1948

Thurlow, G., *Gloucester and Berkeley and the Story of Edward II Martyr King*, Norwich 1977

Tomkinson, A., "Retinues at the Tournament of Dunstaple," *EHR* 74, (1959), pp. 70–89

Tout, T.F., *Chapters in the Administrative History of Medieval England*, 6 vols. Manchester 1920–33

– *The Collected Papers of Thomas Frederick Tout*, 3 vols. Manchester 1932–4, contains in vol. 2:

– "The Tactics of the battles of Boroughbridge and Morlaix," pp. 221–6, *EHR* 19 (1904), pp. 711–15)

– "The Westminster Chronicle attributed to Robert of Reading," pp. 289–304, *EHR* 31 (1916), pp. 450–64) contains in vol. 3:

– "The Captivity and Death of Edward of Carnarvon" (*BJRL* 6 (1921–2), pp. 69–114)

Trabut-Cussac, J-P, *L'Administration anglaise en Gascogne, 1254–1307*, Paris/Geneva 1972

– "Les archives de la Gascogne anglaise (1152–1453)," *Rev. Hist. Bordeaux* 5 n.s. (1956), pp. 69–82

– "Bordeaux dans les rôles gascons d'Edouard II, 1307–17," *Annales du Midi* 77 (1965), pp. 83–98

Trautz, F., *Die Könige von England und das Reich 1272–1377*, Heidelberg 1961

Trease, G.E., "The Spicers and Apothecaries of the Royal Household in the Reigns of Henry III, Edward I and Edward II," *NMS* 3 (1959), pp. 19–52

Treharne, R.F., *The Baronial Plan of Reform , 1258–1263*, Manchester 1932, 1971 imp.

– *Glastonbuty Legends*, London 1967

Treharne, R.F., ed. Fryde E.B., *Simon de Montfort and Baronial Reform: Thirteenth Century Essays*, London/Ronceverte 1986

Tristram, E.W., *English Wall Painting of the Fourteenth Century*, London 1955 [Illustration no. 18 "Execution of Blessed Thomas," no. 25 St Edward and the pilgrim giving ring.]

Trueman, J.H., "The Privy Seal and the Ordinances of 1311," *Speculum* 31 (1956), pp. 611–25

– "The Statute of York and the Ordinances of 1311," *Medievalia et Humanistica* 10 (1956), pp. 64–81

– "The Personnel of Medieval Reform, the English Lords Ordainers," *MS* 21 (1959), pp. 247–71

Tuck, [J.] A., *Crown and Nobility 1272–1461: Political Conflict in Late Medieval England*, Oxford 1986

– "Northumbrian Society in the Fourteenth Century," *NH* 6 (1971), pp. 22–39

Tyerman, C.J., " 'Sed Nihil Fecit?' The Last Capetians and the Recovery of the Holy Land," in *Prestwich Essays*, Gillingham, Holt ed., pp. 170–81

Ullmann, W., "John of Salisbury's *Policraticus* in the Later Middle Ages," in *Geschichtsschreibung und geistiges Leben im Mittelalter*, Hauck and Mordek ed., pp. 520–45

Usher, G.A., "The Career of a Political Bishop: Adam de Orleton (c. 1279–1345)," *TRHS* 5th ser. 22 (1972), pp. 33–47, and see *Institute of Historical Research* MA thesis

Utley, F.L. ed., *The Forward Movement of the Fourteenth Century*, Columbus 1961

Vale, J., *Edward III and Chivalry: Chivalric Society and its Context 1270–1350*, Woodbridge 1982

Vale, M.G.A., "The Gascon Nobility and the Anglo-French War 1294–98," in *Prestwich, Essays*, Gillingham, Holt ed., pp. 134–46

Valente, C., "The Deposition and Abdication of Edward II," *EHR* 113 (1998), pp. 852–81

– "The 'Lament of Edward II': Religious Lyric, Political Propaganda," *Speculum* 77 (2002), pp. 422–39

Vauchez, André, *Sainthood in the Later Middle Ages*, Cambridge 1997

Vercauteran, F., "La Princesse captive: note sur les négotiations entre le pape Jean XXII et le comte Guillaume 1er de Hainaut en 1322–1323," *Le Moyen Âge* 83 (1977), pp. 89–101

Verduyn, A., "The Politics of Law and Order during the Early Years of Edward III," *EHR* 108 (1993), pp. 842–67

Viard, J., "Philippe de Valois avant son avènement au trône," *BEC* 91 (1930)

– "Le titre de roi de France au xive siècle," *BEC* 61 (1900), pp. 447–49

Vinogradoff, P. ed., *Oxford Studies in Legal History* 6, Oxford 1921 rep. New York 1974

Viollet, P., "Comment les femmes ont été exclues, en France, de la succession à la coronne," *Mémoires de l'Académie des Inscriptions et Belles-Lettres* 34 pt 2, pp. 125–78

Walker, D.G., "The Medieval Bishops of Llandaff," *Morgannwg: TGLHS* 6 (1962), pp. 5–32

Walker, D.M., Maxwell, D., *A Legal History of Scotland: 1. The Beginnings to A.D. 1286*, Edinburgh 1988

Walker, R.F., "The Welsh War of 1294–5," in *Book of Prests* (see Collections of Documents)

Walsh, K., *A Fourteenth-Century Scholar and Primate: Richard FitzRalph in Oxford, Avignon and Armagh*, Oxford 1981

Warner, G.F.ed., *The Libelle of Englyshe Polycye*, Oxford 1926

Waters, W.H., *The Edwardian Settlement of North Wales in its Administrative and Legal Aspects, 1284–1343*, Cardiff 1935

Watson, E., "The Minchinhampton Customal and its Place in the History of the Manor," *TB&GAS* 54 (1932), pp. 328–9

Watson, F.J., *Under the Hammer: Edward I and Scotland*, East Linton 1998

Watson, G., "The Black Rood of Scotland," *Trans. Scottish Ecclesiological Society* 2 i, pp. 27–46, especially 37–40

– "The Coronation Stone of Scotland," *Trans. Scottish Ecclesiological Society* 3 (1909–12), pp. 13–31

Watson, J., *Memoirs of the Ancient Earls of Warren and Surrey*, 2 vols. Warrington, 1782

Watt, D.E.R., "A National Treasure? The *Scotichronicon* of Walter Bower," *SHR* 76 (1997), pp. 44–53

Watt., J.A., "Approaches to the History of Fourteenth-Century Ireland," *NHI* chap. 11, pp. 303–13

– *The Church and Two Nations in Medieval Ireland*, Cambridge 1970

– "*Laudabiliter* in Medieval Diplomacy and Propaganda," *IER* 5th ser. 87 (1957), pp. 420–32

– "The Legal Proceedings against the First Earl of Desmond," *AH* 23 (1966), pp. 3–47

– "Medieval Deposition Theory: a neglected Canonist Consultatio from the first Council of Lyons," *Studies in Church History*, G.J. Cuming ed., London 1965, 2, pp 197–214.

– "Negotiations between Edward II and John XXII concerning Ireland," *IHS* 10 (1956), pp. 1–20.

– *The Theory of Papal Monarchy in the Thirteenth Century: the Contribution of the Canonists*, New York 1966 [see also *Traditio* 20 (1964), pp. 179–317]

Watt, J.A., Morrall, J.B., Martin F.X. ed., *Medieval Studies Presented to Aubrey Gwynn*, S.J., Dublin 1961

Watts, J.L., "The Counsels of King Henry VI, *c.* 1435–1445," *EHR* 106 (1991), pp. 279–98.

Waugh, S.L., "For King, Country and Patron: the Despensers and Local Administration 1321–1322," *JBS* 22 (1983), pp. 23–58

– "The Profits of Violence: the Minor Gentry in the Rebellion of 1321–1322 in Gloucestershire and Herefordshire," *Speculum* 52 (1977), pp. 843–69

Webster, B., "The English Occupation of Dumfriesshire in the Fourteenth Century," *TD&GNH&AS* 3rd ser. 35 (1956–7), pp. 64–8

Weinbaum, M., *England unter Edward I und II*, Stuttgart 1933

– and Davis, E. J., "Sources for the London eyre of 1321," *BIHR* 7 (1930), pp. 35–8

Welander, D., *The History, Art and Architecture of Gloucester Cathedral*, Stroud 1991

Wilkinson, B., "The Authorisation of Chancery Writs under Edward III," *BJRL* 8 (1924), pp. 107–39

– *The Chancery under Edward III*, Manchester 1929

– "The Coronation Oath of Edward II," in *Tait Essays*, Edwards et al. ed., pp. 405–16

– "The Deposition of Richard II and the Accession of Henry IV," *EHR* 54 (1959), p. 225 n. 4 (chronology of 1327 parliament)

– "The Negotiations preceding the Treaty of Leake," *Powicke Studies*, Hunt et al. ed., pp. 333–53

– "Notes on the Coronation Records of the Fourteenth Century," *EHR* 70 (1955), pp. 581–600
– "The Protest of the Earls of Arundel and Surrey in the Crisis of 1341," *EHR* 46 (1931), pp. 181–93
– "The Sherburn Indenture and the Attack on the Despensers, 1321," *EHR* 62 (1948), pp. 1–28
– *Studies in the Constitutional History of the 13th and 14th Centuries*, Manchester 1937
Wilks, M., "Corporations and Representation in the Defensor Pacis," in *Post Scripta*, Strayer, Queller ed., pp. 253–92
Willard, J.F., "The Crown and its Creditors', 1327–1333," *EHR* 42 (1927), pp. 12–19
– "The English Church and the Lay Taxes of the Fourtenth Century," *University of Colorado Studies* 4, Colorado 1907, pp. 217–35
– "The Memoranda Rolls and the Remembrances of 1282–1350," in *Tout Essays*, Little, Powicke ed., pp. 215–29
– *Parliamentary Taxes on Personal Property, 1290–1334*, Cambridge Mass. 1934
– "The Scotch Raids and the Fourteenth-Century Taxation of Northern England," *University of Colorado Studies* 5 (1907–8), pp. 237–42
Willard, J.F., Morris W.A. ed., *The English Government at Work, 1327–1336*, Cambridge Mass. 1940
Williams, A. ed., *Prophecy and Milleniarism: Essays in Honour of Marjorie Reeves*, London 1980
Williams, G., *The Welsh Church from Conquest to Reformation*, Cardiff 1962
Wiseman, R.F.E., *Ritual Brotherhood in Renaissance Florence*, New York 1981
Wood, C.T., "Personality, Politics and Constitutional Progress: the Lessons of Edward II," in *Post Scripta:*, Strayer, Queller ed., pp. 521–36
Wood, H., "Letter from Domnal O'Neill to Fineen MacCarthy,1317," *PRIA* 37C pp. 141–8
– "The Muniments of Edmund de Mortimer, third Earl of March, concerning the Liberty of Trim," *PRIA* 40 C (1932), pp. 312–55
Wood, I., Loud, G.A., ed., *Church and Chronicle in the Middle Ages: Essays presented to John Taylor*, London 1991.
Woodcock, B.L., *Medieval Ecclesiastical Courts in the Diocese of Canterbury,* London 1952
Woolf, D.R., "The True Date and Authorship of Henry, Viscount Falkland's History of the Life, Reign and Death of King Edward II," *Bodl. Lib. Record* (1988), pp. 440–52
Wright, J.R., *The Church and the English Crown, 1305–1334: A Study based on the Register of Archbishop Walter Reynolds*, Toronto 1980
– "The Testament or Last Will of Archbishop Reynolds," *MS* 47 (1985), pp. 445–73
Wright, T., "On the Political Condition of the English Peasantry during the Middle Ages," *Archaeologia* 30 (1844), pp. 205–44
Young, A., *Robert Bruce's Rivals: The Comyns, 1212–1314*, East Linton 1997 rep. 1998

Index